Brian Fleming Research & Learning Library
Ministry of Education
Ministry of Training, Colleges & Universities
900 Bay St. 13th Floor, Mowat Block
Toronto, ON M7A 1L2

COMPREHENSION INSTRUCTION

SOLVING PROBLEMS IN THE TEACHING OF LITERACY
Cathy Collins Block, *Series Editor*

RECENT VOLUMES

Reading Assessment and Instruction for All Learners
Edited by Jeanne Shay Schumm

Word Sorts and More: Sound, Pattern, and Meaning Explorations K–3
Kathy Ganske

Reading the Web: Strategies for Internet Inquiry
Maya B. Eagleton and Elizabeth Dobler

Designing Professional Development in Literacy:
A Framework for Effective Instruction
Catherine A. Rosemary, Kathleen A. Roskos, and Leslie K. Landreth

Best Practices in Writing Instruction
Edited by Steve Graham, Charles A. MacArthur, and Jill Fitzgerald

Classroom Literacy Assessment: Making Sense of What Students Know and Do
Edited by Jeanne R. Paratore and Rachel L. McCormack

Fluency in the Classroom
Edited by Melanie R. Kuhn and Paula J. Schwanenflugel

Reading Assessment, Second Edition: A Primer for Teachers and Coaches
JoAnne Schudt Caldwell

Literacy Instruction for English Language Learners Pre-K–2
Diane M. Barone and Shelley Hong Xu

Tools for Matching Readers to Texts: Research-Based Practices
Heidi Anne E. Mesmer

Achieving Excellence in Preschool Literacy Instruction
Edited by Laura M. Justice and Carol Vukelich

Reading Success for Struggling Adolescent Learners
Edited by Susan Lenski and Jill Lewis

Best Practices in Adolescent Literacy Instruction
Edited by Kathleen A. Hinchman and Heather K. Sheridan-Thomas

Comprehension Assessment: A Classroom Guide
JoAnne Schudt Caldwell

Comprehension Instruction, Second Edition: Research-Based Best Practices
Edited by Cathy Collins Block and Sheri R. Parris

The Literacy Coaching Challenge: Models and Methods for Grades K–8
Michael C. McKenna and Sharon Walpole

Creating Robust Vocabulary: Frequently Asked Questions and Extended Examples
Isabel L. Beck, Margaret G. McKeown, and Linda Kucan

Mindful of Words: Spelling and Vocabulary Explorations 4–8
Kathy Ganske

Comprehension Instruction
Research-Based Best Practices

second edition

Edited by
Cathy Collins Block
Sheri R. Parris

Foreword by Lesley Mandel Morrow

THE GUILFORD PRESS
New York   London

© 2008 The Guilford Press
A Division of Guilford Publications, Inc.
72 Spring Street, New York, NY 10012
www.guilford.com

All rights reserved

No part of this book may be reproduced, translated, stored in a retrieval system, or transmitted, in any form or by any means, electronic, mechanical, photocopying, microfilming, recording, or otherwise, without written permission from the Publisher.

Printed in the United States of America

This book is printed on acid-free paper.

Last digit is print number: 9 8 7 6 5 4 3 2 1

Comprehension instruction : research-based best practices / edited by Cathy Collins Block and Sheri R. Parris.—2nd ed.
    p. cm.—(Solving problems in the teaching of literacy)
  Includes bibliographical references and index.
  ISBN 978-1-59385-700-4 (pbk. : alk. paper)
  ISBN 978-1-59385-701-1 (hardcover : alk. paper)
  1. Reading comprehension. 2. Cognitive learning. 3. Action research in education.
I. Block, Cathy Collins. II. Parris, Sheri R.
LB1050.45.C69 2008
428.4′3—dc22
                                          2008002139

About the Editors

Cathy Collins Block, PhD, has served on the graduate faculty of Texas Christian University (TCU) since 1977. She presently serves, has served, or has been elected to serve on the Board of Directors of the International Reading Association, National Reading Conference, Literacy First, New Zealand AWARD Program, U.S. Department of Education Regional Research Laboratory, Pacific Resources for Education and Learning Laboratory, National Center for Learning Disabilities, IBM Education Board of Advisors, National Center for Learning Disabilities, America Tomorrow, and Nobel Learning Communities. Dr. Block has written more than 250 research articles, books, and chapters concerning comprehension development, vocabulary achievement, exemplary teaching practices, and effects of curricular initiatives on student literacy success. She has taught every grade level, from preschool to graduate school, and served as consultant to hundreds of school districts in the United States and around the world. In 2005, she received the highest award bestowed by TCU to a professor for her outstanding teaching and scholarship across the country: the Chancellor's Award for Distinguished Teaching and Scholarship.

Sheri R. Parris, MEd, is currently completing her PhD at the University of North Texas while teaching undergraduate reading courses. Her major area of study is reading education, with a minor in neuroscience. As a former middle school teacher, her emphasis is on secondary reading issues. Currently, she serves as Secretary and Vice President of the Gifted and Talented Special Interest Group of the International Reading Association (IRA) and has recently served on the IRA Adolescent Literacy Committee. Ms. Parris was invited to speak at the 2007 IRA conference to present "The Expertise of Adolescent Literacy Teachers," published in April 2007 in the *Journal of Adolescent and Adult Literacy*. Additionally, she coauthored two chapters in the 2006 book *Collaborative Literacy: Using Gifted Strategies to Enrich Learning for Every Student* (by Susan E. Israel, Dorothy A. Sisk, and Cathy Collins Block), which was nominated for the 2007 Ed Fry Book Award of the National Reading Conference.

Foreword

A Tribute to and Celebration of Michael Pressley

The first edition of *Comprehension Instruction*, which appeared in 2002, was edited by Cathy Collins Block and Michael Pressley. Michael's contributions to that book, and his influence on the teaching of literacy in general, were immense. Thus it is with great pride that I have the honor to celebrate the life and work of Michael Pressley by writing this tribute to him. Michael was a unique and original person. There hadn't been anyone quite like him in the field of literacy before he came onto the scene, nor do I think there will ever be anyone like him in the future. His wife, Donna, referred to him as a "tornado," meaning there was always a rush of activity surrounding him, a huge surge of energy, and never a dull moment. Michael had a sense of urgency throughout the time I knew him. He felt a compulsion to answer the questions about literacy that needed attention, and he felt they needed attention immediately.

I first encountered Michael by reading his work and meeting him at conferences. I got to know him personally when we found common interests. We coedited three editions of *Best Practices in Literacy Instruction*, and presented together at conferences. We were coeditors of the National Reading Conference's *Journal of Literacy Behavior*, now renamed *Journal of Literacy Research*. He graciously invited me to be an investigator on his grant dealing with exemplary teacher practices. Michael was involved in this grant with several colleagues at the State University of New York at Albany in their Center for English Language Arts Assessment and Achievement.

Michael graduated with honors from Northwestern University with a BA in psychology. He received his PhD in child psychology 4 years later from the University of Minnesota. Michael's first academic job was at the University of Wisconsin–Madison, as a visiting Assistant Professor and Assistant Scientist, at the Research and Development Center for Cognitive Learning. From 1978 to 1979, he was an Assistant Professor of Psychology at California State University at Fullerton. As you will see, Michael moved around a bit. He would go to an institution, make his mark working extraordinarily hard with students and his research, and then move on to climb and conquer new mountains.

He was at the University of Western Ontario for a longer period of time than at other institutions. He served the University of Western Ontario from 1979 to 1989, where he started as an Assistant Professor, became a tenured Associate Professor, and soon thereafter was made a full Professor. From Ontario, he went to the University of Maryland at College Park, where he became a Professor of Human Development. After 4 years of leadership there, he then moved on to the State University of New York at Albany, where he was a Professor of Educational Psychology and Statistics. Once again, he served that institution for 4 years and then moved on to another challenge.

In 1997, he became the Inaugural Notre Dame Professor in Catholic Education in the Department of Psychology and Institute for Educational Initiatives at the University of Notre Dame. Michael moved to Michigan State University in 2002 and joined the Department of Teacher Education and the Department of Counseling, Educational Psychology, and Special Education. In 2005, he was awarded the title of University Distinguished Professor, the highest academic honor within the university.

There was a distinct trend in Michael's career, as can be seen from the positions he held at the different universities. He was a cognitive psychologist and scientist who became increasingly more interested in teacher education and teacher practices specifically in the field of literacy.

He received too many professional awards to mention here, but some of the most prestigious follow. It's appropriate to begin with his induction into Phi Beta Kappa. As an academic, he was the recipient of the American Educational Research Association's Award for Outstanding Contribution to Research and Learning, the International Reading Association's Award for Outstanding Research on the Diagnosis and Remediation of Children at Risk for Failure to Learn to Read or Write, and the National Reading Conference's Oscar Causey Award for Outstanding Contributions to Reading Research. He was also inducted into the Reading Hall of Fame.

Why did so many universities want Michael? Why did he receive so many awards, and why was he asked to speak on so many important panels? The reasons are clear; he was a brilliant scholar who articulated his research in a manner that everyone in the profession could understand. He published more than 300 books, book chapters, and journal articles, some of which are still in press, as well as in-process revisions of his work by colleagues. In the early portion of his career he built a reputation based on his research dealing with children's memory and mental imagery. In the 1980s, a time when Michael did some of his most important work, he dealt with children's comprehension, recall of vocabulary, and, of course, his seminal research on cognitive strategy instruction. He always continued with his early themes but added new research, such as helping children to learn to be metacognitive when they read. His work turned more and more toward looking at children and how they learn in the classroom. He was especially interested in comprehension and vocabulary development, and began to attend reading conferences and collaborate with individuals in the field of reading.

In the mid-1990s, Michael began to study teaching practices, and spent hours in classrooms observing teachers for exemplary characteristics that accelerated learning and motivated children to want to learn to read. His work on exemplary practices of teachers has made a strong impact on the field. I am astonished at the wisdom he possessed about teaching in primary grades. Michael was a psychologist who came into the classroom to see what was really there, and he was able to find out from his research what constituted excellent practice. Michael published in journals such as *Reading Research Quarterly; Contemporary Educational Psychology; American Educational Research Journal; Child Development; Journal of Educational Psychology; Educational Communication and*

Technology Journal; National Reading Conference Yearbook; Journal of Experimental Child Psychology; Educational Psychologist; Journal of Learning Disabilities; Elementary School Journal; Applied Cognitive Psychology; Exceptional Children; Journal of Research in Reading; Reading and Writing Quarterly; The Reading Teacher; Educational Leadership; and *Scientific Studies of Reading,* among many others.

Michael was the quintessential professor. He was a wonderful teacher. There weren't enough hours in the day for him to chat with students, advise them, guide them, and mentor them. He would do anything to help them, and they adored him.

Michael was a workaholic. He rarely slept; there was too much to do, too many exciting things to think about and get done. Michael knew how to be a good colleague and friend. He would do anything for those about whom he cared. He came to his friends' presentations to support them even when he had heard them speak many, many times before. He was a "people" person. He loved having folks around; he loved a debate and a good conversation about sports, the arts, and reading. Michael was Passionate, with a capital P, about everything he did, whether it was a book he had just finished writing, a speech he was about to present, or a family trip he was about to take. He approached each one of these with a fresh enthusiasm. He loved life.

When I first met Michael, I was a bit intimidated. There were no secrets with him. He said what he thought, and you knew where you stood. He said what he believed was right even if it was controversial. His abiding priority was doing the best for children when it came to learning to read.

Michael was eccentric and stood out in the crowd, and he loved it. He was a sophisticated man with the enthusiasm of a child. He often looked very much like a "GAP" kid in his t-shirt, baseball jacket, and cap. But he also could be seen in his dapper sports jackets and suits. Some of his unusual outfits were definitely planned. I remember at one National Reading Conference meeting, seeing Michael with a red plaid vest with a matching bow tie. When I admired his outfit, he said, "Wait," as he reached into his backpack and pulled out a red plaid tam that he popped on his head to complete the style statement he was making that night.

Michael was a family man. He dearly loved his wife, Donna, and spoke fondly of her. He was so proud of his son, Tim. A close-knit family, they returned the love to each other. Michael often spoke of good times with his family. He particularly enjoyed his Disney cruises at Christmas. He was the last person I would think of as going on a Disney cruise, but as I said earlier, the enthusiasm and excitement of childhood remained with him.

Michael gave an enormous amount to the world of literacy in such a short time. Many live longer and never contribute nearly what he accomplished. He will be remembered for his contributions that will impact the children of our country and abroad always.

LESLEY MANDEL MORROW
Rutgers, The State University of New Jersey

Contents

Introduction   1
Cathy Collins Block and Sheri R. Parris

I. Theoretical Directions for the Future: What We Have Learned Since the National Reading Panel Report (2000)

1. Beyond Borders: A Global Perspective on Reading Comprehension   9
   Sheri R. Parris, Linda B. Gambrell, and Andreas Schleicher

2. Research on Teaching Comprehension: Where We've Been and Where We're Going   19
   Cathy Collins Block and Gerald G. Duffy

3. Dual Coding Theory: Reading Comprehension and Beyond   38
   Mark Sadoski

4. Cognitive Flexibility and Reading Comprehension: Relevance to the Future   50
   Kelly B. Cartwright

5. Metacognition in Comprehension Instruction: What We've Learned Since NRP   65
   Linda Baker

6. Constructivist Theory and the Situation Model: Relevance to Future Assessment of Reading Comprehension   80
   Donna Caccamise, Lynn Snyder, and Eileen Kintsch

II. Neuroscience: What Brain-Based Research Tells Us about Reading Comprehension

7. Looking at Reading Comprehension through the Lens of Neuroscience   101
   Allan Paivio

8. Using Neuroscience to Inform Reading Comprehension Instruction   114
   Cathy Collins Block and Sheri R. Parris

9. How Neuroscience Informs Our Teaching of Elementary Students 127
Renate N. Caine

10. How Neuroscience Informs Our Teaching of Adolescent Students 142
Sheri R. Parris

III. Improving Comprehension Instruction

11. Transforming Classroom Instruction to Improve the Comprehension of Fictional Texts 159
Mary Helen Thompson

12. Explicit Instruction Can Help Primary Students Learn to Comprehend Expository Text 171
Joanna P. Williams

13. Explanation and Science Text: Overcoming the Comprehension Challenges in Nonfiction Text for Elementary Students 183
Laura B. Smolkin, Erin M. McTigue, and Carol A. Donovan

14. Learning to Think Well: Application of Argument Schema Theory to Literacy Instruction 196
Alina Reznitskaya, Richard C. Anderson, Ting Dong, Yuan Li, Il-Hee Kim, and So-Young Kim

15. Improving Reading Comprehension through Writing 214
Kathy Headley

16. New Insights on Motivation in the Literacy Classroom 226
Jacquelynn A. Malloy and Linda B. Gambrell

IV. Differentiated Comprehension Instruction

17. Comprehension Instruction in Action: The Elementary Classroom 241
Nell K. Duke and Nicole M. Martin

18. Comprehension Instruction in Action: The Secondary Classroom 258
Douglas Fisher and Nancy Frey

19. Comprehension Instruction in Action: The At-Risk Student 271
Michael F. Hock, Irma F. Brasseur, and Donald D. Deshler

20. Comprehension Instruction for English Learners 294
Robert Rueda, Alejandra Velasco, and Hyo Jin Lim

V. Technology and Comprehension Instruction: New Directions

21. Games and Comprehension: The Importance of Specialist Language 309
James Paul Gee

22. Research on Instruction and Assessment in the New Literacies of Online Reading Comprehension 321
Donald J. Leu, Julie Coiro, Jill Castek, Douglas K. Hartman, Laurie A. Henry, and David Reinking

23. Scaffolding Digital Comprehension 347
Bridget Dalton and David Rose

24. Technologically Based Teacher Resources for Designing Comprehension Lessons 362
Jan Lacina

VI. Conclusion

25. Summing Up 381
Sheri R. Parris and Cathy Collins Block

Epilogue: What the Future of Reading Research Could Be 391
Michael Pressley

Author Index 415

Subject Index 431

Contributors 445

COMPREHENSION INSTRUCTION

Introduction

CATHY COLLINS BLOCK and SHERI R. PARRIS

The process of scientific discovery is, in effect, a continual flight that emerges from wonder.
—Albert Einstein

Although the first edition of *Comprehension Instruction: Research-Based Best Practices* was published only 6 years ago, it is important to reflect on how much the world has changed since its release. *Comprehension Instruction* was in its final stages of publication on September 11, 2001. All chapters had been written. Authors who contributed to that volume had not experienced the changes that this single event initiated—a new generation of learners; an increased need to stay connected to family and friends through many technologies not yet on our collective radar (e.g., text messaging, blogging, Facebook, iPhoning); an increased awareness and interest in the global community; the exploding development of new literacies and genres to express our emotions and visions for the future, as well as to break down communication barriers; and, the necessity to develop advanced digital literacies so we could surf among the ever-increasing waves of information that was entering our "Internetted" lives. In 2002, Marie Clay, James Flood, Peter Mosenthal, Mike Pressley, Louise Rosenthal, and Steven Stahl, were still alive and actively researching comprehension instruction.

Although No Child Left Behind legislation had been enacted, there had not been enough time to research either its impact on students' comprehension or the ensuing new comprehension methods that were created to meet the demands of its mandates. J. K. Rowling had not led Harry Potter into the Goblet of Fire, Pluto was still a planet, and only 75% of our classrooms had more than one computer in the room.

When we paused to consider how rapidly our world has changed in the 2,190 days since the first edition of *Comprehension Instruction*, it was exciting to us, as the editors of this book, to read how much the comprehension researchers represented in this second edition have not only embraced the changing landscape but have also led the field in innovations to help students thrive in a society that places increasing demands on their comprehension abilities. The purpose of this volume is to bring together the latest works by many of the leading researchers in the field of reading comprehension. We wanted to update the knowledge that has been created since 2002, and determine how many of the needs in comprehension research and instruction, expressed in the first edition, have now been addressed.

WHAT'S NEW IN THIS EDITION

As Lesley Mandel Morrow so eloquently describes in the Foreword to this book, we mourn the absence of Michael Pressley as an editor of the second edition of this book. However, his voice is not absent. We are honored to provide the written publication of the final speech that he wrote. It is printed in its entirety as an Epilogue in this second edition. His speech alone makes this second edition of *Comprehension Instruction* unique and of value to posterity.

Although this volume contains the same number of chapters as the first edition, every chapter follows a new format and addresses new issues that have emerged since 2002. Within each chapter is a description of what we have done to advance our body of knowledge since the National Reading Panel Report (NICHD, 2000), No Child Left Behind legislation, and the Reading First Act. Most chapters end with projections for classrooms of the future, if the research and best practices described in that chapter become more commonplace in the next two decades. Most authors end their chapters by describing what we still need to do: They ask questions that have not been answered, and challenge future research teams to advance our body of knowledge in new directions.

Every chapter also ends with a series of study questions entitled "Integrate, Investigate, and Initiate: Questions for Discussion." These inquiries can be used by (1) individuals who read and reflect on the contents in the text by themselves, (2) teams of school-based educators that engage in a book study to further their collective knowledge about comprehension and its instruction, or (3) college educators and students who wish to explore newest ways to expand the field's knowledge base through their future work.

The subdivisions in each chapter in this edition reflect the latest directions that have emerged in the field of reading comprehension. "Neuroscientific knowledge" becomes a central focus in this text. This term was never printed in the first edition, and never referenced in the glossary as having been printed on any page in that book. Its intersection with comprehension instruction was not well established in 2002. In the second edition, however, note that 14 chapters report on research that (1) is conducted with neuroscientists, (2) depends upon our understanding of the neurological components of comprehension, (3) engages in brain-based research using digital imagery, and/or (4) creates new brain-compatible instructional methods to improve students' comprehension (e.g., fast mapping, cognitive flexibility, and scaffolded digital instruction).

The need for more dual-coded instructional strategies, based on dual coding theory, is also prominently represented throughout this edition. Its implications for understanding the complexities inherent in making meaning are discussed by numerous researchers. It is important to note that dual coding was cited only once, on page 306, of the first edition. In this volume, numerous researchers report how pictures, hand motions, videotapes, audio inputs, technological stimuli, and virtual or real tutors are being used today to place dual coding theory into practice to the benefit of countless students in classrooms around the world.

This new edition also presents the more inclusive, global nature of comprehension research that exists today and was not prevalent 6 years ago. For example, the contributions of nations outside of the United States were not reflected in the first volume of *Comprehension Instruction*. Of the 40 researchers who contributed to that volume, none lived beyond the boundaries of the 50 states and none reported work that they were doing with citizens in other countries. By contrast, whereas seven of the authors in the second edition represent nations outside of the United States, others have utilized research performed in countries outside the United States.

Moreover, the size of the research teams working to unlock the mysteries of comprehension has expanded since 2002; that is, whereas both the first and second editions of *Comprehension Instruction* contain 24 chapters, in the first edition these chapters were written by 40 researchers. In the second edition, these chapters were authored by 50 people. You might conclude that this expansion in size of research teams was merely a reflection of the people invited to submit their work in the second edition. We did invite over half of the authors of the first edition to participate in the second edition, and three of these had more coauthors working with them on this edition. None of the authors from the first edition decreased the number of people with whom they worked for the second edition. After reviewing the chapters and their respective authors, and the teamwork that went into producing this book, we see a trend toward greater peer collaboration among researchers and larger research teams focusing on comprehension instructional issues than existed 6 years ago. What an uplifting and promising development this is!

In this edition, you may also notice a stronger emphasis on the cumulative effects of high-quality instruction; a closer link between metacognition, comprehension strategy instruction, and motivation. This unity has expanded our understanding of what is needed to truly comprehend. There is also an emerging call for reading comprehension to solve more global issues; derive more research-based benefits from peer instruction, student-led methods, and technological tutorials; and determine why some types of instruction have proven to be more valuable for younger students, whereas other methods have resulted in significantly greater achievement for older students.

In 2002, so much less was known by the field about the age-specific needs in the design of research-based best practices. At that time, we tended to believe that all methods could be equally effective at most grade levels, if we attended to individual learning styles, employed appropriate readability levels, and addressed single reader's interest needs. The information in this second edition challenges these assumptions.

We also believe that one of the most exhilarating realizations that you may experience after having read all the chapters in this edition is that the field of reading research and instruction is now viewing comprehension with the complexity it deserves. For instance, were you to place the tables of contents of the first and second volumes side by side, you would see stark differences between the chapter foci as represented by their titles alone. You would notice how every chapter in the first edition focused on what we were beginning to realize as emerging, separate domains within the field of reading comprehension instruction (e.g., metacognition, self-assessment strategies, individual differences, transactional strategy instruction, comprehending information texts, and imagery).

In contrast, the chapter titles in this second edition demonstrate a more integrative conceptualization as to the nature of comprehension. Each chapter title reflects its research team's insistence on exploring the whole of comprehension as it occurs in real-world environments. The field no longer appears to be trying to view an elephant by touching one part of its body at a time. As you will read within these pages, all chapters look at the whole of what it means to comprehend, without artificial divisions or blindfolds. Contemporary researchers are designing studies that examine how multiple variables (e.g., motivation, dual coding, neuroscientific data, schemas, fast mapping, background knowledge, cognitive flexibility, vocabulary development, constructivism, writing, home language, games and technology, hypertext environments, and/or teacher intervention) coexist to help students learn how to make meaning. All these elements make up the colorful spectrum within the single beam of comprehension. Researchers, acting as prisms, must separate the colors so that they can be seen and studied, all the while knowing that when the prism is removed, these colored components will meld back into their natural state as a single, integrated process that illuminates the path to total understanding.

Throughout this edition, also notice how often chapter authors send out a call for comprehension instruction that occurs systematically throughout the school day. These authors illustrate how methods used to make meaning in one genre may not transfer to another discipline. Similarly, in 2002, it was widely known that working memory was limited in terms of the amount of input it could process and hold as information in a usable form. By 2008, we have learned how we can assist students to preserve working memory space by metacognitively choosing to perform the appropriate cognitive act at certain points in a text. The ability to make such choices matters significantly if deep comprehension is to occur and to be retained. We all have experienced a room full of students who read the same chapter in a textbook. Whereas some students remember most of the information, others cannot discuss in any depth anything that they have read. This volume leads us closer to understanding how, in the future, we can overcome this commonly occurring, contemporary classroom challenge.

WHAT HAVE WE LEARNED SINCE THE FIRST EDITION

In the last chapter of the first edition, Pressley and Block (2002, pp. 383–392) used "What Comprehension Instruction Could Be" as the subtitle for that summation chapter. In writing the introduction to this second edition, we reread in that chapter the proposed actions that needed to be taken, based on the research reported in the first edition of *Comprehension Instruction*, to advance the field of reading comprehension instruction. We are pleased to report that many of the challenges that stood before us at that time no longer exist. We have already taken many of the steps that were suggested in 2002. As you read the list that follows, you may be as delighted as we were to realize that many of the items not present in 2002 are commonplace today. This reflection provides added motivation and confirmation that our recent works in reading comprehension instruction are moving us forward significantly and rapidly. Specifically, within the last 6 years, as a field we have to a large degree accomplished the following actions:

1. Doing all we can to ensure that young readers lean how to decode well (2002, p. 383).
2. Teaching vocabulary more effectively in most classrooms (2002, p. 383).
3. Teaching students to relate relevant prior knowledge to what they read (2002, p. 383).
4. Teaching students to use well-validated comprehension strategies (2002, p. 384).
5. Teaching students to monitor whether what is being read makes sense [as will be demonstrated through more than 15 new research-based best practices in this second edition of *Comprehension Instruction*] (2002, p. 384).

6. Encouraging students to read extensively [with more time allocated to reading instruction today than in 2002] (2002, p. 384).
7. Teaching comprehension strategies early in a student's school career [with significantly more comprehension instruction occurring in elementary schools today than was present in 2002] (2002, p. 384).
8. Teaching comprehension strategies as a coordinated process, such as "prediction of upcoming text, self-questioning, clarifying when confused, and summarizing" [as described in more depth in Chapter 2 of this second edition] (2002, p. 385).
9. No longer facing a paucity of research on comprehension of expository texts (2002, p. 388).
10. Focusing more attention on the study of adolescents' responses to comprehension instruction (2002, p. 389).
11. Embracing the need to depend "on a healthy interaction between qualitative and quantitative approaches, with qualitative studies offering the advantages of naturalism often not afforded by true experiments" (2002, p. 389).

HOW TO READ THIS BOOK

This text is divided into six parts: (1) theoretical directions for the future, what we've learned since the National Reading Panel Report; (2) neuroscience, what brain-based research tells us about reading comprehension; (3) improving comprehension instruction; (4) differentiated comprehension instruction; (5) technology and comprehension instruction, new directions; and (6) conclusions.

We know that you may read this book with many goals in mind, that each of you will likely take different insights from each page. Some may assume a historical perspective. If you are this type of reader, you might want to track the time line of reading comprehension research and instruction, or track what you already know about each chapter's focus. In the process, you may consider both what you have learned in each chapter and what you want to do next, and immediately take a step toward advancing our field in one or more domains of comprehension knowledge reported herein.

Alternatively, you may want to assume an analytical perspective by noting the common themes among chapters and comparing your list to themes that we found to be common among chapters, as reported in Chapter 25 (pp. 382–389). As you discern commonalities, you might feel enlightened by the diversity of directions for future research cited in each chapter. Do you agree with each of these directions or see a pattern among them?

If you choose to assume a futuristic stance, you might list the newly evolving practices reported within this second edition. If this is your purpose, you might also want to compare the number of new practices reported in this edition and that reported in the first edition. How many new terms and research-based best practices have we added to our body of knowledge in 6 years? How many suggestions for future research and advances in comprehension practices did you notice? In the first edition, we noted 75 different suggestions for future research and practice.

Regardless of the stance you choose to take, our goal in this second edition of *Comprehension Instruction* is that, upon the completion of your reading, you will have developed an expanded understanding of the present state and potential for future comprehension instruction and research. In this book, many of the reported research studies are expanding our understanding of how the brain works for individual readers. Many methods can be used reliably and immediately to help countless struggling readers.

We also believe that the directions for future research and projections for tomorrow's classrooms discussed near the end of most chapters deserve careful consideration as new research and curricular programs are designed. When each of the pressing issues that lie before us is examined in the high quality, research-based manner described in this book, all literacy and illiteracy throughout the world can be significantly reduced.

Our goal in writing this second edition remains the same as that established for the first edition. May the work reported herein make the "joys of reading . . . a more permanent state for countless generations to come," and may the work you do in reading this book and thereafter enable comprehension forever to fall more directly and completely under every student's control (Pressley & Block, 2002, p. 392).

REFERENCES

NICHD. (2000). *National Reading Panel Report: Subcommittees Reports and Summaries*. Washington, DC: National Institute for Child Health and Development.

Pressley, M., & Block, C. C. (2002). Summing up: What comprehension instruction could be. In C. C. Block & M. Pressley (Eds.), *Comprehension instruction: Research-based best practices* (pp. 383–392). New York: Guilford Press.

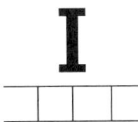

THEORETICAL DIRECTIONS FOR THE FUTURE
What We Have Learned Since the National Reading Panel Report (2000)

1

Beyond Borders
A Global Perspective on Reading Comprehension

SHERI R. PARRIS, LINDA B. GAMBRELL,
and ANDREAS SCHLEICHER

> Literacy educators share a vision and a hope that crosses borders, time zones, and political systems.
> —TIMOTHY SHANAHAN (2006)

This chapter opens this book to bring a needed context to reading comprehension research and instruction. It addresses the important question: Where do each of us, and all of the hard work we do as educational researchers and educators, "fit into" the worldwide literacy agenda? With this overarching perspective, we can more clearly focus our own position on the global map of human literacy.

In an article written for the electronic journal of the International Reading Association, Jan Turbill (2002) speaks to the positioning of comprehension research in the history of the overarching field of reading. She divides the past into five paradigms: (1) the age of reading as decoding (1950s–1970s); (2) the age of reading as meaning making (mid-1970s–late 1970s); (3) the age of reading–writing connections (early to late 1980s); (4) the age of reading for social purposes (early 1990s to the millennium); and, (5) the age of multiliteracies (2000 to the present). However, we propose that yet another stage on this continuum has emerged, not as a replacement of multiliteracies but as its partner. The age of multiliteracies, brought about through advances in technology, has also opened the door to a new era of global literacy discourse that is removing the traditional borders and barriers of the past.

Ripples from this new cultural shift were found in comments made by the incoming editors of *Reading Research Quarterly* (RRQ), David Bloome and Ian Wilkinson, at the 2007 International Reading Association Conference in Toronto, Canada. In their sessions, Bloome and Wilkinson shared the direction they will take RRQ, which is to seek literacy research that crosses geographic and intellectual borders, and fosters new connections among researchers: "We will seek to take RRQ from being a top reading research journal to being one of the top journals in the social sciences in the world" (Wilkinson, 2007).

Moreover, at the turn of the century, and in unprecedented numbers, countries around the world were involved in nationwide efforts to improve their national literacy rates. To name a few, the United States introduced the No Child Left Behind Act of 2001 (NCLB, 2002); the Philippines introduced its Governance of Basic Education Act of 2001 (Republic of the Philippines, 2001), Australia introduced the Adelaide Declaration on National Goals for Schooling in the Twenty-First Century (Ministerial Council on Education, Employment, Training and Youth Affairs, 1999), Japan's Ministry of Education, Culture, Sports, Science, and Technology (MEXT, 2002) began its New Courses of Study; and Great Britain introduced its National Standards for all schools in 1998. For countries that have yet to introduce national standards for literacy, the Programme for International Student Assessment (PISA) provides a way to assess their students' progress on various literacy (and other educational) indicators (to be discussed later in this chapter). PISA also serves as a platform by which all participating countries can compare their students with those of other countries on common educational achievement indicators.

On another front, the United Nations General Assembly is sponsoring the years 2003–2012 as the Literacy Decade—Education for All (United Nations, 2002). The United Nations Educational, Scientific, and Cultural Organization (UNESCO, 2005), is the agency charged with organizing and implementing the Literacy Decade objectives. The Literacy Decade is a manifestation of strong global agreement that the ability to read is a fundamental necessity for full participation in one's society and economy (UNESCO, 2004), and that a joint effort is needed to increase worldwide literacy. It was spurred in part by statistics showing that approximately 860 million adults (20% of the adult population) worldwide are illiterate, and over 100 million children worldwide do not have the opportunity to attend school. But the focus of this Literacy Decade does not end with the plight of the illiterate. It also extends to the majority of countries who want to attain and/or maintain educational competitiveness to participate successfully in the global marketplace. Fortunately, research has shown that there is common ground with which to address these situations, and that the literacy competencies deemed necessary for all people, as defined and measured by the international community, are the same competencies addressed in the field of reading comprehension. Thus, in the new global literacy discourse, reading comprehension is, and will likely continue to be, at the forefront of international educational and economic conversations.

This chapter highlights the following:

- The new global literacy discourse.
- Global literacy research and instruction.
- Future directions and possibilities that enhance a global perspective on reading comprehension.

WHAT'S OUT THERE TODAY: ESTABLISHED RESEARCH AND PRACTICE

To give a broad perspective of the growth in international literacy activity over the past few decades, we have assembled a time line showing some of the most notable events that led up to the current, pervasive global literacy discourse. For the reader's convenience, each entry on the time line is accompanied by a website to access further information on that topic.

- *1959–1962*: The newly formed, and still unofficial, International Association for the Evaluation of Educational Achievement (IEA) conducted a pilot test to determine the feasibility of conducting international assessments of educational achievement. This study, known as the Pilot 12-Country Study, included 13-year-old students in 12 countries. Testing was carried out in five areas: reading comprehension, mathematics, geography, science, and nonverbal ability.
www.iea.nl/brief_history_of_iea.html
- *1966*: International Reading Association's First World Congress on Reading.
eric.ed.gov:80/ericwebportal/custom/portlets/recorddetails/detailmini.jsp?_nfpb=true&_&ericextsearch_searchvalue_0=ed027162&ericextsearch_searchtype_0=eric_accno&accno=ed027162
- *1970–1971*: IEA conducted the first full-scale international student achievement assessment (21 countries participated), the Six Subject Study, which included reading comprehension as one of six major subjects assessed. Reading comprehension has continued to be a central component of these international literacy assessments.
www.iea.nl/brief_history_of_iea.html
- *1990*: International Literacy Year, proclaimed by the UN General Assembly.
www.ericdigests.org/pre-9216/international.htm
- *1990–1991*: IEA conducted the first international study devoted fully to the assessment of literacy abilities, which included 9- to 14-year-old students in 32 counties.
books.nap.edu/html/icse/study_n.html
- *2003–2012*: The Literacy Decade, proclaimed by the UN General Assembly.
portal.unesco.org/education/en/ev.php-url_id=27158&url_do=do_topic&url_section=201.html
- *2005–2015*: The Literacy Initiative for Empowerment (LIFE) is a UNESCO-sponsored, 10-year collaborative action plan (targeting 35 of the world's most challenged countries) designed to achieve 50% improvement in levels of worldwide adult literacy by 2015. This program focuses on implementing research-based literacy programs, as well as a number of other projects designed to improve literacy.
unesdoc.unesco.org/images/0014/001411/141177e.pdf

NEW DEVELOPMENTS IN THIS AREA

Researchers and educators around the globe continue to find ways to collaborate on investigations that provide insights about essential goals for global literacy. Although individual countries differ with respect to social, economic, and literacy goals and practices within their borders, there is much to be learned from comparative studies of reading comprehension from an all-encompassing view, and of literacy and its contributing factors. PISA and the Progress in International Reading Literacy Study (PIRLS) are pioneers in this work.

Programme for International Student Assessment

Since 2000 (and every third year thereafter), PISA has administered standardized tests in reading, math, and science. Over 1 million 15-year-old students in 41 countries (accounting for 90% of the world economy) have participated in this assessment (PISA, 2003), developed by selected literacy experts from these countries. PISA assesses the extent to which students nearing the end of compulsory education have acquired the knowledge and skills essential for full participation in society, focusing on student competencies in the key subject areas of reading, mathematics, and science. It examines the extent to which students are able to extrapolate from what they have learned and apply their knowledge in both familiar and novel settings related to school and nonschool contexts.

In reading, the focus is on the ability of students to use written information in life situations they may encounter. Therefore, "reading literacy" is defined by the interest, attitude, and ability of individuals to use reading appropriately, including digital technology and communication tools, to access, manage, integrate, and evaluate information; to construct new knowledge; to communicate with others to participate effectively in society. The concept of reading literacy in PISA is defined by three dimensions: (1) the format of the reading material, (2) the type of reading task or reading aspects, and (3) the situation or the use for which the text was constructed.

The first dimension, the text format, classifies reading material into continuous and noncontinuous texts. "Continuous texts" typically are comprised of sentences that in turn are organized into paragraphs. They may fit under larger structures, such as sections, chapters, and books. "Noncontinuous texts" are organized differently than continuous texts, require a different reading approach, and can be classified according to their format.

The second dimension is defined by the three reading tasks (i.e., retrieve, interpret, and evaluate). Some tasks require students to retrieve information, that is, to locate single or multiple pieces of information in a text. Other tasks require students to interpret texts, that is, to construct meaning and draw inferences from written information. The third type of task requires students to reflect on and evaluate texts, that is, to relate written information to their prior knowledge, ideas, and experiences.

The third dimension, the situation or context, reflects the categorization of texts based on the author's intended use, the relationship with other persons implicitly or explicitly associated with the text, and the general content. The text situations included in PISA are selected to maximize the diversity of content in the reading literacy assessment and include reading for private use (personal), reading for public use, reading for work (occupational), and reading for education. A full description of the conceptual framework underlying the PISA assessment of reading literacy is provided in *Assessing Scientific, Reading, and Mathematical Literacy: A Framework for PISA 2006* (Organization for Economic Cooperation and Development, 2006).

PISA reading scores are reported according to five levels of proficiency, corresponding to tasks of varying difficulty. The establishment of proficiency levels in reading makes it possible not only to rank students' performance but also to describe what students can do. Each successive reading level is associated with tasks of ascending difficulty. The tasks at each level of reading literacy were judged by panels of experts to share certain features and requirements, and also to differ consistently from tasks at either higher or lower levels. The assumed difficulty of tasks was then validated empirically on the basis of student performance in participating countries.

An analysis of the range of these tasks provides some indication of an ordered set of knowledge construction skills and strategies. For example, the easiest of these tasks requires students to locate explicitly stated information according to a single criterion, when there is little, if any, competing information in the text, to identify the main theme of a familiar text, or to make a simple connection between a piece of the text and everyday life. In general, this information is prominent in the text, and the text itself is less dense and less complex in structure. In contrast, harder retrieval tasks require students to locate and sequence multiple pieces of deeply embedded information, sometimes in accordance with multiple criteria. Often, competing information in the text shares some features with the information required for the answer. Similarly, with tasks requiring interpretation or reflection and evaluation, tasks at the lower end differ from those at the higher end in terms of the process needed to perform them correctly, the degree to which the reading strategies required for a correct answer are signaled in the question or the instructions, the level of complexity and familiarity of the text, and the quantity of competing or distracting information in the text.

Progress in International Reading Literacy Study

Begun in 2001, PIRLS is the successor to the IEA studies that started in 1970 and continued to 1991 through the Reading Literacy Study. This assessment is given every 5 years and currently measures trends in fourth graders' reading achievement in 35 different countries, and obtains information on students' home and school experiences.

PIRLS comprises a written reading comprehension test and a background survey about reading behaviors and attitudes. Assessments are developed by the PIRLS Reading Development Group (RDG) along with National Research Coordinators for each participating country. The RDG includes reading experts from seven different countries. This assessment measures students' ability to understand a wide variety of texts classified under two major categories: acquiring and using information, and applying literary experience. Within these categories, students are asked to use a variety of reading skills that include: (1) Focusing on and retrieving information, (2) making straightforward inferences, (3) interpreting and integrating ideas, and (4) examining or evaluating text features (PIRLS, 2006). These passages are taken from authentic texts (children's storybook and informational texts). Students are given 80 minutes to complete two reading passages (one representing each reading purpose). Then, additional time is allotted to complete a survey.

PIRLS and PISA work together to provide data on students at two key points in schooling: fourth grade and at age 15 (when compulsory education ends for most students worldwide). They also provide countries with data regarding within-school, between-school, and between-country variance, as well the possible factors that account for these variances. These tests also supply data regarding achievement variances among different domains of literacy, including reading comprehension.

HOW THIS NEW KNOWLEDGE
CAN IMPROVE COMPREHENSION INSTRUCTION

One of the stated goals of the Literacy Decade is to support the development of flexible programs that suit people's different needs, and monitor and create evaluations to measure progress (UNESCO, 2004). At the same time, the unifying concept of global literacy is one that, by its very nature, highlights instructional strategies that rely upon a common basic foundation of what works in reading comprehension instruction.

One program that is leading the way to provide a common core of internationally tested comprehension instructional principles is the AWARD Reading program developed by Wendy Pye Publishing in New Zealand. This K–3 reading program combines technology and research-based best practices in reading instruction to meet the national and/or state standards of each country in which it is utilized. The program, developed through a collaboration of international reading experts and researchers, has been (and continues to be) implemented in multiple countries. One of the foremost goals of the AWARD Reading program is to meet students' needs across international borders. It combines high-interest children's books and electronic texts with instruction designed systematically to instill the essential reading (phonemic awareness, phonics, vocabulary, fluency, and comprehension) and writing skills in K–3 curricula. Formative and summative assessments and prescriptions are built into the program, as well as individual, small-group, and whole-group diagnostic evaluations and instruction. Their research projects are based on a train-the-trainer model, or by directly training teachers, who train others, because their research demonstrates that AWARD teachers are what make the crucial difference in students' literacy success.

Research on this program (as of 2008) has been conducted in the United States, New Zealand, Chile, Sri Lanka, and South Africa, with additional countries scheduled for future research. Additionally, the researchers and developers of AWARD Reading are committed to the promotion of information sharing across borders by establishing an international professional learning community. For example, a Sri Lankan school representative shared with the South African school representative how Sri Lankan schools implemented the AWARD program successfully. The Sri Lanka project began with a 20-school study in 1995, and its success has led to AWARD materials being used in 6,000+ Sri Lankan schools today. The development of this reading program is the result of one company's commitment to find out what works in not only its own country but also across borders (see the projections and possibilities section in this chapter for more information).

Reading comprehension instruction is also enhanced through actual student engagement in the global literacy discourse itself. Such interactions foster connections that are both relevant to instructional activities and empowering to students. Advancements in technology will continue to dismantle barriers to multinational student interactions, and a growing number of websites foster such discourse (see the projections and possibilities section in this chapter for more information).

DIRECTIONS FOR FUTURE RESEARCH

1. *What ways can we utilize data from PIRLS and PISA assessments to inform comprehension research and practice in our own countries?* For example, U.S. researchers (Binkley & Kelly, 2003) compared the PIRLS and National Assessment of Educational Progress (NAEP) tests (both of which assess fourth grade reading skills) to see how data from both tests can work together to create a richer understanding of fourth grade reading achievement. We need to create other new ways to utilize this rich data source effectively.

2. *How can classroom instructional practices that have been successful in one country be modified to meet the same needs in another country?* For instance, how can we identify differences in the cultural climate of classrooms or how language differences limit the international transferability of data? Researchers need to explore methods that are working in other countries, then validly transfer such practices into workable formats in their own countries. When this goal is attained, we can more rapidly build a stronger foundation of what comprehension truly entails.

3. *How can research in comprehension instruction (for one language) inform comprehension instruction in another language?* Should language differences be seen as a barrier to providing insightful reading comprehension research data? For instance, Goswami has investigated the ease and difficulty of learning to read across languages (Goswami, 2002, 2006; Goswami, Ziegler, Dalton, & Schneider, 2003; Ziegler & Goswami, 2005) and has compared differences in learning to read across various languages. Such future research projects hold promise for expanding the ability of literacy researchers and practitioners to reduce language barriers, and to increase their opportunities share and learn from each other.

PROJECTIONS AND POSSIBILITIES FOR THE CLASSROOM OF 2030

In the classroom of 2030, students will self-identify as being part of a global community. As they interact in an international arena, comprehending many languages will be commonplace through technologically based instructional translating devices. Facilitating this shift in what reading comprehension means, for example, will be the increasing ease with which students engage in conversations with peers who speak a different language. Language translation software will commonly be used to bridge these gaps. Also, as global literacy discourse becomes more commonplace, the number of students (and teachers) who are multilingual, at least at a conversational level, will grow. The websites listed below show how six forward-thinking groups have already entered into this new global literacy discourse and are impacting how we conceptualize reading comprehension research and practice.

AWARD Reading: *www.awardreading.com*

The AWARD Reading program (discussed in this chapter) is a pioneer, because its entrance into the marketplace marks one of the first complete reading instructional programs developed to participate directly in the new global literacy discourse arena. Serving as both an instructional program and an ongoing research project, AWARD is also leading the way in identifying the most effective cross-cultural teaching and learning processes, many of which are directly applicable to the field of reading comprehension.

Global Nomads Group: *www.gng.org*

Founded in 1998, the Global Nomads Group (GNG) is a nonprofit organization dedicated to heightening children's understanding and appreciation for the world and its people. Using interactive technologies such as videoconferencing, GNG enables young people to meet face-to-face across cultural and national boundaries to discuss (through translation devices) their differences and similarities, and the world issues that affect them. These videoconferences engage critical thinking skills and build background knowledge on international issues. GNG was the winner of the 2005 Goldman Sachs prize for excellence in international education in the media and technology catagory.

Elgin to Elgin Project: *www.u-46.org/ehs/elgintoelgin*

Launched in February 2007, Elgin to Elgin is run by high school students in Elgin, Illinois. It is a community-driven, worldwide reading program based on the idea of unity, with a primary focus of getting all Elgin municipalities in the world to join and host their own reading nights for children. The list is growing, but as of 2008, they have already partnered with schools from Elgin, Scotland and Elgin, Ontario, as well as many other Elgin communities within the United States. Ultimately, the program hopes to encourage schools to start their own similar projects, whether Elgin or not, in an effort to spread the joy of reading and to encourage the improvement of reading comprehension skills in all children.

Kidlink Projects: *www.kidlink.org*

Kidlink, an award-winning website owned by a nonprofit Norwegian organization called the Kidlink Society, is a place where kids collaborate and network with friends around the world and are helped to understand themselves, identify personal interests, and define goals for life. This site is designed to alleviate language barriers and offers translations in many different languages. If a child's language is not found among the 40 translations listed, he or she can request a translation. This site also offers teachers ideas on how to use Kidlink website activities to build reading comprehension skills.

Friendship through Education: *www.friendshiptrougheducation.org*

Friendship through education was launched after the events of September 11, 2001, by the U.S. Department of Education to facilitate interactions between youth and teachers worldwide. This site allows students to interact with students from other countries through letter writing, online interactions, and a variety of projects. There are a multitude of opportunities to build reading comprehension skills through participation in this website.

Global Schoolhouse: *www.globalschoolnet.org*

The Global Schoolhouse is a nonprofit organization that describes itself as "the original virtual meeting place where educators, students, parents, and community members can collaborate, interact, develop, publish, and discover learning resources." This site combines teaching ideas with Web publishing, video conferencing, and other online tools that bridge geographic gaps, allowing young people around the world to learn together. Global Schoolhouse has reached more than 1 million students from 45,000 schools across 194 countries. Among its many choices is a "projects registry," where students and teachers can join international Web-based projects set up by others, or start their own. It also contains links to other globally oriented learning websites.

SUMMARY

Researchers and educators have increasingly focused on individual student differences as they continue their efforts to provide optimal comprehension instruction for each student. This "separating" and "categorizing" effect can be counterbalanced by global literacy discourse, which provides a magnetic force that builds upon and highlights the commonalities in human comprehension, keeping these similarities prominent in the mind of future educators, researchers, and policymakers.

One of our goals in this chapter is to increase the likelihood that research-based best comprehension practices, such as those published in this book, will find their way into the worldwide pipeline of data and discourse concerning how universal human understanding can be built through stronger comprehension instruction. Published research studies from all countries will be increasingly monitored for common, core comprehension research and practice ideas that can be used to combat illiteracy on a global scale. We are each members of not only our communities, our own educational institutions and nations, but also our global family. Our individual efforts and daily hard work are already influencing the worldwide literacy agenda. Our results have already created better comprehenders in our own country and will likely reach farther than we anticipate.

INTEGRATE, INVESTIGATE, AND INITIATE: QUESTIONS FOR DISCUSSION

1. One of our goals in this chapter was to increase your awareness of how individual works in the field of reading comprehension impact the "global literacy discourse." Stop and reflect on your own work and the daily professional responsibilities you perform. In what specific ways has the information in this chapter expanded your understanding of the larger sphere of knowledge and practices that your work influences? List three actions you can take to move beyond the literal and figurative borders of your work, so that you continue to advance a global perspective of reading comprehension for mankind.

2. We have argued that educators' abilities to improve research and instruction on reading comprehension are immediate and increasingly relevant at the international level. Do you agree or disagree that highly effective reading comprehension can lead to greater prosperity, understanding, and peace among and within nations? Why, or why not?

3. As you visit two or more of this chapter's websites, prepare a two-column table. In one column, list the reading comprehension goals that the various projects share. In the other column, list the unique objectives of each project. Share and discuss the items on your table with colleagues.

REFERENCES

Binkley, M., & Kelly, D. A. (2003). A content comparison of the NAEP and PIRLS fourth-grade reading assessments. Washington, DC: U.S. Department of Education. Retrieved July 11, 2007, from *64.233.167.104/search?q=cache:gsLITr6tldAJ:nces.ed.gov/pubs2003/200310.pdf+Marilyn+Binkley&hl=en&ct=clnk&cd=7&gl=us&client=safari.*

Goswami, U. (2002). Phonology, reading development, and dyslexia: A cross-linguistic perspective. *Annals of Dyslexia, 52,* 141–163.

Goswami, U. (2006). Reading and its development: Insights from brain science. *Literacy Today, 46,* 28–29.

Goswami, U., Ziegler, J. C., Dalton, L., & Schneider, W. (2003). Nonword reading across orthographies: How flexible is the choice of reading units? *Applied Psycholinguistics, 24*(2), 235–247.

Ministerial Council on Education, Employment, Training and Youth Affairs. (1999). *The Adelaide Declaration on National Goals for Schooling in the Twenty-First Century.* Retrieved July 25, 2007, from *www.mceetya.edu.au/mceetya/nationalgoals/index.htm.*

Ministry of Education, Culture, Sports, Science, and Technology. (2002). *Implementation of the new courses of study.* Retrieved July 25, 2007, from *www.mext.go.jp/english/org/eshisaku/eshotou.htm.*

No Child Left Behind Act of 2001. (2002). Pub. L. No. 107-110, 115 Stat. 1425. Retrieved July 25, 2007, from *www.ed.gov/policy/elsec/leg/esea02/index.html*.

OECD. (2006). *Assessing scientific, reading, and mathematical literacy: A framework for PISA 2006.* Retrieved November 19, 2007, from *www.oecd.org/document/33/0,3343,en_32252351_32236173_37462369_1_1_1_1,00.html*.

PIRLS. (2006). *PIRLS 2006 Assessment framework and specifications, 2nd Ed.* Retrieved Nov. 19, 2006, from *times.bc.edu/pirls2006/framework.html*.

Programme for International Student Assessment. (2003). *PISA 2003 Technical Report.* Retrieved June 26, 2007, from *www.oecd.org/dataoecd/49/60/35188570.pdf*.

Republic of the Phillipines. (2001). Governance of Basic Education Act (Republic Act No. 9155). Retrieved July 19, 2007, from *www.deped.gov.ph/cpanel/uploads/RA-9155.pdf*.

Shanahan, T. (2006). *Letter of greetings: 21st World Congress on Reading Program.* Available: *www.reading.org/downloads/meetings/wc06_finalprogram_060726.pdf*.

Turbill, J. (2002, February). The four ages of reading philosophy and pedagogy: A framework for examining theory and practice. *Reading Online, 5*(6). Retrieved July 11, 2007, from *www.readingonline.org/international/inter_index.asp?href=turbill4/index.html*.

UNESCO. (2004). *The Literacy Decade: Getting started.* Retrieved July 12, 2007, from *unesdoc.unesco.org/images/0013/001354/135400e.pdf*.

UNESCO. (2005). *United Nations Literacy Decade: Progress Report 2004–2005.* Retrieved July 12, 2007, from *unesdoc.unesco.org/images/0014/001402/140259e.pdf*.

United Nations. (2002). *United Nations Literacy Decade: Education for All: International plan of action; implementation of General Assembly resolution 56/116* (Report of the Secretary General). Retrieved July 12, 2007, from *portal.unesco.org/education/en/file_download.php/f0b0f2edfeb55b03ec965501810c9b6caction+plan+English.pdf*.

Wilkinson, I. (2007). *Wilkinson, Bloome lead Reading Research Quarterly to build knowledge base in literacy.* (OSU College of Education: News and Events). Retrieved July 10, 2007, from *education.osu.edu/newsevents/index.cfm?fuseaction=showevent&eventid=321*.

Ziegler, J., & Goswami, U. (2005). Reading acquisition, developmental dyslexia, and skilled reading across languages: A psycholinguistic grain size theory. *Psychology Bulletin, 131*(1), 3–29.

2

Research on Teaching Comprehension
Where We've Been and Where We're Going

CATHY COLLINS BLOCK and GERALD G. DUFFY

> Let us not be content to wait and see what will happen, but give us the determination to make the right things happen.
> —Peter Marshall

This is a particularly relevant time to be writing about how to teach comprehension. As we began this chapter, the 30th anniversary of Durkin's (1978/1979) landmark comprehension study was upon us. Her findings jarred the profession's consciousness about what it meant to teach comprehension and created a more focused reading comprehension research agenda. May 2008 also marked the 30th anniversary of the first book dedicated solely to research-based comprehension practices, *Teaching Comprehension* (Pearson & Johnson, 1978). Three years later, *Comprehension in Teaching: Research Reviews* (Guthrie, 1981) became the first book to synthesize comprehension research. It contained only 12 chapters.

Since that time, huge strides have been made. Several important books more than 300 pages in length and many landmark studies were completed. Among these works were *Comprehension Instruction: Research-Based Best Practices* (Block & Pressley, 2002); *Explaining Reading: A Resource for Teaching Concepts, Skills, and Strategies* (Duffy, 2003); *Handbook of Research in Comprehension* (Duffy & Israel, 2008); *Improving Comprehension Instruction: Rethinking Research, Theory, and Classroom Practice* (Block, Gambrell, & Pressley, 2002); *Mosaic of Thought: The Power of Comprehension Strategy Instruction* (Keene & Zimmerman, 1997, 2007); *Progress in Understanding Reading* (Stanovich, 2000); *Reading at Risk: A Survey of Literacy Practices in America* (National Endowment for the Arts, 2004); *Reading for Understanding: Towards an R&D Program in Reading Comprehension* (RAND Reading Study Group, 2001);

and, *Verbal Protocols of Reading: The Nature of Constructively Responsive Readings* (Pressley & Afflerbach, 1995).

Let's fast-forward from 1978 to today. Can you determine the year in which the following prominent research team's citation was written?

> There is absolutely no doubt that reading comprehension strategy instruction is a "hot" topic. Entire books are written about it. Journals are publishing a lot of articles, and entire special editions are dedicated to it. . . . The short term goal is to teach children facilitating cognitive processes and when to use them to read for understanding. The long term goal is to encourage "automatic" application of appropriate strategies to appropriate domains.

You may have judged this statement to have been written within the last few years, because its goals are those toward which we strive today. However, Pressley, Symons, Snyder, and Cargilia-Bull (1989, p. 16) wrote these words almost 20 years ago. Our objective for including it here was threefold. First, we wanted to demonstrate that a lot of hard work concerning comprehension strategy instruction occurred between 1978 and 1989. Second, much new research must be completed before the goals stated by Pressley, Symons, and colleagues can be realized. Third, in our review of instructional research in comprehension, we became increasingly aware that progress in this field is moving more slowly than desired. Consequently, our goals in this chapter are as follows:

- To summarize established research findings about comprehension instruction.
- To report more recent insights.
- To describe how evidence can be applied to classrooms.
- To suggest future directions for research and practice.

ESTABLISHED RESEARCH FINDINGS ABOUT COMPREHENSION INSTRUCTION

In 1981, the Center for the Study of Reading at the University of Illinois was the first scientific body to issue a mission statement relative to comprehension instruction: "The challenge is to develop direct methods for teaching basic reading comprehension skills . . . to tens of thousands of children who, in the absence of explicit instruction, are not acquiring these skills today. This is a challenge we accept with enthusiasm" (Anderson, 1981, p. 6). In the years that followed a variety of researchers examined (1) what comprehension strategies should be taught, (2) the impact of directly teaching comprehension strategies, and (3) the process teachers go through in learning to teach comprehension strategies.

What Comprehension Strategies Should Be Taught?

During this early period of research on comprehension instruction, researchers identified what a comprehension strategy is, how many strategies students need to comprehension well, and at what developmental and/or age level a particular strategy should be taught.

Regarding the nature of comprehension strategies, there were efforts to distinguish conceptually between "skills" and "strategies." For instance, Duffy and Roehler (1987) emphasized that whereas skills are procedures applied in the same way every time without conscious thought, strategies are reasoned plans that are applied consciously and adapted to the particular situation. For instance, recognition of sight words is a skill that is learned to automaticity, but comprehension strategies, such as predicting, cannot be done thoughtlessly, because different texts and different reader purposes call for different kinds of background knowledge and must be applied situationally.

Regarding how many strategies to teach, the list of necessary strategies has become shorter in recent years. For instance, from 1987 to 1997, commercial reading materials recommended that as many as 45 different comprehension strategies be taught in a single year (Dewitz, Jones, & Leahy, 2006; Pressley, 1993; Pressley, Johnson, Symons, McGoldrick, & Kurita, 1989). These strategies, listed on the left side of Table 2.l, are still contained in some core reading programs today. More recently, however, the trend has been to teach fewer, rather than more, comprehension strategies in a year, and to teach them thoroughly.

In summary, the research initiated in the 1970s and 1980s by the Center for the Study of Reading, and continued by others, established that comprehension is a strategic process; that is, good readers proactively search for meaning as they read, using text cues and their background knowledge in combination to generate predictions, to monitor those predictions, to repredict when necessary, and generally to construct a representation of the author's meaning. To date, this strategic process has usually been described in terms of individual comprehension strategies, and the focus of instruction has usually been on teaching individual strategies.

Research on the Effect of Directly Teaching Comprehension Strategies

The earliest research on comprehension instruction focused on techniques teachers could use to encourage children to approach text in ways that promoted comprehension. Four early models were of particular importance. The first, called the "experience–text–relationship method," emphasized tying experience background and text cues together to construct meaning (Au, 1979). A second model was called "K-W-L" (for "what you Know already," "what you Want to know," and what you Learned from your reading"), and focused readers on the active thinking required to comprehend (Ogle, 1986). In a third, called "reciprocal teaching," teacher and students queried each other around four specific strategies (predicting, questioning, clarifying, and summarizing; Palincsar & Brown, 1984). In a fourth model, QAR (question–answer relationships), readers were taught to assess whether an author provides information explicitly, or whether the reader will have to infer or go beyond what the author provides (Raphael & Wonnacott, 1985).

Research established that such early instructional techniques were effective. However, because these techniques did not provide students with explicit explanations about how to think their way through text, there was a movement in the 1980s and early 1990s to study the benefits of teaching comprehension strategies more directly. This effort emphasized putting readers in control of how to reason by providing clear and unambivalent information about how strategies work. Subsequently, several studies established that struggling readers particularly benefit from explicit explanations of how to think with strategies, with subjects showing growth in both achievement and metacognitive awareness of what they are doing when comprehending (see e.g., Dewitz, Carr, & Patberg, 1987; Dole, Brown, & Trathen, 1996; Duffy et al., 1987; Pressley et al., 1992).

TABLE 2.1. Recommended Comprehension Strategies to be Taught—Past and Present

Strategies proposed from 1978 through 2000	Strategies that have been researched and validated to be highly successful since 2000
1. Setting a purpose 2. Interpreting text structures 3. Being alert to main ideas 4. Knowing the most important ideas attached to author's goal 5. Relating what one reads to prior knowledge 6. Asking questions 7. Drawing conclusions 8. Changing the hypothesis 9. Adding to themes as the meaning of a text unfolds 10. Predicting 11. Creating mental imagery 12. Making conscious images that relate to what is read in a text and using one's own and the prior knowledge presented in that text 13. Identifying the gist 14. Learning to choose which strategy would be helpful 15. Interpreting author's intentions 16. Paraphrasing 17. Pausing to reflect 18. Interpreting and generating insights using fix-up strategies 19. Monitoring while reading 20. Rereading when something isn't clear 21. Evaluating the text as to how well or how poorly it is written 22. Noting whether one should recommend a text to others 23. Consciously constructing a summary 24. Self-regulating one's own comprehension 25. Internalizing text 26. Corroborating text 27. Contextualizing text 28. Being retrospective about text 29. Actively listening 30. Using mnemonics 31. Organizing text 32. Independently engaging one's own metacognition 33. Using study skills while reading 34. Reorganizing text 35. Completing content analyses 36.–42. Using and being aware of the seven parts of story grammar as aids to comprehending 43. Constructing self-explanations 44. Elaborating on one's understanding 45. Clarifying meanings	1. Predict—Size up a text in advance by looking at titles, text features, sections, pictures, and captions, continuously updating and repredicting what will occur next in a text. 2. Monitor—Activate many comprehension strategies to decode and derive meaning from words, phrases, sentences, and texts. 3. Question—Stop to reread and initiate comprehension processes when the meaning is unclear. 4. Image—Construct meanings expressed in text by wondering, noticing, and generating mental pictures. 5. Look-backs, rereads, and fix-it strategies—Continue to reflect on the text before, during, and after reading, continuously deciding how to shape the knowledge base for personal use. 6. Infer—Connect ideas in text based on personal experiences, knowledge of other texts, and general world knowledge, making certain that inferences are made quickly so as not to divert attention from the actual text but to help the reader better understand it. 7. Find main ideas, summarize, and draw conclusions—Make sure to include information gained from story grammar or textual features; if students can't make a valid summary of information read to date, this is the signal to go back to reread. 8. Evaluate—Approach a fictional text expecting to (and making certain that students do) note the setting, characters, and story grammar early on, with problems, solutions, and resolutions to occur thereafter. 9. Synthesize—Approach an informational text watching for textual features, accessing features, unique types of information, sequence of details and conclusions, and combining all of these to make meaning.

Still other studies established that such direct teaching is effective at various grade levels. For instance, such methods produced highly significant gains in students' achievement by grade 2 (Brown, Pressley, Van Meter, & Schuder, 1996), grades 2–8 (Block, 1993, 1999; Collins, 1991), and grades 6–8 (Anderson, 1992; Anderson & Roit, 1993).

In summary, such studies established that without explicit teacher explanation and intensive scaffolded assistance, many struggling readers fail to comprehend (Duffy, et al., 1987; Pressley, Johnson, et al., 1989; Pressley, Symons, et al., 1989). Comprehension becomes such a challenge for struggling readers that they avoid it, and a downward spiral results.

How Teachers Learn to Teach Comprehension Strategies

Pioneering investigations determined that highly effective teachers monitored their students' understanding, and were " 'reactive-corrective' (i.e., they could observe and redirect pupils who failed to comprehend a text)" (Duffy & McIntyre, 1982, p. 17). However, without professional development, teachers had difficulty implementing explicit comprehension explanations. Even as late as 1999, many educators reported that they did not know how to provide effective comprehension instruction; others believed that students could learn how to comprehend merely by reading a lot (Block & Pressley, 2007).

New professional development programs resulted. For instance, Duffy et al. (1986) examined how to help teachers learn to explain comprehension strategies effectively, teach comprehension, and know when initial instructional lessons did not help students apply comprehension strategies independently. These and other, similar studies used various formats. Some sessions lasted 2 hours, whereas others were conducted 8 hours a day for 6 days, or continued once a month for 4–9 months (e.g., Collins, 1991; Duffy, 1993). Data from these efforts suggested that it took at least 4 months of professional development before teachers' explicit comprehension strategy instruction resulted in significant growth for less able readers (see summaries of research in Collins, 1991; Duffy, 1993; Pressley, 1993). Duffy and Hoffman (1999) concluded that teachers need to be educated to

> "know that good teaching requires doing the right thing in the right way at the right time in response to problems posed by particular people in particular places on particular occasions" (Garrison, 1997, p. 271). No two situations are exactly the same; no two days are the same. Practices that work one day may not work the next; [comprehension] methods that worked on Tuesday with John may not work later the same day with Mary. So, rather than chaining themselves to a particular method or program for all kids, [they] are collectors of methods. They impose harmony on inherently uncertain and ambitious classroom environments by cutting across philosophical lines, combining methodological techniques, and adapting programs and materials to particular needs of students (p. 11).

MORE RECENT RESEARCH FINDINGS ABOUT COMPREHENSION INSTRUCTION

The most recent comprehension research has resulted in increased sophistication and understanding regarding how to teach comprehension. As in the previous section, these understandings are discussed in terms of what has been learned about comprehension strategies, about direct teaching of those strategies, and about how to develop educators' abilities to teach comprehension.

What We Have Recently Learned about Comprehension Strategies

As noted earlier, the trend has been to teach fewer, rather than more, comprehension strategies, because contemporary core reading programs that tend to teach many strategies have been found to interfere with students' ability to comprehend independently (Afflerbach & Walker, 1992; Dewitz et al., 2006; Franks, Mulhern, & Schillinger, 1997; Hoffman et al., 1998; Jitendra, Chard, Hoppes, Renouf, & Gardill, 2001). For instance:

1. Core reading programs promote instruction of more skills and strategies than can be substantiated by empirical evidence (i.e., if present basal manuals were followed explicitly, 18–45 comprehension skills would be taught every year in the curriculum). Research does not support this practice (Afflerbach & Walker, 1992).
2. The same comprehension strategy is identified by two to three different names in a single core program, which confuses students (Dewitz et al., 2006; Schmitt & Hopkins, 1993).
3. Core reading programs limit the amount of comprehension growth that is possible for less able readers (Block, Parris, Reed, Whitley, & Cleveland, in press).

Results from the last 10 years of research demonstrate that only the nine strategies listed in the right column of Table 2.1 have the scientific-basis to be considered essential comprehension strategies. The National Reading Panel (2000) found that the first five on the list to have a strong enough scientific basis for inclusion as part of the comprehension curriculum; the last four were later proven to improve comprehension, after the report of that panel was completed (for summary of this research, see Block & Pressley, 2007).

In summary, the trend regarding strategies is toward teaching fewer, rather than more. Further, there has also been recent emphasis on the importance of combining strategies together. For instance, researchers such as Pearson (2006), Palincsar (2006), and Cummings, Stewart, and Block (2005) have found that teaching multiple strategies to young readers every day for 1 month or more can increase their comprehension of nonfiction. These findings continue to move us away from teaching isolated individual strategies, while also helping to unlock the mysteries about how much mass or distributed practice is needed, and at what age comprehension instruction can most effectively begin.

What We Have Recently Learned about Direct Teaching of Comprehension

The major new finding about direct teaching of comprehension is that it is a much more complex process than was thought at first. Although it involves clearly describing the mental processes needed to comprehend, so that students develop a sense for how to attempt these processes on their own as they read, it is not simply a matter of being explicit in rigid or procedural ways. As with the insights about comprehension strategies noted earlier, much of our understanding in this regard is a result of studies of core reading materials. For instance:

1. Eighty percent of basal readers do not include elements that characterize highly effective comprehension instruction. Instead, such programs often (a) teach only one strategy per week; (b) *do not* provide directions on how to review and gradually release responsibility to students (Pearson & Gallagher, 1983); (c) *do not* encourage students to

practice and apply comprehension strategies independently; and (d) *do not* provide multistrategy instruction with various levels of teacher support to enhance students' transfer of comprehension processes to new texts (Block & Pressley, 2007).

2. Comprehension instruction looks the same from lesson to lesson, and from the first to the last lesson in a program. There is no acknowledgment of (a) growth in readers' expertise; (b) strategies becoming more automatic as readers become more metacognitive; and (c) the need for a transition from using a comprehension strategy first with a simple text, then with a more difficult one.

3. Strategy lessons do not move steadily from teachers' explicit instruction to students' implicit demonstration of a comprehension strategy, even though such models are available (Duffy, 2003).

4. Guided practice is limited, and students have limited opportunity to demonstrate that they are using comprehension strategies independently.

As a result of these kinds of reports, we now think about the direct teaching of comprehension in terms of understanding (1) the classroom environment in which instruction occurs, (2) the complexity of explanations; and (3) the scaffolded nature of instruction.

Understandings about the Classroom Environment

Explicit comprehension instruction occurs in richly contextualized instructional settings (Block et al., in press). Consider, for instance, an expository text lesson. First, students set important, personally relevant themes and choose books they can comprehend or that they are helped to read and to discuss. Second, students read two expository texts on the same topic back-to-back, before they choose to read about another topic. Prior to reading, students are taught how to skim and scan, stop and savor, build content-specific vocabulary, and respond to nonfiction. Last, when students read books of choice silently, they signal as soon as they become confused, and the teacher provides personalized minilessons. Before the end of such silent reading periods, the teacher returns to ask what students would do in the future when facing again the particular challenge they faced that day (Block, 2004; Block et al., in press). In short, a rich learning environment is essential.

To meet No Child Left Behind accountability standards, many schools are adding 20 minutes a day to their literacy programs. However, we still need data to determine which learning environment(s) produce the largest comprehension gains during this additional time (Block, 2006; Braunger & Lewis, 1997; Wade, 2004). We found only one study that analyzed the effects on students' comprehension abilities of adding 20 minutes to the following six most common contemporary learning environments (Block et al., in press): (1) traditional (basal readers), (2) mastery (workbooks), (3) schema-based (silent free voluntary reading [FVR] of a book with teacher monitoring), (4) explicit instruction (silent FVR with explicit teacher instruction), (5) conceptual (silent back-to-back reading of two student-selected, nonfiction books on the same subject), and (6) transactional (silent reading followed by discussion; Chall & Squire, 1999).

Results suggest that different types of learning environments lead to growth in certain types of comprehension abilities for certain types of children, and that comprehension strategy instruction is developmentally sensitive (see also Parris & Block, 2007; Cummings, Stewart, & Block, 2005). Generally, when struggling readers received 20 minutes of instruction in a rich learning environment, their literacy growth was equal to or greater than that of their peers. Furthermore, use of trade, or "little," books produced significantly higher comprehension scores than workbooks or extended basal text treatments. These findings hold true regardless of student's grade-level placement, reading ability level, gender, language spoken at home, or ethnicity (Block et al., in press).

Prior to the previous study, most comprehension instruction was teacher-directed and based on mastery learning theory. No student choice was involved (Hoffman et al., 1998). Based on the data in the previous study, however, the most successful comprehension situations shared three features: (1) allowing student choice of books to be read for guided independent reading practice, (2) reading more than 7 pages of continuous text from fiction–nonfiction trade or "little" books, and (3) 20 minutes of silent reading combined with specific teacher actions. These teacher actions are as follows:

1. Teacher-monitored silent reading periods with direct, explicit scaffolds to assist students to overcome comprehension challenges encountered in individual texts (schema-based learning).
2. Teacher-monitored selection of nonfiction texts, requiring (and making available) two expository books on the same topic, so that students can choose to read both before being allowed to read about another nonfiction topic (conceptual learning).
3. Teacher-provided books from which students may make choices that relate to one aspect of a global class theme.
4. Five minutes of the 20-minute silent reading period spent in an open-ended discussion about insights that students gleaned from reading their selected books (transactional learning).

Additionally, treatments that produced significantly more achievement for less able readers worked equally well for more able readers. Thus, the practice of emphasizing traditional instruction or mastery learning (workbook) exercises needs to be reexamined, because both resulted in the lowest achievement growth.

Another major finding from this study is that selection of teacher actions during guided/independent practice sessions can be similar for all reading levels. Rather than planning different learning environments for different reading levels, environments should change based on what teachers want their students to master. To illustrate, if the goal of instruction is to increase students' ability to retell what they read, then the reading of student-selected books with 5 minutes of thematic discussion is the best 20-minute method for 2nd, 3rd, 4th, and 6th graders at all ability levels. If the objective is for students to learn how better to identify main ideas, the best learning environment is conceptual learning with expository text.

Last, prior to this study, it was theorized that the cause for low literacy achievement was an inadequate number of high-quality fiction and nonfiction trade books in the classroom, and students' limited choices and time to read them (Block & Pressley, 2003; Duke, 2000). If these were the major causes, all treatments that used 200 books per class should have outperformed all non-book-based treatments. This was not the case. Although comprehension abilities increased when students read books rather than workbooks or basal readers silently for independent practice, the highest gains occurred when these reading periods included more than seven pages of text read in student-guided selection of books, and use of the direct teaching actions cited previously.

Understandings about the Complexity of Explanations

The heart of explanation is the modeling provided by the teacher. Duffy (2003) describes such modeling as "think-alouds" and suggests that these include the following steps: (1)

knowing what strategy is needed and the secret to doing the strategy successfully; (2) modeling the thinking, (3) scaffolding from extensive help to no teacher help, (4) assessing a lesson's success, (5) adapting instruction to other situations, and (6) applying the comprehension instruction to students' writing. Keene and Zimmerman (2007) and Block and Israel (2004) describe think-alouds in slightly different ways.

Although virtually all children profit from explicit think-alouds about some aspects of reading comprehension at one time or another, we have learned several things about the nature of such explanation. First, powerful explanations cannot be scripted. Teachers must have the professional expertise to modify their explanations from moment to moment based on student responses (Block & Pressley, 2007; Duffy, 2003). Second, we have learned that teachers must be "relentless." When an explanation does not work the first time, teachers must adjust it and try again. Teachers cannot give up on students. They must give students "multiple opportunities to use what they've learned while in the pursuit of real reading" (Duffy, 2003, p. 13). One technique to accomplish this is fast mapping (Block et al., in press). Fast mapping provides six consecutive instructional experiences in which students generate the use of one comprehension strategy without teacher prompting as they read. Data suggest that fast mapping for some less able readers may need to extend for as many as 10 consecutive, self-initiated applications of a strategy to text before students move on to learn another comprehension strategy.

To illustrate how much more complex comprehension strategy instruction has become over the last 20 years, consider how finding the main idea was taught prior to 1998 (Afflerbach & Walker, 1992; Dewitz et al., 2006; Jitendra et al., 2001; Miller & Blumenthal, 1993) and how it is recommended that it be taught today. From 1980 to 1997, basal texts informed students that a main idea was the theme or most important point in a passage or paragraph, and teachers settled for requiring student memorization of every strategy's definition (e.g., teachers asked and answered their own questions: "What is the main idea? The main idea is the most important point that the author is making. Repeat after me" (Duffy & McIntyre, 1982, p. 18). If students did not know what a main idea was, teachers were not told what to do or how to give students the appropriate reteaching experiences so that they could learn this skill. By contrast, a main idea lesson today may often contain explicit explanation of the mental processing involved, reteaching this thinking procedure as needed, assessing it repeatedly for individual students, and applying main idea thinking to reading and writing with a wide variety of fictional and nonfictional texts (Block, 2004; Block, Rodgers, & Johnson, 2004; Duffy, 2003).

Understandings about the Nature of Scaffolding

"Scaffolding" is the gradual movement from teacher control of an explanation of how to do a strategy to students' control of the strategy as they apply it independently. Researchers have experimented with various forms of scaffolding to help students (1) adjust their depth and breadth of knowledge, (2) consciously and independently use more than one strategy as they read a text, and (3) comprehend literally, inferentially, and applicably (e.g., how to set a purpose for reading, think metacognitively, use fix-up strategies, and continuously self-monitor; see reviews of these studies in Block, 2004; Block, Schaller, Joy, & Gaines, 2002).

Other researchers examined how teachers scaffolded (Vygotsky, 1978) from an introductory skills presentation through a moderate level of teacher support, to the point that no teacher comprehension support was needed. Methods associated with a variety of instructional approaches provide personalized support for individual students at the exact time when comprehension is interrupted (Block & Dellamura, 2001/2002). Regardless of the approach, it is essential for students to be held accountable for (1) comprehension during silent reading, (2) knowing when and why they became confused (Zeckler, Pappas, & Cohen, 1998), and (3) identifying comprehension processes they need and want to learn (Block & Mangieri, 2003).

Summary

In summary, we are learning that direct teaching of comprehension is a sophisticated endeavor. Although sample lessons and explicit examples are available to illustrate a gradual release model of direct explanation (see e.g., Block, Gambrell, et al., 2002; Block & Mangieri, 1996–1997; Duffy, 1993, 2003), teacher thought and adaptation are crucial.

We now understand that direct teaching of comprehension must also include a reduction in the amount of teacher-dominated talk in the classroom, and an increase in the use of authentic tasks with real-world situations and full texts. Data also suggests that comprehension instruction should not be too prescriptive. When instruction is too teacher dominated, students do not learn how to apply the strategies. Nor should instruction be too free flowing. When instruction is too sparse or unmonitored, pupils do not develop the tools necessary to comprehend independently. Also, students who do not need rich, elaborate explanation of strategy use should be exempt, and instruction should be provided only when students are struggling to learn a particular comprehension process (Dewitz et al., 2006; Duffy, 2003).

What We Have Recently Learned about How Teachers Learn to Teach Comprehension

Several crucial characteristics explain effective comprehension instruction (Block & Mangieri, 2003; Duffy, 2003; Parris & Block, 2007): (1) thoughtful, adaptive, and responsive teachers; (2) reteaching; (3) the depth of comprehension lessons; (4) the quality of learning environments; and (5) how teachers relate to and motivate students. These characteristics add complexity to comprehension instruction and, in turn, make professional development more complex.

Many studies conducted during the 1990s to determine how to improve teachers' instruction of comprehension (e.g., Block, Oakar & Hurt, 2002; Duffy, 1993, 2003; Parris & Block, 2007; Pressley, Allington, Wharton-McDonald, Block, & Morrow, 2001) indicated that teachers progress in distinct stages in learning to teach comprehension. Teachers begin in a state of either confusion or rejection before they take conscious control, often teaching strategies by naming them and telling students why they are important. Eventually, they hit a pivotal point in which they either learn to model the strategies, integrate the process of using comprehension strategies and text content together, and view strategies as being useful in "specific ways and [as] a means to an end rather than the end in themselves," or they hit "the wall" (Duffy, 1993, p. 116). Ultimately, some teachers reach a creative, innovative stage in which they are confident and guilt free, and can articulate a clear conceptual understanding of why strategies are important and how to teach them. Striving to achieve that latter stage is where we are in the field of professional development today.

In summary, we now understand that teaching teachers to teach comprehension is much more difficult than we anticipated. It requires much time and effort, and it must be collaborative, gradual, and sensitive to the changing contextual conditions from classroom to classroom.

HOW THIS NEW KNOWLEDGE
CAN IMPROVE COMPREHENSION INSTRUCTION

Collapsing new research, we can begin to think more definitively about how comprehension instruction should occur in classrooms today.

What Strategies to Teach

Listed in the right column of Table 2.1 are the strategies typically recommended today. However, as noted earlier, as we learn more about how comprehension works, we become more aware (1) that comprehension is more a matter of being strategic than of knowing individual strategies, and (2) that learning to be strategic is not a matter of progressing through a scope and sequence as we do with decoding.

First, the awareness that comprehension is more a matter of being strategic than of learning individual strategies is reflected in the shrinking list of strategies. Whereas we used to think there were dozens of comprehension strategies, we see that more current programs list only a few, because of a growing realization that comprehension is mainly a fluid process of predicting, monitoring, and repredicting in a continuous cycle. This strategic process is basically what good readers do for all strategies. For instance, imagery is really a matter of using text cues in combination with background knowledge to predict the image that the author wants the reader to see, with the reader modifying that image as subsequent monitoring reveals new text cues requiring new predictions about that image. Similarly, finding the main idea is primarily a matter of using cues the author provides in the text to predict what is most important, with the reader modifying that idea as subsequent monitoring reveals new text cues requiring new predictions about what is most important.

Second, comprehension strategies cannot be described as a scope and sequence in the way we think about decoding skills, because the fluid cycle of predicting–monitoring–repredicting is the same at all grade levels. Consider a kindergartner listening to a teacher read a story about whales. To comprehend, the listener must predict, monitor, and repredict. Comprehension will not occur if the child only knows how to predict, or only knows how to monitor. The entire strategic process must be in place for comprehension to occur. When the student moves to first grade and begins reading, comprehension is still a process of predicting, monitoring and repredicting. When the student moves on to the upper grades and begins reading more complex expository and narrative material, the process is still one of predicting, monitoring and repredicting. What changes from grade to grade is not the strategies to be taught but the text in which strategies are applied. It is true that comprehension gets progressively more difficult from grade to grade, but it is because the texts become more and more complex, requiring the predicting–monitoring–repredicting cycle to be applied in more sophisticated ways involving more information, more words, more sentences, and more paragraphs. This means that we do not teach one strategy at one time and delay other strategies until a later grade. Instead, we teach the entire comprehension process at each grade level.

Teaching Comprehension Directly

Although teachers are explaining comprehension strategies better today than in the past, they often still teach these strategies in isolation and do not follow the empirically based principles reported earlier in this chapter (Durkin, 1981; Thomas & Barksdale-Ladd, 2000; Wharton, Pressley, & Hampton, 1998). Too many teachers do not state the objective of a comprehension strategy lesson, and write new words and comprehension steps on the board as they teach, so that students can use both verbal and nonverbal input systems, and they do not tell students frequently enough when, why, how, or where to use comprehension strategies. Moreover, when a child gives an incorrect answer, too many teachers either call on another student or merely tell the first student the correct answer themselves, without providing an explanation that helps the child overcome the problem leading to the incorrect answer (Duffy, 2003; Duffy & Roehler, 1987; Duffy et al., 1986).

As recently as last year, there was debate about whether we should directly teach comprehension strategies (Keene & Zimmerman, 2007). Research does substantiate the fact that some students can learn strategies without direct teaching. However, explicit instruction has been demonstrated to increase comprehension for struggling readers. Similarly, as late as 2002, scientists were unclear as to whether students below grades 7 and 8 were metacognitively advanced enough to gain value from multiple strategy instruction (e.g., Israel & Duffy, 2008; Osborn, 1984; Rich & Pressley, 2006), but we now know that multiple strategies can be learned in this lesson sequence by students as young as age 5 (Block, Cummings, & Stewart, under review; Block et al., in press; Roehler & Duffy, 1981).

Consequently, there is little question about the validity of direct teaching of comprehension. However, as noted earlier, delivering direct explanations is a complex process and there are cautions to be observed.

A major caution is that students must first have in place solid conceptual understandings that relate to conditional knowledge—the why and when issues of comprehension (i.e., why are we learning to comprehend? When will it be useful to us? Why should we expend energy on learning to do this?). In short, instruction in comprehension strategies is most effective when students are given authentic reasons for reading in the first place—that is, when they can see that the comprehension strategies they are learning serve a purpose that is important to them, or make it possible for them to achieve an important goal. In summary, teaching comprehension strategies simply to have students learn comprehension strategies is seldom effective.

How We Should Assess

Much research has occurred and much data are still needed to improve the assessment of comprehension strategy instruction. Many newly created instruments that have been, or are being, empirically tested appear in this text and in Israel, Block, Bauserman, and Kinnucan-Welsh (2005).

DIRECTIONS FOR FUTURE RESEARCH

While great progress has been made since the early days, comprehension research is still a relatively young area of study. After all, it was only 37 years ago that the Center for the Study of Reading at the University of Illinois initiated its first studies of comprehension. It is not surprising, therefore, that there is more to be learned. We list some suggested areas below in the same three categories we have used throughout: research on strategies, research on direct teaching, and research on professional development.

Research on Strategies

In the area of strategies, how can we help readers learn how to reassemble separate comprehension strategy instruction into a process that is a coherent, self-initiated whole, under their automatic, independent control? For example, theoretically, story grammar should be taught as a whole process, through fast mapping with six consecutive stories using explanation, modeling, and guided practice. This initial instruction should be followed by six sessions of independent practice, monitored silent reading, and/or written stories. Students should select their best stories and read them in groups of two to six to better assess their knowledge of story grammar by finding it in these writings.

Similarly, how can we encourage teachers to initiate multiple strategies and engage students in using them without teacher prompting at points of need in a text? To do so, we must develop more research methods to teach and assess metacognition (Block, 2005). Presently, nothing in any core program acknowledges the growing expertise of the reader (Dewitz et al., 2006). We need more reciprocal dialogues and transactional strategy lessons in which teachers learn how to lead guided practice toward independent practice transfers. Teachers need more methods in learning how to lead the independent practice of comprehension strategy–process instruction (e.g., PAR: *p*raise, *a*ssist, *r*aise; Block, 2004). Of the time teachers spent in teacher manuals, 18% was focused on independent practice in 1979; it was 10% or less in 2006.

Research on Direct Teaching

In the area of how best to teach comprehension, several things must be considered. What are the most effective methods by which we can teach, model, scaffold, and help students independently apply comprehension strategies to texts? When students, as strategic readers, use more than one strategy, these strategies must unite to become a single comprehension process. This process becomes a fluid ebb and flow of intense and relaxed motivation, focus, and thinking, depending on which strategies and texts are used. We have not yet developed enough methods to make this happen easily for teachers and students in millions of diverse classrooms around the world.

Similarly, what are effective methods by which teachers can transfer responsibility for applying comprehension strategies to students? We need to find better ways to enable students to pass from modeling to guided practice to independent practice. Currently, we usually give an explanation and students then move to independent practice or answering questions. As a part of a new research agenda, we must find ways to keep instruction from looking the same from Lesson 1 to Lesson 6, and instead transfer more and more responsibility for applying strategies to students (e.g., "Here is where you begin, here is what you will notice about your thinking, and here is where you can go in your thinking when you are an expert and have maximum comprehension"). We can vary the density/depth of instruction with each subsequent lesson. We must build more fast mapping into comprehension instruction.

Also, how much mass or distributed practice is best? How can we teach multiple comprehension strategies effectively in a varied and balanced literacy program? How can we better teach students to think metacognitively? How can we develop a more compelling research agenda to ensure that cognitive strategy instruction and direct explicit instruction are components in all K–12 classrooms? What order and chronology are best for teaching comprehension strategies? Should we build on skills that are taught in earlier grades or teach new ones at each new grade level; should we teach a comprehension skill as is needed for a particular text, or should we teach the strategies individual students need, regardless of how "below level" that strategy might be? Because students cannot articulate their thinking about use of higher level strategy use, how can we better measure this ability? Which is better, teaching one strategy over and over in an integrated fashion or teaching separate strategies? Or, as we argue in this chapter, should our question begin to turn away from which strategy to teach when, and focus instead on how to communicate better the complex comprehension process of predicting–monitoring–repredicting across various grade levels and content areas. How can we build better discussion groups, such as Keene and Zimmerman's (2007) invitational groups, or Block and Pressley's (2007) teacher–reader groups?

Research on Professional Development

In the area of professional development, how can we improve teacher education? Teachers explain comprehension more often than they did 30 years ago, but their explanations are not effective enough for all students to reach independent transfer to real reading. Similar to Durkin's 1978–1979 study, asking questions continues to be the dominant practice after a reading. Consequently, we need to improve how we help educators teach all students new, strategic ways of comprehending.

Of primary importance in this area is the need to approach professional development from the perspective of developing professional thinkers as opposed to developing technicians who follow procedures. We know from past studies that effective teaching of comprehension is not tied to any particular method. In fact, different methods work with different students. Consequently, a central issue in effective development of teachers of comprehension is how to focus on developing thinkers rather than on developing a particular method.

PROJECTIONS AND POSSIBILITIES FOR THE CLASSROOM OF 2030

Presently, most struggling readers spend most of their time merely answering teachers' comprehension questions or having stories read to them. For instance, in 2000, the majority of less able kindergarten, grade l, and grade 2 readers spent 70% of their time performing non-reading-related tasks during literacy instructional time. These tasks included cutting and pasting objects from worksheets that were even unrelated to the stories read by their teachers (Block, Schaller, Joy, & Gaines, 2002; Pressley, Allington, Wharton-McDonald, Block, & Morrow, 2001).

By 2030, we want to have moved what we know about comprehension strategy instruction to the larger world—"into many more classrooms and schools, with sophisticated comprehension processing applied to many more types of text by many more learners, and with strategies becoming habits of mind for young readers, teachers of readers, and lifetime readers who both explore new text and return again and again to their favorites" (Pressley et al., 2001, p. 393).

By 2030, we want to have learned how to help students engage in an ongoing, continuous pursuit of meaning, from before they begin, throughout the reading of the entire text, and with the ability to apply it to their lives several years later. Comprehension processes may not be adequately categorized as being useful before, during, and after reading. In this chapter, we wanted to demonstrate how several strategies can be used throughout the ebb and flow of an entire reading experience. Such usage begins before children's eyes reach a printed or computerized text and last for several years after a student comprehends a text. These processes are categorized as knowing (1) what is necessary to understand a word, sentence, paragraph, and complete text; and (2) what is needed to apply the text. Such instruction will occur through rich, explicit 7- to 8-page lessons, in which teachers are masters at delivering how, when, and where to use comprehension strategies, and in which students apply them independently.

By 2030, we will walk into classrooms in which students are selecting the comprehension instruction they need. We want to see more self-initiated student use of comprehension strategies in student-led groups (independently and in pairs). We want to have achieved the goal set in 1981, and move the field of comprehension instruction to its highest level of success, infusing more neuroscientific-based and metacognitive-proven lessons into our classrooms.

Last, in 2030, curricula will have incorporated the research reported in this chapter. When this occurs, no teacher ever again will say,

> My school district requires that the basal be covered in a strict schedule and that the test scores be recorded in the office on a strict schedule. Some of my kids know how to pass the test but they aren't good readers. I know I want to teach them how to improve their reading, but I can't because I have to maintain the coverage schedule. [This quotation could have been made today, unfortunately, because this condition exists in many classrooms across the country (Block & Pressley, 2007). However, this statement was made 20 years ago by a second grade teacher in Michigan who was involved in the research, as cited by Duffy and Roehler (1987, p. 414)].

We hope that the next 22 years moves practice forward more vibrantly and expansively than we have to date.

SUMMARY

In this chapter, we have provided an overview of past and recent research on what has been learned about comprehension strategies, direct teaching of comprehension, and how to teach teachers to teach comprehension. We have indicated several ways that this research has pointed toward more effective instruction in today's schools—methods by which more students may learn how to comprehend between now and 2030. Overall, it is our hope that the mission established in 1981 by the Center for the Study of Reading—for all children to comprehend and to love to read—can become a reality soon.

INTEGRATE, INVESTIGATE, AND INITIATE: QUESTIONS FOR DISCUSSION

1. Select one or more comprehension strategies from the right column of Table 2.1. Develop a lesson plan or professional development activity that would increase students' or teachers' abilities to use that strategy as they read or teach, respectively. Employ the think-aloud methods described in this chapter. Also, demonstrate for students how to predict, monitor, and repredict as a continuous comprehension process, using the clues available in books written at their grade levels. If possible, implement the plan or activity you designed. Where were the effects? Share your results with colleagues.

2. Why do teacher–reader and other small-group discussion procedures apply more comprehension strategies than do whole-class discussions of books read?

3. Write a description of the most effective and the least effective comprehension professional development session that you have led or attended. What made the first one so effective for you? What made the second one less effective for you? Compare and contrast your description

with the experiences of other colleagues and with the information you learned from this chapter. What have you learned that will improve your future abilities to grow as either a leader or participant in comprehension professional development sessions. How can you work to increase what you and others in the group learn?

REFERENCES

Afflerbach, P., & Walker, B. (1992). Main idea instruction: An analysis of three basal reader series. *Reading Research and Instruction, 32,* 11–28.

Anderson, R. C. (1981). *Technical report submitted for funding to the National Institute of Education.* Urbana, IL: Center for the Study of Reading, University of Illinois.

Anderson, V. (1992). A teacher development project in transactional strategy instruction for teachers of severely reading-disabled adolescents. *Teaching and Teacher Education, 8,* 391–403.

Anderson, V., & Roit, N. (1993). Planning and implementing collaborative strategy instruction for delayed readers in grades 6–10. *Elementary School Journal, 94,* 121–137.

Au, K. (1979). Using the experience–text–relationship method with minority children. *Reading Teacher, 32,* 677–679.

Block, C. C. (2006, December). *Discussion of "The research base of comprehension instruction in five basal reading programs" by Peter Dewitx, Jennifer Jones, and Susie Leahy.* Paper presented at the National Reading Conference, Los Angeles, CA.

Block, C. C. (2005). What are metacognitive assessments? In S. E. Israel, C. C. Block, K. L. Bauserman, & K. Kinnucan-Welsh (Eds.), *Metacognition in literacy learning* (pp. 83–100). Mahwah, NJ: Erlbaum.

Block, C. C. (2004). *Teaching comprehension.* Boston: Allyn & Bacon.

Block, C. C. (1993). Strategy instruction in a literature-based program. *Elementary School Journal, 94*(3), 121–132.

Block, C. C. (1999). Comprehension: Crafting understanding. In L. Gambrell, L. Morrow, S. Neuman, & M. Pressley (Eds.), *Best practices in literacy instruction* (pp. 98–118). New York: Guilford Press.

Block, C. C., Cummins, C., & Stewart, M. S. (under review). *Internalization and transfer of comprehension strategies in K–5.*

Block, C. C., & Dellamura, R. Y. (2001/2002). Better book buddies. *Reading Teacher, 54*(4), 364–370.

Block, C. C., Gambrell, L., & Pressley, M. (Eds.). (2002). *Improving comprehension instruction: Rethinking research, theory, and classroom practice.* San Francisco: Jossey-Bass.

Block, C. C., & Israel, S. E. (2004). The ABCs of performing highly effective think alouds. *Reading Teacher, 58*(2), 154–167.

Block, C. C., & Mangieri, J. (1996–1997). *Reason to read: Teaching thinking strategies through literature* (Vols. 1–3). Boston: Pearson.

Block, C. C., & Mangieri, J. (2003). *Exemplary literacy teachers: Promoting success for all children in grades K–5.* New York: Guilford Press.

Block, C. C., Oakar, M., & Hurt, N. (2002). The expertise of literacy teachers: A continuum from preschool to grade 5. *Reading Research Quarterly, 37*(2), 178–208.

Block, C. C., Parris, S., Reed, K. L., Whitley, C. S., & Cleveland, M. (in press). Learning environments that significantly increase reading comprehension. *Journal of Educational Psychology.*

Block, C. C., & Pressley, M. (Eds.). (2002). *Comprehension instruction: Research-based best practices.* New York: Guilford Press.

Block, C. C., & Pressley, M. (2003). Best practices in comprehension instruction. In L. M. Morrow, L. B. Gambrell, & M. Pressley (Eds.), *Best practices in literacy instruction* (pp. 111–126). New York: Guilford Press.

Block, C. C., & Pressley, M. (2007). *Best practices in teaching comprehension.* In L. B. Gambrell,

L. N. Morrow, & M. Pressley (Eds.), *Best practices in literacy instruction* (3rd ed., pp. 220–242). New York: Guilford Press.

Block, C. C., Rodgers, L., & Johnson, R. (2004). *Comprehension process instruction: Creating reading success in grades K–3*. New York: Guilford Press.

Block, C. C., Schaller, J. L., Joy, J. A., & Gaines, P. (2002). Processed-based comprehension instruction: Perspectives of four reading educators. In C. C. Block & M. Pressley (Eds.), *Comprehension instruction: Research-based best practices* (pp. 42–61). New York: Guilford Press.

Braunger, J., & Lewis, J. P. (1997). *Building a knowledge base in reading*. Newark, DE: International Reading Association.

Brown, R., Pressley, M., Van Meter, P., & Schuder, T. (1996). A quasi-experimental validation of transactional strategies instruction with low-achieving 2nd grade readers. *Journal of Educational Psychology, 88*, 18–37.

Chall, J. S., & Squire, J. R. (1991). The publishing industry and textbooks. In R. Barr, M. L. Kamil, P. Mosenthal, & P. D. Pearson (Eds.), *Handbook of reading research* (Vol. 2, pp. 120–146). White Plains, NY: Longman.

Collins, C. (1991). Reading instruction that increases thinking abilities. *Journal of Reading, 34*, 510–516.

Cummings, C., Stewart, M. T., & Block, C. C. (2005). Teaching several metacognitive strategies together to increase students' independent metacognition. In S. E. Israel, C. C. Block, K. L. Bauserman, & K. Kinnucan-Welsh (Eds.), *Metacognition in literacy learning: Theory, assessment, instruction, and professional development* (pp. 227–296). Mahwah, NJ: Erlbaum.

Dewitz, P., Carr, E., & Patberg, J. (1987). Effects of inference training on comprehension and comprehension monitoring. *Reading Research Quarterly, 22*, 99–121.

Dewitz, P., Jones, J., & Leahy, S. (2006, December). *The research base of comprehension instruction in five basal reading programs*. Paper presented at the Annual Meeting of the National Reading Conference. Los Angeles, CA.

Dole, J., Brown, K., & Trathen, W. (1996). The effects of strategy instruction on the comprehension performance of at-risk students. *Reading Research Quarterly, 26*, 62–89.

Duffy, G. G. (1993). Rethinking strategy instruction: Four teachers' development and their low achievers understandings. *Elementary School Journal, 93*(3), 67–78.

Duffy, G. G. (2003). *Explaining reading: A resource for teaching concepts, skills, and strategies*. New York: Guilford Press.

Duffy, G. G., & Hoffman, J. V. (1999). In pursuit of an illusion: The flawed search for a prefect method. *Reading Teacher, 53*(1), 10–16.

Duffy, G. G., & Israel, S. E. (2008). *Handbook of research in comprehension*. Mahwah, NJ: Erlbaum.

Duffy, G. G., & McIntyre, L. D. (1982). A naturalistic study of instructional assistance in primary-grade reading. *Elementary School Journal, 83*(1), 15–23.

Duffy, G. G., & Roehler, L. R. (1987). Teaching reading skills as strategies. *Reading Teacher, 40*(4), 414–418.

Duffy, G. G, Roehler, L. R., Meloth, M. S., Vavrus, L. G., Book, C., Putnam, J., et al. (1986). The relationship between explicit verbal explanations during reading skill instruction and student awareness and achievement: A study of reading teacher effects. *Reading Research Quarterly, 21*(3), 237–252.

Duffy, G. G., Roehler, L. R., Sivan, E., Rackliffe, G., Book, C., Meloth, M. S., et al. (1987). Effects of explaining the reasoning associated with using reading strategies. *Reading Research Quarterly, 22*(3), 347–368.

Duke, N. K. (2003). 3.6 minutes per day: The scarcity of informational texts in first grade. *Reading Research Quarterly, 35*, 202–224.

Durkin, D. (1978–1979). What research observation reveals about reading comprehension instruction. *Reading Research Quarterly, 14*, 481–533.

Durkin, D. (1981). Reading comprehension instruction in five basal reading series. *Reading Research Quarterly, 14*(4), 515–544.

Franks, B. A., Mulhern, S. L., & Schillinger, S. M. (1997). Reasoning in a reading context: Deductive inferences in basal reading series. *Reading and Writing: An Interdisciplinary Journal, 9,* 285–312.

Garrison, J. (1997). *Dewey and Ros: Wisdom and desire in the art of teaching.* New York: Teachers College Press.

Guthrie, J. (Ed.). (1981). *Comprehension in teaching: Research reviews.* Newark, DE: International Reading Association.

Hoffman, J. V., McCarthey, S. J., Elliott, B., Bayles, D. L., Price, D. P., & Ferree, A., et al. (1998). The literature-based basals in first grade classrooms: Savior, Satan, or same-old, same-old? *Reading Research Quarterly, 33,* 28–44.

Hoyt, L. (Ed.). (2005). *Spotlight on comprehension.* Portsmouth, NH: Heinemann.

Israel, S., & Duffy, G. (Eds.). (2008). *Handbook of research on reading comprehension.* Mahah, NJ: Erlbaum.

Israel, S. E., Block, C. C., Bauserman, K., & Kinnucan-Welsh, K. (Eds.). (2005). *Metacognition in literacy learning: Theory assessment, instruction and professional development.* Mahwah, NJ: Erlbaum.

Jitendra, A. K., Chard, D., Hoppes, M. K., Renouf, K., & Gardill, M. C. (2001). An evaluation of main idea strategy instruction in four commercial reading programs: Implications for students with learning disabilities. *Reading and Writing Quarterly, 17,* 53–73.

Keene, E. O. (2006). *Assessing comprehension thinking strategies.* Sonoma, CA: Shell Educational Publishing.

Keene, E. O., & Zimmermann, S. (1997). *Mosaic of thought: The power of comprehension strategy instruction: First edition.* Portsmouth, NH: Heinemann.

Keene, E. O., & Zimmermann, S. (2007). *Mosaic of thought: The power of comprehension strategy instruction: Second edition.* Portsmouth, NH: Heinemann.

Lauber, P. (1983). *Volcano.* New York: Aladdin.

Lysynchuk, L. M., Pressley, M., d'Ailly, H., Smith, M., & Cake, H. (1989). A methodological analysis of experimental studies of comprehension strategy instruction. *Reading Research Quarterly, 24,* 458–479.

Miller, S. D., & Blumenthal, P. C. (1993). Characteristics of task used for skill instruction in two basal reader series. *Elementary School Journal, 94,* 33–47.

National Endowment for the Arts. (2004). *Reading at risk: A survey of literacy practices in America.* Washington, DC: Author.

National Reading Panel. (2000). *Teaching children to read: An evidence-based assessment of the scientific literature on reading and its implications for reading instruction: Reports of the subgroups.* Bethesda, MD: National Institute of Child Health and Human Development.

Ogle, D. (1986). K-W-L: A teaching model that develops active reading of expository text. *Reading Teacher, 39,* 564–570.

Osborn, J. (1984). *Analysis of comprehension instruction provided by basal readers* (Technical Report No. 107). Urbana, IL: Center for the Study of Reading.

Palincsar, A. (2006, December). *Multiple strategy instruction at work in science classrooms.* Paper presented at the Annual Meeting of the National Reading Conference, Los Angeles, CA.

Palincsar, A., & Brown, A. L. (1984). Reciprocal teaching of comprehension-fostering and comprehension-monitoring activities. *Cognition and Instruction, 1,* 117–175.

Parris, S. R., & Block, C. C. (2007). The expertise of adolescent literacy teachers. *Journal of Adolescent and Adult Literacy, 50*(7), 582–598.

Pearson, P. D. (2006, December). *Strategic embedded vocabulary and comprehensive instruction.* Paper presented at Annual Meeting of the National Reading Conference, Los Angeles, CA.

Pearson, P. D., & Gallagher, M. C. (1983). The instruction of reading comprehension. *Contemporary Educational Psychology, 8,* 317–344.

Pearson, P. D., & Johnson, D. (1978). *Teaching comprehension.* New York: Harcourt Brace.

Pressley, M. (1993). Strategy instruction: Thematic issue's introduction. *Elementary School Journal, 94*(3), 17–31.

Pressley, M., & Afflerbach, P. (1995). *Verbal protocols of reading: The nature of constructively responsive reading.* Hillsdale, NJ: Erlbaum.

Pressley, M., El-Dinary, P., Gaskins, I., Schuder, T., Bergman, J., Almasi, L., et al. (1992). Beyond direct explanation: Transactional instruction of reading comprehension strategies. *Elementary School Journal, 92,* 511–554.

Pressley, M., Symons, S., Snyder, B. L., & Carilgia-Bull, T. (1989). Strategy instruction research comes of age. *Learning Disability Quarterly, 12,* 16–31.

Pressley, M., Johnson, C. J., Symons, S., McGoldrick, J. A., & Kurita, J. A. (1989). Strategies that improve children's memory and comprehension of text. *Elementary School Journal, 90*(1), 4–8.

Pressley, M., Allington, R. L., Wharton-McDonald, R., Block, C. C., & Morrow, L. N. (2001). *Learning to read: Lessons from exemplary first grade classrooms.* New York: Guilford Press.

RAND Reading Study Group. (2001). *Reading for understanding: Towards an R&D program and reading comprehension.* Washington, DC: Author.

Raphael, T., & Wonnacott, C. (1985). Heightening fourth grade students' sensitivity to sources of information for answering comprehension questions. *Reading Research Quarterly, 20,* 282–296.

Rich, S., & Pressley, M. (2006). Teacher acceptance of reading comprehension strategy instruction. *Elementary School Journal, 91*(1), 13–17.

Roehler, L., & Duffy, G. (1981). Classroom teaching is more than an opportunity to learn. *Journal of Teacher Education, 32*(6), 7–11.

Smith, M. C., & Hopkins, C. J. (1993). Metacognitive theory applied: Strategic reading instruction in the current generation of basal readers. *Reading Research and Instruction, 32,* 12–24.

Stanovich, K. E. (2000). *Progress in understanding reading.* New York: Guilford Press.

Thomas, K. F., & Barksdale-Ladd, M. A. (2000). Metacognitive processes: Teaching strategies in literacy education courses. *Reading Psychology, 21,* 67–84.

Vygotsky, L. S. (1978). *Mind in society.* Cambridge, MA: MIT Press.

Wade, A. (2004, March). *Effective use of classroom time: What do we really know?* Paper presented at the annual meeting of the American Educational Research Association, Chicago, IL.

Wharton-McDonald, R., Pressley, M., & Hampston, J. M. (1998). Literacy instruction in nine first-grade classrooms: Teacher characteristics and student achievement. *Elementary School Journal, 99,* 101–128.

Zeckler, L., Pappas, C., & Cohen, S. (1998). Finding the "right measure" by explanation for young Latina/o writers. *Language Arts, 76*(1), 49–56.

3

Dual Coding Theory
Reading Comprehension and Beyond

MARK SADOSKI

> I learned very early the difference between knowing the name of something and knowing something.
> —RICHARD FEYNMAN, Nobel Prize winner in Physics

What is the nature of reading comprehension and how can we teach it better? This persistent question remains central to both theory and practice in reading today. Without some functional definition of what we mean by "reading comprehension" beyond a test score, as researchers and teachers we are in the difficult position of not knowing how well we are succeeding at our jobs. Any definition of reading comprehension must ultimately deal with *meaning*, and that is a heavily theoretical construct. Although we may lack precise definitions of these constructs, much progress has been made toward understanding them in recent years.

This chapter deals with some recent progress in theoretically defining and applying the construct of reading comprehension. In particular it reviews the success of dual coding theory (DCT) in defining and applying that construct. I demonstrate that this theory accounts for data that pose basic difficulties for other theories, and opens exciting new areas of reading comprehension research and practice. Specifically, this chapter summarizes:

- The DCT account of reading comprehension and how it differs in important ways from some other theories.
- How certain DCT principles can be applied to teach reading comprehension in new and effective ways.
- The success of both small- and large-scale applications of DCT principles to teaching reading comprehension in schools.

WHAT'S OUT THERE TODAY: ESTABLISHED RESEARCH AND PRACTICE

Recent volumes that deal with the theories of reading comprehension (Ruddell & Unrau, 2004) and teaching reading comprehension (Block & Pressley, 2002; National Reading Panel, 2000) provide convenient benchmarks for determining the current state of theory and practice. The theoretical scene of reading comprehension, like the scene of cognitive theory itself, is pluralistic: There are numerous theories with varying degrees of research support. Likewise, no consensus currently exists about how best to teach reading comprehension. There are numerous instructional strategies with varying degrees of research support. Unfortunately, very few efforts have been made to directly link specific, established theory with specific, established practice.

To illustrate, Rosenshine and his colleagues meta-analyzed reciprocal teaching (Rosenshine & Meister, 1994) and one of its components, student-generated questions (Rosenshine, Meister, & Chapman, 1996). They noted the existence of a gulf between theory and practice in the experiments they reviewed. The studies typically indicated that their theoretical base was to foster active processing, comprehension monitoring, and the like. However, none provided a more specific cognitive theory to explain their results. Rosenshine et al. (p. 197) concluded that the theoretical basis of these studies was "more metaphorical than practical" and that these comprehension strategies did not truly flow from theory.

Likewise, Anderson (2004) proposed the following instructional implications supported by schema theory: (1) Activate relevant personal knowledge before reading; (2) build prerequisite knowledge when it cannot be presupposed; (3) lead children to integrate what they already know with what is presented on the page; (4) highlight text structure through developmentally appropriate advance organizers and structured overviews; and (5) match instructional materials to the cultural knowledge of minority groups. These are surely valuable suggestions, but they are not unique to schema theory and could just as easily have been derived from any theory that emphasizes the structure of knowledge in memory, including DCT.

Therefore, a continuing challenge to researchers and teachers of reading comprehension is to link specific theory more directly with specific practice to better understand reading comprehension, to better account for our instructional successes and failures in teaching it, and to pinpoint productive new directions. To ignore this challenge is to accumulate more, sometimes contradictory, findings that lack an interpretive scientific anchor. In this chapter I propose that DCT can provide a useful interpretive anchor for reading comprehension theory and practice. To set the background for this, I first review a new trend in cognitive theorizing.

NEW RESEARCH IN COGNITION AND READING COMPREHENSION

A new development in the world of cognitive theory is "embodied cognition." This perspective holds that cognitive processes are rooted in the physical body's interactions with the world. For example, Lakoff and Johnson (1999, p. 3) stated three central findings that have emerged from cognitive science: (1) The mind is inherently embodied; (2) thought is mostly unconscious; and (3) because direct sensory experience is concrete, abstract concepts are largely metaphorical (e.g., time is a journey with the past behind us and the future ahead of us). One of the better documented claims of proponents of embodied cognition is that "off-line" (i.e., unconscious) cognition is body-based (Wilson, 2002); that is, many internal, allegedly abstract cognitive activities may make use of sensorimotor representations and processes in a covert way. I present more on this later.

To make light of a serious question, your brain has never been outside your head. How does it know what the world is like? The only logical answers are that (1) knowledge is innate, or that (2) knowledge is derived from the experience of our five sense modalities. Theories that lean toward the first answer include those in which knowledge is a priori, or those in which relatively fixed schemata are abstracted from sensory experience and thereafter exist in a disembodied, amodal state, waiting to render new sensory experience comprehensible (i.e., instantiation). Embodied cognition is the second kind of theory, emphasizing flexible, contextually changing networks of mental representations of sensory experience as the basis of knowledge and thought. DCT is currently the only empirically established, fully embodied theory of reading comprehension.

A basic premise of DCT is that all mental representations retain some of the concrete qualities of the external experiences from which they derive. These experiences are derived from our five senses and can be linguistic or nonlinguistic. Their differing characteristics develop into two separate mental systems, or cognitive codes. One code is specialized for representing and processing language, and the other is specialized for representing and processing nonlinguistic objects and events. The latter is often referred to as the imagery code, because its functions include the generation, analysis, and transformation of mental images in various modalities (i.e., visual, auditory, haptic, olfactory, gustatory). Each code, and each modality within a code, has its own characteristic mental units and organization, and the codes are neurologically based and heavily interlaced. The qualitative differences between the two codes afford great flexibility and diversity to thought.

One can imagine reading comprehension as a contextually constrained, spreading activation in a huge network of modality-specific verbal and nonverbal representations of various sizes, including those for graphemes, phonemes, written and spoken words and phrases, visual images, auditory images, kinesthetic images, and so on. This spreading activation is not random but probabilistically constrained by our life experience and situational contexts. Together, activity within and between the two codes accounts for knowledge of language and knowledge of the world as experienced by the learner.

A basic distinction between DCT and schema theory, or similar single-code theories (e.g., construction–integration theory; Kintsch, 1998), is that such theories assume that knowledge in memory is basically abstract and amodal, existing in a disembodied state that has no objective reality and is associated with no sensory modality. How any knowledge that is not innate becomes divorced from sensory input is an important theoretical and epistemological question that has not been well explained. Schema theory and similar single-code theories propose no apparent answer to this question; rather, they simply postulate the existence of abstract, amodal knowledge.

By contrast, accounts of constructing meaning from text from the DCT perspective have been provided in detail by Sadoski and Paivio (1994, 2001, 2004). As a brief explanation, consider this sentence: *The guard invaded the paint for a dunk.* This may be confusing to some, but to a basketball fan the sentence is immediately clear. A *guard* is a position in basketball, to *invade the paint* is to enter the painted floor area under the basket, and a *dunk* is a leaping shot in which one or both hands are used to deposit the ball over the rim and into the basket. The comprehension of the sentence can be explained entirely in terms of contextually-constrained connections between specific words and phrases, and their contextually relevant mental images drawn or constructed from memory (i.e., verbal and nonverbal prior knowledge).

The word *guard* can mean many different things, but in this verbal context it is constrained with high probability to the name of a basketball position. *Invade the paint* is slang for entering the area under the basket bounded by the foul lanes and the free throw line, and a *dunk* is a short version of *slam dunk*, a shot in which the player leaps up and delivers the ball directly into the basket. However, all this verbal paraphrase and contextual constraint can still fail to be integrated meaningfully unless one enters the nonverbal realm and recalls or imagines a player performing such a shot. This experience may occur consciously, but it may be so fleeting as to be not consciously experienced (i.e., automatic). Also notice how much inference is invited in the comprehension of the sentence: The printed sentence does not literally specify whether the court was indoors or outdoors, whether the player was participating in a game or practicing alone, whether the dunk was performed with one hand or two, and so on. However, people often include such specific details when reporting their interpretations of such texts (e.g., Sadoski, 1983, 1985; Sadoski, Goetz, & Kangiser, 1988; Sadoski, Goetz, Olivarez, Lee, & Roberts, 1990).

This might all seem similar to the schema theory interpretation, but the difference is theoretically and practically critical. The meaning of the sentence can be explained by connections between specific, embodied verbal and nonverbal mental representations, such as written words in a given syntax; their contextually constrained verbal definitions, synonyms, and paraphrases; and images they evoke from our world experience (without such experience the sentence remains vague and elusive). The assumption of a disembodied "basketball shot" schema that governs the instantiation of the episode adds nothing more to the explanation; therefore, it has no necessary role (Sadoski, Paivio, & Goetz, 1991; for more extended examples and explanations see Sadoski & Paivio, 1994, 2001, 2004).

How would a more abstract sentence be understood? Consider this example: *Unanticipated interference interrupted delivery.* In many ways, the topics in this sentence are more familiar than those in the basketball sentence. Surely we have all experienced unplanned interference and delayed deliveries in our lives. However, without some concrete referent, what is this sentence about? E-mail? Having a baby? A basketball dunk? Abstract language without reference to concrete, real-world events produces verbalism, not comprehension. There is a critical difference between knowing the words for something and knowing something.

From a practical educational perspective, DCT translates into strategies that are more specific than simple admonitions to "activate prior knowledge." To illustrate, comprehension instruction in the basketball example becomes a matter of teaching specific vocabulary in context (e.g., *guard, invade the paint, dunk*) and real or imagined experiences with basketball shots through concrete examples. These experiences could be provided vicariously through videos or induced imagery.

This implies that teaching students to form relevant mental images when reading should enhance comprehension, a consistent research finding for decades (see reviews by Denis, 1984; Gambrell & Koskinen, 2002; National Reading Panel, 2000; Pressley, 1977; Rasinski, 1985; Sadoski, 1999; Sadoski & Paivio, 1994, 2001, 2004; Suzuki, 1985). These studies provide a substantial knowledge base that can be stated conclusively: Teaching readers to form mental images when reading is a successful practice in improving reading comprehension. Most of this imagery has been visual imagery in which students were instructed to visualize the objects or events being discussed in the text. Also, presenting pictures, videos, or graphics with matching text has been shown to be effective in multimedia learning (e.g., Kealy & Webb, 1995; Mayer, 2001; Purnell & Solman, 1991).

New Developments: Large-Scale Implementation

Recent developments have extended these educational findings still further. Small-scale studies of instruction in effective comprehension strategies abound in the literature, but very few have been scaled up to the curriculum level for delivery to whole schools or school districts. Recently, a reading comprehension program explicitly based on DCT principles was implemented on a large-scale basis with success (Sadoski & Willson, 2006).

In 1997 Lindamood–Bell Learning Processes began work with Pueblo School District 60 (PSD60) in southern Colorado to implement a DCT-based program to improve reading comprehension on the state-mandated test, the Colorado Student Assessment Program (CSAP). PSD60 is a heavily minority urban district of about 18,000 students. This program focused on grades 3, 4, and 5, in which CSAP testing was conducted most years from 1997 to 2003.

Similar to the National Assessment of Educational Progress (NAEP), the CSAP uses a variety of item formats, including multiple choice and student-constructed responses with a variety of text genres, and divides scores into four ranges: *Unsatisfactory*, *Partially proficient*, *Proficient*, and *Advanced*. The 1997 CSAP results for PSD60 were below the state average, with over half of students scoring in the *Unsatisfactory* or *Partially proficient* ranges.

During implementation years (1997–2003), comprehension was taught through the Verbalizing–visualizing (VV) program (Bell, 1986). The VV instructional program systematically guides students to form mental images and describe them in increasing detail, beginning with pictures and moving on to words, sentences, and longer text passages. Higher-order comprehension skills, such as inference, prediction, and evaluation, are dealt with through mental imagery and verbal elaboration as well. The emphasis on associating language with multisensory mental images in the VV program (i.e., instruction in mentally encoding the information in both verbal and nonverbal form) is a direct application of DCT to reading comprehension instruction. The program was implemented at the school level through extensive inservice teacher and support staff training, and the use of special program materials that scaffolded to standard materials, including basal readers and content area textbooks. Program fidelity monitoring was conducted on site by trained staff. Increasing numbers of PSD60 elementary and middle schools implemented the program during the period 1997 to 2003, providing a robust, large-scale test across years and grades.

The subsequent evaluation study (Sadoski & Willson, 2006) focused on CSAP results in grades 3, 4, and 5. Data were analyzed through a series of repeated measures analyses of covariance between PSD60 schools and the statewide CSAP average, controlling for school size, minority student percentage, socioeconomic status (SES), and the total time a school was included in the intervention. Statistically significant ($p < .0001$) and increasing gains favoring the DCT-based reading comprehension intervention were found in all three grades.

Figure 3.1 illustrates the results for grade 4. As more schools in the district implemented the intervention, the proportion of *Unsatisfactory* and *Partially proficient* scores

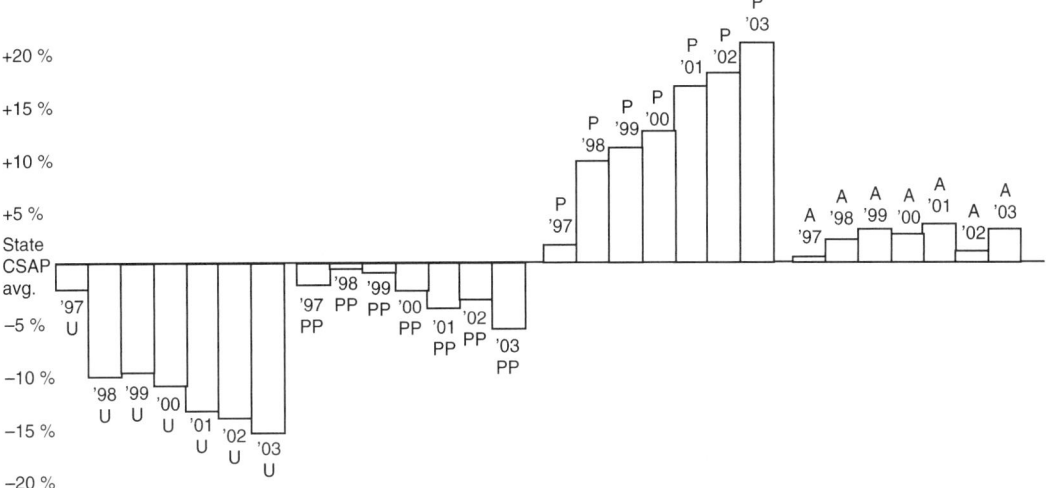

FIGURE 3.1. PSD60 versus Colorado state average on grade 4 CSAP score categories (U, PP, P, A) 1997–2003. Statistically controlled for school size, percent minority, percent free and reduced price lunch (SES), and school years of implementation. U, unsatisfactory; PP, partially proficient; P, proficient; A, advanced. From Sadoski and Willson (2006, p. 146). Copyright 2006 by the American Educational Research Association. Reprinted by permission.

declined relative to the state average, while the proportion of *Proficient* and *Advanced* scores increased relative to the state average. These results show that DCT-based interventions can be successfully explained to teachers and implemented at the district curricular level with success.

New Developments: Kinesthetic Imagery in Reading Comprehension

DCT recognizes mental imagery in modalities other than visual imagery, including kinesthetic and other forms of haptic imagery (Paivio, 1971, 1986, 2007; Sadoski & Paivio, 1994, 2001, 2004). Likewise, a principle of embodied cognition is that cognitive processing may be more sensorimotor than has been previously theorized. Wilson (2002, pp. 632–633) explained:

> Consider the example of counting on one's fingers. In its fullest form, this can be a set of crisp and large movements, unambiguously setting forth the different fingers as counters. But it can also be done more subtly, differentiating the positions of the fingers only enough to allow the fingers to keep track. To the observer, this may look like mere twitching. Imagine, then, that we push the activity inward still further, allowing only the priming of motor programs but no overt movement. If this kind of mental activity can be employed successfully to assist a task such as counting, a new vista of cognitive strategies opens up. Many centralized, allegedly abstract cognitive activities may in fact make use of sensorimotor functions in exactly this kind of covert way.

Cathy Collins Block and her colleagues have developed the Comprehension Process Motions (CPM) method for teaching young readers to learn comprehension processes and initiate them without teacher prompting (Block, Parris, & Whiteley, in press). CPM lessons teach students kinesthetic hand placements and movements that portray the comprehension processes of main idea, inferring, drawing conclusions, clarifying, making predictions, and so on. CPM lessons were designed so that students would internalize comprehension processes, not through verbal repetition and drill, but through dual-coded learning inputs that provide concrete images to help signal how, when, and where to engage specific comprehension processes. In effect, the hand gestures became what was *meant* by the strategies, rather than abstract verbal definitions that might amount to mere verbalism for a child.

In an experimental study, children in grades K–5 from high-minority, low-SES urban schools were taught to use CPMs through teacher introduction and scaffolding as students internalized the strategy. The control group was taught the same comprehension strategies verbally, without the assistance of CPM kinesthetic teaching aids. Teachers were provided 2 days of professional development in the techniques, and teachers delivered the instruction for 12 weeks.

Students were tested on standardized, norm-referenced comprehension tests and specific criterion-referenced tests of (1) drawing conclusions, (2) clarifying, (3) following a story's plot, (4) identifying writing patterns in nonfiction, and (5) finding main ideas. Students receiving CPM instruction significantly outperformed control subjects on every measure. More than 70% of the students' achievement was attributable to the presence or absence of CPM instruction on every measure. For example, the means (and standard deviations) for the main idea test were 79.8 (5.5) for the CPM group and 52.0 (5.9) for the control group. This amounts to a 53% increase in achievement for the CPM group over the control group, and an effect size in standard deviation units of $d = 4.71$ and an r^2 effect size of 0.87. These are very large effect sizes, perhaps among the largest in reading comprehension strategy instruction. Moreover, the largest effects in the study were found for younger learners in grades K–2, those who typically have difficulty in understanding abstract language definitions. What this research may be showing us is how children really think, not how strategies more suitable for adult competencies can be imposed on them.

DCT principles can explain these research results directly. The verbally labeled and explained comprehension strategy (e.g., "main idea") was referentially associated with a nonverbal physical act that gave the label additional, embodied meaning (i.e., dual coding). The strategy was then easier to understand and apply, because there were more and different ways to grasp and remember it. The results of the dual encoding provided very large increases in learning to apply a variety of common comprehension strategies over single coding. Why kinesthetic acts should embody meaning better than language alone is virtually impossible for single-coding, abstract knowledge theories to explain.

HOW THIS NEW KNOWLEDGE
CAN IMPROVE COMPREHENSION INSTRUCTION

There is now a rich and established body of empirical evidence that reading comprehension instruction based on DCT principles can be effectively applied with individual learners, in classrooms, and at the school district level. The theory and its principles have been clearly and successfully communicated to teachers. The practical effects are highly educationally significant, as the previous examples attest.

Actually, DCT principles are consistent with many traditional practices in reading comprehension instruction. But the additional values that it offers include (1) a more specific, concrete, and understandable theoretical account of the concepts of *meaning* and *reading comprehension*, and (2) exciting new vistas in research and practice. DCT is an embodied theory of cognition, and embodied theories have great promise for a better understanding of all cognition. In fact, the nonverbal basis of mind in the form of imagination, augmented later in human history by language, may be one of least understood of the driving forces behind the incredible divergence of human intelligence in evolution (Paivio, 2007). We may be on the verge of a much better understanding of what the mind is really like and, consequently, what cognition in reading is like.

DIRECTIONS FOR FUTURE RESEARCH

The perspective supplied by DCT and an embodied view of cognition opens many new vistas. Here are just a few exciting areas for further research and practice.

1. *How can we improve reading comprehension by exploring imagery in modalities other than the visual modality?* Mental imagery is often a "multimedia event" reflecting the concrete experience of real life. For example, imagine a favorite food such as pizza. Not only will it look various ways depending on the crust and toppings, but it will smell and taste various ways, be eaten in various ways, and even sound various ways as we cut or crunch through the crust. It may be imagined as fresh and sizzling hot or as a cold, morning-after leftover. Imaging in multiple modalities may have increasing effects on meaningful comprehension of topics far less familiar than pizza. This may reflect the Renaissance period of education, in which "things not words" were held prominent, but with the DCT difference that words and things should be more balanced in their importance (Sadoski & Paivio, 2001). Sommer (1978) wrote of the "senseless school" in which sensory world experience was systematically downplayed after the Renaissance in favor of abstractions in the form of words and numbers. The symbolic gestures of CPM are an excellent example of a return to "making sense" and extending imagery beyond the visual.

2. *Can the mental imagery of DCT be found in all aspects of reading, not just comprehension?* For example, both decoding and reader response engage mental imagery to a degree (Sadoski & Paivio, 2004). We may only truly come to understand what individual phonemes are when we learn to pronounce them and make them our own rather than abstracting them from listening to the speech of others; that is, phonology may have a more kinesthetic, sensorimotor basis than an auditory one (Liberman & Mattingly, 1985; Lindamood & Lindamood, 1998). Also, all theories of reader response to literature and even nonfiction involve mental imagery (Sadoski, 2002). Imagery is central to Rosenblatt's (2004) concept of the *aesthetic stance* in reading, and Miall and Kuiken's (1995) factor-analytic dimension of *experiencing* text. If reading is truly interactive, we cannot deal with comprehension alone to fully understand it. Sadoski and Paivio (2007) have proposed DCT as a unified theory of reading, addressing all its aspects using the same basic theoretical principles.

3. *What implications does DCT have for other aspects of literacy?* DCT has recently been extended to account for the effects of word concreteness in spelling (Sadoski, Willson, Holcomb, & Boulware-Gooden, 2005) and written composition (Goetz, Sadoski, Stricker, White, & Wang, 2007; Sadoski, 1992; Sadoski & Goetz, 1998; Sadoski, Goetz, Stricker, & Burdenski, 2000; Sadoski, Kealy, Goetz, & Paivio, 1997; see also the review in Sadoski & Paivio, 2001). Ultimately reading will be best understood

and taught when we understand how it fits into the grand framework of literacy in all its forms.

PROJECTIONS AND POSSIBILITIES FOR THE CLASSROOM OF 2030

The classrooms of the future might be envisioned to be more technologically sophisticated than those of the past. Multimedia materials seem to be very much in our future, and this calls for a much better understanding of how text and both still and animated multimedia presentations of things, people, places, maps, graphics, and other forms of content are best arranged (Rieber, 1995). Mayer's (2001) theory of multimedia learning is consistent with DCT principles, and it serves as one basis for understanding the conjoint effects of multimedia in various combinations.

Another challenge facing classrooms of the future is to eliminate the gap between cultural groups in literacy ability. This is a difficult problem, because its causes are controversial. However, reading instruction based on DCT has a strong record of success in low-SES, high-minority, traditionally low-achieving schools (e.g., Block et al., in press; Sadoski & Willson, 2006). In any case, a better understanding of the nature of reading and its teaching will best serve this need. Ultimately, the best practice emanates from the best theory.

Finally, the neurosciences may open up new vistas for research and practice, although they may also tend to confirm established successful practices. Paivio (2007) has elaborated the extensive neuropsychological support for DCT. See also Chapters 7–10 on neuroscience in this volume.

SUMMARY

This chapter has briefly summarized the DCT account of reading comprehension and its instruction. Although this theory is consistent with current views of embodied cognition, it is in fact one of the oldest and most empirically established theories of cognition, dating from the early days of the cognitive revolution in the 1950s and 1960s (Paivio, 1971). Its principles are well articulated and consistent with current neuroscientific evidence, as well as decades of behavioral evidence on many fronts. This theory provides a tangible, practical definition of reading comprehension that can readily be put into practice by teachers and has had success in doing so. Perhaps most importantly, it offers exciting, expansive, and creative new possibilities for both theory and practice.

INTEGRATE, INVESTIGATE, AND INITIATE: QUESTIONS FOR DISCUSSION

1. In this chapter were several specific terms, such as "dual coding theory," "embodied cognition," "contextually constrained spreading activation," and "multimedia event." Provide a definition for each of these terms that you could present to a layperson such as an administrator or a parent. In constructing this definition, also create an example that you could apply to your classroom environment for your area of professional expertise. Share these definitions and examples with colleagues. Compare the similarities between your understanding and their understanding of dual coding theory and reading comprehension.

2. In this chapter I stated that "the neurosciences may open up new vistas for research and practice, although they may also tend to confirm established successful practices" (p. 46). What is the most convincing argument for you to become more aware of the new research relative to neuroscience and comprehension? What cautions do you have about how neuroscience can be applied in your already established successful practices?

3. What question do you still have relative to dual coding theory? What is your most successful method of answering that question: e-mailing a colleague or researcher, going to the library or the Internet, or discussing your question with a colleague, and so forth? Evaluate how long it took you to find a satisfactory answer to your question. Share the amount of time and effort it took for your investigation with a group of similar colleagues who also completed this exercise. What did you learn about continuing to advance your knowledge in any field independently? What did the sharing experience teach you about other methods of answering specific questions related to comprehension or about your own learning style compared to that of others?

REFERENCES

Anderson, R. C. (2004). Role of reader's schema in comprehension, learning, and memory. In R. B. Ruddell & N. J. Unrau (Eds.), *Theoretical models and processes of reading* (5th ed., pp. 594–606). Newark, DE: International Reading Association.

Bell, N. (1986). *Visualizing and verbalizing for language comprehension and thinking*. Paso Robles, CA: Academy of Reading.

Block, C. C., Parris, S. R., & Whiteley, C. S. (in press). CPMs: Helping primary grade students self-initiate comprehension processes through kinesthetic instruction. *Reading Teacher*.

Block, C. C., & Pressley, M. (Eds.). (2002). *Comprehension instruction: Research-based best practices*. New York: Guilford Press.

Denis, M. (1984). Imagery and prose: A critical review of research on adults and children. *Text, 4*, 381–401.

Gambrell, L., & Koskinen, P. S. (2002). Imagery: A strategy for enhancing comprehension. In C. C. Block & M. Pressley (Eds.), *Comprehension instruction: Research-based best practices* (pp. 305–318). New York: Guilford Press.

Goetz, E. T., Sadoski, M., Stricker, A. G., White, T. S., & Wang, Z. (2007). The role of imagery in the production of written definitions. *Reading Psychology, 28*, 241–251.

Kealy, W. A., & Webb, J. M. (1995). Verbal learning with maps and diagrams. *Contemporary Educational Psychology, 20*, 340–358.

Kintsch, W. (1998). *Comprehension: A paradigm for cognition*. Cambridge, UK: Cambridge University Press.

Lakoff, G., & Johnson, M. (1999). *Philosophy in the flesh*. New York: Basic Books.

Liberman, A. M., & Mattingly, I. G. (1985). The motor theory of speech perception revisited. *Cognition, 21*, 1–36.

Lindamood, P., & Lindamood, P. (1998). *Lindamood phonemic sequencing (LiPS) program*. Austin, TX: PRO-ED.

Mayer, R. E. (2001). *Multimedia learning*. London: Cambridge University Press.

Miall, D. S., & Kuiken, D. (1995). Aspects of literary response: A new questionnaire. *Research in the Teaching of English, 29*, 37–58.

National Reading Panel. (2000). *Report of the National Reading Panel: Reports of the subgroups*. Washington, DC: National Institute of Child Health and Human Development.

Paivio, A. (1971). *Imagery and verbal processes*. Hillsdale, NJ: Erlbaum.

Paivio, A. (1986). *Mental representations: A dual coding approach*. New York: Oxford University Press.

Paivio, A. (2007). *Mind and its evolution: A dual coding theoretical approach*. Mahwah, NJ: Erlbaum.

Pressley, M. (1977). Imagery and children's learning: Putting the picture in developmental perspective. *Review of Educational Research, 47,* 585–622.

Purnell, K. N., & Solman, R. T. (1991). The influence of technical illustrations on students' comprehension of geography. *Reading Research Quarterly, 26,* 277–299.

Rasinski, T. V. (1985). Picture this: Using imagery as a reading comprehension strategy. *Reading Horizons, 25,* 280–288.

Rieber, L. P. (1995). A historical review of visualization in human cognition. *Educational Technology Research and Development, 43,* 45–56.

Rosenblatt, L. M. (2004). The transactional theory of reading and writing. In R. B. Ruddell & N. J. Unrau (Eds.), *Theoretical models and processes of reading* (5th ed., pp. 1363–1398). Newark, DE: International Reading Association.

Rosenshine, B., & Meister, C. (1994). Reciprocal teaching: A review of the research. *Review of Educational Research, 64,* 479–450.

Rosenshine, B., Meister, C., & Chapman, S. (1996). Teaching students to generate questions: A review of the intervention studies. *Review of Educational Research, 66,* 181–221.

Ruddell, R. B., & Unrau, N. J. (Eds.). (2004). *Theoretical models and processes of reading* (5th ed.). Newark, DE: International Reading Association.

Sadoski, M. (1983). An exploratory study of the relationships between reported imagery and the comprehension and recall of a story. *Reading Research Quarterly, 19,* 110–123.

Sadoski, M. (1985). The natural use of imagery in story comprehension and recall: Replication and extension. *Reading Research Quarterly, 20,* 658–667.

Sadoski, M. (1992). Imagination, cognition, and persona. *Rhetoric Review, 10,* 266–278.

Sadoski, M. (1999). Mental imagery in reading: A sampler of some significant studies. *Reading Online* [electronic journal of the International Reading Association]. Available online at *www.readingonline.org/research/sadoski.html.*

Sadoski, M. (2002). Dual coding theory and reading poetic text. *Journal of the Imagination in Language Learning and Teaching, 7,* 78–83.

Sadoski, M., & Goetz, E. T. (1998). Concreteness effects and syntactic modification in written composition. *Scientific Studies of Reading, 2,* 341–352.

Sadoski, M., Goetz, E. T., & Kangiser, S. (1988). Imagination in story response: Relationships between imagery, affect, and structural importance. *Reading Research Quarterly, 23,* 320–336.

Sadoski, M., Goetz, E. T., Olivarez, A., Lee, S., & Roberts, N. M. (1990). Imagination in story reading: The role of imagery, verbal recall, story analysis, and processing levels. *Journal of Reading Behavior, 22,* 55–70.

Sadoski, M., Goetz, E. T., Stricker, A. G., & Burdenski, T. K., Jr. (2003). New findings for concreteness and imagery effects in written composition. *Reading and Writing, 16,* 443–453.

Sadoski, M., Kealy, W. A., Goetz, E. T., & Paivio, A. (1997). Concreteness and imagery effects in the written composition of definitions. *Journal of Educational Psychology, 89,* 518–526.

Sadoski, M., & Paivio, A. (1994). A dual coding view of imagery and verbal processes in reading comprehension. In R. B. Ruddell, M. R. Ruddell, & H. Singer (Eds.), *Theoretical models and processes of reading* (4th ed., pp. 582–601). Newark, DE: International Reading Association.

Sadoski, M., & Paivio, A. (2001). *Imagery and text: A dual coding theory of reading and writing.* Mahwah, NJ: Erlbaum.

Sadoski, M., & Paivio, A. (2004). A dual coding theoretical model of reading. In R. B. Ruddell & N. J. Unrau (Eds.), *Theoretical models and processes of reading* (5th ed., pp. 1329–1362). Newark, DE: International Reading Association.

Sadoski, M., & Paivio, A. (2007). Toward a unified theory of reading. *Scientific Studies of Reading, 11,* 337–356.

Sadoski, M., Paivio, A., & Goetz, E. T. (1991). A critique of schema theory in reading and a dual coding alternative. *Reading Research Quarterly, 26,* 463–484.

Sadoski, M., & Willson, V. L. (2006). Effects of a theoretically based large-scale reading intervention in a multicultural urban school district. *American Educational Research Journal, 43,* 137–154.

Sadoski, M., Willson, V., Holcomb, A., & Boulware-Gooden, R. (2005). Verbal and nonverbal predictors of spelling performance. *Journal of Literacy Research, 36,* 461–478.

Sommer, R. (1978). *The mind's eye: Imagery in everyday life.* Palo Alto, CA: Dale Seymour.

Suzuki, N. S. (1985). Imagery research with children: Implications for education. In A. A. Sheikh & K. S. Sheikh (Eds.), *Imagery in education: Imagery in the educational process* (pp. 179–198). Farmingdale, NY: Baywood.

Wilson, M. (2002). Six views of embodied cognition. *Psychonomic Bulletin and Review, 9,* 625–663.

4

Cognitive Flexibility and Reading Comprehension
Relevance to the Future

KELLY B. CARTWRIGHT

> We keep meaning foremost. But the children still must know the words. It is not a case of words *or* meaning. It is a case of meaning *and* words.
> —DOLCH (1960, p. 189, emphasis added)

Ask beginning or struggling readers what good readers do, and they usually tell you that good readers "get all the words right" or they "don't make mistakes when they read." For many of these children, reading is about accurate decoding, not comprehension (Dewitz & Dewitz, 2003; Gaskins & Gaskins, 1997; Oakhill & Yuill, 1996; Pressley, 2006). In fact, work in developmental psychology shows elementary school-age children have difficulty shifting attention between phonological and semantic aspects of words, with a tendency to focus on phonological aspects of print exclusively (Bialystok & Niccols, 1989). In the words of Dolch (1960) these children focus on *words*, not *meaning*. To focus on only one aspect of a task or situation is the hallmark of cognitive inflexibility (Inhelder & Piaget, 1964; Zelazo & Frye, 1998). Recent research has found that such limits of attention often become significant roadblocks to comprehension for beginning and struggling readers. Their foci on word-level features preclude attending to meaning (Cartwright, 2006, 2008a).

For skilled readers, however, reading comprehension involves the complex orchestration of multiple cognitive attentional variables, such as recognizing phonological, semantic, and syntactic features, while employing strategic and metacognitive processes (e.g., Adams, 1990; Cartwright, 2008b; Pressley & Afflerbach, 1995). Other contemporary studies show that children and adults vary in their ability actively, flexibly, and simultaneously to consider multiple aspects of complex cognitive tasks (Andrews & Halford, 2002; Deák, 2003; Kuhn & Pease, 2006; Zelazo & Frye, 1998). This aspect of executive control, called *cognitive flexibility*, has been fittingly described by Pressley and colleagues as "cognitive juggling" (Pressley et al., in press). Because skilled reading comprehension requires the active coordination of multiple elements, work on the development of cognitive flexibility may be particularly helpful to advance our understanding of reading comprehension processes and instruction (Cartwright, 2008a, 2008b). From this perspective, readers who are less cognitively flexible should be less likely to coordinate the many meaning-making clues necessary for skilled comprehension. Given the potential importance of cognitive flexibility for reading comprehension processes, this chapter highlights the following:

- Contemporary research on the development of cognitive flexibility and its applications to reading comprehension.
- The significant role that reading-specific cognitive flexibility plays in reading comprehension for both beginning and skilled readers.
- Ways to assess and foster cognitive flexibility for improved reading comprehension.

WHAT'S OUT THERE TODAY: ESTABLISHED RESEARCH AND PRACTICE

In recent years, work in cognitive development increasingly has focused on the development of mental representational ability, especially the ability to handle and manipulate multiple aspects of cognitively complex tasks in a flexible manner (e.g., Andrews & Halford, 2002; Deák, 2003; Kuhn & Pease, 2006; Zelazo & Frye, 1998). Such cognitive flexibility is an aspect of executive control and is important to children's development of understanding in a number of different domains, such as social cognition, language, use of symbolic representations, and the distinction between appearance and reality (for a review, see Cartwright, 2008b). For example, to understand that a giant rabbit is actually a human in a bunny suit (and not a frightening menace), young children must be flexible in the way they think about the suited figure. In other words, they must be able to think about both the bunny costume itself (the creature's appearance) and the human inside the costume: They must flexibly consider multiple mental representations of the giant creature standing before them. This kind of flexibility is also apparent and necessary as children develop a conceptualization of phonological awareness. Children must learn to think of words as wholes, while also considering them as symbols composed of different phonological parts (Farrar & Ashwell, 2008; Farrar, Ashwell, & Maag, 2005).

Zelazo and colleagues posited these points in their Cognitive Complexity and Control theory of cognitive development (Frye, Zelazo, & Burack, 1998; Jacques & Zelazo, 2001; Zelazo & Frye, 1998; Zelazo, Müller, Frye, & Marcovitch, 2003). Their framework suggests that children have difficulty thinking about tasks or situations in multiple ways (e.g., thinking about reading as both a phonological and a semantic task), and that they must *learn how* to coordinate flexibly the multiple representations required for successful work on complex tasks. Additionally, even adults vary in their natural abilities to demonstrate cognitive flexibility (Cartwright, 2007; Diamond & Kirkham, 2005). In fact, some adults demonstrate even lower levels of cognitive flexibility than do children (Cartwright, Isaac, & Dandy, 2006; Kuhn & Pease, 2006). These findings are consistent with other contemporary research indicating that cognitive development occurs throughout our lifetimes (Andrews & Halford, 2002; Labouvie-Vief, 1992; Sinnott, 1998; also see Miller, 2006), which updates the initial classic work in this area that argued for full development by the end of the childhood years (Piaget & Inhelder, 1966/1969). Finally, a third important new perspective in cognitive development is the notion that such development is domain-specific (Case, 1992; Case & Okamoto, 1996; Karmiloff-Smith, 1991). For instance, cognitive flexibility that occurs in particular kinds of thinking tasks does not necessarily transfer to other tasks, suggesting that interventions intended to improve flexible thinking in reading must be tailored to the particular demands of reading tasks (for evidence that training in domain-specific cognitive flexibility produces improvements in flexible thinking in particular domains, whereas training in general cognitive flexibility does not; see Bigler & Liben, 1992; Cartwright, 2002).

Because reading comprehension is a cognitive process that requires representation and coordination of multiple elements, contemporary work in cognitive development has important implications for understanding the development of comprehension processes. Unfortunately, these kinds of cross-disciplinary connections occur infrequently (Sternberg, 2000; Sternberg & Lyon, 2002). Thus, the research presented in this chapter is focused at the intersection of work in cognitive development and reading comprehension, producing assessments of reading-specific flexibility to inform understanding of reading processes across the lifespan, and yielding intervention techniques that improve reading-specific cognitive flexibility and reading comprehension (Cartwright, Bock, Guiffré, & Montaño, 2006).

A historical note is in order before I proceed to the review of current research. Flexibility has been considered one of the hallmarks of skilled reading for many decades, and several different perspectives on flexibility have emerged in the reading research literature (for a more detailed review of these perspectives, see Cartwright, 2008b). Although none of these notions was derived from contemporary perspectives on cognitive development, each is consistent with these views. For example, as early as 1944, researchers demonstrated that skilled comprehenders were significantly more cognitively flexible than their less skilled counterparts, with "flexibility" defined as the ability to adjust reading rate according to reading purpose and task difficulty (see Blommers & Lindquist, 1944; for similar perspectives, also see Berger, 1967; Braam, 1963; Dowdy, Crump, & Welch, 1982; Ramsel & Grabe, 1983). In this case, a skilled reader must consider text content and task difficulty, while also maintaining attention to the goal for reading. Thus, consistent with contemporary work in cognitive flexibility, this conceptualization of flexibility requires the coordination of multiple elements.

Since then, other researchers have suggested that skilled reading requires even greater and more flexible (1) attention to multiple cues, such as graphophonological, semantic, and syntactic cues (Goodman, 1973, 1976, 1994); (2) use of cues and strategies (Clay, 1985, 1991, 2001); and (3) representation of and access to knowledge (Spiro, 2004; Spiro, Coulson, Feltovich, & Anderson, 1994; Spiro, Vispoel, Schmitz, Samarapungavan, & Boerger, 1987; Spiro, 2004). Finally, Wagner and Sternberg (1987) offered a description of flexibility in reading that is closely aligned with current cognitive-developmental perspectives. This explanation delineates the ties between reading tasks and mental executive control abilities, suggesting that flexibility is an important aspect of executive processes and cognitive monitoring abilities, which are both necessary for skilled reading comprehension. This view implies that readers are metacognitively aware that flexible cognition is taking place. However, even skilled readers may or may not be aware of the mental representations that must be coordinated during reading comprehension (Masson, 1987), with some text elements represented below the level of conscious awareness (e.g., phonological information in skilled readers). As Forguson and Gopnik

(1988, p. 229) noted, "We typically do not allege that those to whom we ascribe mental representations consciously experience the representations we attribute to them. Indeed, even we language-using adults typically do not experience our own mental representations as such; they are psychologically transparent, not noticed (or perhaps better, beneath notice)." Although each of these historical perspectives on flexibility in reading is consistent with the notion that skilled reading requires flexible coordination of multiple elements, none is explicit about the ways that such flexibility develops across the lifespan, and none offers task-specific ways that such flexibility can be improved. Contemporary perspectives on cognitive development may provide a unifying perspective on flexibility in reading and a theoretical basis for developing empirically testable hypotheses to fill these gaps in reading research and practice (Cartwright, 2008b).

NEW RESEARCH IN THIS AREA (SINCE THE NATIONAL READING PANEL [NRP] REPORT)

Because historical perspectives suggest that our understanding of reading processes may be usefully informed by current work in the field of cognitive development (especially work relative to the assessment and development of cognitive flexibility), recent research has focused on adapting contemporary cognitive-developmental methods for the cognitive demands in reading tasks, particularly those in skilled reading comprehension (e.g., Cartwright, 2002, 2006, 2007). Discussion of this research addresses the following points: (1) the measurement of reading-specific flexibility, (2) the contribution of reading-specific flexibility to reading comprehension, (3) the development of reading-specific flexibility in advantaged and disadvantaged readers, (4) teaching flexibility for improved comprehension, and (5) extensions of this work.

Measuring Reading-Specific Flexibility

Typically, researchers in cognitive development have used classification tasks to assess the flexibility with which individuals can attend to multiple aspects of complex tasks (e.g., Bigler & Liben, 1992; Inhelder & Piaget, 1964; Zelazo et al., 2003). These tasks use items that can be sorted along multiple features, such as pictures of fruit and flowers that can also be sorted by colors, such as yellow and red. Some tasks that assess cognitive flexibility involve sequential sorts of such items and require students first to sort by one dimension (e.g., by color), then switch the sorting rule midtask (e.g., switch to sorting by shape). The Dimensional Change Card Sort task used by Zelazo and colleagues is an example of this kind of sequential flexibility task. (The Wisconsin Card Sorting Test requires similar shifts in rule use as evidence of flexibility in thinking [see Berg, 1948].)

Another kind of task that taps cognitive flexibility is a simultaneous sorting task, the multiple classification task, which requires that students sort items along multiple dimensions at the same time (Inhelder & Piaget, 1964). For example, the stimuli in the previous example would be sorted by color (red or yellow) and type (fruit or flowers) concurrently into a 2 × 2 matrix. Because this multiple classification task requires that students maintain continuous, flexible attention to multiple dimensions at the same time, it seems to be a better assessment of the type of cognitive juggling required in reading comprehension. This task has been successfully adapted in contemporary work for use in assessing and training flexibility in various domains (e.g., Bigler & Liben, 1992; Cartwright, 2002; also see Golbeck, 1983).

Because beginning and struggling readers seem to have particular difficulty considering semantic and phonological features of print flexibly, I (Cartwright, 2002) modified the multiple classification task to tap students' flexibility in considering these particular aspects of printed words. In this reading-specific cognitive flexibility task, students might sort sets of 12 printed words, including words such as *bear*, *toad*, *bus*, and *train*, by initial phoneme (/b/ and /t/) and word meaning (animals and vehicles) into a 2 × 2 matrix (see Figure 4.1), with accuracy and speed of sorting providing an index of the flexibility with which students can consider both word-level features and meaning associated with printed words. Other aspects of print could certainly be tapped with this type of task. However, beginning readers' tendency to focus inflexibly on phonological aspects of words rather than on meaning may be particularly detrimental to developing comprehension. Thus, these particular aspects of print were selected for initial investigations of reading-specific cognitive flexibility; the results of some of these studies are reviewed in the following sections.

Unique Contribution to Comprehension

Across studies and across multiple ages, the ability to consider flexibly the semantic and phonological features of printed words, "graphophonological–semantic flexibility," has contributed significant, unique variance to reading comprehension beyond phonological and semantic processing assessed independently (for reviews, see Cartwright, Bock, et al., 2006; Cartwright, Hodgkiss, & Isaac, 2008). These highly significant findings have been observed in samples as young as beginning first and second grade readers (Cartwright, Marshall, Dandy, & Isaac, 2008), intermediate readers in second to fourth grades (Cartwright, 2002), and even adult readers (Cartwright, 2007). Moreover, across studies, the unique contribution of graphophonological–semantic flexibility to reading comprehension remained significant even when general cognitive ability and age were controlled. These findings indicate that reading-specific flexibility plays an important role in reading

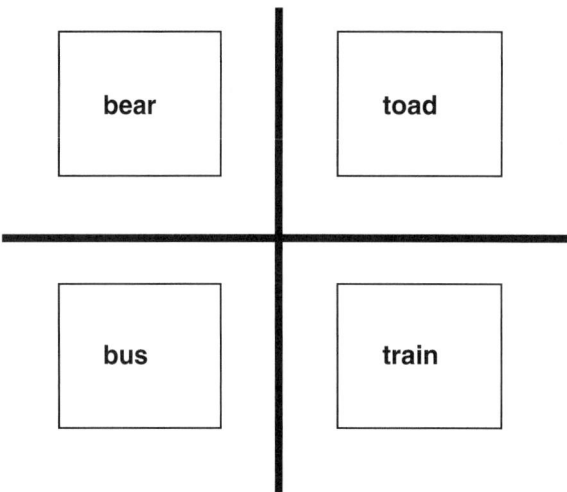

FIGURE 4.1. Example of a correct sort on the graphophonological–semantic flexibility task.

comprehension across skills levels, from beginning readers to adults. Furthermore, this research demonstrates that phonological decoding and semantic processing are not sufficient to explain skilled reading comprehension. Readers must also be able to coordinate flexibly these aspects of print to comprehend successfully.

Development in Advantaged and Disadvantaged Readers

As would be expected, reading-specific cognitive flexibility improves across the lifespan, as shown in a cross-sectional comparison of second graders, fourth graders, and adults (Cartwright, Isaac, & Dandy, 2006). Furthermore, analyses across samples indicate that advantaged and disadvantaged readers differ in the development of reading-specific flexibility. First-, second-, and fourth-grade students from four different samples and studies were included in this particular analysis, because these were the grade levels for which comparison data were available. The disadvantaged readers ($n = 74$) included 49 students from a predominantly Title I sample (Cartwright, Green, & Marshall, 2003) and 25 teacher-identified struggling readers from a Title I school (Cartwright, Schmidt, Clause, Price, & Thomas, 2007). The advantaged readers ($n = 112$) included 44 students from Cartwright's (2002) original reading-specific flexibility study and 68 students from a study of beginning readers' flexibility (Cartwright, Marshall, et al., 2008). A 2 (reader type: advantaged or disadvantaged) × 2 (Grade level: first, second, or fourth) analysis of variance (ANOVA) revealed a main effect of reader type, with advantaged readers ($M = 11.74$, $SD = 10.58$) demonstrating significantly higher levels of reading-specific cognitive flexibility than disadvantaged readers [($M = 6.39$, $SD = 7.89$), $F(1, 180) = 16.32$, $p < .001$]. A main effect of grade level indicated significant improvement in reading-specific cognitive flexibility across first ($M = 5.17$, $SD = 6.55$), second ($M = 9.86$, $SD = 9.10$), and fourth ($M = 16.00$, $SD = 12.69$) grades [$F(2, 180) = 13.29$, $p < .001$]. An inspection of Table 4.1 indicates that disadvantaged readers are about half as flexible as advantaged readers and, not surprisingly, disadvantaged readers also demonstrated significantly lower levels of reading comprehension (assessed with the Woodcock Reading Mastery Test, Passage Comprehension subtest; Woodcock, 1987) than their more advantaged counterparts [$F(1, 180) = 9.22$, $p < .01$].

TABLE 4.1. Cell Sizes, Means, and Standard Deviations for a Comparison of Reading-Specific Cognitive Flexibility in Advantaged and Disadvantaged Readers

Grade level	Cell size	Mean	Standard deviation
First			
Advantaged	33	6.16	6.72
Disadvantaged	24	3.81	6.17
Second[a]			
Advantaged	57	11.83	9.43
Disadvantaged	36	6.73	7.67
Fourth[a]			
Advantaged	22	19.84	12.97
Disadvantaged	14	9.95	9.87

[a]These means are significantly different, $p < .01$.

Teaching Flexibility for Improved Comprehension

Because this initial work indicated that reading-specific cognitive flexibility contributed significant, unique variance to comprehension, I suspected that interventions that target children's reading-specific cognitive flexibility might improve reading comprehension. My theory was based on contemporary work in cognitive development in general, which has demonstrated that cognitive flexibility can be taught, but such teaching is only effective if done with domain-specific flexibility tasks (e.g., Bigler & Liben, 1992). Thus, I assigned students to a reading-specific cognitive flexibility training condition (students sorted words by initial phoneme and word meaning), a general cognitive flexibility training condition (students sorted pictures by color and shape), and a control condition (students played dominoes with the experimenter) to compare the effects of flexibility training on reading comprehension. These interventions occurred with individual students in 15-minute sessions across 5 days, and reading comprehension was assessed before and after the intervention with raw scores on different forms of the Woodcock Reading Mastery Test, Passage Comprehension subtest (Woodcock, 1987).

Children who experienced the reading-specific cognitive flexibility intervention made significant gains in reading-specific flexibility and reading comprehension, as expected, whereas children in the other conditions did not. Recently, this intervention was adapted for small-group administration with a sample of teacher-identified struggling readers, who received five 30- to 40-minute intervention sessions once per week across 5 weeks. Control children received regular, small-group reading instruction. This quasi-experimental comparison indicated that children who experienced a small-group reading-specific flexibility intervention made significant gains on school-administered and researcher-administered measures of reading comprehension (Cartwright, Schmidt, et al., 2007). Taken together, these findings indicate that reading-specific cognitive flexibility training can be delivered in current and future classroom settings, and result in significant increases in reading comprehension for able and less able readers beginning as early as second grade.

Extensions of This Work

Recent extensions of this work by other scholars have expanded our knowledge of the role of cognitive flexibility instruction in reading across cultures and in other instructional formats. For example, Rong and Guo-Liang (2006) found that cognitive flexibility plays an important role in reading comprehension for Chinese children. Additionally, a recent adaptation of Cartwright's (2002) original reading-specific flexibility task was created for computerized administration in a collaborative learning situation. It was demonstrated to be a promising means for improving students' flexibility (Yuill, Kerawalla, Pearce, Luckin, & Harris, 2008). Further work is underway to examine the effects of this instructional format on students' reading comprehension (Yuill, personal communication, March 22, 2007).

HOW THIS NEW KNOWLEDGE CAN IMPROVE COMPREHENSION INSTRUCTION

The research reviewed in this chapter indicates that cognitive flexibility plays an important role in reading comprehension and can be taught. We can use these data to inform classroom instruction in at least two ways: (1) to assess flexibility as an indicator of children's potential success or difficulty with comprehension, and (2) to teach flexibility to improve reading comprehension (for additional information on assessing and teaching flexibility, see Cartwright, 2006, 2008a; Cartwright, Bock, et al., 2006).

Past work indicates that a particular kind of reading-specific flexibility, graphophonological–semantic flexibility, can be assessed in children and adults, and that such flexibility varies across the lifespan (see Cartwright, 2007, 2008a; Cartwright, Isaac, et al., 2006). Thus, we should expect variability in reading-specific flexibility across children at particular grade levels and even across children within classrooms. Additional research shows that this particular kind of reading-specific flexibility is a significant predictor of reading comprehension in beginning readers (Cartwright, Marshall, et al., 2008), intermediate-level readers (Cartwright, 2002), and adults (Cartwright, 2007). Assessment of elementary school children's reading-specific flexibility may therefore provide a useful classroom-based measurement of a cognitive process that is critical for successful comprehension, assisting teachers in the identification of children at risk for comprehension difficulties.

As would be expected, struggling readers show significantly lower levels of reading-specific flexibility and comprehension than their more advantaged peers. However, the research reviewed in this chapter is encouraging in this regard: Experimental and quasi-experimental work reveal that reading-specific flexibility can be taught to elementary school children, changing the way that these children process information about print, and producing significant improvements in reading comprehension (Cartwright, 2002; Cartwright, Schmidt, et al., 2007). Thus, this type of intervention seems to be a promising avenue to assist struggling readers. Additionally, the reading-specific flexibility intervention is relatively brief, occurring over 5 sessions that last approximately 15 minutes for individual intervention and 30–40 minutes for small-group intervention. The individual intervention format, because of its brevity, is ideal for administration by a reading resource teacher, trained tutor, or teachers' aide. However, the small-group intervention might be more practical if several children in a class demonstrate an inflexible focus on phonological aspects of print, with little attention to meaning. Furthermore, the small-group intervention may be a more manageable addition to a reading program than the individual intervention, because small-group instruction is a more typical instructional format for elementary classrooms and reading resource teachers (for more information on the flexibility intervention process, see Cartwright, 2006; Cartwright, Bock, et al., 2006).

DIRECTIONS FOR FUTURE RESEARCH

Contemporary cognitive-developmental work on cognitive flexibility has tremendous implications for understanding the flexibility with which skilled readers process text during successful reading comprehension. However, research applying these perspectives to reading comprehension is in its infancy. There is much room for additional work. The following questions offer possible next steps for future research in this area.

1. *How does reading-specific cognitive flexibility develop throughout one's lifetime?* Consistent with contemporary work in cognitive development, recent research shows that graphophonological–semantic flexibility develops across the lifespan. However, existing data are incomplete: No work has examined graphophonological–semantic flexibility

across all elementary grades, in adolescent readers, or in adults older than traditional college-age students. Additionally, even less work has examined the development of this skill in struggling readers, a population for whom work in cognitive flexibility might be especially beneficial. Thus, future work needs to expand our knowledge of the developmental course of reading-specific flexibility in skilled readers and in other populations for whom flexibility may be particularly relevant, such as struggling readers and English language learners. As noted previously, graphophonological–semantic flexibility is but one type of reading-specific flexibility that may impact reading comprehension processes. Because cognitive development is domain-specific, there is much room to develop assessments of flexibility in reading that tap other, specific elements of reading processes, such as syntactic, orthographic, or strategic features, so that a more complete picture of the role of flexibility in reading may begin to take shape.

2. *How might flexibility interventions be best implemented to improve comprehension?* Although flexibility can be taught, few studies have examined reading-specific flexibility interventions. The experimental (Cartwright, 2002) and quasi-experimental (Cartwright, Schmidt, et al., 2007) work reviewed in this chapter indicates that improvements in reading-specific cognitive flexibility may be achieved in a relatively brief time period, with concomitant increases in reading comprehension. This work is promising and deserves replication. Moreover, other means of intervention should be explored, such as the creation of whole-group instructional procedures or computerized interventions (e.g., the one completed in a collaborative instructional format by Yuill and colleagues, 2008). Furthermore, no work has examined the long-term effects of such interventions.

3. *What role does reading-specific flexibility play in comprehension processes?* The findings reviewed in this chapter indicate that reading-specific cognitive flexibility plays an important role in reading comprehension processes, but the mechanism of flexibility's contribution to comprehension is not yet clear. One potential avenue for this contribution might be to mediate the relation of vocabulary knowledge to comprehension. Although vocabulary knowledge is significantly related to comprehension ability (e.g., Stahl & Fairbanks, 1986), the contribution of vocabulary to reading comprehension is not always reliable (e.g., Mezynski, 1983; Tomesen & Aarnouste, 1998). Cognitive flexibility offers a potential explanation for this inconsistency, as an inflexible focus on phonological features of print (and not meaning) may prevent struggling readers from accessing existing vocabulary knowledge in service of comprehension. In a longitudinal study, Cartwright (2005; Cartwright, Marshall, Isaac, & Hodgkiss, 2006) tested this hypothesis in a sample of 161 first and second graders. Regression analyses indicated that flexibility mediated the relation between vocabulary and comprehension for these children. Moreover, no differences in reading comprehension emerged for children with low and high vocabulary knowledge as long as the children had high levels of reading-specific cognitive flexibility. Less flexible students, however, demonstrated significantly lower levels of reading comprehension; and a follow-up of 31 children 2 years later indicated that these patterns persisted, with pretest flexibility scores contributing uniquely to posttest comprehension scores beyond pretest vocabulary. These findings suggest that cognitive flexibility may enable readers to coordinate vocabulary knowledge with other text features in the comprehension process, but future research is necessary to replicate these findings and further elucidate the nature of this relation.

Understanding of fluency's contribution to comprehension may also be enhanced as we begin to understand better the role of cognitive flexibility in reading comprehension. Kuhn and Stahl's (2003) review of the fluency literature indicates that although we know much about ways to improve fluency, we know less about the cognitive bases for fluency processes. They argue that fluency involves accuracy and automaticity in decoding processes, as well as more meaning-focused processing to produce prosody and expressiveness. Certainly, automaticity in decoding plays an important role in reading fluency (LaBerge & Samuels, 1974). However, automatic decoding does not ensure that one can simultaneously and flexibly attend to meaning, which is required for the prosodic aspects of fluency. A prime example of such inflexible processing is children who have learned to speed through Dynamic Indicators of Basic Early Literacy Skills (DIBELS) passages (i.e., they display accuracy and automaticity), with little evidence of comprehension (Pressley, Hilden, & Shankland, 2006). Thus, the ability to attend flexibly to phonological and semantic aspects of print should be related to fluency beyond automatic word recognition. Bock, Isaac, Montaño, and Cartwright (2006) demonstrated that this is the case in a sample of adult readers. Cognitive flexibility may provide additional explanation for the cognitive basis of fluency beyond automaticity, offering additional insight into the relation between fluency and comprehension, a relation that deserves additional investigation.

4. *What are the implications of cognitive flexibility for theories of reading comprehension?* A final note for future research involves implications of work in cognitive flexibility for theories of reading comprehension. The Simple View of Reading model (e.g., Hoover & Gough, 1990), for example, suggests that skilled reading comprehension is the product of decoding and language comprehension; both of these processes are necessary, but neither by itself is sufficient for reading comprehension to occur. This widely cited theory assumes that skill on both of these components ensures skilled comprehension. However, even with high scores on both language comprehension and decoding assessed independently, there is no guarantee that individuals will be cognitively flexible enough to coordinate these two processes in service of reading comprehension (Pressley et al., in press). In support of this notion, Cartwright (2007) recently showed graphophonological–semantic flexibility contributes significant, unique variance to comprehension beyond the product of decoding and language comprehension in adult readers (even when general cognitive ability was controlled). In other words, flexible coordination of reading processes seems necessary for skilled reading comprehension, which is not as simple as we once assumed.

PROJECTIONS AND POSSIBILITIES FOR THE CLASSROOM OF 2030

Where might these research questions lead us in the future? A more complete picture of the role of cognitive flexibility in reading comprehension processes and a more detailed account of the development of reading-specific cognitive flexibility will provide an empirical foundation to guide classroom assessment. Identification of children who have difficulty coordinating flexibly the many processes involved in reading comprehension will permit targeted intervention for those at risk for comprehension difficulties. Additional research that expands and refines flexibility interventions, especially interventions that target particular demands of comprehension tasks, which children find difficult to manage flexibly, will permit improvement of essential cognitive processes for skilled comprehension. Such differentiated, empirically based interventions are necessary for effective comprehension instruction. Finally, research that further elucidates the role that cognitive flexibility plays in reading comprehension processes will expand our understanding of the complex nature of reading comprehension, fostering more informed research and instructional practice.

SUMMARY

Historically, researchers have recognized the importance of flexibility in skilled reading comprehension, and although various conceptions of flexibility in reading have emerged, they are not unified by a common theoretical foundation. This chapter highlights new cognitive-developmental work on cognitive flexibility, the ability to coordinate flexibly and simultaneously multiple aspects of complex cognitive tasks. This new perspective is consistent with historical conceptions of flexibility in reading and provides a unifying, theoretical foundation for continued work in this area. The primary focus of this chapter is on ways the new cognitive-developmental work on flexibility has been adapted to advance our understanding of reading comprehension processes and instruction. The research described in this chapter shows that reading-specific cognitive flexibility can be assessed, that it develops across childhood into adulthood and is significantly lower for disadvantaged readers, and that it makes a significant contribution to reading comprehension from beginning readers to adults. More importantly, this research shows that reading-specific cognitive flexibility can be taught, and that it produces significant improvements in flexibility and reading comprehension. These findings have important implications for work with struggling readers, who are often inflexible in the ways they approach reading tasks. More broadly, these findings have important implications for the ways we conceptualize reading comprehension, because they indicate that comprehension processes are more complex than we have traditionally assumed.

INTEGRATE, INVESTIGATE, AND INITIATE: QUESTIONS FOR DISCUSSION

1. I began this chapter by asking you to ask a beginning or struggling reader what good readers do. Please perform this action and share your results with colleagues. Make a list of all answers, what they do and do not have in common, and what these answers tell you about the cognitive flexibility of struggling and less able readers.

2. Write three sentences that describe what you consider the most important finding from having read this chapter. Share these summaries with other colleagues who read the same chapter or as a summary for teachers who have not read the chapter. How can this finding be used in your classroom to increase cognitive flexibility in your students?

3. Design a lesson that develops reading comprehension and cognitive flexibility. Share the lesson you designed with colleagues. Compare the similarities and differences between the lessons that were created to foster cognitive flexibility.

REFERENCES

Adams, M. J. (1990). *Beginning to read: Thinking and learning about print*. Cambridge, MA: MIT Press.

Andrews, G., & Halford, G. S. (2002). A cognitive complexity metric applied to cognitive development. *Cognitive Psychology, 45*, 153–219.

Berg, E. A. (1948). A simple objective technique for measuring flexibility in thinking. *Journal of General Psychology, 39*, 15–22.

Berger, A. (1967). Effectiveness of four methods of increasing reading rate, comprehension, and flexibility. *Perceptual and Motor Skills, 24*, 948–950.

Bialystok, E., & Niccols, A. (1989). Children's control over attention to phonological and semantic properties of words. *Journal of Psycholinguistic Research, 18,* 369–387.

Bigler, R. S., & Liben, L. (1992). Cognitive mechanisms in children's gender stereotyping: Theoretical and educational implications of a cognitive-based intervention. *Child Development, 63,* 1351–1363.

Blommers, P., & Lindquist, E. F. (1944). Rate of comprehension of reading: Its measurement and its relation to comprehension. *Journal of Educational Psychology, 35,* 449–473.

Bock, A. M., Isaac, M. C., Montaño, M., & Cartwright, K. B. (2006, March). *The relation of graphophonological–semantic flexibility to reading fluency in university students.* Poster presented at the 77th annual meeting of the Eastern Psychological Association, Baltimore, MD.

Braam, L. (1963). Developing and measuring flexibility in reading. *Reading Teacher, 16,* 247–251.

Cartwright, K. B. (2002). Cognitive development and reading: The relation of reading-specific multiple classification skill to reading comprehension in elementary school children. *Journal of Educational Psychology, 94,* 56–63.

Cartwright, K. B. (2005, December). *The role of flexibility in moderating effects of vocabulary on children's reading comprehension.* Paper presented at the 55th annual meeting of the National Reading Conference, Miami, FL.

Cartwright, K. B. (2006). Fostering flexibility and comprehension in elementary students. *Reading Teacher, 59,* 628–634.

Cartwright, K. B. (2007). The contribution of graphophonological–semantic flexibility to reading comprehension in college students: Implications for a less simple view of reading. *Journal of Literacy Research, 39,* 173–193.

Cartwright, K. B. (Ed.). (2008a). *Literacy processes: Cognitive flexibility in learning and teaching.* New York: Guilford Press.

Cartwright, K. B. (2008b). The role of cognitive flexibility in reading comprehension: Past, present, and future. In S. E. Israel & G. Duffy (Eds.), *Handbook of research on reading comprehension* (Chapter 5). Mahwah, NJ: Erlbaum.

Cartwright, K. B., Bock, A., Guiffré, H., & Montaño, M. (2006). Using classification tasks to assess and improve reading-specific cognitive flexibility. *Cognitive Technology, 11*(2), 23–29.

Cartwright, K. B., Green, S. J., & Marshall, T. R. (2003, December). *Cognitive development and reading: The contribution of reading-specific cognitive flexibility to word identification in first to third grade children.* Paper presented at the 53rd annual meeting of the National Reading Conference, Scottsdale, AZ.

Cartwright, K. B., Hodgkiss, M. D., & Isaac, M. C. (2008). Graphophonological–semantic flexibility: Contributions to skilled reading across the lifespan. In K. B. Cartwright (Ed.), *Literacy processes: Cognitive flexibility in learning and teaching.* New York: Guilford Press.

Cartwright, K. B., Isaac, M. C., & Dandy, K. L. (2006). The development of reading-specific representational flexibility: A cross-sectional comparison of second graders, fourth graders, and college students. In A. V. Mittel (Ed.), *Focus on educational psychology* (pp. 173–194). New York: Nova Science.

Cartwright, K. B, Marshall, T. R., Dandy, K. L., & Isaac, M. C. (2008). *The development of graphophonological–semantic flexibility and its contribution to reading comprehension in beginning readers.* Manuscript submitted to publication.

Cartwright, K. B., Marshall, T. R., Isaac, M. C., & Hodgkiss, M. D. (2006, December). *The role of flexibility in moderating effects of vocabulary on reading comprehension: Two years later.* Paper presented at the 56th annual meeting of the National Reading Conference, Los Angeles, CA.

Cartwright, K. B., Schmidt, K., Clause, J., Price, G., & Thomas, S. (2007). *Small group reading-specific flexibility intervention for struggling readers.* Unpublished data, Christopher Newport University, Newport News, VA.

Case, R. (1992). Neo-Piagetian theories of child development. In R. J. Sternberg & C. A. Berg (Eds.), *Intellectual development* (pp. 161–196). New York: Cambridge University Press.

Case, R., & Okamoto, Y. (1996). The role of central conceptual structures in the development of children's thought. *Monographs of the Society for Research in Child Development, 61*(1–2, Serial No. 246).

Clay, M. M. (1985). *The early detection of reading difficulties* (3rd ed.). Portsmouth, NH: Heinemann.

Clay, M. M. (1991). *Becoming literate: The construction of inner control.* Portsmouth, NH: Heinemann.

Clay, M. M. (2001). *Change over time in children's literacy development.* Portsmouth, NH: Heinemann.

Deák, G. O. (2003). The development of cognitive flexibility and language abilities. *Advances in Child Development and Behavior, 31,* 271–327.

Dewitz, P., & Dewitz, P. K. (2003). They can read the words, but they can't understand. *Reading Teacher, 56,* 422–435.

Diamond, A., & Kirkham, N. (2005). Not quite as grown up as we like to think: Parallels between cognition in childhood and adulthood. *Psychological Science, 16,* 291–297.

Dolch, E. W. (1960). *Teaching primary reading* (3rd ed.). Champaign, IL: Garrard Press.

Dowdy, C. A., Crump, W. D., & Welch, M. W. (1982). Reading flexibility of learning disabled and normal students at three grade levels. *Learning Disability Quarterly, 5,* 253–263.

Farrar, M. J., & Ashwell, S. (2008). The role of representational ability in the development of phonological awareness in preschool children. In K. B. Cartwright (Ed.), *Literacy processes: Cognitive flexibility in learning and teaching.* New York: Guilford Press.

Farrar, M. J., Ashwell, S., & Maag, L. (2005). The emergence of phonological awareness: Connections to language and theory of mind development. *First Language, 25,* 157–172.

Forguson, L., & Gopnik, A. (1988). The ontogeny of common sense. In J. W. Astington, P. L. Harris, & D. R. Olson (Eds.), *Developing theories of mind* (pp. 226–243). New York: Cambridge University Press.

Frye, D., Zelazo, P. D., & Burack, J. A. (1998). Cognitive complexity and control I: Theory of mind in typical and atypical development. *Current Directions in Psychological Science, 7,* 116–121.

Gaskins, R. W., & Gaskins, I. W. (1997). Creating readers who read for meaning and love to read: The Benchmark School reading program. In S. A. Stahl & D. A. Hayes (Eds.), *Instructional models in reading* (pp. 131–159). Mahwah, NJ: Erlbaum.

Golbeck, S. L. (1983). Reconstructing a large-scale spatial arrangement: Effects of environmental organization and operativity. *Developmental Psychology, 19,* 644–653.

Goodman, K. S. (1973). Miscues: Windows on the reading process. In K. S. Goodman (Ed.), *Miscue analysis: Applications to reading instruction.* Urbana, IL: ERIC Clearinghouse on Reading and Communication Skills.

Goodman, K. S. (1976). Behind the eye: What happens in reading. In H. Singer & R. B. Ruddell (Eds.), *Theoretical models and processes of reading* (2nd ed., pp. 470–496). Newark, DE: International Reading Association.

Goodman, K. S. (1994). Reading, writing, and written texts: A transactional sociopsycholinguistic view. In R. B. Ruddell, M. R. Ruddell, & H. Singer (Eds.), *Theoretical models and processes of reading* (4th ed., pp. 1093–1130). Newark, DE: International Reading Association.

Hoover, W. A., & Gough, P. B. (1990). The simple view of reading. *Reading and Writing: An Interdisciplinary Journal, 2,* 127–160.

Inhelder, B., & Piaget, J. (1964). *The early growth of logic in the child* (E. A. Lunzer & D. Papert, Trans.). New York: Humanities Press.

Jacques, S., & Zelazo, P. D. (2001). The Flexible Item Selection Task (FIST): A measure of executive function in preschoolers. *Developmental Neuropsychology, 20,* 573–591.

Karmiloff-Smith, A. (1991). Innate constraints and developmental change. In S. Carey & R. Gelman (Eds.), *The epigenesis of mind: Essays on biology and cognition* (pp. 171–197). Hillsdale, NJ: Erlbaum.

Kuhn, D., & Pease, M. (2006). Do children and adults learn differently? *Journal of Cognition and Development, 7,* 279–293.

Kuhn, M. R., & Stahl, S. A. (2003). Fluency: A review of developmental and remedial practices. *Journal of Educational Psychology, 95,* 3–21.

LaBerge, & Samuels, S. J. (1974). Toward a theory of automatic information processing in reading. *Cognitive Psychology, 6,* 293–323.

Labouvie-Vief, G. (1992). A neo-Piagetian perspective on adult cognitive development. In R. J. Sternberg & C. A. Berg (Eds.), *Intellectual development* (pp. 197–228). New York: Cambridge University Press.

Masson, M. E. (1987). Remembering reading operations with and without awareness. In B. K. Britton & S. M. Glynn (Eds.), *Executive control processes in reading* (pp. 253–277). Hillsdale, NJ: Erlbaum.

Mezynski, K. (1983). Issues concerning the acquisition of knowledge: Effects of vocabulary training on reading comprehension. *Review of Educational Research, 53,* 253–279.

Miller, P. H. (2006). A lot of knowledge is a dangerous thing: Learning in children and adults. *Journal of Cognition and Development, 7,* 305–308.

Oakhill, J., & Yuill, N. (1996). Higher order factors in comprehension disability: Processes and remediation. In C. Cornoldi & J. Oakhill (Eds.), *Reading comprehension difficulties: Processes and intervention* (pp. 69–92). Mahwah, NJ: Erlbaum.

Piaget, J., & Inhelder, B. (1969). *The psychology of the child* (H. Weaver, Trans.). New York: Basic Books. (Original work published 1966)

Pressley, M. (2006). *Reading instruction that works: The case for balanced teaching* (3rd ed.). New York: Guilford Press.

Pressley, M., & Afflerbach, P. (1995). *Verbal protocols of reading: The nature of constructively responsive reading.* Mahwah, NJ: Erlbaum.

Pressley, M., Duke, N. K., Gaskins, I. W., Fingeret, L., Halladay, J., Hilden, K., et al. (in press). Working with struggling readers: Why we must get beyond the simple view of reading and visions of how it might be done. In T. Gutkin & C. R. Reynolds (Eds.), *Handbook of school psychology* (4th ed.). New York: Wiley.

Pressley, M., Hilden, K. R., & Shankland, R. K. (2006). *An evaluation of end-grade-3 Dynamic Indicators of Basic Early Literacy Skills (DIBELS): Speed reading without comprehension, predicting little.* East Lansing: Michigan State University, College of Education, Literacy Achievement Research Center.

Ramsel, D., & Grabe, M. (1983). Attention allocation and performance in goal-directed reading: Age difference in reading flexibility. *Journal of Reading Behavior, 15,* 55–65.

Rong, Y., & Guo-Liang, Y. (2006). Cognitive flexibility of reading-disabled children: Development and characteristics. *Chinese Journal of Clinical Psychology, 14,* 33–35.

Sinnott, J. D. (1998). *The development of logic in adulthood: Postformal thought and its applications.* New York: Plenum Press.

Spiro, R. J. (2004). Principled pluralism for adaptive flexibility in teaching and learning to read. In R. B. Ruddell & N. J. Unrau (Eds.), *Theoretical models and processes of reading* (5th ed., pp. 654–659). Newark, DE: International Reading Association.

Spiro, R. J., Coulson, R. L., Feltovich, P. J., & Anderson, D. K. (1994). Cognitive flexibility theory: Advanced knowledge acquisition in ill-structured domains. In R. B. Ruddell, M. R. Ruddell, & H. Singer (Eds.), *Theoretical models and processes of reading* (4th ed., pp. 602–615). Newark, DE: International Reading Association. (Original work published 1988)

Spiro, R. J., Vispoel, W. P., Schmitz, J. G., Samarapungavan, A., & Boerger, A. E. (1987). Knowledge acquisition for application: Cognitive flexibility and transfer in complex content domains. In B. K. Britton & S. M. Glynn (Eds.), *Executive control processes in reading* (pp. 177–199). Hillsdale, NJ: Erlbaum.

Stahl, S. A., & Fairbanks, M. M. (1986). The effects of vocabulary instruction: A model-based meta-analysis. *Review of Educational Research, 56,* 72–110.

Sternberg, R. J. (2000). The rebirth of children's learning. *Child Development, 71,* 26–35.

Sternberg, R. J., & Lyon, G. R. (2002). Making a difference in education: Will psychology pass up the chance? *Monitor on Psychology, 33*(7), 76.

Tomesen, M., & Aarnoutse, C. (1998). Effects of an instructional programme for deriving word meanings. *Educational Studies, 24*, 107–128.

Wagner, R. K., & Sternberg, R. J. (1987). Executive control in reading comprehension. In B. K. Britton & S. M. Glynn (Eds.), *Executive control processes in reading* (pp. 1–21). Hillsdale, NJ: Erlbaum.

Woodcock, R. W. (1987). *Woodcock Reading Mastery Test—Revised*. Circle Pines, MN: American Guidance Service.

Yuill, N., Kerawalla, L., Pearce, D., Luckin, R., & Harris, A. (2008). Using technology to teach flexibility through peer discussion. In K. B. Cartwright (Ed.), *Literacy processes: Cognitive flexibility in learning and teaching*. New York: Guilford Press.

Zelazo, P. D., & Frye, D. (1998). Cognitive complexity and control II: The development of executive function in childhood. *Current Directions in Psychological Science, 7*, 121–126.

Zelazo, P. D., Müller, U., Frye, D., & Marcovitch, S. (2003). The development of executive function in early childhood. *Monographs of the Society for Research in Child Development, 68*(3, Serial No. 274).

5

Metacognition in Comprehension Instruction
What We've Learned Since NRP

LINDA BAKER

> I don't know how to teach thinking strategies unless I begin with metacognition. Taking time to explore metacognition sets a foundation on which to build. In making kids aware of how they think about their own thinking, I open a channel through which purposeful conversation can flow. With every group of students I teach, no matter the grade level, no matter the subject area, I spend time noticing, naming, and exploring metacognition.
>
> —McGregor (2007, p. 11)

In its 2000 report, the National Reading Panel (NRP) concluded that an important component of metacognition, comprehension monitoring, can be taught, and that it can improve comprehension. The NRP identified 20 instructional studies of comprehension monitoring that met scientifically rigorous criteria for inclusion in its analysis of what works in reading instruction. Further advocacy for incorporating metacognition into reading instruction came from two other national panels in the United States at about the same time. Writing for the National Research Council, Snow, Burns, and Griffin (1998) concluded that "adequate progress in learning to read English beyond the initial level depends on [among other things] control over procedures for monitoring comprehension and repairing comprehension" (p. 223). Similarly, the RAND Reading Study Group (2002, p. 32), tasked with crafting a research agenda on reading comprehension, concluded that "instruction can be effective in providing students with a repertoire of strategies that promote comprehension monitoring and foster comprehension," and called for further research on "the role that cognitive and metacognitive strategies play in accounting for individual differences in acquiring both word-level and comprehension skills" (p. 86).

These three prominent reports by distinguished panels of reading experts have been widely cited in the ensuing years. When John Flavell (1976) first introduced the intriguing construct of metacognition in the mid-1970s, he stimulated a flood of research on individuals' knowledge and control of their own cognitive processes, including reading. Although research on these topics had waned somewhat by the turn of the century, especially in the United States, the importance of metacognition as a construct was still acknowledged. The purpose of this chapter is to review the research on metacognition as it relates to reading comprehension instruction that has been completed since the NRP report was published. Like Tanney McGregor, the K–12 literacy specialist quoted at the beginning of the chapter, my perspective is that strategic reading is only possible if readers are metacognitively aware. This, of course, means that students should receive metacognitively oriented reading instruction.

This chapter highlights the following:

- Cross-sectional and longitudinal research on metacognitive development in reading.
- Cognitive process research illustrating how metacognition contributes to reading comprehension in conjunction with basic processes, such as working memory and decoding skills.
- Research illustrating how self-system variables, such as motivation, interest, and self-efficacy, relate to metacognition and the effectiveness of strategy training.
- Classroom-based intervention research designed to enhance reading comprehension by fostering metacognitive awareness and control.
- Technology-based interventions to foster metacognitive awareness and control.

WHAT'S OUT THERE TODAY: ESTABLISHED RESEARCH AND PRACTICE

Once developmental psychologists began to study metacognition in the 1970s, the construct quickly attracted the attention of researchers seeking to explain why some students were more successful readers than others. The consistent finding at that time was that older and better readers exhibited higher levels of metacognitive knowledge about reading, and were more skilled at monitoring and regulating their own comprehension processes, than younger and less able readers. The early research was primarily of a descriptive and correlational nature (see Baker & Brown, 1984; Garner, 1987). For example, Myers and Paris (1978) interviewed second and sixth graders about their metacognitive knowledge of reading purposes, tasks, and strategies. Younger readers did not seem to realize that they must attempt to make sense of text; they focused on reading as a decoding rather than a meaning-getting process. In addition, older students had more awareness of strategies for dealing with words or sentences they did not understand, such as using a dictionary, asking someone for help, or rereading a paragraph to try to figure out the meaning from context. Students' metacognitive knowledge about reading, as assessed through the interviews, questionnaires, or verbal reports used in the studies cited earlier, remains an active and important area of inquiry today (Mokhtari & Sheorey, 2008; Pressley & Gaskins, 2006).

Also in the 1970s, researchers began to document developmental and individual differences in students' comprehension monitoring abilities, and such research continues today. Many of these studies used the error detection paradigm, in which errors or problems are introduced into texts, and various indices are used to determine whether readers notice the problems and attempt to resolve them. For example, readers may be asked to underline or report detected errors, or online processing measures may reveal longer pauses when readers encounter problematic text.

The early descriptive studies showing differences in metacognitive knowledge and control quickly stimulated interest in the possibility that metacognitive skills might be deliberately fostered, leading to the design and implementation of training studies. In these studies, researchers divided students into groups that received or did not receive some form of instruction designed to promote metacognitive knowledge and/or control. Results were quite consistent in showing that students did learn more about their own reading processes and improve in their ability to monitor their comprehension. More importantly, a few studies (e.g., Bereiter & Bird, 1985) showed that these trained students' reading comprehension also improved.

These small-scale laboratory studies gave way to research conducted in the much more complex environment of real classrooms. Most of these efforts were based on the notion that the best way to promote metacognition is to discuss, model, and practice it explicitly. Many also incorporated Vygotsky's (1978) perspective that in regulating performance there should be a gradual transfer of responsibility from the adult to the child. A landmark study in this area was Paris, Cross, and Lipson's (1984) Informed Strategies for Learning (ISL). Over a 12-week period, third- and fifth-grade children were given lessons in the classroom on the use of various strategies for improving comprehension and comprehension monitoring. They were given opportunities to learn declarative, procedural, and conditional knowledge related to strategy use. The program was effective in promoting metacognitive knowledge about reading and comprehension monitoring. A disappointing outcome was that it did not yield gains on a standardized reading comprehension test relative to comparison classrooms; this issue is revisited later in this chapter.

A second influential intervention study was conducted by Palincsar and Brown (1984), who developed an approach known as reciprocal teaching. Seventh-grade children working within small groups were taught to use the strategies of predicting upcoming text, clarifying unknown words and concepts, summarizing what was read, and generating deep questions about the material. These particular strategies were selected for their potential to help students to comprehend, as well as to monitor that comprehension. The intervention was successful in promoting strategy use and reading comprehension, and it set the stage for many more multiple-strategies interventions (e.g., Collaborative Strategic Reading [CSR], Klingner, Vaughn, & Shumm, 1998; Peer-Assisted Learning Strategies [PALS], Fuchs, Fuchs, Mathes, & Simmons, 1997; Transactional Strategies Instruction [TSI], Brown, Pressley, Van Meter, & Schuder, 1996).

Two meta-analyses based primarily on 1980s research indicated that metacognitively oriented instruction, particularly reciprocal teaching, can improve reading comprehension (Haller, Child, & Walberg, 1988; Rosenshine & Meister, 1994). In other words, a strong consensus had already developed prior to the reports of the national panels around the millennium that promotion of metacognitive knowledge and control was important (Baker, 2002).

Almost from the outset literacy researchers began to share their findings on metacognition with practitioners. Articles written for teachers began to appear in the early 1980s, with recommendations on how to promote metacognition in the classroom and to assess it in students. Too often, these recommendations were made without a solid, supporting research base, and they became a source of concern that metacognition would be taught in isolation, as a goal in itself, rather than as a means to promote better comprehension and learning from text (Baker, 2002; Paris, 2002). Nevertheless, despite the attention given to metacognition in practitioner publications, workshops, and preservice education, and the growing research base indicating how and why to promote metacognition, classroom observations and teacher interviews revealed well into the 1990s that very little metacognitively oriented reading comprehension instruction was actually taking place in schools (Baker, 2005; Pressley & Block, 2002).

NEW RESEARCH ON METACOGNITION IN COMPREHENSION INSTRUCTION

The focus in this section is on research published since the NRP report was released in 2000. Some of the work was no doubt conceived, if not implemented, prior to that, and some of the work was not specifically informed by the panel recommendations, but the year 2000 can be taken as the point in time when metacognition attained full legitimacy as an integral component of reading instruction. Indeed, many researchers now cite the NRP report as validation of their intervention approaches and choice of cognitive and metacognitive strategies (e.g., Guthrie, Wigfield, & Perencevich, 2004; Kim et al., 2006; Lubliner & Smetana, 2005).

Although the emphasis in this section is on applied research that directly examines recent research on the impact of instruction in metacognition on reading comprehension, I first discuss some basic studies that enhance our understanding of how metacognition interacts with other cognitive and motivational processes to affect reading comprehension. Given length constraints, I selectively present only those studies involving elementary and secondary students (for further coverage, see Baker, 2008; Baker & Beall, 2008).

Descriptive and Correlational Research

Cross-Sectional Research on Developmental Differences

Descriptive research continues to examine students' metacognitive knowledge and control. Research outcomes today look remarkably similar to those of 30 years ago, when research on metacognition was in its infancy. For example, Eme, Puustinen, and Coutelet (2006) interviewed third- and fifth-grade students in France about their metacognitive knowledge and their awareness of control strategies, and documented approaches the students used during an authentic reading task. Fifth graders were more likely than third graders to cite understanding as characteristic of a good reader, whereas the younger students described a good reader as one who reads quickly without a mistake. On a reading task, fifth graders did not attempt to correct comprehension difficulties by searching back through the text, even though same-age students had identified rereading as a useful strategy. Students at both levels focused on comprehension difficulties at the word level; only one student identified a whole proposition as a source of misunderstanding. What these results indicate, distressingly, is that little has changed with respect to the metacognitve abilities of elementary schoolchildren; there is still much room for teachers to play a role through instruction.

*Longitudinal Evidence of Stability
in Cognition–Metacognition–Motivation Connections*

Longitudinal studies of metacognitive development are now increasingly available. Data collected from the same children over a period of years are important because they indicate that there is considerable stability in children's metacognition over the long term. In other words, children do not automatically develop increased metacognitive skills simply with age and reading experience. For example, Roeschl-Heils, Schneider, and van Kraayenoord (2003) first examined German children's metacognitive knowledge in grade 3 or 4 in relation to reading motivation and reading comprehension and again in grade 7 or 8. Students who scored higher on assessments of metacognitive knowledge in elementary school continued to do so in middle school. Similarly, relations among reading interest, self-concept, reading ability, and metcognition were statistically significant at both time points. Metacognitive knowledge was a significant predictor of reading comprehension in both elementary and middle school. This study also demonstrated the important links among motivation, metacognition, and comprehension. Children with less interest in reading had weaker metacognitive skills and performed more poorly on reading assessments in grade 3 or 4 and in grade 7 or 8.

Metacognition and Other Basic Processes in Reading

Researchers today are much more cognizant of the fact that metacognition interacts with other cognitive skills to influence reading outcomes. Several studies have illustrated the importance of examining multiple contributors to reading comprehension. For example, Zinar (2000) examined the extent to which comprehension monitoring skills contribute to the prediction of reading comprehension, above and beyond word identification skills. Fourth-grade children's comprehension monitoring was measured online with the error detection paradigm. Students read passages containing embedded inconsistencies, and their reading times and lookbacks were assessed, as were verbalizations of problem detection. Word identification was a powerful predictor of reading comprehension, as expected, but the extent to which children slowed down their reading on encountering inconsistent information was also a significant predictor. In a supplementary analysis, Zinar determined that children who slowed down their reading when encountering the inconsistency, and who looked back at the sentence that set up the inconsistency, had the highest comprehension scores on a standardized test. In other words, those who showed evidence not only of evaluation but also regulation were the best comprehenders.

The contribution of comprehension monitoring to comprehension was examined in conjunction with working memory and inference making by Cain, Oakhill, and Bryant (2004) in a longitudinal study of English children ages 8–11. They assessed comprehension monitoring with error detection tasks, using age-appropriate materials in which students needed to find embedded inconsistencies. Working memory and comprehension monitoring were significant predictors of comprehension. Comprehension monitoring accounted for unique variance once working memory and other background variables (word-reading skill, verbal ability) were controlled. Comprehension monitoring skill was significantly correlated with most measures at the three testing points, providing further evidence of stability in the relations between the cognitive and metacognitive processes.

Oakhill, Hartt, and Samols (2005) focused on the extent to which comprehension predicted comprehension monitoring, rather than vice versa. In two studies, English children ages 9 and 10 were matched for reading vocabulary and word recognition skills. In the first study, the better comprehenders identified more sentence-level anomalies, but not word-level problems, than the poorer comprehenders. In the second study, the better comprehenders detected more inconsistencies in the text, especially when the inconsistent sentences were widely spaced, putting a greater burden on working memory. Working memory ability was related to error detection, but comprehension ability was also a good, and sometimes better, predictor of comprehension monitoring. Of course, the correlational nature of these studies prohibits causal conclusions; most likely, comprehension monitoring and comprehension are reciprocally related.

From the earliest days of research on comprehension monitoring, it was speculated that working memory limitations were responsible for students' difficulties in identifying inconsistencies in text. The work of Oakhill and her colleagues (2005) linking working memory with error detection provides further support for this position. A recent study with adult readers indicates that those with limited working memory can compensate for processing limitations by selectively rereading relevant portions of text (Burton & Daneman, 2007). It has been shown that young readers can also compensate for limited processing abilities (Walczyk, Marsiglia, Johns, & Bryan, 2004); "inefficient" readers compensated by pausing, looking back, rereading, and sounding out words more often than efficient readers, but their literal comprehension scores were comparable.

In summary, basic research since the year 2000 has replicated the developmental and ability-related differences in metacognitive knowledge and comprehension monitoring reported previously. New directions include a greater focus on metacognition in conjunction with other cognitive and motivational processes in reading, and on how comprehension monitoring skills might compensate for limitations in basic processes.

Intervention Research

Classroom-Based Instructional Research

A number of classroom-based intervention studies have been published since the release of the NRP report. Interestingly, much of this work was conducted in Europe, so one cannot directly attribute the research to the influence of the NRP. However, many European countries have been moving in similar directions to those in the United States. For example, Belgium established new standards stipulating that students be taught effective cognitive and metacognitive strategies that facilitate text comprehension (De Corte, Verschaffel, & Van de Ven, 2001). In all but one of the studies discussed in this section, classroom teachers taught multiple strategies, both cognitive and metacognitive, that had previously been documented as effective. And in all but one of the studies, the instructional approach included both teacher-led and student-centered components previously documented as effective (i.e., explicit explanation of how, when, and why to use cognitive and metacognitive strategies, modeling, guided practice, and peer collaboration).

A methodological difference between the post-NRP and earlier studies is that more sophisticated data-analytic techniques are now available, and there is greater recognition of the need to take into account the fact that students are clustered within classrooms. Thus, many of these studies employed multilevel analyses that took into account both classroom (teacher)-level and student-level effects, permitting greater confidence in the conclusions.

One such study was carried out in Belgium (DeCorte et al., 2001) with fifth-grade students. Targeted strategies included activating prior knowledge, clarifying difficult words, forming main ideas, creating schematic representations of text, and regulating one's own reading processes. Four classroom teachers implemented 24 lessons over a 4-month period; eight additional classes served as a comparison group. Students in the intervention classrooms applied the taught strategies more capably than comparison students on a posttest. A transfer test showed that the students were also able to apply the learned strategies in the classroom during a social studies lesson. However, growth on a standardized reading comprehension test did not differ across groups. Students' reading attitudes were assessed pre- and postintervention, but no differential changes were revealed. Follow-up tests 2 months after the intervention revealed continued benefits in strategy application.

A similar, classroom-based intervention project was carried out by Houtveen and van de Grift (2007) in the Netherlands. The goal, again, was to examine the extent to which classroom teachers could enhance students' reading comprehension and metacognitive knowledge about reading strategies. Participants in the study were 10-year-old students enrolled in 20 different intervention or comparison schools. Teachers in the intervention schools provided instruction in cognitive and metacognitive strategies using the approaches previously documented as effective. Students were assessed on metacognitive knowledge and reading comprehension on pre-, post-, and delayed posttests. The metacognitive questionnaire tapped strategies that students can use to check their own reading behavior (monitoring) and strategies to use when they cannot understand a text or paragraph. Teachers in the intervention schools demonstrated better "metacognitive strategy instruction" and devoted more instructional time to their students than those in the comparison schools. Intervention students gained more in metacognitive knowledge and in reading comprehension, as assessed on a standardized test. In addition, they continued to show better comprehension at the beginning of the next school year.

The relative advantages of combining instruction in comprehension strategies with support for cognitive and motivational self-regulation was investigated by Souvignier and Mokhlesgerami (2006). Participants in the study were 20 classes of German fifth graders. The program comprised 20 lessons of 45 minutes each, delivered by the classroom teachers. Strategy knowledge was at the core of the program, and so all intervention students learned cognitive and metacognitive strategies to summarize a text (organization) and to go beyond a text (elaboration). An organizational metacognitive strategy involves checking whether main ideas can be remembered and an elaborative metacognitive strategy involves checking understanding. Students in the cognitive self-regulation condition were also provided with a structure to integrate situational demands, choice of strategies, and the monitoring and regulation of the reading process. A third group of students received not only strategy and cognitive self-regulation supports but also motivation self-regulation supports to help them initiate and maintain the unfamiliar and challenging learning activities. A fourth group served as a no-treatment comparison.

Students were administered pre-, post-, and delayed posttest assessments. All three of the strategy-oriented instructional programs led to improvements in reading comprehension (as assessed on a standardized test) and understanding and application of reading strategies. However, students' changes in self-efficacy did not differ from those in the comparison group. In the long-term follow-up assessments, the program that included not only strategy instruction but also cognitive and motivational self-regulation had the strongest effects. Of particular interest is that effect sizes on the delayed test tended to be even stronger than those on the immediate posttest, suggesting that with the appropriate strategies available, students could continue to improve their skills on their own.

In another large-scale study in Belgium, Van Keer and Verhaeghe (2005) also evaluated the effectiveness of explicit reading comprehension strategies instruction. Again, the strategies were both cognitive and metacognitive, including word- and passage-level comprehension monitoring. The instructional approach of the teachers was consistent with the best practices identified in earlier research. The manipulation of particular interest in this study was how students practiced the strategies they were taught. In one condition, the teacher led whole-class activities; in another condition, practice took place through reciprocal, same-age peer tutoring, and in still another condition, through cross-age peer-tutoring. Second- and fifth-grade students took part in the study. Students were assessed with a standardized reading comprehension test pretest, posttest, and 6 months after study completion, as well as with tests of reading attitudes and self-efficacy. For the cross-age tutoring condition, fifth graders were paired with second graders.

Results revealed that second graders benefited from teacher-led and cross-age tutoring activities, but not from same-age tutoring. Moreover, the effects did not last 6 months after program completion. Fifth graders in all three conditions performed significantly better on the posttest than peers in a comparison group. Results also showed continued growth for the students in the teacher-led and reciprocal teaching conditions 6 months after program completion, but not for students in the cross-age tutoring group. The study did not assess growth in metacognitive knowledge and strategies directly. Students did not show differential growth in reading attitude or self-efficacy, even when they were provided with assistance in promoting motivation self-regulation.

An intervention study carried out in England by de Jager, Jansen, and Reezigt (2005) drew upon a literacy curriculum already in use that emphasizes metacognition. The primary purpose of the study was to compare two different instructional approaches for teaching metacognitive skills to seventh graders: direct instruction or cognitive apprenticeship. Change in student metacognitive knowledge was assessed over the course of instruction and compared to that of students not receiving a metacognitively oriented curriculum. The assessment tapped students' self-reported use of reading strategies and strategies to repair misunderstanding, as well as metacognitive knowledge about effective approaches to reading. Students who received either type of instruction with metacognitive focus gained more in knowledge and skills over the year than students in the comparison group, who showed virtually no growth. The lack of spontaneous metacognitive development in the comparison classrooms illustrates the importance of providing an instructional environment in which metacognition is emphasized. Change in reading comprehension was not assessed in this study.

The final study considered in this section is a small-scale intervention that focused only on comprehension monitoring at the word level (Lubliner & Smetana, 2005). Students in three classrooms were taught strategies to identify words they did not understand in the passages they read, strategies to figure out their meanings, and how to select the appropriate strategy for the specific context. The study was conducted with fifth-grade children in a very low-performing school. Students were first assessed 12 weeks before the intervention started, at which time they received conventional classroom instruction. They were assessed a second time immediately prior to the intervention, and a third time at the end. Students' identification of unknown words and their reading comprehension and vocabulary achievement were assessed. Over the course of the 12-week intervention, students increased the percentage of words they correctly identified as unknown, from 20% on the first assessment to 38% on the third. In addition, their reading comprehension and vocabulary improved.

A conventional comparison group was not included in this study, but data were collected for comparison from students in a high-achieving school. Identification of unknown words was at comparable levels by the end of the intervention, suggesting to the authors that this might be a viable approach for narrowing the achievement gap. It is quite likely, however, that had the students from the high-achieving school participated in the intervention, they too would have benefited, thus perpetuating the gap. Furthermore, it is important to note that the students still failed to identify almost two-thirds of the words whose meanings they did not adequately understand, so there was plenty of room for improvement.

To synthesize, the results of the five multiple-strategies interventions revealed significant increases in metacognitive knowledge and control in the four studies in which it was assessed. Clearly, the instruction effectively did what it was intended to do. More importantly, there were significant gains in comprehension on a standardized test in three of the four studies in which it was assessed. Because such tests are not usually compatible with the time-intensive application of reading strategies, it has previously been difficult to achieve such effects on the kinds of tests that matter for accountability purposes. Finally, there were no significant gains in self-system variables (e.g., reading attitudes, self-efficacy) in the three studies in which they were assessed. Correlational research is clear in showing associations of metacognition and self-system variables (e.g., Roeschl-Heils et al., 2003), but it does not appear that attitudes and efficacy were directly affected by increases in strategic reading skills.

Interventions Using Technology

The turn of the century has seen ever greater availability of technology in schools and increasingly sophisticated software that can facilitate the development of reading comprehension skills. Space constraints do not permit a detailed examination of this topic, but two illustrative studies are presented. Both show how reciprocal teaching of multiple strategies can be facilitated with technology.

A computer-based application of collaborative strategic reading showed promising results for middle school students with reading difficulties (Kim et al., 2006). At the beginning of each lesson, teachers provided explicit strategy instruction tailored to the identified needs of each student. The Computer-Assisted Collaborative Strategic Reading (CACSR) program comprises two parts: learning collaborative strategic reading itself (what each strategy is, when to use it, why it is important, and how to use it) and using collaborative strategic reading to learn (including computer-driven supports to learning). Students in the experimental condition outscored control students in the quality of their composed main ideas and the questions they generated from the text.

Research reviewed earlier in the chapter revealed that one of the reasons younger and less skilled readers do not monitor their comprehension as effectively as older and better readers is that their decoding skills are too weak to permit fluent reading. Engaging in laborious decoding interferes with not only the construction of meaning but also comprehension monitoring. Technology can reduce the processing demands associated with decoding. Having students listen to audiobooks as they follow along in the text is a simple, low-tech option. This has the added advantage of providing struggling older readers access to more engaging stories than those they would be capable of reading without assistance. A compelling demonstration of the effectiveness of tape-assisted reciprocal teaching was provided by LeFevre, Moore, and Wilkinson (2003) with 9-year-old poor readers in New Zealand. In a single-subject design, groups of students engaged in reciprocal teaching either conventionally or with tape assistance. The students who had adequate decoding but poor comprehension learned to engage in the strategies effectively with both approaches, but the poor decoders benefited only with tape assistance. The adequate decoders generalized their learning of strategies to the classroom, but the poor decoders did not. Without support in word recognition, they had difficulty applying the cognitive and metacognitive strategies they had been taught. This instructional intervention, like several of the classroom-based ones, led to gains on a standardized test of reading comprehension.

HOW THIS NEW KNOWLEDGE CAN IMPROVE COMPREHENSION INSTRUCTION

The recent research informs our understanding of how metacognition interacts with other reading processes to affect comprehension, and it demonstrates quite convincingly that many children do not spontaneously develop metacognitive knowledge and control. The instructional interventions provide valuable information with respect to the types of interventions that are effective, and with whom, and they further reinforce the conclusions of the NRP that comprehension monitoring is critical to effective comprehension. These issues are now further elaborated.

New research indicates that comprehension monitoring is an important contributor to reading comprehension, above and beyond basic skills such as word recognition, and that evaluating *and* regulating comprehension are associated with better reading comprehension than evaluating alone. In other words, it is not enough for a child to recognize that he or she does not understand; the child also needs to know what to do about it. Therefore, teachers are on firm ground in teaching students to identify portions of text that are hard to understand, whether at the individual-word level or the sentence or passage level. Furthermore, they should teach students strategies for resolving the comprehension obstacles, such as making inferences, rereading text, and drawing on prior knowledge. Finally, they should teach students how to decide among different strategies or to try alternate strategies depending on the particular situation. These recommendations have been standard in discussions of comprehension monitoring research, but the empirical evidence was not previously so compelling.

New research on the developmental course of metacognition continues to show that older children have better metacognitive knowledge and control than younger children, and that the extent of growth is small over time in the absence of direct instruction. Thus, children who have weak metacognitive skills when they are younger also have weak skills when they are older. Measures of metacognition are strongly correlated over periods as long as 4 years, and there is stability in the magnitude of the metacognition–comprehension correlations over time. The intervention studies, which can be conceptualized as short-term longitudinal studies, also revealed little or no growth over time for children who did not receive metacognitively oriented instruction. Clearly, it cannot be assumed that children will simply "catch up" as they develop. Deliberate instruction is required.

New research examining metacognition in conjunction with more basic reading processes has important implications for instruction. It is well established that working memory plays a role in text comprehension, but working memory is not readily amenable to intervention. Cain et al. (2004) suggested that if working memory and comprehension monitoring are both inadequate, providing instruction in comprehension monitoring should help to circumvent problems in reading comprehension associated with working memory limitations. Burton and Daneman (2007) came up with a similar recommendation for teachers working with students whose working memory capacity is limited: "Instruct them about the value of invoking look-back strategies more frequently, especially when the text deals with unfamiliar and goal-relevant material" (p. 179). We now know that readers can indeed compensate for limited processing abilities (Walczyk et al., 2004). Poor decoders are likely to demonstrate working memory problems because of the additional effort they must expend to identify individual words. As LeFevre et al. (2003) demonstrated, reducing the processing demands by having students listen to texts on tape enables them to use comprehension monitoring strategies more effectively.

Virtually all recommendations coming out of the research on fostering cognitive and metacognitive reading strategies emphasize the importance of beginning with teacher-led explicit instruction, followed by a gradual release of responsibility to the students themselves. The de Jager et al. (2005) study demonstrated that metacognition can be fostered by using more traditional teacher-led instructional approaches, as well as more student-centered ones. The two approaches yielded comparable benefits to the students relative to a traditional approach that was not metacognitively oriented. Thus, it is useful to know that the complex hybrid model incorporating both teacher- and student-led components is not the only approach that can be effective. These findings may be a source of motivation to teachers who think implementing metacognitively oriented reading instruction using the hybrid model is too challenging and are unwilling to try it at all.

The intervention studies demonstrated that students benefited from instruction regardless of ability level. For example, de Jager et al. (2005) found that poor readers and good readers in the seventh grade made comparable gains from the metacognitive curriculum they received, as did Van Keer and Verhaeghe (2005) with second graders. Some have expressed concern that only better students will benefit, but the research shows this is not the case. Nevertheless, poor decoders require additional supports, as shown by LeFevre et al. (2003). The students who were unable to read well independently were not able to benefit from reciprocal teaching in the conventional format, although they benefited when decoding demands were lifted.

Several of the intervention studies demonstrated long-term advantages of metacognitively oriented reading instruction; as much as 1 year later, students who received it still showed better comprehension than those in comparison classrooms. Souvignier and Mokhlesgerami (2006) even found stronger effects of the intervention on delayed relative to immediate assessments, suggesting that continued independent growth was possible once basic tools were in place. It should be noted, however, that maintenance was not always evident for second graders (Van Keer & Verhaeghe, 2005), which reinforces a point made often in the literature: the development of the skills and strategies to be an effective reader requires time and practice. Younger children in particular appear to need continual reinstatement of the cognitive and metacognitive strategies. Nevertheless, we now have stronger evidence that primary level children, even those who are poor readers, can indeed benefit from metacognitive instruction, an issue that the NRP had recommended be further explored.

DIRECTIONS FOR FUTURE RESEARCH

1. *What is the relative importance of comprehension monitoring in multiple strategies interventions?* All of the interventions discussed in this chapter included at least one comprehension monitoring strategy. Van Keer and Verhaeghe (2005) and Houtveen and van de Grift (2007) speculated that comprehension monitoring strategies are the most crucial ones that are taught in the multiple-strategies interventions, but empirical data are not available. The Lubliner and Smetana (2005) study provided evidence that instruction in word-level comprehension monitoring alone can contribute to improved comprehension. Because multiple-strategies instruction is challenging to implement and labor-intensive on the part of teachers and students alike, it would be valuable to begin to tease apart which components of the full implementation model are most critical.

2. *Once students have begun to develop metacognitive awareness and control, how and when do they transition from monitoring their comprehension deliberately, and with effort, to monitoring automatically, with the process arising to consciousness only when troubles arise?* Samuels, Ediger, Willcut, and Palumbo (2005) proposed a model of reading that entails developing automaticity in both comprehension monitoring and decoding. Research suggests that beginning readers have only enough processing capacity to focus on one component at a time, but with repeated experience, they learn to decode and to monitor their comprehension well enough that they do not have to allocate attention to the processes. It is only when an obstacle is noted that attention is directed to the problem area. New research tools such as functional magnetic resonance imaging (as described in Chapters 7–10, this volume) and sophisticated computer software (as described in Chapters 21–24, this volume) may provide empirical data on this question that heretofore has not been readily amenable to investigation.

PROJECTIONS AND POSSIBILITIES FOR THE CLASSROOM OF 2030

Research conducted in the first decade of the 21st century still shows the familiar student limitations in metacognitive knowledge and control that were characteristic of students studied 30 years ago. These patterns are troubling, because they illustrate how slowly advances in research knowledge are translated into changes in classroom practice. We now know more about how to foster metacognitive development than we did at the outset, and classroom-based intervention studies are now far more common (see Israel, Block, Bauserman, & Kinnucan-Welsch, 2005), but the pace with which metacognition is incorporated into routine practice of classroom teachers is slow.

It is my hope that by the year 2030 all students will receive metacognitively oriented reading instruction as a matter of course. This instruction would begin before children are even decoding independently and continue throughout the elementary and secondary years of schooling. Teachers would talk about metacognition itself, much as McGregor (2007) described in the opening quotation for this chapter. Textbooks for students would include explicit discussion of metacognition and comprehension monitoring. The practices at the Benchmark school, described by Pressley and Gaskins (2006), would appear widely throughout the United States and abroad: "Comprehension strategies instruction—and, frankly, all instruction—at the [Benchmark] school is embellished with metacognitive information. Students learn where and when to use the strategies they are acquiring, how and when the strategies are helpful, and how learning and using strategies is part of general competence, not just at the school but in the larger world" (p. 110).

SUMMARY

My purpose in this chapter was to trace the history and present research and best practices in metacognition. Within the last 7 years, research has demonstrated that motivation, decoding efficiency, interest levels, self-efficacy, and age of a reader affect the speed and depth of metacognitive abilities that students can attain through instruction. Most recent classroom-based interventions have significantly increased the comprehension abilities of students both below and above age 9. I discussed why younger and less skilled readers do not monitor their comprehension as effectively as older and better readers. Research has documented that metacognition interacts with other reading motivational and cognitive processes to impact comprehension. Further research is needed to determine the most critical metacognitive strategies to teach, and how these strategies can become more automatic.

INTEGRATE, INVESTIGATE, AND INITIATE: QUESTIONS FOR DISCUSSION

1. This chapter discusses several new bodies of knowledge that have been created since the NRP report (2000) concerning (a) the age at which metacognitively oriented reading instruction can significantly increase students' comprehension abilities, (b) how long the effects of such interventions are sustained, and (c) which methods work most effectively (e.g., teacher-led, student-centered, cross-age tutoring, or same-age pairs) at specific grade levels. Summarize what, according to this latest research, should be occurring in today's classrooms.

2. Make a note of the age range of the students who are the primary focus of your work. Reread, review, and condense the specific information and research findings in this chapter concerning metacognition relative to this age range. Write three of the next steps you will take in your immediate areas of responsibility based on these findings. What do you judge to be the field's next steps to advance our body of knowledge concerning metacognition in comprehension research and instruction? Defend your judgments.

3. Review, reread, reflect, and draw conclusions from the information presented in this chapter concerning less able readers' needs. What does the information in this chapter suggest must occur in more classrooms around the world if more students are going to leave the ranks of struggling readers and join the ranks of the most able readers?

REFERENCES

Baker, L. (2002). Metacognition in comprehension instruction. In C. C. Block & M. Pressley (Eds.), *Comprehension instruction: Research based best practices* (pp. 77–95). New York: Guilford Press.

Baker, L. (2005). Developmental differences in metacognition: Implications for metacognitively-oriented reading instruction. In S. E. Israel, C. C. Block, K. L. Bauserman, & K. Kinnucan-Welsch (Eds.), *Metacognition in literacy learning: Theory, assessment, instruction, and professional development* (pp. 61–79). Mahwah, NJ: Erlbaum.

Baker, L. (2008). Metacognitive development in reading: Contributors and consequences. In K. Mokhtari & R. Sheorey (Eds.), *Reading strategies of first and second language learners: See how they read* (pp. 25–42). Norwood, MA: Christopher Gordon.

Baker, L., & Beall, L. C. (2008). Metacognitive processes in reading comprehension. In S. Israel &

G. Duffy (Eds.), *Handbook of research on reading comprehension* (pp. 373–388). New York: Rougledge.

Baker, L., & Brown, A. L. (1984). Metacognitive skills and reading. In P. D. Pearson, M. Kamil, R. Barr, & P. Mosenthal (Eds.), *Handbook of research in reading* (Vol. 1, pp. 353–395). New York: Longman.

Bereiter, C., & Bird, M. (1985). Use of thinking aloud in identification and teaching of reading comprehension strategies. *Cognition and Instruction, 2*, 131–156.

Brown, R., Pressley, M., Van Meter, P., & Schuder, T. (1996). A quasi-experimental validation of transactional strategies instruction with low-achieving second-grade readers. *Journal of Educational Psychology, 88*, 18–37.

Burton, C., & Daneman, M. (2007). Compensating for a limited working memory capacity during reading: Evidence from eye movements. *Reading Psychology, 28*, 163–186.

Cain, K., Oakhill, J., & Bryant, P. (2004). Children's reading comprehension ability: Concurrent prediction by working memory, verbal ability, and component skills. *Journal of Educational Psychology, 96*, 31–42.

De Corte, E., Verschaffel, L., & Van de Ven, A. (2001). Improving text comprehension strategies in upper primary school children: A design experiment. *British Journal of Educational Psychology, 71*, 531–559.

de Jager, B., Jansen, M., & Reezigt, G. (2005). The development of metacognition in primary school learning environments. *School Effectiveness and School Improvement, 16*, 179–196.

Eme, E., Puustinen, M., & Coutelet, B. (2006). Individual and developmental differences in reading monitoring: When and how do children evaluate their comprehension? *European Journal of Psychology of Education, 21*, 91–115.

Flavell, J. H. (1976). Metacognitive aspects of problem solving. In L. B. Resnick (Ed.), *The nature of intelligence* (pp. 231–235). Hillsdale, NJ: Erlbaum.

Fuchs, D., Fuchs, L. S., Mathes, P. G., & Simmons, D. C. (1997). Peer-assisted learning strategies: Making classrooms more responsive to diversity. *American Educational Research Journal, 34*, 174–206.

Garner, R. (1987). *Metacognition and reading comprehension*. Norwood, NJ: Ablex.

Guthrie, J. T., Wigfield, A., & Perencevich, K. C. (2004). *Motivating reading comprehension: Concept-oriented reading instruction*. Mahwah, NJ: Erlbaum.

Haller, E. P., Child, D. A., & Walberg, H. J. (1988). Can comprehension be taught?: A quantitative synthesis of "metacognitive" studies. *Educational Researcher, 17*(9), 5–8.

Houtveen, A. A. M., & van de Grift, W. J. C. M. (2007). Effects of metacognitive strategy instruction and instruction time on reading comprehension. *School Effectiveness and School Improvement, 18*, 173–190.

Israel, S., Block, C., Bauserman, K., & Kinnucan-Welsch, K. (2005). *Metacognition in literacy learning: Theory, assessment, instruction, and professional development*. Mahwah, NJ: Erlbaum.

Kim, A., Vaughn, S., Klingner, J., Woodruff, A., Reutebuch, C., & Kouzekanani, K. (2006). Improving the reading comprehension of middle school students with disabilities through computer-assisted collaborative strategic reading. *Remedial and Special Education, 27*, 235–249.

Klingner, J., Vaughn, S., & Schumm, J. (1998). Collaborative strategic reading during social studies in heterogeneous fourth-grade classrooms. *Elementary School Journal, 99*, 3–22.

LeFevre, D. M., Moore, D. W., & Wilkinson, I. A. (2003). Tape-assisted reciprocal teaching: Cognitive bootstrapping for poor decoders. *British Journal of Educational Psychology, 73*, 37–58.

Lubliner, S., & Smetana, L. (2005). The effects of comprehensive vocabulary instruction on Title I students' metacognitive word-learning skills and reading comprehension. *Journal of Literacy Research, 37*, 163–200.

McGregor, T. (2007). *Comprehension connections: Bridges to strategic reading*. Portsmouth, NH: Heinemann.

Mokhtari, K., & Sheorey, R. (Eds.). (2008). *Reading strategies of first and second language learners: See how they read.* Norwood, MA: Christopher Gordon.

Myers, M., & Paris, S. (1978). Children's metacognitive knowledge about reading. *Journal of Educational Psychology, 70,* 680–690.

National Reading Panel. (2000). *Teaching children to read: An evidence-based assessment of the scientific research literature on reading and its implications for reading instruction.* Bethesda, MD: National Institute of Child Health and Human Development.

Oakhill, J., Hartt, J., & Samols, D. (2005). Levels of comprehension monitoring and working memory in good and poor comprehenders. *Reading and Writing, 18,* 657–686.

Palincsar, A., & Brown, A. (1984). Reciprocal teaching of comprehension-fostering and comprehension-monitoring activities. *Cognition and Instruction, 1,* 117–175.

Paris, S. G. (2002). When is metacognition helpful, debilitating, or benign? In P. Chambres, M. Izaute, & P. Marescaux (Eds.), *Metacognition: Process, function and use* (pp. 105–120). Boston: Kluwer.

Paris, S. G., Cross, D., & Lipson, M. (1984). Informed Strategies for Learning: A program to improve children's reading awareness and comprehension. *Journal of Educational Psychology, 76,* 1239–1252.

Pressley, M., & Block, C. C. (2002). Summing up: What comprehension instruction could be. In C. C. Block & M. Pressley (Eds.), *Comprehension instruction: Research-based best practices* (pp. 383–392). New York: Guilford Press.

Pressley, M., & Gaskins, I. (2006). Metacognitively competent reading is constructively responsive reading comprehension: How can such reading be developed in students? *Metacognition and Learning, 1,* 99–113.

RAND Reading Study Group. (2002). *Reading for understanding: Towards an R&D program in reading comprehension.* Retrieved July 25, 2007, from *www.rand.org/multi/ achievementforall/reading/readreport.html.*

Roeschl-Heils, A., Schneider, W., & van Kraayenoord, C. E. (2003). Reading, metacognition and motivation: A follow-up study of German students 7 and 8. *European Journal of Psychology of Education, 18,* 75–86.

Rosenshine, B., & Meister, C. (1994). Reciprocal teaching: A review of the research. *Review of Educational Research, 64,* 479–530.

Samuels, S. J., Ediger, K. M., Willcutt, J. R., & Palumbo, T. J. (2005). Role of automaticity in metacognition and literacy instruction. In S. E. Israel, C. C. Block, K. L. Bauserman, & K. Kinnucan-Welsch (Eds.), *Metacognition in literacy learning: Theory, assessment, instruction, and professional development* (pp. 41–59). Mahwah, NJ: Erlbaum.

Snow, C. E., Burns, M. S., & Griffin, P. (Eds.). (1998). *Preventing reading difficulties in young children.* Washington, DC: National Academy Press.

Souvignier, E., & Mokhlesgerami, J. (2006). Using self-regulation as a framework for implementing strategy instruction to foster reading comprehension. *Learning and Instruction, 16,* 57–71.

Van Keer, H., & Verhaeghe, J. P. (2005). Effects of explicit reading strategies instruction and peer tutoring on second and fifth graders' reading comprehension and self-efficacy perceptions. *The Journal of Experimental Education, 73,* 291–329.

Walczyk, J. J., Marsiglia, C. S., Johns, A. K., & Bryan, K. S. (2004). Children's compensations for poorly automated reading skills. *Discourse Processes, 37,* 47–66.

Vygotsky, L. S. (1978). *Mind in society.* Cambridge: Harvard University Press.

Zinar, S. (2000). The relative contributions of word identification skill and comprehension-monitoring behavior to reading comprehension ability. *Contemporary Educational Psychology, 25,* 363–377.

6

Constructivist Theory and the Situation Model

Relevance to Future Assessment of Reading Comprehension

DONNA CACCAMISE, LYNN SNYDER, and EILEEN KINTSCH

> Reading furnishes the mind only with materials of knowledge;
> it is thinking that makes what we read ours.
> —JOHN LOCKE, English empiricist philosopher (1632–1704)

The assessment of reading comprehension serves multiple purposes in today's schools (Carlisle & Rice, 2004). These include large-scale, summative assessments for accountability purposes or for admission to particular programs (e.g., standard achievement test [SAT]), diagnostic testing to determine student placement and intervention options for struggling readers, screening for students at risk for reading failure, and the ongoing monitoring of student progress. Although our subject here is the use of technology in assessing reading comprehension, it would be unwise to view this issue divorced from a broader discussion of how the role of testing and assessment, and its delivery, is quietly undergoing a shift in practice.

With breakthroughs in technology, such as the Internet, as well as advances in cognitive science, the role of assessment is beginning to move from a relatively isolated activity, all too often misaligned with curriculum, to practices that follow a constructivist model of learning that embeds assessment into the actual learning process. The latter kind of assessment takes place as part of classroom activities and is formative, in that it allows immediate judgments about where individuals are in their learning of particular instructed topics. Formative assessment provides specific feedback on gaps in understanding that directs future instruction and allows for optimal progress in mastering a skill or subject. With increasing use of such assessments throughout the learning process, the outcome of a summative assessment becomes a natural progression in the assessment of a student's achievement (Shepard, 2000).

This chapter highlights the following issues:

- The general categories of reading assessment.
- The qualities of an adequate assessment.
- The cognitive theory that drives the design of some of the latest computer-based tools for reading comprehension, learning, and assessment.
- How these issues apply to some of today's most widely used reading assessments.

WHAT'S OUT THERE TODAY: ESTABLISHED RESEARCH AND PRACTICE

We might first ask ourselves, "What do we mean by assessment?" The answer is a complex one. In fact, the National Reading Panel (NRP) formed a committee of leading cognitive scientists, psychometricians, and educators to look at this question. It is generally agreed that assessment is the gathering of information that enables "teachers, administrators, policymakers, and the public [to] infer what students know and how well they know it" (Pellegrino, 2002, p. 2). Although assessments take on the roles identified earlier, many existing assessment vehicles for learning in general, and reading comprehension in particular, are typically more limited than users of this information realize.

In characterizing the nature of assessment of reading comprehension, it is important to be clear about the purpose for which a given assessment has been created. Graesser and Clark (1985) argued that "real" comprehension is defined by those mental activities that take place while one is actually reading. Hence, an assessment that taps into these processes must occur during reading. These sorts of assessments are often developed by researchers to gain a better understanding of the actual cognitive processing during reading. Some of these assessments are transparent to the reading process (e.g., reading times for various activities), and others are more intrusive (e.g., questioning, think-aloud protocols), requiring further consideration as to whether they actually interrupt the reading process or help the reader engage in more expert reading activities (e.g., Gorin, 2005). Assessments that look at comprehension artifacts after reading require further processing after the actual reading has occurred (e.g., questions, summarization, metacognitive querying). The assessments we describe below fall into this category. In addition, some of the newer computer-based reading tutors aim to improve student reading comprehension in the context of particular academic content domains, such as science, history, or social studies, that is, any domain in which some portion of learning is accomplished by reading texts. In this manner, a comprehension support system may serve both as a tutor and as an assessor, embedded in actual curriculum.

Qualities of Good Assessments

Given all of today's advances in learning theory, technology, and measurement, it is surprising that many large-scale assessments rely on static, once-a-year snapshots of a limited number of activities that are thought to represent the full breadth and depth of ability in the domain tested. As a matter of cost and efficiency, these tests typically consist mainly of multiple-choice questions. More recently, some short-answer questions have been added to the items on some measures. This is not sufficient, however, to allow test takers to demonstrate more complex aspects of their reading comprehension skills that could be better reflected in tasks such as writing a critical essay based on the readings or applying the content to a practical activity (e.g., conducting a science experiment) that would demonstrate transfer and generalization of what the test taker gleaned from the text. Clearly, large-scale assessments to determine program effectiveness could not accomplish these more sophisticated test activities in the days of paper-and-pencil tests.

However, the advent of computer-mediated testing, together with advances in statistical and natural language processing, will soon make it possible to deliver and score more sophisticated test protocols based on scientific models of expert abilities. More specifically, advances in cognitive science will guide us in defining explicit learning goals that lead students to become experts in reading comprehension, and advances in technology will help us to better teach and assess student skills in a dynamic, efficient, and accurate manner. In fact, research shows that "formative assessment," assessment that is embedded in instruction with timely feedback and targeted next steps in instruction, provides students with learning tools that can lead to dramatic achievement gains (Black & Wiliam, 1998; Shepard, 2003). Shepard (pp. 124–125) enumerates the following qualities of assessment that are effective for improving learning:

- Activating and building on prior knowledge.
- Making student thinking visible and explicit.
- Engaging students in self-monitoring of their own learning.
- Establishing clear goals and standards for what constitutes good work.
- Providing feedback specifically targeted toward improvement.

Although Shepard's guidelines were intended for classroom assessment in general, they are particularly relevant to reading comprehension assessment. These guidelines represent a radical departure from the traditional assessments based on a behaviorist model of learning still in widespread use today. The behaviorists assumed that learning is a process of accumulating small bits of knowledge; that it proceeds in a set sequential and hierarchical order; and that each objective must be explicitly taught to enable even limited transfer. Moreover, it is assumed that what is tested in this manner is equivalent to what one wants students to know (Shepard, 2000).

Summative versus Formative Assessment

As mentioned earlier, tests serve many purposes, and we should be clear about both the purpose of assessment and the limitations of a given test. Summative assessments are large-scale tests of entire schools, districts, or states, administered at fixed times and intervals to track student progress over longer time spans. In contrast, formative testing is performed more frequently at the classroom level to assess students' competence in particular subject areas.

From a psychometric point of view, we also need to know the extent to which an assessment has criterion validity (i.e., achievement of specific learning goals) versus predictive validity (e.g., an SAT score predicts to some degree how successful one will be in college). Mosher (2004) goes further, claiming that this murky confounding of achievement with aptitude even affects the National Assessment of Educational Progress (NAEP), the "gold standard" of large-scale assessment of academic achievement, including reading achievement. Chudowsky and Pellegrino (2003) argue that the standardized tests used in large-scale assessment are typically based on unclear underlying constructs and lack a theoretical basis. They suggest that assessment would be greatly improved if today's cognitive theories were guiding conceptual refinement and operationalization. However, pragmatic decisions, such as efficient and reliable scoring issues, often drive what we see today in high-stakes standards testing, as well as large-scale standardized assessment, and all too often provide the model for formative testing in the classroom. Advances in technology and cognitive science are changing the options for the better.

The quiet revolution at hand is focused on changing the role of assessment, so that it becomes a dynamic component in a learning culture. In this future, all assessment will be tightly connected to theoretically driven pedagogy and curriculum standards. Rather than a one-time snapshot, like today's summative assessments, future assessment will be an interactive component of learning, guiding students in an individualized manner to greater and greater expertise in every subject domain (Shepard, 2003). If one carries this vision to its logical conclusion, the line between summative and formative assessment may blur, with technology providing reliable data about individual and group comprehension abilities with respect to common curriculum standards.

RESEARCH IN THIS AREA

Comprehension was discovered as a missing link in the achievement of reading competency in educational research in the 1980s and 1990s, and it has slowly made its way into instructional practice, at least in more progressive schools. But it has taken somewhat longer for us to frame research questions in terms of a clear conceptualization of what is meant by "comprehension." With the constructivist viewpoint that now dominates research on learning and instruction has come the realization that comprehension is not a uniform quality that one either has or does not have, say, after reading a text or solving a problem; rather, multiple processes are involved that affect comprehension in qualitatively different ways, with important consequences for learning. More precisely, following Kintsch (1998; van Dijk & Kintsch, 1983), we think in terms of passive, unengaged reading, which results in a shallow mental representation of the text content, versus active, interpretive reading through which a reader creates a mental model of the situation described by the text that fully connects with the reader's existing knowledge. For convenience, we typically speak of "deep" versus "shallow" understanding (e.g., Graesser, 2007; Graesser & Person, 1994). For the most part, this differentiated view of comprehension has yet to be incorporated into our assessment tools, despite the obvious need for transforming both how and why we test according to constructivist principles (Pellegrino, Chudowsky, & Glaser, 2001; Shepard, 2000). The guidelines described below fall far short of the goal Shepard has outlined for designing assessment that can provide useful information to guide and further classroom learning, but they are a step in this direction.

Comprehension Processes

Graesser (2007) provides an overview of representative models of text comprehension. At a general level, current models (e.g., Graesser, Singer, & Trabasso, 1994; Kintsch, 1998; van den Broek, Virtue, Everson, Tzeng, & Sung, 2002; Zwaan & Radvansky, 1998) view reading as a multilevel process by which readers strive (to varying degrees and with varying success) to construct a coherent memory representation of the text being read. Local meaning operations, such as decoding word meanings and determining syntactic relations, typically result in memory for some surface features, such as some of the actual words and phrases used. If reading is unproblematic, what readers mainly remember is the gist of the text, that is, the main ideas, topics, and theme of an expository text or the plot of a story. The need to establish coherence in text meaning drives processing at the local and overall meaning level, because natural texts are never fully explicit: Readers must, for example, figure out the referents for pronouns and synonymous expressions; they must infer how individual sentences are related; and they must understand how groups of sentences, paragraphs, chapters, and sections are related to the overall topic.

The Kintsch model of reading comprehension refers to the resulting memory for text content as the "textbase." This level of understanding is sufficient for many kinds of reproductive tasks, such as providing a summary of the text or a list of the main ideas, and being able to identify particular facts or define key concepts. However, full understanding of the implications of the text requires deeper and often more effortful processing to connect the new content with what one already knows about the topic. The goal here is to form a mental model of the situation implied by the text, called the "situation model." Processing at this level is mainly interpretive and inferential: The reader elaborates the text content with pieces of personal knowledge, forming new connections among text ideas and also beyond what is explicitly stated, for example, by generating causal explanations and analogies, making unique comparisons, forming visual images, exploring consequences, critically evaluating the material, using the material to solve a problem, and so on. Thus, the situation model is a multidimensional meaning representation that may include visual, spatial, temporal, and emotional aspects, as well as abstractions implied by the text.

A major weakness of comprehension instruction in our schools, and of the methods we have developed to assess comprehension, has been the failure to address deep understanding at the level of the situation model. Text comprehension is more complex than we formerly realized, and our ways of assessing understanding and attempts to remedy students' difficulties with learning from instructional text should, but rarely do, reflect this complexity.

Implications for Assessment

A first step, we would argue, is the need to devise tests that differentiate between readers' memory for the text content at different levels of generality and the mental model they have formed. This is easier said than done, because the different comprehension levels described earlier do not comprise discrete entities, but are different aspects of a single meaning representation that is formed during reading. Meaning construction occurs at all levels more or less simultaneously. However, the reader may switch focus from local to global to situational meaning construction as needed to address particular problems (an unfamiliar word, a poorly understood concept or relationship, etc.) or depending on the purpose of reading (e.g., reading for entertainment, to support a strongly held opinion or belief, or to study for a test). To assess whether students' comprehension is fully successful, we need to devise more complete tests that target all levels, but especially we need methods that determine whether students are acquiring deep, lasting, and useful knowledge.

The multiple-choice tests that are the mainstay of standardized testing do a fairly decent job of assessing students' recognition memory for specific facts, that is, for local-level information and, to a limited extent, students' memory for more general, gist-level concepts. It is also possible to construct good multiple-choice items—with appropriate distractors that tap a student's ability to construct inferences—and to apply the content.

However, this is very difficult, especially in less formal domains such as history, literature, biology, or the social sciences. Moreover, the impoverished context of multiple-choice questions and similar closed-entry questions makes them extremely vulnerable to students' misinterpretations. It is not easy to determine the "right" questions to ask and the right way to ask them, although more context helps. Hence, question prompts for open-ended, constructed responses such as essays or short answers are preferable not only for promoting more active learning (e.g., Graesser & Person, 1994; Palincsar & Brown, 1984) but also for assessing deeper, situational understanding.

Giving students a chance to reason about a topic and to express their understanding in an extended written format is more likely to yield an accurate and informative account of what students really do or do not understand from a text and what they can do with the new knowledge (Kintsch, 2005). Summaries and essay questions, for example, that tap the ability to generalize text content, to reason about it, to evaluate it in a critical manner, to generate inferences, and to apply the content in novel contexts reveal not only whether an individual's understanding is faulty or incomplete but also exactly where the problems lie. As Shepard (2000) and others have pointed out, these kinds of informative tests are necessary to guide instruction and further learning.

Good essay prompts may be easier to construct than good multiple-choice items. The trade-off, however, is the labor-intensive effort required to score essay questions, along with lower reliability among scorers, or even consistency within the same scorer over time (e.g., Snyder, Wise, & Caccamise, 2005). For this reason, "objective" questions that can be machine-scored have dominated standardized assessments in this country for generations of students.

HOW THIS NEW KNOWLEDGE CAN IMPROVE COMPREHENSION INSTRUCTION

Large-Scale Reading Comprehension Assessments

As with all good assessment tools, large-scale assessments of reading comprehension should start with a scientific model of how students learn to read, including the activities that expert readers engage in as they deeply process text and competently use that information in subsequent activities. This goes beyond testing the simple components of decoding and vocabulary (the primary focus at the early stages of reading instruction), and into the realm of complex meaning construction activities representing the range and depth of what we expect good comprehenders to do, as described in the previous section.

The focus of our discussion is two popular, large-scale, computer-based assessments used by schools today, though many more are available.[1] These assessments, *Measures of Academic Progress* (*MAP*; Northwest Evaluation Association, 2003) and the *Scholastic Reading Inventory* (*SRI*; Scholastic, 2002, 2006) fall under the rubric of traditional tests and use multiple-choice questions to elicit information regarding students' comprehension of the passages read. The *MAP* can be administered three times a year to document student progress, whereas the *SRI* can be administered multiple times. These two instruments can be contrasted with tutorial-type tools embedded in the curriculum and can be used over and over again throughout the school year. An example of this tutorial-type

---

[1] High-stakes state standards tests that assess reading skills, including comprehension, vary in the manner and in the degree to which they handle this task. Discussion of this type of reading assessment is beyond the scope of this survey chapter (e.g., see Nichols & Berliner, 2005; Sloane & Kelly, 2003).

tool is *WriteToLearn* (Pearson Knowledge Technologies, 2006), which is used throughout the school year as an intervention per se to facilitate the development of reading comprehension and to monitor individual student progress (see further details below). These two types of instrument are probably best viewed as complementary as opposed to competitive options that—when used together—may provide both a thorough assessment of reading comprehension and an instructional plan.

Reading levels for all three instruments are indexed by Lexiles (Stenner, 2003), a readability metric popularly used in school settings. Lexile levels are determined by the total number of words in a selection, word frequencies, and sentence length. In reviewing his own and other studies performed from the 1970s to the 1990s, Kintsch (1998) highlighted the important effects of underlying semantic and organizational aspects of a text on readability and recall, which are largely neglected by lexical feature counts. Nevertheless, pragmatics have prevailed; readability formulas that generally correlate with text difficulty, such as Lexiles, have dominated the industry because they are easy to measure. Until now, determining the underlying semantic structure for even short texts was far too labor-intensive to be useful to publishers of educational materials. We hope that technology today, combined with the science behind reading processes, is poised to change that equation, leading to a more accurate characterization of text difficulty for pedagogical purposes. But for now, many publishers of children's books and reading series index them by Lexiles that have been yoked to existing grade level determinations. As a result, entire school libraries are organized by Lexile levels. The three assessments described earlier provide information about student performance relative to the Lexile levels at which the students are reading. This allows teachers to select instructional materials appropriate to students' skills.

None of these computer-based assessments is sufficiently thorough in sampling the key theoretical features of constructive reading comprehension. Each, however, has strengths that address some of these features.

Measures of Academic Progress

The *MAP* (Northwest Evaluation Association, 2000, 2003) is a Web-based assessment that measures students' performance in reading, language usage, and math. It also has a pencil-and-paper version, the *Achievement Level Tests* (*ALT*; Northwest Evaluation Association, 1996). The reading measure addresses five components of reading: word analysis, literal comprehension, interpretive comprehension, evaluative comprehension, and literary response. A random inspection of some of the test items indicates that these components examine aspects of vocabulary and gist comprehension, inferencing, evaluative thinking, and understanding of literary devices and text genres. From the perspective of constructivist models of comprehension, it samples key skills that contribute to the deep comprehension of text, especially students' ability to build an understanding at different levels of meaning, ranging from the word to the overall text level, and in both expository and literary texts. However a multiple-choice format predominates in the test items, with a response format based on a recognition response. Consequently, it provides less information about students' understanding of what they have read than is provided by short answer responses. On the other hand, the *MAP*'s wide-scale standardization—now based on a participant pool of 1.05 million students—does provide for a reliable assessment and it has been aligned with components of the high-stakes assessments for each state in the United States.

The *MAP* is constructed so that students' levels of performance correspond to a continuum of instructional goals (developed at each level for use by teachers) called the "learning continuum." For example, 3 of 12 sequenced instructional goals identified for students who score within a specified range on the *MAP*'s interpretive reading comprehension subcomponent include the ability to: (1) determine cause and effect in a passage of a specified length, (2) infer conclusions from prior information, and (3) summarize a short passage of 100–150 words. Students taking the test are presented with items that use an adaptive process to establish their individual ability levels. The computational base upon which the program is constructed continues to allow the *MAP* to adjust the reading level after a student's response to each item. The Web-based administration of the *MAP* and its powerful database allow school districts to receive results in a very short time, as rapidly as 48 hours after testing, at the school level. In addition, its large database also allows educators and district administrators to look at student and school performance with reference to groups of students and schools that have similar demographic characteristics.

The psychometric characteristics of the *MAP* are impressive, with strong construct and content validity, as well as reliability. Using Rasch's (1980) item–response theory model, the Northwest Evaluation Association (NWEA) generated a scale that allows teachers and administrators to determine student growth in achievement along a continuum. For example, the ability to respond correctly to items that require students to draw inferences about directionality and character motivations appear at the same growth point on the scale from year to year. Students' scores on this scale are called RIT (Rasch unIT) scores, and they allow educators to measure progress reliably. The RIT score shows a student's current achievement along a curricular/instructional scale. These scores are equal-interval scores, like measurement lines on a ruler, that occur along a learning continuum. They are linked to mastery of curricular content and skills sequenced along that continuum, not to students' positions along the bell-shaped curve like standard scores, which are interpreted with reference to the mean or average score. This means that students who are progressing in the mastery of reading comprehension will have scores that increase as they continue to advance. In addition to the RIT scores, teachers can also use Lexile levels and percentiles as indices of student progress. In short, the *MAP* assesses some key reading comprehension processes in a way that provides teachers with a rough outline of students' skills and some general direction for intervention. Nevertheless, the assessment falls far short of the goal of providing a detailed profile of individual knowledge and skills.

Scholastic Reading Inventory

The *SRI* (Scholastic, 2002, 2006) is a computer-based assessment of reading comprehension that can be used by school districts for accountability purposes, using the District and School Accountability Reports. In addition, it can be administered quarterly for progress monitoring as well as for determining instructional versus mastery levels of students' reading comprehension based on the Lexile method of determining those levels. Its most recent edition uses a computer-based delivery of authentic text fiction and nonfiction reading comprehension passages that students answer using a cloze response format. Their answers then feed into the response database that then presents new items geared to target and determine students' level of mastery, instruction, and frustration. The *SRI* takes only approximately 20 minutes per administration and is also available in a print (i.e., pencil-and-paper) version.

The *SRI*, however, does more than merely determine students' reading levels and report them by class, school, and quarter. It also attends to some components of good text comprehension. Specifically, the program looks at the extent to which a student makes use of background knowledge and context during reading, the effect of the student's vocabulary on comprehension, and whether the student is encountering difficulty with syntax in the targeted passages. It does not address the construction of a gist or the ability to draw inferences in any explicit way as far as we can determine from the publisher's website.

In addition to reporting student performance in terms of Lexile and proficiency levels in the Progress Monitoring Report, the *SRI* also provides indices in terms of percentiles, stanines, and normal curve equivalents (NCEs). More importantly, it provides teachers with Student Action Reports that identify areas or skills on which students need to work and individualized reading materials that take into account both students' instructional levels as indexed by Lexiles and their personal interests. It also provides direct suggestions for general ways in which teachers can work with each student. For example, the *SRI*'s Student Action Report indicates whether an individual student has sufficient control over the syntax, vocabulary, and reading skills needed to read at specified Lexile levels, and makes instructional recommendations. The latter include suggestions such as directing the teacher to focus on using context clues to make story predictions, or on using background knowledge to construct meaning with the particular student.

Finally, the *SRI* has been normed on more than 512,000 students and is supported by reliability and validity studies. It appears to be a remarkably teacher-friendly assessment that does pay attention to some, but not all, of the main constituents of constructive reading comprehension, as discussed in the previous section.

Although the *MAP* and the *SRI* provide some indications of an individual student's level of reading skill or mastery, their reliance on multiple-choice and cloze formats for most items precludes the ability to provide the highly detailed characterizations of the depth of comprehension typical of more active response formats. If we use Shepard's five characteristics of effective assessments as a measuring rod, the *MAP* and the *SRI* do address two of the five to some degree. Specifically, these two tests involve some activation of general background knowledge, especially in the case of the *MAP*'s scale. Both tests do provide clear goals. The instructional goals identified in the *MAP*'s Learning Continuum seem to refer to some aspects of deeper understanding. Neither instrument, however, seems to provide the detailed feedback needed to inform instruction. It must be recognized, however, that these measures were designed with a more traditional, behaviorist perspective of assessment, providing snapshots of student progress across the school year. Nevertheless, from the perspective of constructivist models of comprehension and learning, even the best currently available, large-scale assessments adhere too closely to the closed entry testing format. As we argued previously, although such tests are easy to administer and score by computer, we need more complex kinds of assessment tasks to obtain the kind of rich feedback that is effective for learning.

Broadening the Scope of Computer-Based Assessment

Artificial Intelligence (AI) and Statistical Approaches to Language Processing

Testing with open-ended, constructed response tasks has become increasingly feasible with recent technological advances in automatic language processing methods. These methods enable the semantic content of students' written responses to be scored by a computer, in contrast to earlier methods for automatically scoring essays that focused largely on surface linguistic and lexical features of writing (e.g., Kukich, 2000). More recently, computer scoring technology, using AI, natural language processing (NLP), and statistical methods, singly or in combination, incorporate more authentic writing measures. In addition to counts of lexical features, these tools provide measures of syntactic structure, organization, cohesion, and even ideational content.

For example, newer AI and NPL approaches attempt to infer a human-like scoring model from a large training set of human-scored essays by extracting and quantifying numerous linguistic and discourse indicators (e.g., number of words; vocabulary use and relevance; sentence length; paragraph length; syntactic and rhetorical structure; number of grammatical, punctuation, and spelling errors; and other features). *E-rater*, developed by Educational Testing Service (ETS), and IntelliMetric, for example, have demonstrated impressive scoring accuracy in comparisons with human scorers (Dikli, 2006; Valenti, Neri, & Cucchiarelli, 2003). Nevertheless, ETS supplements automatic assessment with one or two human scorers for use in high-stakes testing, such as the Graduate Management Admission Test (GMAT). Some methods also provide a rubric for supplementary human scoring of more qualitative writing traits (appropriate content, style, voice, logical argument, etc.). In general, NLP-based approaches do not generalize easily to new content and tasks due to their complex and labor-intensive setup requirements: for example, the large sets of human-scored essays or answers needed to train automatic, computer-based scoring models.

A breakthrough in automated essay scoring was achieved by the method called latent semantic analysis (LSA), developed by Landauer and Dumais (1997; Landauer, 1998; for an overview, cf. Landauer, McNamara, Dennis, & Kintsch, 2007). Unlike linguistic-based approaches, LSA focuses on the semantic content of a piece of writing, independent of the particular words used, thus rendering a more direct and more authentic evaluation of writing quality that closely mimics what trained human scorers do. LSA is a statistical method that derives word, term, and document meaning from a large corpus of text documents, representative of the general knowledge one acquires during 14 years of schooling. LSA comparisons of meaning similarity between two documents are as reliable as those made by human judges, even when different words or terms are used to express that meaning. In addition to a holistic score, two LSA-based applications—the Intelligent Essay Assessor (IEA; Landauer, Laham, & Foltz, 2003) and Summary Street (Caccamise, Franzke, Eckhoff, Kintsch, & Kintsch, 2007; Franzke, Kintsch, Caccamise, Johnson, & Dooley, 2005)—provide detailed feedback on various aspects of students' writing, beyond specific topic coverage, that can be used to guide writing and revision. Landauer et al. (2007) provide detailed descriptions of the LSA method, its extensions, and applications in research, instruction, and assessment; interested readers may also explore the websites at *www.lsa.colorado.edu* and *www.pearsonkt.com*. Our interest here is in LSA's potential as an assessment tool to rate writing quality objectively on the basis of the ideas expressed, and how ideas are linked to form a logical argument.

Examples of LSA-Based Educational Applications

In most applications, LSA-based scoring works by comparing students' written summaries or essays with a relevant text passage(s), with an ideal, expert essay, or with a database of representative student essays scored by humans. The input summary or essay can be evaluated on dimensions such as topic coverage, amount of redundant or overly detailed information, plagiarized text, and indicators of style, such as coherence, organization, and sentence fluency.

LSA provides the engine for some novel educational tools such as Summary Street and the IEA. (For descriptions of these tutors see Caccamise et al., 2007; Franzke et al.,

2005; Kintsch, Caccamise, Franzke, Johnson, and Dooley, 2007; and Landauer et al., 2003; respectively.) LSA assessment of content is combined with quantitative analyses of multiple lexical, linguistic, and discourse metrics in Graesser's (2004) AutoTutor. AutoTutor supports learners' attempts to reason through difficult science and technology questions and problems. Computer-based interactive tools (such as these examples) provide students with feedback they can use to remedy conceptual, as well as semantic and syntactic problems with their writing; helps them fill gaps in their understanding of difficult text or challenging problems; and supports deeper level meaning construction.

The detailed, ongoing assessment offered by such tutors can be used by students and teachers alike to detect problems during a learning task: Whereas the capability to self-assess empowers students, the tutor output allows teachers to pinpoint individual students' comprehension and writing problems, as well as to gauge the overall effectiveness of their instruction. LSA scoring of submitted summaries or essays has been shown to match and even exceed the scoring reliability of human graders (Landauer et al., 2003), and impressive gains in college students' essay writing have been documented with use of IEA (Foltz, Gilliam, & Kendall, 2000). Similary, significant improvement in the quality of students' summaries is apparent after only a few practice sessions using Summary Street (Caccamise et al., 2007; Franzke et al., 2005). Note that Summary Street and IEA are now combined in a commercial educational product called WritetoLearn, available from Pearson Knowledge Technologies (2006). Positive effects on college students' deep-level learning and their ability to generate thoughtful questions are also reported for the natural dialogue tutoring system called AutoTutor (e.g., Graesser & McDaniel, 2007; Graesser, McNamara, & VanLehn, 2005; Graesser et al., 2004). In AutoTutor, students engage in interactive problem-solving sessions with an animated "conversational" agent that provides feedback on the quality of a response (agent has facial gesture indicators), coaching (via prompts, hints, explanations, and corrections) and directive questions to guide learners to the expected answers.

Another computer-based learning tool designed to teach reading comprehension strategies but not yet widely used in content curriculum is Interactive Strategy Training for Active Reading and Thinking (*iSTART*; McNamara, Levinstein, & Boonthum, 2004). This Web-based application promotes self-regulated learning by using animated agents to model and teach five expert reading strategies known to help students understand challenging concepts they encounter in difficult material, such as science texts (McNamara et al., 2004). The comprehension strategies taught include comprehension monitoring, paraphrasing and constructing self- explanations, bridging inferences, predictions, and elaborations. This focused strategy learning tool seems to have current constructivist comprehension models at its core. Although both AutoTutor and iSTART are centered on the use of self-explanation as a tool for developing deeper levels of comprehension for science material, they take different paths to reach this objective. AutoTutor promotes the development of inquiry-based questioning, whereas iSTART focuses on deep comprehension using expert learning strategies (Graesser et al., 2005). Both are clearly part of a new generation of comprehension instruction and assessment tools that emphasizes the active role of the reader in meaning constructing during reading.

An additional LSA-based tool designed to facilitate deeper levels of comprehension is the Reading Strategy and Assessment Tool (R-SAT), presently being developed by Magliano and Millis (Magliano, Millis, Ozuru, & McNamara, 2007; Millis, Magliano, Weimer-Hastings, Todaro, & McNamara, 2007). The primary and explicit intent of this computer-driven tool is to promote and to assess deeper levels of comprehension as indexed by the levels of causal coherence and inferential thinking that appear in students' think-aloud protocols (for further details, see sources cited). More than any of the other tools discussed here, this particular measure targets situational understanding: the generation of a locally and globally coherent textbase, and extension of the literal text content through inferences. The R-SAT accomplishes these goals by identifying the strategies that students use in their think-aloud protocols and assessing coherence links and the quality of inferences produced. Students respond in writing to questions about their thinking processes (e.g., "What are you thinking now?") delivered at key points during reading to coach them through the process of uncovering and dealing with gaps in their understanding.

Algorithms driven by LSA and word-matching techniques analyze the written think-aloud protocols and provide a computational index of the quality of strategies being used and the depth of comprehension achieved. R-SAT is unique in that it allows teachers to examine both the processes and products of comprehension. At the present time, R-SAT has been designed and tested with freshman and sophomore college students.

Thus, we have made a major step forward in the development of multipurpose, computer-based tools—systems that make automatic, ongoing substantive assessment and self-assessment feasible, while offering extensive guided practice opportunities for learning high-level writing and reasoning skills. Embedded in classroom instruction, such tools can be used as formative assessment measures that directly and indirectly benefit learning (Shepard, 2003). Automated essay scoring is now being implemented in some national standardized assessments, most notably by ETS (Dikli, 2006), reducing, though not yet entirely replacing, the human resources required for scoring open-ended, constructed responses. These tools will eventually pave the way for more authentic ways to assess students' learning on a broad scale.

Learning from Text and Assessment of Learning

Powerful language processing methods are only one part of the problem facing designers of computer-based learning and assessment tools. Providing content-based feedback is a huge advance in tutoring capability. However, equally important is the design of appropriate tasks according to well-established pedagogic and theoretical principles. At the most basic level, both diagnostic and summative assessments should be able to tell whether students' mastery of new subject matter is deep and lasting or superficial and fragmented, and to direct instruction accordingly.

Assessing Deep Comprehension

Deep comprehension is measured by tasks requiring inferences and problem solving, and is affected by the reader's knowledge and constructive activity; shallow comprehension is passive and reproductive. As previously stated, tests of deep comprehension must assess the quality of the situation model that has been constructed from reading, whereas recall and recognition measures, the mainstay of standardized testing, typically assess the textbase that a reader has formed (Kintsch, 1998; Kintsch & Kintsch, 2005). In fact, many readers who are good at recalling a text often fail on deep comprehension tasks that require inferential reasoning (Mulligan, Rawson, Mangalath, & Kintsch, 2007). Hence, tests that differentiate between these components of the reading process would be highly useful, and a few have recently been proposed (e.g., Hannon & Daneman, 2001; Meneghetti, Carretti, & De Beni, 2007). Open-response questions, which students must answer in their own words, are a good way to assess both content knowledge and situational understanding. Advances in language processing technology, such as those described earlier, will soon provide the automatic response scoring needed to make such tests practical and usable.

Learning from Tests

In her review of assessment practices, Shepard (2003) called for tests that provide accurate assessment of students' skills and knowledge, and from which both teachers and students can learn, that is, tests with substantive content that "embody important learning goals" (p. 143). Advances in language processing technology will soon make it possible to implement this mandate in a cost-effective manner. Tests can be devised that directly involve students in worthwhile learning activities that further their understanding of important curricular topics, and provide practice in higher-level reasoning skills and the use of learning strategies as they assess current understanding. Automatic tutors are ideally suited for this objective: Like a good human tutor, a computer not only coaches the learner in understanding challenging content (e.g., AutoTutor; Graesser et al., 2004) or practicing expert skills (e.g., Summary Street; Caccamise et al., 2007) but also provides dynamic, ongoing assessment that can be used interactively to self-assess and debug comprehension problems, to inform instruction on the spot, and to provide a summative record of achievement (cf. Graesser & McDaniel, 2007).

DIRECTIONS FOR FUTURE RESEARCH

1. *Can statistical approaches, such as LSA or NLP, succeed in developing a satisfactory way to score short answers automatically?* Much has been achieved by semantic models such as LSA, which captures some important aspects of how knowledge is represented in the human brain. However, LSA is by no means a complete model of human knowledge representation, and it has some important limitations that constrain broader usability, both for assessment and for instructional applications. Most notable is that LSA is essentially a word co-occurrence method; unlike humans, LSA is ignorant about syntactic and word-order relationships. However, if the writing sample is long enough, LSA can reliably determine solely on the basis of word use whether a writer knows what he or she is talking about, as described earlier. For humans, likewise, it is often easier and less ambiguous to evaluate longer essays, because they offer more opportunity for a good or poor grasp of content to display itself. However, our knowledge of syntax also makes it possible to detect faulty logic and erroneous responses in brief responses. Because LSA scoring requires texts of 100 words or more, this approach is not well suited for assessments based on short responses to open-ended questions, or for tutors that seek to mimic the interactive exchanges and joint problem solving that characterize good human tutoring. In general, neither statistical approaches such as LSA nor strict NLP approaches have succeeded thus far in developing a satisfactory way to score short answers automatically. Some success has been demonstrated with limited goals, such as judging the correctness of specific content (e.g., fact-finding questions or definitions of key terms) based on key word searches or sentence overlap, with either the appropriate text sentence or an expert answer key (e.g., Text Retrieval Conference [TREC]; Hirschman & Gaizauskas, 2001). Hybrid approaches to scoring constructed responses that use a combination of NLP and semantic analysis are more promising, at least with well-specified content (e.g., C-rater; Leacock & Chodorow, 2003). However, such systems require substantial human effort and large-scale processing resources to implement.

2. *Can computerized assessments be developed to the point so that they can deal with more open-ended kinds of responses?* As discussed earlier, a serious limitation in grading short responses is the inability to deal with more open-ended kinds of responses. For example, what if the answer requires integration across different parts of a text or different knowledge sources, or if it requires inferencing? Even LSA's ability to deal with paraphrased and summarized, as well as literal, content in an answer is not sufficient to evaluate meanings that go beyond the text content—inferences and interpretations (Mulligan et al., 2007)—especially in a brief context. Several quite recent statistical methods that incorporate word-order information in representing meaning offer a promising way to deal with the short-answer dilemma (e.g., Dennis, 2005; Jones & Mewhort, 2006; Mangalath, 2007). These models represent a major theoretical advance in terms of modeling the way humans represent and use knowledge. More work is needed to reduce the computational requirements of this type of model and to enable their application to practical and pedagogical problems. However, such models could potentially be used to automatically score brief constructed answers in a much simpler and more straightforward manner than has hitherto been possible. Such a capability could, for example, support the development of highly useful systems for automated assessment, as well as for diagnostic tutors that provide substantive, individualized feedback online during reading or learning activities. A tutor based on this technology would allow analysis and feedback on answers to a range of questions that target students' grasp of textual content (at different levels) and their ability to infer beyond explicitly stated information.

PROJECTIONS AND POSSIBILITIES FOR THE CLASSROOM OF 2030

As we look ahead, we see a classroom in which reading instruction, particularly reading comprehension instruction, has completely merged with curriculum content area learning. The teacher no longer functions primarily as the dispenser of knowledge, but as a learning guide for students who are actively constructing their own understanding. Crucial to this scenario is the ready availability of automatic tutors that support the students' efforts by modeling expert comprehension strategies, and that require them to test their understanding at each step, to question and evaluate the ideas they encounter, and to be able to communicate their thinking to others. In this manner, these tutors guide students' use of reading strategies that result in deep comprehension by helping them to build connections with prior knowledge and to speculate about possible implications of the material. Theory-to-practice experiences are integrated at appropriate content boundaries by a combination of computer-generated interactive models and actual hands-on exercises guided by teachers. In this classroom computers do not replace teachers, but rather enhance their effectiveness by providing the extensive practice in higher-level thinking, comprehension, and writing skills that underlies the development of expertise in all domains.

In this future classroom, computer-based tutors will supply immediate, individualized feedback at a level that no teacher can provide to a whole classroom of students of differing knowledge and ability levels. Thus, not only have content and reading instruction merged, but also assessment has become an ongoing, dynamic component of learning in this classroom, providing to teachers and students alike feedback that is rich and informative, and that serves to guide the learning process throughout. "High-stakes testing" as we know it will become a thing of the past when summative assessments emerge as a natural outcome of all that has come before in this new learning environment.

Of course, part of what is necessary to make this classroom viable is that all students have networked laptop computers at their desks, with downloaded units that they can take home for homework. In reality, not everyone has a laptop computer; many schools strain today to provide the infrastructure to support even a modest computer lab of 30 networked computers, and many students don't have Internet access as home.

To make all of this happen, we are looking at a challenging convergence of breakthroughs in language processing technology, in our theoretical understanding of comprehension processes, and in fine-tuning learning tutors and their assessment capabilities and strategies. In addition, we need to examine educational policies, budgets, and long-term goals to position our schools to take advantage of all these advances. Perhaps the most difficult task in making this future a reality will be to address natural resistance to change by preparing teachers, school administrators, and parents to expect and plan for a new and better way to teach our children.

SUMMARY

The field of assessment is replete with pencil-and-paper measures of reading comprehension, many of which do not assess these processes in a manner that is accessible for teachers. Because reading comprehension is a dynamic and constructive process, computer-based assessments are often better suited to capture students' performance relative to these features. Technology-based formative and summative assessments can adapt to students' mastery and instructional reading levels, control vocabulary levels, structure the presentation of questions, and query students' ability to construct not only coherence in their understanding of content but also the ability to extend their understanding beyond explicit text content.

We have argued that as a result of advances in technology and test measurement, and theoretical advances in cognitive science, reading comprehension assessments are beginning to look much different than the traditional tests of the past 100 years. We see this as an exciting time for researchers and educators as assessments become a relevant component of the actual day-to-day learning process, providing students and teachers with substantive and timely feedback to drive highly relevant further instruction, as well as provide more accurate conclusions about how and what students comprehend and learn from their reading.

INTEGRATE, INVESTIGATE, AND INITIATE: QUESTIONS FOR DISCUSSION

1. An argument was made in the chapter that real comprehension assessment should take place while students are actually reading. Create an experience for the teachers under your area of responsibility or for the students in your classroom that assesses comprehension while teachers or students are actually reading a selection that you prepared for them. How did your assessment differ from the standardized or informal measures typically used to assess comprehension?

2. Create an assessment experience for teachers or students that reflects the qualities of good assessment reported in this chapter (e.g., activating and building prior knowledge, making students' thinking visible, engaging students in self-monitoring, establishing clear goals and standards, and providing specific, individualized feedback). Allow this test to be as creative and as innovative as possible. Share your results with colleagues who have also experimented with cre-

ating two types of reading comprehension assessments. What did all of your assessments have in common?

3. Examine a reading comprehension test that was administered recently in your school building or that is available on the Internet in one of the standardized reading tests cited in this chapter (e.g., *SRI*, *MAP*). Tally how many of the test questions on that assessment require students to make an inference or to problem-solve to assess deep comprehension. Report your results to a small group of colleagues who performed this same investigation. What does this tell you about innovations that you could make in your area of responsibility to improve or to acknowledge a student's highest level of comprehension ability?

ACKNOWLEDGMENTS

This work was supported by a grant from the Interagency Educational Research Initiative of the National Science Foundation (No. 030.05.0431B).

REFERENCES

Black, P., & Wiliam, D. (1998). Assessment and classroom learning. *Assessment in Education, 5,* 7–61.

Caccamise, D., Franzke, M., Eckhoff, A., Kintsch, E., & Kintsch, W. (2007). Guided practice in technology-based summary writing. In D. S. McNamara (Ed.), *Reading comprehension strategies: Theories, interventions, and technologies* (pp. 375–396). Mahwah, NJ: Erlbaum.

Carlisle, J. F., & Rice, M. S. (2004). Assessment of reading comprehension. In A. Stone, E. Silliman, B. Ehren, & K. Apel (Eds.), *Handbook of language and literacy* (pp. 521–540). New York: Guilford Press.

Chudowsky, N., & Pellegrino, J. W. (2003). Large-scale assessments that support learning: What will it take? *Theory Into Practice, 42*(1), 75–83.

Dennis, S. (2005). A memory-based theory of verbal cognition. *Cognitive Science, 29,* 145–193.

Dikli, S. (2006). An overview of automated scoring of essays. *Journal of Technology, Learning, and Assessment, 5*(1). Retrieved May 21, 2007, from *www.jtla.org*.

Foltz, P., Gilliam, S., & Kendall, S. (2000). Supporting content-based feedback in on-line writing evaluation with LSA. *Interactive Learning Environments, 8*(2), 111–127.

Franzke, M., Kintsch, E., Caccamise, D., Johnson, N., & Dooley, S. (2005). Summary Street[©]: Computer support for comprehension and writing. *Journal of Educational Computing Research, 33*(1), 53–80.

Gorin, J. S. (2005). Manipulating processing difficulty of reading comprehension questions: The feasibility of verbal item generation. *Education and Psychological Measurement, 40,* 351–373.

Graesser, A. C. (2007). An introduction to strategic reading comprehension. In D. S. McNamara (Ed.), *Reading comprehension strategies: Theories, interventions, and technologies* (pp. 3–26). Mahwah, NJ: Erlbaum.

Graesser, A. C., & Clark, L. F. (1985). *Structures and procedures of implicit knowledge.* Norwood, NJ: Ablex.

Graesser, A. C., Lu, S., Jackson, G. T., Mitchell, H., Ventura, M., Olney, A., et al. (2004). AutoTutor: A tutor with dialogue in natural language. *Behavioral Research Methods, Instruments, and Computers, 36,* 180–193.

Graesser, A. C., & McDaniel, B. (2007). Conversation agents can provide formative assessment, constructive learning, and adaptive instruction. In C. A. Dwyer (Ed.), *The future of assessment: Shaping teaching and learning.* Mahwah, NJ: Erlbaum.

Graesser, A. C., McNamara, D. S., & VanLehn, K. (2005). Scaffolding deep comprehension strategies through Point&Query, AutoTutor, and iSTART. *Educational Psychologist, 40*(4), 225–234.

Graesser, A. C., & Person, N. P. (1994). Question asking during tutoring. *American Educational Research Journal, 31*(1), 104–137.

Graesser, A. C., Singer, M., & Trabasso, T. (1994). Constructing inferences during narrative text comprehension. *Psychological Review, 101*, 371–395.

Hannon, N., & Daneman, M. (2001). A new tool for measuring and understanding individual differences in the component processes of reading comprehension. *Journal of Educational Psychology, 93*(1), 103–128.

Hirschman, L., & Gaizauskas, R. (2001). Natural language question answering: The view from here. *Natural Langauge Engineering, 7*(4), 275–300.

Jones, M. N., & Mewhort, D. J. K. (2006). Representing word meaning and order information in a composite holographic lexicon. *Psychological Review, 114*, 1–37.

Kintsch, E. (2005). Comprehension theory as a guide for the design of thoughtful questions. *Topics in Language Disorder, 25*(1), 51–64.

Kintsch, E., Caccamise, D., Franzke, M., Johnson, N., & Dooley, S. (2007). Summary Street©: Computer-guided summary writing. In T. K. Landauer, D. S. McNamara, S. Dennis, & W. Kintsch (Eds.), *Handbook of latent semantic analysis* (pp. 263–277). Mahwah, NJ: Erlbaum.

Kintsch, W. (1998). *Comprehension: A paradigm for cognition.* New York: Cambridge University Press.

Kintsch, W., & Kintsch, E. (2005). Comprehension. In S. G. Paris & S. A. Stahl (Eds.), *Current issues on reading comprehension and assessment* (pp. 71–92). Mahwah, NJ: Erlbaum.

Kukich, K. (2000, September/October). Beyond automated essay scoring. *IEEE Intelligent Systems, 15*(5), 27–31. Retrieved May 21, 2007, from ieeexplore.ieee.org.

Landauer, T. K. (1998). Learning and representing verbal meaning: The latent analysis theory. *Current Directions in Psychological Science, 7*, 161–164.

Landauer, T. K., & Dumais, S. T. (1997). A solution to Plato's problem: The latent semantic analysis theory of the acquisition, induction, and representation of knowledge. *Psychological Review, 104*, 211–240.

Landauer, T. K., Laham, D., & Foltz, P. W. (2003). Automatic scoring and annotation of essays with the Intelligent Essay Assessor. In M. D. Shermis & J. Burstein (Eds.), *Automated essay scoring: A cross-disciplinary perspective* (pp. 87–112). Mahwah, NJ: Erlbaum.

Landauer, T. K., McNamara, D. S., Dennis, S., & Kintsch, W. (Eds.). (2007). *Handbook of latent semantic analysis.* Mahwah, NJ: Erlbaum.

Leacock, C., & Chodorow, M. (2003). C-rater: Automated scoring of short-answer questions. *Computers and the Humanities, 37*, 389–405.

Magliano, J., Millis, K., Ozuru, Y., & McNamara, D. (2007). A multidimensional framework to evaluate reading assessment tools. In D. S. McNamara (Ed.), *Reading comprehension strategies: Theories, interventions, and technologies* (pp. 107–136). Mahwah, NJ: Erlbaum.

Mangalath, P. (2007). *Word-level semantics: Syntacto-semantic analysis with unsupervised latent feature models.* Manuscript in preparation.

McNamara, D. S., Levinstein, I. B., & Boonthum, C. (2004). iSTART: Interactive strategy trainer for active reading and thinking. *Behavioral Research Methods, Instruments, and Computers, 36*, 222–233.

Meneghetti, C., Carretti, B., & De Beni, R. D. (2007). Components of reading comprehension and scholastic achievemnt. *Learning and Individual Differences, 16*, 291–301.

Millis, K., Magliano, J., Weimer-Hastings, K., Todaro, S., & McNamara, D. (2007). Assessing and improving comprehension with Latent Semantic Analysis. In T. Landauer, D. S. McNamara, S. Dennis, & W. Kintsch (Eds.), *Handbook of latent semantic analysis* (pp. 207–225). Mahwah, NJ: Erlbaum.

Mosher, F.A. (2004). What NAEP really could do. In L.V. Jones & I. Olkin (Eds.), *The nation's report card: Evolution and perspectives* (pp. 312–343). Washington, DC: Phi Delta Kappa/American Educational Research Association and National Center for Education Statistics.

Mulligan, E. J., Rawson, K. A., Mangalath, P., & Kintsch, W. (2007). *Designs for a comprehension test.* Manuscript submitted for publication.
Nichols, S. L., & Berliner, D. C. (2005). *The inevitable corruption of indicators and educators through high-stakes testing.* Lansing, MI: Great Lakes Center for Education Research and Practice.
Northwest Evaluation Association. (1996). *Achievement Levels Test (ALT).* Portland, OR: Author.
Northwest Evaluation Association. (2000). *Measures of Academic Progress.* Portland, OR: Author.
Northwest Evaluation Association. (2003). *Measures of Academic Progress.* Portland, OR: Author.
Palincsar, A. M., & Brown, A. L. (1984). Reciprocal teaching of comprehension-fostering and comprehension monitoring activities. *Cognition and Instruction, 1,* 117–175.
Pearson Knowledge Technologies. (2006). *WritetoLearn™.* Boulder, CO. Available online at *www.pearsonkt.com.*
Pellegrino, J. W. (2002). Knowing what students know. *Issues in Science and Technology Online.* Retrieved June 26, 2007, from *www.issues.org/19.2/pellegrino.htm.*
Pellegrino, J. W., Chudowsky, N., & Glaser, R. (Eds.). (2001). *Knowing what students know: The science and design of educational assessment.* Washington, DC: National Academy Press.
Rasch, G. (1980). *Probabilistic models for some intelligence and attainment tests.* Chicago: Mesa Press.
Scholastic. (2002). *Scholastic Reading Inventory.* New York: Author.
Scholastic. (2006). *Scholastic Reading Inventory–Enterprise Edition.* New York: Author.
Shepard, L. A. (2000). The role of assessment in a learning culture. *Educational Researcher, 29*(7), 4–14.
Shepard, L. A. (2003). Reconsidering large-scale assessment to heighten its relevance to learning. In J. M. Atkin & J. E. Coffey (Eds.), *Everyday assessment in the science classroom* (pp. 121–146). Arlington, VA: National Science Teachers Association.
Sloane, F. C., & Kelly, A. E. (2003). Issues in high-stakes testing programs. *Theory Into Practice, 42*(1), 12–17.
Snyder, L., Wise, B., & Caccamise, D. (2005). The assessment of reading comprehension: Considerations and cautions. *Topics in Language Disorders, 25*(1), 33–50.
Stenner, J. (2003). Matching students to text: The targeted reader. *A Scholastic Professional Paper* [Online serial]. New York: Scholastic. Retrieved June 21, 2007, from *www.tomsnyder.com/reports.target_reader_web2.pdf.*
Valenti, S., Neri, F., & Cucchiarelli, A. (2003). An overview of current research on automated essay grading. *Journal of Information Technology, 2,* 319–330.
van den Broek, P., Virtue, S., Everson, M. G., Tzeng, Y., & Sung, Y. (2002). Comprehension and memory of science texts: Inferential processes and the construction of a mental representation. In J. Otero, J. Leon, & A. C. Graesser (Eds.), *The psychology of science text comprehension* (pp. 131–154). Mahwah, NJ: Erlbaum.
van Dijk, T. A., & Kintsch, W. (1983). *Strategies of discourse comprehension.* New York: Academic Press.
Zwaan, R. A., & Radvansky, G. A. (1998). Situation models in language comprehension and memory. *Psychological Bulletin, 123,* 162–185.

11

NEUROSCIENCE
What Brain-Based Research Tells Us about Reading Comprehension

7

Looking at Reading Comprehension through the Lens of Neuroscience

ALLAN PAIVIO

> A primary requirement of a neural representation is that it should be capable of generating activity that matches, in some sense, the sensory input it represents.
> —PETER M. MILNER

Comprehension is a complex behavioral phenomenon. It encompasses the ability to respond to nonverbal situations, as well as to language, in an organized and adaptive way. It varies in the depth or level of processing required for a "sufficient" adaptive response to occur. The shallowest level is recognition that the stimulus has been experienced before. A completely unfamiliar stimulus might elicit only increased attention, which even in infants diminishes to indifference as the stimulus is repeated. Even then, however, the stimulus is remembered better and rated as more familiar when it has been repeated. Deeper levels of comprehension involve learned nonverbal or verbal associative responses to the stimulus; for example, grasping a hammer, saying its name, imaging a hammer when given the word as a cue, or responding with a verbal associate such as "nail." The eliciting stimuli and responses indicative of comprehension can be of any level of complexity.

All cognitive theories assume that the comprehension responses are mediated by direct and indirect activation of mental representations corresponding to the stimuli and responses. Advances in neuroscience have made it increasingly possible to identify such representations with neural structures and connecting pathways located in various areas of the brain. The chapter is focused on the structures and processes that, activated initially by visual language during reading, then spread quickly to other levels that necessarily elicit representations derived from processing of speech and nonverbal objects and events. All of that is interpreted here in terms of neuropsychological correlates of the dual coding approach to comprehension reviewed by Sadoski in Chapter 3, this volume.

The title of this chapter implies that a single neuroscientific lens can be focused on the problems related to reading comprehension. This is unlikely, because such a lens would have to be sufficiently wide angle to provide a general perspective on the diverse behavioral and neuropsychological phenomena that comprise comprehension. Current neuroscientific theories instead offer many narrow lenses that can focus on different tasks used to test for comprehension. Consider, for example, the following two tasks that have often been used to study comprehension: (1) Sentence–picture verification requires the tested person to indicate as quickly as possible whether a sentence truly describes the relations between objects and events in a picture; (2) paraphrase matching requires a judgment about whether two sentences have the same meaning. Thus, sentence–picture verification necessarily engages neural processes involved in dealing with visual language on one hand and nonverbal objects on the other, whereas paraphrase matching begins with two strings of visual language, with no direct activation of perceptual systems involved in object recognition. The two tasks would evoke quite different patterns of brain activity that could be described and evaluated in neuroscientific terms. But there are dozens of different ways of measuring comprehension, and each would require a different neuroscientific lens through which to view and interpret it. A general neuroscientific lens should provide an organized view of common and unique patterns of neural activity involved in the diverse tasks.

Hebb's (1949) cell assembly theory, which was intended to be a general brain-based theory, assumed that behavior is mediated by the activity of organized neural ensembles that are first established during early perceptual learning. Cell assemblies that serve as the representational base for simple ideas and images become progressively elaborated into more complex assemblies involved in perception, learning, memory, thinking, and so on. In general, the theory influenced the development of neuroscience, and in particular, connectionist neural network theories use Hebb's "learning rule" to simulate how neurons become connected. Cell assembly theory has been controversial, and most of its principle assumptions are no longer accepted, although its name continues to serve as a convenient label for neuronal representational structures, the detailed nature of which remains a mystery. While waiting for the mystery to be unraveled, we can at least rely on increasing knowledge of the brain locations with different functions, including those that are activated in reading comprehension.

A neuropsychological extension of multimodal dual coding theory (DCT) described in Chapter 3, this volume, serves as the lens through which we view and interpret a range of reading comprehension phenomena. Recall how DCT assumes that all aspects of cognition are mediated by the separate and cooperative activity of verbal and nonverbal representational systems composed of specific sensorimotor codes. The verbal representations, called "logogens," and the nonverbal ones, called "imagens," both include specialized variants for dealing with different kinds of sensory information and related response demands. Thus, there are visual, auditory, haptic, and motor logogens and imagens. Emotions, tastes, and smells are handled differently in the theory, in that we have no language-like representations constructed from these modalities (Paivio, 2007, p. 35), but we obviously have a rich descriptive vocabulary (thus, a corresponding logogen system) for these experiences. The representations do their cognitive work when they are activated via pathways that connect them relatively directly to the perceptual world on the input side and to response systems on the output side. Importantly, activation can spread between systems and within systems via cross-system referential connection between imagens and logogens or associative connections between representations within each class. These multimodal representational units and their complex (but systematic) interconnections give DCT a high degree of predictive and explanatory power.

The DCT model translates readily into neuropsychological terms that map onto the levels and types of processing involved in reading comprehension. Thus, modality-specific neural representational systems in different areas of the brain correspond to the psychologically defined, modality-specific logogens and imagens. Moreover, these representations are richly interconnected via neural associative pathways. These assumptions have long historical precedents that were based on the behavioral effects of localized brain damage observed by neurologists. For example, Wernicke (1874) proposed that the left posterior superior lobe of the human brain stores "auditory word images" that are translated into "motor word images" in the frontal part of the brain during speech production. Dejerine (1892) similarly proposed a "visual word form system," damage to which resulted in an inability to read. Comparable terms have been used by others over the years, with support coming from brain imaging techniques that were not available to the early neurologists. DCT neural logogens and imagens can now be linked conceptually to such antecedents and their modern variants. We shall see, however, that the DCT representations are more thoroughly modality-specific and nonabstract than those proposed by most neuroscientists.

OVERVIEW OF THE PROBLEM DOMAIN

Reading is initiated by print or writing and the visual system is, therefore, the leading player in this neuropsychological drama. However, both phylogenetically and ontogenetically, reading is completely intertwined with and dependent on all other sensorimotor systems. It is generally accepted that neural systems for word recognition developed from visual systems that had evolved for object recognition. Until recently it was assumed that the same visual brain systems are still used for both object and word recognition, but more refined brain imaging techniques reveal that visual objects and visual words activate separate but closely connected brain regions.

The visual language system is linked to all other sensorimotor systems, both verbal and nonverbal. There are verbal connections to auditory language and speech production systems, because children learn to understand language and speak long before they learn to read. Visual logogens directly activated by print or writing are necessary but not sufficient for deeper levels of comprehension. The deeper levels involve activation of meanings or semantic representations, which are viewed as abstract systems in some theories (more about that later). In DCT, however, there is no abstract semantic level of neural representation; rather, modality-specific imagens and logogens are connected to and can be activated by primary-level logogens or imagens already activated by language or nonverbal sensory stimuli. Thus, deep (meaningful) comprehension during reading entails activation of visual, auditory, haptic, and motor neural imagens or associated logogens, which may or may not be experienced consciously as images, movements, or verbal association. The meanings can include affective reactions associated with memory images of emotional events.

Recent evidence suggests that imagens and logogens are located in brain regions close to the modality-specific sensorimotor systems from which they originate. For example, Martin, Ungerleider, and Haxby (2000) proposed a sensorimotor model of semantic representations, according to which the network of semantic features "that define an object are stored close to the primary sensory and motor areas that were active when information about that object was acquired. Thus, the organization of semantic information parallels the organization of the sensory and motor systems in the primate brain"

(p. 1023). The model is based on modality-specific deficits associated with focal brain lesions and on neural imaging studies. It is especially important that the modality-specific semantic information referred to in the model is associated with language, so that words that refer to color, form, movement, and so on, activate regions close to those activated directly by colors, forms, and movements. In DCT terms, these regions house the modality-specific imagens of objects and events with the relevant sensorimotor properties, which are activated by logogens derived from experience with words that refer to color, form, movement, and so on. Reading comprehension is based on the direct and indirect activation of these sensorimotor neural systems.

The detailed DCT neuropsychological analysis of reading is presented in three sections in the rest of this chapter:

1. Reading based on the DCT verbal system alone.
2. Reading comprehension based on both verbal and nonverbal DCT systems.
3. The application of all DCT options to the analysis of concrete versus abstract language comprehension, a problem viewed here as the crucible of language comprehension theories.

READING IN THE VERBAL BRAIN: NEW RESEARCH

One definition of "reading" is the speaking out loud of printed or written words, with no reference to understanding the meaning of what is read. This happens to parents who read the same story over and over again to young children and find themselves thinking of something else as they automatically mouth the words. It is symptomatic of so-called "hyperlexic" autistic children who become experts at reading aloud but do not understand what they are reading. This is recognized more generally by reading researchers and remedial educators as the distinction between phonemic decoding and comprehension skills. Reading theories generally maintain that it is necessary to decode words fluently as a prerequisite to comprehension. DCT is more of an interactive theory, but skilled decoding is valuable in interactive theories as well. Because there has been considerable neuroscientific research on word decoding, I cover this topic first.

According to DCT, the verbal level of reading involves early activation of visual logogens during recognition, which proceeds quickly to activation of motor logogens that control articulation of printed words. The reading route begins at the retina and passes through several neural processing stations (e.g., the lateral geniculate nucleus) on the way to the cortex and, eventually, the articulatory muscles. The "raw" print information initially reaches the occipitotemporal areas in both hemispheres, then converges on a candidate for a visual logogen area located in the left hemisphere, presumably capitalizing on audiomotor language systems already established in that hemisphere (for relevant brain imaging results, see Cohen et al., 2000).

Evidence for Visual Logogens

The earliest evidence for visual logogens and their left-hemisphere location comes from studies of a neural deficit called "alexia," which refers to an impaired ability to read words that does not affect the ability to recognize auditory words. Pure alexia is a specific variant in which writing also remains intact. For example, Toronto novelist Howard

Engel woke up one morning to find that he could not read the newspaper (see Paivio, 2007, p. 154). After some rehabilitation he "was able to do everything," including write, but he could not read what he had written. The syndrome was first described as "alexia without agraphia" in 1892 by the French neurologist Jules Dejerine, who interpreted it as a disconnection syndrome that isolates the "visual word form system" from the rest of the language zone—also described as " a disconnection of word-form images from early visual analysis" (Sakurai, 2004, p. 35). It is classically associated with a lesion in the left occipitotemporal area. Recent neurimaging studies have identified the area more specifically with the left occipito-temporal sulcus, between the posterior left fusiform and inferior temporal gyri (e.g., see Leff, Spitsyana, Plant, & Wise, 2006; McCandliss, Cohen, & Dehaene, 2003). A lesion in this visual word form area (VWFA) disrupts the "normal" reading system, so that patients characteristically read words slowly, letter by letter, in a left to right sequence, until the entire word can be read correctly. Thus, the overall reading time increases dramatically with word length—as much as 4 or more seconds for each additional letter. By comparison, normal readers can read whole words in less than half a second, with almost no increase with word length up to nine letters. The research articles cited in this chapter provide neuroimages of the precise locations of the brain areas discussed. See Figure 7.1 for the approximate locations of the most pertinent brain regions discussed in this chapter.

Comparisons with naming nonverbal stimuli, such as pictures and colors, are especially relevant here, because they involve the same overt verbal responses as reading and have therefore received critical attention in alexia research. In DCT terms, naming

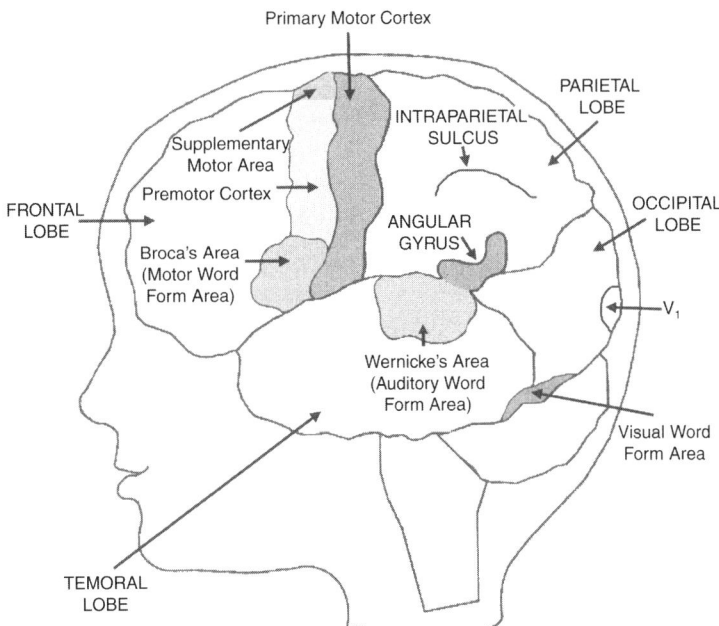

FIGURE 7.1. Approximate locations of left hemisphere brain areas discussed in this chapter. V1 is the primary visual cortex. The VWFA is located deep inside the brain in the medial left hemisphere. The right hemisphere also includes relevant functional areas that are not shown in this Figure.

requires a referential crossover between nonverbal and verbal systems, whereas reading does not, so that naming and reading problems should be functionally independent and dissociable. This appears to be the case according to data summarized in Paivio (2007). For example, adults and reading-age children name pictures and colors slower than they read their printed names, whereas people with alexia are much slower at reading words than naming pictures.

The lesion and brain imaging studies provide strong evidence for the existence of VWFA representations, or logogens, concentrated in the occipitotemporal region of the left hemisphere, as has been classically assumed. Questions remain concerning its other functions (other areas activated early in the reading process that might be candidates for additional visual logogen systems, etc.), but here I address only a few properties of the VWFA that are relevant to this chapter. An important point is that the emergence of the area is associated with the development of reading skills, especially grapheme–phoneme decoding ability (McCandliss et al., 2003). Thus, though functionally specialized, the VWFA results from experience with the sounds and pronunciation of visual words, and not simply passive exposure to the visual patterns.

The neuropsychological evidence also suggests that the VWFA representations are abstract in that, for example, they respond equally strongly to upper- and lowercase words. This is puzzling from the DCT modality–specificity viewpoint and also inconsistent with behavioral evidence, such as the finding that mixing upper- and lowercases disrupts word recognition in both adults' and children's reading (see Maywall, 2002). This disruption indicates that there is competition in activating name responses from upper- and lowercase visual logogens, which suggests that there are separate logogen subsystems for the two print forms within the VWFA. The alternative idea that visual words are represented in a more abstract representational system implies that different mechanisms would be needed to access the common visual lexicon from the different font patterns, which shifts the explanatory burden from multiple word form representations to multiple activation programs that converge on a common representational system. The DCT position is that multiple visual logogen systems result from experience with different kinds of print as well as cursive writing. The variants might be located so close together within the VWFA that the differences (e.g., between upper- and lowercase logogens) are not easily distinguished by current brain imaging techniques, although they are distinguishable psychologically (perceptually, behaviorally) in that, for example, one can quickly decide whether a word is printed in upper- or lowercase letters.

Evidence for Auditory Logogens

The classical model of reading assumes that visual processing of print activates auditory language representations before a printed word can be named. The mediating representations were viewed as auditory word forms (equivalent to DCT auditory logogens) in Wernicke's area in the posterior temporal cortex, which in turn activated motor word forms in secondary motor areas (e.g., Broca's area in the frontal cortex) prior to activating the primary motor system that produces spoken names. However, the theoretical description has become more complex in terms of the brain areas and processing systems involved. Especially important is the angular gyrus of the left parietal lobe, located halfway between Wernicke's area and the visual cortex, which is now seen as an additional important processing area in reading and other types of language activity, especially because it contains multimodal neurons that can process auditory, visual, and somatosensory properties of written and spoken words. Thus, the angular gyrus can play a role in deeper levels of meaningful reading. The classical view was that messages are conducted unidirectionally from Wernicke's area to Broca's area via a large neural bundle called the arcuate fasciculus. It is now known that there is a bidirectional connection between these two areas and still others that connect the parietal angular gyrus to both Wernicke's and Broca's areas, thus allowing for complex interactions, so that, for example, verbal motor activity can influence auditory and visual word processing farther back in the brain.

Motor Logogens

The final stage of reading aloud involves sequential activation of the articulatory muscles (tongue, mouth, larynx, diaphragm, etc.) that produce speech sounds. The articulatory activity is initiated directly by neurons of the primary motor cortex, but it is generally assumed that the pattern of firing is controlled by programs that originate in various regions of the secondary motor cortex (anterior to the primary motor area), especially the supplementary motor area, premotor cortex, Broca's area, and subcortical structures in the basal ganglia. For example, Broca's area near the lower part of the motor cortex in the left hemisphere presumably organizes motor neurons in the nearby facial area of the motor cortex, which help produce speech sounds when accompanied by activity of other areas that control properties of speech such as vocalization.

There are two general interpretations of the organizing "agents." The most common one is that there are motor plans, or organizing programs, that sequentially activate relevant parts of the primary motor cortex to produce the pronounced word. This is a compelling idea, because thousands of different words comprise different arrangements of a small number of phonemes (50 or fewer, depending on the language). Thus, it seems parsimonious to assume that some neural "executive" quickly activates the relevant motor components in the right order for the printed word to be read aloud. A problem with this view is that it would require a different set of rules for rearranging the same set of components to generate different words, which weakens the parsimony argument. The other idea is that each word has a holistic motor representation made up of parts that have become tightly associated through learning. This seems to strain the brain's resources, because it would have to store separate representations for all the syllables, words, stock phrases, idioms, and other overlearned structures that we know and can pronounce fluently after a brief glance at the printed pattern.

Computational connectionist models of reading have used both solutions to verbal output mechanisms. Single-route parallel connectionist models (e.g., Seidenberg & McClelland, 1989) use general rules to map orthography onto phonology. Dual-route models (e.g., Coltheart & Rastle, 1994) complement such mapping rules with lexical knowledge to account for irregular pronunciations not easily captured by mapping rules. I do not consider such models in detail, because their formal character is outside the nonformal DCT framework. Moreover, their computational representations are more abstract than DCT representations. For example, the phoneme is an abstraction for equivalence classes of speech sounds (phones), such as phonetic differences that result from the way r is pronounced in different contexts. Articulatory phonetics, in fact, uses specific pronunciation patterns to define speech sounds as bilabials, dentals, uvulars, glottals, and so on.

DCT motor logogens are more like articulatory phonetic representations than phonemic representations for word components, words, and longer sequences. So defined, they have their antecedents in concepts such as Wernicke's motor word images and neuropsychologist Luria's (1973) "articulemes." Such motor representations develop from childrens's attempts to imitate speech sounds by shaping up the articulatory patterns necessary for producing matching sounds, including those that result from their own babbling ("echolalia"). The patterns are internalized as motor neuronal models or templates. Exactly how this is achieved by the brain is a mystery, but no more so than the mechanisms in abstract computational or other theories.

This ends the discussion of the level of reading involved in going from print to pronunciation using the verbal system alone, which has included more than a hint of the complexity and uncertainty of the nature of the neural structures and processes that control even this apparently simple level of reading. The complexity increases as we move on to consider the deeper levels of comprehension involved in reading for meaning.

READING COMPREHENSION AND THE DUAL CODING BRAIN

Sadoski (Chapter 3, this volume) discusses the complexity of the concept of meaning in reading. What is meant by getting the meaning of what one reads? Cognitive scientists generally suggest that the reader accesses an abstract semantic system in which meaning is defined in terms of combinations of elementary semantic features. Neuropsychological research has identified a "central semantic system" from a selective cognitive disorder called semantic dementia, which is associated particularly with damage caused by neurodegenerative diseases in the inferotemporal regions of one or both temporal lobes. The syndrome entails loss of long-term memory knowledge about meanings of words and attributes that define living and nonliving things. The deficits extend to impaired word comprehension as the disease progresses. Such data have been used to support the argument that there is one central system rather than separate, modality-specific semantic systems (Patterson & Hodges, 2000), thus contrasting specifically with the multimodal DCT view (Paivio, 2007, Chapter 9). Here I focus specifically on brain evidence that is relevant to meaningful reading.

The argument from DCT is that no separate neural semantic or meaning system is accessed and activated when one comprehends text. Instead, meaning consists of the modality-specific dual-coding activity elicited by text during reading. The activity may be experienced as nonverbal imagery or silent verbal associative thoughts, or expressed overtly in, for example, selecting a pictured scene or sentence paraphrase that corresponds most closely to the imagery or verbal thoughts elicited by a sentence, or by performing an act described by the sentence (entailing activation of motor imagens), and so on.

As I have already mentioned, words that refer to colors, shapes, and activities activate brain regions close to the regions activated directly by corresponding sensory stimulation. These word-evoked reactions can be interpreted as neural correlates of modality-specific referential meanings. The correlates also include brain areas associated with the capacity to image complex multimodal objects in response to their names or descriptions. The evidence has come from studies of individuals who showed imagery deficits following damage to the critical areas, as well as activation of those areas, as revealed by brain scans. Much of that research has involved spoken cues for imagery (Paivio, 2007, pp. 162–166), but the results are relevant to reading, because the same areas are activated as part of the pattern of neural reactions that occur when concrete, high-imagery words or sentences are read. Such language-evoked visual imagery is associated particularly with occipital and occipitotemporal areas of the brain, but parietal and inferior temporal lobes are also implicated in some imagery tasks (Thompson & Kosslyn, 2000).

The relevant general conclusion from the neuropsychological imagery results is that the referential meaning of concrete language is experienced as modality-specific images associated with activity of neurons in various brain areas. The results are consistent with DCT, but not with current single-code semantic theories.

CONCRETENESS/IMAGERY EFFECTS: THE CRUCIBLE FOR TESTING READING COMPREHENSION THEORIES

Concrete language is generally easier to understand and remember than abstract language. This is one of the most longstanding and consistent findings in cognitive psychology (reviewed in Paivio, 1986, 2007; Sadoski & Paivio, 2001).The differences are so striking that they can serve as crucial tests for theories of reading comprehension. As already explained by Sadoski (Chapter 3, this volume), the effects are easily interpreted in terms of DCT processes related particularly to the fact that concrete language more readily than abstract language evokes mental images of nonverbal objects and events. The concreteness advantage is explained by the additive effects of nonverbal (imagery) and verbal coding, as well as superiority of images over words as cues for associations that benefit language processing and cognition generally. Alternative explanations suggested by single-code theorists have failed crucial tests. For example, Paivio, Walsh, and Bons (1994) compared memory for lists of words and word pairs that varied in concreteness and associative relatedness of the paired words. They expected that concreteness would have its usual positive effect on memory and, moreover, that this effect would be independent of effects attributable to intrapair relational information that could be based on either imagery or verbal processes. It turned out, as predicted from DCT, that concreteness and relatedness had independent (additive) positive effects on associative memory, a result that is inconsistent with an alternative theory that attributes concreteness effects to relational processing rather than to imagery (for a more detailed summary of the theoretical arguments and results, see Paivio, 2007, pp. 84–85). Other studies have supported DCT predictions using sentences and longer texts. For example, Sadoski, Goetz, and Avila (1995) experimentally compared concrete and abstract extended paragraphs carefully matched for a host of variables suggested by other theories. They found that DCT explained their results best.

I focus next on recent neuropsychological studies designed to reveal brain correlates of concreteness effects in reading comprehension. Several experiments by John Kounios, Philip Holcomb, and their colleagues compared neuropsychological predictions from DCT and common coding theories, using electroencephalographic event-related potentials (ERPs) to identify cortical regions activated by concrete and abstract words presented in sentence and other contexts. Interest centered on a component of ERPs known to be sensitive to semantic variables—a negatively changing component (N400) that peaks about 400 ms after the crucial stimulus event. The researchers predicted that concrete and abstract materials would be processed by different brain regions rather than by a single region, as would be predicted from single-coding theories.

The results supported the general prediction, with some variation over experiments in the specific locations of the concrete–abstract differences. Kounios and Holcomb's

(1994) subjects classified nouns as concrete or abstract, or distinguished them from nonwords. The main result was that concrete words elicited more ERPs in the N400 range than did abstract words, especially in anterior brain sites and in the right hemisphere. Holcomb, Kounios, Anderson, and West (1999) showed participants concrete and abstract sentences in which the final word was either congruent or incongruent with the prior context (e.g., "Armed robbery implies that the thief used a *weapon* [versus a *rose*]"). Participants judged whether a sentence made sense or not. The crucial results were that anomalous sentences elicited more N400 ERPs than congruent sentences, as did concrete compared to abstract sentences. Moreover, the concrete–abstract difference was larger at more anterior sites for anomalous sentences but not congruent sentences. Holcomb et al. concluded that these results are more consistent with dual coding than an alternative single-code theory.

West, O'Rourke, and Holcomb (1998) used sentence processing tasks that did or did not require use of imagery to determine whether the sentence was true or false. For example, to respond appropriately, subjects presumably had to image to the sentence, "It is easy to form a mental image of a canoe," whereas imagery was not required to decide whether a similar sentence (e.g., "It is common for people to have a canoe") made sense. A further control group simply decided whether a probe letter was present in the final word of the sentence (e.g., "There is a *t* in the word canoe"). Among other notable results, a concrete–abstract ERP difference showed up in frontal sites regardless of word imageability, whereas imageable and nonimageable words differed mostly at posterior regions. The pattern of results was again interpreted as strong support for the dual-coding model of mental representation over single-code models that reject imagery as a significant symbolic system underlying language.

This conclusion has been supported in experiments using other brain scanning procedures. Binder, Westbury, McKiernam, Possing, and Medler (1995) obtained functional magnetic resonance imaging (fMRI) recordings from participants who viewed concrete words, abstract, words, and nonwords, and indicated whether each item was a word or a nonword by pressing one of two keys. The fMRI results showed overlapping but partly distinct patterns of neural activity, such that a bilateral network of association and posterior multimodal cortices were activated during processing of concrete words, whereas a strongly left-lateralized network was activated during processing of abstract words. The authors conclude that the results provide firm evidence for a dual coding model of concrete and abstract concepts.

Using regional blood flow (positron emission tomography [PET]) as a measure of activation, Mellet, Tzourio, Denis, and Mazoyer (1998) found that overlapping but partly distinct patterns of neural activity were elicited when subjects imaged while listening to definitions of concrete words compared to definitions of abstract words. Just, Newman, Keller, McKelney, and Carpenter (2004) used fMRI to study brain activation during more complex comprehension tasks involving sentences that varied in imagery value. Participants read or heard high-imagery sentences (e.g., "A circle placed at the top of the capital letter *v* resembles the outline of an ice cream cone") or low-imagery sentences (e.g., "Horsepower is the unit for measuring the power of engines or motors"). Participants were asked to respond "True" or "False" to the sentences. They were also told that on some trials they would have to visualize the sentence to answer, and they were presented an example of such a sentence. The following are the pertinent results for my purposes in this chapter. High-imagery sentences resulted in more activation than low-imagery sentences in the parietal cortex (particularly the left intraparietal sulcus), whereas low-imagery sentences produced more activation of the left temporal cortex.

Both regions also showed coactivation with frontal regions generally involved in language processing. These generalizations hold for both visual and auditory presentation.

The coactivation of parietal and language-processing areas in the case of high-imagery sentences in the Just et al. (2004) experiment suggests a dual-coding involvement in the form of verbal–imaginal referential processing. The authors interpret the temporal lobe processing of abstract sentences in terms of retrieval and processing of semantic and world knowledge, but a DCT alternative is that the effect simply reflects verbal associative processing encouraged by strong associative connections between key words in the abstract sentences (Paivio, 2007, p. 196).

This procedure was extended to the study of imagery effects in sentence comprehension in autism. Kana, Keller, Cherkassky, Minshew, and Just (2006) predicted from a theory of cortical underconnectivity in autism that the interregional collaboration between linguistic and imaginal processing in the sentence imagery task described earlier would be underutilized in autism. They tested this by comparing fMRI activation patterns of individuals with autism with age- and IQ-matched controls while subjects processed high- and low-imagery sentences. The functional connectivity analysis showed that the language and spatial brain centers were less synchronized among participants with autism than among control participants. In addition, however, whereas the control group showed imagery-related activation primarily with the high-imagery sentences, the autistic group showed activation of parietal and occipital brain regions associated with imagery for comprehending both low- and high-imagery sentences. The authors concluded that, in addition to their general brain underconnectivity, people with autism are more reliant on visualization to support language comprehension (cf. Grandin, 1995). All these studies provide crucial neuropsychological support for concreteness–abstractness differences at the word and sentence levels, as predicted by DCT—results that are very difficult for common code theories to explain.

Neuropsychological studies at the story level are few, but they tend to be supportive of DCT and the spontaneous formation of mental images of key story events. For example, Sadoski (1983, 1985) and Sadoski, Goetz, Olivarez, Lee, and Roberts (1990) found that people of various ages tended to report an image of the climax of a short story much more than any other part of the story. Xu, Kemeny, Park, Frattali, and Braun (2005) used fMRI to determine brain activity at the word, sentence, and narrative levels using Aesop's fables as narratives. Consistent with the Sadoski et al. (1990) results, they found that brain activation in the early stages of reading a short story was mainly, but not completely, in the left perisylvian language cortices associated with word and sentence processing. However, the climactic outcomes of the stories showed additional brain activation far beyond areas that could be associated with lexical and syntactic processing. The additional brain areas stimulated as the story progressed were an array of extralinguistic centers in the right perisylvian and extrasylvian centers associated with multimodal integration, mental imagery, and emotional responses. These areas included the angular gyrus and superior temporal sulcus mentioned earlier.

In conclusion, by default, the case for imagery and DCT as explanations of reading comprehension is accepted as a possibility by Walter Kintsch, one of the best known proponents of single-code (propositional) theories of comprehension (see Sadoski's summary in Chapter 3, this volume). His theory includes a situational model that is intended to account for the same phenomenal domain as imagery, but the representational base of the model is entirely propositional. He concedes that "situation models may be imagery based, in which case the propositional formalism currently used by most models fails us" (Kintsch, 2004, p. 1284). He nonetheless argues for their feasibility and future research success. However, propositional situation models have not explained the concreteness effects to which they should be most applicable, and they are unlikely to do so as long as they remain linked only to an abstract propositional code.

INTEGRATE, INVESTIGATE, AND INITIATE: QUESTIONS FOR DISCUSSION

1. This chapter has described how recent research enables scientists to isolate neural structures and connecting neurological, mental pathways that process comprehension. How would you suggest that future research in this field be directed to improve comprehension of less able readers? What do you judge to be our own next most important step?

2. What is the most memorable information you gained from reading this chapter? Envision your professional realms of responsibilities (e.g., your classroom, administrative team, university research center). Describe a concrete action you can take in your environment to implement the new perspective neuroscience lends to one or more of the actions you take.

3. Take a position concerning the reason why concrete ideas are easier to comprehend than abstract ones. What future instructional methods hold the greatest potential to increase less able readers' abilities to comprehend abstract concepts?

REFERENCES

Binder, J. R., Westbury, C. F., McKiernan, K. A., Possing, E. T., & Medler, D. A. (2005). Distinct brain systems for processing concrete and abstract language. *Journal of Cognitive Neuroscience, 17,* 905–917.

Cohen, C. L., Dehaene, S., Naccache, L., Lehéricy, Dehaene-Lambertz, G., Hénaff, M. A., & Michel, F. (2000). The visual word form area: Spatial and temporal characterization of an initial stage of reading in normal and posterior split-brain patients. *Brain, 123,* 291–307.

Coltheart, M., & Rastle, K. (1994). Serial processing in reading aloud: Evidence for dual-route models of reading. *Journal of Experimental Psychology: Human Perception and Performance, 20,* 1197–1211.

Dejerine, J. (1892). Contribution à l'étude anatomo–pathologique et clinique des differentes variétés de cécité-verbale [A contribution to the anatomical–pathological and clininal study of different varieties of word blindness]. *Mémoires Societé Biolique, 4,* 61–90.

Grandin, T. (1995). *Thinking in pictures.* New York: Doubleday.

Hebb, D. O. (1949). *The organization of behavior.* New York: Wiley.

Holcomb, P. J., Kounios, J., Anderson, J. E., & West, W. C. (1999). Dual-coding, context-availability, and concreteness effects in sentence comprehension: An electrophysiological investigation. *Journal of Experimental Psychology: Learning, Memory, and Cognition, 25,* 721–742.

Just, M. A., Newman, S. D., Keller, T. A., McKelney, A., & Carpenter, P. A. (2004). Imagery in sentence comprehension: An fMRI study. *NeuroImage, 21,* 112–124.

Kana, R. K., Keller, ST. A., Cherkassky, V. L, Minshew, N. J., & Just, M. A. (2006). Sentence comprehension in autism: Thinking in pictures with decreased functional connectivity. *Brain, 129*(9), 2484–2493.

Kintsch, W. (2004). The construction–integration model of text comprehension and its implications for instruction. In R. B. Ruddell & N. J. Unrau (Eds.), *Theoretical models and processes of reading* (5th ed., pp. 1270–1328). Newark, DE: International Reading Association.

Kounios, J., & Holcomb, P. J. (1994). Concreteness effects in semantic processing: ERP evidence supporting dual-coding theory. *Journal of Experimental Psychology: Learning, Memory, and Cognition, 20,* 804–823.

Leff, A. P., Spitsyana, G., Plant, G. T., & Wise, R. J. S. (2006). Structural anatomy of pure and hemianopic alexia. *Journal of Neurology, Neurosurgery, and Psychiatry, 77*, 1004–1007.

Luria, A. R. (1973). *The working brain: An introduction to neuropsychology*. New York: Penguin.

Martin, A., Ungerleider, L. G., & Haxby, J. V. (2000). Category specificity and the brain: The sensory/motor model of semantic representation of objects. In M. Gazzaniga (Ed.), *The new cognitive neurosciences* (pp. 1023–1035). Cambridge, MA: MIT Press.

Maywall, K. (2002). Case-mixing effects on children's word recognition: Lexical feedback and development. *Quarterly Journal of Experimental Psychology, 55A*, 525–542.

McCandliss, B. D., Cohen, L., & Dehaene, S. (2003). The visual word form area: Expertise for reading in the fusiform gyrus. *Trends in Cognitive Sciences, 7*, 293–299.

Mellet, E., Tzourio, N., Denis, M., & Mazoyer, B. (1998). Cortical anatomy of mental imagery of concrete nouns based on their dictionary definition. *Neuroreport, 9*, 803–809.

Paivio, A. (1986). *Mental representations: A dual coding approach*. New York: Oxford University Press.

Paivio, A. (2007). *Mind and its evolution: A dual coding theoretical approach*. Mahwah, NJ: Erlbaum.

Paivio, A., Walsh, M., & Bons, T. (1994). Concreteness and memory: When and why? *Journal of Experimental Psychology: Learning, Memory, and Cognition, 20*, 1196–1204.

Patterson, K., & Hodges, J. R. (2000). Semantic dementia: One window on the structure and organization of semantic memory. In F. Boller & J. Grafman (Eds.), *Handbook of Neuropsychology* (2nd ed., Vol. 2, pp. 313–333). Amsterdam: Elsevier.

Sadoski, M. (1983). An exploratory study of the relationships between reported imagery and the comprehension and recall of a story. *Reading Research Quarterly, 19*, 110–123.

Sadoski, M. (1985). The natural use of imagery in story comprehension and recall: Replication and extension. *Reading Research Quarterly, 20*, 658–667.

Sadoski, M., Goetz, E. T., & Avila, E. (1995). Context effects in text recall: Dual coding or context availability? *Reading Research Quarterly, 30*, 278–288.

Sadoski, M., Goetz, E. T., Olivarez, A., Lee, S., & Roberts, N. M. (1990). Imagination in story reading: The role of imagery, verbal recall, story analysis, and processing levels. *Journal of Reading Behavior, 22*, 55–70.

Sadoski, M., & Paivio, A. (2001). *Imagery and text: A dual coding theory of reading and writing*. Mahwah, NJ: Erlbaum.

Sakurai, Y. (2004). Varieties of alexia from fusiform, posterior inferior temporal and posterior occipital gyrus lesions. *Behavioral Neurology, 15*, 35–50.

Seidenberg, M. S., & McClelland, J. L. (1989). A distributed developmental model of word recognition and naming. *Psychological Review, 96*, 523–568.

Thompson, W. L., & Kosslyn, S. M. (2000). Neural systems activated during visual mental imagery: A review and a meta-analysis. In A. W. Toga & J. C. Mazziota (Eds.), *Brain mapping: III. The systems* (pp. 535–560). San Diego: Academic Press.

Wernicke, K. (1874). *Der Aphasische Symptomencomplexe* [*The aphasia symptom-complex*]. Breslau: Cohn & Weigert.

West, W. C., O'Rourke, T. B., & Holcomb, P. J. (1998). Event related brain potentials and language comprehension: A cognitive neuroscience approach to the study of intellectual functioning. In S. Soraci & W. J. McIlvane (Eds.), *Perspectives on fundamental processes in intellectual functioning* (pp. 133–168). Stamford, CT: Ablex.

Xu, J., Kemeny, S., Park, G., Frattali, C., & Braun, A. (2005). Language in context: Emergent features of word, sentence, and narrative comprehension. *NeuroImage, 25*, 1002–1015.

8

Using Neuroscience to Inform Reading Comprehension Instruction

CATHY COLLINS BLOCK and SHERI R. PARRIS

> By examining reading comprehension at the most basic, cellular level, we can begin to fill the gaps that exist in our understanding of comprehension.
> —SHERI R. PARRIS (2007)

This chapter discusses the neuroscientific influences that are transforming our understanding of how reading comprehension occurs. Our knowledge of these meaning-making processes, like most other topics of educational interest and research, have evolved as a product of the cumulative integration of many discoveries outside of educational research. In the last part of the 20th century, the emergence of neuroscience caused the fields of philosophy, psychology, linguistics, education, and others to merge in new and previously unconceivable ways. This movement was fueled in the last two decades by advancements in technology that better enabled researchers to monitor subjects' brain activity while reading. By 2006, these advancements led Edelman (2006) to declare that the field of neuroscience so integrated biological sciences of the brain into what was once the exclusive domain of philosophers that a "paradigm shift" in cognitive science had occurred. The result of these recent works is the ability to understand more deeply the cognitive and emotional processes involved in reading comprehension.

This chapter highlights the following:

- Historical perspective of neuroscience as applied to reading comprehension
- Neuroimaging tools used to quantify and identify reading comprehension processes in the brain
- Neuroimaging research findings related to reading comprehension processes
- Future implications for using neuroscientific research to understand reading comprehension

WHAT'S OUT THERE TODAY: ESTABLISHED RESEARCH

Jean Piaget (1963), pioneer of the theory and research that support the tenet that cognitive development occurs in stages, has greatly influenced thinking in the field of reading comprehension today. He labeled his body of work "genetic epistemology" (Edelman, 2006, p. 47). His goal was to explain knowledge and how we acquire it. Unlike others of his time and earlier, Piaget chose not to rely on single, isolated observations to formulate conclusions. He insisted that research concerning mental processes needed to be triangulated to ensure that conclusions could be transferable, valid, and reliable. He challenged the position that knowledge is a static entity. Instead, Piaget showed that information is developed in the brain over a period of time. His work led the way for educators today to view reading comprehension through the lens of neuroscience. Such a lens requires a relationship between thought and language, psychology and linguistics (Piaget, 1963; Piaget & Kamii, 1978). Until the recent advent of neuroimaging technology, however, we could not document Piaget's theory. We now know that multiple language centers in the brain are indeed activated during the reading comprehension process.

Cognitive Neuroscience Meets Reading Comprehension

The term "cognitive neuroscience," coined in the late 1970s (Cognitive Neuroscience Society, n.d.), defines the branch of neuroscience that intersects with cognitive psychological research. Its focus is to determine "how brain function[s] give rise to mental activity" (Kosslyn & Shin, 1992, p. 146). The study of reading processes and other intellectual activities is a component of this domain within neuroscience.

In the early 1980s, reading researchers and cognitive neuroscientists began working together to investigate the processes of reading. P. David Pearson (1985) attributed this union to three forces:

1. In early reading instruction, an overwhelming consensus was reached by experts in the field to support the need to teach phonics. Thus, the mental energies of the reading field were free to turn their attention toward the next level of reading instruction, comprehension.
2. The 1981 National Assessment of Educational Progress (NAEP) report found that 13- to 17-year-olds struggled with inferential and interpretive comprehension, centering attention on the need for more insight in this area.
3. The relatively new field of cognitive psychology began to recognize the reading process as an important object of study.

In the 1990s, with the widespread use of neuroimaging technologies, cognitive psychologists' ushered in the use of formal neuroscientific study as an important component within the realm of reading research. This fact is documented by the growing number of research studies (using neuroimaging to document reading processes in the brain) that have appeared in both psychology and reading-related, peer-reviewed journals over the past two decades. In addition, neuroimaging technology has continued to become increasingly sophisticated year after year. That said, another common use of neuroimaging is to identify subjects with damage in specific areas of the brain. These subjects can then be given a variety of reading comprehension tasks to determine how damage to a particular part of the brain affects these thinking processes. The most common types of brain imaging used by cognitive researchers today are discussed below.

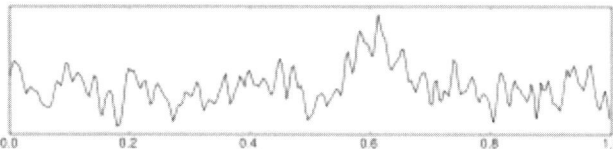

FIGURE 8.1. Example of EEG recording showing the sound waves that cross different regions of the brain at distinct points as a child comprehends a text.

Three Types of Neuroimaging

The first type of neuroimaging, electroencephalography (EEG), is a diagnostic test used to create an audio recording of the electrical activity within the brain. The recording is generated by attaching electrodes to the scalp that can detect electrical noise variations within the brain as the subject performs specific thinking tasks. For example, researchers can use these electrodes to collect data during silent reading episodes. The audio recordings are called event-related potentials (ERPs). Each ERP, or experimental mental "event," is recorded as a visual image that shows how brain activity changes when students read. The resulting collection of ERPs measures three changes in a brain's activity during reading comprehension: (1) the amount of time needed to comprehend (latency); (2) the depth of thoughts and amount of brain activity that occurs as each new sentence is decoded (amplitude or magnitude or brain activity); and (3) the distribution of various sound waves across all regions of the brain that emerges at different points during comprehension. See Figure 8.1 for an example of an EEG recording.

The second type of neuroimaging, magnetoencephalography (MEG), is a diagnostic test used to create an image of the brain that allows researchers to measure its magnetic activity during specific thinking tasks (magnetic activity is a by-product of the electrical activity within the brain). Because nerves send messages via electrical impulses, MEGs can measure the latency, amplitude, and distribution of these electrical impulses through the magnetic data that are retrieved. This method has become increasingly popular with cognitive neuroscientists in the past few years, because advances in magnetic technology

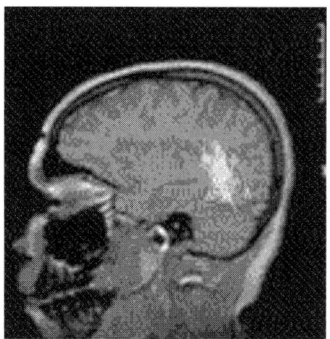

FIGURE 8.2. Example of a magnetoencephalography image of the brain that is used as a diagnostic test to measure the magnetic activity in the comprehension of text.

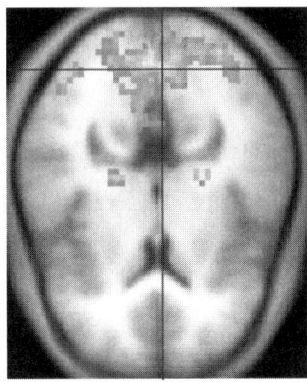

FIGURE 8.3. Example of a functional magnetic resonance image that measures blood flow to specific regions in the brain during different comprehension tasks.

enable more precise measurements of distinct nerve impulses. See Figure 8.2 for an example of an MEG image.

The third type of neuroimaging, functional magnetic resonance imaging (fMRI), introduced in 1990 (Moffett, 2006), is a diagnostic brain imaging procedure that combines radio waves and a strong magnetic field to illuminate areas with increased blood flow during specific types of thinking tasks (e.g., specific types of reading comprehension tasks). Thuse, fMRI creates a "map" of the most active regions of the brain during various mental processes. See Figure 8.3 for an example of an fMRI image.

NEW RESEARCH IN NEUROSCIENCE THAT RELATES TO READING COMPREHENSION

In the past decade, neuroimaging has allowed scientists to identify brain regions that are engaged when successful text processing occurs. Thus, we can now "see" (through neuroimaging) that reading comprehension comprises many dynamic subprocesses. Some major recent findings follow. Figure 8.4 provides a visual reference to each of the subprocessing components discussed below.

Highly Effective Reading Comprehension Activates Most Major Regions in the Brain

Neuroscience has shown that at specific points in a reading comprehension episode, the brain utilizes most of its major regions, even those previously thought to be uninvolved in the reading process. For instance, Fulbright et al. (1999) proved that the cerebellum plays a role in reading. This is a surprising finding, because the cerebellum (see lower region in Figure 8.4) had long been thought to be concerned mainly with motor control and balance. In another study, Ferstl and von Cramon (2001) found that the emotional structures of the brain are indeed activated during story reading at emotional moments in the story. One of the main emotional structures of the brain is the amygdala (see Parris, Chapter 10, this volume, for more information on the amygdala).

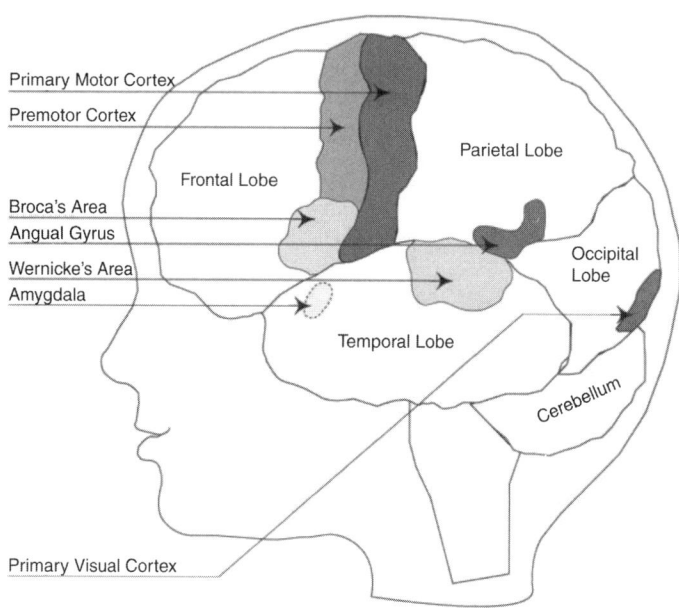

FIGURE 8.4. Diagram of regions of the brain that are activated when successful comprehension occurs.

Brain Differences by Reading Level

Brain imaging has also shown that the depth, scope, and location of mental activity vary by a students' reading ability levels. Molfese et al. (2006) found that above average readers process text faster than average and below-average readers. They also found that above-average readers show more right-hemisphere activity (right side of the brain) during reading, whereas average and below-average readers show more activity in the left hemisphere (left side of the brain). There is also less differentiation in brain activity as reading ability levels go down. Therefore, it seems that whereas the best readers have developed more highly specialized and differentiated processing systems, less advanced readers' brains have not developed such processing speed or mental specializations to enlist the power in various regions of the brain to comprehend better.

The Importance of Working Memory

fMRI research has revealed that the brain region most activated during sentence comprehension is the left frontotemporal lobe (including the basal ganglia [thought to help the brain choose the best of several available meaning-making options; Copland, Chenery, & Murdoch, 2001] and thalamus; Fiebach, Vos, & Friederici, 2004; Friederici, 2002; Kaan & Swaab, 2002). Fiebach et al. (2004) found that the right basal ganglia and thalamus are more strongly activated in poor readers who have a low level of working memory. The thalamus serves as the central switchboard for most of the information entering into the brain. It routes incoming messages to the appropriate place. These data suggest that a less able reader's basal ganglia and thalamus must work harder to interpret meaning from text and help to explain why a less able reader has more difficulty finding correct responses. These data also show why, in general, readers with a low working memory have more difficulty comprehending syntactically difficult sentences (Caplan & Waters, 1999; Friederici, Steinhauer, Mecklinger, & Meyer, 1998; Just & Carpenter, 1992; MacDonald, Just, & Carpenter, 1992; Mitchell, 1994). Reading syntactically similar sentences together, though, increases reading fluency for everyone in general, because the brain adapts itself to the similarly styled sentences; thus, less effort is required as each additional sentence is read (Noppeney & Price, 2004). This new finding helps explain why young readers can more quickly comprehend patterned books. It also supports the need to use high-quality literature in comprehension instruction. Award-winning authors have their own distinctive styles, based on the masterful repetition of similarly styled sentences.

Word Identification and Decoding

Through neuroimaging studies, we have learned that fluent word identification and decoding occur in the left posterior cortical region (temporal, parietal, and occipital lobes of the brain, with both dorsal [top] and ventral [bottom] components; Fiez & Peterson, 1998; Henderson, 1986; Nobre, Allison, & McCarthy, 1994; Puce, Allison, Asgari, Gore, & McCarthy, 1996; Pugh, Mencl, Jenner, Lee, et. al., 2001). In normal development of fluent decoding skills, the temporoparietal area predominates, along with the premotor cortex, for analytic processing. This union is essential if readers are to integrate word recognition and meaning of printed words (Pugh, Mencl, Jenner, Lee, et al., 2001). The need for these left posterior regions of mental activity is further supported by the discovery that some students with reading disabilities rely on the inferior (lower) frontal and right-hemisphere posterior (rear) regions, suggesting that the normal pathways do not efficiently allow fluent word identification. The normal pathways utilize the posterior left-hemisphere areas. Shaywitz et al. (2002) found that activation in the occipitotemporal lobes (which largely overlaps the posterior left hemisphere) increases as word decoding skill increases, further substantiating the importance of this area of the brain for reading ability.

Comprehension

Neuroscience has also informed us that different reading comprehension processes activate different types of mental activity. For example, Ferstl, Guthke, and von Cramon (2002) used fMRI to determine that the left prefrontal lobe of the brain is active during inferencing tasks. In another study, Guthke and von Cramon (2001) gave subjects with brain-damage a story comprehension test. Results showed that whereas subjects with left-hemisphere damage had more problems remembering details, subjects with right-hemisphere damage had more problems finding main ideas, and those with prefrontal damage (an area of the brain associated with executive function) had more difficulty determining implicit main ideas. Ni et al. (2000) found that grammar (syntactic) errors (e.g., "Trees can grew") and meaning (semantic) errors (e.g., "Trees can eat") are also processed in different areas of the brain. Syntactic errors were processed in Broca's area, whereas semantic errors were processed in Wernicke's area. The latter study, however, used verbal rather than text-based cues (i.e., the sentences were read aloud to participants rather than having participants read sentences in a silent reading format). It is necessary for future research to examine whether Broca's area is still a major source of brain activity for processing text-based syntactic properties during silent reading sentence comprehension.

Additionally, analyses of neuroimaging studies has shown there are multiple neural pathways through which reading comprehension can be achieved:

> Kaan and Swaab (2003) found that distinct types of syntactic processing in sentence comprehension is transmitted from the primary visual cortex [when we see the printed words] to the angular gyrus where the message is somehow matched with the sounds of the words when spoken. The auditory form of the word is then processed for comprehension in Wernicke's area as if the word had been heard.... [Other studies, however,] using positron emission tomography (PET) have demonstrated that some reading tasks performed by normal people activated neither Wernicke's area nor the angular gyrus. These results suggest that there is [also] a direct reading route that does not involve speech sound recoding of the visual stimulus before the processing of either meaning or speaking. (Carey, 2002, p. 19)

These new data provide new hope for struggling readers. As more information is obtained, new methods may be used to create future instruction and curricula to strengthen those regions of the brain that are necessary for certain types of comprehension subprocessing. These neuroscientific findings also support dual coding theory (DCT; Paivio, 1971, 1986, 1991; Sadoski, Paivio, & Goetz, 1991; also see Sadoski, Chapter 3, this volume); that is, words can be encoded through two avenues of input. These input systems, linguistic (verbal) and nonlinguistic (nonverbal), function either independently or together to form vivid mental representations of text. Neuroimaging also provides support for cognitive flexibility theory, which demonstrates that readers attend to print through multiple pathways (e.g., phonological, semantic, etc.) simultaneously for comprehension to occur (Cartwright, 2002), as described by Cartwright in Chapter 4, this volume.

HOW THIS KNOWLEDGE CAN IMPROVE COMPREHENSION INSTRUCTION

To review, we know that different areas of the brain are called upon to handle specific reading comprehension process(es). Thus, excellent comprehenders are able concurrently to pool all of the aforementioned subprocessing regions more rapidly than less able readers, so that various comprehension strategies operate almost simultaneously as a seamless whole. Those who research reading comprehension through the vehicle of neuroscience must stay abreast of the burgeoning flow of information that is published in journals from a variety of interrelated fields, continuously assemble this new data into the increasingly complex model of how we comprehend text, then build theoretical bridges to bring this information into the field of reading, so that we can produce more effective, practical learning guidelines and applications. For instance, Pugh, Mencl, Jenner, Lee, et al. (2001; Pugh, Mencl, Jenner, Katz, et al., 2001) examined a large number of neuroimaging studies of reading and created a tentative model of the neural circuitry for reading. They have not updated this model since 2001. Much new neuroscientific data have been added to the literature in the last 7 years, so researchers must constantly update their own models of reading comprehension to include new data to push our understanding of comprehension further. Moreover, even though we can make some general assumptions about the brain through neuroscientific studies, each brain is still as unique as the individual it represents. With over 100 billion nerve cells in every brain, no two brains ever think exactly alike. Neuroscience, like any other aspect of reading research, can give us a general framework for how the brain functions during comprehension, but in the end, as with all other approaches to teaching and learning, we must treat each student as an individual. That said, neuroscience applied to comprehension instruction can provide scientific supporting data to validate new and existing instructional practices that exemplary teachers have used for generations. We would like to describe four of these applications.

Eliminating Inefficient Thinking Processes

Neuroscientists have proven that the elimination of responses that fail to serve a useful purpose during reading comprehension can enable a student to focus on more purposeful mental subprocesses (Kandel, 2006, p. 168). Therefore, an activity used to keep less able readers from repeatedly relooping through unfruitful mental subprocesses would become more effective if such students learned to eliminate responses they have used to try to understand a word, sentence, or paragraph. For instance, such readers could use the checklist below. By checking off the things that they have tried, students are focused toward a more specific, higher-level type of thinking and obtain more control of their thinking processes to resolve a specific comprehension problem. For example, our checklist could include the following:

What I've already done to try to figure out this word I didn't know

1. _____ Sound it out.
2. _____ What would make sense that begins with this letter?
3. _____ Substitute a word that could make sense.
4. _____ Read on.
5. _____ If there is a prefix or suffix, try to break the word into smaller, meaning related parts.
6. _____ Is it a content-specific word? If so, it will most likely be a noun that names one very specific thing related to the subject of the paragraph.
7. _____ Reread by starting at the beginning of the paragraph to pick up and add together all clues to meaning.

We could then teach students to reorder this list in the order of items that they personally use most habitually or find themselves most often checking off first. Over time, students could consciously rechannel their mental pathways to a "check off" list, then later, subconsciously and automatically, pull themselves out of useless mental relooping.

Fastmapping for Long-Term Memory

Scientists have shown that nerve synapses can undergo large and enduring changes in strength (through protein synthesis) after only a relatively small amount of training. Thus, memory is built and strengthened through repetition. Practice does make perfect, in other words (Kandel, 2006). Thus, we can convert short-term learning of a comprehension strategy into long-term memory through "fastmapping," which is defined as a minimum of six consecutive, in-depth mental experiences in which readers generate one application of a major comprehension concept or strategy before being asked to learn a second one (Block, Parris, & Whiteley, 2008). Fastmapping builds long-term memory by allowing synapses to send the same connecting mental impulses with enough repetitions that they become permanent synaptic connections. The benefit of allowing students time to build such long-term synaptic connections (which hold long-term memories) was demonstrated when subjects' memories of lists were tested at various intervals after they had formed long-term memories of these lists. It was found that relearning to repeat the contents of a list took less time and fewer trials than did the original learning (Kandel, 2006). Alternatively, when initial learning experiences are not repeated enough times to initiate protein synthesis (i.e., form a long-term synaptic connection), the process of forgetting can be observed by a rapid initial decline in the first hour after learning. This initial forgetting is followed by a very gradual decline over a period that lasts about a month.

In Chapter 3, this volume, Sadoski provides a description of one research-based, instructional method that fastmapped several comprehension strategies for K–5 readers (Block, Rodgers, & Johnson, 2004). We are in the process of researching other such neuroscientifically based classroom applications. In theory, most comprehension strategies can be fastmapped as long as the lessons meet the following essential qualities to fastmap synaptic connections and build long-term memory. The lesson must contain at least six of a teacher's expertly modeled demonstrations (think-alouds) of a strategy's use during the reading of an authentic text with students. Some struggling readers may need as many as 10 of these think-aloud, teacher-led experiences.

These modeling sessions describe each mental step taken to complete the comprehension process, why the steps are necessary, how students will know that the strategy is needed for full comprehension at specific points in a text, and how students will know they have used the strategy successfully. Students must be allowed to ask questions about how to perform all steps in the strategy after each demonstration. Teachers use these questions as an informal assessment to judge which students are ready to fastmap their own independent application of that strategy while they read authentic text orally or silently. For those determined to need more fastmapped demonstrations of the actual strategy itself, the teacher plans time to deliver them in a more interactive, small-group setting in which students have more time to express exactly what part of a strategy they cannot do and to participate in peer explanations of various steps.

Whenever students demonstrate the ability and desire to use the strategy by themselves, they can read alone, in pairs, or in small groups under teacher monitoring. At these sessions, students read (and record) each incident of a strategy use. Many varieties of recording formats can be used, including simply writing the page and paragraph number where students used a specific strategy as they read.

Regardless of the record-keeping format used, as soon as students judge themselves to have read long enough to have fastmapped a strategy's automatic application to text (at least six uses for most students), they meet with their teacher alone or in groups. Each student is required to describe the strategy and how he or she used it at a specific time in a text. Preferably, these explanations are given six times for every student, five of which occur on consecutive days when students apply the strategy to different and slightly more difficult text.

Make Reading an Emotional Experience

Neuroscientists have proven that an emotional response of fear occurs at the cellular level before it actually is manifest as a behavior (Campeau et al., 1991; Pasco & Kapp, 1985). Therefore, a student's dislike of reading can occur instantly and become permanent from the brain's chemical point of view. One mistake or a tiny fear that a student is going to make a mistake while reading activates his or her amygdala, the fear center of the brain. Either one is just as powerful, because both chemical changes lead to a biological neural connection that causes the student to perceive reading as a fearful experience. Therefore, comprehension instruction should reduce the mistakes students make: more comprehension instruction and more open-ended lessons must be created to reduce students' fear of making a mistake (Kandel, 2006). Examples of how to do so are described in detail by Malloy and Gambrell in Chapter 16, this volume.

Create an Emotionally Risk-Free Environment

In reference to Leo Tolstoy's novel about the tragic consequence of a socially unacceptable love affair, happy or good readers (Tolstoy referred to families) are all alike. However, every unhappy, or less able reader (or family) is disabled or unhappy in its own way. Neuroscientists have proven that this occurs during comprehension because of learned fear or learned safety. These data can transfer to future comprehension instruction, in that an "Aha" moment needs to occur in each new reading experience before students initiate a contemplation that reading will not cause fear and pain (Kandel, 2006).

DIRECTIONS FOR FUTURE RESEARCH

Based on the neuroscientific data to date, we pose three considerations for future research.

1. *Are there specific patterns of brain processes that can be developed into an organized, systematic set of principles that will translate into useful guidelines for reading comprehension instruction?* We are only beginning to discover the complex array of brain activities that take place during reading comprehension, and much of the research is still "scattered." Very few meta-analyses tailored to the field of reading comprehension have been performed to identify more reliable, universally applicable mental patterns and links that we can strengthen by brain-nurturing, fastmapped, emotionally pleasing, "aha"-filled, and pain-free instruction.

2. *Does brain activity change based on the type of text that a student is reading?* For example, with the growing emphasis on utilizing technology in teaching practices, would different areas of the brain become activated based on whether a student was reading from Web-based text or a book? How does the more interactive style of reading on the Web affect reading comprehension? If so, what are these neuroscientific processing differences, and how might they improve teaching in the future?

3. *How can we take neuroscientific findings and integrate them into new or current theoretical models to inform reading research and instruction?* Allan Paivio and Mark Sadoski have been leaders in this area by bringing neuroscientific findings into DCT (Paivio, 1986), which has been shown to be an effective model for explaining reading processes. More work needs to be done to tie neuroscientific data to other theories that guide the field of reading.

PROJECTIONS AND POSSIBILITIES FOR THE CLASSROOM OF 2030

The classrooms of 2030 will contain the children of children who are in classrooms today. Many of us often find ourselves comparing today's classrooms with those in which we were students. Yet it is likely there will be even more of a difference between the classrooms of today and those 25 years into the future. Just as the technological revolution has changed the landscape of our lives faster than at any previous time in history, technology and its contributions to the field of neuroscience have the potential to change classrooms at a faster pace than ever before. As the choices and possibilities for productive learning environments grow and expand, the rows of desks will give way to more dynamic, exploratory, and interactive learning activities in which technology replaces dictionaries and encyclopedias as the first "go to" places to gain new information. Reading comprehension will be seen as a dynamic, fluid process of brain-based events that vary depending on the context in which the reading is taking place. Thus, definitions of reading comprehension may need to be extended to account for the growing number of ways we will have learned to help children's brains learn to read.

SUMMARY

To date, the growing body of neuroscientific knowledge can tell us fairly precisely what parts of the brain are operating during specified mental tasks and how neurons interact during various types of mental tasks. In this chapter we have highlighted some aspects of this mushrooming database. We also suggested that we already know enough to improve comprehension in very specific ways to become more brain-friendly and compatible with individual, unique neuroprocessing styles of learning. We described four such applications that have been demonstrated to (1) eliminate inefficient thinking processes; (2) fastmap new strategy learning for long-term memory growth; (3) increase the positive emotional qualities inherent in comprehension experiences; and (4) create a more emotionally risk- and pain-free learning environment. We provided three areas for future research and a projection of the qualities that are likely to shape classrooms in 2030. It will be up to us to create and interpret these new neurologically based findings, to develop more effective learning tools, then to test both in learning environments specifically designed to bridge the gap between brain research and reading comprehension classroom instruction.

INTEGRATE, INVESTIGATE, AND INITIATE: QUESTIONS FOR DISCUSSION

1. This chapter discusses the neuroscientific influences that are transforming our understanding of how reading comprehension occurs. Reflect on the overall message in this chapter. In 50 words or less, summarize the main message this chapter communicates to educators as they begin to design classrooms for the future.

2. Design a teaching activity that implements the most important finding from this chapter, in your opinion, that can be used today to improve reading comprehension instruction. Explain how this activity was derived from the information in this chapter. Share these activities with others of like responsibility or another group of educators.

3. Based on what you've learned in this chapter, what changes will you make to your own teaching practices and why?

REFERENCES

Block, C. C., Rodgers, L. L., & Johnson, R. B. (2004). *Comprehension process instruction: Creating reading success in grades K–3*. New York: Guilford Press.

Block, C. C., Parris, S. R., & Whiteley, C. S. (2008). CPMs: Helping primary grade students self-initiate comprehension processes through kinesthetic instruction. *The Reading Teacher, 61*(6), 440–448.

Campeau, S., Hayward, M. D., Hope, B. T., Rosen, J. B., Nestler, E. J., & Davis, M. (1991). Induction of the *c-fos* proto-oncogene in rat amygdala during unconditioned and conditioned fear. *Brain Research, 565,* 349–352.

Caplan, D., & Waters, G. (1999). Online syntactic processing in aphasia: Studies with auditory moving window presentation. *Brain and Language, 69,* 330–333.

Carey, J. (2002). *Brain facts: A primer on the brain and nervous system.* Washington, DC: Society for Neuroscience.

Cartwright, K. B. (2002). Cognitive development and reading: The relation of reading-specific multiple classification skill to reading comprehension in elementary school children. *Journal of Educational Psychology, 94,* 1–7.

Cognitive Neuroscience Society. (n.d.). *What's in a name?* Retrieved December 2, 2006, from *www.cogneurosociety.org/content/cognitive%20neuroscience.*

Copland, D. A., Chenery, H. J., & Murdoch, B. E. (2001). Discourse priming of homophones in individuals with dominant nonthalamic subcortical lesions, cortical lesions and Parkinson's disease. *Journal of Clinical and Experimental Neuropsychology, 23,* 538–556.

Edelman, G. M. (2006). *Second nature: Brain science and human knowledge.* New Haven, CT: Yale University Press.

Ferstl, E. C., Guthke, T., & von Cramon, D. Y. (2001). Text comprehension after brain injury: Left prefrontal lesions affect inference processes. *Neuropsychology, 16*(3), 292–308.

Ferstl, E. C., & von Cramon, D. Y. (2001). The role of coherence and cohesion in text comprehension: An event-related fMRI study. *Cognitive Brain Research, 11,* 325–340.

Fiebach, C. J., Vos, S. H., & Friederici, A. D. (2004). Neural correlates of syntactic ambiguity in sentence comprehension for low and high span readers. *Journal of Cognitive Neuroscience, 16*(9), 1562–1575.

Fiez, J. A., & Peterson, S. E. (1998). Neuroimaging studies of word reading. *Proceedings of the National Academy of Science USA, 95,* 485–497.

Friederici, A. D. (2002). Towards a neural basis of auditory sentence processing. *Trends in Cognitive Sciences, 6,* 78–84.

Friederici, A. D., Steinhauer, K., Mecklinger, A., & Meyer, M. (1998). Working memory constraints on syntactic ambiguity resolution as revealed by electrical brain responses. *Biological Psychology, 47,* 193–221.

Fulbright, R. K., Jenner, A. R., Mencl, W. E., Pugh, K. R., Shaywitz, B. A., Shaywitz, S. E., et al. (1999). The cerebellum's role in reading: A functional MR imaging study. *American Journal of Neuroradiology, 20*(10), 1925–1930.

Henderson, V. W. (1986). Anatomy of posterior pathways in reading: A reassessment. *Brain and Language, 29,* 119–133.

Just, M. A., & Carpenter, P. A. (1992). A capacity theory of comprehension: Individual differences in working memory. *Psychological Review, 99,* 122–149.

Kaan, E., & Swaab, T. Y. (2002). The brain circuitry of syntactic comprehension. *Trends in Cognitive Sciences, 6,* 350–356.

Kaan, E., & Swaab, T. Y. (2003). Repair, revision, and complexity in syntactic analysis: An electrophysiological investigation. *Journal of Cognitive Neuroscience, 15,* 98–110.

Kandel, E. R. (2006). *In search of memory: The emergence of a new science of mind.* New York: Norton.

Kosslyn, S. M., & Shin, L. M. (1992). The status of cognitive neuroscience. *Current Opinion in Neurobiology, 2,* 146–149.

MacDonald, M. C., Just, M. A., & Carpenter, P. A. (1992). Working memory constraints on the processing of syntactic ambiguity. *Cognitive Psychology, 24,* 56–98.

Mitchell, D. C. (1994). Sentence parsing. In M. A. Gernsbacher (Ed.), *Handbook of psycholinguistics* (pp. 375–409). San Diego: Academic Press.

Moffett, S. (2006). *The three-pound enigma: The human brain and the quest to unlock its mysteries*. Chapel Hill, NC: Algonquin Books.

Molfese, D. L., Key, A. F., Kelly, S., Cunningham, N., Terrell, S., Fergusson, M., et al. (2006). Below-average, average, and above-average readers engage different and similar brain regions while reading. *Journal of Learning Disabilities, 39*, 352–363.

Ni, W., Constable, R., Mencl, W., Pugh, K. R., Fulbright, R. K., Shaywitz, S. E., et al. (2000). An event-related neuroimaging study distinguishing form and content in sentence processing. *Journal of Cognitive Neuroscience, 12*, 120–133.

Nobre, A. C., Allison, T., & McCarthy, G. (1994). Word recognition in the human inferior temporal lobe. *Nature, 372*, 260–263.

Noppeney, U., & Price, C. J. (2004). An fMRI study of syntactic adaptation. *Journal of Cognitive Neuroscience, 16*, 702–713.

Paivio, A. (1971). *Imagery and verbal processes*. New York: Holt, Rinehart.

Paivio, A. (1986). *Mental representations: A dual coding approach*. New York: Oxford University Press.

Paivio, A. (1991). Dual coding theory: Retrospect an current status. *Canadian Journal of Psychology, 45*, 255–287.

Pasco, J. P., & Kapp, B. S. (1985). Electrophysiological characteristics of amygdaloid central nucleus neurons during Pavlovian fear conditioning in the rabbit. *Behavioral Brain Research, 16*, 117–133.

Pearson, P. D. (1985). Changing the face of reading comprehension instruction. *Reading Teacher, 38*(8), 724–738.

Piaget, J. (1963). *The origins of intelligence in children*. New York: Norton.

Piaget, J., & Kamii, C. (1978). What is psychology? *American Psychologist, 33*(7), 648–652.

Puce, A., Allison, T., Asgari, M., Gore, J., & McCarthy, G. (1996). Differential sensitivity of human visual cortex to faces, letters strings, and textures: A functional magnetic resonance imaging study. *Cerebral Cortex, 6*, 600–611.

Pugh, K. R., Mencl, W. E., Jenner, A. R., Katz, L., Frost, S. J., Lee, J. R., et al. (2000). Neurobiological studies of reading and reading disability. *Journal of Communication Disorders, 34*(6), 479–492.

Pugh, K. R., Mencl, W. E., Jenner, A. R., Lee, J. R., Katz, L., Frost, S. J., et al. (2001). Neuroimaging studies of reading and reading disability. *Learning Disabilities Research and Practice, 16*(4), 240–250.

Sadoski, M., Paivio, A., & Goetz, E.T. (1991). A critique of schema theory in reading and a dual coding alternative. *Reading Research Quarterly, 26*, 463–484.

Shaywitz, B., Shaywitz, S., Pugh, K., Mencl, W., Fulbright, R., Skudlarski, P., et al. (2002). Disruption of posterior brain systems for reading in children with developmental dyslexia. *Biological Psychiatry, 54*(1), 101–110.

9

How Neuroscience Informs Our Teaching of Elementary Students

RENATE N. CAINE

> Neither anguish nor the elation that love or art can bring about are devalued by understanding some of the myriad biological processes that make them what they are. Precisely the opposite should be true: Our sense of wonder should increase before the intricate mechanisms that make such magic possible.
> —ANTONIO DAMASIO, *Descartes' Error*

Neuroscience research is literally rewriting our collective understanding of learning, including reading comprehension (Sousa, 2005; Wolfe & Nevills, 2004). Yet it would be a mistake for educators simply to integrate this research into a model of teaching that still largely emphasizes transmission and memorization. Helping students "learn" from the perspective of the brain leads to an entirely new vision of what it means to have understood text, one that is most readily described as constructivism. Here are some examples:

- Research on neural plasticity (Begley, 2007; Conlan, 1999; Diamond, 1988; Doige, 2007; Greenough, Black, & Wallace, 1987) shows that the brain is extraordinarily malleable and that many areas of the cortex are literally shaped by experience.
- Research on the vast degree of interconnectedness between different regions of the brain, and on the nature of neural networks, indicates that academic learning and comprehension are never separate from emotions, meaning, motivation, past experience, recognition, and memory (Fuster, 2003).
- Research on what are called "mirror neurons" (Iacoboni et al., 1999; Rizzolatti

& Craighero, 2004) demonstrates that children continuously and largely unconsciously learn from what is modeled by events and others around them.
- Research on emotions and the brain documents that some types of comprehension are inhibited by fear and helplessness (LeDoux, 1996; Wiedenfeld et al., 1990), and how the more positive emotions can affect and enhance certain types of learning (Panksepp, 1998; Peterson, Maier, & Seligman, 1996).

My colleague and I realized how critical this emergent research could be for educators. Yet we also recognized that this information had little chance of getting to teachers and administrators given the focus of their past professional development activities and the intensity of the day-to-day classroom responsibilities. My goal in this chapter is to begin the process of assisting literacy educators to rewrite the traditional view of reading comprehension instruction in elementary schools. Specifically, this chapter highlights the following:

- Basic learning principles that impact learning and comprehension.
- A process that helps teachers translate the principles into practice.
- Documentation of how the process was used in one K–5 school to move teachers to a more constructivist approach to teaching and simultaneously to raise test scores.

WHAT'S OUT THERE TODAY: ESTABLISHED RESEARCH AND PRACTICE

In 1990, Geoffrey Caine and I sought to integrate research from neuroscience, perceptual psychology, behaviorism, cognitive psychology, biology, and a large number of other fields. We did this to determine a set of brain/mind learning principles, which we most recently updated in 2005 (Caine, Caine, McClintic, & Klimek, 2005). The principles we delineated were based on a view of human beings as living systems. They had to meet four basic criteria:

1. *The phenomena described by a principle should be universal.* A brain/mind learning principle must therefore be true for all human beings, despite individual genetic variations, unique experiences, and developmental differences.

2. *Research documenting any one specific principle should be evidenced in, and its influence must span, more than one field or discipline.* Because a learning principle describes a systems property, one would expect it to withstand validation and confirmation by triangulation of research that crosses multiple fields and disciplines.

3. *A principle should anticipate future research.* It should be expected and anticipated that research will continue to emerge that refines and confirms each brain-based learning principle. For example, much of the brain research on the links between emotion and cognition was published after we first formulated our principles in 1990. That research was added in 2005; thus, a principle is a continuous work in progress, in the sense that new perspectives and ongoing research constantly shape and advance our understanding of each truth a principle addresses.

4. *The principle should provide implications for practice.* By their nature, principles are general, so they cannot be expected to tell educators precisely what to do. However, as a minimum, effective learning principles ought to provide the basis for an effective gen-

eral framework to guide decisions about teaching and help in the identification and selection of appropriate methods and strategies. Principles illuminate new sparks of *capacities for learning*, which can be translated into further enhancements of comprehension instructional practices.

NEW RESEARCH SINCE THE NATIONAL READING PANEL: BRAIN/MIND LEARNING PRINCIPLES

Based on our research, meta-analyses, and syntheses, we formulated a set of 12 brain/mind learning principles (Caine & Caine, 1990, 1994; Caine et al., 2005). They do not follow a sequential or hierarchical pattern. I present them here because they hold a primary value for learning in general, and for literacy educators in particular. Each principle explains a capacity that all students have for learning language and comprehending text.

Principle 1: *All learning engages the physiology.*

One reason so much traditional comprehension teaching involves students sitting in their assigned seats is the belief that the brain is somehow separate from the body, and that the body is not very involved in learning. The research on neural plasticity, as well as other research (Capra, 1996; Damasio, 1994; Diamond & Hobson, 1998; Thelen & Smith, 1994), tells us that the body and mind are totally interconnected. Cognitive scientists often refer to this in terms of embodied cognition (e.g., see Lakoff & Johnson, 1999). The brain is a parallel processor in which body, emotions, senses, memory, motivation, and action are deeply interconnected.

Capacity 1: *All students have the capacity to comprehend more effectively when involved in experiences that naturally call on the use of their senses and their bodies.*

Principle 2: *The brain/mind is social.*

Every individual on this planet comes complete with what Gopnik, Meltzoff, and Kuhl (1999) have called the "contact urge." Social relationships, with an emphasis on belonging, being recognized, listened to, and noticed, all contribute to an optimal state of mind we call "relaxed alertness" (Azar, 2002; Brothers, 1997; Sternberg & Grigorenko, 2001). Recent research on mirror neurons confirms that the social nature of human beings is grounded in biology. The social nature of learning is sometimes described in terms of situated learning (e.g., see Lave, Wenger, Pea, Brown, & Heath, 1991).

Capacity 2: *All students have the capacity to comprehend more effectively when their needs for social interactions and relationship are engaged and honored.*

Principle 3: *The search for meaning is innate.*

The need to make sense of things is characteristic of every human being from infancy to adulthood. It has been called the "explanatory drive" (Gopnik et al., 1999). One aspect of even young students' search for meaning is illustrated by the way that all people respond to novelty. For example, in reading a text on one of Christopher Columbus's voyages, imagine yourself as a rat on the ship. What is your point of view of the voyage? Another dimension of the mind's innate search for meaning has to do with the compelling power of purpose. For example, a girl about 9 years old recently described what she understood to be the causes and best treatment for breast cancer. She was extremely articulate. Her interest had been sparked by the fact that her mother had been diagnosed with the disease, prompting her to read as much as she could find on the subject.

Learning that is reducible to memorizing facts that are true or false is different from learning that engages actor-centered, adaptive decision making (Goldberg, 2001). This kind of decision making, the result of an authentic question generated by the learner, inevitably requires more complex thinking. It is the search for meaning that organizes actor-centered questions and encourages the use of higher order functions.

Capacity 3: *All students have the capacity to comprehend more effectively when their interests, purposes, and ideas are engaged and honored.*

Principle 4: *The search for meaning occurs through patterning.*

"Patterning" refers to the meaningful organization and categorization of information. A person makes sense of experience by the mind's drive to find and create patterns and relationships. The brain is designed to perceive and generate patterns, and it resists having meaningless patterns imposed on it by others. Cognitive scientists have developed a large number of terms to describe patterning, such as "categories," "frames," and "schemas." All decision making, before, during, and after one reads, is based on the patterns that a person perceives and the choices he or she makes about where to focus attention in a text. Education in reading comprehension should be about increasing patterns that students can use, recognize, and communicate to gain new knowledge and ideas.

Capacity 4: *All students have substantial unused capacities to perceive and create patterns, and to link those new patterns to what they already understand.*

Principle 5: *Emotions are critical to patterning.*

Emotions are central to human life. Neuroscience now shows (Damasio, 1999; Pert, 1997) that emotions are involved in every thought, decision, and response. Powerful learning is enhanced by rich emotional experiences, guided and moderated by higher-order functions. In fact, emotions and physical reactions are so much a part of understanding (and comprehending text) that psychologist Eugene Gendlin (1981) described the link with the term "felt meaning."

Capacity 5: *All students can comprehend more effectively when appropriate emotions are elicited before, during, and after their experiences with a text.*

Principle 6: *The brain/mind processes parts and wholes simultaneously.*

The brain/mind is designed to make sense of the world. Making sense of experience requires both perceiving a big picture and paying attention to the individual parts. The experience of the whole provides a story, a model, or a fascinating example of what can be achieved. Gestalt psychology (Sternberg, 2006) explicitly shows how the mind connects parts to make these wholes. And, some of the most recent brain research is exploring this relationship between parts and wholes in terms of neural networks—lattices of individual neurons that fire together as one reads (Fuster, 2003).

Capacity 6: *All students can comprehend more effectively when details (specific facts and information) are embedded in wholes that they understand, such as a real-life event, a meaningful story, or a project that they create or witness.*

Principle 7: *Learning involves both focused attention and peripheral perception.*

Every human being is continuously immersed in a field of stimuli and constantly attends to a selected part of that field. Attention is a natural phenomenon guided by interest, novelty, emotion, and meaning, and paying attention is critical. What is less understood is the fact that human beings also learn from the background—the context to which people do not consciously attend. This is illustrated by research on implicit memory (Schacter, 1996) and on mirror neurons (Rizzolatti & Craighero, 2004), which shows how children "pick up" behaviors, beliefs, intentions, and preferences or dislikes while engaging in life experience. Implicit memories include unconscious memories that influence one's thinking and behavior without conscious awareness. Mirror neurons enable this kind of unconscious learning that is activated by the actions or modeling of an individual who is significant in the learner's eyes.

Capacity 7: *All students can comprehend more effectively when their attention is deepened and multiple layers of the context are used to support learning.*

Principle 8: *Learning is both conscious and unconscious.*

Learning involves layers of consciousness. Some learning requires that a person attend consciously to a problem that needs to be solved or analyzed. Some learning at a deeper level requires unconscious incubation in the same way that the creative insights of artists and scientists sometimes occur after the mind has done some conscious processing. Beyond that, really successful comprehenders are also capable of monitoring themselves by means of the executive functions of their brains (Denkla, 1999), a central feature of higher-order functions, so that they know their own strengths and weaknesses and can take charge of how they process text.

Capacity 8: *All students can comprehend more effectively when given time to reflect on and to process those experiences they live and about which they read.*

Principle 9: *There are at least two approaches to memory.*

Researchers have identified many different memory systems. These tend to be organized into two primary categories—declarative and procedural memories. However, of more value to the literacy educator's viewpoint is the separation of memories in a slightly different way. One type of memory is designed to store or archive isolated facts, skills, and procedures that individuals read or are taught as strategies to comprehend a text. The other type of memory is very dynamic, in that it engages multiple mental systems to make sense of the reading experience itself, as well as the experiences about which one reads. The key distinction that educators need to make and understand is between rote memorization, which is the hallmark of traditional approaches to comprehension teaching, and the dynamic memory is engaged in everyday experience. Sometimes facts and comprehension procedures or steps in strategies do need to be memorized, but rote learning is different from dynamic memory. Dynamic memory is likely to be engaged naturally as learners sift through the ideas that they recognize to make sense in new contexts.

Capacity 9: *All students can comprehend more effectively when immersed in experiences that engage multiple ways to remember.*

Principle 10: *Learning is developmental.*

All human beings develop in several somewhat predictable ways, though rarely in precisely the same way or at exactly the same rate. There are stages in brain development (Bransford, Brown, & Cocking, 2000; Sylwester, 2007) for instance, and in the formation of identity, that impact reading comprehension. In addition, all new learning builds on previous learning. We now know that this additive/cumulative process is accompanied by changes in the physiology (Huttenlocher, 2002) of the brain. This mental alteration is in turn altered by new experiences with text, and the cycle continues throughout life. Unfortunately, the traditional age/grade organization of students does not adequately deal with the realities of their mental development. Performance, not age or grade level, provides a much better foundation for teaching reading.

Capacity 10: *All students can comprehend more effectively if individual differences in maturation, development, and prior learning are taken into consideration.*

Principle 11: *Complex learning is enhanced by challenge and inhibited by threat associated with helplessness and/or fatigue.*

A great deal of research from disciplines such as neuroscience (e.g., LeDoux, 1996), creativity theory (Deci & Ryan, 1987), stress theory (Lazarus, 1999; Sapolsky, 1998), and perceptual psychology, (Combs, 1999) shows that effective mental functioning can be sabotaged by fears associated with helplessness. Thus, both inferential and applied reading comprehension can be sabotaged. One consequence of such hightened negative emotions is that higher-order executive functioning has been hijacked. That is why the optimal state of mind for reading comprehension is relaxed alertness, a combination of low threat and high challenge.

Capacity 11: *All students can comprehend more effectively in a supportive, empowering, and challenging environment.*

Principle 12: *Each brain is uniquely organized.*

The paradox facing education is that human beings are both similar and different. For example, every human being is an expression of DNA. Yet every individual has a unique genetic blueprint. Everyone has a lifetime of experience, yet some experiences of every person are unique. All of this complexity is compounded by a wide variety of social, ethnic, gender, and economic differences.

Capacity 12: *All students can comprehend more effectively when their unique individual talents, abilities, and capacities are engaged.*

When used and understood, these brain/mind learning principles challenge traditional views of learning and teaching. Neuroscience has proven that although direct instruction is important, constructivism is fundamental. In effect, neuroscientists have shown that even young elementary-age learners really do make sense of their own reading experience and construct meanings by themselves and in association with others (Wolfe & Nevills, 2004).

HOW NEUROSCIENTIFIC PRINCIPLES CAN BE INTRODUCED INTO ELEMENTARY SCHOOL COMPREHENSION INSTRUCTION

When the No Child Left Behind law became a reality in 2001, we were provided an opportunity to test the 12 brain/mind learning principles in an elementary school. The law emphasized results on standardized tests as the primary indicator of reading ability. Many teachers and schools felt the pressure to demonstrate almost instant results.

Two administrators at a low-performing K–5 school approached my coauthor and me because they were concerned that, in an effort to implement district standards, teachers at their school were sacrificing the more complex, constructivist teaching advocated by the *California Standards for the Teaching Profession* (California Commission on Teacher Credentialing, 1997). Teachers were opting for direct instruction, focusing extensively on memorization of isolated, decontextualized facts and skills through rote practice and rehearsal, or "teaching to the test." The administrators felt that our work with schools and the principles, cited in this chapter, could help teachers maintain a constructivist focus even as they attempted to raise reading comprehension test scores.

The School

Redwood School in Fontana, California, was a low socioeconomic status (SES), low performing K–5 elementary school with over 1,000 students (89% Hispanic students). The school operated on a multitrack, year-round calendar. The school was located in an industrial environment, with a fertilizer factory next door.

As with other schools in California, it was also ranked by the Academic Performance Index (API). The API ranks schools in two ways: statewide and similar schools rankings. The California Department of Education (CDE) takes the SAT9 (Stanford Achievement Test) results for all public schools in California and ranks them from highest to lowest. Then schools are grouped into a 10-decile performance ranking, with 10 being the highest and 1 the lowest rank. In the past two ranking years, Redwood was in the bottom decile, with a rank of 1. The second measure takes the demographics of each school into consideration and finds similarities between sites in the domains of SES, ethnicity, and parent level of education, to name a few. The CDE then reranks the schools by comparing the SAT9 results of schools with similar demographics. This ranking is also in deciles, with 10 being the highest and 1 the lowest rank. In 2000/2001, Redwood was reranked with 1.

Overview of Our Approach

Geoffrey Caine and I developed a small-group approach to professional development, working with what we call "process learning circles" (Caine, Caine, & Crowell, 1999; Caine et al., 2005). I set out to use these circles as the basic method for building a learning community among teachers and some of the administrators.

Within the context of that community, I introduced one principle and capacity each month as the focal point for professional development. Participants were exposed to the theory, developed practical implications and strategies to try out in their classrooms, and returned to their process learning circles to share feedback (documentation) and their reflections. It was not possible to cover the entire set of 12 principles in 1 year, though it remains our ideal. We dealt with the first seven principles and their corresponding capacities.

The Group Process

At our first meeting, teachers were placed in process learning circles. Each group comprised 6–7 participants across grade levels (at group members' request, groups were later changed to reflect grade levels). I also explained and modeled the group process, which has four distinct phases:

1. *Ordered sharing*: The purpose is to help participants learn to listen deeply and speak their own truth, and to *optimize the social–emotional conditions for their own learning*. They do this by speaking on an issue one at a time, without interruption, around the circle, until everyone is finished.
2. *Reflective study*: The purpose of the "reflective study" phase is to help the participants make sense of new material (in this case, a new brain/mind learning principle). Participants are provided with relevant research and have time to relate to, and dissect, the new material to clearly identify essential elements and connect to their own understanding and experience as learners.
3. *Implications for practice*: In this phase, participants explore how to translate their new understanding of a principle and capacity into practice. They are given examples and models of things to do, but are encouraged to develop their own.
4. *Regrouping*: Participants come briefly to review the meeting and recall what they thought, felt, and remembered, and to clarify what they intend to do to implement the principle.

Additional Procedures

After the first extensive introductory meeting, I set up a series of monthly meetings. Tuesdays had been designated minimum school days, and students were dismissed around noontime, leaving the teachers the rest of the day to meet in teams and plan together. I met on the first Tuesday each month with all teachers and staff members who had volunteered to participate. We followed the procedure described above.

Although there were incentives for teachers to attend the workshops and to participate in the program, ultimately participation was voluntary. Because the school was year-round, almost all teachers missed the introduction to at least one principle. Several teachers, however, chose to attend these workshops while they were officially off campus.

They had two process learning circles meetings per month—the first and third weeks. During the second and fourth Tuesdays they had meetings on school business, but nevertheless connected informally to discuss their teaching.

On a Tuesday other than the first one in each month, I again visited the school. I was available for classroom observations in the morning. Discussions and feedback were handled on a sign-up basis in the afternoon.

Documenting the Impact of the Process

I had made four basic predictions that I wanted to test.

Prediction 1: *There would be a clear movement to learner-centered teaching—a critical implication inherent in the principles and an aspect of constructivism.* Constructivist teaching tends to be more complex than direct instruction, in the sense that it is more directly student centered. While allowing for direct instruction and a standards-based curriculum, it deviates greatly from more prescriptive teaching.

We had developed an instrument called the Teacher/Student Responsibility Questionnaire. The T/S R Questionnaire was administered three times during the year. The questionaire comprised a piece of paper with a line down the middle. On the left side, teachers listed what they had to do to ensure a good teaching day. On the right side, teachers listed what students had to do to ensure a good learning day. Over the period of a year, there was a clear indication of teacher changes in philosophies and actions when the data in these questionnaries were compared.

All answers on the first set indicated that teachers' teaching relied on their own decision making, and student compliant behavior was indicative of teaching for transmission. On the pretest questionnaire, teachers initially described their responsibilities as follows:

- Planning
- Making copies
- Having a clean room
- Making lessons fun, entertaining, and easy to learn
- Rewarding students appropriately
- Disciplining appropriately
- Communicating with parents

On this same pretest, student responsibilities were basically viewed as "doing whatever would let the teachers do their job." We particularly looked at how passively or actively students were being engaged. According to pretest questionnaire teacher responses, what students had to do to ensure a good learning day included the following:

- Come to school ready to learn
- Get plenty of sleep the night before
- Come to school with a positive attitude
- Behave appropriately
- Dress comfortably for class
- Respect all rules and classmates
- Make an effort
- Smile at the teacher
- Try

Almost all pretest teacher responses lacked reference to actual strategies, active learning, or engagement in learning on the part of the students. Students were seen as passive learners. References to teaching concepts or teaching for depth also were not evident.

Although little change was evident when the questionnaire was given in the middle of the year, at the end of 12 months, the third time the questionnaire was given, major shifts in teachers' beliefs and actions became evident. Here are some examples of how teachers saw students' responsibilities in the learning process:

- Raise questions
- Get involved
- Work effectively in a group
- Listen actively, participate, and question
- Call on prior knowledge
- Collect data from peers
- Be willing to take risks
- Be an independent worker

Many teachers' beliefs about their own responsibilities also changed after 12 months of professional development. The third time the instrument was given, responses ranged from little change to responses that described what *should happen*, to actual examples that documented application of the principles:

"I have students socially engaged as part of every subject."

"I allow students to teach each other and answer questions without my feeling a constant need to press on."

"I try to have lessons that fit the standards but also fit the kids."

"I provide a climate for social collaboration on [specific] topics."

"I try to spark interest by using motivational activities."

Prediction 2: *There would be a steady change in teacher professional dialogue centered around the principles.* This prediction held true. One overriding comment made by teachers 2 months into the study referred to the shift in conversations that teachers had with each other. Frequently comments such as the following were made: "I truly feel like a professional because we find ourselves talking about learning and what we are doing with students." Such statements were accompanied by others that reflected a change in the nature of how teachers listened to and worked with each other. Here are two typical examples: "My colleagues and I have begun listening to each other more quietly and carefully in meetings (I'm still working on it)" and "My colleagues have begun to team-teach."

Prediction 3: *There would be documentable evidence that teaching would begin to incorporate the principles and the capacities.* Our prediction was that as the additional capacities for learning became obvious to teachers, they would more easily see opportunities for teaching in different ways. I developed two instruments that allowed teachers to record changes in teaching. The first was the Brain/Mind Constructivism Checklist.

This instrument was administered before embarking on the next principle to identify changes in teachers' practices that directly incorporated the previous principle. This questionnaire comprised items such as the following:

Given Principle 2, "The brain/mind is social," please check the following:
- I have changed the way I interact or communicate with my students.
- I have observed that others interact differently with their students.
- Please give specific examples.

Here are some of those examples:

> "The third-grade 'POD' (students are divided among staff into groups of 6–10 to study something students care about) is now collaborating weekly about students rotating activities every Friday."
>
> "I have seen more students working together as partners and in groups."
>
> "I have students working on various issues together, looking for means of validating each other's experiences, and relying on each other for support."
>
> "I use lots of counseling style prompts, like 'Can you explain this to me?'; 'Show me?'; 'Where would you use this?' "

The second instruction that allowed teachers to record changes in teaching was the Teacher Research Questionnaire. This questionnaire had three open-ended inquiries and was administered 1 month after each principle had been introduced. It was administered six times. Participants were invited to write their answers and observations anonymously:

> 1. What evidence do you see that you and your fellow teachers are beginning to understand the brain/mind learning principles? Give specific examples if at all possible.
> 2. What evidence do you see that teacher(s) understand Principle _____ (different every month)?
> 3. How are teachers putting the principle(s) into action in their teaching?

The responses included the following:

> "We searched the campus for evidence of animals living or having lived on campus. We found birds nests, wasps nests, and gopher holes." [This statement came from a teacher on a campus with little vegetation, surrounded mostly by cement.]
>
> "I use more 'into' activities and work harder to tap into [students'] prior knowledge."
>
> "[Understanding] that learning is innate seems to have given some teachers permission to elaborate—to allow their students to think outside of the box."

Prediction 4: *At the end of the school year, test scores on the SAT9 would improve significantly.* We were delighted with the improvement of student scores on standardized tests. The original goals for the school included a growth target gain of 16 points on the SAT9 for the 2001/2002 school year, as measured by the API (state standards). The school's actual growth amounted to 48 points—far exceeding its target. In addition, Hispanic students, who made up 89% of students (and whose target growth base had been set at 13 points) ended up with actual growth of 54 points. Moreover, students identified as coming from low SES and disadvantaged environments also exceeded their target. Their target had been set at 13 points and their actual growth was 47 points.

Also, Redwood School moved out of the bottom decile in the similar schools ranking and since then has continued to maintain the original rise in achievement every year for 5 years. There were additional, indirect indicators that teachers, the school, and students were functioning more effectively, including reductions in faculty and student absenteeism, in faculty and student attrition, and in disciplinary referrals.

Perspective

Since our work together at Redwood School, my coauthor and I have continued to use the process learning circles in helping teachers work with the principles. Here are two quotes from our most recent summer workshop:

> "My overall response is that I feel as though I have grown in wisdom as a human being. My thought process was challenged beyond what I had originally known to be my capacity. As participants we joined together, bringing totally different backgrounds and experiences, but were able to bond and work together to digest and process the same information."

> "As an educator, I can see how learning and the work of schools have to be reworked and reconfigured to align with how the brain does its work. As I train teachers and supervise their development, I will need to show them how vital their role is and how enriched their own practice can become when they shift their paradigm and look at how [this approach] can inform their development as catalysts in their school and as people."

We are convinced that the principles and the process learning circles combine to shift the teacher's view of the learner as someone whose primary role is to follow instructions, to someone who needs to be deeply engaged in the learning and writing process as a creative individual, seeking to express his or her own meaningful ideas and connections. This can be done while students are held to high standards and are expected to do well on tests.

SUGGESTIONS FOR FUTURE RESEARCH

- Identify more clearly which parts of the group process are critical to change and why.
- Document more thoroughly changes in teacher beliefs about learning and how these are related to shifts in practice.
- Document long-term change over 4–5 years.
- Use performance standards in addition to standardized testing as student outcome measure.

PROJECTIONS AND POSSIBILITIES FOR THE CLASSROOM OF 2030

We predict that the alignment between schools and what is understood about the brain's natural, biological approach to learning will force education to face great challenges. I suggest that the educational community must come to understand and address what neuroscience is revealing—that children are whole individuals whose emotions, motivation, past learning, and beliefs about themselves as learners all interact with the curriculum and develop their comprehension.

In practical terms we can expect to see the following:

1. Educators will ensure that learners are constantly immersed in experience in which the content standards are embedded, and in which students have the following opportunities:

- *Physically interact* with what is to be learned or understood.
- *Make associations* with what they already know.
- *Ask their own questions.*
- *Adapt to real-world situations* through what neuroscientist Goldberg (2001) calls actor-centered adaptive decision making.
- *Research* and find what experts know about their questions.
- *Receive guidance, instruction, and feedback* tied to real-world standards.
- *Demonstrate real-world knowledge and competence* in both formal and spontaneous ways.

2. Educators will strive to create a social–emotional climate of relaxed alertness. This consists of low threat on the one hand, and high challenge and high expectations on the other. Healthy relationships based on respectful and coherent procedures will be considered to be essential.

3. There will be extensive and active processing of student experiences. This will range from the deliberative practice and rehearsal, in which all experts engage, to responding to respectful but challenging questions. Active processing will provide feedback for both teachers and students at the same time that it expands and deepens student thinking. This provides both formative and summative assessment.

Over the last 100 years the educational system has segmented and divided learning into distinct disciplines that are studied in equally fragmented environments, largely limited to "classrooms." The change to a more integrated environment and curriculum will not be easy, but both technology and neuroscience are providing evidence that will require educators to do so.

SUMMARY

My purpose in this chapter was to describe how 12 brain/mind learning principles can inform the teaching of reading comprehension at the elementary school level. If standards are to be raised, and if success is to be sustained, then the professional development of teachers is paramount in this age of critical research. Educators need to access *their own* additional capacities, because the brain/mind learning principles in this chapter apply to *all* learners, including the teachers themselves. In the last few years, Redwood School has continued to thrive and to raise its API, despite the fact that the school has had a new principal almost every year. Grade-level teams are powerful, and the current principal assures me that the entire learning environment has been transformed by the school's continued implementation and "living by" the principles described in this chapter.

INTEGRATE, INVESTIGATE, AND INITIATE: QUESTIONS FOR DISCUSSION

1. This chapter proposed that the educational community "must come to understand and address what neuroscience is revealing—that children are whole individuals whose emotions, motiva-

tion, past learning, and beliefs about themselves as learners all interact with the curriculum and develop their comprehension" (p. 138). List four principles you learned in this chapter that can assist you to integrate the theory of neuroscience into your comprehension instruction.

2. Select one of the 12 learning principles that you have witnessed occurring in your school building or school district. Select another principle that you want to take a step to begin to implement more completely. Describe the action you would like to take and share that action with others who might support you or describe similar actions that they would take.

3. Based on what you learned in this chapter and your own experiences, what changes would you like to see made in current curricula in schools, and why do you judge these changes to be necessary?

REFERENCES

Azar, B. (2002, January). At the frontier of science: Social cognitive neuroscience merges three distinct disciplines in hopes of deciphering the process behind social behavior. *APA Monitor, 33*(1), 40–43.

Begley, S. (2007). *Train your mind, change your brain.* New York: Ballantine Books.

Bransford, J., Brown, A. L., & Cocking, R. R. (Eds.). (2000). *How people learn: Brain, mind, experience, and school: Expanded edition* (Paperback). Washington, DC: National Academy Press.

Brothers, L. (1997). *Friday's footprint: How society shapes the human mind.* New York: Oxford University Press.

Caine, G., Caine, R., & Crowell, S. (1999). *Mindshifts* (2nd. ed.). Chicago: Zephyr Pres.

Caine, R., Caine, G., McClintic, C., & Klimek, K. (2005). *12 brain/mind learning principles in action: The field book for making connections, teaching, and the human brain.* Thousand Oaks, CA: Corwin Press.

Caine, R. N., & Caine, G. (1990). Understanding a brain-based approach to learning and teaching. *Educational Leadership, 48*(2), 66–70.

Caine, R. N., & Caine, G. (1994). *Making connections: Teaching and the human brain.* Menlo Park, CA: Addison-Wesley.

Caine, R. N., & Caine, G. (1997). *Unleashing the power of perceptual change: The potential of brain-based teaching.* Alexandria, VA: Association for Supervision and Curriculum Development.

California Commission on Teacher Credentialing. (1997, July). *California standards for the teaching profession.* Sacramento: California Department of Education.

Capra, F. (1996). *The web of life: A new understanding of living systems.* New York: Doubleday.

Combs, A. W. (1999). *Being and becoming.* New York: Springer.

Conlan, R. (Ed.). (1999). *States of mind: New discoveries about how our brains make us who we are.* New York: Wiley.

Damasio, A. R. (1994). *Descartes' error: Emotion, reason, and the human brain.* New York: Avon.

Damasio, A. R. (1999). *The feeling of what happens: Body and emotion in the making of consciousness.* New York: Harcourt Brace.

Damasio, A. R. (2005). The neurobiological grounding of human values. In J. P. Changeux, A. R. Damasio, W. Singer, & Y. Christen (Eds.), *Neurobiology of human values* (pp. 47–56). Heidelberg: Springer.

Deci, E. L., & Ryan, R. M. (1987). The support of autonomy and the control of behavior. *Journal of Personality and Social Psychology, 53*(6), 1024–1037.

Denckla, M. B. (1999). A theory and model of executive function: A neuropsychological perspective. In G. Lyon & N. Krasnegor (Eds.), *Attention, memory, and executive function* (pp. 263–298). Baltimore: Brookes.

Diamond, M. C. (1988). *Enriching heredity: The impact of the environment on the anatomy of the brain*. New York: Free Press.
Diamond, M. C., & Hobson, J. (1998). *Magic trees of the mind*. New York: Penguin/Putnam.
Fuster, J. M. (2003). *Cortex and mind: Unifying cognition*. New York: Oxford University Press.
Doige, N. (2007). *The brain that changes itself*. New York: Penguin.
Gendlin, E. T. (1981). *Focusing* (2nd ed.). New York: Bantam.
Goldberg, E. (2001). *The executive brain: Frontal lobes and the civilized mind*. New York: Oxford University Press.
Gopnik, A., Meltzoff, A. N., & Kuhl, P. (1999). *The scientist in the crib: Minds, brains, and how children learn*. New York: Morrow.
Greenough, W. T., Black, J. E., & Wallace, C. S. (1987). Experience and brain development. *Child Development, 58*, 539–559.
Hurley, S., & Charter, N. (Eds.). (2005). *Perspectives on imitation: From neuroscience to social science* (Vols. 1 and 2). Cambridge, MA: MIT Press.
Huttenlocher, P. R. (2002). *Neural plasticity: The effects of environment on the development of the cerebral cortex* (Perspectives in cognitive neuroscience series). Cambridge, MA: Harvard University Press.
Iacoboni, M., Woods, R., Brass, M., Bekkering, H., Mazziotta, J. C., & Rizzolati, G. (1999). Cortical mechanisms of human imitation. *Science, 286*, 2526–2528.
Lakoff, G., & Johnson, M. (1999). *Philosophy in the flesh: The embodied mind and its challenge to western thought*. New York: Basic Books.
Lave, J., Wenger, E., Pea, R., Brown, J. S., & Heath, C. (1991). *Situated learning: Legitimate peripheral participation*. London: Cambridge University Press.
Lazarus, R. S. (1999). *Stress and emotion: A new synthesis*. New York: Springer.
LeDoux, J. E. (1996). *The emotional brain*. New York: Simon & Schuster.
Panksepp, J. (1998). *Affective neuroscience*. New York: Oxford University Press.
Pert, C. (1997). *Molecules of emotion*. New York: Scribner.
Peterson, C., Maier, S., & Seligman, M. (1996). *Learned helplessness*. New York: Oxford University Press.
Rizzolatti, G., & Craighero, L. (2004). The mirror-neuron system. *Annual Review in the Neurosciences, 27*, 169–192.
Sapolsky, R. (1998). *Why zebras don't get ulcers: An updated guide to stress, stress-related diseases, and coping*. New York: Freeman.
Schacter, D. (1996). *Searching for memory: The brain, the mind, and the past*. New York: Basic Books.
Sousa, D. (2005) *How the brain learns to read*. Thousand Oaks, CA: Corwin Press.
Sternberg, R. (2006). *Cognitive psychology* (4th ed.). Belmont, CA: Wadsworth.
Sternberg, R. & Grigorenko, E. (2001). *Environmental effects on cognitive abilities*. London: Erlbaum.
Sylwester, R. (2007). *The adolescent brain: Reaching for autonomy*. Thousand Oaks, CA: Corwin Press.
Thelen, E., & Smith, L. (1994). *A dynamic systems approach to the development of cognition and action*. Cambridge, MA: MIT Press.
Wiedenfeld, S. A., O'Leary, A., Bandura, A., Brown, S., Levine, S., & Roska, K. (1990). Impact of perceived self-efficacy in coping with stress on components of the immune system. *Journal of Personality and Social Psychology, 59*(5), 1082–1094.
Wolfe, P., & Nevills, P. (2004). *Building the reading brain*. Thousand Oaks, CA: Corwin Press.

10

How Neuroscience Informs Our Teaching of Adolescent Students

SHERI R. PARRIS

> Sometimes we give up on kids early and feel that they are already doomed for certain fates, but from the biological perspective there are still lots and lots of opportunities for change during the teen years.
> —JAY GEIDD, MD, Chief of the Brain Imaging Unit—Child Psychiatry Branch, U.S. National Institute of Mental Health

One of the most common questions asked by secondary teachers is, "How can I meet the literacy needs of students who possess widely varied reading levels, linguistics differences, cultures, and backgrounds?" (Zwiers, 2004). Research has established that students profit from different types of instruction at various stages in their literacy development (Anders, Hoffman, & Duffy, 2000; Block, Oakar, & Hurt, 2002; Snow, Burns, & Griffin, 1998); therefore, it is reasonable to assume that the distinct developmental brain stages that occur during childhood and adolescence are one factor in this phenomena. Identifying the neurological traits that explain these specific adolescent peculiarities holds the potential to help numerous educators learn how to make the most of their instructional time.

Although, by adolescence, the brain has basically reached its adult size (e.g., Blakemore & Choudhury, 2006; Casey, Geidd, & Thomas, 2000; Dahl, 2004) significant changes still occur until about age 25. Yet brain-based research, through increasingly sophisticated neuroimaging technology, is continually expanding our knowledge about the inner workings of the adolescent brain. This constant influx of new information helps us design instructional programs that most effectively meet the needs of secondary students. This chapter addresses some specific challenges that are faced by secondary educators and how neuroscience may help resolve some of these issues in the future.

This chapter highlights the following:

- Established brain research pertaining to adolescents.
- Reading comprehension and its relationship to adolescent thinking processes.
- Ways to improve adolescent reading comprehension and to promote brain development.
- Directions for future brain-based research concerning comprehension.
- Projections for future adolescent comprehension instruction.

WHAT'S OUT THERE TODAY: ESTABLISHED RESEARCH AND PRACTICE

Many other chapters in this book provide information about how to optimize learning through our ever-expanding knowledge of the brain. Whereas most of these instructional directives are applicable to both elementary and secondary students, in this chapter I highlight factors that make the teenage brain unique with regard to learning processes involved in reading comprehension. This section provides a brief overview of some of the major aspects of adolescent brain development. Figure 10.1 is provided as a reference to demonstrate the approximate location of the brain areas discussed in this chapter.

Myelinization and Pruning

Neuroimaging studies show that a sudden proliferation of gray matter (nerve cell bodies and unmyelinated nerve fibers) occurs in the frontal lobe at the onset of puberty (approximately age 11 for girls; age 12 for boys; Geidd et al., 1999). These billions of new nerve fibers, created as part of a developmental growth spurt in the brain, are followed by a longer period, lasting throughout adolescence (usually ending in the early 20s), in which the brain slowly reorganizes itself through pruning and myelinization (Changeux & Dehaene, 1989; Geidd et al., 1999; Huttenlocher, 1979, 1990; Huttenlocher, deCourten, Garey, & van der Loos, 1982; Sowell, Thompson, Holmes, Jernigan, & Toga, 1999); that is, these new nerve fibers are either retained and specialized to perform specific tasks

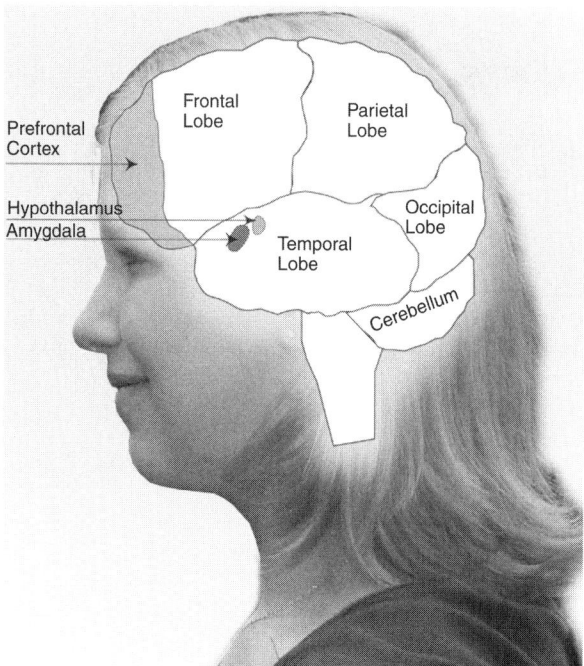

FIGURE 10.1.

(resulting in myelinization), or they are deemed unnecessary and discarded by the brain (pruned).

Myelinization is the process whereby layers of insulating fat are wrapped around the axons of neurons (axons are the wire-like extensions that connect neurons). Myelinated nerve cell fibers are often referred to as "white matter," because of the layer of fat that gives these fibers a white appearance (as opposed to unmyelinated fibers, which have a gray appearance). This insulation acts much like the insulation around an electrical wire, helping the electrical messages that are sent between neurons move faster and more efficiently (e.g., Barkovich, Kjos, Jackson, & Norman, 1988; McArdle et al., 1987). Neurons that are not used by the brain during this period do not get myelinated and are purged or "pruned." The Nobel Prize–winning neuroscientist Gerald Edelman describes this myelinization and pruning process as "neural Darwinism"—survival of the fittest (or most used) synapses (Wallis & Park, 2004). In essence, this means that adolescence is the period in which the brain forms specializations for certain cognitive processes by eliminating unused connections and strengthening those that are used most often (Geidd, 2004; Goldman-Rakic, 1987).

Thus, Geidd et al. (1999) postulated that the teenage years are a critical stage of development, because the depth of mental challenges and cognitive activities during this time influence the neural selection process and will likely have long-term cognitive effects. On the one hand, teenagers who exercise the higher-level thinking processes involved in reading comprehension literally "install the wiring" in their brains that enables them to become more and more adept readers, and this wiring lasts their lifetime. On the other hand, wiring needed for reading comprehension processes is stripped from teenagers whose brains do not partake in this activity. And once stripped of this particular type of wiring, it is difficult, if not impossible, to regain what has been lost after the pruning process stops in the early 20s.

Development of Higher Cognitive Processes

Whereas the adolescent developmental process of pruning affects higher cognitive processes and sensory systems development (Bruer, 1997; Iran-Nejad, 1998; Iran-Nejad & Gregg, 2001), it does not affect all cognitive processes. Neville (1995) determined that there is no critical period for the acquisition of new vocabulary or for memorization processes, which continue throughout a lifetime. In summary, although information acquisition and storage processes are not bound to a developmental timetable, higher-level thinking processes, such as those necessary for reading comprehension, go through a crucial stage of development during the teenage years. Figure 10.2 shows how myelinization changes the brain over time.

This myelinization and pruning process has important and lifelong implications for secondary students who are not encouraged to progress along the literacy continuum throughout their secondary school years. The Matthew effect (i.e., the rich get richer, and the poor get poorer; Stanovich, 1986) is certainly a viable concept when viewed from the lens of adolescent literacy achievement! This leads to important implications with respect to traditional thinking about secondary students and reading. In general, schools typically drop direct reading instruction from the curriculum just before the onset of adolescence, a time when the brain is choosing which neural connections will stay and become more efficient, and which will be pruned. This practice, although well established in most educational systems worldwide, may be counterproductive to the achievement of literacy success for all.

Three of the main areas of the brain that influence adolescent cognition and behavior during this maturation process are (1) prefrontal cortex, (2) amygdala, and (3) hypo-

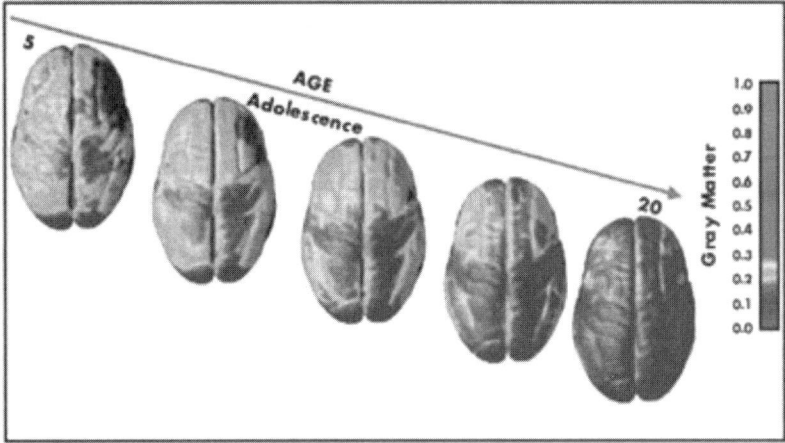

FIGURE 10.2. Time-lapse sequence showing the dramatic myelinization process as it occurs in the brain between the ages of 5 and 20 (with most changes occurring during the teenage years), ending with the majority of myelinization completed by age 20. From Gogtay et al. (2004). Copyright 2004 by the National Academy of Sciences, U.S.A. Reprinted by permission.

thalamus. A description of these areas and their implications for adolescent reading comprehension growth are discussed next.

Prefrontal Cortex

The prefrontal cortex (PFC) occupies the anterior portion of the frontal lobe and contains the neural connections between the reasoning and emotion centers of the brain. As stated earlier, myelinization and pruning in the frontal lobe are not largely complete until about age 20; thus, the PFC undergoes its most significant development during adolescence.

Interestingly, the fully developed frontal lobe (including the PFC) is the main differentiator that separates the thinking abilities of the human brain from the brains of all other animal species; the fact that the PFC is still underdeveloped during adolescence warrants our consideration. Duties of the PFC include executive functions such as planning, judgment, attention, working memory (holding a thought or object briefly in the forefront of our minds while we proceed with another thought), thought organization, impulse control (self-control), new or complex goal-directed action, higher-level and complex thinking, empathy, the ability to understand the motivations of others, and emotional regulation. This neuroscientific evidence is consistent with typical adolescent behavior in that, compared to adults, teenagers engage in more risk-taking, sensation-seeking, and novelty-seeking behavior. When fully developed, the PFC helps us to evaluate a situation carefully, weigh the options logically, and determine which action (or behavior) is most reasonable.

To demonstrate how the thinking processes of the PFC overlap with those required for reading comprehension, I have included a general description of the reading comprehension process:

> Comprehension is both a product and a process, something that requires purposeful, strategic effort on the reader's part—anticipating the direction of the text (predicting), seeing the action of the text (visualizing), contemplating and then correcting whatever confusions we encounter (clarifying), connecting what's in the text to what's in our mind to make an educated guess about what's going on (inferencing). (Beers, 2003, pp. 45–46)

Amygdala

Also known as the emotional center of the brain, the amygdala causes reactionary behavioral responses based on emotions (fear, anger, etc.). Such responses commonly take the form of fight, flight, approach, or freeze. The amygdala promotes impulsive behaviors that are not grounded in the logic-based PFC. During adolescence, signals from the amygdala override the underdeveloped neurons in the PFC, causing the amygdala to be more influential than it is in the adult brain (Blakemore & Choudhury, 2006; Monk et al., 2003).

Hypothalamus

For all age groups, the hypothalamus is a hormone-producing gland that controls our drive for basic survival needs (eating, sleeping, reproduction, etc.) and also directly influences the amygdala's emotional response system. The increased hormone production during adolescence significantly increases the influential effect of the hypothalamus on the amygdala, especially since the PFC is not yet fully capable of mediating the behaviors ignited by this hormonal surge.

NEW RESEARCH IN THIS AREA (SINCE THE NATIONAL READING PANEL REPORT)

Although neuroscientific studies of the teenage brain do much to enhance our understanding of how teenagers think, as educators we must link this brain-based information with what works in the classroom to inform future decisions regarding the design of secondary reading comprehension instruction. Next, I examine a few recent neuroscience studies and how we can use our knowledge of the adolescent brain and our firsthand knowledge of what works in the secondary classroom to make informed decisions to improve instruction.

Considering Perspectives

In one recent study, Choudhury, Blakemore, and Charman (2006) found that, compared to adults, teenagers take others' feelings less into account. Often, they fail to imagine different perspectives. Neuroimaging data show that the underdeveloped PFC denies adolescents the ability to think about others' emotions and thoughts; therefore, such information is unavailable for decision-making purposes.

In another study (Blakemore, den Ouden, Choudhury, & Frith, 2007), teenagers (ages 12–18) and adults (ages 22–38) were asked questions about the actions they would take in a given situation. At the same time, their brains were monitored by functional magnetic resonance imaging (fMRI). Sample questions included "You want to go to the cinema. Do you look at the newspaper?" and "You are at the cinema and have trouble seeing the screen. Do you move to another seat?" A second set of questions asked what subjects would expect to happen as a result of a natural event, for example, "A huge tree comes crashing down in a forest. Does it make a loud noise?"

Although members of both groups gave similar responses, the PFC was significantly more active in adults than in teenagers when questions were about intended actions. Teenagers showed more activity in a specific area of the temporal lobe of the brain—an area that's involved in predicting future actions based on past actions. Blakemore (Leadbeater, 2006) has concluded that because "[this area] is usually used in making simple actions, or watching other people make actions, we think adolescents are performing this task by simply thinking about the action they're going to take. The part of the brain that the adults are using more is involved in much higher-level thinking, such as thinking about the consequences of your actions in terms of other people's emotions and feelings" (p. 1). She also added that "the brain of, for example, a typical 15-year-old boy is very much still developing; he's a very different person from himself at 25. His brain is very different" (p. 1).

Interpreting Facial Expressions

In another study, Yurgelun-Todd (2002) found that teens differ from adults in their ability to interpret emotions on the faces of others. They also use different areas of their brain when responding to these tasks. In this study Yurgelun-Todd showed photos of people with fearful facial expressions to teenagers between the ages of 11 and 17 (an fMRI scan was taken of their brains at the same time). When compared to the adults' reactions, the teens had less frontal lobe activity and more amygdalar activity. In addition, the teens often misread the facial expressions. For example, those under the age of 14 were more likely to report sadness, anger, or confusion instead of fear (which was the correct response) on the faces. Older teenagers answered correctly more often, exhibiting a progressive shift of activity away from the amygdala toward the frontal lobes as they became older.

McGivern, Anderson, Byrd, Mutter, and Reilly (2002) also found that teenagers have more difficulty matching facial expressions to words describing those emotions. In this study, a group of 246 participants ages 10–17 years, and another group of 49 participants ages 18–22 years, were shown either faces with emotional expressions (e.g., happy, sad, angry) or words describing these emotions (e.g., *happy, sad, angry*). On this task, participants were asked to give a response, as quickly as possible, indicating the emotion represented on the face, or the emotion written on the card. On another task, participants were shown a face and a word, and had to decide whether the facial expression matched the word. Results showed that there was a decline in the ability to perform both tasks in participants at the onset of puberty (ages 11–12) compared to the youngest participants (ages 10–11) (e.g., lowered response time, lowered ability to match facial expression with the correct word). However, at ages 13–14, performance improved again, and continued to improve until ages 16–17. The researchers found that this result correlated with neuroimaging studies showing that the sudden proliferation of synapses at the onset of puberty creates a sudden period of inefficient neural processing, followed by a longer period throughout adolescence in which the brain slowly reorganizes itself through pruning and myelinization.

Additionally, Monk et al. (2003) found that once adolescents have engaged the amygdala during a facial expression task (e.g., viewing faces with a fearful expression), they cannot disengage the activated amygdala to switch to a nonemotional task (e.g., being asked to ignore the fearful expression on a particular face and think about the width of the nose on that face). Adult participants, but not the adolescents, were able to disengage the amygdala and engage the PFC for the nonemotional task.

Studies such as these show us specific brain functions (e.g., exhibiting empathy, reading emotion on faces) that are still developing in the teenage years and provide information to guide our choices when developing adolescent reading comprehension activities. Although more research is needed, neuroscientists are beginning to propose that utilizing thinking processes that engage the PFC, including those that develop social cognition, will enable these processes to develop more fully at this critical time. Students who do not adequately engage these thinking processes (many of the same processes that are necessary for reading comprehension) during adolescence may miss the critical period to fully develop these brain networks, which can lead to permanent deficiencies in these higher-level thinking processes (Blakemore & Choudhury, 2006). The brain has already established a precedent for the "use it or lose it" process of maturation. For instance, this same phenomena occurs during the first 12 months of life, in which infants develop the ability to distinguish all of the sounds of the language spoken in their home. At the end of 12 months, which marks the end of neural pruning and myelinization in the sensory areas of the brain that have been correlated with sound identification, infants lose the ability to distinguish new sounds that are introduced (for a review, see Kuhl, 2004).

Classroom instruction that strengthens the developing neurons associated with these underdeveloped PFC functions increases these neurons' chances of survival and myelinization. It is important to give students opportunities to engage in comprehension processes that ignite the types of PFC thinking activities that encourage maximum growth in this part of the brain. In turn, because these higher-level thinking functions are also associated with reading comprehension ability, the level of reading comprehension ability achieved during the secondary years will likely last a lifetime. Research is needed to establish these links empirically, but a growing body of evidence is leading us in this direction.

Implications for Practice

In a recent study, Parris and Block (2007) conducted a randomized survey of state- and local-level secondary literacy supervisors, including (1) 27 directors or coordinators of adolescent reading programs (representing 27 U.S. state departments of education, (2) 22 district-based supervisors of literacy or language instruction, and (3) 21 professors of literacy education, master teachers of reading or English, or site-based administrators. Through this study, we were able to construct a rich description of expert adolescent teaching practices embedded within eight general domains. These commonly accepted traits of excellent secondary teaching practices can assist us in building a bridge between the fields of neuroscience and secondary comprehension instruction.

First, I provide an overview of the Parris and Block (2007) findings. In addition to ongoing professional development and the ability to meet the diverse needs of adolescent students, excellent secondary teachers were also excellent classroom managers. They also demonstrated the personality characteristics and teaching practices I describe in the next section of this chapter. These results came from experienced educators who were simply sharing practices that they knew worked with adolescents, based on years of experience in secondary classrooms. It is interesting to note how this information naturally correlates with what we are learning about the teenage brain through neuroscience.

Teacher: Personality Characteristics

Respondents noted that exemplary secondary literacy teachers genuinely care about all students and possess a love of learning and reading themselves. These teachers are trustworthy, demonstrate good rapport with students, create time to give personal attention to each student, communicate that each student is valued and accepted, and create mutual respect between themselves and their students. With neuroscientific data indicating that adolescents are highly susceptible to distractions from emotional input, it is easy to see why such a positive emotional environment is critical for adolescents to be able to focus on (and comprehend) what they are reading.

Although negative emotional experiences can be especially detrimental in a secondary classroom, this does not imply that students in such classrooms should be without emotion. Research has already established that memories (a vital component of learning) are formed through connections with the limbic system (the emotional center of the brain that includes the amygdala). Bonding with others (both students and teachers) and motivation are found to be interrelated with the ability to learn (Corrigan, 2000; Kandel, Schwartz, & Jessell, 1991; Kolb & Whishaw, 1990). Emotions, even without relationship attachments, are still found to be significant factors in the growth of cognitive skills (Ames, 1987; Ames & Archer, 1988; Gambrell, Dromsky, & Mazzoni, 2000; Pekrun, 1992; Ruff, 1993). Additionally, our survey respondents noted that humor is a necessary component in highly effective secondary classrooms. Finally, as Nichols, Jones, and Hancock (2003) stated, regarding a study of eighth graders, teachers who encourage students to adopt goals that engage emotional responses also promote a greater increase in the development of cognitive growth, which in turn paves the way for higher levels of comprehension and academic achievement at the secondary level.

Teaching: Pedagogy and Practices

Respondents from the Parris and Block (2007) study noted that the practices of exemplary secondary literacy teachers allow students to (1) use critical thinking skills, (2) ask questions, (3) participate in decision making, and (4) become increasingly independent learners. They also use multiple forms of input systems (visuals, hands-on methods, technology) and expression (peer share, publishing), inatate book-sharing activities, allow time to read and write independently, and promote group activities.

Data from many research studies show that assignments should guide students to articulate their thoughts and feelings either through writing (Scales, 2003) or a wide variety of other modalities. In addition, adolescents should be encouraged to examine the options (as well as the consequences) of various behaviors they encounter through reading (Kellough & Kellough, 2008).

HOW THIS NEW KNOWLEDGE CAN IMPROVE COMPREHENSION INSTRUCTION

In examining neuroscientific data on adolescents and comparing it to known best practices in secondary classrooms, we can begin to find those methods that are corroborated by both areas of research and lead us to develop more effective teaching practices for the future. Regarding the data presented thus far in this chapter, the following three instructional components emerge that likely provide the type of thinking skills adolescents need to nourish both their developing brains and their reading comprehension abilities.

Problem Solving

Adolescence is a period when mental pruning enables youth to progress from thinking concretely to gaining the ability to think more abstractly, problem-solve, analyze options, tackle complex concepts, and think reflectively (Manning, 2002). Activities that promote these thinking processes help to ensure that the neurons responsible for these mental abilities are myelinized and become part of the permanent repertoire of thinking processes for each student. Comprehension lessons (using fiction or nonfiction) in which students read about, enact, and/or discuss solutions to problems encountered in the text should be encouraged in the secondary classroom. For instance, these lessons can be applied to character dilemmas in fiction, historical or scientific dilemmas in nonfiction, or even to thoughtful discussion of which comprehension strategy is best for a particular type of text, and for a particular juncture within the text.

Additionally, secondary teachers need to plan assignments in which students contemplate real-life dilemmas (Scales, 2003) and consider possible responses. These dilemmas can include thinking activities that involve making and defending decisions by using the types of logic and reasoning skills that utilize neurons in the PFC. Also, because adolescents often overreact to emotional prompts, they are also more vulnerable to the influences of media and advertisements (Kellough & Kellough, 2008; Scales, 2003). Assignments that allow teenagers to analyze various types of media and texts from more than one point of view are encouraged.

Exploration

Adolescents' comprehension instruction should satisfy their need to have opportunities for exploration in a variety of ways. Teenagers' brains need reading experiences that bring out their emotions and cause them to think about situations in which emotion and logic are at odds, then allow them to observe or explore the possible consequences. Such thinking activities build vital neurological connections in the brain. Students should also be allowed the time to explore topics deeply and utilize their higher-level thinking processes. They should also be encouraged to make authentic connections to their own lives to give personal meaning to learning experiences. Exploration can include experimentation, data collection, and/or analysis to find answers to students' questions or to spark discussions. Because the sensorimotor area of the adolescent brain is also still developing, exploration experiences that allow for student involvement and practice of motor skills are doubly beneficial. Such activities include labs, artistic expression, presentations, group activities, and so forth. Although it is not possible to scan the brain of every student to ensure that certain instructional activities are promoting optimal brain development, we *can* observe the brain-building results of such instruction through student artifacts, discussions, and assessments.

Identity Development

A major component of adolescent growth is the process of developing a sense of individuality and of seeking an adult identity (Knowles & Brown, 2000). All this is done while the adolescent also strives to maintain peer approval and deal with conflict between competing family and peer alliances (Wiles, Bondi, & Wiles, 2006). Secondary comprehension instruction should encourage students not only to think about their developing self-identity but also to consider the future, to anticipate future needs, and to develop personal goals (Kellough & Kellough, 2008). This type of forward thinking that activates the PFC engages positive, logically motivated thinking and encourages development of the PFC's capacity to override the influence of the amygdala.

Identity development and PFC brain functions may also be supported through character studies. Through literature, and literary characters, students can place themselves vicariously in a variety of situations. As Roser and Martinez (2005) point out in their informative book *What a Character!: Character Study as a Guide to Literary Meaning Making in Grades K–8*, character study allows students to consider characters' traits and perspectives, understand their motivations and goals, explore their feelings, and probe their relationships. Roser and Martinez recommend that students be guided to "consider character thoughtfully using tools such as writing, visual representations, and drama" (p. vi). Not only does character study enhance reading comprehension skills, but also the more that students develop the ability to empathize with characters in books, the more this ability becomes a permanent part of their PFC brain structure, which in turn strengthens their own character. The neurological need for this type of thinking activity can be drawn from the Choudhury, Blakemore, and Charman (2006) study described earlier in this chapter. Also, characters' moods in literature are often portrayed through written descriptions of their facial expressions and/or body posture. Students' ability to recognize certain facial expressions as belonging to particular moods is greatly enhanced through character study. The neurological need for this type of thinking activity can be drawn from the Yurgelun-Todd (2002) study described earlier in this chapter. Finally, even though the title of the Roser and Martinez book (described earlier) mentions that it is for grades K–8, neuroscience is leading us to understand that this would be an excellent teaching resource for all secondary teachers, grades 9–12 included.

DIRECTIONS FOR FUTURE RESEARCH

1. *Can brain imaging studies empirically establish that becoming adept at certain reading comprehension skills also promotes development of the PFC areas known to process these thinking skills?* Because higher-level thinking functions are also associated with reading comprehension ability, activities designed to aid development of the PFC likely increase reading achievement, and vice versa. More research is needed to establish these links empirically, but a growing body of evidence is leading us in this direction.

2. *What is the complete list of PFC thinking processes that can be enhanced through reading comprehension instruction, and vice versa?* We are just beginning to make connections to instructional practices that enhance the development of the PFC, and in particular, the specific thinking processes used in reading comprehension. We need researchers to develop a more complete list of the thinking processes that should be used in reading comprehension instruction in secondary classrooms.

3. *Can gender be used as a covariate in studies of adolescent reading comprehension?* We know that the PFC develops sooner in girls than in boys, yet we do not know how this difference, or how other brain-based gender differences, might affect the acquisition of reading comprehension skills in boys and girls. Research is needed in this area to determine the implications of these differences relative to instruction.

PROJECTIONS AND POSSIBILITIES FOR THE CLASSROOM OF 2030

The secondary classroom of 2030 will be a place where students are given many opportunities specifically to utilize still developing areas of their brains. Literacy assignments will often include solving problems, grappling with complex concepts, and exploring options. Students will participate in projects they care about, and learning environments will by design be emotionally supportive to all students. Additionally, we have only begun to scratch the surface regarding the significant, stimulating effects that literature has on adolescent brain development. Teachers and researchers in 2030 will more fully understand the implications of using literature to encourage adolescent brain development, and I foresee that it will be commonly utilized as a very vital part of secondary education curricula.

SUMMARY

In studying neuroscience as it relates to instruction, we cannot separate the cognitive, emotional, and physical: They are all interrelated parts of a whole. Instruction based on neuroscience, by definition, must include all of these processes that are controlled by the brain. In the past, scientists believed the adolescent brain was somehow less capable of learning than a child's brain (that an important window of learning had somehow passed). We now know that the adolescent brain is still developing, and still very capable of abundant learning.

A unique feature of adolescent students is that they are more distracted learners due to the combination of an underdeveloped PFC, which gives increased control to the amygdala, and the increase in hormone production through the hypothalamus, which also leads to more influence from the amygdala. These factors cause teenagers to be driven more by emotion than by reason. Therefore, it is more challenging to keep the adolescent learner focused on academic learning. Rich learning experiences that are tailored for the developing adolescent brain and a positive learning environment will provide the optimal learning situation.

As we progress down the path to corroborating instructional approaches that work with brain-based research findings, we will continue to develop more precise teaching practices tailored to the particular needs of adolescent learners. We will experience more productive research efforts in the future because we will be able to explain not only *what* works but also *why* certain practices work. Finally, secondary educators and researchers should deeply consider how efforts to engage students to stretch the capacity of their minds also serve a vital function in a life-or-death situation for the higher-level thinking processes in the brain.

INTEGRATE, INVESTIGATE, AND INITIATE: QUESTIONS FOR DISCUSSION

1. Compare the information about how neuroscience informs the teaching of our adolescent students to the information you learned in Caine (Chapter 9, this volume) about teaching comprehension to elementary students. How are they different and how are they alike?

2. This is the last chapter in Part II of this book: Neuroscience: What Brain-Based Research Tells Us about Reading Comprehension. Write a paragraph that describes how you were taught to comprehend. Write a paragraph that summarizes what this section of the book has reported as the newest research-based methods of teaching comprehension. What action can you take to advance comprehension in your classroom to move beyond the comprehension experiences you had?

3. The next section of this book, Part III, describes how we can improve comprehension instruction for different types of text and content areas. Write a statement to predict one activity that you expect to read about in the next section. Base your prediction on a synthesis of the information you have learned through reading the first 10 chapters of this book.

REFERENCES

Ames, C. (1987). The enhancement of student motivation. In M. L. Maehr & D. Kleiber (Eds.), *Advanced in motivation and achievement: Enhancing motivation* (Vol. 5, pp. 123–148). Greenwich, CT: JAI Press.

Ames, C., & Archer, J. (1988). Achievement goals in the classroom: Student learning strategies and motivation processes. *Journal of Educational Psychology, 80*, 260–267.

Barkovich, A. J., Kjos, B. O., Jackson, D. E., & Norman, D. (1988). Normal maturation of the neonatal and infant brain: MR imaging at 1.5 T. *Radiology, 166*, 173–180.

Beers, K. (2003). *When kids can't read what teachers can do*. Portsmouth, New Hampshire: Heinemann.

Blakemore, S., & Choudhury, S. (2006). Development of the adolescent brain: Implications for executive function and social cognition. *Journal of Child Psychology and Psychiatry, 47*(3/4), 296–312.

Blackmore, S., den Ouden, H., Choudhury, S., & Frith, C. (2007). Adolescent development of the neural circuitry for thinking about intentions. *Social Cognitive and Affective Neuroscience, 2*(2), 130–139.

Block, C. C., Oakar, M., & Hurt, H. (2002). The expertise of literacy teachers: A continuum from preschool to grade 5. *Reading Research Quarterly, 37*(2), 178–206.

Bruer, J. T. (1997). Education and the brain: The bridge too far. *Educational Researcher, 26*(8), 4–16.

Casey, B. J., Geidd, J. N., & Thomas, K. M. (2000). Structural and functional brain development and its relation to cognitive development. *Biological Psychology, 54*, 241–257.

Changeux, J. P., & Dehaene, S. (1989). Neuronal models of cognitive functions. *Cognition, 33*, 63–109.

Choudhury, S., Blakemore, S., & Charman, T. (2006). Social cognitive development during adolescence. *Social Cognitive and Affective Neuroscience, 1*(3), 165–174.

Corrigan, S. Z. (2000, September 22). *Biology, neuroscience, and education*. Second Annual UVSC Faculty Conference, Biology in the 21st Century: Genetics, Economics, and Ethics, Utah Valley State College, Orem, Utah.

Dahl, R. E. (2004). Adolescent brain development: A period of vulnerabilities and opportunities [Keynote address]. In R. E. Dahl & L. P. Spear (Eds.), Adolescent brain development: Period of vulnerabilities and opportunities. *Annals of the New York Academy of Sciences, 1021*, 1–22.

Gambrell, L. B., Dromsky, A. J., & Mazzoni, S. A. (2000). Motivation matters: Fostering full access to literacy. In K. D. Wood & T. S. Dickinson (Eds.), *Promoting literacy in grades 4–9: A handbook for teachers and administrators* (pp. 128–138). Needham Heights, MA: Allyn & Bacon.

Geidd, J. N. (2004). Structural magnetic resonance imaging of the adolescent brain. *Annals of the New York Academy of Sciences, 1021*, 77–85.

Geidd, J. N., Blumenthal, J., Jeffries, N. O., Castellanos, F. X., Liu, H., Zijdenbos, A., et al. (1999). Brain development during childhood and adolescence: A longitudinal MRI study, *Nature Neuroscience, 2*, 861–878.

Gogtay, N., Geidd, J. N., Lusk, L., Hayashi, K. M., Deanna, G., Vaituzis, A. C., et al. (2004). Dynamic mapping of human cortical development during childhood through early adulthood. *Proceedings of the National Academy of Sciences of the United States of America, 101*(2), 8174–8179.

Goldman-Rakic, P. S. (1987). Circuitry of primate prefrontal cortex and regulation of behavior by representational memory. In F. Plum (Ed.), *Handbook of physiology: The nervous system: Section 1, Vol. 5. Higher functions of the brain* (pp. 373–417). Bethesda: American Physiological Society.

Huttenlocher, P. R. (1979). Synaptic density in human frontal cortex—Developmental changes and effects of aging. *Brain Research, 163*, 195–205.

Huttenlocher, P. R. (1990). Morphometric study of human cerebral cortex development. *Neuropsychologia, 28*, 517–527.

Huttenlocher, P. R., deCourten, C., Garey, L. J., & van der Loos, H. (1982). Synaptogenesis in human visual cortex—Evidence for synapse elimination during normal development. *Neuroscience Letters, 33*, 247–252.

Iran-Nejad, A. (1998). *Brain-based education: A reply to Bruer* (Report No. SP038393). (ERIC Document Reproduction Service No. ED429063)

Iran-Nejad, A. & Gregg, M. (2001). *The brain–mind cycle of reflection*. New York: Teachers College, Columbia University.

Kandel, E. R., Schwartz, J. H., & Jessell, T. M. (1991). *Principles of neuroscience* (3rd ed.). New York: Elsevier Science.

Kellough, R. D., & Kellough, N. G. (2008). *Teaching young adolescents: Methods and resources for middle grades teaching* (5th ed.). Upper Saddle River, NJ: Merrill/Prentice Hall.

Knowles, T., & Brown, D. F. (2000). *What every middle school teacher should know*. Portsmouth, NH: Heinemann.
Kolb, B., & Whishaw, I. Q. (1990). *Fundamentals of human neuropsychology* (3rd ed.). New York: Freeman.
Kuhl, P. K. (2004). Early language acquisition: Cracking the speech code. *Nature Reviews Neuroscience, 5*(11), 831–843.
Leadbeater, E. (2006, September 8). Seeing the teenager in the brain. BBC News. Retrieved January 31, 2008, from *http://news.bbc.co.uk/2/hi/science/nature/5327550.stm*.
Manning, M. L. (2002). *Developmentally appropriate middle level schools* (2nd ed.). Olney, MD: Association for Childhood Education International.
McArdle, C. B., Richardson, C. J., Nicholas, D. A., Mirfakhraee, M., Hayden, C. K., & Amparo, E. G. (1987). Developmental features of the neonatal brain: MR Imaging: Part 1. Gray–white matter differentiation and myelination. *Radiology, 162*, 223–229.
McGivern, R., Anderson, J., Byrd, D., Mutter, K., & Reilly, J. (2002). Cognitive efficiency on a match to sample task decreases at the onset of puberty in children. *Brain and Cognition, 50*, 73–89.
Monk, C. S., McClure, E. B., Nelson, E. E., Zarahn, E., Bilder, R. M., Leibenluft, et al. (2003). Adolescent immaturity in attention-related brain engagement to emotional facial expressions. *NeuroImage, 20*(1), 420–428.
Neville, H.J. (1995). Developmental specificity in neurocognitive development in humans. In M. S. Gazzaniga (Ed.), *The cognitive neurosciences* (pp. 219–231). Cambridge, MA: MIT Press.
Nichols, W. D., Jones, J. P., & Hancock, D. R. (2003). Teachers' influence on goal orientation: Exploring the relationship between eighth graders' goal orientation, their emotional development, their perceptions of learning, and their teachers' instructional strategies. *Reading Psychology, 24*(1), 57–86.
Parris, S. R., & Block, C. C. (2007). The expertise of adolescent literacy teachers. *Journal of Adolescent and Adult Literacy, 50*(7), 582–596.
Pekrun, R. (1992). The impact of emotions on learning and achievement: Towards a theory of cognitive/motivational mediators. *Applied Psychology: An International Review, 41*(4), 359–376.
Roser, N. L., & Martinez, M. G. (2005). *What a character!: Character study as a guide to literacy meaning making in grades K–8*. Newark, DE: International Reading Association.
Ruff, T. P. (1993). Middle school students at risk: What do we do with the most vulnerable children in American education? *Middle School Journal, 24*(5), 10–12.
Scales, P. C. (2003). Characteristics of young adolescents. In National Middle School Association (Ed.), *This we believe: Successful schools for young adolescents* (pp. 43–51). Westerville, OH: National Middle School Association.
Snow, C. E., Burns, M. S., & Griffin, P. (Eds.). (1998). *Preventing reading difficulties in young children*. Washington, DC: National Academy Press. (ERIC Document Reproduction Service No. ED416465)
Sowell, E. R., Thompson, P. M., Holmes, C. J., Jernigan, T. L., & Toga, A. W. (1999). In vivo evidence for post-adolescent brain maturation in frontal and striatal regions. *Nature Neuroscience, 2*, 859–861.
Stanovich, K. E. (1986). Matthew effects in reading: Some consequences of individual differences in the acquisition of literacy. *Reading Research Quarterly, 21*, 360–406.
Wallis, C., & Park, A. (2004). What makes teens tick: Dr. Jay Geidd. *Time, 163*(19), 56.
Wiles, J., Bondi, J., & Wiles, M. T. (2006). *The essential middle school* (4th ed.). Upper Saddle River, NJ: Pearson Prentice Hall.
Yurgelun-Todd, D. (2002). Frontline interview: Inside the teen brain. Full interview available at *www.pbs.org/wgbh/pages/frontline/shows/teenbrain/interviews/todd.html*.
Zwiers, J. (2004). *Building reading comprehension habits in grades 6–12*. Newark, DE: International Reading Association.

III

IMPROVING COMPREHENSION INSTRUCTION

11

Transforming Classroom Instruction to Improve the Comprehension of Fictional Texts

MARY HELEN THOMPSON

> Reading instruction is all about the choices you make. . . . It is the fine art of weaving all of those choices together to create a meaningful experience from your students' own personal reading.
> —AMY SAUNDERS, third-grade teacher

For many people, understanding stories is almost a natural process. Repeated early childhood exposure to stories told, read, and viewed develops a strong framework to understand most of the fictional texts encountered throughout elementary schooling. However, once those printed narratives become more complex, that internalized structure ceases to be an adequate tool, and comprehension instruction becomes necessary. Although there has been much research into comprehending fictional texts, some educators still struggle to construct effective comprehension lessons for fiction.

Although schools increasingly are placing greater emphasis on instruction designed to ease the comprehension of nonfiction texts, fiction continues to serve as the major source of curricula in the educational process. From *Charlotte's Web* to *Hamlet*, fictional texts abound throughout K–12 education and even into higher education. With increased accountability in education today, teachers are focusing on ways to improve instruction, especially comprehension instruction, as a way to meet federal mandates. Meanwhile, comprehension is among the most difficult reading processes to teach (Block, Gambrell, & Pressley, 2002). This current high-stakes environment accentuates the critical importance of using research-based best practices in narrative reading instruction. However, many teachers are at a loss for how to teach fiction effectively. This has led some researchers to develop more effective fictional text instructional frameworks to enhance comprehension. Moreover, many frameworks designed to teach nonfiction text are effective with fiction as well.

This chapter highlights the following:

- Established research on instructional frameworks used to build narrative comprehension.
- New research related to the effects of using those instructional frameworks to teach comprehension of fiction.
- Recommended directions for future research on instruction in comprehension of fiction.

ESTABLISHED RESEARCH OF INSTRUCTIONAL FRAMEWORKS

When planning classroom instruction, teachers often use an instructional framework to guide the process and to sequence lessons. Over the years, frameworks in comprehension instruction have taken several forms. In this section, I discuss a few established instructional frameworks and provide an overview of the concept of scaffolding as it relates to comprehension instruction.

Two Early Instructional Frameworks

One of the earliest instructional frameworks in reading instruction was Directed Reading Activity (DRA). Used as the basis of many basal reading lessons, Betts (1946) developed DRA as a framework for teachers to provide highly sequenced comprehension instruction aimed at the specific needs of a particular group of students. The primary steps of DRA are readiness, silent reading, discussion, rereading, and follow-up. Students were not provided direct comprehension instruction relative to the stories read in this model. Rather, students were presented key terms and background material related to a story's content, silently read the story, and engaged in discussion of the text. Those who already possessed strong comprehension abilities prior to reading the story usually did well on the questions; those who did not usually failed to supply the correct answers.

Much like DRA, Directed Reading–Thinking Activity (DR–TA; Stauffer, 1969) provided a framework for instruction, but focused more directly on developing critical reading skills. Students examined a text by looking at the title, illustrations, and the first few pages, then hypothesized what the passage would be about. Subsequently, they read the passage and confirmed or disconfirmed their predictions. This cycle continued until the full selection had been read. Following the reading–prediction–evaluation phases, a skills-training phase took place. For many years, DRA and DR-TA were the primary instructional frameworks used by classroom teachers; however, they were not without criticism.

Two of the primary criticisms were that DRA and DR-TA both were highly teacher-dominated and didactic, not lending themselves to transfer of responsibility from the teacher to the student. They also did not provided opportunities for students to learn how to generalize the comprehension processes independently across contexts. These weaknesses created a need for instructional frameworks that scaffolded student learning, gradually releasing responsibility to students as they became more proficient in their understanding of and ability to construct meaning on their own.

Instructional Scaffolding

Based in part on Vygotsky's (1967, 1978) research into the zone of proximal development, the concepts of constructivism and scaffolding became the foundation for many instructional frameworks. In constructivistic models, scaffolds provide a structural framework that enables students (like construction workers) to work at higher levels than they could independently. The temporary comprehension scaffolds from their teachers remain only as long as they are needed; then, they are gradually removed.

In education, the term "scaffolding" was first used by Wood, Bruner, and Ross (1976) to mean the "process that enables a child or novice to solve a problem, carry out a task, or achieve a goal which would be beyond his unassisted efforts" (p. 90). Central to scaffolded instruction is the gradual removal of the scaffold and the transference of learning to other, less controlled, contexts (Palincsar, 1986). More recent instructional frameworks seek to provide a scaffold that allows students to work with the assistance of their teacher, a tutor, or another, more capable peer to construct an understanding of the text and gradually take on more of the responsibility for that task.

Reciprocal Teaching: A Brief Overview

Driven to improve student capacity to learn from text, Palincsar and Brown (1984) developed an interactive instructional framework that focuses on sharing the teaching of assigned texts among the teacher and the students. Based on the concept of scaffolding to increase competence, reciprocal teaching comprises four key activities: summarizing, questioning, clarifying, and predicting. After determining who will "teach" a passage, the selection is read. The "teacher" (student leader) then summarizes the passage, asks test-like questions, discusses and clarifies difficulties, and finally makes predictions about content that is likely to occur in the next section of the passage. Initially, the adult teacher models each activity and provides extensive scaffolding until students become more adept at completing the activities without outside assistance: then, they become the "teachers."

In their three-phase study of the reciprocal teaching framework, Palincsar and Brown (1984) found that students gradually grew more proficient at asking clarifying questions and creating summaries of the main ideas of passages. Through assessments of generalizability and transfer, researchers determined that students were also able to use the framework independently when reading other passages, and even to generalize their knowledge to new contexts.

Substantial and significant improvements in comprehension were shown for students with and without reading difficulties. Reciprocal teaching proved effective in providing comprehension instruction that allowed students to understand a particular text. The next instructional framework focuses on instruction of various comprehension strategies.

Transactional Strategies Instruction: A Synopsis

As described in greater detail in Sadoski (Chapter 3, this volume) and as summarized below, Transactional Strategies Instruction developed from Duffy and Roehler's (Duffy et al., 1987) direct explanation of the Strategic Instructional Model. Transactional Strategies Instruction (Pressley et al., 1992) provides dynamic instruction through a wide range of reading strategies in interactive settings. Although Transactional Strategies Instruction is not limited to one particular instructional model, all models that fall under this category have the same basic goal and include the same key components. The primary goal of Transactional Strategies Instruction is students' self-regulated use of the strategies (Pressley et al., 1992). Components of Transactional Strategies Instruction include strategy instruction, strategy use, and extensive interaction between teacher and student. A key element of strategy instruction and use in this framework is direct explanation of the purpose, benefits, and times to use various strategies (Brown, Pressley, Van Meter, & Schuder, 1996).

Anderson (1992) studied Transactional Strategies Instruction with severely disabled adolescent readers. By the end of the 3-month study, a significant number of students in the treatment group performed substantially better than the control group on standardized comprehension assessments. A previous study (Collins, 1991) of fifth- and sixth-grade readers showed similar results. In a yearlong quasi-experimental study of the impact of Transactional Strategies Instruction on at-risk second-grade readers, Brown et al. (1996) found that students receiving Transactional Strategies Instruction performed better on various comprehension assessments than did students receiving typical classroom instruction. Brown et al. also found that students continued using the strategies they learned long after the initial instruction. These studies show the efficacy of Transactional Strategies Instruction in enhancing higher-level comprehension abilities and the transfer of strategic thinking processes to new contexts.

Summary of Established Research

Although other research-based instructional frameworks are available (e.g., Concept-Oriented Reading Instruction (Guthrie et al., 1998) or Collaborative Strategic Reading (Vaughn, Hughes, Schumm, & Kingner, 1998), many of these focus primarily on content area reading or special needs populations. While students still struggle to comprehend fiction, many contemporary researchers have shifted their focus away from fiction to nonfiction and electronic text. Still, there are a few recent studies examining the impact of instructional frameworks on student comprehension of fictional texts. Those studies are the focus of the next section of this chapter.

USING INSTRUCTIONAL FRAMEWORKS TO ENHANCE COMPREHENSION

Although nonfiction has captured much of the attention of researchers in recent years, a few studies have used instructional frameworks to teach and to comprehend fiction. In this section, I discuss studies related to two frameworks: reciprocal teaching and Scaffolded Reading Experiences.

Using Reciprocal Teaching with Kindergarten Students

After successful utilization of reciprocal teaching (Palincsar & Brown, 1984) with older students, Pamela Ann Myers (2005) felt that it could be effectively modified for use with her kindergarten students. In an anecdotal account of her action research, Myers describes the modifications she made to the reciprocal teaching framework and their impact on student understanding.

Because her students were beginning to learn how to decode texts, Myers decided to use read-alouds instead of asking her students to read passages silently. This decision allowed her to utilize more sophisticated texts for instruction, although the specific titles used were not provided. Students were already familiar with the texts, because they had heard them several times. Myers does not indicate in her account the amount of instruction, if any, that had already taken place using the selected texts. It is assumed that the texts were used primarily for enjoyment before their inclusion in reciprocal teaching lessons.

Another modification to traditional reciprocal teaching was the utilization of puppets to model each stage of the process. Myers (2005) also notes that the puppets helped some of her more shy students "find their voice" in the lessons. Princess Storyteller was the summarizer of the stories. Asking literal comprehension questions fell to Quincy Questioner, with more inferential and clarifying questions falling to Clara Clarifier. Prediction was the responsibility of the Wizard. Myers noted that each student had an opportunity to assume each role at least once a week during the 3-month project.

To make the instructional framework more effective for kindergarten students, Myers (2005) introduced two of the four stages individually, allowing her students fully to understand each stage before moving to the next. Myers found that predicting was the easiest stage for students to master, because they were already familiar with the texts. Retelling, on the other hand, was the most difficult stage for students. Clarifying and questioning stages were introduced simultaneously, with "questioning" defined as asking easy questions, and "clarifying" as a means to understand the story.

Using interviews with four students of differing abilities, along with anecdotal records of student responses during the lessons and teacher-generated rubrics, Myers (2005) examined not only student performance but also student growth over the course of the project. Findings show that students became reflective learners who engaged in self-monitoring of their comprehension. At the beginning of the study, all of the focus students indicated they did not have any problems understanding stories. By the end of the study, the students knew when they were unable to understand something and were able to ask appropriate questions to eliminate confusion. Myers also notes an increase in students' ability to retell the stories effectively over the course of the study. One additional finding was that student learning of the reciprocal teaching stages transferred to content area lessons.

Although these findings are promising, there are several limitations to the study (Myers, 2005) that must be addressed in future studies. The primary limitation was the design of the study. As with other action research studies; the findings are not generalizable to other populations. It would be beneficial to conduct a study with a control group that received standard classroom literacy instruction, and an experimental group that received the modified reciprocal teaching treatment.

Another primary limitation was the use of familiar texts for the lessons. Whereas this might be an effective way of introducing kindergarten students to reciprocal teaching, additional empirical studies must be conducted concerning the efficacy of using familiar and unfamiliar texts in reciprocal teaching of primary-age students. However, even with the limitations, the study provides an intriguing and promising look at the utilization of reciprocal teaching as an instructional framework for comprehension development of narrative texts with young readers.

Scaffolded Reading Experiences

First introduced in the mid-1990s, the Scaffolded Reading Experience (SRE) (Graves & Graves, 2003) was, until recently, supported more by anecdotal accounts than empirical evidence. An SRE is a flexible "set of prereading, during-reading, and postreading activities designed to assist a particular group of students in successfully reading, understanding, learning from, and enjoying a particular selection" (p. 5) of text.

Underlying SREs is the concept of scaffolding. As utilized in SREs, instructional scaffolding provides the foundation for this flexible framework. Although research into the effectiveness of SREs as an entire instructional framework has only recently been conducted, the primary SRE components—the prereading, during-reading, and postreading activities—are extensively recommended (Graves & Graves, 2003).

An SRE comprises two phases: planning and implementation (Graves & Graves, 2003). In the planning phase, teachers use their knowledge of their students, the reading passage, and the purpose for reading to create an SRE of prereading, during-reading, and postreading activities that meets students' instructional needs. Prereading activities may include, but are not limited to, creating interest, activating prior knowledge, and vocabulary instruction. Guided reading, silent reading, and read-alouds are some of the activities available for the during-reading stage. Postreading includes a variety of activities that allow students to assess their comprehension of fiction and respond to the text. During the implementation phase, the teacher puts the plan into action, using the chosen prereading, during-reading, and postreading activities. Careful planning and implementation ensure that each SRE is crafted to cater to the needs of a specific group of students reading a particular text.

Cooke (2002) examined the impact of SRE instruction on student comprehension of multicultural fictional stories using a quasi-experimental research design. Over the 5-week study, Cooke chose as the basis for instruction four selections from a collection of short stories. Each selection provided some characteristic that the researcher felt would prove challenging for the seventh-grade students participating in the study.

Cooke designed activities for each SRE component and each of the four selections. Each nontreatment lesson was also planned around prereading, during-reading, and postreading activities. However, the actual instruction did not involve teacher modeling and scaffolding of the narratives. The same short stories used in the SRE treatment were used in the nontreatment lessons. Evaluation of student comprehension was accomplished by multiple-choice and short-answer assessments. An interrater reliability of 98% was achieved for the informal, short-answer assessment.

Cooke found that students who received the SRE treatment demonstrated significantly greater comprehension of the stories than those who received nontreatment instruction. These results were the same whether the question was implicit or explicit in nature. Cooke concluded that SREs had a positive impact on students' deep thinking about short stories, aiding them in developing a more in-depth understanding of the text.

Although the Cooke (2002) study produced promising results, it had several limitations. One limitation that Cooke noted was the population of the school. Overall, the school population was 95% white, which calls into question the generalizability of the study to more ethnically diverse populations. Another limitation concerns the lack of a control group. Students received either the SRE treatment or a non-SRE treatment, both of which comprised prereading, during-reading, and postreading activities.

Whereas these three components might be the norm for the classes involved in the study, other schools do not consistently use these activities in their everyday reading instruction. One final limitation that might have impacted results was the inability to assign research subjects randomly to treatment groups. This particular limitation, however, is a consistent issue in educational research. Although the study had limitations, the results were promising for the use of SREs as a new, up-and-coming instructional framework to increase students' comprehension of fiction.

Much like Cooke, Liang (2004; Liang, Peterson, & Graves, 2005) examined the impact of SRE instruction on student comprehension of short stories. However, in both of her studies, Liang changed the focus of the final aspect of SRE planning; the purpose for reading. The first focus used a cognitive orientation with the SRE, and the second focus was response-oriented. Lessons using the cognitive orientation emphasize "both teaching students how to employ their cognitive processes to be more active and successful readers, and providing them with opportunities to successfully understand text through scaffolding that fosters their participation as more active readers" (Liang, 2004, p. 20). Response-oriented lessons focus on students' responses to stories when using an aesthetic stance to reading. While both studies examined the change of focus on student comprehension and response, the population was different in each study.

The first study (Liang, 2004) involved 85 mixed-ability, sixth-grade students in four classrooms. Two experienced middle school teachers selected to participate in the study received training on the control instruction, the SRE cognitive-oriented instruction, and the SRE response-oriented instruction. They prepared lessons using short stories for each instructional focus, basing the control lesson on typical instructional activities found in basal readers. Instruction using the control and two experimental treatments took place over a period of 3 weeks, with assessment taking place on the last instructional day of each week.

Findings from the first study (Liang, 2004) showed that student understanding of the short stories was higher during the SRE treatments than during the control lesson. However, the cognitive-oriented instruction showed an increase in comprehension only slightly higher than that of the response-oriented instruction. The reverse was the result when examining student response. Response-oriented instruction had a slightly more positive impact on students' engagement with the text than did cognitive-oriented instruction. The author concluded that there is a place for both cognitive-oriented and response-oriented SREs in an effective reading program.

In the second study, Liang et al. (2005) used cognitive-oriented and response-oriented SRE instruction with a population of 54 third-grade students across two classrooms. Much like the first study, lessons created for each instructional focus used short stories. A primary difference in this study was the lack of a control lesson. An examination of the lessons revealed that both cognitive-oriented and response-oriented lessons unintentionally shared the SRE framework. As such, findings from this study showed that both orientations fostered comprehension of the short stories.

The studies (Liang, 2004; Liang et al., 2005) share similar limitations. One such limitation is the population. Both studies took place in urban schools with ethnically and linguistically diverse populations, in which approximately 40% of students received free or reduced lunch. This calls into question the ability to generalize the results to other populations. The short duration of both studies is another shared limitation. A final limitation in the study of third-grade students involves the absence of a control group. Even with these limitations, both studies show promising results for Scaffolded Reading Experiences as a new instructional framework to build students' comprehension of fiction.

Summary of New Research

Much of the more recent research into instructional frameworks has focused on the impact of students' comprehension of nonfiction. However, there is still a need to examine their efficacy with fiction. Whereas students reading from fourth grade on is primarily nonfiction, the focus in students' formative years is on reading fictional texts. As such, it is imperative to continue studying the impact of particular instructional frameworks on student comprehension of fictional texts.

IMPROVING COMPREHENSION INSTRUCTION

Based on the discussion of new research into the use of instructional frameworks with fictional text, three immediate applications for improving classroom comprehension instruction arise and fall into three broad areas: (1) Know your students; (2) plan effective, engaging instruction; and (3) scaffold appropriately. Although these ideas are not groundbreaking, they continue to be critically important in creating classroom instruction that enhances comprehension and engagement with text. As such, they deserve reexamination.

To create effective, engaging comprehension instruction, it is imperative that teachers have an in-depth knowledge of their students' instructional needs, personal interests, and academic strengths. Prior to planning the instructional treatments, Liang (2004) met with participating middle school teachers to identify and record "any special strengths or needs of the students" (p. 53) who would be involved in the study. This allowed her to plan more effective treatment and control lessons.

By focusing on academic strengths and needs, Myers (2005) planned opportunities for Melissa, one of her focus students who was very shy, to showcase her developing understanding of a story through retelling, while increasing her leadership and oral communication skills. To identify stories that might be of interest, Cooke (2002) asked non-participating sixth-grade students to read 10 carefully selected stories and comment on their appeal to sixth graders. These few examples show how researchers capitalized on students' strengths, needs, and interests to plan effective instruction. Classroom teachers must capitalize on their insider knowledge of their students when planning classroom instruction to provide appealing, successful learning opportunities for them.

Using their extensive knowledge of their students, teachers must also plan effective, engaging lessons that provide opportunities for cooperation and collaboration. For example, by examining Myers's (2005) study of reciprocal teaching with kindergartners, we find an excellent illustration of one classroom teacher who planned engaging lessons. Knowing that her students enjoyed puppets, Myers crafted reciprocal teaching lessons, using the puppets to "assist [her] children in generating language and finding their 'voices' when learning the strategies" (p. 316).

This approach actively engaged students who would otherwise typically be reluctant to participate in classroom discussions. It also proved to be an effective means of teaching students how to summarize stories, to identify and clarify problem areas within a story, and to generalize their learning to other academic subjects. As the description of Myers's classroom shows, effective instruction does not necessitate boring drill and practice; instead it is engaging, providing opportunities for lively discussion and collaboration in building a shared understanding of the text.

A final implication of the research presented is the need to scaffold instruction appropriately. A thorough understanding of the students' strengths and instructional needs is crucial to scaffold their understanding of new concepts. A teacher's modeling of his or her thought processes using think-alouds is one way to provide instructional scaffolding for comprehension. Block and Israel (2004) and Duffy (2003) provide more than 50 such think-alouds to assist readers before, during, and after reading fiction.

Cooke (2002) describes in her study the use of discussion guides to scaffold fiction. Story maps proved to be an effective scaffolding technique for students in one study (Liang et al., 2005). More capable peers also provide effective scaffolding for other students. An example of this is found in Myers (2005) study when she describes how other students assisted a peer by retelling parts of a story and clarifying the parts that were confusing. These are just a few examples of scaffolded instruction in the studies discussed earlier. By scaffolding a student's developing understanding, teachers can use slightly more complex texts than texts the student could understand independently. This provides more challenging instructional activities that build students' confidence in their abilities to learn successfully. This is a critical part of effective classroom instruction that builds on what students already know and helps them develop the knowledge and skills they will need in the future.

Although the ideas in this section are not revolutionary, they are foundational ideas that should be second nature for classroom teachers. Unfortunately, some teachers neglect to consider these ideas when planning lessons. If student growth and achievement are the primary goals of classroom instruction, it is imperative that teachers remember to plan lessons that take advantage of their students' strengths and scaffold their developing knowledge and skills in effective and engaging ways.

WHAT WE STILL NEED TO KNOW ABOUT COMPREHENDING FICTION

Interest in researching comprehension of fictional texts seems to have waned over the past decade, yet scores of children still struggle with understanding fiction. Three questions for future research are examined in this section:

1. *What instructional frameworks are best suited for primary age readers?* Most classroom teachers use a general instructional framework to guide their content-area and literacy lessons (Tierney & Readence, 2000). Much of the research on instructional frameworks, however, has been conducted with populations of students that are in third grade and older. Very few empirical studies have been conducted with K–2 students. One example discussed earlier was the Brown et al. (1996) study that examined the effectiveness of transactional strategies instruction with second-grade readers. Myers's (2005) description of her success with reciprocal teaching indicates that modifying that framework for beginning readers might be a successful strategy. Still, not much is known about the efficacy of instructional frameworks with beginning readers. As such, more research into the effectiveness of using various instructional frameworks with K–2 students should be conducted.

2. *Which instructional frameworks are most beneficial for comprehending fictional texts?* Much of the instructional frameworks research has examined their use with nonfiction texts. As noted at the beginning of this chapter, although greater emphasis is generally placed on understanding nonfiction text in schools, learning to comprehend fiction still plays a valuable role in students' overall education. Further research is needed to expand the knowledge base about the usefulness of instructional frameworks in teaching reading comprehension of fictional texts.

3. *How should comprehension instruction related to fictional texts change as a result of increased use of electronic texts?* Whereas some teachers already make use of electronic storybooks and other electronic texts in their classrooms, others have access to

these texts but do not know how to incorporate them into their instruction. In anticipating the classroom of the future, it becomes imperative that researchers extend the current knowledge base related to electronic texts and examine how comprehension instruction should change as classroom use of electronic texts becomes a more widely accepted practice. This research must extend to the use of electronic and animated storybooks in the early grades. Although much research has related to student processing of hypertext and other electronic texts, the possibilities for how these texts may be employed in the classroom are limitless. There is much we still need to know about how children—especially young children—process these texts. With greater understanding of these processes, it will become necessary to research effective ways to make use of electronic texts, including electronic and animated storybooks, during comprehension instruction.

PROJECTIONS AND POSSIBILITIES FOR THE CLASSROOM OF 2030

If Thorndike had been asked to anticipate the types of instructional materials and tools that would be available at the end of the 20th century, it is doubtful that he would have imagined classrooms with personal computers and electronic texts. It seems equally challenging for me to envision what the classroom of 2030 will be like. Currently, most teachers still use books—textbooks, trade books, picture books, and so on—as the basis of their classroom instruction. However, with rapidly advancing technologies, and the decreasing cost of those technologies, the possibility of many more teachers employing electronic texts grows. As such, continued research into comprehension of electronic texts is a necessity. I envision classroom instruction routinely involving electronic and animated storybooks. With the ability to hyperlink text and images, vocabulary and background information will be more readily accessible within one text, and only one click away. Teachers and students alike will need to understand how to utilize effectively the features of electronic texts to prevent possible blocks to comprehension.

Along with electronic texts, I see the continued use of electronic whiteboards and other, yet unknown technologies as tools for classroom instruction. Students will be able to access fictional text outlines, class-generated questions and diagrams, and other resources wirelessly. However, regardless of the vehicle of delivery, it will remain critically important that teachers understand how to utilize these technologies to plan and implement effective comprehension instruction for narrative texts. There will continue to be a crucial need for professional development to instruct teachers on how to use electronic instructional tools, and to create engaging and effective comprehension instruction around those tools.

Finally, the potentially isolating effect of technology use increases the need to discover ways of engaging students with one another, either face-to-face or through electronic media to discuss the fictional text that they read. Teachers must be aware of the sociological impact of changing technology so they can prepare instructional activities that both enhance comprehension and facilitate social learning.

While the classroom of 2030 seems a long way off, it will be upon us before we know it. The time to plan is now! Research that anticipates changes in the classroom of tomorrow is crucial. Philip Crosby (1995) once said, "If anything is certain, it is that change is certain. The world we are planning for today will not exist in this form tomorrow." As literacy researchers, we do not have the luxury of planning for today. We must plan for the future.

SUMMARY

The possibilities for the future of classroom instruction are limitless. However, before those possibilities become reality, there are still students who must learn how to comprehend fictional text. Research has shown that various instructional frameworks are useful for teaching children to comprehend nonfiction texts (e.g., see Concept-Oriented Reading Instruction [Guthrie et al., 1998], Collaborative Strategic Reading [Vaughn et al., 1998], and Questioning the Author [Beck, McKeown, Worthy, Sandora, & Kucan, 1996]). Research must still examine the use of instructional frameworks with fictional texts, especially with beginning readers who use fictional texts as the basis of much of their classroom instruction. In the future, crafting effective comprehension lessons using fictional texts will be made easier by further research into instructional frameworks.

INTEGRATE, INVESTIGATE, AND INITIATE: QUESTIONS FOR DISCUSSION

1. Describe the typical manner in which fictional texts are taught to students in the school or school district in which you work. How can this traditional model be improved based on what you have read in this chapter?
2. I suggested that two effective ways to rapidly advance the comprehension of fiction is to use reciprocal teaching and SREs more frequently. Do you agree that these are effective methods? What others would you like to add to the list?
3. Interview a colleague or parent. Ask what he or she does to help a student or child to comprehend a fictional text while reading. Before you conduct this interview, however, prepare a list of three points from this chapter to suggest for consideration and use in their present practices.

REFERENCES

Anderson, V. (1992). A teacher development project in transactional strategy instruction for teachers of severely reading-disabled adolescents. *Teaching and Teacher Education, 8*(4), 391–403.

Beck, I. L., McKeown, M. G., Worthy, J., Sandora, C. A., & Kucan, L. (1996). Questioning the Author: A year-long classroom implementation to engage students with text. *Elementary School Journal, 96*, 385–414.

Betts, A. A. (1946). *Foundations of reading instruction*. New York: American Book Company.

Block, C. C., Gambrell, L. B., & Pressley, M. (2002). *Improving comprehension instruction: Rethinking research, theory, and classroom practice*. San Francisco: Jossey-Bass.

Block, C. C., & Israel, S. E. (2004). The ABCs of performing highly effective think-alouds. *Reading Teacher, 58*(2), 154–167.

Brown, R., Pressley, M., Van Meter, P., & Schuder, T. (1996). A quasi-experimental validation of Transactional Strategies Instruction with low-achieving second-grade readers. *Journal of Educational Psychology, 88*(1), 18–37.

Collins, C. (1991). Reading instruction that increases thinking abilities. *Journal of Reading, 34*(7), 510–516.

Cooke, C. L. (2002). *The effects of scaffolding multicultural short stories on students' comprehension and attitudes*. Unpublished doctoral dissertation, University of Minnesota, Twin Cities, MN.

Crosby, P. B. (1995). *Philip Crosby's reflections on quality: 295 inspirations from the world's foremost quality guru*. New York: McGraw-Hill.

Duffy, G. G. (2003). *Explaining reading: A resource for teaching concepts, skills, and strategies*. New York: Guilford Press.

Duffy, G. G., Roehler, L. R., Sivan, E., Rackliffe, G., Book, C., Meloth, M. S., et al. (1987). Effects of explaining the reasoning associated with using reading strategies. *Reading Research Quarterly, 22*(3), 347–368.

Graves, M., & Graves, B. (2003). *Scaffolding Reading Experiences: Designs for student success*. Norwood, MA: Christopher-Gordon Publishers.

Guthrie, J. T., Van Meter, P., Hancock, G. R., Alao, S., Anderson, E., & McCann, A. (1998). Does concept-oriented reading instruction increase strategy use and conceptual learning from text? *Journal of Educational Psychology, 90*(2), 261–278.

Liang, L. A. (2004). *Using scaffolding to foster middle school students' comprehension of and response to short stories*. Unpublished doctoral dissertation, University of Minnesota, Twin Cities, MN.

Liang, L. A., Peterson, C. A., & Graves, M. F. (2005). Investigating two approaches to fostering children's comprehension of literature. *Reading Psychology: An International Quarterly, 26*(4–5), 387–400.

Myers, P. A. (2005). The Princess Storyteller, Clara Clarifier, Quincy Questioner, and the Wizard: Reciprocal teaching adapted for kindergarten students. *Reading Teacher, 59*(4), 314–324.

Palincsar, A. S. (1986). The role of dialogue in providing scaffolded instruction. *Educational Psychologist, 21*(1–2), 73–98.

Palincsar, A. S., & Brown, A. L. (1984). Reciprocal teaching of comprehension-fostering and comprehension-monitoring activities. *Cognition and Instruction, 1*(2), 117–175.

Pressley, M., El-Dinary, P. B., Gaskins, I., Schuder, T., Bergman, J. L., Almasi, J., et al. (1992). Beyond direct explanation: Transactional instruction of reading comprehension strategies. *Elementary School Journal, 92*(5), 513–555.

Stauffer, R. G. (1969). *Directing reading maturity as a cognitive process*. New York: Harper & Row.

Tierney, R. J., & Readence, J. E. (2000). *Reading strategies and practices: A compendium*. Boston: Allyn & Bacon.

Vaughn, S., Hughes, M. T., Schumm, J. S., & Kingner, J. (1998). A collaborative effort to enhance reading and writing. *Learning Disability Quarterly, 21*, 57–74.

Vygotsky, L. S. (1967). Play and its role in the mental development of the child. *Soviet Psychology, 5*, 6–18.

Vygotsky, L. S. (1978). *Mind in society: The development of higher psychological processes*. Cambridge, MA: Harvard University Press.

Wood, D., Bruner, J. S., & Ross, G. (1976). The role of tutoring in problem solving. *Journal of Child Psychology and Psychiatry, 17*, 89–100.

12

Explicit Instruction Can Help Primary Students Learn to Comprehend Expository Text

JOANNA P. WILLIAMS

> The sciences of grammar and logic are little more than attempts methodically to classify ideas and to trace certain laws of relationship among them. The forms of relation between them, becoming themselves in turn noticed by the mind, are treated as conceptions of a higher and more abstract order.
> —WILLIAM JAMES, *Talks to Teachers on Psychology* (1899)

The ultimate goal of reading is to get meaning from the printed page. Readers use the information in a text, along with other information that they have already acquired, to construct a meaningful representation of the text. Some small but important amount of the textual information has to do not with the text's content, but with its structure. This structural information helps readers organize the content information and construct their mental representation (i.e., the meaning of the text).

There are different types of structural information in a text. Sometimes explicit markers in the surface text may guide the reader, such as the signal terms *first* or *as a result*. These terms identify the particular genre of the text (narrative or expository) and the particular type of structure within a genre. There may also be titles or headings that cue the overall organization of the text. But even without such obvious signals, structure is inherent in a text's organizational pattern, which reflects the logical connection among the ideas in the text (Meyer & Poon, 2001).

Proficient readers have a sense of the structures that exist, so that even when there are no surface cues to the text's structure, and even with text that is not organized effectively, they can organize the information presented in text into a well-structured mental representation. Of course, these organizational patterns are not merely text structures; they represent general rhetorical structures (Dickson, Simmons, & Kame'enui, 1998).

My purpose in this chapter is to examine what we have learned about helping students take advantage of the structure that in fact exists in text, and thereby improve their reading comprehension. Specifically, this chapter highlights the following:

- How we can make students aware that text has structure.
- How we can teach them to identify the cues that exist in text.
- How we can provide practice, so that all students learn to respond to those cues.
- How we can teach students to apply their knowledge of structure when they come upon texts that are not well organized.

WHAT'S OUT THERE TODAY: ESTABLISHED RESEARCH AND PRACTICE

Use of structural information is usually an automatic process, but sometimes it is not. Readers must be able to apply their knowledge consciously on occasions when they run into comprehension difficulties. Thus instruction becomes a matter of teaching students strategies that they will be able to apply when they become aware of the need to do so (Pressley & McCormick, 1995).

Many studies have indicated that knowledge of text structure is related to reading achievement, and difficulties arising from a lack of understanding of text structure have been described (Gersten, Fuchs, Williams, & Baker, 2001). Problems occur more often with expository text than with narrative text. Narrative text generally follows a single structural pattern, story grammar (Mandler & Johnson, 1977). Young children, before they start school, have developed sensitivity to narrative structure. They can identify the basic elements of a simple story (i.e., setting, main character, major actions and reactions of the characters, and story resolution). Although their comprehension of narrative does not ordinarily reach the more advanced level of theme until they are older (Williams, Brown, Silverstein, & de Cani, 1994), most kindergarten and first-grade students are successful at the plot level.

Expository text, on the other hand, often presents problems. One reason is that expository text typically involves unfamiliar content in complex logical relationships (Stein & Trabasso, 1981). Moreover, there are several different types of expository structure: description, sequence, listing, comparison, cause–effect, and problem–solution (Meyer & Poon, 2001).

Past instructional studies are few, but the results are promising. They usually focus on students in middle school or beyond. For example, Armbruster, Anderson, and Ostertag (1987) gave middle school students either instruction in the problem–solution structure or more traditional instruction that included general comprehension questions and summarization. Compared to other students, structure-trained students recalled more of what they read and also identified more main ideas. Dickson (1999) found that the comparison structure could be taught successfully in middle school general education classrooms. Bakken, Mastropieri, and Scruggs (1997) found that eighth-grade students with learning disabilities who were explicitly taught relevant strategies were better able to recall important information from expository text.

However, very little research on text structure instruction focuses on young children. Indeed, rather little attention is given to expository text in the elementary school classroom. Only a very small amount of expository text has been included in basal readers (Hoffman et al., 1994). Teachers rarely read such books aloud to students (Campbell,

Kapinus, & Beatty, 1995). Chall, Jacobs, and Baldwin (1990) suggested that this lack of experience with expository text contributes to the commonly observed fourth-grade slump in reading achievement.

Over the past several years there have been calls for a greater emphasis on expository texts in elementary school. For example, Pappas (1993) has shown that young children recognize expository language and can recall the content of expository trade books. On the basis of this and similar evidence, the National Research Council (Snow, Burns, & Griffin, 1998) has recommended that there be more exposure to expository text in the first years of schooling. The term *exposure* is critical here; most of the interest is in providing primary grade students with more opportunities to listen to expository text.

NEW RESEARCH IN COMPREHENSION OF EXPOSITORY TEXT

Developmental issues are of major concern at the primary level. Smolkin and Donovan (2001, 2003) described the course of learning to read in terms of Krashen's monitor theory of second language acquisition and learning. According to Krashen (1976), two knowledge systems underlie children's second language performance. The first, *acquisition*, operates in an unconscious fashion, and the second, *learning*, operates during formal instruction. Smolkin and Donovan conceptualized the development of reading and reading comprehension as following the same pattern. They compare the stage of emergent literacy to Krashen's *acquisition* system; children pick up some awareness of print simply through exposure to their environment. In the first grade, they learn letter–sound relationships and writing, which typically they would not pick up on their own without instruction. These tasks are based on simple associative learning, which first graders can handle developmentally.

However, according to Smolkin and Donovan (2001, 2003), children are not developmentally ready for comprehension *learning* at the first-grade level and into the second grade. At that point, they are responsive to texts read to them, so they can benefit from informal read-alouds and discussions, but not from formal comprehension instruction.

This is a very different point of view from that taken in other areas of the curriculum, where explicit instruction has been found to be highly effective. The National Reading Panel (2000) has shown that such instruction is very effective in beginning reading, which covers alphabetics and word recognition. This type of instruction follows classic principles of good instructional design (i.e., content is introduced in small increments, moving from the simple to the complex), providing (1) modeling by the teacher; (2) scaffolding that fades as instruction progresses; and (3) at each step, substantial practice and feedback, first guided and then independent. Such a systematic, explicit approach to comprehension instruction in the primary grades has not yet been undertaken seriously.

The design of any instructional program, whether explicit and systematic or not, involves another critical decision: What is the nature of the content of the texts that are to be used? Several investigators, including Guthrie and Ozgungor (2002), Pressley (2002), and Williams, Hall, and Lauer (2004), have suggested that it would be effective to teach reading comprehension even to young students within the context of content area learning. Texts would then be selected at least partly on the basis of the information they provide about social studies, science, or other content areas.

This suggestion has been welcomed by many educators in the reading field (Gersten et al., 2001). However, the actual increase in the amount of time spent on reading (and mathematics) over the last few years has led to a substantial reduction in the amount of attention given to other subject areas. In fact, the Center on Education Policy (2006) reported that three-fourths of the school districts they polled in a national survey now spend less time on teaching the content areas, notably social studies and science. Investigators have pointed out that this not only limits the acquisition of the social studies and science content but also reduces opportunities to develop critical thinking and problem-solving skills usually acquired when studying these topics (Ferretti & Okolo, 1996; Lee, Buxton, Lewis, & LeRoy, 2006).

Thus, embedding reading comprehension training within social studies or science instruction might be an attractive proposition for both reading and content area educators. However, if doing so resulted in diminished acquisition of the social studies or science content, the value of that instruction would be lessened considerably. A challenge, then, is to embed reading comprehension training within content instruction in such a way that there is no loss in the amount of content taught.

CLOSE ANALYSIS OF TEXTS WITH STRUCTURE (CATS): CAUSE AND EFFECT

For the past few years my students and I have been involved in developing and evaluating instruction that embeds comprehension training within instruction in social studies or science. We developed a program that provides instruction in the cause–effect structure, embedded within the social studies domain. The program followed an explicit instructional model that included explanation and modeling by the teacher, and guided, then independent, practice. The content goal was to teach students about three historical communities in the United States (colonists, pioneers, and immigrants at the turn of the 20th century)—specifically, about homes, schools, and jobs in those communities.

Most second-grade instruction involves a great deal of speaking and listening; many students at that level are not yet fluent readers. We included in our program a typical second-grade mix of listening–speaking and reading–writing tasks. The same cognitive processes are basic to both listening and reading comprehension (Perfetti, Marron, & Foltz, 1996), and our goal was to improve comprehension, as demonstrated in either oral or written language.

An important element of our training was the close analysis of specially written, well-structured target paragraphs to serve as exemplars of the cause–effect text structure. Students analyzed these paragraphs using three strategies: (1) clue words to identify a text as a cause–effect text; (2) a graphic organizer to lay out the relevant information in the text; and (3) a series of questions that would help students focus on the important information in the text. This training was incorporated into a CATS program that featured biographies and informational trade books related to the social studies content that was taught, classroom discussion, and vocabulary work. In this study (Williams et al., 2007) we asked the following questions: (1) Will our instructional program help second graders at risk for academic failure improve their comprehension? and (2) Can this goal be accomplished without a decrease in the amount of content knowledge that students acquire from the program?

Fifteen classroom teachers from three elementary schools in New York City volunteered to participate in the study. Almost all of the students in these schools were members of minorities (75% of them were Hispanic), and 93% of them received state aid in the form of free or reduced-price lunch. Approximately 5% were enrolled in either part-time or full-time special education services.

The teachers were randomly assigned to one of three experimental conditions: our text structure program; a content program that used the same materials (including the target paragraphs) and required the same amount of training time but did not focus on the cause–effect instruction (treated control); or a no-instruction control. Conditions were blocked by school. All statistical analyses were performed with the classroom as the unit of analysis.

All of the students in the 10 instructed classrooms received their instruction from their classroom teacher. The students who returned letters from their parents/guardians granting permission to participate in our study were given a pretest and a posttest. We randomly selected 12 students from each classroom for the statistical analysis.

The Target Paragraphs

Ten short, well-structured cause–effect paragraphs were written specifically for the program. In the first unit of the program (on colonists), each target paragraph comprised several causation sentences; each sentence included one cause, one effect, and a clue word. In the second unit (on pioneers), each paragraph contained one cause and multiple effects. The cause and each effect appeared in separate sentences. The third unit (on immigrants) included both types of paragraphs. Examples of the two types of paragraphs are as follows:

> From Lesson 3—One cause–one effect paragraph:
>
> *Houses in early colonial days were simple. At first, the keeping room was the only main room in the house; therefore, the family cooked, ate, and worked in that room. Later, colonists built more rooms, since they needed more space for their growing family. Babies stayed in the keeping room, because the parents needed to take care of them.*

> From Lesson 12—One cause–multiple effects paragraph (this paragraph also contained one sentence with noncausal information):
>
> *Schools on the prairie had very little money. Thus, in the schoolhouse there was only one teacher who taught kids of all ages. Children would study reading, writing, spelling, math, history, and geography. Kids had to bring their own books to the schoolhouse. Schools did not have heaters.*

Readability of the target paragraphs was at the third-grade level according to the Dale–Chall Readability Scale—rather high, because some of the words in the text (i.e., words relevant to the program content and some of the clue words) are unfamiliar words on the Dale–Chall Reading List. However, our students were quite familiar with these words, because they were taught as vocabulary words. The mean readability level calculated with our vocabulary words considered as familiar words was at the second-grade level.

Overview of the Text Structure Program

The CATS program contained three units, each of which focused on one historical community. There were 22 lessons. First, an introductory lesson introduced both the concept of cause–effect and program content through a trade book that follows a boy and his mother as they explore their community (Caseley, 2002). Then, for each unit, a lesson introduced the focus community via a biography of a young person living in that community. This lesson included a read-aloud and discussion, and an introduction to the relevant vocabulary. There were six additional lessons in each unit: two lessons each on home, schools, and jobs. Each pair of lessons was organized around a target paragraph and included further read-alouds from a second trade book. The first lesson on each feature included instruction on the following:

1. *Concepts of cause and effect.* The students were introduced to the definition of *cause* and *effect*. *Effect* was defined as a thing or event that happens, and *cause*, as the person, thing, or event that makes the effect happen. Students developed their understanding of these concepts through picture cards, matching, and cloze activities.

2. *Cause–effect clue words.* In Lesson 1, students were introduced to four cause–effect clue words—*because*, *since*, *therefore*, and *thus*. As the program continued, they memorized the clue words and used them to identify paragraphs as cause–effect paragraphs.

3. *Vocabulary.* The 15 vocabulary words were related to the content of the program (e.g., *community, colonist, immigrant, keeping room, tenement, blacksmith*) and were embedded in the target paragraphs; they were also presented as a list of words that were explained and illustrated through examples.

4. *Trade book read-aloud and discussion.* Specific passages from a trade book were read aloud. Students were encouraged to ask questions and share comments.

5. *Community chart.* A chart for each unit listed the vocabulary words organized by feature (*home*, *school*, *job*) for further review. During the second and third units, words from previous charts were reviewed.

6. *Cause–effect questions (beginning in the second unit).* With the introduction of the second type of paragraph (one cause–multiple effects), the students learned two generic questions designed to help them focus on the cause–effect information in the text rather than on irrelevant details or prior knowledge: What is the cause? and What is the effect?

7. *Read-aloud and analysis of the target paragraph.* Students read the target paragraph first silently and then aloud. The class analyzed the cause–effect structure of the first type of paragraph (one cause–one effect) by circling the clue word and underlining the part of the sentence that followed the clue word (the cause or the effect). Causes and cause clue words were marked with a blue crayon, and effects and effect clue words, with a green crayon. For the second type of paragraph (one cause–multiple effects), the students circled the clue word and underlined what followed it. Then they used the cause–effect questions to guide the analysis of the rest of the paragraph. Sentences that included noncausal information were introduced in Lesson 12 and identified as irrelevant to the causal analysis.

The second lesson on each feature included instruction on the following:

1. *Graphic organizer.* The students completed a graphic organizer for the target paragraph. There were two organizers, one for each paragraph type (for examples, see Chambliss & Calfee, 1998). This helped the students visually organize the three elements in a cause–effect sentence: *cause*, *effect*, and *clue word*.

2. *Comprehension questions.* Students answered three types of questions abut the target paragraph. The first was noncausal (e.g., How many teachers worked in a schoolhouse?). The second type asked about causes (e.g., Why did a schoolhouse have only one teacher?), and the third asked about effects (e.g., What are the effects of having very little money for schools?). We showed students that they could find the answers to the comprehension questions in the completed graphic organizer, as well as in the target paragraph.

3. *Lesson review*. Each lesson ended with a review of the strategies (clue words, cause–effect questions, and graphic organizer), as well as the content covered.

Overview of the Content Program

The Content program represented a more conventional approach and was used in our treated control group. It taught the same social studies content and used the same materials (target paragraphs, trade books, and charts) as the CATS Text Structure program, but it did not focus on cause–effect structure. As in the other program, there were 22 lessons: one introductory lesson; three lessons introducing each historical community via the biography; and two lessons on each of the three features within each unit.

The lessons in this program began with a discussion of the students' background knowledge about the community (colonist, pioneer, or immigrant) and the feature (home, school, or job) that were the foci of the lesson. This was done through a K-W-L procedure (what I Know, what I Want to know, and what I Learned). The teacher recorded responses to "what I Know" on a chart. Then, with the help of the teacher, the students generated questions about what they wanted to know, and the teacher recorded these. The "what I Learned" portion of the chart was completed during the second half of each lesson. At this point, the students attempted to answer the questions they had generated at the beginning of the lesson and added other details discussed during the course of the lesson.

The graphic organizer used in this program was an information web. In the center of the web was a labeled depiction of a home, school, or job, surrounded by several blank circles connected by a line to the center picture. Students filled in the circles with information that they learned during the lesson.

When students read, first silently and then aloud, the target cause–effect paragraph, they did not identify it as such. Rather, the paragraph was presented as another opportunity to read and learn about the community, and about the feature that was targeted in the lesson.

The students in the Content program answered the same noncausal questions as the students in the CATS Text Structure program. They also answered additional, noncausal questions pertaining to the information in the target paragraph. Content students also kept a journal, in which they each drew a picture of something related to the lesson's topic (e.g., immigrant jobs) and wrote a paragraph about the drawing.

When we introduced teachers to the program they were to teach in individual sessions of 30–45 minutes, we discussed the program's overall goals and reviewed each section of the lesson. One of the strengths of our program is that it does not take an inordinate amount of explanation to familiarize teachers with its features. We have found that after being guided through the details of just one of the lessons, teachers are able to work through all the lessons on their own. All the materials needed during the instruction are available in the lessons. We encouraged teachers to use their own judgment and expertise to decide how best to present each section of the lessons.

Assessing Performance

We gave a short pretest comprising five of the measures that were also administered on the posttest. No differences among the three treatment groups were found on the pretest. We observed each of the 10 instructed classrooms twice during the course of the instruction to assess fidelity to treatment. We found that teachers taught every section of every lesson except the review, which was taught in about half of the lessons we observed. (The review may have been omitted due to the length of the lessons.)

The posttest comprised individual, audiotaped interviews. It included an extensive array of strategy and outcome measures. First, we evaluated how well the students learned the strategies that the program taught. The four strategy measures required students to locate clue words in texts, to identify cause clauses and effect clauses in sentences, to use the graphic organizer appropriately, and to recall the generic cause–effect questions. On all four of these measures, the CATS Text Structure group outperformed the other two groups, which did not differ from each other. This pattern of findings reached statistical significance on the first two of these measures. Thus, the students were successful at learning the strategies.

There were three content outcome measures designed to determine how much of the social studies content had been acquired. We asked questions that tapped the information presented in the target paragraph pertaining to the three main features of the communities (home, school, job—the principal content that the program taught), and that tapped other information presented in the target paragraphs and vocabulary questions. On all three of these measures, the CATS Text Structure and the Content groups did not differ, and both groups were significantly superior to the no-instruction control group. These findings indicated that the cause–effect training did not result in a diminished amount of content acquisition.

The rest of the outcome measures pertained to comprehension: what the students had learned from the cause–effect instruction. These measures for the most part involved paragraphs with social studies content. Both one cause–one effect and one cause–multiple effects paragraphs were represented in the posttests. Students were required to answer both cause questions and effect questions.

The first of these measures assessed the effect of explicit teaching and required a written response. There was no effect of treatment on the cause question. On the effect question, the CATS Text Structure group significantly outperformed the Content group, which did not differ from the no-instruction group.

The other four measures, all of which required oral responses, assessed transfer. Two of these measures assessed performance on paragraphs that although not seen in training were written in the same well-structured format as the target paragraphs. The other two measures assessed performance on paragraphs taken from trade books (i.e., they were authentic texts and as such were not as well structured as the other paragraphs). For three of these four transfer paragraphs, the same pattern was found as that seen on the explicitly taught paragraph: There was no effect of treatment condition on the causal question, but the text structure group significantly outperformed the content and the no-instruction groups on the effect question. (The fourth transfer measure, one of the two authentic texts, showed no differences among the groups on either the cause or the effect question, probably because the content of the paragraph was rather abstract.)

Effect sizes on these measures were substantial. The lowest effect size among the significant effects was 1.57, indicating that all of the significant effects could be considered large effects.

Results and Conclusions

The results of this study confirmed our expectations, except for the fact that the text structure group did not outperform the other groups on the cause question. Perhaps the students were sufficiently familiar with the cause concept to be able to deal with it successfully at the level of difficulty inherent in the content of the paragraphs we used. Our instruction, however, did improve performance on the more difficult effect concept.

Overall, the results indicated that second graders at risk for academic failure can benefit from explicit comprehension instruction. These results extend our earlier findings from a series of studies focused on the compare–contrast structure (Williams et al., 2004, 2005). Those studies also showed that explicit training in comprehension embedded in content area instruction can be effective, without detracting from the amount of content acquired.

How This New Knowledge Can Improve Comprehension Instruction

Although this study showed that our cause–effect program was effective, we are not yet completely satisfied. Data we collected during classroom observations and feedback from the teachers suggested places where our program might be improved. We have undertaken a revision. One important change we have made is at the beginning of the instruction, where we now introduce the cause–effect structure in the context of individual sentences instead of entire paragraphs. We also provide more practice on everyday content before moving into the less familiar content of social studies. (The cause–effect structure is considered one of the most challenging of the basic text structures [Ciardiello, 2002]). In addition, we have simplified the graphic organizer and the generic questions, and we include only the one cause–one effect pattern.

We are also in the process of developing instruction in other structures. Our ultimate goal is to develop an evidence-based, whole-year curriculum that covers all the basic expository text structures.

DIRECTIONS FOR FUTURE RESEARCH

Our work to date has convinced us that young students' comprehension abilities can be improved substantially. We encourage others to take up some of the issues that we have been addressing:

1. *How can teacher–researcher collaborations be designed to maximize the expert contributions that each can make to a study?* Our instructional programs and evaluations have benefited a great deal from our consultations with the teachers who have worked with us over the years. Their insights have provided valuable ideas for improving the programs. We encourage more teacher–researcher collaborations.

2. *How can text structure training be effectively transferred to all content area courses?* In this chapter we have discussed research demonstrating the positive effects of infusing text structure training into social studies content. In other work we have also shown such effects using science content (Williams et al., 2005). Some of these techniques might well be suitable for certain aspects of mathematics instruction, such as word problems.

3. *How effective is each step in the process of explicit comprehension instruction outlined in this chapter?* We would like to see more empirical studies of the effects of instructional programs such as ours. Our research to date has focused on evaluating our programs in their entirety, as the programs would be presented in the classroom. It would be of value to undertake studies that focus on one element at a time, to determine which are the (more) effective instructional components.

PROJECTIONS AND POSSIBILITIES FOR THE CLASSROOM OF 2030

As of 2007, one of the hopes I most often hear expressed is that the professional development of classroom teachers of reading comprehension will be improved. We have begun to research better methods of accomplishing this challenging task, and it seems likely that we will have made great strides in this pursuit by 2030. I believe that the work involved in the design of instructional programs such as those I have described here will contribute to reaching the crucial goal of excellent professional development.

I also expect that there will be positive changes in the use of technology to deliver reading comprehension instruction to young children, as well as to assess their achievement. Although at present there is still controversy about the effectiveness of reading technology products at the elementary school level (Dynarski et al., 2007), it is difficult to believe that we will not find effective means of using technology in the early grades. Because one of the virtues of using technology in instruction is the fact that technology requires clarity and explicitness, I believe that the use of educational technology will help keep alive the emphasis on explicit, structured instruction that has proved so valuable in so many areas of education over the years, including beginning reading (Fletcher, Lyon, Fuchs, & Barnes, 2007), and that is just beginning to take hold in the area of comprehension instruction.

SUMMARY

Second graders are often not fluent readers. But they can benefit from the type of explicit comprehension instruction described in this chapter that combines listening and reading. Our research has shown that an explicit, structured approach to primary grade comprehension instruction can be effective.

Many of the strategies and activities included in our programs have been adapted from similar successful instruction at higher grades. What is more unusual here is the prominent position given to well-structured texts in our programs. Students spend a considerable amount of time reading, analyzing, and discussing short texts that have been written expressly for the purpose at hand (i.e., to model the particular structure under study). This is one of the critically important elements of our instruction.

Of course, it will take more than one research program to resolve the issue of how to provide effective, explicit comprehension instruction to primary grade children. I hope that others will address this issue and contribute to the evidence base.

INTEGRATE, INVESTIGATE, AND INITIATE: QUESTIONS FOR DISCUSSION

1. Discuss with colleagues the challenges that exist in the instruction of expository texts.

2. An argument was made in this chapter that providing explicit instruction can increase children's comprehension of nonfictional material. Please describe the five most important steps in explicit instruction that you will use and encourage others to use in the future instruction of nonfictional texts.

3. Prepare a lesson that contains the features described in this chapter. Select a specific content area, trade book, or textbook on which to base this lesson. Share your lessons with colleagues. Discuss how use of the features described in this chapter can improve students' comprehension of nonfictional texts.

REFERENCES

Armbuster, B. B., Anderson, T. H., & Ostertag, J. (1987). Does text structure/summarization instruction facilitate learning from expository text? *Reading Research Quarterly, 22*, 331–346.

Bakken, J. P., Mastropieri, M. A., & Scruggs, T. E. (1997). Reading comprehension of expository science material and students with learning disabilities: A comparison of strategies. *Journal of Special Education, 31*, 300–324.

Campbell, J. R., Kapinus, B., & Beatty, A. S. (1995). *Interviewing children about their literacy experiences: Data from NAEP's integrated reading performance at grade 4*. Washington, DC: U.S. Department of Education.

Caseley, J. (2002). *On the town: A community adventure*. New York: Greenwillow.

Center on Education Policy. (2006). *From the capitol to the classroom: Year 4 of the No Child Left Behind Act*. Washington, DC: Author.

Chall, J. S., Jacobs, V. A., & Baldwin, L. E. (1990). *The reading crisis: Why poor children fall behind*. Cambridge, MA: Harvard University Press.

Chambliss, M. J., & Calfee, R. C. (1998). *Textbooks for learning*. Malden, MA: Blackwell.

Ciardiello, A. V. (2002). Helping adolescents understand cause/effect text structure in social studies. *Social Studies, 93*, 31–36.

Dickson, S. (1999). Integrating reading and writing to teach compare–contrast text structure: A research-based methodology. *Reading and Writing Quarterly, 14*, 49–79.

Dickson, S. V., Simmons, D. C., & Kame'enui, E. J. (1998). Text organization: Research bases. In D. C. Simmons & E. J. Kame'enui (Eds.), *What reading research tells us about children with diverse learning needs* (pp. 239–277). Mahwah, NJ: Erlbaum.

Dynarski, M., Agodini, R., Heaviside, S., Novak, T., Carey, N., Campuzana, L., et al. (2007). *Effectiveness of reading and mathematics software products: Findings from the first cohort*. Washington, DC: U.S. Department of Education, Institute of Education Sciences.

Ferretti, R. P., & Okolo, C. M. (1996). Authenticity in learning: Multimedia design projects in the social studies for students with disabilities. *Journal of Learning Disabilities, 29*, 45–60.

Fletcher, J. M., Lyon, G. R., Fuchs, L. S., & Barnes, M. A. (2007). *Learning disabilities: From identification to intervention*. New York: Guilford Press.

Gersten, R., Fuchs, L. S., Williams, J. P., & Baker, S. (2001). Teaching reading comprehension strategies to students with learning disabilities: A review of research. *Review of Educational Research, 71*, 279–320.

Guthrie, J., & Ozgungor, S. (2002). Instructional contexts for reading engagement. In C. C. Block & M. Pressley (Eds.), *Comprehension Instruction: Researcher-based best practices* (pp. 275–288). New York: Guilford Press.

Hoffman, J. V., McCarthy, S. J., Abbott, J., Christian, C., Corman, L., Curry, C., et al. (1994). So what's new in the new basals?: A focus on first grade. *Journal of Reading Behavior, 26*, 47–73.

James, W. (1899). *Talks to teachers on psychology: And to students on some of life's ideals*. New York: Holt.

Krashen, S. (1976). Formal and informal linguistic environments in language acquisition and language learning. *TESOL Quarterly, 10*, 157–168.

Lee, O., Buxton, C., Lewis, S., & LeRoy, K. (2006). Science inquiry and student diversity: Enhanced abilities and continuing difficulties after an instructional intervention. *Journal of Research in Science Teaching, 43*, 607–636.

Mandler, J. M., & Johnson, N. S. (1977). Remembrance of things parsed: Story structure and recall. *Cognitive Psychology, 9*, 111–151.

Meyer, B. J. F., & Poon, L. W. (2001). Effects of the structure strategy and signaling on recall of the text. *Journal of Educational Psychology, 93*, 141–159.

National Reading Panel. (2000). *Teaching children to read: An evidence-based assessment of the scientific research literature on reading and its implications for reading instruction*. Washington, DC: National Institute of Child Health and Human Development.

Pappas, C. C. (1993). Is narrative "primary"?: Some insights from kindergarteners' pretend reading of stories and information books. *Journal of Reading Behavior, 25,* 97–129.

Perfetti, C. A., Marron, M. A., & Foltz, P. W. (1996). Sources of comprehension failure: Theoretical perspectives and case studies. In C. Cornoldi & J. V. Oakhill (Eds.), *Reading comprehension difficulties: Processes and remediation* (pp. 137–165). Mahwah, NJ: Erlbaum.

Pressley, M. (2002). What should comprehension instruction be the instruction of? In M. L. Kamil, P. B. Mosenthal, P. D. Pearson, & R. Barr (Eds.), *Handbook of reading research* (Vol. 3, pp. 545–561). Mahwah, NJ: Erlbaum.

Pressley, M., & McCormick, C. (1995). *Advanced educational psychology.* New York: Harcourt Brace.

Smolkin, L. B., & Donovan, C. A. (2001). The contexts of comprehension: The information book read aloud, comprehension acquisition and comprehension instruction in a first-grade classroom. *Elementary School Journal, 102,* 97–129.

Smolkin, L. B., & Donovan, C. A. (2003). Supporting comprehension acquisition for emerging and struggling readers: The interactive information book read-aloud. *Exceptionality, 11,* 25–38.

Snow, C. E., Burns, M. S., & Griffin, P. (Eds.). (1998). *Preventing reading difficulties in young children.* Washington, DC: National Academy Press.

Stein, N. L., & Trabasso, T. (1981). What's in a story: An approach to comprehension and instruction. In R. Glaser (Ed.), *Advances in instructional psychology* (Vol. 2, pp. 213–267). Hillsdale, NJ: Erlbaum.

Williams, J. P., Brown, L.G., Silverstein, A. K., & de Cani, J. S. (1994). An instructional program for adolescents with learning disabilities in the comprehension of narrative themes. *Learning Disabilities Quarterly, 17,* 205–221.

Williams, J. P., Hall, K. M., & Lauer, K. (2004). Teaching expository text structure to young at-risk learners: Building the basics of comprehension instruction. *Exceptionality, 12,* 129–144.

Williams, J. P., Hall, K. M., Lauer, K. D., Stafford, K. B., DeSisto, L. A., & de Cani, J. S. (2005). Expository text comprehension in the primary grade classroom. *Journal of Educational Psychology, 94,* 235–248.

Williams, J. P., Nubla-Kung, A. M., Pollini, S., Stafford, K. B., Garcia, A., & Snyder, A. E. (2007). Teaching cause–effect text structure through social studies content to at-risk second graders. *Journal of Learning Disabilities, 40,* 111–120.

13

Explanation and Science Text
Overcoming the Comprehension Challenges in Nonfiction Text for Elementary Students

LAURA B. SMOLKIN, ERIN M. McTIGUE, and CAROL A. DONOVAN

> If we wish students to gain insights and understanding of the manner and nature of scientific reasoning, we must offer them opportunity to use and explore that language, i.e. to read science, to discuss the meaning of its texts, to argue how ideas are supported by evidence, and to write and communicate in the language of science.
> —JONATHAN OSBORNE (2002)

Even when the science is well presented, as Graesser, Leon, and Otero (2002) have commented, "it is hardly a secret that students find most science texts very difficult to comprehend" (p. 1). Science text comprehension is made difficult by many factors, including, but not limited to, prior knowledge (both its absence and its inaccuracies), the abstract nature of certain science topics, unfamiliar text structures at both macro- and microlevels, as well as children's degree of reading and graphical interpretation abilities, including metacognition (Otero, Leon, & Graesser, 2002).

With the education field's increased attention to knowledge building and nonfiction text reading in the primary grades (e.g., Duke, 2000; Neuman, 2001; Pappas, 1991; Purcell-Gates, Duke, & Martineau, 2007; Smolkin & Donovan, 2001; Williams, 2007), the use of expository science texts has now spread from the upper elementary grades to children as young as preschool age (Leung, 2004). Although this change has been important in terms of exposing children to text structures, concepts, and vocabulary that may aid in overcoming Chall, Jacobs, and Baldwin's (1990) "fourth-grade slump," it has meant that the complexities of science text comprehension now present themselves to teachers and students across the elementary grades. At the same time, elementary science textbooks and trade books themselves have changed, reflecting an increasingly heavy use of graphics (e.g., Martins, 2002; Moss, 2001) and presenting new challenges to elementary readers (Walpole, 1998–1999) and their teachers (Walpole & Smolkin, 2004).

From the viewpoint of science educators, helping students to seek and to understand explanations should be an essential focus in science instruction (National Research Council, 2000). However, the results of studies over time (e.g., Dagher & Cossman, 1992; Newton & Newton, 2000; Russell, 1983) suggest that teachers, in their presentation of science, offer limited instruction in how to recognize—nor do they themselves model—explanatory statements (but see new work on scientific explanation writing; e.g., McNeill, Lizotte, Krajcik, & Marx, 2006). Given the importance of explanations in science and their absence in teachers' science-related talk, Newton, Newton, Blake, and Brown (2002) suggested that explanations in science text merit increased attention. With the many changes to the visual aspects of science textbooks, we posit that visual explanations also merit increased attention. In this chapter, we report on two of our recent studies that have focused on increasing readers' interactions with explanatory aspects of science text in both verbal and visual forms.

This chapter highlights the following:

- Verbal explanations in primary grade science trade books and teachers' explanations during science trade book read-alouds.
- Graphical explanations in upper elementary science texts and students' ability to comprehend those graphics.
- Suggestions for elementary teachers to increase their students' comprehension of science texts.

WHAT'S OUT THERE TODAY: ESTABLISHED RESEARCH AND PRACTICE

The place of text in elementary science instruction has long been controversial, with many science educators advocating for a heavier weighting of experience over textual encounters (e.g., National Education Association, 1893; Rutherford, 1991). As Yore, Craig, and Maguire (1998) explained, these calls for a diminished presence of text in elementary classrooms generally arose from perceptions of science reading as "a passive, text-driven, meaning-taking process, while science learning was perceived as an active, hands-on, meaning-constructing process" (p. 28). Science textbooks continue to come under particular criticism, for their overly heavy emphasis on science as fact and description rather than explanation (e.g., Newton et al., 2002), their failure to address students' commonly held misconceptions (e.g., Kesidou & Roseman, 2002) and the actual integrity of the presented information (e.g., Hubisz, 2001, 2003).

Increasing Presence of Graphics in Students' Science Texts

Additionally, Hubisz (2001, 2003), in his review of middle school (sixth through eighth grade) textbooks, pointed to an overabundance of visual representations, including "diagrams and drawings that represent impossible situations" (Hubisz, 2001, p. 305).

> The depictions of light passing through a prism were often incorrect. Electrical circuits were frequently drawn improperly, as were mirror and lens figures.... In our study, we found mostly pictures, sidebars, and capsules that interrupted what little text there was. Apparently, text is seen as much too slow a medium for disseminating information. (Hubisz, 2003, p. 51)

This heavy increase in graphics, which may have followed the Dorling Kindersley model for informational text presentations (see Moss, 2001), appears designed to increase student interest. Dorling Kindersley, a British publishing company (now owned by Pearson), began its unique visual style with the publication of the *First Aid Manual* (St. John Ambulance, St. Andrew's Ambulance Association, & British Red Cross Society, 1982). This work featured a multitude of pictures on a glossy white background to support a modest amount of text. Unfortunately, as Walpole (1998–1999) has shown, children can become confused in their navigation of multiple graphical representations on a page, struggle to determine their meaning, and be unclear about how the text and the visual representations work together. In fact, increasing numbers of studies suggest that even in the upper elementary grades, children have trouble interpreting the graphical representations typically found in science textbooks (e.g., Stylianidou, Ormerod, & Ogborn, 2002; Watkins, Miller, & Brubaker, 2004). This problem is further compounded in textbooks published within the last few years. These newer works often use graphics to present new information rather than to reiterate or duplicate information that can be gained from the text alone (see Mayer, 1997; but for an author/illustrator's perspective on picture–text relationships, see Smolkin & Donovan, 2005).

Presence of Texts and Textbooks in Elementary Science Instruction

Nonetheless, elementary teachers have continued to rely upon science texts and, in particular, on science textbooks (Shymansky, Yore, & Good, 1991). In a recent survey (Weiss, Banilower, McMahon, & Smith, 2001), 85% of fifth- through eighth-grade teachers reported employing textbooks in their science instruction, generally relying upon a single textbook. Though similar, that picture was somewhat different in kindergarten through fourth-grade classrooms, where 64% of surveyed teachers reported using a science textbook. In those earlier elementary grades, however, teachers more frequently reported using multiple texts for science instruction, some of which no doubt include science trade books given that the National Science Teachers Association and the Children's Book Council have collaborated in publishing the Outstanding Science Trade Book lists since 1973, and that science publications have been assessing and recommending children's science-related trade books since at least the 1930s (e.g., Billig, 1930).

Elementary Teachers and Explanations in Science

It seems likely that elementary teachers' strong attraction to science textbooks arises, at least to some degree, from insecurities about their own scientific content knowledge base (e.g., Harlen & Holroyd, 1997; King, Shumow, & Lietz, 2001; Schoon & Boone, 1998). This self-perceived weakness leads many teachers to limit their science instruction to the topics with which they feel most comfortable, generally life sciences (Appleton, 2007). Also, as Harlen and Holroyd (1997) suggested, it may lead teachers to avoid questions and discussion. In fact, observations of elementary science teaching reveal that the science instruction of elementary school teachers lacks an emphasis on explanation (Newton & Newton, 2000) or, for that matter, on higher-order thinking (King et al., 2001). In Britain, Newton and Newton (2000) found that teachers with stronger science backgrounds tended to ask upper elementary students for more explanations than did those without such backgrounds, but they found no such similar difference in the primary grades, leading them to suggest that teachers may view younger children as unable to understand the reasons underlying scientific phenomena. Here in the United States, this lack of attention to explanation has been found to persist even when teachers have been engaged in professional development created by the National Science Foundation (Banilower, Boyd, Pasley, & Weiss, 2006).

Explanations in Science Texts

Concerned by the lack of explanatory teaching they had observed, Newton et al. (2002) suggested that there might "be other 'teachers' in a classroom and that these might show a concern for knowing why" (p. 229). Accordingly, they turned their attention to explanatory passages in a sample of science texts produced by all major education publishers in Britain. (See Table 13.1 for examples of explanatory and descriptive science texts we have created or selected.) In that work, they divided the text of 53 books into clauses, then coded the clauses as *condition, consequence* (effect), *causal explanation, purpose, prediction, aim, directing attention*, or *irrelevant* to the subject matter. Their final category, *not differentiated*, contained clauses that might more commonly be thought of as fact and description. By far, the majority of clauses fell into this last category, with percentages ranging from a low of 70.9 in a text on electricity to a high of 100.0 in a book on earth in space. Of interest to us were the categories *condition, consequence* (effect), and *cause*, which are particularly important in the development of children's scientific reasoning (see Zimmerman, 2000). Clauses of condition ranged from a low of 0% to a high of 12.2% in a text. Clauses of consequence (effect) ranged from a low of 0% to a high of 12.5%. Clauses of cause ranged from a low of 0% to a high of 6.7%. Newton and colleagues (2002) concluded that most science texts, like the teaching of elementary teachers, focused on facts and description. They did, however, note that not all the books were like this, that certain books reflected "some concern for explanatory understanding" (p. 237). If teachers used such books in their science instruction, they suggested, it "could help them change their practices" (p. 237).

Also concerned with explanatory aspects of science texts, Mayer and Gallini (1990) turned their attention to particular types of diagrams that explain how a physical process in science works. The participants in this study, in contrast to the elementary focus of the Newtons' studies, were college-age skilled readers, with varying knowledge about the subject matter—the braking system of automobiles. Mayer and Gallini prepared one verbal text with a written explanation of how a braking system works. Working with a single drawing of the braking system, they then created four conditions, in which each subject read the same text but was presented with a different diagram condition. In the *parts*

TABLE 13.1. Descriptive versus Explanatory Text

Descriptive	Explanatory
A glacier moves a few inches to several yards each day. Snow gathers at its higher end. The leading edge of the glacier is the end that is at a lower elevation. This part of the glacier often starts to melt. As glaciers advance, they get wider and thicker.	A glacier moves a few inches to several yards each day. Whenever more snow gathers at its higher colder end, the added weight helps push the glacier down the mountainside. The leading edge of the glacier is the end that is at a lower elevation where the temperature is warmer. This part of the glacier often starts to melt. If snow is added to the high end of the glacier faster than it melts from the leading edge, the glacier **advances** [emphasis in the original]. It gets wider and thicker, and its leading edge moves farther downhill (Winner, 1999, p. 15).

condition, the parts of the braking system were labeled; in the *steps condition*, the steps (i.e., processes) of the braking system were labeled; in the *parts and steps condition*, both the parts and steps were labeled. Finally, in the control condition, subjects read only the text. The results indicated that the only diagram condition that facilitated comprehension of the text was the *parts and steps diagram*. Merely having the components of the system (*parts*), or the processes labeled (*steps*) did not help readers' comprehension. These findings led to the realization that not every diagram (even accurate diagrams) enhances comprehension, and that apparently minor changes to a diagram design can greatly alter the effectiveness of an instructional graphic.

NEW RESEARCH IN THIS AREA

Intrigued by these two studies on explanation and science text, we decided to create two very different studies, both of which would focus on science text and give us further understanding of the explanatory aspects of elementary school science instruction. In Study 1, using a typical read-aloud format for science text presentation in the primary grades, we pursued the Newton et al. (2002) suggestion that teachers' acts of explanation might be greater than had been observed during instruction if they were to read a text containing many explanatory passages. In Study 2, using a student reading situation typical of science text use in the upper elementary grades, we replicated Mayer and Gallini's (1990) study to determine whether improved graphics enhance students' comprehension of explanatory science text. Because of the significance of the text in these two studies, we begin each study's section with a description of the materials.

Study 1: Primary-Grade Teachers' Explanatory Efforts during a Science Trade Book Read-Aloud

Prior to this study, we had replicated the Newton et al. (2002) study with a corpus of highly recommended science trade books (Smolkin, Donovan, McTigue, & Coleman, 2005). From that work, we found that physical science trade books were more likely to contain what we termed "science reasoning clauses" than were life science trade books (our science reasoning included all Newton et al. [2002] categories except for *direct attention* and *facts and description*). Given these findings (and despite our awareness that elementary teachers are more challenged by earth science), we selected for Study 1 an earth science trade book, *Planet Earth/Inside Out*, by Gail Gibbons (1995), a well known, highly regarded children's information book writer. We analyzed the clauses of this book with our adaptation of Newton et al.'s (2002) coding system. Our analysis revealed the book to contain 61.4% *fact and description* clauses; the remainder we coded as *condition*, *effect*, or *cause*. This trade book, therefore, had significantly less emphasis on facts and descriptions, and more emphasis on explanation than any book in Newton et al.'s (2002) study.

Participants and Procedures

Eleven primary grade—three first-grade, four second-grade, and four third-grade—teachers participated in the study. All teachers were given a copy of *Planet Earth/Inside Out* and a tape recorder. Their instructions were to turn on the tape recorder before they began, to read the book as they would usually conduct a read-aloud, then turn off the tape recorder.

Data Analysis

We transcribed the teachers' audiotapes, then divided all their commentary and questions regarding the book into clauses, following Halliday's (1994) attention to the clause as critical in oral communication. Working together, two raters coded all teacher comments and questions regarding the text; differences were resolved though discussion. To aid us in examining explanatory aspects of the teachers' talk, we relied upon Blank, Rose, and Berlin's (1978) Discourse Analysis System. As applied to adults, Level 1 of that system, *Matching Perception*, represents adult moves (both questions and comments) that focus children's attention on text and pictures to notice, label, locate, or practice a term. Level 2, *Selective Analysis*, represents adult moves that support children's understanding through descriptions of objects. Level 3, *Reordering Perception*, entails adult moves designed to help children synthesize information through summarization and integration of personal experiences. Level 4, *Reasoning*, addresses adult efforts at formulating "explicitly the reasons and logic responsible" (Blank et al., 1978, p. 32) for relationships among objects or events. Although researchers (Hammett, van Kleeck, & Huberty, 2003; Price, van Kleeck, & Huberty, 2006; van Kleeck, Gillam, Hamilton, & McGrath, 1997) consider both Levels 3 and 4 as higher-order reasoning, we have been particularly interested in Level 4, with its stress on cause, condition, and effect, seen by Zimmerman (2000) as critical to science understanding.

Results and Discussion

Our goal was descriptive in nature; we sought to determine the types and amounts of discourse teachers would produce when interacting with a book with a strong emphasis on explanation. Our coding at Level 3 revealed many efforts by teachers to assist children in integrating prior knowledge or current science studies with the text. Level 3 discourse increased from 34.6% for first-grade teachers to 38.9% for second-grade teachers to 55.9% for third-grade teachers. Given that third graders in this school had engaged in greater amounts of earth science, this increase in Level 3 activity by their teachers made considerable sense.

In terms of teacher discourse at Level 4, such clauses accounted for 25.3% of first-grade teachers' discourse, 19% of second-grade teachers' discourse, and 15% of third-grade teachers' discourse. Although these percentages seem to reflect a decline in attention to reasoning about text across the three grades, we believe they must be considered in light of the increasing Level 3 activity across the grades to integrate text information with children's prior knowledge. When considered together, Levels 3 and 4 accounted for 59.9% of first-grade teachers' discourse, 57.9% of second-grade teachers' discourse, and 70.9% of third-grade teachers' discourse. No matter the interpretation, these Level 4 percentages reveal a significantly greater emphasis on explanatory discourse than the 8% explanatory talk reported by Newton and Newton (2000) in their observations of teachers. These data suggest that children could come to consider explanation as critical to science text comprehension through a low road to transfer of learning (see Salomon & Perkins, 1989; see also Smolkin & Donovan, 2002), in which well-practiced routines (e.g., discussing explanations) are triggered by similar situations.

Study 2: Sixth-Grade Students Reading Explanatory Science Texts with Graphics

As explained earlier, we decided to replicate Mayer and Gallini's (1990) work on explanatory graphics with upper elementary school students. We knew that elementary students were less likely to have studied physical science than life science (e.g., Martin, Mullis, Gonzalez, & Chrostowski, 2004). We were interested to see whether the science discipline had an impact on students' comprehension. Our goal in this study was to determine which type of diagram best supported sixth graders' understanding of explanatory text (for a description of the complete study, see McTigue, 2006).

Text Creation

We created two verbal texts, one life science and the other physical science, from existing informational science passages, then employed Coh-Metrix (Graesser, McNamara, Louwerse, & Cai, 2004) to make the texts as comprehensible as possible. Coh-Metrix is a "Web-based software tool . . . [that] analyzes texts on over 50 types of cohesion relations and over 200 measures of language, text, and readability" (p. 194). The life science text explained the life cycle of a sporozoan, whereas the physical science text explained the workings of a heat combustion engine. We then adapted the diagrams for both the sporozoan and engine texts from the original informational science passages. For each diagram, following Mayer and Gallini (1990), we created three conditions that differed only by inserted text boxes to address (1) labeled *parts*, (2) labeled *steps*, and (3) labeled *parts and steps*. Our final condition was a control in which no diagrams were present in the text.

Comprehension Measures

The comprehension questions we created were either explicit, addressing the factual details of the texts, or implicit, assessing students' conceptual understanding of the main principles and their applications. Post- and pretest measures differed in that the posttest contained additional items that asked students specific questions endemic to the passage.

Participants and Procedures

The participants were 180 sixth-grade students recruited from 11 sixth-grade language arts classes in a suburban, middle-class, school system in the mid-Atlantic region. One week prior to the experiment, the students completed a pretest on the subject matter as a control for prior knowledge. The day of the experiment, each child read one version of both the life cycle text and the physical science text, answering questions after each, with controls for order effects.

Results and Discussion

Regarding the life cycle texts, the students with the *steps* diagram performed best. We speculate that this diagram design helped to emphasize the "verbs" of science, therefore focusing readers on the major interactions of the system rather than simply on the "nouns" of science, enabling them to answer our implicit questions. This finding contrasted with Mayer and Gallini's (1990) results in which the *parts and steps diagram* group was the only condition to outperform the control, a disparity that was likely the result of differences in the overall reading ability and science knowledge of Mayer and Gallini's participants (college students) and ours (sixth graders). As a result, the most complex diagram design, with both the parts and steps labeled, may have created a scenario of cognitive overload rather than a helpful instructional support for our upper elementary school readers (Sweller, van Merriënboer, & Paas, 1998). Alternatively, the readers may simply have judged the *parts and steps diagram* as too formidable and avoided it entirely (e.g., Halliday, 1976).

The results from the physical science text differed markedly from those of the life science text. In short, the diagrams showed no effect on students' comprehension of the physical science text. Although there are multiple potential reasons for the diagrams' failure, including cognitive overload as the students struggled to comprehend a text and graphic on their less familiar topic, here we turn our attention to the diagram itself.

Our physical science text, which depicted the transformation of energy, in contrast to our life science text, is abstract and difficult to visualize (e.g., try to make a mental picture of "energy"). Although the diagram's purpose was to make the text more tangible, it seems likely that for students who had never seen a steam turbine engine, the symbolic representation in the diagram did not correspond to a preexisting, tangible understanding. Although they could see from the label that the purple rectangle represented the turbine, this likely did not activate a mental image of an actual turbine. This lack of concreteness would make the impact of the diagram less effective (Sadoski, 2001). In contrast, the life science text dealt with the human body and mosquitoes, both quite familiar, visible aspects of life. As a result, that text might have been more visually accessible and, therefore, illustrated in a less ambiguous manner.

HOW THIS NEW KNOWLEDGE CAN IMPROVE COMPREHENSION INSTRUCTION

These two studies provide much to think about in terms of science text comprehension in elementary classrooms. The results of the primary grade read-aloud study suggest that science text selection can play a critical role in determining teacher discourse and explanative reasoning with young children. Our attention on teacher discourse derives from our own (Smolkin & Donovan, 2002) and others' (e.g., Dickinson & Smith, 1994) contention that children learn to reason about text as they engage in read-alouds with parents and teachers. Given van Kleeck et al.'s (1997) finding that levels of parental reasoning influence their children's levels of reasoning 1 year later, it is reasonable to conclude that teachers' talk about reasoning in science will later affect students' ability to reason about the concepts presented in science text. To us, this suggests that the texts selected for information book read-alouds related to science instruction merit a new kind of attention from science educators as they assess trade books to recommend for teachers—attention that focuses on the explanatory aspects of those texts.

Regarding the results of our study of graphics and science text, we believe there are several classroom implications. First, these results, as do others examining children's comprehension of graphics, suggest that comprehension instruction needs to include attention on how to read and to make meaning from graphics. Second, children's inability to find strong support for comprehension from the most complex diagram, *parts and steps*, suggests that science textbook designers may need to revise their current irrationally exuberant stance that more graphical information on a page is a desirable trait. In the absence of such revisions, teachers will need to be equipped to teach comprehension strategies that guide their students in dealing with a situation we have come to think of as "graphical dismay."

DIRECTIONS FOR FUTURE RESEARCH

These two studies suggest many possibilities for future research. Below we present some of our favorites.

1. *What is the impact of primary grade teachers' read-alouds of explanatory rich science trade books on their students' future comprehension of science text, as well as their ability to provide scientific explanations in oral and written forms (e.g., Rowan, 1990)?* For example, would children from such primary grade classrooms have better comprehension of their upper elementary science textbooks than students who had not participated in such read-alouds? During their upper-grade science instruction, would these students be more likely to offer explanations of science phenomena than students who had not participated in explanatory-rich science trade book read-alouds?

2. *How best can we teach graphics to elementary school students to enhance their comprehension of science texts?* This line of work would address which diagrams are most developmentally appropriate for which ages of children, and which instructional techniques best enable children not only to interpret graphical representations but also to integrate visual and verbal text information. This line of work would also determine which instructional techniques are best for struggling readers and whether new types of teaching supports/aids are necessary for English language learners.

3. *What would controlled experiments reveal if we compared elementary school students' comprehension of current science textbooks, representing today's irrational exuberance, to those of the past, with their more limited graphical presence (e.g., Moss, 2001)?* For example, would we find students' comprehension to be improved when a single, well-designed graphic accompanies text, as opposed to a Dorling Kindersley–like page on which multiple graphical representations appear with text describing each representation?

4. *Which types of graphical study would best prepare elementary students for their future comprehension of science text, including the reading of high school science textbooks and popular science articles (e.g., Parkinson & Adendorff, 2004)?* Such work would begin by categorizing and quantifying the frequencies of graphic representations in high school science textbooks and in popular science articles. Instruction for an experimental group of elementary science students would include the interpretation of such graphics, whereas students in a control group would not receive this specific graphical emphasis. Knowledge of graphics and their influence on science text comprehension could then be measured in later years, once science knowledge, reading skill, and reading strategy knowledge have been controlled (O'Reilly & McNamara, 2007).

PROJECTIONS AND POSSIBILITIES FOR THE CLASSROOM OF 2030

As we consider the future of elementary school students' science text comprehension, we see primary grade classrooms in which teachers read science trade books rich in explanatory passages and discuss with students the meanings of the graphical, as well as explanatory, aspects of these texts. We see these teachers not only reading aloud and explaining the ideas in the text and graphics but also encouraging students to share their own understandings of the text ideas. We see them guiding their students in presenting explanations for science experiments' results, both in verbal and visual manners. Such practice will provide students with additional exposure to the macro- and microlevel text structures endemic to science writing and support their understanding of the multimodal nature of science discourse.

As children progress through the elementary grades, we will see them working with textbooks whose graphics have been carefully researched and feature strong explanations for science phenomena, including phenomena that children have examined through classroom experiments. We see teachers providing developmentally based instruction in how to interpret the various diagrams most commonly found in the texts children will encounter in future science studies and encouraging their students to include appropriate graphical representations in their own science writing. In our ideal classroom, students would move comfortably between explanation-rich visual and verbal representations of science far more frequently than they do now. Although the preferred order of visual and verbal presentations is not presently clear, we might envision students transforming their knowledge from verbal (perhaps the scientists' notebook genre created by Palincsar & Magnusson, 2001; Magnusson & Palincsar, 2004) to visual (science experiments or narrated multimedia, see Moreno & Mayer, 2002) to verbal presentations (both teacher-led discussions that focus on conceptual development and explanation, as well as well-designed textual presentations). Ultimately, students would demonstrate their new understandings in visually enhanced text representations.

SUMMARY

This chapter has explored some of the issues related to explanatory science text comprehension. We have presented two of our current studies examining the impact of text type and graphical representations on teachers and students in the elementary grades, and have considered the implications of that work for text-related science instruction. Importantly, these studies suggest that it may be possible to change the nature of elementary school teachers' science-related talk by providing instructional materials that focus on the explanatory talk sought by science educators, and that we must pay particular attention to graphical representations in the science texts created for K–6 students.

INTEGRATE, INVESTIGATE, AND INITIATE: QUESTIONS FOR DISCUSSION

1. Given your professional experience, and your present educational role and responsibility, what are the challenges to providing the best instruction of nonfictional texts for elementary students under your care? Based on what you've learned in this chapter, what first step can you take this week to begin to overcome that challenge? Share the results of what you did with colleagues. Go to a bookstore or your school library and ask the librarian to show you a nonfictional science book written within the last 5 years. Ask the librarian to also give you one of the books written on the same topic in the 1980s or 1990s. Skim through both books. What differences are publishers trying to incorporate into the newest trade books to help students comprehend sciences, based on the principles you've learned in this chapter?

2. Create a lesson that you could use to complete a read-aloud more effectively using a science trade book. If possible, incorporate as many innovations from this chapter as you can. After you complete that lesson, share with colleagues both your successes and the improvements and adaptations you will make in future read-aloud experiences using nonfictional texts.

REFERENCES

Appleton, K. (2007). Elementary science teaching. In S. K. Abell & N. G. Lederman (Eds.), *Handbook of research on science education* (pp. 493–535). Mahwah, NJ: Erlbaum.

Banilower, E. R., Boyd, S. E., Pasley, J. D., & Weiss, I. R. (2006). *Lessons from a decade of mathematics and science reform: A capstone report for the local systemic change through teacher enhancement initiative*. Chapel Hill, NC: Horizon Research.

Billig, F. (1930). Review of the book *Green Magic*. *Science Education, 15*(1), 70.

Blank, M., Rose, S. A., & Berlin, L. J. (1978). *The language of learning: The preschool years*. New York: Grune & Stratton.

Chall, J. S., Jacobs, V. A., & Baldwin, L. E. (1990). *The reading crisis: Why poor children fall behind*. Cambridge, MA: Harvard University Press.

Dagher, Z., & Cossman, G. (1992). Verbal explanations given by science teachers: Their nature and implications. *Journal of Research in Science Teaching, 29*, 361–374.

Dickinson, D. K., & Smith, M. W. (1994). Long-term effects of preschool teachers' book readings on low-income children's vocabulary and story comprehension. *Reading Research Quarterly, 29*(2), 104–122.

Duke, N. K. (2000). 3.6 minutes per day: The scarcity of informational texts in first grade. *Reading Research Quarterly, 35*, 202–224.

Gibbons, G. (1995). *Planet earth/inside out*. New York: Morrow Junior Books.

Graesser, A. C., Leon, J. A., & Otero, J. (2002). Introduction to the psychology of science text comprehension. In J. Otero, J. A. Leon, & A. C. Graesser (Eds.), *The psychology of science text comprehension* (pp. 1–15). Mahwah, NJ: Erlbaum.

Graesser, A. C., McNamara, D. S., Louwerse, M. M., & Cai, Z. (2004). Coh-Metrix: Analysis of text on cohesion and language. *Behavior Research Methods, Instruments, and Computers, 36*, 193–202.

Halliday, M. A. K. (1994). *An introduction to functional grammar* (2nd ed.). London: Arnold.

Holliday, W. G. (1976). Teaching verbal chains using flow diagrams and texts. *Audio–Visual Communication Review, 24*, 63–78.

Hammett, L. A., van Kleeck, A., & Huberty, C. J. (2003). Patterns of parents' extratextual interactions during book sharing with preschool children: A cluster analysis study. *Reading Research Quarterly, 38*(4), 442–468.

Harlen, W., & Holroyd, C. (1997). Primary teachers' understanding of concepts of science: Impact on confidence and teaching. *International Journal of Science Education, 19*, 93–105.

Hubisz, J. (2001). Report on a study of middle school physical science texts. *Physics Teacher, 39*, 304–309.

Hubisz, J. (2003). Middle-school texts don't make the grade. *Physics Today, 56*(5), 50–54. Available: *www.physicstoday.org/vol-56/iss-55/p50.html*.

Kesidou, S., & Roseman, J. E. (2002). How well do middle school science programs measure up?: Findings from Project 2061's curriculum review. *Journal of Research in Science Teaching, 39*, 522–549.

King, K., Shumow, L., & Lietz, S. (2001). Science education in an urban elementary school: Case studies of teacher beliefs and classroom practices. *Science Education, 85*(2), 89–110.

Leung, C. B. (2004). *Preschoolers' acquisition of vocabulary from participation in repeated read-aloud events and retellings involving informational picture books about light and color*. Paper presented at the 54th annual conference of the National Reading Conference. San Antonio, TX.

Magnusson, S., & Palincsar, A. S. (2004). Learning from text designed to model scientific thinking in inquiry-based instruction. In W. Saul (Ed.), *Crossing borders in literacy and science instruction: Perspectives on theory and practice* (pp. 316–333). Newark, DE: International Reading Association.

Martins, I. (2002). Visual images in school science texts. In J. Otero, J. A. Leon, & A. C. Graesser (Eds.), *The psychology of science text comprehension* (pp. 73–90). Mahwah, NJ: Erlbaum.

Martin, M. O., Mullis, I. V. S., Gonzalez, E. J., & Chrostowski, S. J. (2004). *TIMMS 2003 international science report: Findings from IEA's trends in international mathematics and science study at the eighth and fourth grades*. Chestnut Hill, MA: Boston College.

Mayer, R. E. (1997). Multimedia learning: Are we asking the right questions? *Educational Psychologist, 32*, 1–19.

Mayer, R. E., & Gallini, J. K. (1990). When is an illustration worth ten thousand words? *Journal of Educational Psychology, 82*, 715–726.

McNeill, K. L., Lizotte, D. J, Krajcik, J., & Marx, R. W. (2006). Supporting students' construction of scientific explanations by fading scaffolds in instructional materials. *Journal of the Learning Sciences, 15*, 153–191.

McTigue, E. M. (2006). *Graphical support for comprehending science texts: The contributions of diagram design and text directives*. Unpublished doctoral thesis, University of Virginia, Charlottesville.

Moreno, R., & Mayer, R. E. (2002). Learning science in virtual reality multimedia environments: Role of methods and media. *Journal of Educational Psychology, 94*, 598–610.

Moss, G. (2001). To work or play?: Junior age nonfiction as objects of design. *Reading, 35*, 106–110.

National Education Association. (1893). *Report of the Commission on Secondary School Studies*. Washington, DC: Author.

National Research Council. (2000). *Inquiry and the national science education standards: A guide for teaching and learning*. Washington, DC: National Academy of Sciences.

Neuman, S. (2001). The role of knowledge in early literacy: A review of selected technical reports from the Center for the Improvement of Early Reading Achievement. *Reading Research Quarterly, 36*, 468–475.

Newton, D. P., & Newton, L. D. (2000). Do teachers support causal understanding through their discourse when teaching primary science? *British Educational Research Journal, 26*, 601–613.

Newton, L. D., Newton, D. P., Blake, A., & Brown, K. (2002). Do primary school science books for children show a concern for explanatory understanding? *Research in Science and Technological Education, 20*, 227–240.

O'Reilly, T., & McNamara, D. S. (2007). The impact of science knowledge, reading skill, and reading strategy on more traditional "high-stakes" measures of high school students' science achievement. *American Educational Research Journal, 44*, 161–196.

Otero, J., Leon, J. A., & Graesser, A. C. (Eds.). (2002). *The psychology of science text comprehension*. Mahwah, NJ: Erlbaum.

Palincsar, A. S., & Magnusson, S. J. (2001). The interplay of first-hand and second-hand investigations to model and support the development of scientific knowledge and reasoning. In S. Carver & D. Klahr (Eds.), *Cognition and instruction: Twenty-five years of progress* (pp. 151–194). Mahwah, NJ: Erlbaum.

Pappas, C.C. (1991). Fostering full access to literacy by including information books. *Language Arts, 68*, 449–462.

Parkinson, J., & Adendorff, R. (2004). The use of popular science articles in teaching science literacy. *English for Specific Purposes, 23*, 379–396.

Price, L. H., van Kleeck, A., & Huberty, C. J. (2006). *Patterns of parents' extratextual utterances during book sharing with preschool children: A comparison between storybook and expository book conditions*. Unpublished manuscript, University of North Carolina, Chapel Hill, Chapel Hill, NC.

Purcell-Gates, V., Duke, N. K., & Martineau, J.A. (2007). Learning to read and write genre-specific text: Roles of authentic experience and explicit teaching. *Reading Research Quarterly, 42*, 8–45.

Rowan, K. E. (1990). Cognitive correlates of explanatory writing skill: An analysis of individual differences. *Written Communication, 7*, 316–341

Russell, T. L. (1983). Analyzing arguments in science classroom discourse: Can teachers' questions distort scientific authority? *Journal of Research in Science Teaching, 20*(1), 27–45.

Rutherford, F. J. (1991). Vital connections: Children, books, and science. In W. Saul & S. A. Jagusch (Eds.), *Vital connections: Children, science, and books*. Washington, DC: Library of Congress.

Sadoski, M. (2001). Resolving the effects of concreteness on interest, comprehension, and learning important ideas from text. *Educational Psychology Review, 13*, 263–281.

Salomon, G., & Perkins, D. N. (1989). Rocky roads to transfer: Rethinking mechanisms of a neglected phenomenon. *Educational Psychologist, 24*(2), 113–142.

Schoon, K. J., & Boone, W. J. (1998). Self-efficacy and alternative conceptions of science of preservice elementary teachers. *Science Education, 82*, 553–568.

Shymansky, J. A., Yore, L. D., & Good, R. (1991). Elementary school teachers' beliefs about and perceptions of elementary school science, science reading, science textbooks, and supportive instructional factors. *Journal of Research in Science Teaching, 28*, 437–454.

Smolkin, L. B., & Donovan, C. A. (2001). The contexts of comprehension: The information book read aloud, comprehension acquisition, and comprehension instruction in a first-grade classroom. *Elementary School Journal, 102*, 97–122.

Smolkin, L. B., & Donovan, C. A. (2002). "Oh excellent, excellent question!": Developmental differences and comprehension acquisition. In C. C. Block & M. Pressley (Eds.), *Comprehension instruction: Research-based best practices* (pp. 140–157). New York: Guilford Press.

Smolkin, L. B., & Donovan, C. A. (2005). Looking closely at a science trade book: Gail Gibbons and multimodal literacy. *Language Arts, 83*, 52–62.

Smolkin, L. B., Donovan, C. A., McTigue, E. M., & Coleman, J. M. (2005, December). *Scientific reasoning included in science trade books used for elementary science instruction*. Paper presented at the National Reading Conference, Miami, FL.

St. John Ambulance, St. Andrew's Ambulance Association, & British Red Cross Society. (1982). *First aid manual*. London: Dorling Kindersley.

Stylianidou, F., Ormerod, F., & Ogborn, J. (2002). Analysis of science textbook pictures about energy and pupil's readings of them. *International Journal of Science Education, 24*, 257–283.

Sweller, J., van Merriënboer, J. J. G., & Paas, F. (1998). Cognitive architecture and instructional design. *Educational Psychology Review, 10*, 251–295.

van Kleeck, A., Gillam, R., Hamilton, L., & McGrath, C. (1997). The relationship between middle-class parents' book sharing discussion and their preschoolers' abstract language development. *Journal of Speech, Language, and Hearing Research, 40*, 1261–1271.

Walpole, S. (1998–1999). Changing texts, changing thinking: Comprehension demands of new science textbooks. *Reading Teacher, 52*, 358–369.

Walpole, S., & Smolkin, L. (2004). Teaching the page: Teaching learners to read complex text. In A. Peacock & A. Cleghorn (Eds.), *Missing the meaning: The development and use of print and non-print materials in diverse school settings* (pp. 197–212). New York: Palgrave-Macmillan.

Watkins, J. K., Miller, E., & Brubaker, D. (2004). The role of the visual image: What are children really learning from pictorial representations? *Journal of Visual Literacy, 24*, 23–40.

Weiss, I. R., Banilower, E. R., McMahon, K. C., & Smith, P. S. (2001). *Report of the 2000 National Survey of Science and Mathematics Education*. Chapel Hill, NC: Horizon Research.

Williams, J. P. (2007). Literacy in the curriculum: Integrating text structure and content area instruction. In D. S. McNamara (Ed.), *Reading comprehension strategies: Theories, interventions, and technologies* (pp. 199–219). New York: Erlbaum.

Yore, L. D., Craig, M. T., & Maguire, T. O. (1998). Index of science reading awareness: An interactive–constructive model, test verification, and grades 4–8 results. *Journal of Research in Science Teaching, 35*, 27–51.

Zimmerman, C. (2000). The development of scientific reasoning skills. *Developmental Review, 20*, 99–149.

14

Learning to Think Well
Application of Argument Schema Theory to Literacy Instruction

ALINA REZNITSKAYA, RICHARD C. ANDERSON, TING DONG,
YUAN LI, IL-HEE KIM, and SO-YOUNG KIM

> Thought is not merely expressed in words; it comes into existence through them.
> —VYGOTSKY (1962)

A voting booth and a jury box are among the many staples of American democracy. However, democracy implies not only the opportunity to have a choice but also the ability to make sound choices regarding political, social, scientific, and personal dilemmas. Students need to be able to interact critically with the information they receive from a variety of sources, and to use the process of rational argument to form and to justify their choices. Becoming proficient in the skills of argument should enable students "not just to think, but to think well" (Kuhn, 1991, p. 1).

The use of dialogue to promote argumentation development, long explored by theorists (Bakhtin, 1981; Mead, 1962; Vygotsky, 1962), has recently become the focus of empirical investigations (Anderson et al., 2001; Billings & Fitzgerald, 2002; Chinn & Anderson, 1998; Kumpulainen & Mutanen, 1999). Many of these empirical studies, however, have focused on argumentation development *during* group interactions, and have not fully addressed the transfer potential of engagement in a dialogue. An important question to consider next is whether dialogic interaction can promote what Perkins and Salomon (1987) call "far transfer," or an ability to use reasoning skills in contextually different situations. According to Perkins and Salomon, far transfer ought to be the desired goal of an educational enterprise, because it allows students to address "a wide range of intellectual challenges" (p. 287).

To date, research has determined that successful transfer is largely governed by the surface and structural similarities between the learning environment and transfer tasks

(Detterman, 1993; Druckman & Bjork, 1994; Gentner, 1989; Gick & Holyoak, 1987). It is not clear, however, which elements of these two situations must be similar and to what extent. In the four studies discussed in this chapter, we examine the effects of engagement in group oral argumentation on students' ability to produce a better argument individually and in writing. Specifically, we do the following:

- Present the theoretical assumptions motivating our research.
- Describe a pedagogical environment that embodies our theoretical assumptions.
- Review empirical studies investigating the transfer from oral to written argumentation conducted in the United States, China, and Korea.
- Discuss implications for classroom instruction.
- Suggest directions for future research.

ARGUMENT SCHEMA THEORY

Our work is influenced by several independent theoretical traditions that are integrated to form a new model that we call argument schema theory (AST; Reznitskaya & Anderson, 2002). Following structural theories of cognition (Anderson, 1977; Reed, 1993; Rumelhart, 1980), we propose that knowledge is organized and stored in memory symbolically as generic structures or schemas. Successful transfer entails accessing and applying appropriate mental schemas, which must be "sufficiently abstract as to characterize both the training and transfer task" (Gick & Holyoak, 1987, p. 31). For example, in a classic book, Schank and Abelson (1977) described a restaurant schema, or a knowledge structure abstracted from multiple experiences with eating out. A restaurant schema contains elements such as ordering, eating, and paying for food. To specify the elements involved in an argument schema, we draw upon the normative models proposed by argumentation theorists (e.g., Govier, 1985; Toulmin, 1958; Walton, 1996). In an influential book, Toulmin (1958) suggested a model of a rational argument, pioneering the effort to define nonoverlapping functions of the premises, including data, a warrant, and a qualifier. Other theorists expanded Toulmin's model to incorporate additional elements, such as a counterargument (Walton, 1996).

An important structural difference between the restaurant schema and the argument schema is that the restaurant schema typically would not include any explanatory knowledge associated with the process of visiting a restaurant. In contrast, separate elements of an argument schema are related through a theory explaining and justifying the meaning, configuration, and uses of a rational argument. In other words, argumentation ability relies, implicitly or explicitly, on one's theory of knowledge and knowing (King & Kitchener, 1994; Kuhn, 1992).

An example of an "explanatory framework" (Mishra & Brewer, 2003) that connects and justifies the elements of an argument schema is an *evaluatist* type of epistemology described by Kuhn (1991). Similar to others' conceptions of the higher stages of epistemological commitment (Dewey, 1933; Hofer & Pintrich, 1997; King & Kitchener, 1994; Perry, 1970), the evaluatist stance assumes that knowledge is relative and contextual, while also recognizing that some judgments are more reasonable than others. Evaluatists view knowledge as tentative and evolving through a reasoned justification of claims (Kuhn, 1991).

Our assumptions about the acquisition of argumentative knowledge are heavily influenced by the theoretical perspectives that emphasize the priority "in time and in fact" (Vygotsky, 1979, p. 30) of social interaction in individual learning (e.g., Luria, 1981; Mead, 1962; Rogoff, 1990; Vygotsky, 1962; Wertsch, 1985; Wertsch & Bivens, 1992). Through the process of internalization, children adopt and transform external processes experienced in social settings, thus advancing their cognitive development to higher levels (Vygotsky, 1981).

The educational value of the engagement in a social activity is derived from its *dialogic* organization (Bakhtin, 1981, 1986; Mead, 1962; Vygotsky, 1981). "It is in argumentation, in discussion, that the functional moments appear that will give rise to the development of reflection" (Vygotsky, as cited in Wertsch, 1985, p. 112). Deemphasizing the distinction between public argument and private thinking, Bakhtin writes that "our thought itself . . . is born and shaped in the process of interaction and struggle with others' thought, and this cannot but be reflected in the forms that verbally express our thought as well" (Bakhtin, 1986, p. 92). Similarly, Mead viewed individual reasoning as a process of internal argumentation, a dialogue with a "generalized other" (Mead, 1962, p. 156). The ability to incorporate the voices of "others" into one's own thinking should come from participating in dialogic discussions, where participants collectively formulate, defend, and scrutinize each other's claims.

Thus, according to our theory, argument schemas are developed through socialization into argumentative discourse in a collective setting. Pedagogically effective group discussions may potentially allow participants to use the discourse of reasoned argumentation in a variety of situations. While every discussion has unique features, AST postulates that dialogic discussions share important structural elements, such as formulating a claim, providing relevant reasons, questioning assumptions, and offering counterarguments. We project that by engaging in arguments during group discussions, students are provided with multiple instances from which the principles of argumentation can be abstracted. In other words, students generate mental representations of argument tactics, strategies, and principles, or argument schemas. Abstract properties of an argument schema should enable successful transfer of the acquired knowledge to new situations. Just as entering a new restaurant activates a restaurant schema that guides and directs an experience of eating out (Schank & Abelson, 1977), an encounter with a task requiring the use of argumentation should trigger a set of cognitive and social practices that constitute an argument schema.

AST also assumes that it is possible to postulate general, "field-invariant" characteristics of an argument. Although different domains (i.e., moral, scientific, legal) may have their own argumentation standards (Toulmin, 1958), even these "field-dependent" rules can be generalized across multiple contexts. Thus, we can think of argumentative knowledge as an aggregation of field-invariant and field-dependent rules, principles, and informal heuristics that together comprise an argument schema. Generalizing from research on various types of schemas and discourse structures (Anderson & Pichert, 1978; Bransford & Johnson, 1972; Brewer & Treyens, 1981; Chambliss, 1995; Cheng & Holyoak, 1985; Meyer, Brandt, & Bluth, 1980; Reed, 1993), students with developed argument schemas should be more proficient in retrieving, generating, and processing argument-relevant information (Reznitskaya & Anderson, 2002).

To summarize, AST provides an account of argumentative knowledge acquired through dialogic interaction. The theory allows for the generation of testable predictions regarding the acquisition and transfer of argumentative discourse. In the rest of the chapter, we discuss four studies that were designed to test our theory of argumentative knowledge transfer. According to AST, a student will apply knowledge of argumentation acquired in group oral discussions to a new written task performed individually and independently. We realize that a switch in communication modality can reduce the possibility of transfer (Pellegrini, Galda, & Rubin, 1984). In fact, some scholars suggest that oral argumentation provides "no model" for written discourse because, in an oral argument, "each idea is produced in response to the immediately preceding point," whereas a written argument requires "a new solitary ability" to generate the material (Freedman & Pringle, 1988, p. 79). On the other hand, Bakhtin (1986) argues for the absence of boundaries between oral and written communication, suggesting that "however monological the utterance may be . . . it cannot but be . . . a response to what has already been said about the given topic . . . , even though this responsiveness may not have assumed a clear-cut external expression" (p. 92). These existing theoretical disagreements, as well as the scarcity of research examining the issue of transfer from oral to written argumentation (cf. Kuhn, Shaw, & Felton, 1997), supported the need to conduct empirical investigations of the underlying assumptions of AST.

PEDAGOGICAL FRAMEWORK FOR PROMOTING ARGUMENTATIVE KNOWLEDGE

We examined implications of AST using a pedagogical model called collaborative reasoning (CR), an educational environment that embodies the structural and social leaning theoretical perspectives integrated through AST. CR is designed to promote argumentation development by engaging elementary school students in meaningful dialogue. During a typical CR discussion, students gather in small groups to discuss "big questions" raised in their readings. CR discussions typically last 15–25 minutes. Stories are carefully chosen to contain dilemmas that are central and common to students' experience, and that can provoke a lively controversy among the discussion participants. For example, *Paper Bag Princess* (Munsch, 2001) is a story about a princess who is going to marry a prince. One day, a dragon comes and burns down their castle and takes away the prince. The princess outwits the dragon and rescues the prince. She has nothing to wear but a paper bag, which is the only thing left after the castle burns. When the prince sees her, he tells her to go away and come back when she dresses herself like a princess. The question is: Should the princess marry the prince?

The contestable nature of CR discussion questions, in which nobody, not even the teacher, knows the "right answers," allows establishment of a truly egalitarian classroom community. In such a community, authority is shared and fluid rather than a role given to the teacher. This absence of authority based on institutionalized rules is an essential characteristic of genuine dialogue (e.g., Bakhtin, 1984; Burbules, 1993; Dewey, 1933; Freire, 1970).

During CR discussions, students take a position on the issue, support it with reasons and evidence from the story, and challenge other participants with counterarguments and rebuttals. They manage the discussions with little help from the teacher. Students don't have to raise their hand and can communicate freely without being nominated to speak by the teacher. Such open participation promotes a genuine dialogue and may thereby stimulate students' intellectual development. The teacher provides scaffolding for students' development, leading and supporting the inquiry into the issues raised by the students. Characteristic teaching strategies include (1) prompting students for their positions and reasoning; (2) demonstrating reasoning processes by thinking aloud; (3) challenging students with countering ideas; (4) acknowledging good reasoning; (5) summing up what students have said; and (6) using the vocabulary of critical and reflective thinking (Waggoner, Chinn, Yi, & Anderson, 1995).

Thus, CR pedagogy brings both a substantive and a procedural focus to bear on the subject of promoting higher-order thinking in a context of literacy instruction. It provides a much needed context for investigating influential yet under researched assumptions of social learning theories.

EMPIRICAL STUDIES OF ARGUMENT SCHEMA THEORY

The four studies described in this chapter employed the same posttest-only, quasi-experimental design in which intact elementary school classrooms were assigned to treatment conditions. Across the four studies, argumentation development was examined in 14 experimental classrooms that participated in CR and in 10 control classrooms that did not. Experimental and control classrooms were matched based on relevant demographic characteristics, including age, geographic location, and socioeconomic level. In three studies (Kim, 2001; Reznitskaya, Anderson, & Kuo, 2007; Reznitskaya et al., 2001), participants came from grades 4 and 5 in public schools in central Illinois. In one study (Dong, Anderson, Li, & Kim, 2006), participants were fourth-grade students from two public schools in China and one public school in South Korea.

Table 14.1 presents information regarding the number of participants in each study.

In Studies 1 and 2, students were assigned to one of two treatment conditions: CR or routine. Students in the CR condition participated in small-group discussions using the CR pedagogy described earlier. Students in the routine condition engaged in their regular reading instruction. In Study 1, students from the experimental condition participated in 10 CR discussions; In Study 2, students engaged in 4 CR discussions.

In Studies 3 and 4, there were three treatment conditions: CR, CR+, and routine. Children in the CR condition participated in four CR discussions, whereas students in the routine condition engaged in their regular reading instruction. In addition to participating in four CR discussions, children in CR+ conditions received either explicit instruction in argumentation (Study 3) or participated in group monitoring activities (Study 4).

TABLE 14.1. Number of Participants in Each Study

	CR	CR+	Routine (control group)	Total
Study 1 (Reznitskaya et al., 2001)	52	0	62	114
Study 2 (Dong, Anderson, Li, & Kim, 2006)	42	0	42	84
Study 3 (CR + direct instruction) (Reznitskaya, Anderson, & Kuo, 2007)	41	47	40	128
Study 4 (CR + group monitoring) (Kim, 2001)	31	32	39	102
Total	166	79	183	428

In Study 3, explicit instruction was delivered in two scripted lessons. During the lessons, children were presented with the definition, purpose, and uses of an argument. The teacher described parts of an argument, including position, reasons, supporting facts, objection, and response to objection; explained the relations among the parts; and gave examples. To help students see the relevance of presented abstract principles of argumentation, the teachers delivered explicit instruction after students participated in the first two CR discussions. The lessons employed the basic argument schema depicted in Figure 14.1.

Following the lessons, children in the CR + direct instruction condition participated in the remaining two CR discussions. At the end of these discussions, students classified propositions from the discussions into the basic argument schema (Figure 14.1) displayed in front of them. This activity was designed to further familiarize students with the elements of the schema, following Gick and Holyoak's (1987) suggestion that students need practice with instantiation of abstract structures.

In Study 4, following each discussion, students in CR + group monitoring participated in a metacognitive group monitoring activity designed to review the contributions of participants that were helpful for substantive and social aspects of the discussion. During the 5-minute group monitoring activity, students shared their reflections on questions such as "Did we talk about important ideas?", "Did we respond to others' different views?", "Was everyone able to participate?", and so on. Being aware of one's cognitive and social functioning is viewed as fundamental for generating well-reasoned arguments, because it permits ongoing evaluation of both processes and products of thinking (Ander-

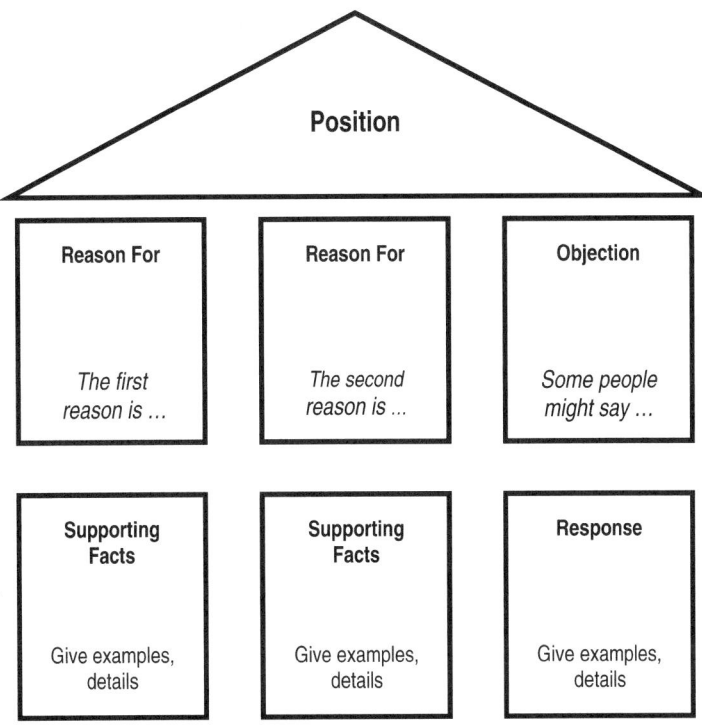

FIGURE 14.1. Basic argument schema.

son et al., 2001; Kuhn, 1991; Means & Voss, 1996). Metacognitive skills are also suggested to be important for facilitating transfer performance (Perkins & Salomon, 1989).

Within 1 or 2 weeks of participating in their respective interventions, students in all four studies were given the same posttest. The posttest was a reflective essay, written in response to a three-page story that was 816 words long. The story was similar to those that served as a basis for CR discussions, although students did not discuss this particular story or a story presenting the same type of moral dilemma. In the posttest story, an unpopular boy named Thomas wins the school Pinewood Derby Race, but he breaks the rules by not making his car by himself. He confides to his classmate Jack that he has received help from his older brother in making his car. The students were asked to write an essay reflecting on whether or not Jack should tell on Thomas. Children were given 40 minutes to work on the essay.

DATA ANALYSIS

The analysis of the essays was performed in several steps. First, all essays were transcribed and given an anonymous identification number to keep researchers blind to treatment differences when evaluating students' responses. In the following step, each document was parsed into *idea units*. An "idea unit," as defined by Mayer (1985), "expresses one action or event or state, and generally corresponds to a single verb clause" (p. 71). More detailed rules for chunking student essays into idea units are discussed elsewhere (Reznitskaya, Anderson, & Kuo, 2007; Reznitskaya et al., 2001).

Next we used QSR Nvivo software (Qualitative Solutions and Research, 1999) to organize, search, code, and evaluate the data. With QSR Nvivo, one can assign a particular code to a selected text and perform various searches of coded text patterns. An identified and coded word string, such as an idea unit in a reflective essay, can be effortlessly placed back into its original context. This allows for the examination of not only the linguistic form of an utterance but also its function, meaning, and conditions of use. This in turn permits the required contextual sensitivity, which is often absent when natural discourse is fragmented into easily quantifiable segments.

Different codes were assigned to idea units representing (1) statements supporting a chosen position, or supporting reasons; (2) statements opposing a chosen position, or counterarguments; and (3) statements given in response to anticipated objections, or rebuttals. Thus, each student essay received three scores corresponding to these outcome variables. In addition, we combined the categories representing distinct argument elements to form a summary measure, indicating the total number of argument-relevant propositions.

In three of the four studies reviewed here, we selected a random sample of student essays (Studies 1 and 3, $n = 30$; Study 2, $n = 42$) to evaluate interrater reliability of the assigned scores. The second rater was trained in applying the scoring system and received written scoring criteria. The interrater reliability coefficients in every study were high, all exceeding .89.

RESULTS AND DISCUSSION

Descriptive statistics from the four studies are presented in Table 14.2. Students who participated in CR discussions generally wrote essays that contained a greater number of

TABLE 14.2. Means and Standard Deviations for Outcome Variables

	Method					
	CR		CR+		Routine (control group)	
Variable	M	SD	M	SD	M	SD
Number of supporting reasons						
Study 1	8.70	6.74	n/a	n/a	6.95	4.41
Study 2	12.74	6.66	n/a	n/a	8.62	4.97
Study 3 (CR + direct instruction)	11.05	8.09	6.51	3.17	6.28	3.41
Study 4 (CR + group monitoring)	6.80	8.60	5.66	5.39	5.97	4.44
Number of counterarguments						
Study 1	2.02	2.63	n/a	n/a	0.94	1.62
Study 2	4.00	4.34	n/a	n/a	2.88	4.30
Study 3 (CR + direct instruction)	1.98	2.50	0.89	1.22	1.74	2.27
Study 4 (CR + group monitoring)	1.26	2.86	3.13	3.55	0.57	1.24
Number of rebuttals						
Study 1	0.88	1.68	n/a	n/a	0.50	0.97
Study 2	1.98	2.52	n/a	n/a	1.17	2.17
Study 3 (CR + direct instruction)	1.09	1.48	0.51	0.75	0.64	0.93
Study 4 (CR + group monitoring)	0.26	1.04	1.78	3.63	0.29	0.83
Total number of argument components						
Study 1 [a]	11.60	7.92	n/a	n/a	8.39	5.02
Study 2 [a]	18.72	9.70	n/a	n/a	12.67	7.94
Study 3 (CR + direct instruction) [a]	14.12	10.80	7.91	3.63	8.66	5.29
Study 4 (CR + group monitoring) [a]	8.32	4.16	10.57	4.19	6.83	2.17
Total number of argument components pooled over four studies	13.41	8.84	n/a	n/a	9.09	6.12

[a]Significant Method effects were found at $p < .05$.

arguments, counterarguments, and rebuttals than the essays of similar students who did not experience CR. In all studies, the analysis of variance (ANOVA) indicated a statistically significant effect of CR discussions versus routine condition ($p < .05$), although not all multiple comparisons conducted to examine group differences within individual schools or on separate outcome variables reached statistical significance.

Table 14.3 presents the effect sizes for the differences between CR, CR+, and routine conditions, using Cohen's *d* measure with pooled variance estimates. With the exception of the CR + direct instruction condition, treatment differences were in the expected direction, with medium to large treatment effects. Contrary to our expectation, the tendency to present more argument-related elements in writing disappeared when students were also given direct instruction in argumentation in Study 3. Thus, direct instruction resulted in negative transfer.

One explanation for negative transfer is that at the initial stages of learning, the rules that are being acquired interfere with ability to perform the transfer task (Mandler, 1962). Negative effects may be more evident when learners have some competence in performing the transfer task before learning the new principles. In this case, students need to learn not only to apply the new principles but also to abandon partially successful strate-

TABLE 14.3. Effect Sizes for Treatment versus Routine Conditions

Variable	Effect size (Cohen's *d*)	
	CR versus routine	CR+ versus routine
Total number of argument components		
Study 1	0.48	n/a
Study 2	0.68	n/a
Study 3 (CR + direct instruction)	0.64	−0.17
Study 4 (CR + group monitoring)	0.45	1.12
Total number of argument components pooled over four studies	0.57	n/a

gies. With additional learning and practice, students can master principles and may eventually exhibit enhanced performance on transfer tasks (Gick & Holyoak, 1987; Mandler, 1962; Morehouse & Williams, 1998).

Students in the CR + direct instruction condition were given additional instruction in constructing good arguments. Their experience with argumentation was more structured and cognitively demanding, because it incorporated additional rules to be learned and applied. The newly acquired awareness of the rules, and the attempt to apply them, might have interfered with student ability and motivation to generate more argument-relevant statements, resulting in negative transfer. As other researchers have noted, there are "costs and benefits associated with the use of schemata in learning" (Thorndyke & Hayes-Roth, 1979, p. 87). One may suppose that as students acquire a better grasp of the argument schema, the benefits could outweigh the costs.

The addition of group monitoring activity to CR discussions resulted in students presenting a greater number of counterarguments and rebuttals in their essays compared to students without the activity. During the group monitoring activity, students reflected on whether they had considered alternative perspectives and invited everyone to share their ideas. This apparently prompted students to become more dialogical in their thinking, and this enhanced ability transferred to the postintervention task in which students engaged in argumentative writing after reading a novel text.

To examine treatment differences in more detail, we conducted a qualitative analysis of selected student compositions. Consider, for example, a composition written by a fourth-grade student from the CR condition (Study 1). This essay was selected as an example because its total number of coded units approximated the mean for the respective treatment.

> I say yes Jack should tell on Thomas yet, I also say no, too. *I say yes because* Jack worked really hard on his car and Thomas didn't. *I say No because* this is probably the first time Thomas ever actually felt good about himself. *A way someone might disagree with me on yes*, because like it said in the book, nobody likes a tattletale. *A way someone might disagree with me on a reason for no* is maybe that's not true.
>
> I'd feel bad for Thomas if Jack told on him. Also if Jack told on Thomas, Jack would probably feel bad too. If Thomas worked on his own, his pinewood race car would be worse. So, it is partly good that his brother did his race car for him, but mostly not.

A distinctive feature of the preceding composition is its dialogic quality. The student is consistently shifting her frame of reference, arguing with the imagined "someone" (italicized). Although the assignment was completed silently and individually, the student's thinking processes appear to be modeled after discussions with others, with multiple points of view present (in italics) and each given careful consideration.

The student's comfort with uncertainty and willingness to entertain multiple solutions may represent an important progression from an absolutist, right-or-wrong view of the world. Granted, the student's ability to resolve the controversial issues she entertains needs further refinement. Yet it is encouraging to observe the fundamental shift from monological to dialogical thinking in this composition, especially since studies consistently document students' tendency to favor propositions that support their own opinions (e.g., Kuhn & Udell, 2003; Kuhn et al., 1997; Pontecorvo & Girardet, 1993; Voss & Means, 1991).

An essay of another fourth-grader represents a typical performance in the routine condition in terms of its quality and the number of coded units:

> I think Jack should tell because his brother helped him, and his teacher said to work by himself. Also, because he did little, like putting on the sticker. His brother made sure that the wheels were straight and he also helped with the car, made the wheels round, and helped shape the car. Thomas also cheated because he wasn't supposed to have help to make the car, the wheels, and the design.

In this composition, a student clearly states his position, presents several supporting reasons, and refers to the story information for evidence. However, the student only discusses one side of the issue. The essay is constructed not to explore alternatives but to defend a fixed point of view. It is more representative of typical performance by schoolchildren, who frequently exhibit the "my-side bias" documented by other researchers (e.g., Crowhurst, 1988; Dolz, 1996; Gleason, 1999; McCann, 1989; Means & Voss, 1996).

Similar benefits of engagement in dialogic discussions of controversial issues were evident in cross-cultural studies, as shown in the writings of Asian students (Study 2). Chinese and Korean children were able rapidly to assimilate the discourse practices introduced by the CR model, even though such practices are not common in Asian schools (Davin, 1991). Study participants in both China and Korea made a surprisingly smooth adaptation to CR and were able to transfer the acquired discourse practices to a new writing task they performed individually. Our study challenges the conception that children's history of language socialization determines their success with unfamiliar discourse practices (Heath, 1991; Street, 1984), suggesting that students can flexibly change their experiential, cultural, and cognitive frames, as well as benefit from the opportunities offered by new forms of discourse.

Next, we would like to present the essay from CR + direct instruction condition. This essay was chosen not because it represents typical performance, but because it helps to demonstrate the possible benefits of additional instruction in argumentation that are evident in the performance of some, although not all, students.

> I think Jack should tell on Thomas. *One reason is* Thomas should have worked on the car by himself. *For example*, in the story the teacher called Mr. Howard said that you need to work by yourself, and that is one of the most important rules. *Another good reason is* Jack worked really hard and put a lot of work into his car. *For example*, the story said that Jack worked on it every night for 3 weeks. Also, if Thomas' brother made the car he should get the credit, and if he isn't in the class Thomas should have done it by himself. *Some people might say* that Jack

shouldn't tell, because Thomas finally got noticed, but it would be better if Thomas did it by himself. This is why I believe that Jack should tell the teacher Mr. Howard what Thomas did.

This essay presents an unambiguous position on the issue. It contains reasons elaborated with relevant examples from the story, as well as a counterargument and a rebuttal. Importantly, the essay replicates the structure of an argument explicitly taught to students in the CR + direct instruction condition (Figure 14.1); that is, the essay starts with the position and is followed by the first reason, supported with an example. It then presents the second reason, the corresponding example, the counterargument, and the rebuttal. The student effectively uses linguistic markers (in italics) to introduce various argument components (i.e., "One reason is," "Another reason is," "For example," and "Some people might say"). These devices called *argument stratagems* (Anderson et al., 2001) are expected to facilitate argument construction. In this case, they might have prompted the student to include relevant components, as well as to edit or suppress the propositions that came to mind while, or after, reading the story but were inappropriate for argumentative writing.

The student's application of the argument schema in the preceding composition is flexible in two respects. First, while the underlying function of the argument stratagems taught during the intervention was preserved, the student could change the surface form. For example, the second reason in the argument frame presented during the lessons was introduced with "The second reason is [REASON]." The student modified this to "Another good reason is [REASON]." Second, although the argument frame used during instruction contained only two reasons (Figure 14.1), the student provided a third reason (i.e., "Also, if Thomas' brother made the car he should get the credit"), adding to the breadth of her argument. While not all students in the CR + direct instruction condition were as successful in applying the explicitly taught argument schema to their writing, this essay demonstrates that adding explicit instruction to group discussions has the potential for further disciplining and focusing students' argumentative writing.

Another addition to CR discussions was a group monitoring activity. Below, we present an essay that demonstrates the potential effects of this activity on a child's awareness of his own cognitive functioning:

> I think Jack should tell because Thomas could at least try to make his own. But it was good he did a little bit. He should have done the whole thing. Jack already feels bad for him so if Thomas gets in trouble Jack will feel even worse for him. *I guess I do not know* because Jack could be right this might be the first time he has won anything in his life. *I still cannot make up my mind* because they are both good reasons. Though he did do some work into it and he does deserve the credit. Besides he won the racing part. But I still think the best thing to do is to tell.

This essay again demonstrates the dialogic quality of writing exhibited by many CR students. For example, the second sentence (i.e., "But it was good he did a little bit") represents the voice of a person with a different point of view, which the student is able to rebut successfully ("He should have done the whole thing"). In addition, there is evidence of the student's attentiveness to his own thinking processes. After presenting two opposing perspectives, he pauses to indicate his confusion about the issue ("I guess I do not know"). Later in his essay, he again reflects on his position, stating "I still cannot make up my mind." It is plausible that drawing attention to the quality of their discussions during the group monitoring activity, helps students to become more attuned to their thinking processes. This "habit of mind" could then manifest itself in new contexts and communicative modes.

IMPROVING LITERACY INSTRUCTION THROUGH DIALOGIC INTERACTION

The consistency of results across different sampling occasions and cultural contexts supports the pedagogical potential of dialogic interaction for the development of individual competence in argumentation. We suggest that students who participate in group discussions that focus on making reasoned judgments are able to generalize some common elements of argumentation, which includes formulating a position, supporting it with reasons, anticipating counterarguments, and offering rebuttals. In other words, engagement in a genuine dialogue with others helps students develop and refine their argument schemas. Armed with an argument schema, students are better able to generate argument-relevant propositions, to consider alternatives, and to reconcile opposing perspectives. Four replications of this finding are especially noteworthy considering that the research was done in authentic classroom settings.

Because an argument schema is abstract, it enables transfer between different contexts and communicative modes, from an oral group discussion to a new written task performed individually. We further predict that its abstract properties should make the schema a powerful tool for reading comprehension in a variety of domains. A schema for a well-formed argument, the disposition to reflect on issues from several angles, and the standard that explanations and justifications must be comprehensive, internally consistent, and well supported are integral to comprehension of many kinds of texts, including not only argumentative texts in the narrow sense of polemical, win-the-debate-by-any-means communications but also most texts that children are expected to read beyond primer stories. Genuine philosophical, historical, legal, or scientific writing always contains arguments, as does much popular writing and many works of literature, in the broad sense of a thoughtful consideration of the case for one or several explanatory theories or policy options. But the arguments in texts may be invisible to schoolchildren, and even to their teachers, because elementary textbooks are compiled without a clear author's voice. It may not be apparent that behind the history text is an historian, and behind the science text is a scientist, so children profit from assistance in "questioning the author" (Beck & McKeown, 2001).

Participation in a dialogue with others can provide students with opportunities to develop a critical stance toward the information they receive, alerting them to the fact that they can scrutinize every conclusion based on the rules of rational argument. Our findings support the position that elementary schoolchildren are developmentally ready to become acquainted with argumentation (see also Crowhurst, 1988; Stein & Trabasso, 1982) and that the teaching of argumentative discourse ought not to be delayed until later grades (see also Anderson, Chinn, Waggoner, & Nguyen, 1998; Crowhurst, 1988; Lipman, 1997; Paul, 1986). As a civil society in which citizens can play an active role in shaping their own destinies, we can only benefit from helping students develop "the values and habits of mind to use reasoned discourse as means for choosing among competing ideas" (Anderson et al., 1998, p. 172). From the early grades on, literacy instruction that emphasizes dialogic interaction offers a useful context in which applications of rational argument can be experienced, practiced, and learned.

DIRECTIONS FOR FUTURE RESEARCH

Applying AST to literacy instruction opens a new door to advance our understanding of the pedagogical potential of social interaction in the development of higher-order thinking. Below, we present several directions for future research inspired by our theoretical and empirical investigations:

1. Future studies should further examine the dialogic quality of group interactions. Because genuine dialogic discussions are difficult to achieve, they are a rare occurrence in classrooms (Almasi, O'Flahavan, & Arya, 2001; Alveraman, O'Brien, & Dillon, 1990; Nystrand, Wu, Garmon, Zeiser, & Long, 2003). Although teachers in all CR studies were provided with training and in-class supervision, the quality of the discussion varied. Future studies can attempt to link specific properties of discussion in which students participated to students' postintervention performance on argumentative tasks.

2. In addition, new professional development models need to be developed and tested to ensure that classroom teachers are capable of supporting students' argumentation development through the skillful use of dialogue.

3. Alternative ways of assessing individual argumentation should also be explored. In the four studies reviewed here we evaluated student argumentative writing in terms of the number of acceptable argument components. Other scoring frameworks and assessment instruments should be employed in future studies to examine further the link between oral and written argumentation and to provide a broader base for conclusions.

4. Another direction for future research is to explore the social aspects of discussions that lead to improved individual argumentation. Li et al. (2007) took a step in this direction in a study that examined the important role of emergent child leaders in 12 CR discussion groups. Comparison of the number and kind of leadership moves made by the children showed that one primary child leader emerged in 6 out of the 12 groups, and that in all but one of the remaining groups, leadership was shared among several children. Li et al. (p. 79) explained the emergence of leadership in terms of the acquisition of a *leadership schema*. Future studies should further examine the properties, functions, and applications of the leadership schema, which is theorized to incorporate knowledge about the overall structure of group processes, including the roles played by members, the functions served by leadership moves, the contingencies under which moves may be useful, the complementary relationships between leading and following, the problems that may arise and possible remedies, and the temporal–causal flow of group activities (Li et al., 2007).

SUMMARY

Our broader goal in this chapter was to outline and evaluate the tenets of AST in relation to literacy instruction. Integrating schema theories with social learning perspectives via AST has made it possible to specify what argumentative abilities are being developed and how social interaction affects their development. We propose that group argumentation externalizes the rational processes we would like to foster within individual students, socializing them into the new ways of thinking. Our analysis of students' written productions generally supported the tenets of AST. Students were able to acquire and, in general, to transfer successfully structural and functional discourse principles they learned through their experience with oral argumentation. The transfer occurred even though students did not engage in argument-related writing during the intervention. These findings are consistent with the research conducted by Kuhn and colleagues, in which young adolescents who participated in peer dialogues showed improvements in the quantity and quality of their postintervention individual arguments (Kuhn & Udell, 2003; Kuhn et al., 1997).

The role of dialogue in the development of argument skills is an important topic with both theoretical and practical implications. "If discourse is indeed the social scaffold from which individuals' argumentative reasoning develops, it stands to reason that analysis of its development is of interest not only in its own right but because of the insight it promises into the developing cognitive competence of individuals" (Kuhn & Udell, 2003, p. 1258). Unfortunately, intervention studies in the domain of argumentation typically focus on evaluating the overall effect of multifaceted instructional programs (e.g., Dolz, 1996; Gleason, 1999; Hidi, Berndorff, & Ainley, 2002; Morehouse & Williams, 1998), and do not isolate components of the intervention and their relative contribution to the acquisition of intended skills.

The paucity of studies that examine the connections between group and individual argumentation is troublesome given the importance of such research for understanding the mechanism by which social functions give birth to individual learning. Social learning theories of cognition (e.g., Bakhtin, 1981; Rogoff, 1995; Vygotsky, 1962) continue to inspire educators who call for the restructuring of traditional school practices (e.g., Lipman, 1991; Paul, 1986). Yet educators who wish to expand or modify their pedagogies have little to go on, except the highly theoretical ideas of scholars such as Vygotsky or the largely unsubstantiated practical suggestions championed by his supporters. Systematic, theoretically driven research, capable of expanding our knowledge regarding the social origins of individual cognition, represents a clear need and a responsibility.

INTEGRATE, INVESTIGATE, AND INITIATE: QUESTIONS FOR DISCUSSION

1. We have provided research examples of how to use AST to improve comprehension instruction. Conduct an experiment; teach a lesson as it is described in either the basal reader or a content area textbook. Follow the explicit instructions provided for building students' comprehension of that material. With the next lesson in that book, prepare an AST-driven lesson. Explain the differences you found as to the depth and breadth of students comprehension. What did this experiment teach you about future comprehension lessons that you might want to conduct?

2. Create a graphic organizer that best depicts the important information you learned from this chapter. How does this graphic organizer assist your comprehension? How can an activity in which students create a graphic organizer as they read, or after they read, increase their comprehension?

3. The last few chapters have presented several theories, research studies, and activities on how to increase students' comprehension of fiction and nonfiction. In Chapter 15, this volume, Headley examines how we can increase student's abilities to write based on the latest neuroscientific evidence. Predict one direction in the field of reading and writing instruction that you anticipate will be presented in that chapter.

REFERENCES

Almasi, J. F., O'Flahavan, J. F., & Arya, P. (2001). A comparative analysis of student and teacher development in more or less proficient discussions of literature. *Reading Research Quarterly, 36*(2), 96–120.

Alveraman, D. E., O'Brien, D. G., & Dillon, D. R. (1990). What teachers do when they say they're having discussions of content area reading assignments: A qualitative analysis. *Reading Research Quarterly, 25*, 297–322.

Anderson, R. C. (1977). The notion of schemata and the educational enterprise. In R. C. Anderson, R. J. Spiro, & W. E. Montague (Eds.), *Schooling and the acquisition of knowledge* (pp. 415–431). Hillsdale, NJ: Erlbaum.

Anderson, R. C., Chinn, C., Waggoner, M., & Nguyen, K. (1998). Intellectually stimulating story discussions. In J. Osborn & F. Lehr (Eds.), *Literacy for all: Issues in teaching and learning* (pp. 170–186). New York: Guilford Press.

Anderson, R. C., Nguyen-Jahiel, K., McNurlen, B., Archodidou, A., Kim, S., Reznitskaya, A., et al. (2001). The snowball phenomenon: Spread of ways of talking and ways of thinking across groups of children. *Cognition and Instruction, 19*(1), 1–46.

Anderson, R. C., & Pichert, J. W. (1978). Recall of previously unrecallable information following a shift in perspective. *Journal of Verbal Learning and Verbal Behavior, 17*, 1–12.

Bakhtin, M. M. (1981). *The dialogic imagination: Four essays by M. M. Bakhtin*. Austin: University of Texas Press.

Bakhtin, M. M. (1984). *Problems of Dostoevsky's poetics* (Vol. 8). Minneapolis: University of Minnesota.

Bakhtin, M. M. (1986). *Speech genres and other late essays* (V. W. McGee, Trans.). Austin: University of Texas Press.

Beck, I. L., & McKeown, M. G. (2001). Inviting students into the pursuit of meaning. *Educational Psychology Review, 13*(3), 225–241.

Billings, L., & Fitzgerald, J. (2002). Dialogic discussion and the Paideia Seminar. *American Educational Research Journal, 39*(4), 907–941.

Bransford, J. C., & Johnson, M. K. (1972). Contextual prerequisites for understanding: Some investigations of comprehension and recall. *Journal of Verbal Learning and Verbal Behavior, 11*, 717–726.

Brewer, W. F., & Treyens, J. C. (1981). Role of schemata in memory for places. *Cognitive Psychology, 13*, 207–230.

Burbules, N. (1993). *Dialogue and teaching: Theory and practice*. New York: Teachers College Press.

Chambliss, M. J. (1995). Text cues and strategies successful readers use to construct the gist of lengthy written arguments. *Reading Research Quarterly, 30*(4), 778–807.

Cheng, P., & Holyoak, K. J. (1985). Pragmatic reasoning schemas. *Cognitive Psychology, 17*, 391–416.

Chinn, C. A., & Anderson, R. C. (1998). The structure of discussions that promote reasoning. *Teachers College Record, 100*(2), 315–368.

Crowhurst, M. (1988). *Research review: Patterns of development in writing persuasive/argumentative discourse* (Report No. 506374). Vancouver: University of British Columbia. (ERIC Document Reproduction Service No. ED299596)

Davin, D. (1991). The early childhood education of the only child generation in urban China. In I. Epstein (Ed.), *Chinese education: Problems, policies, and prospects* (pp. 42–65). New York & London: Garland.

Detterman, D. K. (1993). The case for the prosecution: Transfer as an epiphenomenon. In D. K. Detterman & R. J. Sternberg (Eds.), *Transfer on trial: Intelligence, cognition, and instruction* (pp. 1–24). Norwood, NJ: Ablex.

Dewey, J. (1933). *How we think: A restatement of the relation of reflective thinking to the educative process*. Lexington, MA: Heath.

Dolz, J. (1996). Learning argumentative capacities. A study of the effects of a systematic and intensive teaching of argumentative discourse in 11–12 year old children. *Argumentation, 10,* 227–251.

Dong, T., Anderson, R. C., Li, Y., & Kim, I. (2006). Collaborative reasoning in Asia: Mismatch reconsidered. Manuscript submitted for publication. *Reading Research Quarterly.*

Druckman, D. Q., & Bjork, R. A. (1994). *Learning, remembering, believing: Enhancing human performance.* Washington, DC: National Academy Press.

Freedman, A., & Pringle, I. (1984). Why students can't write arguments. *English in Education, 18,* 73–84.

Freire, P. (1970). *Education for critical consciousness.* New York: Herder & Herder.

Gentner, D. (1989). The mechanisms of analogical reasoning. In S. Vosniadou & A. Ortony (Eds.), *Similarity and analogical reasoning* (pp. 197–241). Cambridge, UK: Cambridge University Press.

Gick, M. L., & Holyoak, K. J. (1987). The cognitive basis of knowledge transfer. In S. M. Cormier & J. D. Hagman (Eds.), *Transfer of learning: Contemporary research and applications* (pp. 9–47). San Diego: Academic Press.

Gleason, M. M. (1999). The role of evidence in argumentative writing. *Reading and Writing Quarterly, 14,* 81–106.

Govier, T. (1985). *A practical study of argument.* Belmont, CA: Wadsworth.

Heath, S. B. (1991). The sense of being literate: Historical and cross-cultural features. In P. D. Pearson, R. Barr, M. L. Kamil, & P. Mosenthal (Eds.), *Handbook of reading research* (pp. 3–25). White Plains, NY: Longman.

Hidi, S., Berndorff, D., & Ainley, M. (2002). Children's argument writing, interest and self-efficacy: An intervention study. *Learning and Instruction, 12,* 429–446.

Hofer, B. K., & Pintrich, P. R. (1997). The development of epistemological theories: Beliefs about knowledge and knowing and their relation to learning. *Review of Educational Research, 67*(1), 88–140.

Kim, S. (2001). *The effects of group monitoring on transfer of learning in small group discussions.* Unpublished doctoral dissertation, University of Illinois at Urbana–Champaign.

King, P. M., & Kitchener, K. S. (1994). *Developing reflective judgment: Understanding and promoting intellectual growth and critical thinking in adolescents and adults.* San Francisco: Jossey-Bass.

Kuhn, D. (1991). *The skill of argument.* Cambridge, UK: Cambridge University Press.

Kuhn, D. (1992). Thinking as argument. *Harvard Educational Review, 62*(2), 155–177.

Kuhn, D., Shaw, V., & Felton, M. (1997). Effects of dyadic interaction on argumentative reasoning. *Cognition and Instruction, 15*(3), 287–315.

Kuhn, D., & Udell, W. (2003). The development of argument skills. *Child Development, 74*(5), 1245–1260.

Kumpulainen, K., & Mutanen, M. (1999). The situated dynamics of peer interaction: An introduction to an analytic framework. *Learning and Instruction, 9,* 449–473.

Li, Y., Anderson, R. C., Nguyen-Jahiel, K., Dong, T., Archodidou, A., Kim, I., et al. (2007). Emergent leadership in children's discussion groups. *Cognition and Instruction, 25*(1), 75–111.

Lipman, M. (1991). *Thinking in education.* Cambridge, UK: Cambridge University Press.

Lipman, M. (1997). Education for democracy and freedom. *Wesleyan Graduate Review, 1*(1), 32–38.

Luria, A. R. (1981). *Language and cognition.* New York: Wiley.

Mandler, G. (1962). From association to structure. *Psychological Review, 69*(5), 415–427.

Mayer, R. E. (1985). Structural analysis of science prose: Can we increase problem solving performance? In B. K. Britton & J. B. Black (Eds.), *Understanding of expository text* (pp. 65–87). Hillsdale, NJ: Erlbaum.

McCann, T. M. (1989). Student argumentative writing knowledge and ability at three grade levels. *Research in the Teaching of English, 23*(1), 63–77.

Mead, G. H. (1962). *Mind, self, and society from the standpoint of a social behaviorist.* Chicago: University of Chicago Press.

Means, M. L., & Voss, J. F. (1996). Who reasons well?: Two studies of informal reasoning among children of different grade, ability, and knowledge levels. *Cognition and Instruction, 14*(2), 139–178.

Meyer, B. J., Brandt, D. M., & Bluth, G. J. (1980). Use of top-level structure in text: Key for reading comprehension of ninth-grade students. *Reading Research Quarterly, 1,* 72–103.

Mishra, P., & Brewer, W. F. (2003). Theories as a form of mental representation and their role in the recall of text information. *Contemporary Educational Psychology, 28,* 277–303.

Morehouse, R., & Williams, M. (1998). Report on student use of argument skills. *Critical and Creative Thinking, 6*(1), 14–20.

Munsch, R. (2001). *Paper bag princess.* Buffalo, NY: Annick Press.

Nystrand, M., Wu, L., Garmon, A., Zeiser, S., & Long, D. A. (2003). Questions in time: Investigating the structure and dynamics of unfolding classroom discourse. *Discourse Processes, 35*(2), 135–200.

Paul, R. W. (1986). Dialogical thinking: Critical thought essential to the acquisition of rational knowledge and passions. In J. B. Baron & R. J. Sternberg (Eds.), *Teaching thinking skills: Theory and practice* (pp. 127–148). New York: Freeman.

Pellegrini, A. D., Galda, L., & Rubin, D. (1984). Persuasion as a social-cognitive activity: The effects of age and channel of communication on children's production of persuasive messages. *Language and Communication, 4*(4), 285–293.

Perkins, D. N., & Salomon, G. (1987). Transfer and teaching for thinking. In D. N. Perkins, J. Lochhead, & J. C. Bishop (Eds.), *Thinking* (pp. 285–303). Hillsdale, NJ: Erlbaum.

Perkins, D. N., & Salomon, G. (1989). Are cognitive skills context-bound? *Educational Researcher, 18,* 16–25.

Perry, W. G. (1970). *Forms of intellectual and ethical development in the college years: A scheme.* New York: Holt, Rinehart & Winston.

Pontecorvo, C., & Girardet, H. (1993). Arguing and reasoning in understanding historical topics. *Cognition and Instruction, 11*(3/4), 365–395.

Qualitative Solutions and Research. (1999). *QSR Nvivo* [Computer software]. Victoria, Australia: Author.

Reed, S. K. (1993). A schema-based theory of transfer. In D. K. Detterman & R. J. Sternberg (Eds.), *Transfer on trial: Intelligence, cognition, and instruction* (pp. 39–67). Norwood, NJ: Ablex.

Reznitskaya, A., & Anderson, R. C. (2002). The argument schema and learning to reason. In C. C. Block & M. Pressley (Eds.), *Comprehension instruction* (pp. 319–334). New York: Guilford Press.

Reznitskaya, A., Anderson, R. C., & Kuo, L. (2007). Teaching and learning argumentation. *Elementary School Journal, 107*(5), 449–472.

Reznitskaya, A., Anderson, R. C., McNurlen, B., Nguyen-Jahiel, K., Archodidou, A., & Kim, S. (2001). Influence of oral discussion on written argument. *Discourse Processes, 32*(2–3), 155–175.

Rogoff, B. (1990). *Apprenticeship in thinking: Cognitive development in social context.* New York: Oxford University Press.

Rogoff, B. (1995). Observing sociocultural activity on three planes: Participatory appropriation, guided participation, and apprenticeship. In J. V. Wertsch, D. Rio, & A. Alvarez (Eds.), *Sociocultural studies of mind* (pp. 139–164). Cambridge, UK: Cambridge University Press.

Rumelhart, D. E. (1980). Schemata: The building blocks of cognition. In R. J. Spiro, B. C. Bruce, & W. F. Brewer (Eds.), *Theoretical issues in reading and comprehension* (pp. 33–58). Hillsdale, NJ: Erlbaum.

Schank, R. C., & Abelson, R. P. (1977). *Scripts, plans, goals, and understanding: An inquiry into human knowledge structures.* Hillsdale, NJ: Erlbaum.

Stein, N. L., & Trabasso, T. (1982). Children's understanding of stories: A basis for moral judgment and dilemma resolution. In C. J. Brainerd & M. Pressley (Eds.), *Verbal processes in children: Progress in cognitive development research* (pp. 161–188). New York: Springer-Verlag.

Street, B. V. (1984). *Literacy in theory and practice.* New York: Cambridge University Press.

Thorndyke, P. W., & Hayes-Roth, B. (1979). The use of schemata in the acquisition and transfer of knowledge. *Cognitive Psychology, 11,* 82–106.

Toulmin, S. E. (1958). *The uses of argument.* Cambridge, UK: Cambridge University Press.

Voss, F. J., & Means, M. L. (1991). Learning to reason via instruction in argumentation. *Learning and Instruction, 1,* 337–350.

Vygotsky, L. S. (1962). *Thought and language.* Cambridge, MA: MIT Press.

Vygotsky, L. S. (1979). Consciousness as a problem in the psychology of behavior. *Soviet Psychology, 17,* 5–35.

Vygotsky, L. S. (1981). The genesis of higher-order mental functions. In J. V. Wertsch (Ed.), *The concept of activity in Soviet psychology* (pp. 144–188). Armonk, NY: Sharpe.

Waggoner, M., Chinn, C. A., Yi, H., & Anderson, R. C. (1995). Collaborative reasoning about stories. *Language Arts, 72,* 582–589.

Walton, D. (1996). *Argument structure: A pragmatic theory.* Toronto: University of Toronto Press.

Wertsch, J. V. (1985). *Vygotsky and social formation of mind.* Cambridge, MA: Harvard University Press.

Wertsch, J. V., & Bivens, J. A. (1992). The social origins of individual mental functioning: Alternatives and perspectives. *Quarterly Newsletter of the Laboratory of Comparative Human Cognition, 14*(2), 35–44.

15

Improving Reading Comprehension through Writing

KATHY HEADLEY

My own words, when I am at work on a story, I hear too as they go, in the same voice that I hear when I read in books. When I write and the sound of it comes back to my ears, then I act to make my changes. I have always trusted this voice.
—EUDORA WELTY (1985, p. 13)

"When students are skilled in reading and writing and their motivation is maintained through appropriately challenging literacy experiences, they read and write more" (Pressley, 2002, p. 355). This reading–writing relationship motivates strategic readers and writers of text in making meaning and meaning making within our pre-K–12 classrooms. In the 21st century, the research designed to improve reading comprehension through writing has moved from merely putting pen to paper to more technology supported writing aids for comprehension.

In looking at reading–writing yesterday, today, and tomorrow, this chapter highlights the following:

- Balanced literacy for reading comprehension and writing composition instruction in today's classrooms.
- Reading and writing development as complementary ways of knowing and communicating.
- How technology has changed, and continues to change, the relationship between reading comprehension and writing processes.

ESTABLISHED RESEARCH/PRACTICE

Is writing a process or product? The answer to this question was the source of intense debate waged among literacy educators during the 1970s and even into the 1980s.

Teachers of English language arts were initially cautious about moving the instructional focus even slightly away from standard writing domains, such as grammar and conventional formats of compositions, toward teaching and using writing processes as tools to advance comprehension. Truthfully, grammar still holds writing hostage, but more and more educators embrace the fundamentals of engaging students in the processes of writing.

Today's discussions cross many different literacy landscapes. The writing workshop has rooted its way into elementary- and middle-level classrooms and gained much momentum within secondary classrooms. Thanks to leaders such as Donald Graves (1983), Lucy Calkins (1983, 1986), and Regie Routman (1988, 1994), and James Gray's conception of the National Writing Project (1985), teachers are urged to be readers and writers as they provide guidance to literacy learners within their own classrooms. Balanced literacy, as defined by Frey, Lee, Tollefson, Pass, and Massengill (2005), emphasizes daily, sustained reading and writing, cooperative learning for positive experiences, realistic and high expectations for all students, and integrated reading and writing across all content areas. Past research has affirmed that the "balance of literacy" takes place within the classroom and across the school setting, with "can do, will do" inspiration to improve literacy for all students. According to Frey et al., balanced literacy includes the following strategies and activities: guided reading, independent reading, independent writing, read-alouds, shared reading, accountable talk (about learning), conferencing, pair–share, and prediction. Through modeling and direct instruction, teachers support these skills, strategies, processes, and activities. Importantly, students are engaged in the literacy learning process, and instructional support is scaffolded as the learner moves toward independence in both reading comprehension and composition.

Providing balanced literacy instruction entails that teachers know their students' varied levels of literacy development. Fitzgerald and Shanahan (2000) were among the first to delineate the multiple ways in which composition builds reading comprehension. They proposed that the following inherent critical knowledge stages provide synergistic benefits when reading comprehension and writing abilities are developed jointly:

Stage 1: Literacy Roots (Birth–Age 6)
Stage 2: Initial Literacy (Grades 1–2, Ages 6–7)
Stage 3: Confirmation, Fluency, Ungluing from Print (Grades 2–3, Ages 7–8)
Stage 4: Reading and Writing for Learning the New: A First Step (Grades 4–8, Ages 9–13)
Stage 5: Multiple Viewpoints (High School, Ages 14–18)
Stage 6: Construction and Reconstruction—A Worldview (College, Age 18 and Above) (p. 45)

In Stage 1, students grapple with their emerging literacy as they learn about the functions and components of reading and writing. Learning how language works and beginning to manipulate language for difference purposes are predominant in Stage 2. Automaticity, or fluency in receiving and creating information, is a cornerstone for Stage 3, which prepares the learner for the more complex literacy demands of Stage 4. In this developmental level, reading and writing increasingly involve comprehension of informational text. In Stage 5, differences in viewpoints, both as readers and as writers, demand that learners think critically and openly. Such comprehension requires greater depths of understanding, which often do not fully develop until the construction–reconstruction period of Stage 6. These developmental stages (as outlined by Fitzgerald and Shanahan, 2000) have been used by teachers to assess students' literacy progress and to provide appropriate instruction for increased comprehension and achievement.

To receive the full benefits of balanced literacy, schools and districts must assume responsibility to support their teachers' ongoing professional development. Onsite administrators must also provide continued classroom support for the most effective comprehension and comprehension implementation. With such professional support, teachers can continue to advance their students' literacy and their own professional expertise.

NEW RESEARCH

In a recent investigation by Brooks (2007), four fourth-grade teachers who were nominated as exemplary reading and writing teachers responded to three questions:

> How did they describe themselves as readers and writers?
> What factors were most influential in their reading and writing?
> How did they describe any relationships, or lack thereof, between their reading and writing and their reading and writing teaching? (p. 177).

These exemplary language arts teachers self-reported that their instructional practices did not rely primarily upon their own personal reading and writing experiences. Instead, they focused on knowing their students and how to optimize total literacy development. This teacher-knowledge base is vital in establishing a writing workshop environment within a balanced literacy framework, if such a classroom is to advance reading comprehension.

Literacy development, in and out of the classroom, has been reshaped as we have come to view reading and writing as social and cultural practices (Landis, 2003). With this redefinition, reading and writing have merged and exploded into "new literacies" as we have used written language for different purposes, in different settings, in multiple ways. These new literacies confront us as we surf Internet sites, listen to and/or view podcasts, and read/respond to blogs and other online postings.

To keep pace with today's reading comprehension demands and to prepare for those in our future, reading and writing should be taught using cohesive text and as an integrated process (Parodi, 2007). According to Stevens (2003),

> Using research-based instructional procedures, good literature as the basis for instruction, cooperative learning processes, and integrating reading and writing instruction, can result in significantly higher student achievement. The components, particularly the use of cooperative learning and the writing process, cause students to get more actively engaged in and take more responsibility for their own learning. (p. 155)

Recently, in *Writing Next*, Graham and Perin (2007) listed 11 elements of writing instruction that are effective, research supported components for improving middle and high school students' writing:

1. Writing Strategies, which involve teaching students strategies for planning, revising, and editing their compositions
2. Summarization, which involves explicitly and systematically teaching students how to summarize texts
3. Collaborative Writing, which uses instructional arrangements in which adolescents work together to plan, draft, revise, and edit their compositions
4. Specific Product Goals, which assign students specific, reachable goals for the writing they are to complete

5. Word Processing, which uses computers and word processors as instructional supports for writing assignments
6. Sentence Combining, which involves teaching students to construct more complex sophisticated sentences
7. Prewriting, which engages students in activities designed to help them generate or organize ideas for their composition
8. Inquiry Activities, which engage students in analyzing immediate, concrete data to help them develop ideas and content for a particular writing task
9. Process Writing Approach, which interweaves a number of writing instructional activities in a workshop environment that stresses extended writing opportunities, writing for authentic audiences, personalized instruction, and cycles of writing
10. Study of Models, which provides students with opportunities to read, analyze, and emulate models of good writing
11. Writing for Content Learning, which uses writing as a tool for learning content material (p. 4).

Viewing these 11 elements of effective writing instruction through a reading comprehension lens reveals critical thinking strengths. Even during the stages of the writing process, writers dually function as readers as they reread, multiple times, their own words and those of their peers. Likewise, summarization requires, of course, the analysis of text for important ideas and critical understandings. This critical analysis also extends to the study of models when students and teachers select texts that provide an array of models for their writings. Often the study of models is embedded within genre studies; in other instances, it may be rooted within direct strategy instruction for types of writing. Last, but importantly, reading comprehension bonds with writing for content learning when writing is used as a tool (1) before reading content area text to activate prior knowledge of concepts and related vocabulary, (2) during reading to clarify information, and (3) after reading to stimulate reflective thinking that goes beyond literal understandings.

To reinforce comprehension and its subsequent application during writing instruction, teachers guide students' implementation of writing strategies by directly teaching and modeling the stages of the writing process (planning, drafting, revising, editing, publishing) and supporting students' engagement during each step of the process (Graham & Perin, 2007). Relatedly, cognitive strategy instruction (e.g., think-alouds, scaffolded instruction for gradual achievement of student independence, and mnemonic devices for strategy sequence remembrance) is taught through the same methods and has demonstrated a positive impact upon student learning (De La Paz & Graham, 2002; Graham, 2006). As reiterated by De La Paz (2007), "cognitive strategy instruction programs have consistently been found effective in promoting impressive gains in students' writing performance and self-efficacy for writing, regardless of the student's academic functioning or grade level" (p. 262). Recently, such types of instruction have also consistently provided significant gains in reading comprehension (see other chapters in this volume for examples).

Another cognitive support, setting purposes for reading, helps to focus students' understanding of text. Likewise, establishing specific product goals for writing supports students' understanding and successful completion of writing assignments. Such specific product goals go beyond merely selecting a general purpose for writing; instead, students must understand the writing assignment task, as well as the key elements or characteristics that comprise the composition's message and process (Graham & Perin, 2007). To illustrate, if students are writing a comparison text on cable television and Direct TV, they must first determine the primary elements in each delivery system (benefits, costs, programming choices, service support, etc.), then contrast the differences and draw a final conclusion or make recommendations for potential customers.

Although more narrow in scope and focused predominately on writing composition support, sentence combining helps students create more complex sentences by reconfiguring two or more simple sentences into one interesting, informative statement (Graham & Perin, 2007). Although this activity can begin with linking two basic sentences into one compound sentence, models from literature and informational text provide more challenging sentence-combining tasks for student application. This simple strategy, when applied to narrative and expository texts, transforms the conventional rote learning of grammar into an interactive tool that students can use with the mechanics of language to create, translate, and communicate their comprehension of text.

Since we know that traditional grammar instruction does not improve students' writing, and that it may even negatively impact struggling writers (Anderson, 1997; Saddler & Graham, 2005), effective writing instruction should begin with engaging students in the writing process through prewriting as an initial transition to the planning and drafting stages (Graham & Perin, 2007). As a scaffolded activity, prewriting requires that students understand their writing goals, brainstorm known or needed information, and organize their ideas into a beginning format for initial writing. Prewriting is thought provoking and motivational, establishing momentum for critical thinking and launching a beginning platform for further inquiry into the selected and/or assigned topic.

To be counted as an effective component of writing instruction that facilitates critical reading and thinking, the process writing approach cannot be interpreted to mean "just let students write." Instead, teachers must establish classroom environments that allow risk taking and exploration, provide opportunities for self- and peer feedback along with teacher conferences, offer crucial skill and strategy instruction for writing development, monitor student goals and progress, and develop avenues for sharing with real audiences. In classrooms that employ the process writing approach, composing is a regular, sustained component of the curriculum that cuts across all content areas. Within such classrooms, students reflect upon a variety of models from literature and from informational text, analyze the writer's craft from their study of these models, and emulate the resulting characteristics in their own writing. The process writing approach links a seamless cycle of learning to write and writing to learn as students read, discuss, and create print in all of its diverse forms. "Writing is a means of extending and deepening students' knowledge; it acts as a tool for learning subject matter.... *Reading Next* recommended that language arts teachers use content-area texts to teach reading and writing skills and that content-area teachers provide instruction and practice in discipline-specific reading and writing" (Graham & Perin, 2007, pp. 9–10).

To summarize effective writing instruction in simple terms, knowledge about writing facilitates writing development (Saddler & Graham, 2007). As such, writing development can be supported by increasing opportunities for reading comprehension development; creating more authentic writing experiences; providing direct instruction on writing skills, strategies, and processes; modeling the composing process; and applying strategic knowledge to the processes of writing. This stance is supported by the National Commission on Writing for America's Families, Schools, and Colleges (2003), which recommends that elementary students spend more time writing (that the current writing time in fact be doubled); use writing as a learning tool across the curriculum, especially in math, science, and social studies; and write more often during their out-of-school time (even using composing activities as homework counts).

HOW NEW KNOWLEDGE IMPROVES COMPREHENSION INSTRUCTION

Effective research-based practices have provided insights into student learning. Supported by professional development activities, today's teachers are armed with instructional techniques and strategies that better reach the needs of individual students. Instead of accumulating stacks of completed worksheets, many students are now active participants in reading and writing for real purposes and real audiences. In programs with such authentic reading comprehension instructional foci, participants read and write in both in-school and out-of-school contexts. With purposeful reading and writing engagements, students interact with more complex text as they envision meaningful ways to use their developing literacy powers (Duke, Purcell-Gates, Hall, & Tower, 2006/2007).

Moreover, students' reading, writing, and thinking extend beyond classrooms into their daily lives and community activities. One of my personal images of reading and writing across schools and communities comes from my travel to Carpi, Italy. In Carpi, a local preschool engaged the toddlers with family members in reading, drawing, and "writing" episodes to develop their literacy comprehension. The arts were used as basic elements to encourage these children's literacy development. On any given day, adults and children side-by-side were busy with books, clay, and paint as they transcribed their discoveries into beautiful evidence of learning. Outside the expansive windows grew the abundant community gardens the adults and children had planted. Learning possessed no age limits or classroom wall barriers.

Such early literacy exchanges can translate successfully to upper grade levels. For instance, Fisher and Frey (2003) experimented with various collaborative forms of writing instruction for struggling adolescents who could not comprehend. The Language Experience Approach (LEA), a traditional method, was used with a first-year section of "genre studies" in the low-performing urban high school examined in this research study. The writing component of LEA created an opportunity for the students to "talk" about a chosen topic, which was then transcribed into their own written language to be more easily read and comprehended. The teacher modeled and taught writing processes and conventions when needed while transcribing the students' discussion. These adolescent learners' next progressive step was Interactive Writing (IW), a collaborative writing technique similar to LEA, in which students used a dry-erase board to capture their ideas into visible, meaningful text for repeated readings by the group. During IW, the teacher relinquished the transcribing role to the students. As with LEA, IW resulted in the group's creation of a single class composition. Because IW stimulated more risk taking than LEA, the teacher fostered an encouraging environment of acceptance and growth. Power Writing (writing as many words as possible on a single topic within a short time limit), Generative Sentences (short activities in which students are given a single letter, generate words using that letter, then compose a sentence using their particular words, and finally generate a paragraph that incorporates the sentence), and Independent Writing (individual, scaffolded student compositions based on teacher-provided writing prompts) were additional instructional activities in which the students engaged. The outcomes of these daily, interactive writing experiences were increased writing fluency and length of written responses, decreased writing errors, and improved reading achievement, particularly comprehension.

As with narrative and personal memoir writing, content area writing skill development needs instruction and teacher support with models, examples, realistic expectations, decision-making scenarios, constructive feedback, and adequate time for writing, if reading comprehension is to be affected (Knipper & Duggan, 2006). Additionally, rubrics and checklists for content writing provide students with guidance, levels of expectations, and evaluative goals, just as pre-, during-, and postreading instruction requires. These supports and strategies, such the guided writing procedure, learning logs, quick writes, structured note taking, and Listen–Stop–Write, assist students in understanding their reading assignments. Framed paragraphs, cloze-like paragraphs that students complete with words that "connect the dots" on their understanding of informational text, and use of key vocabulary in composing a one-sentence synthesis of the main idea are two examples of strategies that guide students through reviewing and summarizing content text after reading (Knipper & Duggan, 2006). Even quick, efficient minilessons that focus young writers' attention on the author's craft support reading comprehension and writing to learn. Such minilessons for nonfiction may include author's purpose and point of view (and how one knows); text structures, such as question–answer, problem–solution, descriptive, cause–effect, sequential, and compare–contrast; as well as how punctuation guides the reader through the text (Rickards & Hawes, 2006). (Refer to Table 15.1 for a list of reading comprehension and writing composition strategies and activities that facilitate balanced literacy.)

Whereas writing is an important school-related skill, it is also a critical skill for the workplace (Graham & Perin, 2007). Our current and future job markets are raising the bar on reading and composing competencies (Knipper & Duggan, 2006). Breaching this knowledge gap, technology provides the cornerstone for day-to-day life experiences and forecasts career possibilities. More and more, our youth are using technology that incorporates writing for communication on some level (e.g., blogs, instant messaging, text

TABLE 15.1. Balanced Literacy Emphases for Strategies and Approaches That Focus on Reading Comprehension, Writing Composition, and Integrated Reading and Writing

Focus on reading comprehension	Focus on writing composition	Integrated reading and writing
Guided reading	Guided writing procedure	Pair–share
Independent reading	Independent writing	Summarizations
Read-alouds	Planning, revising, editing compositions	Inquiry activities
Shared reading		Language Experience Approach (LEA)
Prediction	Conferencing	
Purpose(s) for reading	Collaborative writing	Interactive Writing (IW)
Text structures (question–answer, problem–solution, descriptive, cause–effect, sequence, compare–contrast)	Specific product goals	Learning logs
	Sentence combining	Author's craft (text structures, purpose, point of view, punctuation as a reader's guide)
	Power Writing	
	Generative Sentences	
Author's purpose and point of view		Listen–Stop–Write
		Quick writes
		Framed paragraphs
		Cloze text
		Vocabulary synthesis for main idea
		Think-alouds and modeling
		Structured note taking

messaging). When we talk about the use of technology in writing instruction, two perspectives impact our discussion: "research on the use of technology to support traditional writing outcomes, and research on new forms and contexts for writing" (MacArthur, 2006, p. 259). Media and information and communication technologies (ICTs; e.g., Internet, e-mail) can provide viable, meaningful reading–writing links between young people and their new literacies (Alvermann, 2004).

Navigating this fast-paced, networked world of new literacies requires that teachers use technology both as an instructional tool and topic (Biancarosa & Snow, 2004). Research on the use of technology to support traditional writing informs us that word processing alone does not significantly affect written products, but when word processing is supported by writing instruction, students do improve their writing skills. Improved writing is not the only outcome of such instruction; reading comprehension benefits as well (Biancarosa & Snow, 2004).

Technology-supported instruction has the potential for greater student independence with the writing process (Montgomery & Marks, 2006). In the technological cycle for reading–writing improvement, key elements are quality software and integration of instruction with computer capabilities (MacArthur, 2006). Programs such as Inspiration and Kidspiration (*www.inspiration.com*) lend organizational structures for brainstorming and summarizing. Word prediction software programs, for instance, Co:Writer (*www.donjohnston.com*) and Aurora (*www.aurora-systems.com*), assist with spelling difficulties and content-specific vocabulary. Voice output programs permit students to hear what's been written. In this way, students, especially students with learning disabilities, may identify more errors and improve word identification. As currently used, spell checker, thesaurus, and grammar checker continue to smooth the revision process, enabling students to focus on the content, with technology tools for writing conventions.

The instructional issue, according to Lacina (2003/2004), is not merely "whether a teacher uses technology in the classroom, but rather how well he or she integrates the technology into classroom instruction in order to enhance student learning and promote active learning" (p. 102). Technology penetrates the writing workshop when teachers use an LCD (liquid crystal display) projector to model writing processes; e-mail, chat room sessions, and the Internet offer students opportunities to share their work with others. When we talk about improving reading comprehension through writing, we must project beyond the traditional pen-and-paper image and envision the myriad possibilities that technology creates.

DIRECTIONS FOR THE FUTURE

The future directions and possibilities for writing should include instructional integration and development of the following stances:

1. *What are the best instructional practices for merging the sequential, print-based notion of reading (Jewitt, 2005) with technologically driven writing formats?* Technology tools, specifically the computer, the Internet, and CD-ROM software, have contributed to the transformation of reading into a multimodal practice. For instance, the Internet's hypertext transforms the slick pages of books into multiple layers of information. It is no longer adequate to teach reading only through printed texts such as books.

2. *As Yancey (2004) urges, in what ways can educators engage in envisionment (Leu, Kinzer, Coiro, & Cammack, 2004) as we experiment and explore new uses for*

technology tools? This may involve students sharing preliminary research findings with fellow students through slide presentations for organizing thinking and learning prior to composing final drafts of research papers. Likewise, we need to test how such adorned writing affects students' comprehension and investigate how components of critical comprehension are advanced.

3. *How will this computerized transformation of writing impact the instructional content and delivery of composition?* Composing with a pen and composing with a computer engage the writer in different cognitive and motor abilities (Ardila, 2004), causing left-brain and right-brain debates to merge into discussions of "interhemispheric integration" (p. 65). As we replace computer labs and two or three outdated computers at the rear of the classroom with technology that's readily available to all students, teachers will add an additional layer of knowing and learning about the writing process to their repertoires. Online texts can be accessed and read, with students' technology-supported responses offered as evidence of their cognitive understandings.

4. *How will the social and cultural impact of technology-assisted writing advance our current definitions of "sharing" and "publishing" student writing?* Peer feedback, now possible across classrooms, schools, and even countries, engages a richer, more extensive network of readers and writers. This new context for peer response requires a research lens that examines the quality, along with the quantity, of these communications.

5. *How can technology-assisted writing formats be used as efficient tools for assessment?* An important application of formative assessment is the use of computer software to identify patterns of errors in student writing (Kuriloff, 2004). In using computers both for composing and for assessing students' writing, teachers can transform writing instruction to target individualized needs of students for additional support. Future research directions regarding technology-supported assessment should focus on discovering the most effective impacts upon students' composing process and subsequent connections to improved reading comprehension.

PROJECTIONS AND POSSIBILITIES FOR THE CLASSROOM OF 2030

Will walls encapsulate the classroom in 2030? I don't believe so. Working—and learning—at home may be the wave of the future. Less dependent on fossil fuels, students can remain within the comfortable surroundings of home, local communities, and neighborhoods as they learn new knowledge, skills, and strategies. Writing will be more than letters, words, sentences, and paragraphs. Instead, graphics, images, and audio will punch up the interest quota. Engaging in reading, writing, and thinking will involve classmates nearby and far away. "The sky's the limit" may be a realized truth. Authentic literacy tasks, catchwords in today's conversations about reading and writing, are finally realized in the classroom of 2030. Real-world, or perhaps real-universe, conversations among readers and writers through immediately interchanged communications will certainly and dramatically "motivate" our futurized readers and writers.

SUMMARY

Balanced literacy in today's classrooms involves reading comprehension and composition development as complementary ways of knowing and communicating. As such, reading and writing—for real purposes and real audiences—engage students in literacy learning both in and out of school. Writing can improve comprehension as students do the following:

1. Connect with text.
2. Experience a variety of text forms and composition formats.
3. Engage in reading, thinking, and writing for regular, sustained periods of time.

Reflecting on the important, balanced literacy relationship between reading comprehension and writing composition returns us to Michael Pressley's (2002) reminder that "when students are skilled in reading and writing and their motivation is maintained through appropriately challenging literacy experiences, they read and write more" (p. 355). In nurturing readers and writers who read and write more, with greater meaning and understanding, effective comprehension and composition instruction integrated with technology can arm students with tools for school, home, and the workplace, enabling them to envision, explore, and inhabit their own places in society. These comprehension and composition tools are rapidly changing as technology moves education, business, and industry forward at rapid paces. To survive and thrive, teachers and students must come together as colearners who engage in the evolution of reading and writing processes across the 21st century.

INTEGRATE, INVESTIGATE, AND INITIATE: QUESTIONS FOR DISCUSSION

1. I have presented 11 elements of writing instruction that improve students writing abilities. Observe a writing instructional lesson or analyze a writing lesson that is offered on the Internet or through a printed curriculum. How many principles are included in this lesson? What did this analysis tell you about the most important step we need to take in the future to improve writing instruction?
2. Summarize the ways that writing instruction improves reading comprehension.
3. Reread the projections and possibilities for a 2030 classroom. Draw a graphic image, describe, or write a summary about a specific classroom at a specific grade level, in which you envisioned the principles you have learned thus far in this book being implemented in the year 2030.

REFERENCES

Alvermann, D. E. (2004). Media, information communication technologies, and youth literacies: A cultural studies perspective. *American Behavioral Scientist, 48*(1), 78–83.

Anderson, A. A. (1997). *The effects of sociocognitive writing strategy instruction on the writing achievement and writing self-efficacy of students with disabilities and typical achievement in an urban elementary school.* Unpublished doctoral dissertation, University of Houston, Houston, TX.

Ardila, A. (2004). There is not any specific brain area for writing: From cave-paintings to computers. *International Journal of Psychology, 39*(1), 61–67.

Biancarosa, G., & Snow, C. E. (2004). *Reading next: A vision for action and research in middle and high school literacy: A report of the Carnegie Corporation of New York.* Washington, DC: Alliance for Excellent Education.

Brooks, G. W. (2007). Teachers as readers and writers and as teachers of reading and writing. *Journal of Educational Research, 100*(3), 177–191.

Calkins, L. M. (1983). *Lessons from a child: On the teaching and learning of writing*. Portsmouth, NH: Heinemann.

Calkins, L. M. (1986). *The art of teaching writing*. Portsmouth, NH: Heinemann.

De La Paz, S. (2007). Managing cognitive demands for writing: Comparing the effects of instructional components in strategy instruction. *Reading and Writing Quarterly, 23*, 249–266.

De La Paz, S., & Graham, S. (2002). Explicitly teaching strategies, skills, and knowledge: Writing instruction in middle school classrooms. *Journal of Educational Psychology, 94*, 687–698.

Duke, N. K., Purcell-Gates, V., Hall, L.A., & Tower, C. (2006/2007). Authentic literacy activities for developing comprehension and writing. *Reading Teacher, 60*, 344–355.

Fisher, D., & Frey, N. (2003). Writing instruction for struggling adolescent readers: A gradual release model. *Journal of Adolescent and Adult Literacy, 46*, 396–406.

Fitzgerald, J., & Shanahan, T. (2000). Reading and writing relations and their development. *Educational Psychologist, 35*(1), 39–50.

Frey, B. B., Lee, S. W., Tollefson, N., Pass, L., & Massengill, D. (2005). Balanced literacy in an urban school district. *Journal of Educational Research, 98*(5), 272–280.

Graham, S. (2006). Strategy instruction and the teaching of writing: A meta-analysis. In C. MacArthur, S. Graham, & J. Fitzgerald (Eds.), *Handbook of writing research* (pp. 187–207). New York: Guilford Press.

Graham, S., & Perin, D. (2007). *Writing next: Effective strategies to improve writing of adolescents in middle and high schools—A report to Carnegie Corporation of New York*. Washington, DC: Alliance for Excellent Education.

Graves, D. (1983). *Writing: Teachers and children at work*. Exeter, NH: Heinemann.

Gray, J. (1985). Joining a national network: The National Writing Project. *New Directions for Teaching and Learning, 24*, 61–68.

Jewitt, C. (2005). Multimodality, "Reading," and "Writing" for the 21st century. *Discourse: Studies in the Cultural Politics of Education, 26*, 315–331.

Knipper, K. J., & Duggan, T. J. (2006). Writing to learn across the curriculum: Tools for comprehension in content area classes. *Reading Teacher, 59*, 462–470.

Kuriloff, P. C. (2004). Rescuing writing instruction: How to save time and money with technology. *Liberal Education, 90*(4), 36–41.

Lacina, J. G. (2003/2004). Technology and the writing workshop. *Childhood Education, 80*(2), 101–103.

Landis, D. (2003). Reading and writing as social, cultural practices: Implications for literacy education. *Reading and Writing Quarterly, 19*, 281–307.

Leu, D. J., Kinzer, C. K., Coiro, J., & Cammack, D. (2004). Toward a theory of new literacies emerging from the Internet and other information and communication technologies. In R. Ruddel & N. Unrau (Eds.), *Theoretical models and processes of reading* (5th ed., pp. 1570–1614). Newark, DE: International Reading Association.

MacArthur, C. A. (2006). The effects of new technologies on writing and writing processes. In C. A. MacArthur, S. Graham, & J. Fitzgerald (Eds.), *Handbook of writing research* (pp. 248–262). New York: Guilford Press.

Montgomery, D. J., & Marks, L. J. (2006). Using technology to build independence in writing for students with disabilities. *Preventing School Failure, 50*(3), 33–38.

National Commission on Writing for America's Families, Schools, and Colleges (2003). *The neglected "R": The need for a writing revolution*. New York: College Entrance Examination Board. (ERIC Document Reproduction Service No. ED 475856)

Parodi, G. (2007). Reading–writing connections: Discourse-oriented research. *Reading and Writing, 20*, 225–250.

Pressley, M. (2002). *Reading instruction that works: The case for balanced teaching*. New York: Guilford Press.

Rickards, D., & Hawes, S. (2006). Connecting reading and writing through author's craft. *Reading Teacher, 60*, 370–376.

Routman, R. (1988). *Transitions: From literature to literacy*. Portsmouth, NH: Heinemann.

Routman, R. (1994). *Invitations: Changing teachers and learners K–12*. Portsmouth, NH: Heinemann.

Saddler, B., & Graham, S. (2005). The effects of peer-assisted sentence-combining instruction on the writing performance of more and less skilled young writers. *Journal of Educational Psychology, 97*, 43–54.

Saddler, B., & Graham, S. (2007). The relationship between writing knowledge and writing performance among more and less skilled writers. *Reading and Writing Quarterly, 23*, 231–247.

Stevens, R. J. (2003). Student team reading and writing: A cooperative learning approach to middle school literacy instruction. *Educational Research and Evaluation, 9*, 137–160.

Welty, E. (1985). *One writer's beginnings*. Cambridge, MA: Warner Books.

Yancey, K. B. (2004). Using multiple technologies to teach writing. *Educational Leadership, 62*(2), 38–40.

16

New Insights on Motivation in the Literacy Classroom

JACQUELYNN A. MALLOY and LINDA B. GAMBRELL

> Motivation does not reside solely in the child; rather it is in the interaction between students and their literacy environments.
> —TURNER AND PARIS (1995, p. 672)

It's Monday morning, and as Angie sits at her desk looking over her daily plan, students begin filing into the classroom.

"Good morning! How was your weekend?" She smiles, greeting students as they enter.

"Can we read a little since we're early?" asks Ben. "I found a book last Friday that might help me with my PowerPoint on meteorites. I think it would also be a great one for book sharing, if I finish it today!"

"Sure," Angie replies, glad to see Ben interested in reading. "Knock yourself out!" As Ben settles in with his book, a gaggle of girls approaches Angie's desk.

"Can we print out the information we gathered on dog breeds? We saved it on the computer last week and want to get started on our 'How to Choose the *Totally* Right Dog' brochure. We want to publish it and take it to the animal shelter before spring break."

"Absolutely," Angie replies. "I think your brochure will help a lot of people to choose the right pet. Go ahead and print it out—you can talk about how to synthesize the info a little later on."

After all of her students are seated and accounted for, and the announcements have been read, Angie begins the class with, "OK! What are *you* looking forward to working on today?"

Highly motivated students come into the classroom ready to work on projects they've started, books they've discovered, and projects they've left unfinished. Most teachers would agree that motivation is the Holy Grail of effective comprehension instruction. Creating a motivating instructional climate, where students are ready and willing to learn, to read, to comprehend, and to compose, requires a willingness on the teacher's part to get to know students' interests and needs. With this knowledge, teachers can assist students in setting goals, finding resources, developing strategies, and negotiating ways to engage with topics in personally relevant ways. When students are supported in cognitively and socially engaging ways with text, they make meaningful connections that have the potential to build their knowledge base—and by broadening and deepening their knowledge base, students are equipped to make connections with newly presented material. It is a wonderfully replenishing cycle that happens every day in classrooms where high motivation exists.

Clearly, teachers would prefer a room full of students who are engaged in the instruction provided, and who progress in their ability and willingness to read and write for school and for personal enjoyment. The most basic goal of any comprehension program is the development of highly motivated readers who *can* read, and who *choose* to read for pleasure and information. However, because motivation is not currently one of the "five pillars" of reading instruction identified by the National Reading Panel Report (2000)—that is, phonemic awareness, phonics, vocabulary, fluency, and comprehension—it does not receive the same focus or emphasis as the instructional goals. While all students deserve high-quality instruction in these areas, it is clear that if our students are not motivated to read, they will never reach their full literacy potential. We believe that motivation exerts a tremendous influence on comprehension development. In an attempt to place motivation at the heart of comprehension instruction, this chapter explores the following:

- The theories of achievement motivation and their influence on our developing understanding of literacy engagement.
- What research has to say about the factors that influence an individual student's motivation to engage in literacy tasks and the potential for this engagement to enhance comprehension.
- A theoretical framework for incorporating research findings in the literacy classroom.

ESTABLISHED THEORIES OF ACHIEVEMENT MOTIVATION

In the field of literacy research, a fair amount of activity has been aimed toward understanding the construct of literacy motivation and the components of that construct. In so doing, a number of factors that seem to be related to an individual student's motivation have been delineated. "Motivation for literacy," defined for the purposes of this discussion as the likelihood of engaging in a literacy task, and persisting in the activity despite challenges, grew out of decades of research by behavioral, humanistic, cognitive, and social–cognitive psychologists. Therefore, to ground the current state of our understanding of literacy motivation, we begin at the beginning with pertinent theories of achievement motivation.

In the early part of the 20th century, *behaviorists* maintained that our motivations grow from interactions with our environment—meaning that we are driven by things we want to attain (e.g., a reward or incentive) or avoid (e.g., an unpleasant consequence; Skinner, 1953; Thorndike, 1910; Watson, 1913). In today's classroom, whenever you see students reading *solely* for the purpose of receiving points, pizzas, or parties, they are responding to an environment that treats literacy as something that is externally controlled and quantifiable, as in the number of books read or tests taken. Of course, there are some who question the quality of the student's interaction with text when using these methods and the value of these extrinsic motivators in our attempts to encourage students to read intrinsically for information or for pleasure (Labbo, 1999; Lepper, Greene, & Nisbeit, 1973; Mallette, Henk, & Melnick, 2004). However, there are teachers (and parents) who argue that these extrinsic rewards are the only reason some students pick up a book.

Proposing that the source of human motivation is more internal than external, the view of *humanistic psychologists* is that we are driven by our internal needs and our quest to control our lives. For example, Maslow's hierarchy (1943) delineated four *deficiency* needs and three *growth* needs. The deficiency needs include *survival* (food, shelter, water), *safety* (free from emotional or physical threat or harm—such as bullies!), *belonging* (connections to others like oneself), and *self-esteem* (positive regard for oneself). If these deficiency needs are not met—and many of us can think of students for whom these needs are woefully unfulfilled—the growth needs of *intellectual achievement, aesthetic appreciation*, and *self-actualization* cannot be addressed.

Similarly, Deci and Ryan (1985) described in their *self-determination theory* that we have a need to experience control in our lives. Students who feel they have some control over their learning have been found to engage more meaningfully with learning tasks (Turner, 1995) and to be willing to accept greater challenges in learning (Csikszentmihalyi, 1990). In classrooms, for example, students may be offered a choice of three different assessments at the end of a unit, such as a taking a multiple-choice test, writing a paper, or presenting a project. In this way, students can engage with and respond to the material in a manner that provides for them an internal locus of control and a choice in how they express their knowledge.

Cognitive psychologists (Atkinson, 1964; Festinger, 1957; Vroom, 1964) would agree that the source of our motivation is internal. In their view, we are motivated by what we think—our attitudes, beliefs, ideas and goals. One such subtheory of these cognitive views, *attribution theory*, was developed by Weiner (1979, 1985), who proposed that individuals explain events in their lives by assigning an attribution to the expected outcome of engaging in an activity. These attributions are described by three continua of causality: *internal to external locus of control*, or the degree to which a student perceives ownership or direction of a behavior, or cedes it to others; *stability to instability*, indicating the reliability of a behavior to elicit similar results; and *controllability to uncontrollability*, which describes the perceived potential for influencing or changing the behavior. According to this theory, a student might explain a poor test grade with a remark such as "My teacher hates me!" (external, stable and uncontrollable) or "I didn't study enough!" (internal, unstable and controllable). This focus on student expectations for success heralded an interest in cognitive and affective factors of motivation.

A second cognitive subtheory, which involves an interest in how and why students set goals for achievement, stimulated research that has settled on two broad categories of goals that might be valued by students (Ames, 1992; Dweck & Leggett, 1988). These include *task* (or *mastery*) goals, described as a desire for personal improvement and mastery of a skill, and *ability* (or *performance*) goals that focus on one's performance in relation to others. Broadly related to the developing understanding of goal theory are the constructs of intrinsic and extrinsic motivation (Lepper et al., 1973). "Intrinsic motivation" can be described as self-generated interest in an activity that brings a pleasure that is inherent in engaging the activity itself. Describing a heightened form of intrinsic involvement, Csikszentmihalyi (1978) cited the experience of being totally absorbed in an activity as "flow," such as when reading a book that is so interesting that one loses the perception of place or of time passing. This can be differentiated from "extrinsic motivation," which is more closely associated with other-oriented aspects of goal setting, such as rewards, recognition, and approval or obedience, as are the ability goals previously described.

A more contemporary view of motivation is expressed by the social-cognitive theorists, who believe that we are driven by what we think of ourselves (internal source) and the task presented (external source). In 1983, Eccles and her colleagues introduced a theory of motivation that has been highly influential in current literacy motivation research. The *expectancy–value* theory of motivation has its roots in the work of Atkinson (1957) and, broadly defined, poses that an individual's perception of potential success (*expectancy*) in performing a task and the perceived *value* attributed to the activity are determinants of the person's willingness to engage in achievement behaviors. Eccles and her colleagues (1983) posited three essential components of an individual's perceived value of engaging in a task: *importance* (attainment value), *intrinsic value* (personally generated), and *utility value* (usefulness). These aspects are described as *subjective task values* (Eccles & Wigfield, 2002) and refer to the individual's incentive or reason for engaging in the task. Perceptions of expectancy, thought to be influenced by the individual's sense of competence in completing a specific task successfully, are based on Bandura's (1977, 1982) work on self-efficacy, which he describes as a self-judgment of a domain-specific ability to perform a task successfully. The expectancy–value theory serves as a suitable initial framework for organizing the more specific research on literacy motivation.

ESTABLISHED RESEARCH ON LITERACY MOTIVATION IN THE CLASSROOM

Reading is an activity that is initially full of effort. In learning to read, children make a purposeful transition from a world of oral language to one of printed language. In so doing, the relationship of letters to sounds and the visual negotiation of symbols situated on pages that beg to be decoded into meaningful words seems a monumental task, but one they have seen others successfully accomplish. If children perceive a value in learning to read and write, and if the environment provides resources and opportunities to guide the endeavor, it is quite likely they will attain some level of comprehension. But what then? Once the code is broken and the mystery is solved, what maintains their interest and engagement in the process of developing into mature and discerning literate beings?

Perhaps the most concentrated and foundational effort to understand literacy motivation and instruction was the research conducted through the National Reading Research Center (NRRC), which received funding from the Office of Educational Research and Improvement of the U.S. Department of Education in the 5-year period from 1992 to 1997. During this time the *engagement perspective* of literacy motivation guided investigations into reading instruction that would develop "motivated and strategic readers who use literacy for pleasure and learning" (National Reading Research Center, 1997, p. 5). Drawing on the body of research that led up to the 5-year research initiative, the engagement perspective assumes that desire to read, strategies to improve reading ability, knowledge, and social interactions are key components to cultivating "highly engaged, self-determining readers who are architects of their own learning" (Alvermann & Guthrie, 1993, p. 2). Several studies explored home, school, and community contexts of literacy motivation for preschool-, elementary-, and secondary-age students. A sampling of this research across grade levels follows.

The 1997 NRRC report indicated that preschool children can become engaged readers when the following factors are present: Their homes contain an abundance and variety of print materials; they are given opportunities to read and to be read to; they see caregivers modeling reading behaviors; they have opportunities to play, to interact with environmental print, and to gain knowledge by exploring their world inside and outside of the home; they have caring interactions and discussions with adults and older siblings, and make connections with schools (p. 22).

NRRC researchers Gambrell, Codling, and Palmer (1996) explored the reading motivation of elementary students and found that access to books, choice of reading materials, and discussion of readings (e.g., through book clubs) were highly motivating factors in the school setting. Furthermore, students are motivated to engage in reading when teachers and students share books together. Palmer, Codling, and Gambrell (1994) found that when teachers read selections from high-quality literature aloud to the class and discuss what they like about the books, students are more motivated to read those selections than to read books not introduced by teachers. Research evidence also suggests that children benefit from opportunities to discuss books with others, and the social interactions have been found to have a positive effect on reading engagement (Almasi, 1995; Oldfather & McLaughlin, 1993).

At middle and high school levels, NRRC researchers investigated reading for pleasure through programs designed to encourage students to read for pleasure with their peers in Read and Talk Clubs (Alvermann, Young, & Green, 1997). In each instance, students were permitted to choose materials that reflected their personal interests or preferences and social interactions with others—two personally relevant aspects of literacy involvement.

The importance of the NRRC initiative was that it incorporated motivation to read into a broader understanding of reading engagement as it affected social and instructional contexts for learning to read. NRRC research findings, especially with regard to classroom contexts and instructional methods, highlighted the interrelatedness of values, beliefs, and social factors for reading engagement and rich comprehension.

HOW MOTIVATION CAN IMPROVE COMPREHENSION INSTRUCTION

Research into the effects of instruction on reading engagement suggests that certain aspects of the classroom environment and the instructional practices used by teachers can encourage reading engagement and increase comprehension. Classroom environments that provide appropriate materials, strategic support, and instructional resources are more likely to nurture literacy engagement (Anderman & Midgley, 1992; Gambrell & Morrow, 1996). Several researchers (e.g., Morrow, 1992; Neuman & Celano, 2001) have suggested that classrooms with an abundance and variety of print materials positively affect the quality and frequency of literacy behaviors in the classroom.

In continuing research on the effects of Concept-Oriented Reading Instruction (CORI), Guthrie and his colleagues (Guthrie & Cox, 2001; Guthrie, McGough, Bennett, & Rice, 1996; Guthrie, Wigfield, & Von Secker, 2000) explored the features of classroom contexts that were related to long-term comprehension growth and reading engagement in fifth graders. The CORI program introduced by Guthrie et al. (1996) was designed to merge reading comprehension strategy instruction and content material, such as science or social studies, to produce a combined positive effect on both reading comprehension and motivation. Their results suggested that strategic instruction that utilizes text-to-self connections, interesting trade books, student choice in reading, and small-group collaborations results in significantly higher measures of motivation for fifth-grade students (based on the Motivation for Reading Questionnaire; Wigfield & Guthrie, 1997).

Designing Engaging Literacy Tasks

Brophy (2004) and Cunningham and Allington (1999) found that children are more motivated to engage in literacy activities that are authentic—based on real-world purposes—and that connect them to their home cultures. Students are also more engaged in tasks that permit them to choose materials for reading and to set their own goals (Cambourne, 1995; Schunk & Zimmerman, 1997, Turner, 1995), and children report a higher level of interest and enjoyment in books they personally have chosen (Schiefele, 1991; Spaulding, 1992). Supporting these findings, Turner and Paris (1995), stated: "The most reliable indicator of motivation for literacy learning is not the type of reading program that districts follow, but the actual daily tasks that teachers provided in their classrooms" (p. 662).

In her research with 84 6-year-olds, Turner (1995) utilized classroom observations and student interviews to understand the effects of classroom tasks on student engagement with literacy tasks. Based on a view that intrinsic motivation to learn is key to literacy engagement, Turner found that certain tasks increased students' internal locus of control and intrinsic motivation to participate. These *open tasks* were distinguished from *closed tasks*. Open tasks involved several of the factors found in previous research to be motivating, such as choice of topics, partners, or materials; personally relevant or authentic tasks that related to students interests, goals, and abilities; enough challenge to make the outcome personally rewarding; and social collaboration, in which interactions expand students' knowledge and point of view. When tasks were "closed," students were forced to find the "one right answer" or to complete a task that was not relevant or connected to their lives, or that involved a product or outcome determined by the teacher. Turner found that open tasks predisposed students to associate literacy with cognitive involvement and provided a focus for the uses and purposes of literacy.

Literacy Engagement and Reading Comprehension

Reading comprehension can be thought of as a cognitive act; that is, without a cognitive investment on the part of the student, comprehension is not likely to occur. The strategies and self-regulation required to understand text—especially at an instructional reading level—necessitate a continued effort on the part of the student. Cognitive engagement occurs when the student voluntarily accesses higher-order skills, such as self-regulation and monitoring strategies (Blumenfeld & Meece, 1988). So the question becomes, how do we use what research has shown us regarding contexts, tasks, and literacy motivation to entice our students to *cognitively engage* in comprehension, and how do we encourage them to continue when the search for meaning becomes effortful?

To answer these important questions, we must recall the basic framework of expectancy–value theory. We are all more likely to involve ourselves in activities when we feel we can participate successfully and value the process or the outcome. Teachers already know a great deal about how to assist students in experiencing success with literacy tasks: They provide students with strategies for decoding and comprehension, processes for writing, and metacognitive awarenesses to monitor their progress. Teachers model these strategies, present opportunities for practice, and provide feedback.

To increase the value of literacy activities, teachers should create classroom climates that encourage intrinsic motivations for learning, and a task or mastery orientation. They should surround students with books and other types of text, online computer access, and opportunities to share with each other in pairs, or in literacy groups or workshops. Teachers want their students to feel that they are literate souls within a *community* of literate souls. But even with this attention rightfully focused on value and expectancy factors, there may be an aspect of value that is left unattended; however, it is one that can be thoughtfully addressed, with hopes of rounding out a student's motivation to *cognitively* engage in literacy tasks and improve the quality of their learning.

Teasing Out the Utility Value of Tasks

In his 1999 theoretical piece, Brophy proposes that we mirror the progress we have made in matching content to cognitive strategies by creating optimal matches between content and motivational strategies. Here Brophy agrees with Turner (1995) and Turner and Paris (1995) that the source of a student's engagement with the content we present does not exist solely within the student, but in the interaction between the student and the material. Students might be predisposed to learn material in which they already are interested or for which they currently hold some level of curiosity, but what about the things we feel students should learn that have no intrinsic value to them at all? Brophy proposes that we tease out the *utility value* of the material and scaffold the student toward some appreciation for the worth of the learning target. Here are some of Brophy's suggestions for increasing students' interest in and comprehension of content when they are not intrinsically predisposed to the topic:

1. *Create some situational interest in the learning domain by presenting enough information to make the topic familiar and relevant to the student.* The initial goal of many comprehension strategies is to assist the student in accessing some prior knowledge of the topic, but it's important to do so in a way that connects to students' lives or their sense of self. This has been done in the CORI research (Guthrie et al., 1996, 2001) on science topics by involving the students in natural observations or experiments that pique their interest and entice them to know more. When you have matched the topic or learning target to some aspect of the student's lives and made it relevant in some way, you move into what Brophy terms "the Motivational Zone of Proximal Development" (1999, p. 77).

2. *Encourage the development of curricula that tie learning outcomes to student's lives.* Although curricular development is often determined by school districts and administrators or coordinators, teachers are often asked to assist on curricular development committees. Consider how much easier it would be to motivate interest in a topic if the learning outcomes were tied to some aspect of our students' lives outside of the classroom. For example, the learning target, "recognize and discriminate among a variety of informational texts" could be tied to the purposes and uses of the genre in school and home environments. [Examples of how this might be done are provided in the paragraph that follows.] Not every curricular standard is easily transposed into a relevant and authentic purpose, but if we take the time to know more about our students and their lives, their communities and their interests, we can make connections between learning and living. And if the learning target is *not* easily tied to some aspect of living in society, perhaps we should question why we must teach it.

3. *Once curricular goals are set and the learning targets are established, it is incumbent upon the teacher to create an "optimally mediated learning experience."* Teachers can scaffold a student's appreciation of the material by stimulating interest and connecting the learning outcome to the student's life and to previous learning.

To continue the example of introducing the genre of informational text to your third graders: After defining the genre briefly and passing around a few examples of these types of reading materials, you might want to poll the students for types of informational texts they've seen or used before—such as newspapers that carry information about what's going on in the world; directions for putting together a new bicycle; Web pages on the Internet where they might search topics of interest; and course books and trade books that provide specific information from which they might learn. Perhaps after discussing times when they needed to find specific information to answer a question or to know more about a subject of interest, students could survey various informational texts to determine features they have in common, such as headings, pictures, diagrams, and sidebars. By being entirely explicit in your comprehension instruction, you model for your students how you access these features to realize your goal of finding general or specific information, depending on your goal in using the text. In this way, you have begun to teach students comprehension strategies for accessing a particular genre in a manner that should lead to their successful interactions with text and ability to engage cognitively with the materials. This is done by modeling what you're thinking as you access new material ("Because I don't have to read expository text straight through like a story, I can just look at the headings and zero in on the information I want right now"), providing opportunities for practice ("Choose a book on a topic that you already know something about. Did they lay out the information in a way that makes sense to you? How would you do it?"), and feedback ("I think your idea of putting the map on the first page would help a lot! Now, where would you put the text that describes what the map shows?"). Ultimately, students can choose projects that showcase the ways they might utilize their knowledge, such as creating a brochure on choosing a dog as a pet and donating it to the animal shelter, or creating a slide show presentation on sites where meteorites have landed on the earth.

When we move the utility value of a comprehension target out into the open, such as in the examples discussed previously, we create for the student a *clear path* from their existing knowledge and experiences to new knowledge and experiences. Clear paths are created when the content is made relevant to our students' present and future lives, and when they are given strategies to comprehend and to apply the knowledge gained from this new comprehension. It is in these connections and interactions between the content we present and the lives of our students that comprehension and understanding can flourish, and where we can allow our students to build some intrinsic interest and measure of competence in moving toward the motivated and strategic learners that we (and they!) hope they become.

DIRECTIONS FOR FUTURE RESEARCH

1. *How do literacy practices and teacher interactions influence student expectancies for literacy tasks—particularly for students with varying levels of ability?* Chapman and Tunmer (2003) reviewed studies that indicate the self-concepts and self-efficacy related to reading in young children develop in response to their initial successes or failures with

learning to read. Students who experience early difficulties in learning to read may begin to label themselves as "poor readers" and, with this reduced self-efficacy, may be less willing to engage in or value reading comprehension tasks. As predicted by the Matthew effect (Stanovich, 1986), the poor indeed do become poorer. Research that documents the development and trajectory of these attitudes, such as through repeated interviews with students by gender and varying levels of ability across the early grades, would help educators to visualize where the "clear path" to valuing and expecting literacy attainment is being obstructed, and to consider how best to intervene.

2. *What classroom contexts and instructional practices facilitate the growth of intrinsic motivation for students from various cultural and linguistic backgrounds and varying levels of ability?* Turner's (1995) work involving open versus closed tasks, and the work of Guthrie and his colleagues (1996, 2000; Guthrie & Cox, 2001) in developing CORI, present evidence that literacy engagement is enhanced when comprehension instruction offers choice, relevance, explicit strategy instruction, and access to resources. Additional research that explores the efficacy of these promising instructional practices with an expanded array of grade levels, subject areas, and diversity of participants would provide much-needed information regarding the specific needs of certain individuals and particular sub-groups of the student population.

3. *What formative comprehension assessments or practices can be designed to help teachers stay attuned to students' changing interests, values, and self-concepts as readers?* At present, measures exist that are helpful in determining students' school and recreational reading interests, such as the Elementary Reading Attitude Scale (McKenna & Kear, 1990), and students' value and self-concept of reading, as with the Motivation to Read Profile (Gambrell, Palmer, Codling, & Mazzoni, 1996). Although these instruments help teachers to assess important elements of motivation, they do not assist in determining the effect of the interface between students' needs and the comprehension instruction offered—the utility value. Interestingly, Vroom (1964) posits a strikingly similar construct, using the term *instrumentality*, as being differentiated from value and expectancy. The addition of instrumentality to the existing constructs of value and expectancy may provide an avenue for exploring what we described earlier as utility value. His VIE theory of motivation (Motivation = Valence × Instrumentality × Expectancy), sometimes used in business applications, may find its way into the field of educational research. For example, there is a need to develop assessment measures that, when administered periodically throughout the school year, validly and reliably target a student's perceived value, instrumentality, and expectancy for reading comprehension activities and tasks. Such an instrument would assist teachers in fine-tuning instruction and providing suitable materials and resources to meet individual student needs and interests.

PROJECTIONS AND POSSIBILITIES FOR THE CLASSROOM OF 2030

In the year 2030, motivation will be seen as a crucial component of teaching and learning in all areas of instruction, such as phonemic and phonological awareness, phonics, fluency, vocabulary, and comprehension. Teachers in highly motivating classrooms will create opportunities to become familiar with their students' interests and goals through cooperative projects and individualized tasks in which students use the knowledge they have to delve brain-first into the knowledge they crave. Teachers will view themselves as colearners with their students as they cognitively engage in learning tasks that are instrumental to their current lives as well as their perceived future lives.

Furthermore, research that investigates new instructional practices will be required to consider the possible motivational influences in addition to student mastery of comprehension targets. For a preview of what these classrooms might look like, please see the work of McCombs (2003) and her discussion of learner-centered psychological principles. These principles involve cognitive and metacognitive factors, such as strategic thinking and contexts for learning, motivational and affective factors that highlight intrinsic motivations to learn and the effects of motivation on effort, as well as developmental and individual factors that consider social factors and individual differences (p. 95). These hopeful predictions are based on the assumption that in the year 2030, educators and administrators will see the value of basing policy on well-researched and agreed-upon principles.

SUMMARY

Our knowledge of literacy engagement has its roots in the study of general achievement motivation, and the research of numerous, past educational psychologists continues to inform our comprehension practices today. Reading comprehension instruction in classrooms is both a cognitive and social enterprise that requires thoughtful intervention to suit a variety of student interests and needs. Comprehension necessitates a connection between what is already known and new content in a strategic and self-regulated manner. However, as one student's background knowledge, intrinsic involvement, ability, and efficacy for a particular comprehension task will likely be quite different than that of nearly every other student in the classroom, effective instruction should incorporate some manner of choice, collaboration, and situated interest with which students engage and persist in the specific meaning-making activity.

Although curricula are often set by district policies—sometimes with little teacher input—teachers can position themselves as change agents in connecting students' lives to the content presented, and their minds to the texts. The NRRC initiative provided the field of literacy research with a valuable standard: to evaluate our practices in terms of how they promote motivated, strategic, knowledgeable, and socially interactive learners. Although the NRRC has concluded its 5-year effort, we would do well as educators and researchers to continue striving to provide well-integrated and engaging reading comprehension instruction to all of our students.

INTEGRATE, INVESTIGATE, AND INITIATE: QUESTIONS FOR DISCUSSION

1. Describe the three most important actions that you will initiate to increase the amount of motivation that you build into your reading lessons to improve students' comprehension.

2. Observe a reading comprehension lesson. Decide which theoretical influences in this chapter were incorporated into that lesson: (a) designing engaging literacy tasks, (b) using literacy engagement with reading comprehension, or (c) teasing out the utility value of tasks. Document your findings with specific anecdotes that occurred during this lesson.

3. Create a method of teaching that teases out the utility value of a task, using one of the three suggestions cited in this chapter to do so. Share the idea you created with colleagues. Summarize how the information from this shared experience can improve comprehension in your school or school district.

REFERENCES

Almasi, J. F. (1995). The nature of fourth graders' socio-cognitive conflicts in peer-led and teacher-led discussions of literature. *Reading Research Quarterly, 30*(3), 314–351.

Alvermann, D. A., & Guthrie, J. T. (1993). *Themes and directions of the National Reading Research Center* (Project Report No. 1). Athens, GA: National Reading Research Center.

Alvermann, D. A., Young, J. P., & Green, C. (1997). *Adolescents' negotiations of out-of-school reading discussions* (Research Report No. 77). Athens, GA: National Reading Research Center.

Ames, C. A. (1992). Classrooms: Goals, structures, and student motivation. *Journal of Educational Psychology, 84*(3), 261–271.

Anderman, E. M., & Midgley, C. (1992). Changes in achievement goal orientations, perceived academic competence, and grades across the transition to middle-level schools. *Contemporary Educational Psychology, 22*(3), 269–298.

Atkinson, J. W. (1964). *An introduction to motivation*. Princeton, NJ: Van Nostrand.

Atkinson, J. W. (1957). Motivational determinants of risk-taking. *Psychological Review, 64*, 359–372.

Bandura, A. (1977). *Social learning theory*. New York: General Learning Press.

Bandura, A. (1982). Self-efficacy mechanism in human agency. *American Psychologist, 37*(2), 122–147.

Blumenfeld, P. C., & Meece, J. L. (1988). Task factors, teacher behavior, and students' involvement and use of learning strategies in science. *Elementary School Journal, 88*(3), 235–250.

Brophy, J. (1999). Toward a model of the value aspects of motivation in education: Developing appreciation for particular learning domains and activities. *Educational Psychologist, 34*(2), 75–85.

Brophy, J. (2004). *Motivating students to learn*. Mahwah, NJ: Erlbaum.

Cambourne, B. (1995). Towards an educationally relevant theory of literacy learning: Twenty years of inquiry. *Reading Teacher, 49*(3), 182–192.

Chapman, J. W., & Tunmer, W. E. (2003). Reading difficulties, reading-related self-perceptions, and strategies for overcoming negative self-beliefs. *Reading and Writing Quarterly, 19*(1), 5–24.

Csikszentmihalyi, M. (1978). Intrinsic rewards and emergent motivation. In M. Lepper & D. Greene (Eds.), *The hidden costs of reward: New perspectives on the psychology of human motivation* (pp. 205–216). Hillsdale, NJ: Erlbaum.

Csikszentmihalyi, M. (1990). *Flow: The psychology of optimal experience*. New York: Harper & Row.

Cunningham, P. M., & Allington, R. L. (1999). *Classrooms that work: They all can read and write* (2nd ed.). Reading, MA: Addison-Wesley/Longman.

Deci, E. L., & Ryan, R. M. (1985). *Intrinsic motivation and self-determination in human behavior*. New York: Plenum Press.

Dweck, C. S., & Leggett, E. L. (1988). A social-cognitive approach to motivation an personality. *Psychological Review, 95*, 256–273.

Eccles, J., Adler, T., Futterman, R., Goff, S. B., Kaezala, C. M., Meece, J. L., et al. (1983). Expectancies, values, and academic behaviors. In J. T. Spence (Ed.), *Achievement and achievement motives: Psychological and sociological approaches* (pp. 75–146). San Francisco: Freeman.

Eccles, J. S., & Wigfield, A. (2002). Motivational beliefs, values, and goals. *Annual Review of Psychology, 53*, 109–132.

Festinger, L. (1957). *A theory of cognitive dissonance*. Evanston, IL: Row, Peterson & Company.

Gambrell, L. B., & Morrow, L. M. (1996). Motivating contexts for literacy learning. In L. Baker, P. Afflerbach, & D. Reinking (Eds.), *Developing engaged readers in school and home communities* (pp. 115–136). Mahwah, NJ: Erlbaum.

Gambrell, L. B., Codling, R. M., & Palmer, B. M. (1996). *Elementary students' motivation to read*

(National Reading Research Center Report No. 52). Athens, GA: National Reading Research Center.

Gambrell, L. B., Palmer, B. M., Codling, R. M., & Mazzoni, S. A. (1996). Assessing motivation to read. *Reading Teacher, 49*(7), 518–533.

Guthrie, J. T., & Cox, K. E. (2001). Classroom conditions for motivation and engagement in reading. *Education Psychology Review, 13*(3), 283–302.

Guthrie, J. T., McGough, K., Bennett, L., & Rice, M. E. (1996). Concept-oriented reading instruction: An integrated curriculum to develop motivations and strategies for reading. In L. Baker, P. Afflerbach, & D. Reinking (Eds.), *Developing engaged readers In school and home communities* (pp. 165–190). Hillsdale, NJ: Erlbaum.

Guthrie, J., Wigfield, A., & VonSecker, C. (2000). Effects of integrated instruction on motivation and strategy use in reading. *Journal of Educational Psychology, 92*(2), 331–341.

Labbo, L. (1999). Five more questions worth asking. In *Reading online*. Retrieved October 20, 2006, through the International Reading Association at *www.readingonline.org*.

Lepper, M. R., Greene, D., & Nisbeit, R. E. (1973). Undermining children's intrinsic interest with extrinsic reward: A test of the overjustification hypothesis. *Journal of Personality and Social Psychology, 28*(1), 129–137.

Mallette, M. H., Henk, W. A., & Melnick, S. A. (2004). The influence of Accelerated Reader on the affective literacy orientations of intermediate grade students. *Journal of Literacy Research, 36*(1), 73–84.

Maslow, A. H. (1943). A theory of human motivation. *Psychological Review, 50*, 370–396.

McCombs, B. L. (2003). A framework for the redesign of K–12 education in the context of current educational reform. *Theory Into Practice, 42*(2), 93–102.

McKenna, M. C., & Kear, D. J. (1990). Measuring attitudes toward reading: A new tool for teachers. *Reading Teacher, 43*(8), 626–639.

Morrow, L. M. (1992). The impact of a literature-based program on literacy achievement, use of literature and attitudes of children from minority backgrounds. *Reading Research Quarterly, 27*(3), 251–275.

National Reading Panel Report. (2000). *Teaching children to read: An evidence-based assessment of the scientific research literature on reading and its implications for reading instruction.* Washington, DC: National Institute of Child Health and Human Development.

National Reading Research Center. (1997). *Engaged reading for pleasure and learning: A report from the National Reading Research Center* (J. F. Baumann & A. M. Duffy, Eds.). Athens, GA: Author.

Neuman, S. B., & Celano, D. (2001). Access to print in low-income and middle-income communities: An ecological study of four neighborhoods. *Reading Research Quarterly, 36*(1), 8–26.

Oldfather, P., & McLaughlin, J. (1993). Gaining and losing voice: A longitudinal study of students' continuing impulse to learn across elementary and middle school contexts. *Research in Middle Level Education, 17*(1), 1–25.

Palmer, B. M., Codling, R. M., & Gambrell, L. B. (1994). In their own words: What elementary students have to say about motivation to read. *Reading Teacher, 48*(2), 176–178.

Schiefele, U. (1991). Interest, learning, and motivation. *Educational Psychologist, 26*(3–4), 299–323.

Schunk, D. H., & Zimmerman, B. J. (1997). Social origins of self-regulatory competence. *Educational Psychologist, 32*(4), 195–208.

Skinner, B. F. (1953). *Science and human behavior.* New York: Free Press.

Spaulding, C. L. (1992). *Motivation in the classroom.* New York: McGraw-Hill.

Stanovich, K. E. (1986). Matthew effects in reading: Some consequences of individual differences: I. The acquisition of literacy. *Reading Research Quarterly, 21*(4), 360–407.

Thorndike, E. L. (1910). The contribution of psychology to education. *Journal of Educational Psychology, 1*, 5–12.

Turner, J. (1995). The influence of classroom contexts on young children's motivation for literacy. *Reading Research Quarterly, 30*(3), 410–441.

Turner, J., & Paris, S. G. (1995). How literacy tasks influence children's motivation for literacy. *Reading Teacher, 48*(8), 662–673.

Vroom, V. H. (1964). *Work and motivation.* New York: Wiley.

Watson, J. B. (1913). Psychology as the behaviorist views it. *Psychological Review, 20,* 158–177.

Weiner, B. (1979). A theory of motivation for some classroom experiences. *Journal of Educational Psychology, 71*(1), 3–25.

Weiner, B. (1985). An attributional theory of achievement motivation and emotion. *Psychological Review, 92*(4), 548–573.

Wigfield, A., & Guthrie, J. T. (1997). Relations of children's motivation for reading to the amount and breadth of their reading. *Journal of Educational Psychology, 89*(3), 420–432.

IV

DIFFERENTIATED COMPREHENSION INSTRUCTION

17

Comprehension Instruction in Action

The Elementary Classroom

NELL K. DUKE and NICOLE M. MARTIN

> If reading is about mind journeys, teaching reading is about outfitting the travelers, modeling how to use the map, demonstrating the key and the legend, supporting the travelers as they lose their way and take circuitous routes, until, ultimately, it's the child and the map together and they are off on their own.
> —Keene and Zimmermann (1997, p. 28)

If this quotation captures the task of teaching reading comprehension, then elementary educators can be seen as both the travel agents and the tour guides. When students begin their elementary education, most have never comprehended a text they have read themselves (rather than one read to them). Elementary educators are the travel agents responsible for helping students understand the journey toward reading comprehension they are about to take and helping them want to take it. Then, as throughout the journey, they serve as tour guides, providing the dispositions, background knowledge, and ways of thinking that students need to become, we hope, increasingly sophisticated comprehenders, confident travelers.

So, indeed, the elementary years play, or should play, a critical role in the development of reading comprehension. It is widely agreed that elementary educators, even primary grade educators, are responsible for more than developing students' ability to read individual words and connected text fluently (National Reading Panel, 2000; Snow, Burns, & Griffin, 1998). They are also charged with:

- *Developing students' disposition to comprehend.* We have all met students who view reading primarily as recognizing words on the page rather than comprehending their collective meaning(s). Elementary educators are responsible for ensuring that students do not adopt this stance, even in the first few years of schooling, when learning to recognize words is a major focus, and certainly in the time thereafter.
- *Developing students' disposition to comprehend deeply.* We have all met the test or instruction that implies comprehension is about recalling trivial details from text. Elementary educators have to work vigorously against any such forces to ensure that students do not enter middle school with this stance toward reading.
- *Developing the habits of mind to comprehend.* Good comprehenders engage in certain ways of thinking when they comprehend (e.g., Pressley & Afflerbach, 1995)—integrating prior knowledge and material in the text, asking themselves questions as they read, attending to the structure of the text, and so on. Elementary educators are the *force majeure* for developing these habits of mind.
- *Developing the knowledge base for comprehension.* Wilson and Anderson (1986) once wrote that when it comes to reading comprehension, "what you don't know can hurt you." A lack of substantial knowledge and vocabulary base impedes comprehension; thus, elementary educators are charged with sending students to middle and high school with the knowledge base that texts and teachers assume.
- *Developing the ability to "do" something with comprehension.* In many standards documents, not simply comprehending, but "doing" something with that comprehension is expected—the ability to engage in sophisticated discussion of text, to compare one text to another, to write a report drawing from a range of texts, and so on. Helping students learn to do this is an enormous task for the elementary educator.
- *Developing students' desire to comprehend.* None of these dispositions, none of this knowledge, none of these habits of mind or abilities will be of value if students do not form a deep desire to comprehend texts they encounter. The elementary years are traditionally marked by a steady decline in positive attitudes toward reading (McKenna, Kear, & Ellsworth, 1995), a decline that elementary educators are charged with counteracting.

Elementary educators who are successful in all this position students to spend their later years of formal schooling learning to meet the growing comprehension demands of more complex, specific academic disciplines and occupational fields, and coping with the more difficult and unfamiliar reading tasks, technologies, and genres they encounter.

Given this multifaceted and formidable task, it is easy to feel overwhelmed when contemplating comprehension instruction in elementary school—and it was easy to feel overwhelmed trying to capture it in a single chapter! After providing a summary of some of the established knowledge bases about comprehension instruction in the elementary years, we focus on five trends in comprehension research and development in these years:

- Developing students' background knowledge.
- Increasing attention to genre.
- Teaching to the demands of new technologies.
- Using authentic contexts for comprehension instruction.
- Attending to the needs of English Language Learners (ELLs).

We conclude with a summary, and some directions and visions for future research and development in this area.

WHAT'S OUT THERE TODAY: ESTABLISHED RESEARCH AND PRACTICE

Reading comprehension at the elementary level is a well-established and thriving area of research. This may be due in part to the fact that it is foregrounded in many current theories of reading; that is, many theories (e.g., Rosenblatt, 2004; Ruddell & Unrau, 2004; Rumelhart, 2004) cite meaning making as the ultimate end product of reading. Because reading comprehension is not taught in schools as often as we might like (Durkin, 1978/1979; Kurth & Greenlaw, 1980; Wendler, Samuels, & Moore, 1989), a desire to draw more attention to comprehension instruction may also be contributing to the impetus in this area.

Whatever the reason, researchers have learned much about comprehension in elementary school. Among other things, it is long and well established that comprehension instruction in the elementary years

- *Should occur.* That is, various deliberate and explicit approaches to teaching children to comprehend what they read do in fact help elementary-age children to comprehend better (National Reading Panel, 2000). Good comprehension does not necessarily happen automatically, even given good word recognition and oral language skills (for a review, see Duke, Pressley, & Hilden, 2004).
- *Should Start Early.* Although there is far less research on comprehension instruction in the primary grades, the research we have indicates that teaching comprehension at these grade levels can produce improvements for children (for reviews, see Pearson & Duke, 2002; Stahl, 2004), and without detracting from their decoding development (Brown, Pressley, Van Meter, & Schuder, 1996). Indeed, studies of highly effective teachers and schools consistently find that primary grade teachers give their attention to comprehension, as well as to decoding and encoding (Block & Mangieri, 2003; Knapp & Associates, 1995; Pressley, Rankin, & Yokoi, 1996; Pressley et al., 2001; Taylor, Pearson, Clark, & Walpole, 2000; Wharton-McDonald, Pressley, & Hampston, 1998).
- *Should Attend to Language Knowledge.* Although, as noted earlier, good reading comprehension is not simply a matter of strong oral language skills, there is also no doubt that comprehension relies heavily on language knowledge and skills. Language difficulties are strongly linked to reading comprehension problems in the elementary years (for a review, see Scarborough, 2001), and reading comprehension and vocabulary knowledge are integrally related (for reviews, see National Reading Panel, 2000; Stahl, 1998).
- *Should Include Strategy Instruction.* A robust body of research demonstrates that explicitly teaching children strategies for understanding what they read improves their comprehension (for reviews, see Block & Duffy, Chapter 2, this volume; Duke & Pearson, 2002; National Reading Panel, 2000), with much of this research conducted with elementary-age children. Although the list of which strategies should be taught, and/or the names for these strategies, differs somewhat from study to study and review to review, they generally include those cited by Block and Duffy, (Chapter 2, this volume) and some variation of teaching students to activate and apply background knowledge relevant to the text, preview text, attend to text structure, make predictions, monitor their understanding, generate questions related to text, visualize, use graphic organizers, and summarize.
- *Should Include Rich Discussion and Writing.* It is also well accepted that particular kinds of discussion and writing can improve comprehension (for reviews, see

Nystrand, 2006; Shanahan, 2006). For example, Saunders and Goldenberg (1999) demonstrated that a form of discussion called instructional conversations, combined with regular writing in literature logs improved the narrative reading comprehension of fourth- and fifth-grade students, including ELLs.

These long- and well-established insights, if implemented fully, would go a long way toward improving reading comprehension in the elementary years and beyond. But some newer research emphases in this area can further deepen and refine our ability to improve reading comprehension; we turn to these newer emphases in the next section of the chapter.

NEW RESEARCH IN THIS AREA

It is beyond the scope of this chapter to review all recent research in reading comprehension in the elementary years. Some of this research is addressed in other chapters of this volume, or in recent or forthcoming reviews (e.g., Block & Pressley, 2007; reviews for the upcoming fourth volume of the *Handbook of Reading Research*). Here we have chosen to focus on five trends in this area. Not all of these trends represent new insights, but all have received particular attention in recent years. Of course, the list is not exhaustive, although within this list alone are many new and exciting developments:

- The importance of developing students' background knowledge as a part of comprehension instruction.
- The need to increase attention to the role of genre in reading comprehension.
- The need to teach to the demands of new technologies.
- The value of using authentic contexts for comprehension instruction.
- The importance of understanding reading comprehension in ELLs.

The Importance of Developing Students' Background Knowledge as a Part of Comprehension Instruction

The notion that one's knowledge base impacts one's comprehension has a long history, flourishing in particular during the development of schema theory (e.g., Anderson, 1984). In the 1980s, Stanovich proposed that individual differences in reading could be attributed in part to "Matthew effects," or "the rich-get-richer" phenomenon: Better readers tend to have a stronger knowledge base and more opportunities for practice, allowing them to continue to race ahead, thereby further building their knowledge base (Stanovich, 2004, p. 481). Despite these insights, however, relatively little reading comprehension research has focused on building background knowledge or on the impact of reading comprehension instruction focused heavily on knowledge building.

In recent years various commentators (Chall & Jacobs, 2003; Hart & Risley, 2003; Hirsch, 2003, 2006; Neuman, 2006) have underscored the importance of background knowledge in reading comprehension, arguing that schools have been underattentive to this—that schools have a responsibility to help children acquire the world knowledge and vocabulary they need to comprehend text in part by simulating young children's informal home experiences that often build oral vocabulary and conceptual stores (Hirsch, 2003, 2006; Neuman, 2006). In recent years several researchers (e.g., Anderson, West, Beck,

MacDonnell, & Frisbie, 1997; Guthrie, Wigfield, & Perencevich, 2004; Palincsar, Magnusson, Collins, & Cutter, 2001; Romance & Vitale, 2001) have developed and tested reading comprehension interventions that focus heavily on building world knowledge, along with teaching reading comprehension strategies or related skills. These studies seem to support the commentators' arguments that addressing students' conceptual knowledge base—by focusing on the world and how it works—during instructional activities can improve students' reading comprehension. For example, Guthrie and his associates developed the Concept-Oriented Reading Instruction (CORI) model, in which teachers teach coherent, thematic units in life science and help students to develop reading strategies, collaborate with others, and direct their own learning. In CORI, students move through four phases, in which they notice and connect to a targeted phenomenon, spend time reading about and experimenting with it, pull together what they have learned, and make public their knowledge (Guthrie, Wigfield, & Perencevich, 2004). CORI is used in place of a portion of the classroom's regular reading–language arts instruction, yet this heavily science-focused instruction—for the third and fifth graders with whom it has been tested—results in significantly better performance on measures of reading comprehension and reading motivation, even when compared to students receiving comprehension strategy instruction (Guthrie, 2003; Guthrie, Anderson, Alao, & Rinehart, 1999; Guthrie, Wigfield, & VonSecker, 2000; Guthrie et al., 1996, 1998; Guthrie, McRae, & Klauda, 2007, for a review). Similarly, Romance and Vitale's (1992, 2001) In-Depth Expanded Application of Science (or IDEAS) model, which conducts reading–language arts instruction in the context of a 2-hour block focused on science learning, produced significantly better performance in both reading comprehension and science achievement, and more positive attitudes toward reading and science, than a control providing basal-based reading instruction. It seems that contextualizing reading comprehension instruction within a strong focus on knowledge-building yields considerable benefit.

The Need to Increase Attention to the Role of Genre in Reading Comprehension

Students encounter a variety of different genres—or types of text with a particular purpose, and linguistic features to meet that purpose—in and out of school. These include different kinds of narratives, such as fables and realistic fiction; informational text, which teaches about the natural and social world; procedural text, which tells how to do something (e.g., recipes, how-to books, etc.); persuasive text, which is intended to persuade someone of a particular action or belief; and so on (Duke & Tower, 2004). In recent years there is a growing realization that reading comprehension does not occur in the same way with these different kinds of text. Genre affects the comprehension strategies readers use (Kucan & Beck, 1996), the inferences they make (van den Broek, Everson, Virtue, Sung, & Tzeng, 2002), and their overall approach to text (Langer, 1985). Students who comprehend one kind of text well may not comprehend another equally well (e.g., Hidi & Hildyard, 1983; Langer, Applebee, Mullis, & Foertsch, 1990). Thus, although we often refer to "comprehension" as a monolithic entity, it is not a unitary construct (Duke, 2005), and comprehension instruction in one genre may not transfer entirely or even in part to another genre.

This idea has sparked a flurry of research. Some researchers (e.g., Donovan, 2001; Duke & Kays, 1998; Kamberelis, 1999; Langer, 1985; Pappas, 1991; Wollman-Bonilla,

2000) have examined children's development of genre knowledge, usually by asking students to produce the genre or genres of interest. Together, these studies have supported the idea that children's knowledge varies across the genres. For example, Kamberelis (1999) analyzed students' stories, reports, and poems for prototypicality; he found that the majority of K–2 students he studied were able to write prototypical stories, with fewer successfully producing reports, and children's poems being "less prototypic and less rhetorically effective" (p. 433). Researchers have also found that an individual's genre knowledge develops over time; that is, as students progress through the school year and through the elementary grades, they exhibit more sophisticated structures and organizations in their stories and reports (Chapman, 1994; Donovan, 2001; Newkirk, 1987). This has also led some researchers to express concern about neglect of some important genres in elementary curricula—the concern being that ability to comprehend those genres suffers if instruction does not include *those* genres (e.g., Duke, 2000).

There are also signs of an uptick in studies of reading comprehension interventions that make genre particularly salient (e.g., Purcell-Gates, Duke, & Martineau, 2007; Williams et al., 2005). It may be that reading comprehension instruction will go the way that a considerable body of work on writing instruction has gone (Graham & Harris, 2005), toward developing instructional approaches tailored to developing skill with a particular genre.

The Need to Teach to the Demands of New Technologies

Closely related to the growth in attention to genre in general is increased attention to comprehension of digital genres in particular. Technology has changed rapidly in the last few decades, with more people using computers and other digital devices at their jobs and during their leisure hours to accomplish a variety of goals. This has given rise to a huge array of new genres. As we might expect given the research reviewed earlier, comprehension processes for these genres are not entirely the same as those for other genres. For example, a study of sixth graders' reading of informational websites revealed not only similarities but also differences between comprehension strategies used in these contexts and those used with informational texts on paper (Coiro & Dobler, 2007). The purpose for which websites are being read also seems to impact comprehension processes (Zhang & Duke, in press).

Given the uniqueness and importance of digital genres, there have been many calls for more attention to these genres throughout schooling (e.g., Bruce & Levin, 2003; Kinzer & Leander, 2003; Leu, Kinzer, Coiro, & Cammack, 2004). The literacy field has responded with professional books that provide guidance about teaching and using digital technologies in the elementary grades (e.g., Eagleton & Dobler, 2006; Taffe & Gwinn, 2007; Wood, 2004) and research on everything from comprehension of talking books (Labbo & Kuhn, 2000) to processes of searching for information to comprehend (e.g., Kuiper, Volman, & Terwel, 2005). Still needed, however, are additional studies that examine the impact of specific instructional approaches to building reading comprehension of and with digital genres, and help students grapple with the texts of their increasingly digital world.

The Value of Using Authentic Contexts for Comprehension Instruction

A concern circulating in conversations at many conferences we attend, if not yet a great deal in print, is that comprehension strategy instruction is increasingly being provided in an isolated fashion—comprehension strategies more for strategies' sake than for the sake of actually comprehending text for a larger purpose. We have observed extreme examples of this in recent years, such as having students make predictions with a text they have already read, or having students apply comprehension strategies to a text so empty of meaning there is really little to nothing for students to comprehend. A counter to this concern is greater attention, or renewal of attention, to the context of comprehension instruction. The studies we discussed earlier contextualize comprehension instruction very heavily in efforts to build content area knowledge, as in the IDEAS model (Romance & Vitale, 1992, 2001), in which comprehension instruction occurs entirely in the context of student learning in science units, such as processes that shape the earth, and energy, force, and motion. Students are being taught to comprehend in the service of learning important information in the content area. Another example lies in research and development around literature circles and book clubs in the elementary grades (e.g., Certo, Moxley, Reffitt, Miller, & Flam, 2007; Goatley, Brock, & Raphael, 1995). In a number of respects, these contexts are meant to mimic book or literary clubs that have long flourished outside schooling. Students select a text they would like to read and meet to discuss their understanding, interpretation, and response to the text. Comprehension instruction can be provided within and in the service of this social context, though the impact of this needs further study.

Research is highlighting what many educators have long espoused—that students need to be motivated to employ the comprehension strategies they have been taught (Dole, Brown, & Trathen, 1996; Guthrie, Wigfield, & Perencevich, 2004; Hall, 2006). The CORI approach, which is designed to enhance motivational processes, produced better results than comprehension strategy instruction outside that context (Guthrie, Wigfield, Barbosa, et al., 2004). A recent study links the degree to which teachers have elementary students read and write texts in authentic contexts to students' growth in reading comprehension (Purcell-Gates et al., 2007). Specifically, second- and third-grade students whose teachers had them read and write informational and procedural science texts that were very much like informational and procedural texts found in the world outside of school, and for the reasons people read and write those kinds of texts outside of school (e.g., rather than simply for the sake of fulfilling school assignments), showed higher growth in their reading comprehension and writing abilities. Across these studies is a strong sense that comprehension instruction is being presented as a means to an end, rather than as an end unto itself.

Very much tied to this issue of authenticity is the question of whether comprehension strategies should be taught singly or one at a time, or whether they should be taught collectively or as groups. Certainly, outside of schools, it is clear that good readers coordinate a multiplicity of comprehension strategies simultaneously (Pressley & Afflerbach, 1995), but does this mean that instruction in school should begin with this approach as well? Increasingly it seems that this is the case. Reviews of literature have noted that effects of interventions involving multiple-strategy approaches tend to be stronger than those for interventions involving single-strategy instruction (Duke & Pearson, 2002; National Reading Panel, 2000), and in a head-to-head comparison of single-strategy instruction versus multiple strategies instructional approaches with second graders, students in the multiple-strategies group outperformed their peers on certain school tasks, such as recalling details from science books, remembering science content, and taking curriculum-based reading tests, although performance across groups on other tasks (e.g., standardized tests, motivation surveys, etc.) was similar (Reutzel, Smith, & Fawson, 2005).

The Importance of Understanding Reading Comprehension in ELLs

With the increasing diversity of modern U.S. classrooms, teaching reading to ELLs is a growing concern. When the National Research Council published *Preventing Reading Difficulties in Young Children* (Snow et al., 1998), for example, the authors discussed several findings that related to ELLs. In the last few years research synthesis reports focusing solely on the literacy development of ELLs have included *Double the Work: Challenges and Solutions to Acquiring Language and Academic Literacy for Adolescent English Language Learners* (Short & Fitzsimmons, 2007) and *Developing Literacy in Second-Language Learners: A Report of the National Literacy Panel on Language-Minority Children and Youth* (August & Shanahan, 2006).

Even though these commissions discuss many aspects of reading, such reports often highlight reading comprehension. In particular, August and Shanahan (2006) had a lot to say about reading comprehension, as follows:

- They listed it as an important instructional component for ELLs.
- They pointed out the persistent reading comprehension performance gap between ELLs and native speakers of English.
- They found links between reading comprehension and ELLs' oral proficiency, in which four aspects of language appear to play important roles: vocabulary knowledge, listening comprehension, syntactic abilities, and metalinguistic skills.
- They endorsed "greater attention to word-level skills early in the process and more direct and ambitious attention to reading comprehension later on. However, vocabulary and background knowledge, ... should be targeted intensively throughout the entire sequence" (pp. 4–5).
- They suggested a relationship between first language literacy and English reading comprehension, and recommended that when teaching children who have already become literate in their first language, teachers take into account the "transferability of some literacy skills" (p. 5).

This area of research has grown, particularly in the last several years. We've discovered, for instance, that vocabulary knowledge appears to be central to ELLs' comprehension, at least for those whose native language is Spanish (Proctor, August, & Carlo, 2006; Proctor, Carlo, August, & Snow, 2005). Attending to their vocabulary knowledge may improve ELLs reading comprehension. If presented in meaningful, varied contexts, supported by their Spanish reading comprehension skills, and undergirded by a belief in multifaceted word knowledge, for instance, we can help native Spanish speakers learn academic word meanings while we teach them about context clues, morphology, multiple meanings, and cognate-based inference making (August, Carlo, Dressler, & Snow, 2005; Carlo et al., 2004).

Furthermore, instructional techniques may boost ELLs' reading comprehension. For example, Instructional Conversations and literature logs can be effective tools, and using the two together helped students with limited English proficiency, although more proficient speakers did not benefit significantly (Saunders & Goldenberg, 1999).

Other efforts have the potential to improve reading comprehension as well. Strategy instruction (Klingner & Vaughn, 1996; Proctor, Dalton, & Grisham, 2007); instruction that combines vocabulary, fluency, and error correction (Tam, Heward, & Heng, 2006); and supplemental instruction that includes fluency, phonemic awareness, word study, and short, instructional-level reads (Linan-Thompson, Vaughn, Hickman-Davis, & Kouzekanani, 2003) show promise. The focus of research and development on addressing reading comprehension in this important and growing sector of U.S. students is encouraging.

Summary

In summary, recent research into reading comprehension instruction in the elementary years reveals at least five insights about which we need to think carefully as we build our practices (or help others build theirs). We need to extend students' background knowledge, our attention to genre, and our instruction to meet the demands of new technologies. We need a new, or renewed, focus on providing authentic contexts for comprehension and techniques that improve the comprehension of ELLs. Ideally, these efforts, combined with more long- and well-established practices for building reading comprehension, will yield more proficient comprehenders among elementary-age students.

HOW THIS NEW KNOWLEDGE CAN IMPROVE COMPREHENSION INSTRUCTION

The five insights we have discussed have the potential to help us expand the reach of comprehension instruction—into specific genres and new technologies; into content area learning and more motivating, real-world contexts for literacy; and to both ELLs and those for whom English is the first language. Research seems to be pushing us ever further away from reading comprehension instruction that comprises spending a few minutes asking and answering questions about a passage in the basal reader, and ever closer to comprehension instruction that permeates the entire elementary curriculum and addresses our entire school population.

These insights can also help us improve comprehension by bringing it closer to the real comprehension demands that students face later in school, addressing, perhaps, the age-old problem of students' difficulties in transferring skills from the contexts in which they were learned to the contexts in which they are needed. These insights can also help us improve comprehension by further persuading educators that comprehension instruction is everyone's job—the job of the content area educator, who, even in elementary schools, increasingly often is not the regular classroom teacher; the job of the technology teacher and media specialist; and the job of the English as a second language (ESL) teacher. And these insights can improve comprehension by reminding us that creating situations in which students actually want to comprehend is fundamental to comprehension instruction.

Of course, these insights can only improve comprehension if they influence preservice teacher education and professional development for teachers throughout their careers. Integrating these insights into policies (e.g., creating policies that require a certain amount of attention to building content area knowledge, even in the primary grades), assessments (e.g., including digital texts in assessments), and curricular materials (e.g., establishing authentic contexts for comprehension instruction within materials) will also influence the degree to which these insights affect and improve comprehension instruction.

DIRECTIONS FOR FUTURE RESEARCH

As in many areas, when it comes to reading comprehension instruction it seems that the more we know, the more we don't know. For example, even as we realize that comprehension instruction with one genre will not necessarily transfer to another, we realize that we need to know how to provide different comprehension instruction for different kinds of text. Below are six research directions that address just some of the things we don't yet know, drawing closely on the trends discussed in this chapter.

1. How do we integrate reading comprehension instruction and knowledge-building throughout the school day? With today's ever-expanding demands on instructional time, integration, in which multiple domains are addressed simultaneously, seems like a highly promising direction. Some studies suggest that integration can benefit both reading comprehension and knowledge development, as with the IDEAS and CORI models discussed earlier. However, in general the research literature on integration reveals a plentitude of anecdotal and opinion pieces and a shortage of empirical research (Gavelek, Raphael, Biondo, & Wang, 2000). To supplement this, future studies could examine approaches to integrating reading comprehension instruction and the teaching of other subjects (e.g., science, social studies) and skills (e.g., writing) in the elementary years. Successful approaches could be studied to provide a closer look at the skills and practices required to accomplish that feat; to pinpoint natural connections between subjects that could function as a springboard for integration; to identify inexpensive but educationally worthwhile resources that could be used during integration; to develop scaffolds for teachers that make integration more doable; and to define further the appropriateness of different types and demands of integration activities.

2. How do children develop their knowledge of different genres, and how can teachers support this process? As mentioned earlier, this line of inquiry is still developing, and future research could add to current efforts by including the following: continued exploration of the theoretical construct of genre and its role in current reading theories; longitudinal tracking of individual students' genre development; investigations into elementary children's knowledge of less-researched genres (persuasive essays, procedural texts, etc.); examinations of teachers' current knowledge, attitudes, and instructional activities around genre; interventions designed to encourage genre knowledge development in both students and their teachers; and close scrutiny of the role that teacher education programs might play in fostering genre knowledge development.

3. What digital literacy skills do elementary teachers possess, and how can they teach their students to comprehend in digital environments? Researchers are beginning to identify the reading skills needed to cope with new media and to speculate about the kinds of instruction needed to prepare today's students to comprehend tomorrow's evolved technologies (for more information, see Castek et al., Chapter 22, and Lacina, Chapter 24, this volume, Kamil, Intrator, & Kim, 2000; Leu, 2000; Leu et al., 2004). As this line of inquiry expands, researchers will need to explicate carefully the skills sets needed by both students and teachers, to examine the gaps in teachers' and students' current skills, and to address these needs. We need to know more about what students and adults do when they are and are not successful at comprehending in digital environments, what instructional practices teachers already use successfully and/or adapt to develop students' comprehension in a variety of new technologies, and what specific instructional interventions improve comprehension of digital texts.

4. How can we develop students who not only can comprehend but also want to and do so? Although many researchers have worked on this question, there is still more to be done. Research is needed that works within a triangle of specific instructional practices, reading comprehension development, and students' reading habits inside and outside of school. Are there specific approaches or practices in reading comprehension instruction that result in gains in reading comprehension over time *and* in students engaging in more reading outside of school with a variety of texts? Are there approaches to reading comprehension instruction that over the long-term counteract the decline in reading attitudes we so often see across the elementary years? These are questions we need to pursue in multifaceted, longitudinal research studies.

5. In classrooms in which elementary students make huge gains in their comprehension abilities, what do teachers believe and do? Although a great deal of energy has been spent on researching individual approaches to improving students' reading comprehension performance, less attention has been allocated to in-depth examinations of how teachers piece together approaches to create an entire school day and school year of reading comprehension instruction and experiences (let alone how a whole school does so). Following the tradition of research on effective teachers cited earlier in this chapter, and based on the idea that some teachers appear to hold certain beliefs and engage in specific instructional behaviors that foster elevated levels of student growth (Ruddell, 2004), the daylong, yearlong practices of highly effective reading comprehension teachers should be studied. Future research could engage in long-term, multicase studies of such educators by comparing their beliefs, background experiences, and practices to those of other educators, and by developing and testing professional development programs to help other literacy teachers become highly accomplished reading comprehension practitioners.

PROJECTIONS AND POSSIBILITIES FOR THE CLASSROOM OF 2030

We hope for an elementary classroom of 2030 that looks profoundly different from many—though certainly not all—elementary classrooms today. We picture students working in small groups and individually, on the floors and at tables, on interdisciplinary projects that require both reading and writing, that involve both content area learning and literacy skills, and a wide range of different genres. We imagine that a variety of digital technologies are available to students as they work: One small group is watching a videoclip related to its project; another is conducting a online search to address a key question that has arisen in the project; another is interviewing an expert via video conference; and yet another is using a simulation tool to understand better the phenomenon it is studying. All of these students are deeply engaged in the work they are doing, and eager for any instruction from the teacher that might help them grapple with the texts they are reading.

The classroom we imagine has students of many different hues, backgrounds, and interests. All are seen as bringing important knowledge and skills to the table—one student in a group is translating a website on the project topic into English for the others; a student who struggles with word reading is using her extensive knowledge of a digital interface to assist her peers—and as capable of developing new knowledge and skills. In this classroom the teacher holds in mind a catalog of the strengths and needs of each of these students and tailors instruction accordingly. One student has a poor vocabulary and requires reading comprehension instruction that focuses heavily on vocabulary building.

Another struggles with understanding informational texts and needs instruction designed to address that challenge. In this teacher's mind, every student is a "special case" requiring an individualized instructional plan. The teacher's extensive professional development in comprehension learning and instruction informs the formation of those individualized plans. At the same time, researchers in schools throughout the country work diligently to address additional questions that this teacher and others raise about effective comprehension instruction practices.

SUMMARY

The quotation at the beginning of this chapter likened reading comprehension instruction to guiding travelers on journeys they will eventually carry out on their own. As with traveling, becoming a highly effective instructor of comprehension is an exciting, challenging venture, with moments of peril and fatigue, paths that dead-end, majestic vistas, unexpected surprises, and—ultimately—the joys of success. In this chapter, we have discussed both longstanding and emerging knowledge that can inform these travels, including insights about how attention to world knowledge, genre knowledge, new technologies, and authentic contexts, has the potential to improve comprehension. We hope this continually growing body of research will help you and the next generation of travelers you teach to conquer the world of texts.

INTEGRATE, INVESTIGATE, AND INITIATE: QUESTIONS FOR DISCUSSION

1. In this chapter we have discussed the need to teach comprehension strategies in a less isolated fashion—to go beyond teaching strategies for "strategies' sake" and to teach them for "the sake of actually comprehending text for a larger purpose." List three actions you can take to advance comprehension strategy instruction to reach this goal, using what you have learned in this and previous chapters.
2. What new types of strategy instruction do you envision could be created to assist students to comprehend more genres and digital texts? How can you use the information in this chapter to create new instructional strategies to advance students' comprehension of more diverse texts? What elements of the methods found in this and prior chapters could you combine and expand to meet the new comprehension needs of your students?
3. Compare the research, instructional needs, and new methods being created to advance the comprehension of ELLs in this chapter and those presented by Rueda, Velasio, and Kim in Chapter 20 (this volume). What does the information in both of these chapters have in common? On what points do they disagree?

REFERENCES

Anderson, R. C. (1984). Role of the reader's schema in comprehension, learning, and memory. In R. C. Anderson, J. Osborn, & R. J. Tierney (Eds.), *Learning to read in American schools: Basal readers and content texts* (Vol. 29, pp. 243–257). Mahwah, NJ: Erlbaum.

Anderson, T. H., West, C. K., Beck, D. P., MacDonnell, E. S., & Frisbie, D. S. (1997). Integrating reading and science education: On developing and evaluating WEE science. *Journal of Curriculum Studies, 29,* 711–733.

August, D., Carlo, M., Dressler, C., & Snow, C. E. (2005). The critical role of vocabulary development for English language learners. *Learning Disabilities Research and Practice, 20,* 50–57.

August, D., & Shanahan, T. (Eds.). (2006). *Developing literacy in second-language learners: Report of the National Literacy Panel on language-minority children and youth.* Mahwah, NJ: Erlbaum.

Block, C. C., & Mangieri, J. N. (2003). *Exemplary literacy teachers: Promoting success for all children in grades K–5.* New York: Guilford Press.

Block, C. C., & Pressley, M. (2007). Best practices in teaching comprehension. In L. B. Gambrell, L. M. Morrow, & M. Pressley (Eds.), *Best practices in literacy instruction* (3rd ed., pp. 220–242). New York: Guilford Press.

Brown, R., Pressley, M., Van Meter, P., & Schuder, T. (1996). A quasi-experimental validation of transactional strategies instruction with low-achieving second-grade readers. *Journal of Educational Psychology, 88,* 18–37.

Bruce, B., & Levin, J. (2003). Roles for new technologies in language arts: Inquiry, communication, construction, and expression. In J. Flood, D. Lapp, J. R. Squire, & J. M. Jensen (Eds.), *Handbook of research on teaching the English language arts* (pp. 649–657). Mahwah, NJ: Erlbaum.

Carlo, M. S., August, D., McLaughlin, B., Snow, C. E., Dressler, C., Lippman, D. N., et al. (2004). Closing the gap: Addressing the vocabulary needs of English-language learners in bilingual and mainstream classrooms. *Reading Research Quarterly, 39,* 188–215.

Certo, J., Moxley, K., Reffitt, K., Miller, J., & Flam, E. (2007, April). *Enjoyment, social outcomes and learning in literature circles: Children's perspectives across grades and abilities.* Presentation to the Annual Conference of the American Educational Research Association, Chicago, IL.

Chall, J. S., & Jacobs, V. A. (2003). Poor children's fourth-grade slump. *American Educator, 27,* 14–15, 44.

Chapman, M. L. (1994). The emergence of genres: Some findings from an examination of first-grade writing. *Written Communication, 11,* 348–380.

Coiro, J., & Dobler, E. (2007). Exploring the online reading comprehension strategies used by sixth-grade skilled readers to search for and locate information on the Internet. *Reading Research Quarterly, 42,* 214–257.

Dole, J. A., Brown, K. J., & Trathen, W. (1996). The effects of strategy instruction on the comprehension performance of at-risk students. *Reading Research Quarterly, 31,* 62–88.

Donovan, C. A. (2001). Children's development and control of written story and informational genres: Insights from one elementary school. *Research in the Teaching of English, 35,* 394–447.

Duke, N. K. (2000). 3.6 minutes per day: The scarcity of informational texts in first grade. *Reading Research Quarterly, 35,* 202–224.

Duke, N. K. (2005). Comprehension of what for what: Comprehension as a non-unitary construct. In S. Paris & S. Stahl (Eds.), *Current issues in reading comprehension and assessment* (pp. 93–104). Mahwah, NJ: Erlbaum.

Duke, N. K., & Kays, J. (1998). "Can I say 'once upon a time'?": Kindergarten children developing knowledge of information book language. *Early Childhood Research Quarterly, 13,* 295–318.

Duke, N. K., & Pearson, P. D. (2002). Effective practices for developing reading comprehension. In A. E. Farstrup & S. J. Samuels (Eds.), *What research has to say about reading instruction* (3rd ed., pp. 205–242). Newark, DE: International Reading Association.

Duke, N. K., Pressley, M., & Hilden, K. (2004). Difficulties with reading comprehension. In C. A. Stone, E. R. Silliman, B. J. Ehren & K. Apel (Eds.), *Handbook of language and literacy development and disorders* (pp. 501–520). New York: Guilford Press.

Duke, N. K., & Tower, C. (2004). Nonfiction texts for young readers. In J. Hoffman & D. Schallert (Eds.), *The texts in elementary classrooms* (pp. 125–144). Mahwah, NJ: Erlbaum.

Durkin, D. (1978/1979). What classroom observations reveal about reading comprehension instruction. *Reading Research Quarterly, 14,* 481–533.

Eagleton, M. B., & Dobler, E. (2006). *Reading the web: Strategies for Internet inquiry.* New York: Guilford Press.

Gavelek, J. R., Raphael, T. E., Biondo, S. M., & Wang, D. (2000). Integrated literacy instruction. In M. L. Kamil, P. B. Mosenthal, P. D. Pearson, & R. Barr (Eds.), *Handbook of reading research* (pp. 587–607). Mahwah, NJ: Erlbaum.

Goatley, V. J., Brock, C. H., & Raphael, T. E. (1995). Diverse learners participating in regular education "book clubs." *Reading Research Quarterly, 30,* 352–380.

Graham, S., & Harris, K. R. (2005). *Writing better: Effective strategies for teaching students with learning difficulties.* Baltimore: Brookes.

Guthrie, J. T. (2003). Concept-Oriented Reading Instruction: Practices of teaching reading for understanding. In A. P. Sweet & C. E. Snow (Eds.), *Rethinking reading comprehension* (pp. 115–140). New York: Guilford Press.

Guthrie, J. T., Anderson, E., Alao, S., & Rinehart, J. (1999). Influences of Concept-Oriented Reading Instruction on strategy use and conceptual learning from text. *Elementary School Journal, 99,* 344–366.

Guthrie, J. T., McRae, A., & Klauda, S. L. (2007). Contributions of Concept-Oriented Reading Instruction to knowledge about interventions for motivations in reading. *Educational Psychologist, 42,* 237–250.

Guthrie, J. T., Van Meter, P. V., Hancock, G. R., Solomon, A., Anderson, E., & McCann, A. (1998). Does Concept-Oriented Reading Instruction increase strategy use and conceptual learning from text? *Journal of Educational Psychology, 90,* 261–278.

Guthrie, J. T., Van Meter, P., McCann, A. D., Wigfield, A., Bennett, L., Poundstone, C. C., et al. (1996). Growth of literacy engagement: Changes in motivations and strategies during Concept-Oriented Reading Instruction. *Reading Research Quarterly, 31,* 306–332.

Guthrie, J. T., Wigfield, A., Barbosa, P., Perencevich, K. C., Taboada, A., Davis, M. H., et al. (2004). Increasing reading comprehension and engagement through Concept-Oriented Reading Instruction. *Journal of Educational Psychology, 96,* 403–423.

Guthrie, J. T., Wigfield, A., & Perencevich, K. C. (2004). *Motivating reading comprehension: Concept-Oriented Reading Instruction.* Mahwah, NJ: Erlbaum.

Guthrie, J. T., Wigfield, A., & VonSecker, C. (2000). Effects of integrated instruction on motivation and strategy use in reading. *Journal of Educational Psychology, 92,* 331–341.

Hall, L. (2006). Anything but lazy: New understandings about struggling readers, teaching, and text. *Reading Research Quarterly, 41,* 424–426.

Hart, B., & Risley, T. R. (2003). The early catastrophe: The 30 million word gap. *American Educator, 27,* 4–9.

Hidi, S. E., & Hildyard, A. (1983). The comparison of oral and written productions in two discourse types. *Discourse Processes, 6,* 91–105.

Hirsch, E. D., Jr. (2003). Reading comprehension requires knowledge—of words and the world: Scientific insights into the fourth-grade slump and stagnant reading comprehension. *American Educator, 27,* 10–13, 16–22, 28–29, 48.

Hirsch, E. D., Jr. (2006). Building knowledge: The case for bringing content into the language arts block and for a knowledge-rich curriculum core for all children. *American Educator, 30,* 8–21, 28–29, 50–51.

Kamberelis, G. (1999). Genre development and learning: Children writing stories, science reports, and poems. *Research in the Teaching of English, 33,* 403–460.

Kamil, M. L., Intrator, S. M., & Kim, H. S. (2000). The effects of other technologies on literacy and literacy learning. In M. L. Kamil, P. B. Mosenthal, P. D. Pearson & R. Barr (Eds.), *Handbook of reading research* (pp. 771–788). Mahwah, NJ: Erlbaum.

Keene, E. O., & Zimmermann, S. (1997). *Mosaic of thought: Teaching comprehension in a reader's workshop.* Portsmouth, NH: Heinemann.

Kinzer, C. K., & Leander, K. (2003). Technology and the language arts: Implications of an expanded definition of literacy. In D. L. J. Flood, J. R. Squire, & J. M. Jensen (Ed.), *Hand-*

book of research on teaching the English language aArts (pp. 546–565). Mahwah, NJ: Erlbaum.

Klingner, J. K., & Vaughn, S. (1996). Reciprocal teaching of reading comprehension strategies for students with learning disabilities who use English as a second language. *Elementary School Journal, 96,* 275–293.

Knapp, M. S., & Associates. (1995). *Teaching for meaning in high-poverty classrooms.* New York: Teachers College Press.

Kucan, L., & Beck, I. L. (1996). Four fourth graders thinking aloud: An investigation of genre effects. *Journal of Literacy Research, 28,* 259–287.

Kuiper, E., Volman, M., & Terwel, J. (2005). The web as an information resource in K–12 education: Strategies for supporting students in searching and processing information. *Review of Educational Research, 75,* 285–317.

Kurth, R. J., & Greenlaw, M. J. (1980). *Research and practices in comprehension instruction in elementary classrooms* (Report No. CS 005 736). Paper presented at the annual meeting of the American Reading Conference, Sarasota, FL. (ERIC Document Reproduction Service No. ED195931)

Labbo, L. D., & Kuhn, M. R. (2000). Weaving chains of affect and cognition: A young child's understanding of CD-ROM talking books. *Journal of Literacy Research, 32,* 187–210.

Langer, J. A. (1985). Children's sense of genre: A study of performance on parallel reading and writing tasks. *Written Communication, 2,* 157–187.

Langer, J. A., Applebee, A. N., Mullis, I. V. S., & Foertsch, M. A. (1990). *Learning to read in our nation's schools: Instruction and achievement in 1998 at grades 4, 8, and 12.* Princeton, NJ: Educational Testing Service.

Leu, D. J. (2000). Literacy and technology: Deictic consequences for literacy education in an information age. In M. L. Kamil, P. B. Mosenthal, P. D. Pearson, & R. Barr (Eds.), *Handbook of reading research* (pp. 743–770). Mahwah, NJ: Erlbaum.

Leu, D. J., Kinzer, C. K., Coiro, J. L., & Cammack, D. W. (2004). Toward a theory of new literacies emerging from the Internet and other information and communication technologies. In R. B. Ruddell & N. J. Unrau (Eds.), *Theoretical models and processes of reading* (5th ed., pp. 1570–1613). Newark, DE: International Reading Association.

Linan-Thompson, S., Vaughn, S., Hickman-Davis, P., & Kouzekanani, K. (2003). Effectiveness of supplemental reading instruction for second-grade English language learners with reading difficulties. *Elementary School Journal, 103,* 221–238.

McKenna, M. C., Kear, D. J., & Ellsworth, R. A. (1995). Children's attitudes toward reading: A national survey. *Reading Research Quarterly, 30,* 934–956.

National Reading Panel. (2000). *Teaching children to read: An evidence-based assessment of the scientific research literature on reading and its implications for reading instruction* (National Institute of Health Publication No. 00-4769). Washington, DC: National Institute of Child Health and Human Development.

Neuman, S. (2006). How we neglect knowledge—and why. *American Educator, 30,* 24–26, 51.

Newkirk, T. (1987). The non-narrative writing of young children. *Research in the Teaching of English, 21,* 121–144.

Nystrand, M. (2006). Research on the role of classroom discourse as it affects reading comprehension. *Research in the Teaching of English, 40,* 392–411.

Palincsar, A. S., Magnusson, S. J., Collins, K. M., & Cutter, J. (2001). Making science accessible to all: Results of a design experiment in inclusive classrooms. *Learning Disability Quarterly, 24,* 15–32.

Pappas, C. C. (1991). Young children's strategies in learning the "book language" of information books. *Discourse Processes, 14,* 203–225.

Pearson, P. D., & Duke, N. K. (2002). Comprehension instruction in the primary grades. In C. C. Block & M. Pressley (Eds.), *Comprehension instruction: Research-based best practices* (pp. 247–258). New York: Guilford Press.

Pressley, M., & Afflerbach, P. (1995). *Verbal protocols of reading: The nature of constructively responsive reading.* Hillsdale, NJ: Erlbaum.

Pressley, M., Rankin, J. L., & Yokoi, L. (1996). A survey of instructional practices of primary teachers nominated as effective in promoting literacy. *Elementary School Journal, 96,* 363–384.

Pressley, M., Wharton-McDonald, R., Allington, R., Block, C. C., Morrow, L., Tracey, D., et al. (2001). A study of effective grade-1 literacy instruction. *Scientific Studies of Reading, 5,* 35–58.

Proctor, C. P., August, D., & Carlo, M. S. (2006). The intriguing role of Spanish language vocabulary knowledge in predicting English reading comprehension. *Journal of Educational Psychology, 98,* 159–169.

Proctor, C. P., Carlo, M., August, D., & Snow, C. E. (2005). Native Spanish-speaking children reading in English: Toward a model of comprehension. *Journal of Educational Psychology, 97,* 246–256.

Proctor, C. P., Dalton, B., & Grisham, D. L. (2007). Scaffolding English language learners and struggling readers in a universal literacy environment with embedded strategy Instruction and vocabulary support. *Journal of Literacy Research, 39,* 71–93.

Purcell-Gates, V., Duke, N., & Martineau, J. A. (2007). Learning to read and write genre-specific text: Roles of authentic experience and explicit teaching. *Reading Research Quarterly, 42,* 8–45.

Reutzel, D. R., Smith, J. A., & Fawson, P. C. (2005). An evaluation of two approaches for teaching reading comprehension strategies in the primary years using science information texts. *Early Childhood Research Quarterly, 20,* 276–305.

Romance, N. R., & Vitale, M. R. (1992). A curriculum strategy that expands time for in-depth elementary science instruction by using science-based reading strategies: Effects of a year-long study in grade four. *Journal of Research in Science Teaching, 29,* 545–554.

Romance, N. R., & Vitale, M. R. (2001). Implementing an in-depth expanding science model in elementary schools: Multi-year findings, research issues, and policy implications. *International Journal of Science Education, 23,* 373–404.

Rosenblatt, L. M. (2004). The transactional theory of reading and writing. In R. B. Ruddell & N. J. Unrau (Eds.), *Theoretical models and processes of reading* (5th ed., pp. 1363–1398). Newark, DE: International Reading Association.

Ruddell, R. B. (2004). Researching the influential literacy teacher: Characteristics, beliefs, strategies, and new research directions. In R. B. Ruddell & N. J. Unrau (Eds.), *Theoretical models and processes of reading* (5th ed., pp. 979–997). Newark, DE: International Reading Association.

Ruddell, R. B., & Unrau, N. J. (2004). Reading as a meaning-construction process: The reader, the text, and the teacher. In R. B. Ruddell & N. J. Unrau (Eds.), *Theoretical models and processes of reading* (5th ed., pp. 1462–1521). Newark, DE: International Reading Association.

Rumelhart, D. E. (2004). Toward an interactive model of reading. In R. B. Ruddell & N. J. Unrau (Eds.), *Theoretical models and processes of reading* (5th ed., pp. 1149–1179). Newark, DE: International Reading Association.

Saunders, W. M., & Goldenberg, C. N. (1999). Effects of instructional conversations and literature logs on limited- and fluent-English-proficient students' story comprehension and thematic understanding. *Elementary School Journal, 99,* 277–301.

Scarborough, H. S. (2001). Connecting early language and literacy to later reading (dis)abilities: Evidence, theory, and practice. In B. Neuman & D. K. Dickinson (Eds.), *Handbook of early literacy research* (pp. 97–110). New York: Guilford Press.

Shanahan, T. (2006). Relations among oral language, reading, and writing development. In C. A. MacArthur, S. Graham, & J. Fitzgerald (Eds.), *Handbook of writing research* (pp. 171–183). New York: Guilford Press.

Short, D. J., & Fitzsimmons, S. (2007). *Double the work: Challenges and solutions to acquiring language and academic literacy for adolescent English language learners: A report to Carnegie Corporation of New York*. Washington, DC: Alliance for Excellent Education.

Snow, C. E., Burns, M. S., & Griffin, P. (Eds.). (1998). *Preventing reading difficulties in young children*. Washington, DC: National Academy Press.

Stahl, K. A. D. (2004). Proof, practice, and promise: Comprehension strategy instruction in the primary grades. *Reading Teacher, 57*, 598–609.

Stahl, S. A. (1998). Four questions about vocabulary knowledge and reading and some answers. In C. R. Hynd (Ed.), *Learning from text across conceptual domains* (pp. 73–94). Mahwah, NJ: Erlbaum.

Stanovich, K. E. (2004). Matthew effects in reading: Some consequences of individual differences in the acquisition of literacy. In R. B. Ruddell & N. J. Unrau (Eds.), *Theoretical models and processes of reading* (5th ed., pp. 454–516). Newark, DE: International Reading Association.

Taffe, S. W., & Gwinn, C. B. (2007). *Integrating literacy and technology: Effective practice for grades K–6*. New York: Guilford Press.

Tam, K. Y., Heward, W. L., & Heng, M. A. (2006). A reading instruction intervention program for English-language learners who are struggling readers. *Journal of Special Education, 40*, 79–93.

Taylor, B. M., Pearson, P. D., Clark, K. F., & Walpole, S. (2000). Effective schools and accomplished teachers: Lessons about primary-grade reading instruction in low-income schools. *Elementary School Journal, 101*, 121–165.

van den Broek, P., Everson, M., Virtue, S., Sung, Y., & Tzeng, Y. (2002). Comprehension and memory of science texts: Inferential processes and the construction of a mental representation. In J. Otero, J. Leon, & A. C. Graesser (Eds.), *The psychology of science text comprehension* (pp. 131–154). Mahwah, NJ: Erlbaum.

Wendler, D., Samuels, S. J., & Moore, V. K. (1989). Comprehension instruction of award-winning teachers, teachers with master's degrees, and other teachers. *Reading Research Quarterly, 24*, 382–401.

Wharton-McDonald, R., Pressley, M., & Hampston, J. M. (1998). Literacy instruction in nine first-grade classrooms: Teacher characteristics and student achievement. *Elementary School Journal, 99*, 101–128.

Williams, J. P., Hall, K. M., Lauer, K. D., Stafford, B., DeSisto, L. A., & deCani, J. S. (2005). Expository text comprehension in the primary grade classroom. *Journal of Educational Psychology, 97*, 538–550.

Wilson, P. T., & Anderson, R. C. (1986). What they don't know will hurt them: The role of prior knowledge in comprehension. In J. Oransano (Ed.), *Reading comprehension from research to practice* (pp. 31–48). Hillsdale, NJ: Erlbaum.

Wollman-Bonilla, J. E. (2000). Teaching science writing to first graders: Genre learning and recontextualization. *Research in the Teaching of English, 35*, 35–65.

Wood, J. M. (2004). *Literacy online: New tools for struggling readers and writers*. Portsmouth, NH: Heinemann.

Zhang, S., & Duke, N. K. (in press). Strategies for Internet reading with different reading purposes: A descriptive study of twelve good Internet readers. *Journal of Literacy Research*.

18

Comprehension Instruction in Action
The Secondary Classroom

DOUGLAS FISHER and NANCY FREY

> . . . a very complex procedure, involving the weighing of each of many elements in a sentence, their organization in the proper relations to one another, the selection of certain connotations and the rejection of others, and the cooperation of many forces to produce the final response.
> —EDWARD THORNDIKE (1917)

At the risk of stating the obvious, secondary students who cannot comprehend will in all likelihood fail to achieve in school. Although we have known this for decades, the emergence of high-stakes high school exit exams has put struggling readers at greater risk than ever before (Jacob, 1991). It is imperative that we focus on reading comprehension across the middle and high school day. As Thorndike (1917) noted, comprehension requires a "cooperation of forces." He was referring to the interaction between the structures of language and the knowledge of the reader. The National Reading Panel (NRP; 2000) also focused our attention on the forces required for comprehension: phonemic awareness, phonics, fluency, and vocabulary. We might add to this list background knowledge (as Lacina describes in Chapter 24, this volume) and oral language skills.

Since the NRP's (2000) report, new forces have been identified for improving comprehension for adolescents. In addition to the NRP literacy processes, we know that comprehension at the secondary school level requires a systemic focus and a link between current performance and instruction. These newer forces, which also require a great deal of cooperation, are the focus of this chapter.

As such, this chapter highlights the following:

- What we already know about adolescent literacy, including effective strategies for teaching and learning.
- Promising new research on how we can "go to scale" to elevate literacy rates and raise achievement.
- Changing technologies that will transform literacy education and schooling into something very different from what we have today.

WHAT'S OUT THERE TODAY: ESTABLISHED RESEARCH AND PRACTICE IN SECONDARY SCHOOLS

Adolescent literacy is hot, at least according to literacy researchers surveyed in *Reading Today* ("Adolescent literacy," 2007). Why is that? Adolescent literacy isn't new. More than 40 years ago, Strang (1964) recognized the need to attend to the unique challenges of adolescents, especially those who struggled to read. So, as a profession, we've known for decades that literacy is critical to understanding content area texts (e.g., Herber, 1970). Could it be that adolescent literacy instruction is hot because we haven't gotten very good at it yet?

In the days when we thought of adolescent literacy as "content literacy," middle and high school teachers were regularly told that "every teacher is a teacher of reading." Fisher and Ivey (2005) note that this mantra, now decades old, has not resulted in the expected changes in achievement. Alvermann (2002) acknowledged that we must not only attend to the literacy demands of subject area classes but also recognize the profound need to "address issues of self-efficacy and student engagement with a variety of texts (e.g., textbooks, hypermedia texts, digital texts) in diverse settings" (p. 2) if we expect to see changes.

But changes are occurring. We know more today than we have ever known about improving adolescent's comprehension achievement. Some specific, compelling areas of evidence include the following:

- Word knowledge and vocabulary are critical to comprehension in every discipline (Allen, 1999; Whipple, 1925).
- Students don't learn from simply being told, yet "telling" is common in middle and high school classrooms (Alvermann, O'Brien, & Dillon, 1990).
- Engagement and motivation play a powerful role in reading comprehension (Guthrie & Wigfield, 2000).
- Family literacy practices can have a significant positive effect on the level of an adolescent's engagement in reading (Kirsch et al., 2002).
- Students arrive at school with experiences and background knowledge that await activation and use for learning (Marzano, 2004).
- Content literacy strategies are effective in helping students to comprehend (Fisher, Brozo, Frey, & Ivey, 2007).

The International Reading Association's position statement on adolescent literacy acknowledges what we know and what we still need to accomplish:

> Adolescents entering the adult world in the 21st century will read and write more than at any other time in human history. They will need advanced levels of literacy to perform their jobs, run their households, act as citizens, and conduct their personal lives. They will need literacy

to cope with the flood of information they will find everywhere they turn. They will need literacy to feed their imaginations so they can create the world of the future. In a complex and sometimes even dangerous world, their ability to read will be crucial. (Moore, Bean, Birdyshaw, & Rycik, 1999, p. 99)

Biancarosa and Snow (2004) have described two ways to improve the literacy of adolescents: instruction and infrastructure. Effective comprehension instruction comprises much of what we describe earlier as the enduring forces. Information about effective infrastructure is less clear, but it is emerging (e.g., Fisher & Frey, 2007). These new forces are the focus of the remainder of this chapter.

"NEW FORCES" IN RESEARCH ON IMPROVING ADOLESCENT LITERACY

Given all we know, the question at this point is, "What will it take to radically improve comprehension abilities and achievement at the middle and high school levels?" Our answer to this question comes in three big ideas. As teachers and teacher–leaders, we need to do the following:

- Develop a level of instructional consistency.
- Internalize an effective instructional infrastructure or framework.
- Examine student work, with colleagues, on a regular basis.

These ideas represent some of the most exciting "new forces" in improving adolescent literacy. Each builds on the enduring forces in comprehension research for secondary students. We examine the idea, history, and current thinking of each of these in turn.

Develop a Level of Instructional Consistency

Our first big idea scares a lot of people. On the surface, it sounds like we're recommending a scripted program or teacher-proof curriculum. We are not. There are simply too many comprehension strategies to force a group of teachers to use a specific subset of them. The problem is that each teacher chooses different strategies; thus, students don't achieve proficiency in any of them.

Consider note taking, for example. It's easy to imagine that the first-period science teacher requires outlining, the second-period art teacher requires graphic/visual notes, the third-period math teacher requires Cornell notes, the fourth-period social studies teacher requires outlining, and the fifth-period English teacher lets students choose any style they want. As a result, students spend too much time attending to the *ways* in which they are taught and not *what* they are taught. Furthermore, students are not developing a note-taking habit.

In reading this chapter and recognizing the problem, some readers might argue that mandating specific comprehension strategies is the solution. Although this may be appealing, it probably won't work. Top-down solutions are often short-lived and highly contested. Sarason (1990) acknowledged that billions of dollars have been spent on top-down reforms, with little to show for it. Goodlad (1992) noted that "top-down, politically driven education reform movements are addressed primarily to restructuring. The have little to say about educating" (p. 238).

Instead of mandating specific strategies, we know that individual schools or districts need to develop literacy frameworks such that teachers own and implement content literacy instructional strategies (Fisher, 2001; Frey, 2002, 2006). Through professional development, coaching, accountability, and the like, teachers can begin to develop students' thinking within and across the school day.

Our review of research, our own research, and our experience working in schools suggest that students need to develop habits. These habits must be transportable from content area to content area for students to incorporate them into their repertoires. For instance, at Hoover High School in San Diego, California, teachers agreed on seven instructional strategies that would permeate the school day, including (Fisher, Frey, & Williams, 2002) anticipatory activities (building background), read-alouds and shared reading, vocabulary development, graphic organizers, Cornell note taking, writing to learn, and reciprocal teaching. Definitions of these strategies can be found in Figure 18.1.

Staff members at Hoover are careful to point out that their success is based on the agreements they reached, the professional development they designed and delivered, and the administrative support they garnered for their initiative. They state very clearly that although these are good content literacy strategies, they are not the only ones that

---

Anticipatory activities. Such strategies as bellwork, anticipation guides, and K-W-L charts (i.e., what I *know*, what I *want* to know, what I *learned*) are designed to activate background knowledge and make connections between what students already know and what they are learning. These strategies also help students see the relevance of the curriculum.

Cornell note taking. Students use split pages to take notes on the right side, identify key ideas on the left, and write a summary at the bottom. This strategy improves listening comprehension and provides students with a study tool.

Graphic organizers. Any number of tools are used to display information in visual form. Common graphic organizers include semantic webs, cause-and-effect charts, Venn diagrams, matrices, and flowcharts.

Read-alouds and shared reading. On a daily basis, the teacher reads aloud material connected with the content standards being taught. This short, 3- to 5-minute reading provides students with a context for learning, builds their background knowledge, improves vocabulary, and provides them with a fluent reading model.

Reciprocal Teaching. In groups of four, students read a piece of text and engage in a structured conversation in which they summarize, clarify, question, and predict. In doing so, they learn to use strategies that good readers use while reading for information.

Vocabulary development. In addition to the incidental vocabulary learning that is done through read-alouds and anticipatory activities, students are taught specific content vocabulary words required in various disciplines.

Write-To-Learn. These brief writing prompts provide students an opportunity to clarify their understanding of the content, as well as provide the teacher a glimpse into the students' thinking. As a result, teachers know when reteaching or clarifications are necessary.

FIGURE 18.1. Schoolwide content literacy strategies. From Fisher and Frey (2006). Copyright 2006 by the National Association of Secondary School Principals. Reprinted by permission. (For more information on NASSP products and services to promote excellence in middle level and high school leadership, visit *www.principals.org*.)

would have worked to improve achievement. Having said that, they also acknowledge that achievement has increased as a result of the habits they have fostered in their students.

Waianae High School in Hawaii also developed a schoolwide literacy plan that comprised four major elements: daily silent, sustained reading; read-alouds and shared readings; note taking; and writing to learn. The staff at Waianae, after 1 year of implementation, began to see changes in student engagement and achievement. At both Hoover and Waianae, the intent was to make comprehension strategies *transparent* and *transportable* (Fisher et al., 2002), which means that students recognize when and why their teachers are providing this type of instruction (transparent) and know how to apply what they have learned in other content areas (transportable).

Although more research is needed on schoolwide literacy initiatives, the idea is gaining momentum. Several national organizations have published guidelines for the development and implementation of schoolwide approaches to improving adolescent literacy:

- National Association of Secondary School Principals (NASSP): *Creating a Culture of Literacy: A Guide for Middle and High School Principals* (2005).
- Association for Supervision and Curriculum Development: *Creating Literacy-Rich Schools for Adolescents* (Ivey & Fisher, 2006).
- WestEd: Strategic Literacy Initiative, *Reading Apprenticeship* (Schoenbach, Greenleaf, Cziko, & Hurwitz, 2000).

Having said this, if we could move from using a variety of strategies to create a level of instructional consistency—predictable for students—within a school, we might be able to move to the next level of achievement. Our intention is not to minimize the fact that there are discipline-specific literacy strategies. We know that reading like a scientist is different from reading like a historian or art critic. However, there are simply far too many students who read, write, and think far below grade level to assume that generic strategies won't help. Having said this, we also believe that as students incorporate these basic content literacy habits into their practices, we should also focus on discipline-specific literacy. One of the ways we know that teachers can do this is through their modeling, which brings us to our second big idea.

Internalize an Instructional Framework

One of the unintended consequences of the proliferation of instruction strategies is that many teachers are overwhelmed and feel the need to collect strategies and then shove them into their already full class periods. In the absence of a instructional framework, teachers are at risk of become "strategy junkies." There are a number of instructional frameworks that have been proposed and studied, including the commonly known reading instructional framework: before reading, during reading, and after reading (B-D-A; Laverick, 2002) and the Concept-Oriented Reading Instruction (CORI; Swan, 2003) framework for adolescents.

Our work focuses on a different instructional framework: the gradual release of responsibility model (Pearson & Gallagher, 1983). We have documented success with this framework in middle and high school classrooms as teachers internalize components, use strategies purposefully, and monitor student progress (Fisher & Frey, 2003, 2007). Our work on this framework has focused on four interrelated components:

1. *Focus lessons*, in which teachers establish purpose and model their own comprehension. This brief (5–15 minutes) instructional event is designed to ensure that students understand the point of the lesson and are provided with an expert model. Our experience suggests that teachers often do not provide modeling of comprehension strategies and instead question students about their comprehension (Ivey & Fisher, 2005). Although questioning is important, we know that teachers must explain their thinking, so that students can incorporate these comprehension strategies into their own behaviors (Duffy, 2003).

2. *Guided instruction*, in which the teacher meets with small groups of students, is based on their assessed needs. During guided instruction, the teacher uses cues, prompts, and questions to validate and to extend students' comprehension and comprehension strategy use. Although a number of instructional strategies are useful during guided instruction, we know that direct observation of students as they read and attempt to comprehend allows for the identification of problem areas. Teachers can use these teachable moments to further students' understanding.

3. *Collaborative learning* includes opportunities for students to work with one another to apply what they have learned in focus lessons and guided instruction. The key to quality collaborative learning is the product that each student produces as a result of the group interaction. We have seen too many group projects go wrong when a single product is required (the one student who does all of the work does all of the comprehension/thinking). Consistent with social learning theory, scaffolding, cognitive development, and interaction theory (Bandura, 1965, 1977; Vygotsky, 1962, 1978; Wood, Bruner, & Ross, 1976), we believe that students need opportunities to consolidate their understanding with peers before being asked to complete tasks alone. Unfortunately, this doesn't happen very often in most middle and high school classrooms.

4. *Independent learning tasks* comprise the final component of the gradual release of responsibility model of instruction—the full release to the student. Students must be provided opportunities to apply the skills, strategies, knowledge, and ideas to novel tasks. Importantly, independent learning tasks should follow rather than replace instruction. One caution is in order here: Independent learning tasks are not rote memorization tasks or worksheets. Instead, these tasks should be directly related to the unit of study. The higher the degree of internal consistency between the components in the gradual release of responsibility, the more likely it is that students will learn.

Over time and across units of instruction, teachers apply the gradual release of responsibility model recursively and iteratively (Fisher & Frey, 2007). This ensures that students learn new knowledge through focus lessons that provide modeling by expert, guided instruction that creates space for teachers to differentiate experiences, collaboration with peers as students refine their understanding, and independent learning through tasks that require students to synthesize and evaluate.

Examine Student Work, with Colleagues, on a Regular Basis

Our final big idea focuses on the collaborative analysis of student work (Langer, Colton, & Goff, 2003). There is a significant and growing body of evidence that collaboratively developed, common formative assessments focus teachers on the standards and what their students can and cannot do or have and have yet to master (Fisher, 2005; Fisher, Frey, Farnan, Fearn, & Peterson, 2004; Fisher & Johnson, 2006). In addition, common

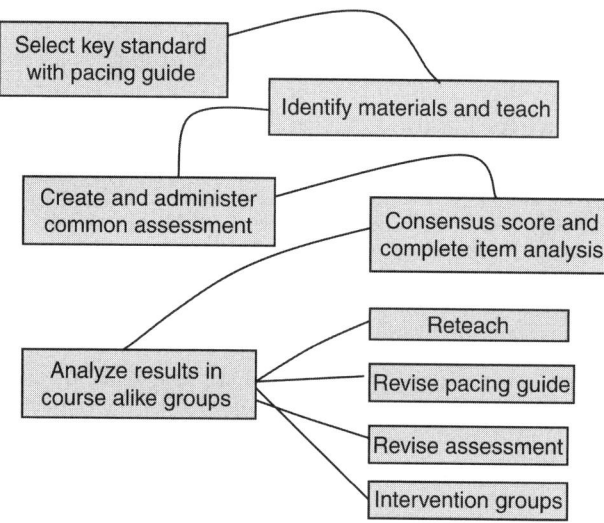

FIGURE 18.2. The process of common formative assessments.

formative assessments provide an opportunity for teachers to talk with one another, sharing instructional ideas and innovations (Ainsworth & Viegut, 2006). The process we use comprises a number of steps, as outlined in Figure 18.2.

The process starts with a group of teachers who teach the same course meeting to develop pacing guides. These guides outline which standards will be taught, as well as when. They also identify a range of instructional materials and approaches that might be used to teach this particular content. Importantly, teachers' work should incorporate schoolwide literacy strategies into their pacing guides.

Along the way, teachers who teach the same course meet to develop a common assessment. Typically, these assessments are brief and mirror the type of tasks students are required to do both in class and on state accountability assessments. As Langer (2001) demonstrated, schools can "beat the odds" when they provide students with regular test format practice. We have learned that the process of assessment development results in increased understanding of grade-level standards by teachers. This is an important lesson learned in the era of standards-based reform.

Upon completion of the unit of study, all students in the particular course participate in the common assessment. After the results are aggregated, an item analysis is conducted. During their course-alike meetings, teachers discuss their hypotheses for the correct and incorrect answers and plan "next steps" instruction. They can also make decisions to change the pacing guide, change the assessment, and/or form an intervention group. For example, one of the sixth-grade language arts common formative assessments included the following question:

> Directions: Read the words in the box very carefully. Look at the part that is underlined. If the underlined part is correct, mark answer D (*Correct as written*). If the underlined part is *not* correct, read all the answer choices carefully. Find the answer that shows the *best* way to write the underlined part and mark that answer. There is only one correct answer for each item.

> 4. <u>She and I</u> are going to the park.

A. She and me
B. Her and I
C. Me and her
D. Correct as written

Of the 242 students who attempted this item, only 16% answered it correctly (answer D). Of the incorrect answers, A was most commonly selected (38%), C was the second most common choice (27%), and B was third (19%). This was the most missed item on the assessment and served as the basis for a great deal of discussion among the English language arts teachers. Given the number of students who got this wrong, these educators knew that they had to reteach this concept. They also discussed the need to introduce language registers and focus their work on the difference between informal speech and formal writing. One of the teachers suggested that they look at students' authentic writing for such errors and use those samples for instruction.

Together, these three new forces—schoolwide comprehension strategies, a gradual release of responsibility framework of instruction, and common assessments and consensus scoring of student work—can work together with the assumed forces of adolescent literacy to meet the needs of more students.

HOW THIS NEW KNOWLEDGE CAN IMPROVE COMPREHENSION INSTRUCTION

Imagine that the three big ideas we have discussed are in place in schools across the country. Suddenly, "adequate yearly progress" isn't such a problem. Of course, there are students who challenge our ability to teach, newcomers to the language, students who have histories of failure, and so on. But if these three big ideas were enacted, could we collectively raise our expectations for adolescent literacy achievement? Could we begin to dream of a community in which members engage in complex reading, writing, and thinking tasks as a matter of fact?

Fullan, Hill, and Crévola (2006) have such a dream. To reach the dream, they argue, we don't need more prescriptive teaching. Instead, we need increased precision teaching that requires teachers to know their content well, to know their students well, to know how their students are performing, and to apply strategies to facilitate learning. This precision, when applied systemwide, results in improved comprehension (i.e., improved achievement) for middle and high school students.

DIRECTIONS FOR FUTURE RESEARCH

1. *How can we accelerate the literacy learning of adolescents who are reading and writing significantly below grade level?* Secondary students at the lowest levels of literacy achievement are at profound risk, because the clock is ticking for them. Whereas adults may internalize an academic calendar that extends through 12th-grade, in truth these students often possess a timetable that ends on the day they turn 16. That means that we

have until sometime in 9th or 10th grade to get them near grade level, or they will likely drop out. Therefore, we need to be able to triage their treatment, without making school seem even more restrictive to them. Doubling down on literacy and math instruction to the exclusion of other curricular experiences is proving to be a disincentive for these students. The answers likely lie in a better understanding of what engages young adults.

2. *What does effective secondary literacy learning look like for English language learners and students with disabilities?* Whereas student demographics continue to change, teacher demographics have remained largely unchanged for decades. The California Department of Finance (2005) projected that by 2040, 50% of all California schoolchildren will be English language learners. In addition, presently students with disabilities are accessing general education curriculum and instruction with their peers without disabilities. For example, in 2002, 80% of all students with disabilities spent 80% or more of their day in general education classrooms (U.S. Department of Education, 2005). However, literacy achievement for too many English language learners and students with disabilities stalls at the late elementary level of achievement, which is considered the minimum for functional literacy (Kutner, Greenberg, Jin, Boyle, Hsu, & Dunleavy, 2007).

3. *What will constitute "functional literacy" in the future?* Current definitions of a functional level of literacy are far removed from what will be needed to understand, interact, and develop information sources that have yet to be developed, such as Tim Berners-Lee's Web 3.0, the so-called "Semantic Web." (This hypothetical Internet of the future will not use Hypertext, but instead will allow databases to interact directly with one another rather than be dependent on humans to link them. For more information, see *semanticwebfaq.com/index.php?title=main_page*.) It is difficult to foresee what our students will need to be able to do in the future; it is certain that higher levels of literacy are equated with more degrees of choice in one's life.

4. *How do we prepare adolescents to be literate users of technologies that don't yet exist?* You probably recall your early attempts at using the technology that allows you to do your work—laptop computers, personal data assistants, information databases. In each case, you had to draw upon your considerable literacy skills to master the new device or process (and even then, it was probably a strain). How will our students of today fare with the technology of tomorrow? Much has been written about the urgency for producing sophisticated consumers and generators of information in an increasingly digital world. The digital divide grows with each innovation, especially for the poor, the aged, and the unskilled. In a postindustrial society, adolescents of today will find themselves on one side or the other of that divide. Some already do so.

5. *How do we shift the structure of schools and the instructional practices of teachers that are predicated on 20th century learning?* This may be the most challenging question of all. A body of research, some of it dating back nearly a century, identifies the components of sound instruction, especially as it relates to adolescent literacy. Yet, if you removed the obvious artifacts that signal an era, such as fashion and technologies, it would be difficult to discern any significant changes from those that we used at the turn of the previous century. Comprehensive high schools abound, in which students are grouped by chronological age and sit in rows, and the teacher's primary job is to transmit knowledge, while the students' job is to regurgitate it on demand. Yet who sits in the classroom has changed a great deal, and the world on the other side of the window is nearly unrecognizable. Although it is not possible to transform the way school is structured in one fell swoop, it should be a part of the conversation. School reform should be more that just "new wine in old bottles"—it may need to include rethinking the bottle itself.

PROJECTIONS AND POSSIBILITIES FOR THE CLASSROOM OF 2030

It seems clear that secondary schools will look significantly different by 2030, as the vestiges of the industrial revolution continue to transform global economies and societies. The information transmission model that was essential for much of the 20th century is giving way to new ways of learning information. As with the Web 3.0 example, the future of literacy research may focus on knowledge creation rather than transmission (Natriello, 2004). "Knowledge creation" is the phenomenon of learners coming together to form new understandings. This is already occurring in the lives of our students as they blog, post on Facebook, and collaborate with peers overseas to compose fanzines. The appetite for knowledge creation experiences can be witnessed in the success of Second Life, a virtual world with over 5 million residents and a monetary system of lindens that sell for real dollars on eBay. We predict that the traditional classroom of the past (and today) will fade as other new learning experiences are created to meet future societal needs.

The literacy skills for knowledge creation will become more sophisticated as well, because students will need to communicate with others in order to participate. Therefore, the importance of synthesizing and evaluating information will become more important than ever, because interactions will not be constrained by distance and time. Literacy educators will need to facilitate these knowledge-creation experiences and guide learning by using some of the very same enduring forces we mentioned at the beginning of this chapter—vocabulary, strategic learning, building background knowledge, motivation, and engagement.

Literacy educators will likewise need to engage in knowledge creation through collaboration with colleagues as they identify and refine strategies and approaches, and utilize instructional frameworks. Just as schools of the future will not need to segregate children from the rest of a society to educate them, teachers will not be able to continue to segregate themselves from each other. The "cooperation of forces" first proposed by Thorndike nearly a century ago serves as an appropriate metaphor for the present and the future of adolescent literacy research. The knowledge creation for future learners will happen as we create knowledge with one another.

SUMMARY

The future of adolescent comprehension research must incorporate what is already known about what works, while focusing on how to go to scale, so that all students can profit. As classroom composition changes, so must the ways we conceive of the creation of understanding. This means working together as never before, not only to identify the enduring data of our field but also to create new knowledge that will help our students keep pace with changes in the ways we communicate. Thus, schoolwide commitments to strategic learning, changing the ways content is designed and delivered, and collaborating with fellow educators to understand our students' learning will yield the new knowledge we need to support adolescents' growth as successful comprehenders in the 21st century.

INTEGRATE, INVESTIGATE, AND INITIATE: QUESTIONS FOR DISCUSSION

1. Compare the information you learned in this chapter about secondary classrooms to the information that Duke and Martin presented (Chapter 17, this volume) about improving compre-

hension in the elementary classroom. Create a Venn Diagram to show the similarities between highly effective comprehension across all grade levels and the differences that exist at the elementary and secondary classrooms. Share your diagrams with colleagues and compare their findings with yours.

2. Describe the preventive accelerated and long-term support that is provided in your school district or through state-level policies for adolescent literacy comprehension instruction. Prepare this description by using the state education agency website for your state or the school district website. After you have examined one or both of these websites, write a paragraph to describe how much information was available concerning comprehension instructional supports at the secondary level.

3. If you are a professional with responsibility at the secondary level, how many of the goals in this chapter do you include in your area of responsibility? If you are not a secondary school educator, summarize the actions you have learned in this chapter that you would like to share with a colleague who teaches at the secondary level but has not had an opportunity to read this chapter.

REFERENCES

Adolescent literacy: The hottest topic. (2007, February). *Reading Today, 24*(4), 12.

Ainsworth, L., & Viegut, D. (2006). *Common formative assessments: How to connect standards-based instruction and assessment*. Thousand Oaks, CA: Corwin.

Allen, J. (1999). *Words, words, words: Teaching vocabulary in grades 4–12*. York, ME: Stenhouse.

Alvermann, D. E. (2002). Effective literacy instruction for adolescents. *Journal of Literacy Research, 34*(2), 189–208. Retrieved April 2, 2007, from *www.coe.uga.edu/reading/faculty/alvermann/effective2.pdf*.

Alvermann, D. E., O'Brien, D. G., & Dillon, D. R. (1990). What teachers do when they say they're having discussions of content area reading: A qualitative analysis. *Reading Research Quarterly, 25*, 296–322.

Bandura, A. (1965). Influence of models' reinforcement contingencies on the acquisition of imitative responses. *Journal of Personality and Social Psychology, 1*, 589–595.

Bandura, A. (1977). *Social learning theory*. Englewood Cliffs, NJ: Prentice-Hall.

Biancarosa, G., & Snow, C. E. (2004). *Reading next: a vision for action in middle and high school literacy* (A report to the Carnegie Corporation of New York, 2nd ed.). Washington, DC: Alliance for Excellent Education.

California Department of Finance. (2005). *Population projections by race/ethnicity, gender, and age for California and its counties 2000–2050*. Sacramento, CA: Author.

Duffy, G. G. (2003). *Explaining reading: A resource for teaching concepts, skills, and strategies*. New York: Guilford Press.

Duke, N. K., & Pearson, P. D. (2002). Effective practices for developing reading comprehension. In A. E. Farstup & S. J. Samuels (Eds.), *What research has to say about reading instruction* (pp. 205–242). Newark, DE: International Reading Association.

Fisher, D. (2001). We're moving on up: Creating a schoolwide literacy effort in an urban high school. *Journal of Adolescent and Adult Literacy, 45*, 92–101.

Fisher, D. (2005). The missing link: Standards, assessment, *and* instruction. *Voices From the Middle, 13*(2), 8–11.

Fisher, D., Brozo, W. G., Frey, N., & Ivey, G. (2007). *50 content area strategies for adolescent literacy*. Upper Saddle River, NJ: Merrill/Prentice-Hall.

Fisher, D., & Frey, N. (2003). Writing instruction for struggling adolescent readers: A gradual release model. *Journal of Adolescent and Adult Literacy, 46*, 396–407.

Fisher, D., & Frey, N. (2006). Majority rules: A schoolwide literacy success. *Principal Leadership, 6*(7), 16–21.

Fisher, D., & Frey, N. (2008). *Better learning through structured teaching: A gradual release of responsibility framework*. Alexandria, VA: Association for Supervision and Curriculum Development.

Fisher, D., & Frey, N. (2007). A tale of two middle schools: The role of structure and instruction. *Journal of Adolescent and Adult Literacy, 51*, 204–211.

Fisher, D., Frey, N., Farnan, N., Fearn, L., & Petersen, F. (2004). Increasing achievement in an urban middle school. *Middle School Journal, 36*(2), 21–26.

Fisher, D., Frey, N., & Williams, D. (2002). Seven literacy strategies that work. *Educational Leadership, 60*(3), 70–73.

Fisher, D., & Ivey, G. (2005). Literacy and language as learning in content area classes: A departure from "ever teacher a teacher of reading." *Action in Teacher Education, 27*(2), 3–11.

Fisher, D., & Johnson, C. (2006). Using data to improve student achievement. *Principal Leadership, 7*(2), 27–31.

Frey, N. (2002). Literacy achievement in an urban middle-level professional development school: A learning community at work. *Reading Improvement, 39*(1), 3–13.

Frey, N. (2006). "We can't afford to rest on our laurels": Creating a district-wide content literacy instructional plan. *NASSP Bulletin, 90*(1), 37–48.

Fullan, M., Hill, P., & Crévola, C. (2006). *Breakthrough*. Thousand Oaks, CA: Corwin.

Goodlad, J. (1992). On taking school reform seriously. *Phi Delta Kappan, 74*(3), 232–238.

Guthrie, J. T., & Wigfield, A. (2000). Engagement and motivation in reading. In M. L. Kamil, P. B. Mosenthal, P. D. Pearson, & R. Barr (Eds.), *Handbook of reading research* (Vol. III, pp. 403–422). Mahwah, NJ: Erlbaum.

Herber, H. L. (1970). *Teaching reading in the content areas*. Englewood Cliffs, NJ: Prentice-Hall.

Ivey, G., & Fisher, D. (2005). Learning from what doesn't work. *Educational Leadership, 63*(2), 8–17.

Ivey, G., & Fisher, D. (2006). When thinking skills trump reading skills. *Educational Leadership, 64*, 16–21.

Jacob, B. A. (1991). Getting tough?: The impact of high school graduation exams. *Educational Evaluation and Policy Analysis, 23*(2), 99–121.

Kirsch, I., de Jong, J., LaFontaine, D., McQueen, J., Mendelovits, J., & Monseur, C. (2002). *Reading for change: Performance and engagement across countries: Results from PISA 2000*. Paris: Organization for Economic Cooperation and Development.

Kutner, M., Greenberg, E., Jin, Y., Boyle, B., Hsu, Y., & Dunleavy, E. (2007). *Literacy in everyday life: Results from the 2003 National Assessment of Adult Literacy* (NCES2007–480). Washington, DC: U.S. Department of Education, National Center for Education Statistics.

Langer, G. M., Colton, A. B., & Goff, L. S. (2003). *Collaborative analysis of student work: Improving teaching and learning*. Alexandria, VA: Association for Supervision and Curriculum Development.

Langer, J. A. (2001). Beating the odds: Teaching middle and high school students to read and write well. *American Educational Research Journal, 38*, 837–888.

Laverick, C. (2002). B-D-A strategy: Reinventing the wheel can be a good thing. *Journal of Adolescent and Adult Literacy, 46*, 144–147.

Marzano, R. J. (2004). *Building background knowledge for academic achievement*. Alexandria, VA: Association for Supervision and Curriculum Development.

Moore, D. W., Bean, T. W., Birdyshaw, D., & Rycik, J. A. (1999). Adolescent literacy: A position statement. *Journal of Adolescent and Adult Literacy, 43*, 97–112.

National Association of Secondary School Principals (NASSP). (2005). *Creating a culture of literacy: A Guide for middle and high school principals*. Reston, VA: Author.

National Reading Panel. (2000). *Teaching children to read: An evidence-based assessment of the scientific research literature on reading and its implications for reading instruction*. Washington, DC: National Institute of Child Health and Human Development and U. S. Department of Education.

Natriello, G. (2004). *Beyond courses: The search for new forms of education online.* Retrieved April 4, 2007, from *edlab.tc.columbia.edu/files/edlab_beyondcourses.pdf.*

Pearson, P. D., & Gallagher, G. (1983). The gradual release of responsibility model of instruction. *Contemporary Educational Psychology, 8,* 112–123.

Sarason, S. B. (1990). *The predictable failure of educational reform: Can we change course before it's too late?* San Francisco: Jossey-Bass.

Schoenbach, R., Greenleaf, C. L., Cziko, C., & Hurwitz, L. (2000). *Reading for understanding: A guide to improving reading in middle and high school classrooms.* San Francisco: Jossey-Bass.

Strang, R. (1964). *Diagnostic teaching of reading.* New York: McGraw-Hill.

Swan, E. A. (2003). *Concept-Oriented Reading Instruction: Engaging classrooms, lifelong learners.* New York: Guilford Press.

Thorndike, E. L. (1917). Reading as reasoning: A study in mistakes in paragraph reasoning. *Journal of Educational Psychology, 8,* 323–332.

U.S. Department of Education. (2005). *26th annual (2004) report to Congress on the implementation of the Individuals with Disabilities Education Act.* Washington, DC: Office of Special Education Programs.

Vygotsky, L. S. (1962). *Thought and language.* Cambridge, MA: MIT Press.

Vygotsky, L. S. (1978). *Mind in society.* Cambridge, MA: Harvard University Press.

Whipple, G. (Ed.). (1925). *The 24th yearbook of the National Society for the Study of Education: Report of the National Committee on Reading.* Bloomington, IL: Public School Publishing Company.

Wood, D., Bruner, J. S., & Ross, G. (1976). The role of tutoring and problem solving. *Journal of Child Psychology and Psychiatry, 17,* 89–100.

19

Comprehension Instruction in Action
The At-Risk Student

MICHAEL F. HOCK, IRMA F. BRASSEUR, and DONALD D. DESHLER

> It wasn't just the obvious things . . . that made me feel anxious or worried and ate away at my confidence and self-esteem during high school. It was the small things that unnerved me, the seemingly simple concepts that I couldn't forgive myself for not comprehending.
> —SAMANTHA ABEEL, *My Thirteenth Winter* (2005, pp. 135–136)

For years, many educators and policymakers have made a compelling case for early identification and intervention of at-risk students on the assumption (or hope) that if these things happen at a young age, many of the manifestations of learning problems would be minimized or avoided altogether in later years. Although such goals are important and laudable, there is a potential danger in overemphasizing early remediation *at the expense of* interventions at later ages; that is, such calls for early diagnostic/prescriptive efforts may be misinterpreted as implying that early instruction will ameliorate the learning difficulties in older students. Indeed, the most recent National Assessment of Educational Progress (NAEP) of the National Center for Education Statistics (NCES; 2005) results underscore the fact that the reading problems of a significant number of older students continue to exist in staggering numbers. Specifically, 26% of eighth-grade students cannot read material essential for daily living, such as road signs, newspapers, or bus schedules. Overall, 68% of secondary-level students score below the proficient level.

Fortunately, increased efforts have been made during the past decade to understand better the characteristics of older students who continue to struggle in becoming proficient readers. Building on the findings of these efforts, instructional programs have been designed and data that are beginning to emerge point to promising practices for struggling adolescent readers. Among the attributes that appear to be important for yielding positive outcomes are direct and explicit comprehension instruction, engagement with reading materials that motivate students, formative assessments to help shape instruction in a timely fashion, extended time for intensive literacy instruction, deliberate linkage of strategy instruction to subject matter curricular demands, and comprehensive, coordinated literacy programs (Snow & Biancarosa, 2003).

To understand better some recent advancements in adolescent literacy, we designed this chapter to address three main objectives:

1. Describe what's out there in terms of an emerging research and practice base.
2. Describe some of what's out there in terms of new research.
3. Discuss how this new knowledge can inform comprehension instruction designed for middle and high school struggling readers.

WHAT'S OUT THERE: AN EMERGING RESEARCH AND PRACTICE BASE

Some adolescents leave elementary school unprepared for the rigors of the secondary school curricular demands that await them (Hock & Deshler, 2003). For example, nearly 60% of struggling adolescent readers in poor urban settings fall between the 5th and the 30th percentiles in reading performance; that is, they have some basic reading skills but not at a sufficient level to deal fluently with subject matter reading demands, and they lack the skills and strategies necessary to meet comprehension expectations (Curtis, 2002; Snow, 2002; Snow & Biancarosa, 2003). Some of these same students were proficient readers in early elementary school but were unable to make the fourth-grade shift from learning to read to reading to learn (Cutting & Scarborough, 2006).

Reading comprehension results from proficiency in key, text-based reading skills, the acquisition of a wide-ranging knowledge base, and proficiency in the strategic use of comprehension strategies. These attributes allow the learner to create and apply knowledge to novel learning situations. Whereas decoding is essential for proficient reading at the secondary level, it is not sufficient (Gersten, Fuchs, Williams, & Baker, 2001; Kamil, 2003; Pressley, 2002; Snow, 2002; Snow & Biancarosa, 2003). What is required is fluent decoding *and* linguistic knowledge (vocabulary and general knowledge of the world) for readers to be able effectively to deploy reading strategies that allow them to bring meaning to text (Gersten et al., 2001; Hoover & Gough, 1990; Kamil, 2003; Pressley, 2000; Snow, 2002).

In light of these assumptions, reading comprehension initiatives must address the complex nature of literacy as content demands increase, vocabulary knowledge becomes essential to understanding various disciplines, and materials become more difficult to read. In short, adolescent readers must be able to decode, read with fluency, understand an increased vocabulary, build background knowledge, and be critical comprehenders of difficult and diverse text and text structures (Snow, 2002). Additionally, they must be motivated to put forth time and energy to improve their reading proficiency (Curtis, 2002; Guthrie, Wigfield, & Perencevich, 2004; Kamil, 2003; National Institute for Child Health and Human Development [NICHD], 2000; Snow, 2002).

A growing number of intervention initiatives aimed at struggling adolescent readers have emerged in the past several years. The instructional approaches described below have shown promise in improving outcomes for struggling adolescent learners.

Reading for Understanding

Using Reading Apprenticeship as a framework for reading instruction, researchers have developed a ninth-grade course, Academic Literacy (Greenleaf, Schoenbach, Cziko, & Mueller, 2001). In contrast to typical skills-based remedial reading courses, here students engage in ongoing, collaborative discussion of text-based information, have scheduled time for independent reading, and are able to access a variety of engaging materials directly related to content class curricula. Subject-area teachers deliver the interventions in their classes. One study showed pre- to posttest gains on a standardized reading measure. When compared to national norm data in the Degrees of Reading Power assessment, these gains were statistically significant, and the students moved from an average seventh-grade reading level at pretest to an average ninth-grade level at posttest; that is, on average, students made progress in closing the reading achievement gap (Greenleaf et al., 2001).

Language!

Language! is a comprehensive reading program that integrates reading, spelling, and writing instruction (Greene, 1998). Designed for students who struggle with literacy skills and who are 2 or more years below grade placement, the program is highly structured, and instruction is explicit. Language! was intended be used in general or special education settings and as a mastery-based program, with students progressing at their own pace. Instruction is provided to students in small groups, and students also engage in independent practice. Specific units of instruction include vocabulary, prereading activities, written expression, and questioning techniques related to reading. Specific reading skills units include phonemic awareness, word recognition, and reading comprehension.

Several studies conducted with Language! yielded treatment group gains that were both statistically and socially significant. Thus, students in the treatment group gained an average of three grades in word identification and reading comprehension.

Read 180

Read 180 is a comprehensive reading intervention for struggling readers in grades 4 through 12. The program comprises four major components: (1) whole-group instruction (with the teacher modeling fluent reading and the application of various reading strategies); (2) intensive small-group instruction; (3) computer instruction designed for building background information, vocabulary, reading comprehension, fluency, and word study; and (4) silent reading in engaging, leveled books supported with audiobooks. The initial project design for Read 180 was based on research conducted on students with mild disabilities (Hasselbring, 1996; Hasselbring & Bottge, 2000).

Most studies on Read 180 have employed quasi-experimental pre- to posttest designs. A large study of low-performing middle school students in Dallas, Houston, and Boston reported a significant advantage on Stanford Achievement Test (SAT-9) results for students instructed with Read 180. Similar trends were found in a study conducted in the Los Angeles Unified School District. Scores on both the Nation's Report Card: Reading 2002 (NCES, 2002) and Reading and Language Arts SAT-9 subsections showed significant gains for the experimental groups (Scholastic, 2005). Although these findings are encouraging, caution should be exercised in interpreting the data because of a lack of random assignment to instructional conditions or appropriate quasi-experimental matching (Smith, Rissman, & Grek, 2004).

Reciprocal Teaching

Reciprocal Teaching (Palincsar & Brown, 1984) is an instructional model that emphasizes teaching students key cognitive reading comprehension strategies for predicting, clarifying, summarizing, and questioning in the context of authentic text. The strategies are taught explicitly with scaffolded guided practice to engage students in conversations about what they are reading and learning. Discussion gradually moves from teacher- to student-mediated interactions. After a while, students assume the role of teacher as they use the strategies to support comprehension. Thus, instruction is reciprocal between teacher and students. Numerous evaluation studies have shown that Reciprocal Teaching effectively improves reading comprehension (e.g., Alfassi, 1998; Lysynchuk, Pressley, & Vye, 1990; Rosenshine & Meister, 1995; Taylor & Frye, 1992; Westera & Moore, 1995).

Science Research Associates (SRA) Corrective Reading

Corrective Reading is another comprehensive reading intervention program designed to improve word-level reading and comprehension (Adams & Engelmann, 1996). Intended for students in grades 4–12 who are reading one or more grade levels below grade placement, Corrective Reading may be implemented in general or special education classrooms with small groups of students or in a whole-class format. The program is highly structured, sequenced, and scripted. Teachers follow a direct instruction model as they teach decoding skills that focus on word attack skills, group reading, and individual mastery. A comprehension strand includes instruction in thinking strategies and oral group exercises (Adams & Engelmann, 1996).

The effectiveness of Corrective Reading is supported by a sizable research base (Adams & Engelmann, 1996; Borman, Hewes, Overman, & Brown, 2003; M. L. Campbell, 1984; Gersten & Keating, 1987; Thorne, 1978). However, to date, the research with adolescents has not been conducted in a random assignment of treatment and control group designs. Thus, although initial findings are encouraging, they are somewhat limited.

Strategic Instruction Model

Since 1978, researchers at the University of Kansas Center for Research on Learning (KUCRL) have developed a broad array of interventions called the Strategic Instruction Model (SIM) designed to improve literacy outcomes for struggling adolescent learners, including those with learning disabilities (e.g., Deshler et al., 2001; Schumaker & Deshler, 2006). In one line of research, content-enhancement routines (CERs) enable subject matter teachers in secondary schools to select and present critical content information that is potentially difficult to learn in a way that is understandable and memorable to all students in an academically diverse class, regardless of literacy levels (Bulgren, Deshler, & Schumaker, 1997; Bulgren, Deshler, Schumaker, & Lenz, 2000; Bulgren, Schumaker, & Deshler, 1988; Bulgren, Schumaker, Deshler, Lenz, & Marquis, 2002; Lenz & Bulgren, 1995; Lenz & Deshler, 2004).

In a second line of research, teachers instruct students to use various learning strategies that enable them to negotiate successfully the demands of the curriculum, teaching them how to learn (Lenz, Ehren, & Deshler, 2005). Two major questions have guided this line of programmatic work: (1) Can adolescents be taught to use complex learning strategies? and (2) does their use of the strategies result in improved performance on academic tasks? Over 20 studies have been completed (e.g., for a review, see Schumaker & Deshler, 2006). Each learning strategy intervention includes the instructional procedures and materials teachers need to teach adolescents to apply a given strategy using an eight-stage explicit instructional methodology (Brownell, Mellard, & Deshler, 1993; Ellis, Deshler, Lenz, Schumaker, & Clark, 1991).

In general, this research has shown that adolescents greatly improve their use of a particular strategy when the eight-stage instructional methodology is implemented. Furthermore, in all of the studies, students generalized their application of the strategy across stimulus materials (Clark, Deshler, Schumaker, Alley, & Warner, 1984; Lenz & Hughes, 1990; Schumaker, Deshler, Alley, Warner, & Denton, 1982).

NEW RESEARCH IN READING COMPREHENSION FOR AT-RISK STUDENTS

Theoretical Underpinnings of Comprehension

Established research and practice is best understood in the context of reading theory, because theory in large measure determines what comprehension is and how it is operationalized and measured (Cutting & Scarborough, 2006). The *Simple View of Reading* model proposes that reading comprehension is a product of word recognition and linguistic comprehension (Gough & Tunmer, 1986; Hoover & Gough, 1990). This view recognizes the complexities of reading and divides them into two parts: word recognition and comprehension. The word recognition component is responsible for translating print into language, and the comprehension component makes sense of this linguistic information. While multiple theories about reading exist, the Simple View of Reading has garnered interest and support through multiple studies (Catts, Adlof, & Ellis-Weismer, 2006; Cutting & Scarborough, 2006; Leach, Scarborough, & Rescorla, 2003; Vellutino, Tunmer, Jaccard, & Chen, 2007).

Balanced Instructional Needs of Adolescent Struggling Readers

Given the theoretical underpinnings of comprehension described earlier, reading instruction for adolescents should encompass a comprehensive approach; that is, all components of reading that are related to the two critical strands identified in the Simple View of Reading need to be considered as interventions are designed and struggling readers' needs are addressed. This point is highlighted in recent descriptive research on struggling adolescent readers (Catts et al., 2006; Cutting & Scarborough, 2006; Hock et al., in press; Leach et al., 2003; Vellutino et al., 2007). This research has shown the need for balanced instruction that includes attention to word-level skills, language comprehension, acquisition of key reading comprehension strategies, and student motivation for reading. Descriptive studies help to inform researchers and practitioners about the reading profiles of struggling adolescent readers. These studies highlight the comprehensive nature of such profiles and their potential to inform instruction.

What Are the Reading Skills of Adolescent Struggling Readers?

In a recently completed descriptive study to determine the reading component skills profiles of struggling adolescent readers in urban high schools, 345 adolescents were administered a battery of reading measures (Hock et al., in press). The average age of students in this study was 14.9 years. Fifty-five percent of students were male and 45% were female. The race and ethnicity profile of the sample was 52% African American, 15% Hispanic, 29% European American, and 4% reporting in other categories. Fifty-one percent of the students received free/reduced-cost lunch, and 47% of the students paid for lunch. Struggling readers were defined as those who scored at or below the 40th percentile (standard score of 96) on the Woodcock Language Proficiency Battery—Revised (WLPB-R). Using this criterion, the sample included 195 "struggling" readers and 150 "proficient" readers.

Instruments were selected and grouped within a reading component framework identified in the literature as essential to the reading success of younger and adolescent readers (Curtis, 2002; NICHD, 2000). The measures comprised a battery of language and literacy tasks, and selected student characteristics. Multiple measures of each construct were included so that the relations among latent abilities could be examined independent of task-specific factors or measurement error (Kline, 2005). Component skills differences between proficient and struggling readers were identified and found to be significant. Data also showed that the majority (63%) of struggling readers scored poorly on all reading component measures. These results contradict some of the information commonly used to describe struggling adolescent learners. For example, Buly and Valencia (2003) concluded that poor student performance on the state reading assessment was due primarily to issues related to reading fluency and comprehension. Furthermore, they stated that word-level problems contributed minimally to poor reading performance, and only about 9% of the students in the sample were poor readers in terms of word recognition, fluency, and meaning. Thus, most struggling readers in the study needed instruction primarily in comprehension and fluency, with very few needing instruction in all three areas.

The Hock et al. (in press) study provides a comprehensive set of descriptive data that has not previously been available. In all component domains of reading (alphabetics, fluency, vocabulary, and comprehension), struggling readers were found to score statistically lower than their proficient reader counterparts. Specifically, less able readers were approximately 1 standard deviation below the mean in each reading domain and 20 to 25 or more standard score points lower than the good readers in some areas. Although the domains of greatest deficit were fluency, vocabulary, and comprehension, many struggling readers demonstrated significant deficits at the word level as well (i.e., word attack, decoding, and word recognition). These data have many implications for assessment, instruction, and policy.

Additional descriptive analyses for students who scored at or below the standard score of 96 on at least one of the components were conducted. Examination of the resultant group of 193 struggling readers with low scores on at least one reading domain showed that 121 (63%) of them were low on every domain. Another 25 were low on every skill except alphabetics. The two reading domains with the largest number of persons below the mean standard score of 96 were comprehension (91%) and fluency (89%) (Hock et al., in press). Thus, more than half of the struggling reader sample was deficient in word level *and* comprehension skills (see Figure 19.1). A list of the measures used to describe the reading component skills of adolescent readers in this sample is found in Figure 19.2.

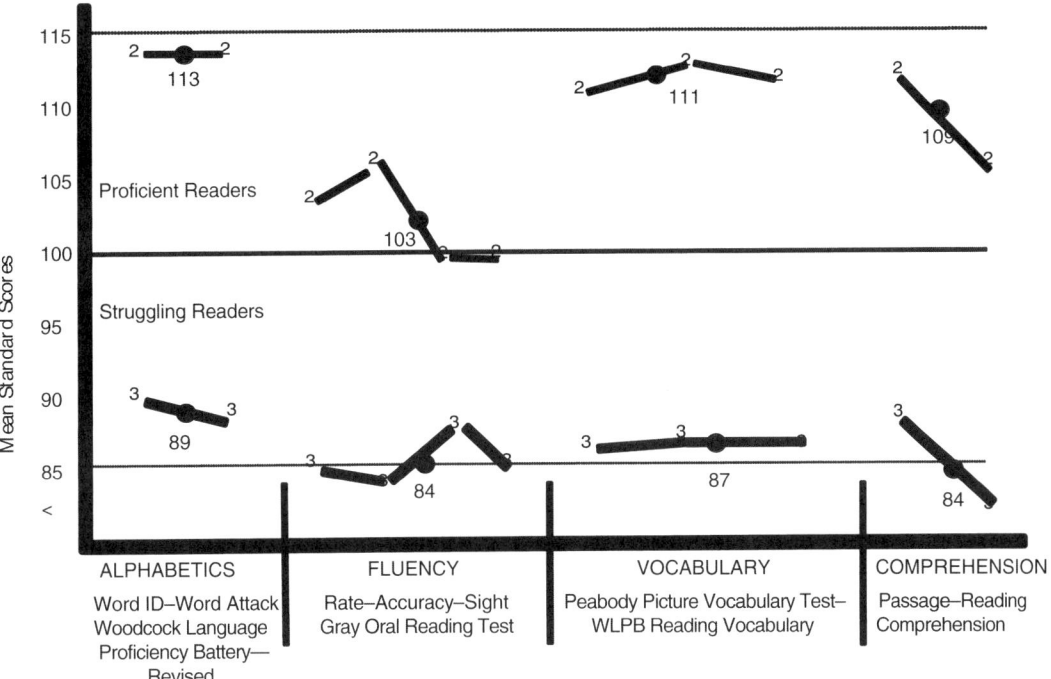

FIGURE 19.1. Reading component skills scores.

Assessment Area	Measure

Alphabetics
  Decoding
  Word identification
	Woodcock Language Proficiency Battery—Revised (WLPB-R)
	  WLPB-R: Word Attack
	  WLPB-R: Word Identification

Fluency
  Pace/rate
  Accuracy
	Test of Word Reading Efficiency (TOWRE)
	  Phonetic Decoding Efficiency
	  Sight Word Efficiency
	Gray Oral Reading Test–4 (GORT-4)

Vocabulary
  Expressive
  Receptive
	Peabody Picture Vocabulary Test III (PPVT-III)
	  WLPB-R: Reading Vocabulary

Comprehension
  Reading
  Listening
	WLPB-R: Passage Comprehension
	GORT-4: Passage Comprehension
	WLPB-R: Listening Comprehension

FIGURE 19.2. Reading component measures.

A Comprehensive Response to Adolescent Struggling Readers: Fusion Reading

In response to the challenges faced by many adolescent struggling readers, and in line with current reading theory and research data described earlier, researchers at the KUCRL have developed and tested the effects of a 2-year-long course for struggling readers who enter middle or high school reading 2 years or more below grade level. The course is called Fusion Reading (Hock, Brasseur, & Deshler, 2007). "Fusion" is defined as the merging, blending, or resulting blend of two or more things. This simple definition exemplifies the instructional and curricular development of the Fusion Reading program. The program is designed to focus on the integration and application of multiple reading and motivational strategies necessary to improve the reading comprehension of struggling adolescent readers.

Previous work with our own interventions and those of other researchers supports specific instructional principles that help to define the science of highly effective instruction. The principles include (1) direct or explicit instruction, (2) student engagement, (3) transactional strategy instruction (metacognition), (4) elaborated feedback, (5) multiple controlled and independent practice opportunities, (6) teacher modeling, (7) scaffolded support, and (8) the use of small interactive learning groups (Dole, Duffy, Roehler, & Pearson, 1991; Ellis et al., 1991; Gersten et al., 2001; Kline, Schumaker, & Deshler, 1991; NICHD, 2000; Schumaker & Deshler, 1992; Snow, 2002; Swanson & Hoskyn, 1999; Torgesen, 2002).

Fusion Reading comprises newly developed reading interventions and has been designed for teaching classes of 12–15 students. The course is grounded in highly engaging literature that teens find motivating. Through this literature, students are taught a set of key reading strategies that have been organized or bundled into three main components: (1) the Motivation Component, (2) the Bridging Component, and (3) the Reading Comprehension Component. The Motivation Component, Possible Selves, a validated motivation intervention (Hock, Deshler, & Schumacher, 2006), focuses students' attention on the importance of becoming an expert reader and how the benefits of doing so help them reach their hopes and dreams (Hock, Schumaker, & Deshler, 2003). For example, during Possible Selves instruction, students participate in a structured interview, describing themselves as persons and learners in a desired career area. They also identify their hopes, expectations and fears for the future in each of these areas. Then they draw a Possible Selves Tree that visually depicts all their hopes, expectations, and fears. A careful examination of the "tree" and the desire to keep the tree strong and healthy brings to the surface the student's specific goals for maintaining and nurturing the tree and, in a sense, him- or herself. From this examination of what is possible for each individual, an action plan is developed that clearly shows the linkage between reading and the attainment of the desired goals identified by the student. Reading is now seen as something that supports the hopes and expectations of the student, and not as an abstract, required course with seemingly little relevance to the student's personal goals. In short, the Possible Selves program serves as the "pillar" on which all other instruction is supported and is designed to nurture student motivation for positive academic performance in general and motivation for reading specifically—all while being taught within the context of engaging literature.

The Bridging Component comprises four core elements: decoding/phonics skills, word identification, reading fluency, and vocabulary. Bridging is designed to address the needs of students who struggle with word-level reading skills. When students apply the bridging strategy, they use multiple skills and strategies to help them quickly and accurately recognize words in connected text. For example, a student who did not recognize the word *peripheral* while reading a passage would use the PART strategy. First she would *P*ronounce any letter sounds within the word. In this case the student might recognize "per" and "her." She would underline those letter sounds and attempt to say each combination of letters and blend them into a word. In this case, the groups of letters do not lend themselves to word recognition, so the student would continue to attack the word using the next step of the strategy, *A*nalyze for beginnings and endings. In the case of the word *peripheral* the student would separate "per" and "er" and "al" (a compound suffix). Again, the student would say each word part and blend them together. If the word was still unrecognizable, then she would proceed to the next step of the strategy, *R*eview the remaining letters to find the syllable(s). The remaining letters include *iph*. Students locate the vowel *i* and place a dot under it. Next, she would look for consonants that might follow the vowel, such as the "ph" consonant blend. Next, the student would look for the type of syllable represented by a vowel followed by a consonant, and in this case the syllable is closed, so the vowel makes a short-*i* sound. She would say each part of the word per-iph-er-al, then blend the parts to say *peripheral*. If she recognizes the word, she then rereads the word in context to check of meaning. If the student still does not recognize the word, then she uses the last step of PART, the *T*ry another resource step. The student would ask another person, or use a dictionary or computer to figure out how to say the word and what the word means. As the student works her way through the PART steps, she may find that she recognizes a word just using the first step, or after using the first two steps of PART. In other words, students are taught to work their way through the PART steps as needed to identify the unknown word. Throughout the process of applying the PART steps students are guided to think about what the word means by rereading the word in context and using their knowledge of word beginning and ending meanings. Once students demonstrate proficiency in the "PART" steps, they engage in fluency activities that build accuracy, rate, and prosody.

Finally, the Comprehension Component comprises two key strategies that include multiple substrategies to support comprehension. For example, the Summarization Strategy includes strategies for finding clues in reading material, linking the material to prior knowledge, reading short chunks of information, finding main ideas, paraphrasing, and summarizing sections of text material. The Prediction Strategy is designed for making and confirming predictions, and involves the following steps (CLUE): *C*heck for clues that give an idea what the selection is about, *L*ink that information to what is already known about the topic, *U*ncover predictions about the information in the selection, and *E*valuate your predictions.

Two additional overall program components, Thinking Reading and Book Study, were developed to increase the amount of time students are engaged in the reading process. First, Thinking Reading is an instructional process that teachers use to demonstrate expert reading behaviors, to forecast strategy application, and to provide opportunities for students to practice strategy application in the context of authentic reading material. Highly engaging reading materials are used during Thinking Reading. For example, when students are engaged in Possible Selves activities during Thinking Reading, they might read a novel and discuss the main character's hopes, expectations, and fears. In addition, they might describe the main character as a person and as a learner. In this fashion, students are given examples of hopes, expectations, and fears in the context of what they are reading.

Second, a Book Study component designed for extension and application of learned strategies is completed outside the classroom. Students choose books that they like to complete, and Book Study assignments that are directly related to the strategies and vocabulary being taught. Book Study assignments present opportunities for wide-ranging reading experiences that support student practice of skills and strategies, and the development of vocabulary.

During Book Study, students choose their own books within a structure that requires that they read both challenging materials and easier material. Once students have selected a book, they read and apply reading strategies independently. For example, a student might read a rather challenging book that has several unfamiliar, multisyllabic words. The student would apply the word recognition strategy PART to unfamiliar words. In his Book Study portfolio, the student would show evidence that he had "attacked" the word using the PART strategy. The portfolio is then scored with the Book Study rubric (see Figure 19.3). Thus, students read books independently and apply the strategies they learned in the reading class.

A key element used with each component of the Fusion Reading program is a structured procedural format (see Figure 19.4) designed to teach each of the reading strategies to classes of 12–15 students.

Throughout each lesson in the course, the teacher engages students in a teacher-led reading activity for a part of each class period, wherein the class reads aloud a series of engaging novels and short stories. During this activity, the teacher models expert reader behaviors for approximately 15–20 minutes (e.g., asks questions, makes inferences, talks about the images in her mind) and prompts the students to use steps of the strategies (e.g., asks the students what they are wondering about to prompt them to ask questions). This Thinking Reading practice is scaffolded across time, so that students become more and more independent in using the strategy being taught; that is, initially the teacher takes the lead in reading the text and modeling expert reader behaviors. Later, and after students become comfortable and have learned some reading strategies, they begin to read more during Thinking Reading and actually ask questions and guide discussion, much as the teacher did. Meanwhile, during the remainder of each class hour (for approximately 20–25 minutes), and in addition to Thinking Reading, explicit instruction of strategies and vocabulary takes place. Each strategy is described and modeled, and the teacher ensures that students can name the steps of the strategy by engaging them in small-group, rapid-fire verbal practice of naming the steps. For instance, the teacher displays the steps of the strategy and discusses each step. During this discussion, the teacher models how to apply each step of the strategy and enlists students to participate. Once the strategy has been described and modeled, the teacher guides students through a variety of activities, such as the Cooperative Learning Activity, Numbered Heads Together, or "The Jeopardy Game," both to help students memorize the steps of the strategy and to expand their understanding of how to apply each step. Then, students are engaged in a variety of carefully scaffolded practice activities. For example, students work with a partner using a list of words to apply the Bridging strategy, then work with a partner using 200- to 400-word passages to eventually apply the strategy to a student-selected book or novel. In each configuration, teachers meet with individual students for the purpose of providing individual, detailed feedback. While students are working with their partners, the teacher circulates around the room and in a sense takes on the role of a coach. During this coaching time, the teacher provides positive feedback, along with some reteaching or modeling to ensure that students are practicing the strategy in the proper fashion.

As students practice using a strategy, they begin with narrative and informational passages written at their instructional reading level. As they progress and become more and more skillful in using the strategy and in understanding the passages that they are

Objectives	1 point	2 points	3 points	4 points	Earned Points
Book Selection	1 point Selected an easy challenge book	2 points Selected an average challenge book	3 points Selected a challenging book	4 points Selected an exemplary book	
Application of Reading Strategies	1 point No evidence of reading strategy application	2 points Applies some reading strategies but inconsistently	3 points Applies reading strategies consistently	4 points Applies reading strategies regularly and with skill	
Quality of Work	1 point Activities are completed at a level not consistent with high school work	2 points Completes activities as expected	3 points Completes activities with above average quality	4 points Completes activities that are exemplary in quality and content	
Deadline	1 point Turns in book study late	2 points Turns in book study on time	3 points Completes the book study 1 day early	4 points Completes the book study 1 week early	
TOTAL POINTS	1	2	3	4	/16

Student Name:

Block:

Date:

FIGURE 19.3. Fusion Reading book study scoring rubric.

Time	Lesson Format
5	**Warm-Up**
15	**Thinking Reading/Vocabulary** • Engaging novels • High interest informational text • Words selected from content, novels, and Tier 2 level
2	Transition
20	**Explicit Instruction** • Classroom Procedures • Vocabulary Process • Book Study • Reading Strategies • Practice with Feedback
3	Transition
15	**Vocabulary/Thinking Reading**

FIGURE 19.4. Fusion Reading lesson format.

reading, they advance to a series of new reading ability levels. The final phase of instruction in a strategy is called Generalization and Integration. Within this stage, and initially under the direction of the teacher, students apply the strategy to a variety of materials, including newspapers, magazines, course textbooks, and novels. They also use *all* the strategies they have learned in combination. The teacher monitors student application of the strategies using the Integration Checklist (see Figure 19.5). The teacher and/or peer–partner uses this checklist as the student reads the material chosen for the day.

In essence, Fusion Reading is a structured course that allows for individualized instruction both in targeted strategies and in large-group activities. Depending on students' needs, instruction involves teacher-led, whole-group discussions and guided practice activities, as well as lessons in which students work independently or in pairs. Classroom activities might include the following: (1) The teacher meets with one student to measure his or her progress, while a pair of students practice a targeted reading strategy aloud; (2) students work individually, practicing the strategies they have learned; (3) pairs of students engage in fluency practice activities; (4) students design aids and study cards for vocabulary words and test each other; and (5) students practice integrating several strategies simultaneously, adapting a strategy, or applying a strategy to subject area assignments.

All instruction involves high-interest reading materials chosen to ensure that they engage students and address their academic needs. Progress measures are gathered as part of instruction for each strategy during the various practice activities. The progress measures are embedded within the curriculum. Some are administered by student partners during partner practice, and others are administered by the teacher during independent practice. The measures inform the learner and teacher as to the level of student understanding of the strategy, mastery of skills being taught, and comprehension of reading material, and are used to provide immediate, individualized, and corrective feedback. These data allow the teacher to decide when a student has mastered a strategy. Scores for

1. **Preview** the reading and decide which strategies you would use. Circle the strategies you plan to use: PS (Possible Selves)   TBS (Bridging Strategy)   TPS (Prediction Strategy)
   TSS (Summarization Strategy)

Monitor the effectiveness of the strategy(ies) (e.g., Is this strategy working? Do I need a different one?) Pause and reflect on the strategy(ies) you selected.

2. **Read** the passage with a goal of understanding the text and integrating it with what you already know about the topic.

Directions: For each strategy, check off the completed step or provide the needed information.

Strategy Monitoring

Possible Selves	Vocabulary	Bridging Strategy	Prediction Strategy	Summarization Strategy
Hopes:	1. 2. 3. 4. 5.	P A R T 1 2 3 4 5	C L U E	R E A
Expectations:	1. 2. 3. 4. 5.	P A R T 1 2 3 4 5	C L U E	R E A
Fears:	1. 2. 3. 4. 5.	P A R T 1 2 3 4 5	C L U E	R E A
Goals:	1. 2. 3. 4. 5.	P A R T 1 2 3 4 5	C L U E	R E A
	1. 2. 3. 4. 5.	P A R T 1 2 3 4 5	C L U E	R E A
	1. 2. 3. 4. 5.	P A R T 1 2 3 4 5	C L U E	

(continued)

FIGURE 19.5. Integration Checklist.

3. Reread

_____ # of words in the passage

1st Read:	_____ words read correctly	_____ words per minute
2nd Read:	_____ words read correctly	_____ words per minute
3rd Read:	_____ words read correctly	_____ words per minute
4th Read:	_____ words read correctly	_____ words per minute

FIGURE 19.5. *(continued)*

each practice session are plotted on a progress chart graph. Then, the teacher meets with each student to discuss the student's progress and goals for future practice attempts. These meetings occur during partner practice sessions and while other students are involved in partner practice activities. The teacher circulates and periodically joins each partner practice session, and takes the lead in providing feedback to the student reader and the partner "coach." Thus, feedback on reading performance is provided to the reader, and feedback on providing good feedback is given to the student coach.

Foundational Empirical Support for Fusion Reading

During the past 25 years, a growing body of knowledge has emerged from the KUCRL concerning the design and delivery of effective interventions for adolescents (Deshler & Lenz, 1989; Deshler & Schumaker, 1986; Fisher, Schumaker, & Deshler, 2002; Peterson, Caverly, Nicholson, O'Neal, & Cusenbary, 2000; Pressley, Graham, & Harris, 2006; Pressley & Hilden, 2005; Schumaker & Deshler, 1992; Swanson & Deshler, 2003; Swanson & Hoskyn, 1998). Two major questions have guided this line of work:

1. Can struggling adolescent readers be taught to use complex learning strategies?
2. Does their use of the strategies result in improved performance on academic tasks?

In general, this research has shown that adolescents dramatically improve their use of a particular strategy when the instructional methodology of Fusion Reading is implemented. In the studies that focused on reading strategies (e.g., Clark et al., 1984; Lenz & Hughes, 1990; Schumaker & Deshler, 2006; Schumaker et al., 1982), generalization occurred across written materials at varying reading levels in middle and high school settings. Several studies showed that performance on reading comprehension tasks also improved when students used the strategies (Bulgren, Hock, Schumaker, & Deshler, 1995).

The Intervention Study: Preliminary Findings

We have collected and analyzed data from one experimental teacher and three control teachers involving 72 randomly assigned students. Data on another experimental teacher and additional control teachers are incomplete as the teacher joined the project 1 year after the start of the study. (The previous experimental teacher resigned from the district.) The design calls for evaluation of a 2-year intensive reading program and instruction is still in progress. Thus, only preliminary results can be shared.

Students in the experimental condition were taught a series of reading strategies and skills in an explicit instruction program that included highly engaging reading materials, student goal setting, strategies and skills for decoding, word attack, word identification, fluency, and comprehension (prediction and summarization). In addition, students learned to apply the strategies and skills to a variety of narrative and informal texts. Students in the control condition were taught reading skills through a reading program called Second Chance Reading. Second Chance is a research-based, balanced adolescent reading program that includes instruction targeted at increasing student comprehension, fluency, higher-order thinking skills, spelling, word analysis skills, writing, and motivation through explicit instructional activities. Second Chance was supported through required professional development activities and ongoing student assessment (Swartz, 1998).

After 1 of 2 years of planned instruction students in the experimental condition ($n = 37$) made statistically significant gains on certain subtests of the Group Reading and Diagnostic Evaluation test battery (GRADE), a standardized measure of reading proficiency (Williams, 2001), and on a researcher-designed reading comprehension measure (Hock & Brasseur, 2005) than did control students ($n = 37$). An ANOVA was conducted to measure the degree of significance, if any, between the experimental and control groups. On the GRADE, significant differences were found for the experimental group on the subtest for Passage Comprehension ($F(1.936)$, $p < 0.05$, Sig. 0.048). Calculated effect sizes (ES) were large for this subtest (Cohen's $d = 0.73$). The subtests ANOVA for sentence comprehension (SC), and vocabulary (V) indicated no significant statistical differences between the experimental and control conditions (SC = $F(0.71)$, $p < .05$, Sig. 0.74 and V = F0.99, Sig. 0.47). Given the small number of cases in this preliminary analysis, the ANOVA may well be underpowered. When effect sizes are calculated for SC and V using Cohen's d, we found an ES of 0.20 for SC, a small effect and an ES of 0.96 for V, a large effect. In addition, t-tests were calculated for the developer-made reading comprehension test. The comprehension test has three subtest scores that measure specific steps of *The Prediction Strategy* (Hock, Deshler, & Brasseur, 2005). According to an analysis of student scores obtained on this measure, statistically significant differences were found for subtest A, a measure of prediction making from clues embedded in text (t 2.085, df 37, Sig (2-tailed) 0.044, mean difference 2.55). The effect size for this measure was 0.90, which is considered a large effect.

The results from a preliminary analysis of data indicated that the Fusion Reading Program is effective in improving struggling adolescent readers' reading proficiency as measured by a subtest for passage comprehension on standardized reading measure and for comprehension using a developer-created prediction strategy measure. Effect sizes for both measures were large. While no significant differences were found on other measures of reading proficiency, effect sizes for those subtest measures also indicated large gains.

In Xtreme Reading, students are taught a set of key reading strategies, including the Word Identification Strategy, the Self-Questioning Strategy, the Visual Imagery Strategy, the Paraphrasing Strategy, and the Inferencing Strategy. These reading strategies are closely aligned with the individual reading strategies originally developed in support of the SIM and are distinct from Fusion Reading strategies. Additionally, students are taught key classroom skills, such as how to behave in the classroom, participate in discussions, work within small groups, and work with partners. Students also learn in the SCORE Skills program basic social skills for use in school, and especially in work in cooperative groups (Vernon, Schumaker, & Deshler, 1996). Finally, they work through the *Possible Selves program* (Hock et al., 2003).

HOW THIS NEW KNOWLEDGE CAN INFORM READING COMPREHENSION INSTRUCTION

The search for solutions to improve outcomes for struggling adolescent readers has generally focused on the design and validation of instructional practices that produce large effect sizes. Although this target is both foundational and necessary for student growth, it is by no means sufficient; that is, a host of other considerations must be taken into account to ensure that evidence-based instructional practices are enthusiastically embraced and used over a sustained period of time.

Faggella-Luby and Deshler (in press) have articulated six questions that curriculum designers and intervention researchers should ask to determine the degree to which their interventions would be found acceptable to practitioners. Tending to the issues embodied in these questions will determine, to a large degree, whether any sets of new instructional practices (designed to improve reading comprehension) are ultimately embraced and successfully implemented as commonplace, daily features in classrooms across the world in other, English-speaking nations.

These questions are as follows:

- To what degree is the intervention considered reasonable, appropriate, and unobtrusive to teachers? (general acceptability)
- To what degree do teachers have the necessary background knowledge and skills needed to use the intervention? (understanding)
- To what degree do teachers believe it is practical or reasonable to use the intervention? (feasibility)
- To what degree do teachers believe that the intervention could be implemented as prescribed? (integrity)
- To what degree do teachers feel positive about implementing the intervention? (personal enthusiasm)
- To what degree are the necessary instructional conditions and supports in place (administrative, school culture, etc.) to enhance the chances of teachers being successful in implementation? (support systems)

DIRECTIONS FOR FUTURE RESEARCH

The list of research needs for older struggling learners is extensive. Others have outlined proposed topics for study (e.g., Curtis, 2002; Partnership for Reading, 2002; Snow, 2002; Snow & Biancarosa, 2003). Drawing upon those recommendations, we suggest the following areas as foundational in advancing the knowledge base and enhancing the quality of practice in the classrooms of less advanced adolescent readers.

1. *We know a lot about effective reading instruction for struggling adolescent readers* (Biancarosa & Snow, 2006; Pressley & Block, 2002). Although our knowledge of evidence-based practice, programs, and strategies is growing, we continually need basic research that proves and extends theory and contributions of individual reading components to improved reading comprehension. There is, in our opinion, a critical need to support rigorous research in applied settings, with all the challenges they present in the conduct of research. Additionally, there is a need to test the efficacy and scalability of comprehensive and multistrategy interventions under a variety of conditions, such as

those found in the often-changing world of school. Considerable evidence supports the notion that comprehensive solutions are necessary to impact the lives of some of the neediest students. Therefore, the number one research priority from our perspective is to study the effects of multicomponent interventions under real-world conditions, and with teachers and students who learn in the context of school, home, and community.

2. *Rigorous research should reflect the notion that multiple research designs can inform researchers, practitioners, administrators, and policy leaders.* Reliance upon one design limits our ability to conduct research in environments where random assignment experimental designs are not always practical. Quality research, whether experimental, quasi-experimental, single-subject, or qualitative, can inform the field with regard to what works, with whom, under what conditions, *and* with a qualitative richness and robustness often lost in quantitative designs. A balanced research portfolio would lead to greater understanding of intervention effectiveness and student outcomes.

3. *Other research efforts should reflect questions related to literacy and student outcomes.* One such critical question is, "What are the reading component characteristics of struggling adolescent readers, and which components best predict reading comprehension?" The Hock et al. (in press) article mentioned in this chapter focused on adolescents from a poor urban environment. Descriptive studies are needed on adolescents in other environments (e.g., rural and suburban settings, predominantly English language learner settings, out-of-school environments) to study the effects of language and other environmental conditions on reading achievement. Predictive studies, on the other hand, are needed to determine which reading components (e.g., fluency, vocabulary) in the theory of adolescent reading are most predictive of good reading comprehension, and with which subgroups of readers.

4. *Effecting change in applied settings is challenging, and comprehensive interventions must be tested.* One key question is, "What are the effects of explicit and comprehensive interventions designed to close the achievement gap for struggling adolescent readers?" We propose that, whereas much is known about the effects of interventions involving only a single reading component, much less information is available that measures the effects of courses or programs designed to close the entire gap. Applied research studies should be conducted in schools (with all their inherent challenges) to test the robustness of basic research findings. For example, intervention studies are needed to determine which combination of theory-driven reading components (e.g., decoding + prediction; questioning + summarizing + vocabulary) are effective. Although research suggests the merit of teaching multiple strategies (Biancarosa & Snow, 2006; Block & Pressley, 2007; Pressley & Block, 2002), it is unclear which combination of multiple strategies should be matched with which type of learner. It is also important to determine *how* these components should be taught. In particular, the effects of various instructional methodologies and instructional conditions (e.g., amount of scaffolding, group size, opportunities for student responding) on student rates of growth and ultimate outcomes need to be determined.

5. *Learning is not exclusive to school environments.* Significant questions need to be answered, such as "What is the impact of alternative literacies on the academic performance of struggling adolescent readers?" Some have argued that use of alternative literacies can influence student attitudes toward traditional literacies and school in general (e.g., Tannock, 2001; Witkin, 1994). We suggest that studies on alternative literacies and contexts (e.g., Alvermann & Heron, 2001; Moje et al., 2004) be conducted outside of classroom and text environments to determine the effects on student outcomes.

6. *Another critical research and development area is assessment.* The question "How can formative and summative assessment be used to inform instruction that is timely and responsive to students needs?" complements our research agenda. The primary source of assessment data available to teachers is often student results from state assessments, but this neither informs instruction nor monitors students' short- and long-term progress. Thus, there is a need to build and norm screening and diagnostic instruments that may be administered as students enter secondary school to identify students' various reading needs.

This research agenda is ambitious. The overriding goal we must keep in mind as we think about an adolescent research and development agenda is that adolescents must be prepared to read, and to read critically, so that they attain new knowledge and their creative thinking is nurtured. We believe this research agenda targets these critical skills areas.

PROJECTIONS AND POSSIBILITIES FOR THE CLASSROOM OF 2030

Somewhere, someplace, expert teachers have created learning environments in which many aspects of *great* instruction and learning are in place. However, we have yet to observe a classroom in which *all* the essential elements associated with great learning exist. We hope that by the year 2030 such learning environments will be common, and that many good schools will become *great* schools (Collins, 2001).

Our vision of the learning environment of 2030 follows. It is characterized first and foremost by student engagement in high-quality, challenging learning activities in the school, the home, and the community, and in an Internet-connected world. Thus, *great* learning is found beyond traditional classroom walls.

Foundational to all education in 2030 is learning that is tied directly to what students see as their future selves or what they desire and believe is possible for them. Such learning follows a path identified by self-determined learners and is focused on individual goals and life aspirations. In short, this learning and instruction are directly related to and supportive of student-determined "Possible Selves" (Markus & Nurius, 1986).

Self-determined reading classrooms, an aspect of the learning environment described earlier and relevant to this chapter, are characterized by four critical elements: (1) an environment that embraces risk taking and student learning; (2) a diverse library of engaging and challenging reading materials, tools, and learning contexts; (3) evidence-based and explicit literacy instruction and practice; and, (4) a core literacy curriculum that has a clear and dramatic impact on struggling adolescent literacy outcomes.

Furthermore, the 2030 classroom environment is anchored in "conscious relationship building," in which students' voices are heard, and in whose surroundings literacy-rich learning takes place within the school and community. Students are able to reengage in learning and risk taking to achieve their identified possible selves. In addition, set routines and procedures are in place to provide order and opportunity to work collaboratively with classmates and teachers. The classroom is organized to provide a literacy-rich environment, with reading materials available in online formats or soft and hardback copies. A variety of genres, informational textbooks, and culture-specific readings are available and have been carefully chosen to provide exposure to a wide range of topical, cultural, and general knowledge. Finally, handheld computers, camcorders, and recorders are the tools used by students to perform reading tasks and to demonstrate their comprehension of material.

In the classroom of 2030, the teacher's role is markedly different than the role played by many current teachers. First, the teacher is considered a literacy and relationship builder. His or her role becomes that of student coach, assisting students in determining and achieving their personal goals as they relate to literacy and overall academic achievement. Explicit instruction is provided for text-specific comprehension strategies, along with student-centered activities and projects for practice and mastery of strategies. Student progress is guided by corrective, explicit feedback. Purposeful assessment and student progress monitoring inform instruction and curricular adjustments.

In summary, the reading classroom of 2030 engages all students and provides critical learning processes and instruction that become relevant tools that in turn support the attainment of students' hopes for the future.

SUMMARY

Although significant progress has been made on behalf of struggling adolescent readers in terms of legislative initiatives, development efforts, and research, much remains to be learned. Of particular importance is learning how better to translate research findings relative to effective instructional practices into broadscale adoption in a host of school settings. Many questions about generalization of practices to varying school environments remain to be answered. Central to any solution, however, is Elmore's (2004) contention that until both administrators and teachers focus in an unrelenting fashion on core issues in the instructional process, student outcomes will not improve markedly.

INTEGRATE, INVESTIGATE, AND INITIATE: QUESTIONS FOR DISCUSSION

1. List each of the programs cited in this chapter. Create a 2 × 2 table. List in one column the benefits of using each program; in the second column, rank-order the programs. Which would you recommend first to your school or school district, and why?
2. We have described six questions that curriculum designers and intervention researchers should ask to determine the degree to which their intervention would be found acceptable to practitioners. Reread those six questions. What do they help you to understand about the level of innovation that is present in your school or school district? Specifically, based on these questions, do you judge your environment to be one that is innovative enough to provide the type of comprehension instruction that at-risk students need?
3. How would you suggest that we measure the effects of any type of intervention that is designed to close the comprehension–achievement gap? Share your results with colleagues.

REFERENCES

Abeel, S. (2005). *My thirteenth winter: A memoir.* New York: Orchard Books.
Adams, G. L., & Engelmann, S. (1996). *Research on direct instruction: 25 years beyond DISTAR.* Seattle, WA: Educational Achievement Systems.
Alfassi, M. (1998). Reading for meaning: The efficacy of reciprocal teaching in fostering reading

comprehension in high school students in remedial reading classes. *American Educational Research Journal, 35*(2), 309–332.

Alvermann, D. E., & Heron, A. H. (2001). Literacy identity work: Playing to learn with popular media. *Journal of Adolescents and Adult Literacy, 45*(2), 118–122.

Biancarosa, G., & Snow, C. (2006). *Reading next: A vision for action and research in middle and high school literacy: A report to the Carnegie Corporation of New York* (2nd ed.). Washington, DC: Alliance for Excellent Education.

Block, C. C., & Pressley, M. (2007). Best practices in teaching comprehension. In L. B. Gambrell & L. M. Morrow (Eds.), *Best practices in literacy instruction*. New York: Guilford Press.

Borman, G. D., Hewes, G. M., Overman, L. T., & Brown, S. (2003). Comprehensive school reform and achievement: A meta-analysis. *Review of Educational Research, 73*(2), 125–226.

Brownell, M. T., Mellard, D. F., & Deshler, D. D. (1993). Differences in the learning and transfer performance between students with learning disabilities and other low-achieving students on problem-solving tasks. *Learning Disability Quarterly, 16*(23), 138–156.

Bulgren, J., Deshler, D., & Schumaker, J. (1997). Use of a recall enhancement routine and strategies in inclusive secondary classes. *Learning Disabilities Research and Practice, 12*(4), 198–208.

Bulgren, J. A., Deshler, D. D., Schumaker, J. B., & Lenz, B. K. (2000). The use and effectiveness of analogical instruction in diverse secondary content classrooms. *Journal of Educational Psychology, 92*(3), 426–441.

Bulgren, J. A., Hock, M. F., Schumaker, J. B., & Deshler, D. D. (1995). The effects of instruction in a paired associates strategy on the information mastery performance of students with learning disabilities. *Learning Disabilities Research and Practice, 10*(1), 22–37.

Bulgren, J. A., Schumaker, J. B., & Deshler, D. D. (1988). Effectiveness of a concept teaching routine in enhancing the performance of LD students in secondary-level mainstream classes. *Learning Disability Quarterly, 11*(1), 3–17.

Bulgren, J. A., Schumaker, J. B., Deshler, D. D., Lenz, B. K., & Marquis, J. (2002). The use and effectiveness of a comparison routine in diverse secondary content classrooms. *Journal of Educational Psychology, 94*(2), 356–371.

Buly, M., & Valencia, S. (2003). *Meeting the needs of failing readers: Cautions and considerations for state policy*. Seattle: University of Washington.

Campbell, M. L. (1984). Corrective reading program evaluated with secondary students in San Diego. *ADI News, 7*, 15–17.

Catts, H., Adlof, S., & Ellis-Weismer, S. (2006). Language deficits in poor comprehenders: A case for the Simple View of Reading. *Journal of Speech, Language, and Hearing Research, 49*(2), 278–293.

Clark, F. L., Deshler, D. D., Schumaker, J. B., Alley, G. R., & Warner, M. M. (1984). Visual imagery and self-questioning: Strategies to improve comprehension of written material. *Journal of Learning Disabilities, 17*(3), 145–149.

Collins, J. C. (2001). *Good to great*. New York: HarperCollins.

Curtis, M. B. (2002). *Adolescent reading: A synthesis of research*. Boston: Lesley College, Center for Special Education.

Cutting, L. E., & Scarborough, H. S. (2006). Prediction of reading comprehension: Relative contributions of word recognition, language proficiency, and other cognitive skills can depend on how comprehension is measured. *Scientific Studies of Reading, 10*(3), 277–299.

Deshler, D. D., & Lenz, B. K. (1989). The strategies instructional approach. *International Journal of Disability, Development and Education, 36*(3), 203–224.

Deshler, D. D., & Schumaker, J. B. (1986). Learning strategies: An instructional alternative for low achieving adolescents. *Exceptional Children, 52*(6), 583–590.

Deshler, D. D., Schumaker, J. B., Hock, M. F., & Bulgren, J. B. (2005). *The Xtreme Adolescent Reading Program*. Lawrence: University of Kansas, Center for Research on Learning.

Deshler, D. D., Schumaker, J. B., Lenz, B. K., Bulgren, J. A., Hock, M. F., Knight, J., et al. (2001). Ensuring content-area learning by secondary students with learning disabilities. *Learning Disabilities Research and Practice, 16*(2), 96–108.

Dole, J. A., Duffy, G. G., Roehler, L. R., & Pearson, P. D. (1991). Moving from the old to the new: Research on reading comprehension instruction. *Review of Educational Research, 61*(2), 239–264.

Ellis, E. S., Deshler, D. D., Lenz, B. K., Schumaker, J. B., & Clark, F. L. (1991). An instruction model for teaching learning strategies. *Focus on Exceptional Children, 23*(6), 1–24.

Elmore, R. (2004). *School reform from the inside out.* Cambridge, MA: Harvard University Press.

Faggella-Luby, M. N., & Deshler, D. D. (in press). The importance of instructional dosage in reading comprehension instruction. *Learning Disability Research and Practice.*

Fisher, J. B., Schumaker, J. B., & Deshler, D. D. (2002). Improving the reading comprehension of at-risk adolescents. In C. C. Block & M. Pressley (Eds.), *Comprehension instruction: Research-based best practices* (pp. 351–364). New York: Guilford Press.

Gersten, R., Fuchs, L. S., Williams, J. P., & Baker, S. (2001). Teaching reading comprehension strategies to students with learning disabilities: A review of research. *Review of Educational Research, 71*(2), 279–230.

Gersten, R., & Keating, T. (1987). Long-term benefits from direct instruction. *Educational Leadership, 44,* 28–31.

Gough, P. B., & Tunmer, W. E. (1986). Decoding, reading, and reading disability. *Remedial and Special Education, 7*(1), 6–10.

Greene, J. F. (1998, Spring/Summer). Another chance: Help for older students with limited literacy. *American Educator,* pp. 1–6.

Greenleaf, C. L., Schoenbach, R., Cziko, C., & Mueller, F. L. (2001). Apprenticing adolescent readers to academic literacy. *Harvard Educational Review, 71*(1), 30–39.

Guthrie, J. T., Wigfield, A., & Perencevich, K. C. (2004). Scaffolding for motivation and engagement in reading. In *Motivating reading comprehension: Concept-oriented reading instruction* (pp. 55–86). Mahwah, NJ: Erlbaum.

Hasselbring, T. S. (1996). Looking at technology in context: A framework for understanding technology and education research. In D. C. Berliner & R. C. Calfee (Eds.), *The handbook of educational psychology* (pp. 807–840). New York: Simon & Schuster/MacMillan.

Hasselbring, T. S., & Bottge, B. A. (2000). Planning and implementing a technology program in inclusive settings. In J. D. Lindsley (Ed.), *Technology and exceptional individuals, 3rd edition* (pp. 91–113). Austin, TX: PRO-ED.

Hock, M. F., Brasseur, I. F., & Deshler, D. D. (2007). *Fusion reading: A comprehensive reading program for adolescents.* Lawrence, KS: University of Kansas Center for Research on Learning.

Hock, M. F., Brasseur, I. F., Deshler, D. D., Catts, H. W., Marques, J., et al. (in press). What is the nature of struggling adolescent readers in urban high schools? *Learning Disability Quarterly.*

Hock, M. F., & Deshler, D. D. (2003). Adolescent literacy: Ensuring that no child is left behind. *Principal Leadership, 13*(4), 55–61.

Hock, M. F., Deshler, D. D., & Schumaker, J. B. (2006). Enhancing student motivation through the pursuit of possible selves. In C. Dunkel & J. Kerpelman (Eds.), *Possible selves: Theory, research, and applications* (pp. 205–221). New York: Nova Science Publishers.

Hock, M. F., Schumaker, J. B., & Deshler, D. D. (2003). *Possible selves: Nurturing student motivation.* Lawrence, KS: Edge Enterprises.

Hoover, W. A., & Gough, P. B. (1990). The simple view of reading. *Reading and Writing: An Interdisciplinary Journal, 2,* 127–160.

Kamil, M. L. (2003). *Adolescents and literacy: Reading for the 21st century.* Washington, DC: Alliance for Excellent Education.

Kline, F. M., Schumaker, J. B., & Deshler, D. D. (1991). Development and validation of feedback routines for instructing students with learning disabilities. *Learning Disability Quarterly, 14*(3), 191–207.

Kline, T. (2005). *Psychological testing: A practical approach to design and evaluation.* Thousand Oaks, CA: Sage.

Leach, J. M., Scarborough, H. S., & Rescorla, L. (2003). Late-emerging reading disabilities. *Journal of Educational Psychology, 95*(2), 211–224.

Lenz, B. K., & Bulgren, J. A. (1995). Promoting learning in content classes. In P. T. Cegelka & W. H. Berdine (Eds.), *Effective instruction for students with learning disabilities* (pp. 385–417). Boston: Allyn & Bacon.

Lenz, B. K., & Deshler, D. D., with Kissam, B. R. (2004). *Teaching content to all: Evidence-based inclusive practices in middle and secondary schools.* Boston: Pearson Education.

Lenz, K., Ehren, B. J., & Deshler, D. D. (2005). The content literacy continuum: A school reform framework for improving adolescent literacy for all students. *Teaching Exceptional Children,* 37(6), 60–63.

Lenz, K. B., & Hughes, C. A. (1990). A word identification strategy for adolescents with learning disabilities. *Journal of Learning Disabilities, 23*(3), 149–158, 163.

Lysynchuk, L. M., Pressley, M., & Vye, N. J. (1990). Reciprocal teaching improves standardized reading-comprehension performance in poor comprehenders. *Elementary School Journal, 90*(5), 469–484.

Markus, H., & Nurius, P. (1986). Possible selves. *American Psychologist, 41,* 954–969.

Moje, E. B., McIntosh-Ciechanowski, K., Kramer, K., Ellis, L., Carrillo, R., & Collazo, T. (2004). Working toward third space in content area literacy: An examination of everyday funds of knowledge and discourse. *Reading Research Quarterly, 39*(1), 38–71.

National Center for Educational Statistics. (2002). *The Nation's Report Card: Reading 2002.* Washington, DC: U.S. Department of Education.

National Center for Education Statistics. (2005). *Mapping 2005 state proficiency standards onto the NAEP scales* (NCES 2007-482, U. S. Department of Education, National Center for Education Statistics). Washington, DC: U. S. Government Printing Office.

National Institute for Child Health and Human Development (NICHD). (2000). *Report of the national reading panel. Teaching children to read: An evidence-based assessment of the scientific research literature on reading and its implications for reading instruction* (Publication No. 00-4769). Washington, DC: U.S. Government Printing Office.

Palincsar, A. S., & Brown, A. L. (1984). Reciprocal teaching of comprehension fostering and monitoring activities. *Cognition and Instruction, 1,* 117–175.

Partnership for Reading. (2002, May). *Adolescent literacy: Research informing practice.* Washington, DC: National Institute for Literacy, National Institute of Child Health and Human Development, U. S. Department of Education.

Peterson, C. L., Caverly, D. C., Nicholson, S. A., O'Neal, S., & Cusenbary, S. (2000). *Building reading proficiency at the secondary level: A guide to resources.* Austin, TX: Southwest Educational Development Laboratory.

Pressley, M. (2000). What should comprehension instruction be the instruction of? In M. Kamil, P. Mosenthal, P. D. Pearson, & R. Barr (Eds.), *Handbook of reading research* (Vol. III, pp. 545–561). Mahwah, NJ: Erlbaum.

Pressley, M. (2002). *Reading instruction that works: The case for balanced teaching.* New York: Guilford Press.

Pressley, M., & Block, C. (2002). Summing up: What reading comprehension could be. In C. C. Block & M. Pressley (Eds.), *Comprehension instruction: Research-based practices* (pp. 383–392). New York: Guilford Press.

Pressley, M., Graham, S., & Harris, K. (2006). The state of educational intervention research as viewed through the lens of literacy intervention. *British Journal of Educational Psychology, 76*(1), 1–19.

Pressley, M., & Hilden, K. (2006). Cognitive strategies: Production deficiencies and successful strategy instruction everywhere. In D. Kuhn & R. Siegler (Vol. Eds.) & W. Damon & R. Lerner (Series Eds.), *Handbook of child psychology: Vol. 2. Cognition, perception, and language* (6th ed., pp. 511–556). Hoboken, NJ: Wiley.

Rosenshine, B., & Meister, C. (1995). Direct instruction. In L. Anderson (Ed.), *International encyclopedia of teaching and teacher education* (2nd ed., pp. 143–148). Oxford, UK: Elsevier Science.

Scholastic. (2005). *The compendium of Read 180 research: 1999–2004.* New York: Author.

Schumaker, J. B., & Deshler, D. D. (1992). Validation of learning strategy interventions for students with learning disabilities: Results of a programmatic research effort. In B. Y. L. Wong (Ed.), *Contemporary intervention research in learning disabilities: An international perspective* (pp. 22–46). New York: Springer-Verlag.

Schumaker, J. B., & Deshler, D. D. (2006). Teaching adolescents to be strategic learners. In D. Deshler & J. B. Schumaker (Eds.), *Teaching adolescents with disabilities: Accessing the general education curriculum* (pp. 121–156). New York: Corwin Press.

Schumaker, J. B., Deshler, D. D., Alley, G. R., Warner, M. M., & Denton, P. H. (1982). MultiPass: A learning strategy for improving reading comprehension. *Learning Disability Quarterly, 5*, 295–304.

Smith, S., Rissman, L., & Grek, M. (2004). *Evaluation of Read 180*. Tallahassee: Florida Center for Reading Research.

Snow, C. E. (2002). *Reading for understanding: Toward an R&D program in reading comprehension*. Santa Monica, CA: Science and Technology Policy Institute, RAND Education.

Snow, C. E., & Biancarosa, G. (2003). *Adolescent literacy and the achievement gap: What do we know and where do we need to go from here?* (Adolescent Literacy Funders Meeting Report). New York: Carnegie Corporation of New York.

Swanson, H. L., & Deshler, D. D. (2003). Instructing adolescents with disabilities: Converting a meta-analysis to practice. *Journal of Learning Disabilities, 36*(2), 124–135.

Swanson, H. L., & Hoskyn, M. (1998). Experimental intervention research on students with learning disabilities: A meta-analysis of treatment outcomes. *Review of Educational Research, 68*(3), 277–321.

Swartz, S. L. (1998). California early literacy learning and reading recovery: Two innovative programs for teaching children to read and write. In P. Dreyer (Ed.), *Reading, writing, and literacy*. Claremont, CA: Claremont Graduate University.

Tannock, S. (2001). The literacies of youth workers and youth workplaces. *Journal of Adolescent and Adult Literacy, 45*(2), 140–143.

Taylor, B. M., & Frye, B. J. (1992). Comprehension strategy instruction in the intermediate grades. *Reading Research and Instruction, 21*(1), 39–48.

Thorne, M. T. (1978). "Payment for reading": The use of the corrective reading scheme with junior maladjusted boys. *Remedial Education, 13*, 87–89.

Torgesen, J. K. (2002). The prevention of reading difficulties. *Journal of School Psychology, 40*, 7–26.

Vellutino, F. R., Tunmer, W. E., Jaccard, J. J., & Chen, R. (2007). Components of reading ability: Multivariate evidence for a convergent skills model of reading development. *SSSR Journal, 11*(1), 3–32.

Vernon, D. S., Schumaker, J. B., & Deshler, D. D. (1996). *The score skills: Social skills for cooperative groups*. Lawrence, KS: Edge Enterprises.

Westera, J., & Moore, D. W. (1995). Reciprocal teaching of reading comprehension in a New Zealand high school. *Psychology in the Schools, 32*(3), 225–232.

Williams, K. T. (2001). *GRADE: Group Reading Assessment and Diagnostic Evaluation*. Circle Pines, MN: American Guidance Service.

Witkin, M. (1994, January). A defense of using pop media in the middle-school classroom. *English Journal, 83*(1), 30–33.

20

Comprehension Instruction for English Learners

ROBERT RUEDA, ALEJANDRA VELASCO, and HYO JIN LIM

> ... Analyzing the reading comprehension performance of English language learners is a complex endeavor because of the multiple program, instructional, language, cultural, and affective factors that may intersect and affect their reading development.
> —GARCIA (2003, p. 31)

Recent work suggests that reading and literacy, including comprehension, are dynamic and multidimensional in nature. Kucer and Silva (2006), for example, describe the dimensions of literacy as being represented by concentric cognitive, linguistic, sociocultural, and developmental domains. Recent attempts to improve reading achievement, however, have tended to focus largely on the cognitive domain. The National Reading Panel (2000), for example, concluded that the following strategies have sufficient empirical foundations for effectiveness: comprehension monitoring; cooperative learning; graphic and semantic organizers, including story maps; question answering; question generation; story structure; and summarization (National Reading Panel, 2000). For those who work with English learners, this influence has been reflected in their instructional practices. Reflecting this orientation, there now exist resources that help teachers apply this cognitive, strategy-focused approach to English learners and students from diverse backgrounds (Bouchard, 2005; Herrell & Jordan, 2008).

Subsequent to the National Reading Panel work, the RAND Reading Study Group (2002) focused on comprehension specifically and defined it as

> the process of simultaneously extracting and constructing meaning through interaction and involvement with written language. Comprehension has these elements: the reader, the text, and the activity, or purpose for reading. These elements define a phenomenon—reading comprehension—that occurs within a larger sociocultural context that shapes and is shaped by the reader and that infuses each of the elements. All are influenced by the broader context. (p. xi)

Whereas work in reading is focused increasingly on comprehension, the predominant focus in research and intervention efforts tend to favor the cognitive aspects of the comprehension process. Thus, although the teaching of strategies is extremely valuable, much less attention has been paid to the other dimensions of reading and literacy. Yet the surge in school populations of students from diverse linguistic and cultural backgrounds is beginning to shift researchers' and practitioners' attention to aspects of comprehension that may need attention as well (Portes, 1996). In this chapter, therefore, we focus on two dimensions that have been relatively overlooked with English learners: the motivational aspects and the cultural aspects of comprehension. This chapter highlights the following:

- Recent work in motivation, with applicability to English learners.
- What is currently known about cultural factors in the acquisition of reading and literacy for English learners.
- Characteristics of English learners that should be taken into account in comprehension instruction.

WHAT'S OUT THERE TODAY: ESTABLISHED RESEARCH AND PRACTICE

English language learners (ELLs) are a diverse group, especially in large urban school districts. In California, for example, the Los Angeles Unified School District serves over 300,000 ELLs who speak over 90 different languages. Whereas the majority speak Spanish, there is great diversity not only in terms of country of origin and length of residence but also in terms of bilingualism and biliteracy abilities. Other factors that contribute to this within-group diversity include socioeconomic status (SES), immigration status, family constellations, acculturation, and so forth. (Zentella, 2005). All of these factors may be correlated, and they may have both independent and interactive effects on reading and literacy acquisition.

Although there has been much study of monolingual native English readers, less is known about the particulars of reading comprehension for ELLs (Sweet & Snow, 2003). However, based on both standardized test scores and anecdotal classroom evidence, we do know that ELLs face many obstacles in the journey to become competent and fluent readers in their second language. Many struggle with literacy in general, and with vocabulary and reading comprehension in particular. Contextual influences, such as prior schooling, home literacy practices, and print access, strongly influence the facility with which ELL students meet the challenging demands of learning to read. We also know that ELLs are a not a homogenous group, and that these differences should be taken into account to provide optimal instruction.

Many researchers and educators alike believe that quality instruction in the native language facilitates the development of English literacy skills and, consequently, overall academic achievement. Research suggests that students who have the opportunity to draw on knowledge in their first language are more likely to comprehend what they read in the second language. Jimenez, Garcia, and Pearson (1996), for example, found that successful bilingual readers were able to approach reading comprehension problems by using a variety of strategies, such as invoking prior knowledge, inferencing, questioning, and monitoring. Less successful readers were unable or did not know how to use their bilingual skills to enhance English comprehension skills (Jimenez et al., 1996). Although the effects of primary language instruction are not exceedingly large, they are great enough to be instructionally significant, on the order of about 12–15 percentile points. This is only slightly less than the overall effects of phonics instruction, as reported by the National Reading Panel (2000).

It is important to keep in mind that there is no separate theory of learning or development that explains how ELLs acquire school content differently than their English-speaking counterparts. Effective instruction for ELLs is similar to effective instruction for English-speaking students (Goldenberg, 2006). As Goldenberg (2006) notes, this includes general instructional practices, such as clear goals and objectives, clearly structured routines, motivational considerations to foster engagement, strategic opportunities for practice, accurate and detailed feedback, opportunity for application of material learned to meaningful problems, frequent formative assessment, and so forth. Similarly, in the specific domain of reading, ELLs need to master phonemic awareness, decoding words (phonics), vocabulary, fluency (accurate and automatic word recognition and passage reading), and comprehension (literal and inferential understanding of what is read). Vocabulary is particularly important because it is a major determinant of reading comprehension and, during the fourth grade, ELLs begin to encounter content areas in which academic language poses particular challenges.

It is also important to note that ELLs may often require instructional accommodations. This need does not stem from any inherent deficiencies within students. Rather, it has to do with limited English proficiency, which often—but not always—accompanies fewer learning opportunities, oftentimes due to factors such as SES. Students from less affluent backgrounds may have less print access (in the first or second language), less exposure to adults who have advanced schooling, less occasions to develop specialized academic vocabulary and school-based background knowledge, and fewer overall opportunities related to reading and school achievement. Additionally, diverse linguistic and economic backgrounds, methods of language instruction, years of schooling, literacy levels, and motivational factors all contribute to the challenges of learning to read in a second language. For instructional practices to be effective, the context in which non-native English readers exist must be taken into account, so that by understanding how they approach each reading task, we can tailor instruction accordingly.

NEW RESEARCH

The most recent and comprehensive synthesis of work on the reading of English as second language (ESL) and ELL students was conducted by the National Literacy Panel (August & Shanahan, 2006). The review included all empirical work on several subtopics related to reading and literacy for language minority students, incorporating work from 1980 forward. In the area of reading comprehension specifically, factors that were reviewed because of the links to the development of comprehension (Lesaux, Koda, Siegel, & Sanan, 2006) included the following:

- Precursor and word-level skills (phonological awareness, letter knowledge, decoding, print concepts, word reading proficiency and oral proficiency).
- Understanding of literacy (including the connections between school literacy and everyday functional literacy).
- Experience with context-independent and formal uses of language as opposed to informal, out-of-school language use.
- Metalinguistic awareness (awareness of language structures, including syntactic

and pragmatic awareness, and ability to analyze and reflect on language forms and functions).
- Reader strategies (both cognitive and metacognitive strategies, including rereading, concentrating, predicting outcomes).
- Background knowledge.
- Motivational variables (e.g., instrumental motivation, learning the new language to accomplish a specific purpose such as getting a job vs. integrative motivation, learning the language to become more integrated in to a host society).
- Acculturation.
- Text factors (plot structure, pronoun reference, text content and difficulty, organization, vocabulary, density, syntactic complexity, discourse style, and genre).
- Demographic factors (SES and amount of ESL schooling).

In short, the multiple and varied factors that impact comprehension for ELLs are more similar than different from the factors that influence comprehension for English-speaking students. Yet there is a need for caution. Many of the domains we listed have been examined in only a very small number of studies, and the robustness of these conclusions remains to be determined.

The Role of Cultural Factors

There is a longstanding assumption (Rueda, 2006) regarding the importance of cultural factors in reading instruction and reading comprehension. Specifically, cultural factors are widely believed to be important mediators of reading comprehension and achievement. This area was given significant attention in the National Literacy Panel Report (Goldenberg, Rueda, & August, 2006). The variety of sociocultural and contextual factors considered in the review included the following questions:

- What is the influence of immigration (generation status and immigration circumstances) on literacy development, defined broadly?
- What is the influence of differences in discourse and interaction characteristics between children's homes and classrooms?
- What is the influence of other social and cultural characteristics of students and teachers?
- What is the influence of parents and families?
- What is the influence of policies at the district, state, and federal levels?
- What is the influence of language status or prestige?

Although a review of this work is beyond the scope of this chapter, the most widely studied question, and the one most germane to the present discussion, relates to the second question: What is the nature of differences between school and home (or community) settings? There is a longstanding notion that classroom instruction and students' sociocultural characteristics should be brought into close alignment—and that doing so improves student learning, including reading comprehension. Although the National Literacy Panel Report excluded qualitative studies, it did not exclude any design, provided that the study was without serious design flaws and included any outcome measures—not just formal or informal test data, but *any* outcome data linking factors under study to some student outcome. Surprisingly, the panel found that most of the work was purely descriptive. A significant number of studies describe specific cultural settings and cultural practices, but few tie practices to student (measured) outcomes. The evidence is strong and clear in terms of the existence of differences in cultural norms, practices, expectations, and interactional and discourse forms in the homes and classrooms of many ELLs. The impact of attempts to minimize or otherwise address those differences is much less clear. However, the hypothesis that accommodation to cultural differences impacts reading comprehension remains highly plausible but relatively untested. In all fairness, culture as a construct is difficult to operationalize and manipulate; moreover, the goal of work in the field has more often been to describe cultural processes in a valid fashion rather than to test cultural interventions. The best evidence for cultural effects on reading comprehension is in the area of culturally relevant or meaningful text.

The Role of Motivational Factors

There is increasing recognition that reading is not governed by cognitive factors alone, but also by motivational and affective factors (Guthrie, Wigfield, & Perencevich, 2004; Pintrich, 2003). In the area of reading comprehension specifically, for example, Guthrie and Wigfield (1999) and Guthrie, Wigfield, and Perencevich (2004) proposed a motivational–cognitive model that depicts cognitive processes (activating prior knowledge, forming text representations, constructing causal inferences, and integrating prior knowledge and text) and motivational processes (task mastery goals, intrinsic motivation, self-efficacy, personal interest, and transactional beliefs) influencing text comprehension. In cognitive processes, readers activate prior knowledge at the outset of reading a text and form a mental representation of information. During the text comprehension process, readers build causal inferences and integrate prior knowledge with the text representation. The authors also support both direct and indirect connections between motivational processes and reading comprehension (Guthrie & Wigfield, 2005). For example, students with high task mastery goals have higher intentions for a reader–text interaction. Students with intrinsic motivation tend to participate in reading for its own sake, enjoying the knowledge built from text. Readers with high self-efficacy sense that they have the capability to read effectively, which is related to reading more and to better reading comprehension. Also, individuals who value and have positive affect about specific topics in a text may have more personal interest in the text content, which leads to deep conceptual processing and increased comprehension. Finally, readers' transactional beliefs about reading influence text comprehension, because they are convinced that their knowledge and values are relevant to their understanding of text (for a more complete description of this model, See Guthrie, Wigfield, Barbosa, et al., 2004). Taking into account the motivational dimensions of reading comprehension, Concept-Oriented Reading Instruction (CORI; Guthrie, Wigfield, & Perencevich, 2004; Guthrie & Wigfield, 1999; Guthrie, Wigfield, & VonSecker, 2000) and related approaches have been successful in promoting reading comprehension.

Although this work demonstrates the clear role of motivational factors in reading comprehension, research in this area with ELLs is almost nonexistent (Goldenberg et al., 2006). Most of the work on motivational and affective factors has examined parental attitudes and beliefs, and findings have been mixed in terms of student outcomes. Additionally, little of this work has targeted reading comprehension directly. For example, in a recent study Loera and Rueda (2007) found that parental aspirations and literacy practices were related to student reading engagement in a sample of 128 Latino elementary and middle school children.

Although there is good evidence that motivation has both direct and indirect influences on reading comprehension (Guthrie & Wigfield, 2005) for native English-speaking students, little of the existing work has targeted ELLs specifically. A reasonable hypothesis is that motivational factors should be equally important for these students, and much work needs to be done to extend and examine the robustness of current research and theory.

HOW THIS NEW KNOWLEDGE CAN IMPROVE COMPREHENSION INSTRUCTION

Considering the preceding discussion, it is reasonable to ask, "Where might comprehension break down for students from diverse language or cultural backgrounds?" A preliminary list might include the following:

- *Attention.* There may be differences in the cues students attend to in classroom instruction or text, because of the lack of connection and meaningfulness to their everyday lives. Culturally unfamiliar materials might play a role in this process.
- *Encoding.* The input from text, the teacher, or peer discussions may not be comprehensible because of language differences, differences in genre or vocabulary, the formal register used in academic contexts or "academic English" (Bailey, 2007), or typical classroom discourse and interactional patterns that conflict with home and community norms (Cazden, 1988; Mehan, 1979).
- *Strategic behavior.* Because of the complex interplay among race, ethnicity, and especially SES, students from some households may not be exposed to large numbers of schooled adults who can model useful strategies in processing text.
- *Background knowledge.* The knowledge and skills that students have acquired may not map easily onto that in curricular materials, books, or activities. This may be a function of differences in cultural practices between home and school, and/or a function of reduced opportunity to learn because of restricted socioeconomic circumstances.
- *Motivational factors.* Students may come to school with different learning goals (Goldenberg, Gallimore, Reese, & Garnier, 2001; Ogbu & Simmons, 1998), poor self-efficacy due to past academic experiences, or, as suggested earlier, low task value for school activities, because the structure or purpose of instructional activities does not parallel known experiences and abilities and interests.

An additional, often overlooked factor is that many ELLs are provided remedial and unchallenging activities, materials, and learning environments. From a motivational perspective, it has long been known that many students who are poor readers receive motivationally impoverished materials and activities (Stanovich, 1986). Quirk and Schwanenflugel (2004) conducted a motivational analysis of five popular supplemental reading programs commonly provided to struggling readers. These authors argued that the three most relevant aspects of motivation to the instruction of remedial readers include reading self-efficacy, making internal and controllable attributions for successes and failures associated with reading, and establishing personally relevant value in becoming a better reader. The analysis suggested serious shortcomings in the materials provided, and the authors argued for more attention to motivational considerations in instructional environments and materials for students who need special attention in reading.

In general, there is a reason to be optimistic that increased attention to cultural and motivational factors shows promise in improving reading comprehension outcomes for ELLs. Thus, teachers, publishers, and policymakers need to be more informed regarding not only the cognitive aspects of materials, activities, practices, and policies that they construct or use, but also the motivational aspects. Knowing that cultural and motivational factors are present in the classroom is important. However, knowing how the factors we listed earlier impact performance in specific areas, such as literacy and reading comprehension, is more critical, because steps can be taken to overcome these barriers to improved reading comprehension.

DIRECTIONS FOR FUTURE RESEARCH

A great deal more is known about how ELLs become proficient readers than was the case even 5 years ago, but there are significant gaps in the research. As the National Literacy Panel Report (August & Shanahan, 2006) illustrates, much of the knowledge is based on a very small number of studies in any single area. In terms of directions for future research, there are unresolved issues and questions both for ELLs in general and reading comprehension for this group. Some of these questions are detailed below.

1. *Are there instructionally relevant subgroups within the ELL population?* Although ELLs are often considered a homogenous group, it is likely that differences among ELLs require different instructional approaches. These differences may be related to a host of mediating variables, such as SES, home language environment, age when learning a second language, and so forth. Artiles, Rueda, Salazar, and Higareda (2005), for example, found differential rates of special education placement related to, among other factors, language proficiency status (proficiency in one or both languages) and type of language support program. Students proficient in neither their native language nor English were the most vulnerable.

In practice, school districts have to make instructional decisions about ELLs on a daily basis, but there is not a good research base for providing guidance in distinguishing subgroups for optimal instructional design.

2. *What is the impact of cultural accommodations on student academic outcomes? And what types of accommodations work best with which learners?* As the review in the National Literacy Panel suggests (Goldenberg et al., 2006), currently there is inadequate evidence regarding the impact of classroom cultural accommodations on student outcomes, although the impact of home and school differences is well-documented. The descriptive studies that exist have been extremely valuable in providing detailed accounts about how these differences play out in day-to-day interaction in the classroom. It is now important to begin to examine how these differences affect student outcomes, and how student and family strengths can be appropriated for academic learning goals.

3. *What are the optimal instructional approaches for teaching comprehension in multilingual classrooms with ELLs from a variety of different language groups?* Although much of the research on pedagogy for ELLs has been carried out in or has assumed a bilingual context, it is increasingly the case that classrooms contain students who speak multiple languages. This is especially true in large urban schools. In Los Angeles Unified School District (2006), as one example, 91 primary languages were reported during the 2005–2006 period. The research does not offer extensive guidance in these circumstances, yet these classrooms likely represent unique language and literacy learning environments.

4. *What is the impact of motivational and cultural as opposed to cognitive factors in comprehension?* As noted earlier, cognitive factors have been given primary attention in reading comprehension research and practice, because there is strong evidence that this is

an effective means of improving student comprehension. However, there are strong reasons to believe that, especially for ELLs, attention to cultural and motivational factors might be equally important. This is not a case of an "either–or" approach; rather, the main question is how to provide cognitively rich instruction in engaging and culturally relevant ways.

5. *What are the best assessment procedures and indicators to capture "true" competence?* Reading comprehension assessment has received much less attention than some other early literacy skills that are relatively more straightforward to measure. Comprehension assessments are challenging, especially for very young students (e.g., K–1) and for ELLs (because of language and other confounds). The lack of reliable, valid, and widely used measures of comprehension is a problem both for classroom instruction and research purposes. Although progress has been made (Paris, 2005), this remains an open area of investigation.

Whereas all of these problems are significant, a more fundamental need is the lack of a comprehensive theoretical framework(s) that relates basic reading skills and comprehension processes to the multiple dimensions of literacy, including not only cognitive but also cultural, motivational, and social dimensions (Kucer & Silva, 2006). Although it is convenient and often necessary to dissect these elements to study them more carefully, it is important to remember that children are whole beings in which these processes interact seamlessly.

PROJECTIONS AND POSSIBILITIES FOR THE CLASSROOM OF 2030

An exciting and intriguing possibility for future work in reading comprehension, especially for ELLs, focuses on the role that technology will play. In a recent study, Proctor, Dalton, and Grisham (2007) reported that fourth-grade ELLs made great use of the digitally embedded features (e.g., vocabulary supports, and text-to-speech and read-aloud functionality), in a way that enhanced both learning novel lexical items and effectively applying reading comprehension strategies. The authors found that students who showed significant gains in reading scores frequently accessed the hyperlinked glossary items and coaching avatars that provided support in the use of comprehension strategies.

Thus, virtual environments, bilingual speech recognition, and the ability to measure individual cognitive and affective processes in real time promise to change the nature of this area. Imagine, for example, the role of virtual environments in comprehension instruction and comprehension assessment, where linguistically informed and learner-sensitive virtual environments can provide on-demand scenarios and real-life-like contexts and conversational partners. Such technology could provide much needed individual and responsive assistance to those students who need it most. Virtual environments, for example, could facilitate the creation of background knowledge by providing students with exposure to virtual activities and experiences that might not otherwise be affordable or practical.

At the same time, new technologies might be able to gauge an individual learner's basic cognitive processes (such as cognitive load during a specific task) (Paas, Renkl, & Sweller, 2003) and task engagement (by monitoring physiological indicators) and communicate instantaneous data to a teacher. This offers the possibility of providing information "just in time" (Novak, Patterson, Govrin, & Christian, 1999) that a teacher could use to adjust the challenge level, content or pace of a lesson, or to monitor and adjust students' reading materials based on levels of engagement and cognitive load. Because much of the motivation work relies on self-report or observational measures that are subject to intentional or unintentional inaccuracies, and many cognitive measures of comprehension are confounded by language and cultural factors, more direct measures would be a significant advance for research and classroom practice.

SUMMARY

Although comprehension is a complex process, we have focused here on two dimensions that we feel offer potential for improving student outcomes yet have been understudied, specifically, cultural and motivational factors. With respect to reading comprehension, it is reasonable to expect that the same basic underlying processes operate for ELLs as for students who are native speakers of English. However, two areas in which differences may be important are cultural and motivational factors.

As we noted, there are well-documented differences in what many ELLs experience at home and at school. Although the National Literacy Panel did not find substantial evidence to date for the impact of culturally compatible teaching practices, this is most likely a function of the descriptive way that cultural factors have been studied. The example of students with access to *funds of knowledge* (González, Moll, & Amanti, 2005) shows that there is a possible way to build on students' cognitive, linguistic, and cultural resources and provide excellent guidelines for their literacy development. It should be kept in mind that limited evidence is not the same as negative evidence. Thus, it is important to continue to evaluate the connection between these factors and eventual student outcomes.

With respect to motivation, there are many areas in which ELLs may encounter problems, from lack of self-efficacy due to poor English language skills (Monzo & Rueda, 2003) to lack of task value due to unchallenging or boring remedial activities, or limited prior knowledge. These and many other factors have received relatively little consideration in the design or study of programs, materials, or learning environments for ELLs, especially related to reading comprehension instruction.

Finally, and perhaps most important in making advances in reading comprehension instruction for ELLs, is the necessity for additional comprehensive models and theories that link the multiple dimensions of reading, literacy, and comprehension in a more coherent fashion.

INTEGRATE, INVESTIGATE, AND INITIATE: QUESTIONS FOR DISCUSSION

1. Comprehension instruction for ELLs is a large and important topic. In one paragraph, summarize the new information you learned from reading this chapter.
2. This is the last chapter in Part IV ("Differentiated Comprehension Instruction") of this book. What is the most important insight you gained from reading Chapters 17–20? What specific action will you take to ensure that this new research-based innovation can be applied within a true educational area of responsibility in your classroom in the next week? Research demonstrates that highly effective educators implement the newest information they have learned and judged to be relevant to their situation within 7 days from the time that they first learned and validated its importance.

3. Part V of this book is entitled "Technology and Comprehension Instruction: New Directions." Please place a check mark in the column Agree or Disagree below and write the reason for your answer on the line that follows. These questions act as an anticipatory guide to prepare you for the information presented in the next section of this book.

    A. It is important that we teach children through the use of games, if we want comprehension to improve in the schools. Reasons why I agree or disagree with this statement: Agree   Disagree

_____
_____

    B. Students in schools of the future must spend 50% of the time reading from the Internet and 50% reading from texts. Reasons why I agree or disagree with this statement:

_____
_____

    C. The most effective comprehension lessons of the future must use Web-based lesson plan formats. Reasons why I agree or disagree with this statement:

_____
_____

REFERENCES

Artiles, A. J., Rueda, R., Salazar, J., & Higareda, I. (2005). Within-group diversity in minority disproportionate representation: English language learners in urban school districts. *Exceptional Children, 71*(3), 283–300.

August, D., & Shanahan, T. (2006). *Developing literacy in second language learners: Report of the National Literacy Panel on language-minority children and youth.* Mahwah, NJ: Erlbaum.

Bailey, A. L. (2007). *Language demands of school: Putting academic English to the test.* New Haven, CT: Yale University Press.

Bouchard, M. (2005). *Comprehension strategies for English language learners.* New York: Teaching Resources.

Cazden, C. B. (1988). *Classroom discourse.* New York: Heinemann.

Garcia, G. (2003). The reading comprehension development and instruction of English language learners. In A. P. Sweet & C. E. Snow (Eds.), *Rethinking reading comprehension* (pp. 30–38). New York: Guilford Press.

Goldenberg, C. (2006). Improving achievement for English-learners: What the research tells us. *Education Week, 25*(43), 34–36.

Goldenberg, C., Gallimore, R., Reese, L., & Garnier, H. (2001). Cause or effect?: A longitudinal study of immigrant Latino parents' aspirations and expectations and their children's school performance. *American Educational Research Association Journal, 38,* 547–582.

Goldenberg, C., Rueda, R., & August, D. (2006). Synthesis: Sociocultural contexts and literacy development. In D. August & T. Shanahan (Eds.), *Developing literacy in second language learners: Report of the National Literacy Panel on language-minority children and youth* (pp. 249–268). Mahwah, NJ: Erlbaum.

González, N., Moll, L. C., & Amanti, C. (2005). *Funds of knowledge: Theorizing practice in households, communities, and classrooms.* Mahwah: NJ: Erlbaum.

Guthrie, J. T., & Wigfield, A. (1999). How motivation fits into a science of reading. *Scientific Studies of Reading, 3*(3), 199–205.

Guthrie, J., & Wigfield, A. (2005). Roles of motivation and engagement in reading comprehension assessment. In S. G. Paris (Ed.), *Current issues in reading comprehension and assessment* (pp. 187–213). Mahwah, NJ: Erlbaum.

Guthrie, J. T., Wigfield, A., Barbosa, P., Perencevich, K. C., Taboada, A., Davis, M. H., et al., (2004). Increasing reading comprehension and engagement through Concept-Oriented Reading Instruction. *Journal of Educational Psychology, 96*(3), 403–423.

Guthrie, J. T., Wigfield, A., & Perencevich, K. C. (2004). *Motivating reading comprehension: Concept-Oriented Reading Instruction*. Mahwah, NJ: Erlbaum.

Guthrie, J. T., Wigfield, A., & VonSecker, C. (2000). Effects of integrated instruction on motivation and strategy use in reading. *Journal of Educational Psychology, 92*(2), 331–341.

Herrell, A. L., & Jordan, M. (2008). *50 strategies for teaching English language learners* (3rd ed.). Upper Saddle River, NJ: Merrill/Prentice-Hall.

Jimenez, R. T., Garcia, G., & Pearson, P. (1996). The reading strategies of bilingual Latina/o students who are successful English readers: Opportunities and obstacles. *Reading Research Quarterly, 31*(1), 90–112.

Kucer, S. B., & Silva, C. (2006). *Teaching the dimensions of literacy*. Mahwah, NJ: Erlbaum.

Lesaux, N., Koda, K., Siegel, L., & Sanan, T. (2006). Development of literacy. In D. August & T. Shanahan (Eds.), *Developing literacy in second language learners: Report of the National Literacy Panel on language-minority children and youth* (pp. 75–122). Mahwah, NJ: Erlbaum.

Loera, G., & Rueda, R. (2007, April). *Latino parental aspirations and literacy practices related to childrens' reading engagement*. Paper presented at the Annual Meeting of the American Educational Research Association, Chicago, IL.

Los Angeles Unified School District. (2006). *R-30 Language Census Report, Los Angeles Unified School District 2005–2006* (Publication No. 313). Los Angeles: Planning, Assessment, and Research, School Information Branch.

Mehan, H. (1979). *Learning lessons: The social organization of classroom instruction*. Cambridge, MA: Harvard University Press.

Monzo, L., & Rueda, R. (2003, April). *Passing as English fluent: Strategies of Latino immigrant children*. Presented at the Annual Meeting of the American Educational Research Association, Chicago, IL.

National Reading Panel. (2000). *Report of the National Reading Panel: Teaching children to read: An evidence-based assessment of the scientific research literature on reading and its implications for reading instruction: Reports of the subgroups* (NIH Publication No. 00-4754). Washington, DC: U.S. Government Printing Office.

Novak, G. M., Patterson, E. T., Gavrin, A. D., & Christian, W. (1999). Just in time teaching. *American Journal of Physics, 67*(10), 937–938.

Ogbu, J., & Simmons, H. D. (1998). Voluntary and involuntary minorities: A cultural-ecological theory of school performance with some implications for education. *Anthropology and Education Quarterly, 29*(2), 155–188.

Paas, F., Renkl, A., & Sweller, J. (2003). Cognitive load theory [Special issue]. *Educational Psychologist, 38*(1).

Paris, S. G. (2005). *Current issues in reading comprehension and assessment*. Mahwah, NJ: Erlbaum.

Pintrich, P. R. (2003). A motivational science perspective on the role of student motivation in learning and teaching contexts. *Journal of Educational Psychology, 95*(4), 667–686.

Portes, P. (1996). Ethnicity and culture in educational psychology. In D. C. Berliner & R. C. Calfee (Eds.), *Handbook of educational psychology* (pp. 331–357). New York: Macmillan.

Proctor, C. P., Dalton, B., & Grisham, D. L. (2007). Scaffolding English language learners and struggling readers in a universal literacy environment with embedded strategy instruction and vocabulary support. *Journal of Literacy Research, 39*(1), 71–93.

Quirk, M. P., & Schwanenflugel, P. J. (2004). Do supplemental remedial reading programs address the motivational issues of struggling readers?: An analysis of five popular programs. *Reading Research and Instruction, 43*(3), 1–19.

RAND Reading Study Group. (2002). *Reading for understanding: Toward an R & D program in reading comprehension.* Washington, DC: RAND Education.
Rueda, R. (2006). Motivational and cognitive aspects of culturally accommodated instruction: The case of reading comprehension. In D. M. McInerney, M. Dowson, & S. Van Etten (Eds.), *Effective schools: Vol. 6. Research on sociocultural influences on motivation and learning* (pp. 135–158). Greenwich, CT: Information Age.
Stanovich, K. E. (1986). Matthew effects in reading: Some consequences of individual differences in the acquisition of literacy. *Reading Research Quarterly, 21,* 360–407.
Sweet, A., & Snow, C. (Eds.). (2003). *Rethinking reading comprehension.* New York: Guilford Press.
Zentella, A. C. (2005). *Building on strength: Language and literacy in Latino families and communities.* New York: Teachers College Press/Covina, CA: California Association of Bilingual Education.

TECHNOLOGY AND COMPREHENSION INSTRUCTION
New Directions

21

Games and Comprehension
The Importance of Specialist Language

JAMES PAUL GEE

> Words are, of course, the most powerful drug used by mankind.
> —RUDYARD KIPLING

The argument in this chapter is as follows: Success in school requires children to comprehend the complex academic language found in the content areas (e.g., science, math, social studies). This in turn requires a good school-based vocabulary and familiarity with the syntactic and discourse features of such language. It is best to get ready for these language demands early in life at home, before coming to school, and to sustain home-based support for such academic language development thereafter, because it is difficult to develop a good school-based vocabulary starting late, without such early and on ongoing home-based support (Gee, 2004). To remedy such a vocabulary problem requires lots of reading, which people with a poor vocabulary are often not motivated to do, but, unfortunately, lots of reading, although important, is neither highly efficient nor totally effective by itself as a way to learn vocabulary (Gersten, Fuchs, Williams, & Baker, 2001).

So what can we do? Decades of research show that we need to teach comprehension strategies overtly in school from the early grades (Pressley, 2006). We need, as well, to teach as much vocabulary as we can, with the most effective methods (Pearson, Hiebert, & Kamil, 2007). Both matters are covered elsewhere in this book. Here I suggest an unorthodox, third possible source of help: to learn from and even use popular culture practices for literacy development. I concentrate here on video games and games that have both face-to-face and video forms (Gee, 2003, 2007; Hawisher & Selfe, 2007). Similar arguments could and have been made for using other popular culture practices (e.g., fan fiction writing; see Black, 2005, 2007).

TYPES OF WORDS

We can divide vocabulary into three types of words (Beck, McKeown, & Kucan, 2002). First, there are "everyday," "vernacular," or "informal words," such as *hot*, *nice*, *happy*, and so forth. Everyone knows such words as part of the process of becoming a native speaker. Second, there are "technical words," such as *generative* in mathematics or linguistics, *mitocondria* in biology, *quark* in physics, or *power up* in video gaming. Such words are best learned as part of the process of learning the domains in which they are technical terms. Third, are what I will call "formal words" such as *perceive*, *assertion*, *insinuate*, *advocate*, *simultaneous*, and so forth, which are found in a variety of different specialist areas or public sphere activities (e.g., philosophy or social activism), in literature, in the content areas of school, and in the more formal vernacular of some speakers (i.e., those heavily influenced by school-based sorts of books).

Formal words have a wider application than technical terms, though they sometimes have more technical uses within a given specialist area (e.g., *sensitivity* in physiological psychology or *assertion* in linguistics—in fact, even informal words can have a technical meaning in some domains, e.g., *work* in physics). "Formal words" are the ones most important to teach in school as part of "language arts" and the content areas to increase student comprehension.

Formal words—like all words—take on somewhat different meanings in different contexts (Gee, 2005). In particular, they may mean somewhat different things in different sorts of situations, activities, texts, or academic or specialist areas of concern (e.g., consider the different meanings that words such as *process*, *system*, and *formal* might take on in different contexts of use). Thus, it is not effective to teach these words out of context and leave things at that. Children need in-school and out-of-school-based activities to see and hear these words in a variety of different contexts.

Many children see and hear formal words in various texts and content areas in school far more than they hear them in everyday forms of talk at home or in their communities (though children from highly educated homes hear a good number of them in talk). I suggest below, however, that many children, rich and poor, see and hear a good number of both technical terms and formal words in some of their popular culture practices.

Specifically, in this chapter I do the following:

- Define specialist language and its impact on students comprehension.
- Report early oral vocabulary correlates with school success.
- Identify informal specialist language lessons that could occur at school and home.
- Describe the implications of specialist language comprehension research and instruction.

WHAT WE KNOW NOW: SPECIALIST LANGUAGE

I refer to forms or styles of language that use lots of technical terms or formal words, or both (and recruit characteristic forms of complex syntactic and discourse structures), as "specialist language." Academic content areas (e.g., biology or literary criticism) use specialist forms of language. School content areas (e.g., social studies, math, language arts, or science) use specialist forms of language. Some types of literature—the types we tend to use in school—use a good many formal words, as well as complex syntactic and discourse patterns, so I call this specialist language as well. Some popular cultural practices also use lots of technical and formal words, as well as complex syntactic and discourse patterns, so these too are specialist forms of language. Remember, though, that people who, in some contexts, use lots of formal words in their everyday vernacular speech when they are not talking as specialists of any sort have picked up this vocabulary because of their exposure to the sorts of specialist texts and talk often found in school and books.

NEW RESEARCH: EARLY ORAL VOCABULARY CORRELATES WITH SCHOOL SUCCESS

Phonemic awareness and early practice with literacy are the most important factors before school that predict a child's success in first grade (Dickinson & Neuman, 2006). However, the most important factors that predict a child's success past the first grade, essentially for the rest of schooling, are the child's early, home-based oral vocabulary and early skills with complex oral language (Dickinson & Neuman, 2006; Senechal, Ouellette, & Rodney, 2006).

There is an important qualification that I need to make here. Research in linguistics has for decades shown that every normal child develops a perfectly adequate oral language, the child's "native language" (Chomsky, 1986; Pinker, 1994)—and, of course, sometimes children develop more than one native language. When I say that children's early vocabulary and skills with complex language are crucial correlates of success in school, I am not talking about children's everyday ("vernacular") language, but about their early preparation for language that is not "everyday," for language that is "school-based," "specialist," or "academic" (Gee, 2004; Schleppegrell, 2004). I am talking about the difference between saying something like "Hornworms sure vary a lot in how well they grow" (vernacular) and "Hornworm growth displays a significant amount of variation" (specialist).

INFORMAL SPECIALIST LANGUAGE LESSONS AT HOME

Let me give an example of what I am talking about in terms of getting ready early in life for the demands that school will eventually make for specialist language. Kevin Crowley has talked insightfully about quite young children developing what he calls "islands of expertise" (Crowley & Jacobs, 2002). Crowley and Jacobs (p. 333) define an island of expertise as "any topic in which children happen to become interested and in which they develop relatively deep and rich knowledge." In this respect, then, consider, a mother talking to her 4-year-old son, who has an island of expertise around dinosaurs (the transcript below is adapted from Crowley & Jacobs [2002, pp. 343–344]). The mother and child are looking at a replica fossil dinosaur and a replica fossil dinosaur egg. The mother places a little card in front of the boy that reads:

- Replica of a Dinosaur **Egg**
- From the Oviraptor
- Cretaceous Period
- Approximately 65 to 135 million years ago
- The actual fossil, of which this is a replica, was found in the Gobi Desert of Mongolia

The child says, "This looks like this is a egg," and the mother responds, "That's exactly what it is! How did you know?" The child says, "Because it looks like it," and the mother responds, "That's what it says [on the card], see look **egg**, **egg** . . . replica of a dinosaur **egg**. From the oviraptor." Here the mother asks the child the basis of his knowledge ("How did you know?"). Then she publicly displays the technical text, even though the child cannot yet read, using print to confirm the child's claim to know, showing one way that this type of print (descriptive information) can be used in an epistemic game of confirmation, and demonstrates the primacy of print as evidence. Specialist domains are almost always "expert" domains that involve claims to know and evidence for such claims, evidence that is very often tied to print.

Here and elsewhere in the interaction, the mother also uses elements of nonvernacular, specialist language. For example, here this includes "**replica** of a dinosaur egg," "from the **oviraptor**"; and later it includes "from the **Cretaceous period**," "the **hind claw**," "their **prey**."

As the interaction proceeds, the mother makes a number of other moves that facilitate the early development of specialist language. For instance, the mother relates the current talk and text to other texts with which the child is familiar, when at one point she says, "You have an oviraptor on your game! You know the egg game on your computer?" and at another point, "And remember they have those, remember in your book, it said something about the claws." This sort of intertextuality helps the child to connect words, the world, images, technologies, and written texts.

The mother explicates hard concepts by saying things like "And that's from the Cretaceous Period. And that was a really, really, long time ago." This signals to the child that "Cretaceous Period" is a technical term and displays how to explicate such terms in the vernacular. She also offers technical-like definitions when she says things like "And this is . . . the hind claw. What's a hind claw? (pause) A claw from the back leg from a velociraptor." This demonstrates a common language move in specialist domains, that is, giving relatively formal and explicit definitions (not just examples of use).

This interaction is a language lesson, but not primarily a lesson on vernacular language, though, of course, it thoroughly mixes vernacular and specialist language. This lesson on specialist language is early preparation for the sorts of school-based language children see ever more increasingly, in talk and in texts, as they move on in school.

All this, however, raises the issue of what happens to children who come to school without such informal specialist language teaching, and, often, without other important aspects of emergent literacy. My view is that this deficit cannot be ignored. We cannot just move on to reading instruction of the "decode and literally comprehend" sort as if it just doesn't matter that these children have missed out on early specialist language learning. For these children language teaching for "academic language" (one form of specialist language) needs to start with and sustain itself throughout the course of reading instruction (Zwiers, 2007).

HOW THIS NEW KNOWLEDGE CAN IMPROVE COMPREHENSION INSTRUCTION: IF YOUR VOCABULARY IS POOR, IT IS NOT EASY TO GET A BETTER ONE

When children end up with poor vocabularies late in their schooling, the problem is very difficult to remedy. In fact, vocabulary learning involves a paradox: if a child has poor vocabulary, the only way to remedy the matter is for him or her to engage in lots of independent reading (something people with poor vocabularies often don't want to do). However, reading is really not all that effective a way to learn vocabulary:

> The variety of contexts in which words can appropriately be used is so extensive, and the crucial nuances in meaning so constrained by context, that teaching word meanings in an abstract and decontextualized manner is essentially futile and potentially misleading. . . . The only realistic chance students with poor vocabularies have to catch up to their peers with rich vocabularies requires that they engage in extraordinary amounts of independent reading (Baker, Simmons, Kame'enui, n.d.; see also Anderson & Nagy, 1991).
>
> It may be somewhat surprising to learn that most researchers agree that although students do learn word meanings in the course of reading connected text, the process seems to be fairly inefficient and not especially effective (Beck & McKeown, 1991). Beck and McKeown state that "research spanning several decades has failed to uncover strong evidence that word meanings are routinely acquired from context." (Gersten et al., 2001)

So we face an interesting problem: How do we get children to learn academic or specialist vocabulary when they may not want to engage in lots of reading, and when that reading will not necessarily be highly effective in solving the problem. As I pointed out earlier, research has shown that we need to teach and practice comprehension strategies overtly in school from the early grades on (Pressley, 2006). We need as well to teach and practice as much vocabulary as we can, with the most effective methods (Pearson et al., 2007). In addition, I want to suggest an unorthodox supplement to these approaches: to learn from and even use popular culture practices for literacy development.

Specialist Language in Popular Culture

Something very interesting has happened in children's popular culture. It has gotten very complex, and it contains a great many activities that involve highly specialist styles of language (Gee, 2003, 2004, 2007). For example, consider the text below, which appears on a Yu-Gi-Oh card. Yu-Gi-Oh is a card game involving quite complex rules. It is often played by two players, face-to-face, sometimes in formal competitions, more often informally, though it can be played as a video game as well.

> **Armed Ninja**
> **Card-Type:** Effect Monster
> **Attribute:**: Earth/**Level:** 1
> **Type:** Warrior
> **ATK:** 300/**DEF:**: 300
> **Description:** FLIP: Destroys 1 Magic Card on the field. If this card's target is face-down, flip it face-up. If the card is a Magic Card, it is destroyed. If not, it is returned to its face-down position. The flipped card is not activated.
> **Rarity:** Rare

The "description" is really a rule. It states what moves in the game the card allows. Whereas this text has little specialist vocabulary (though it has some, e.g., *activated*), it contains complex specialist syntax, for instance, three straight conditional clauses (the "if" clauses). Note how complex this meaning is: First, if the target is face-down, flip it over. Now check to see if it is a Magic Card. If it is, destroy it. If it isn't, return it to its face-down position. Finally, the child is told that even though he or she flipped over the opponent's card, which in some circumstances would activate its powers, in this case, the card's powers are not activated. This is "logic talk," a matter really of multiple related "either–or", "if–then" propositions. It is the type of explicit specialist language children see often in school in the later grades.

Consider another Yu-Gi-Oh card:

Cyber Raider

Card-Type: Effect Monster

Attribute: Dark/**Level:** 4

Type: Machine

ATK: 1400/**DEF:** 1000

Description: When this card is Normal Summoned, Flip Summoned, or Special Summoned successfully, select and activate 1 of the following effects: Select 1 equipped Equip Spell Card and destroy it. Select 1 equipped Equip Spell Card and equip it to this card.

Rarity: Common

This card has the following technical words (some are compound words) on it: *effect monster, dark, machine type, normal summoned, flip summoned, special summoned, successfully, select, activate, effects, equipped, Equip Spell Card, destroy, rarity*, and *common*. These all have special meanings within the game rules. Children don't really know exactly what they mean unless they know the game. These words are, for the most part, what I called "formal words" earlier, here being used as technical terms in the game. Although they have specialized uses within the game, their uses there are related to their more common meanings in other activities and areas.

I have watched 7-year old children play Yu-Gi-Oh with great expertise. They must read each of the cards. They endlessly debate the powers of each card by constant contrast and comparison with other cards when they are trading them. They discuss and argue over the rules and, in doing so, use lots of specialist vocabulary, syntactic structures, and discourse features. They can go to websites to learn more or to settle their disputes. If and when they do so, here is the sort of thing they see: "The effect of '8-Claws Scorpion' is a Trigger Effect that is applied if the condition is correct on activation." Note *effect, applied, condition, activation*, and the conditional "if" clause.

Lucidly Functional Language

Let's consider for a moment what Yu-Gi-Oh involves. First and foremost, it involves what I call "lucidly functional language." The language on Yu-Gi-Oh cards, websites, and in children's discussions and debates is quite complex, but it relates piece by piece to the rules of the game, to the specific moves or actions one takes in the game. Here, language—complex specialist language—is married closely to specific and connected actions. The relationship between language and meaning (here meaning is the rules and the actions connected to them) is clear and lucid.

Situated Meaning and Verbal Meanings

There are two ways to understand words. I call one way "verbal" and the other "situated" (Gee, 2004, 2005). People have situated understandings of words when they can associate them with images, experiences, actions, or dialogue with which the words are associated. They have merely verbal understandings when they can only associate the words with other words (e.g., a paraphrase or a definition). Although verbal understandings may facilitate passing certain sorts of information-focused tests, they do not necessarily facilitate actual problem solving, in which learners have to apply words to the world to accomplish goals and actions.

Situated understandings are, of course, the norm in everyday life and in vernacular language. Even the most mundane words take on different meanings in different contexts of use, and we can associate the words with different images and actions in the different contexts. For instance, people construct different meanings for a word like *coffee* when they hear something like "The coffee spilled. Get the mop" versus "The coffee spilled. Get a broom" versus "The coffee spilled. Stack it again."

Situated Meanings and Video Games

We can see the nature and importance of situated meanings if we consider video games for a moment (Gee, 2003, 2007). Written texts associated with a video game are not very meaningful, certainly not very lucid, unless and until one has played the game. Let me take the small booklet that comes with the innovative game Deus Ex as an example. In the 20 pages of this booklet, there are 199 boldface references that represent headings and subheadings (one small, randomly chosen stretch of headings and subheadings that appears at the end of page 5 and the beginning of page 6 is as follows: **Passive Readouts, Damage Monitor, Active Augmentation & Device Icons, Items-at-Hand, Information Screens, Note, Inventory, Inventory Management, Stacks, Nanokey Ring, Ammunition**). Each of these 199 headings and subheadings is followed by text that gives information relevant to the topic and relates it to other information throughout the booklet. So, though the booklet is small, it is just packed with concise technical information.

Here is a typical piece of language from this booklet:

> Your internal nano-processors keep a very detailed record of your condition, equipment, and recent history. You can access this data at any time during play by hitting F1 to get to the Inventory screen or F2 to get to the Goals/Notes screen. Once you have accessed your information screens, you can move between the screens by clicking on the tabs at the top of the screen. You can map other information screens to hotkeys using Settings, Keyboard/Mouse. (p. 5)

This makes perfect sense at a literal level, but that just goes to show how worthless the literal level is. First, when you comprehend this sort of passage at only a literal level, you have only an illusion of understanding, one that quickly disappears as you try to relate the information in this passage to the hundreds of other important details in the booklet. This passage means nothing real to you if you have no situated idea about what *nano-processors, condition, equipment, history, F1, Inventory screen, F2, Goals/Notes screen* (and, of course, *Goals* and *Notes*), *information screens, clicking, tabs, map, hotkeys*, and *Settings, Keyboard/Mouse* mean in and for playing games like Deus Ex.

Second, though you know literally what each sentence means, the sentences raise a plethora of questions if you have no situated understandings. For instance: Are the same data (condition, equipment, and history) on both the Inventory screen and the Goals/Notes screen? If so, why are they on two different screens? If not, which type of information is on which screen, and why? The fact that I can move between the screens by clicking on the tabs (but what do these tabs look like, and will I recognize them?) suggests that some of this information is on one screen and some is on the other. But, then, is my "condition" part of my Inventory or my Goals/Notes? It doesn't seem to be either, but, then, what is my "condition" anyway? If I can map other information screens (and what are these?) to hotkeys using "Setting, Keyboard/Mouse," does this mean there is no other way to access them? How will I access them in the first place to assign them to my own chosen hotkeys? Can I click between them and the Inventory screen and the Goals/Notes screens by pressing on "tabs"?

Of course, all these terms and questions can be defined and answered if you closely check and cross-check information over and over again through the little booklet. You can constantly turn the pages backwards and forwards. But once you have one set of links relating various items and actions in mind, another drops out just as you need it, and you're back to turning pages. Is the booklet poorly written? Not at all. In fact, it is written just like any of myriad school-based texts in the content areas.

When I first read this booklet before playing Deus Ex, I was sorely tempted to put the game on a shelf and forget about it. I was simply overwhelmed with details, questions, and confusion. So I decided just to play the game—however badly—for several hours. After playing, when I went back to the booklet, something marvelous had happened. Now all the language in the booklet was lucidly clear and easy to understand. Why? Because now I had an image, action, experience, or piece of dialogue from the game to associate with words—had situated meanings for the words. Then, at last, the booklet makes good sense.

Content at School: Situated Meanings through Playing the "Game."

So now I could make just the same claim about any school content domain as I have just made about the video game Deus Ex: Specialist language in any school domain (e.g., math, science, or social studies) has no situated meaning (thus, no lucid or applicable meaning) *unless and until one has "played the game,"* that is, engaged in and with the images, actions, goals, experiences, practices, and dialogue that give situated meaning to words in these domains.

Good video games not only support situated meanings for the written materials associated with them in manuals and on fan websites—and these are copious—but also for all language within the game itself (Gee, 2003, 2007). The meaning of such language is always associated with actions, goals, experiences, images, and dialogue. Furthermore, players always and only get verbal information (words) "just in time," when they can apply it or see it apply, or "on demand," when they feel the need for it and are ready for it (then, in some cases, games will give the player walls of print, e.g., as in Civilization IV).

So my claim is this: What I call "game-like learning" leads to situated and not just verbal meanings. In turn, situated meanings make specialist language lucid, easy, and useful.

DIRECTIONS FOR FUTURE RESEARCH

Implications: Make Meaning Lucidly Functional

My point is not just to use popular culture for literacy learning, but to learn from popular culture how better to teach traditional content. Whenever we can, we should seek to make the meanings of specialist language in school lucidly functional, much in the way that language is in Yu-Gi-Oh.

For example, the science educator Andrea diSessa (2000) has successfully taught children in sixth grade and beyond the algebra behind Galileo's principles of motion by teaching them a specific computer programming language called Boxer. Using Boxer, students write into the computer a set of discrete steps in the programming language. For example, the first command in a little program meant to represent uniform motion might tell the computer to set the speed of a moving object at 1 meter per second. The second step might tell the computer to move the object. A third step might tell the computer to repeat the second step over and over again. Once the program starts running, the student will see a graphical object move 1 meter each second repeatedly, a form of uniform motion. Now the student can elaborate, play with, and change the model in various ways, for example, by adding a fourth step that tells the computer to add a value a to the speed of the moving object after each movement the object has taken (let us just say, for convenience, that a adds 1 more meter per second at each step), a step that models the concept of acceleration.

Here students are creating and observing quite direct links between actions they take in the programming language, the meanings of technical words (e.g., *uniform motion*, *acceleration*), and images they see on the screen. This is one powerful form of situated meaning.

Implications Continued: Situate Meanings

Beyond creating lucid functionality, there are, of course, other ways to situate meanings to enhance comprehension. Specialist language should be associated with images, actions, experiences, goals, and dialogue, not just verbal explications, summaries, definitions, and texts. Verbal information should be given "just in time"—near the time when learners will use it—or "on demand"—when learners are ready for it, and know they need it and why they need it.

For example, the learning scientist David Shaffer (2007) runs workshops in which middle school children are given an urban planning challenge: They are asked, working as teams, to create and then report on a detailed redesign plan for a major pedestrian thoroughfare in their own town. Like real professional urban planners, the students' plans must meet the social, economic, and physical needs of their communities. Students not only talk to real urban planners, study their communities, and read about urban planning, but they also have simulation software (using a global positioning systems [GPS] device) that lets them see a virtual representation of the street they are going to replan.

The simulation has two components: a decision space and a constraint table. The decision space displays address and zoning information using official two- or three-letter zoning codes to designate changes in land use for property parcels on the street. As students make decisions about changes they wish to make, they receive immediate feedback about the consequences of changes in the constraint table. The constraint table shows the effects of changes on six planning issues raised in the original information packet and the video: crime, revenue, jobs, waste, car trips, and housing.

Here, lots and lots of common language in the social sciences is placed in a context of image, action, experiences, goals, and dialogue, not just texts. Meaning is fully situated. Shaffer's work has demonstrated that such an approach leads to large language and thinking gains.

PROJECTIONS AND POSSIBILITIES FOR CLASSROOMS OF 2030: USING POPULAR CULTURE

Although I advocate using popular culture for language, comprehension, and literacy development, I do not advocate turning it into a school subject used for grading and sorting. This is just a way to co-opt what the children own and take a feeling of ownership away from them. Rather, in tomorrow's schools, I advocate finding children's areas of expertise in popular culture and helping them to use these areas to build, practice, and identify with specialist vocabulary and language skills (Shaffer, 2007). This can be done in a number of ways, a few of which follow:

1. Have children teach and explicate their areas of expertise to parents, teachers, and other children.
2. Engage children with research projects that involve their areas of expertise, projects that encourage extended talk, discussion, argumentation, and writing in various genres.
3. Have children explicate vocabulary in their areas of expertise and encourage them to relate these words to other uses these words have in other areas and activities.
4. Have children read and write challenging texts from their areas of expertise for real purposes that do not just recruit these areas for "doing school" (engage with reading and writing on chats, boards, forums, reviews, and websites; also have children talk and write about such engagement to parents and at school to teachers and other children, as well).
5. Encourage children to develop a new area of expertise (perhaps one related to an old area of expertise), all the while helping them to pay overt attention to words and language in this area.
6. Encourage children to engage in discussions and to make arguments about their areas of expertise with other children who share their expertise, including extended and explicit talk and writing that is responsive to other people's questions and concerns.
7. Encourage children to read what others—including adults—have said about their areas of expertise and how these areas relate to larger social and cultural issues.

SUMMARY

The most important thing we can do for children in the area of popular culture is first to encourage them to develop areas of expertise that recruit specialist language and thinking, then to get them to think, talk, and write at a "meta" level about this area to their peers, parents, and teachers. We also need to encourage them to think about the relationships that exist between their area of expertise and other, related and unrelated areas and activities in the world. Our ultimate goal for literacy comprehension instruction and research is to understand better how we can get students to think about how language works in their local worlds and the larger global world.

INTEGRATE, INVESTIGATE, AND INITIATE: QUESTIONS FOR DISCUSSION

1. Give yourself a grade as to how knowledgeable you were prior to reading this chapter about the importance of specialist language in teaching comprehension for this new generation of students. Grade yourself as to how knowledgeable you feel you are now that you have completed the reading of this chapter.

2. Create an informal, specialized language lesson at your school or school district that could increase children's comprehension.

3. Project what effect technology and games will have upon future students' comprehension and give your reasons why.

REFERENCES

Anderson, R. C., & Nagy, W. E. (1991). Word meanings. In R. Barr, M. L. Kamil, P. B. Mosenthal, & P. D. Pearson (Eds.), *Handbook of reading research* (Vol. 2, pp. 690–724). New York: Longman.

Baker, S. K., Simmons, D. C., Kame'enui, E. J. (n.d.). Vocabulary acquisition: Synthesis of the research. Retrieved March 2, 2003, from *idea.uoregon.edu/~ncite/documents/techrep/tech13.html*.

Beck, I. L., & McKeown, M. G. (1991). Conditions of vocabulary acquisition. In R. Barr, M. Kamil, P. Mosenthal, & P. D. Pearson (Eds.), *Handbook of reading research* (Vol. 2, pp. 789–814). New York: Longman.

Beck, I. L., McKeown, M. G., & Kucan, L. (2002). *Bringing words to life: Robust vocabulary instruction*. New York: Guilford Press.

Black, R. W. (2005). Access and affiliation: The literacy and composition practices of English language learners in an online fanfiction community. *Journal of Adolescent and Adult Literacy, 49,* 118–128.

Black, R. W. (2007). Digital design: English language learners and reader feedback in online fanfiction. In M. Knobel & C. Lankshear (Eds.), *A new literacies sampler* (pp. 115–136). New York: Peter Lang.

Chomsky, N. (1986). *Knowledge of language*. New York: Praeger.

Crowley, K., & Jacobs, M. (2002). Islands of expertise and the development of family scientific literacy. In G. Leinhardt, K. Crowley, & K. Knutson (Eds.), *Learning conversations in museums* (pp. 333–356). Mahwah, NJ: Erlbaum.

Dickinson, D. K., & Neuman, S. B. (Eds.). (2006). *Handbook of early literacy research: Volume 2*. New York: Guilford Press.

diSessa, A. A. (2000). *Changing minds: Computers, learning, and literacy*. Cambridge, MA: MIT Press.

Gee, J. P. (2003). *What video games have to teach us about learning and literacy*. New York: Palgrave/Macmillan.

Gee, J. P. (2004). *Situated language and learning: A critique of traditional schooling*. London: Routledge.

Gee, J. P. (2005). *An introduction to discourse analysis: Theory and method* (2nd ed.). London: Routledge.

Gee, J. P. (2007). *Good video games and good learning: Collected essays on video games, learning and literacy*. New York: Peter Lang.

Gersten, R., Fuchs, L. S., Williams, J. P., & Baker, S. (2001). Teaching reading comprehension strategies to students with learning disabilities: A review of research. *Review of Educational Research, 71,* 279–320.

Hawisher, G. E., & Selfe, C. L. (2007). *Gaming lives in the twenty-first century: Literate connections*. New York: Palgrave/Macmillan.

Pearson, P. D., Hiebert, E. H., & Kamil, M. L. (2007). Vocabulary assessment: What we know and what we need to learn. *Reading Research Quarterly, 42,* 282–296.

Pinker, S. (1994). *The language instinct. How the mind creates language.* New York: William Morrow.

Pressley, M. (2006). *Reading instruction that works: Third edition: The case for balanced teaching.* New York: Guilford Press.

Schleppegrell, M. (2004). *Language of schooling: A functional linguistics perspective.* Mahwah, NJ: Erlbaum.

Senechal, M., Ouellette, G., & Rodney D. (2006). The misunderstood giant: Predictive role of early vocabulary to future reading. In D. K. Dickinson & S. B. Neuman (Eds.), *Handbook of early literacy research: Volume 2* (pp. 173–182). New York: Guilford Press.

Shaffer, D. W. (2007). *How computer games help children learn.* New York: Palgrave/Macmillan.

Zwiers, J. (2007). *Building academic language: Essential practices for content classrooms, grades 5–12.* San Francisco: Jossey-Bass.

22

Research on Instruction and Assessment in the New Literacies of Online Reading Comprehension

DONALD J. LEU, JULIE COIRO, JILL CASTEK,
DOUGLAS K. HARTMAN, LAURIE A. HENRY, and DAVID REINKING

> The knowledge economy is about how the new technologies have transformed the way we think and act.... To thrive in the global knowledge economy, it is going to be important to change the whole educational system to ensure a wide base of knowledge workers who understand and use information technologies.
> —RILEY (2003, paragraphs 8–10)

The Internet has rapidly become the defining medium for information, communication, and reading comprehension in the twenty-first century (Friedman, 2005; The New Literacies Research Team, 2007; Partnership for 21st Century Skills, 2004, 2006). Moreover, research indicates that online reading comprehension is not isomorphic with offline reading comprehension; proficient readers offline are not always proficient readers online (Coiro, 2007; Leu, Reinking, et al., 2007). Additional reading comprehension skills are required to be a successful online reader (Castek et al., 2008; Coiro & Dobler, 2007; Henry, 2006; Leu et al., 2005). The emergence of new online reading comprehension skills has profound consequences for instruction as reading has moved from page to screen (Coiro, 2003). These new literacies have redefined many aspects of traditional comprehension instruction.

In this chapter, we explore online reading comprehension, instruction, and assessment. The chapter:

- Provides data to establish that the Internet is now a central context for reading comprehension.
- Defines the new literacies of online reading comprehension and reviews research in this area.

- Defines the emerging outlines of Internet Reciprocal Teaching (IRT), an instructional model used to teach online reading comprehension.
- Explores emerging assessment practices in online reading comprehension.
- Identifies key public policy and research questions to direct upcoming work.
- Describes what classroom instruction in the new literacies of online reading comprehension might be like in the future.

THE INTERNET IS THIS GENERATION'S DEFINING TECHNOLOGY FOR INFORMATION, READING COMPREHENSION, AND LEARNING

It is increasingly clear that online reading comprehension has become central to success in the 21st century. Consider some of the evidence for this claim:

1. Over 1 billion readers are reading online today, one-sixth of the world's population (de Argaez, 2006; Internet World Stats, n.d.).

2. Internet use at work to read, write, communicate, and solve problems increased by nearly 60% in the United States during 2002 among all employed adults 25 years of age and older (U.S. Department of Commerce, 2002).

3. Many of the productivity gains realized during the past decade in the economies of the world are due to the rapid integration of the Internet into the workplace to share information, communicate, and solve problems (Matteucci, O'Mahony, Robinson, & Zwick, 2005; Van Ark, Inklaar, & McGuckin, 2003).

4. In the United States, students from 8–18 years of age report spending more time reading online per day, 48 minutes, than reading offline, 43 minutes per day (Kaiser Family Foundation, 2005).

5. More than 90% of adolescent students in the United States with home access to the Internet report using the Internet for homework (Pew Internet & American Life Project, 2001). Over 70% of these students used the Internet as the primary source for information on their most recent school report or project, whereas only 24% of these students reported using the library for the same task.

6. The first international assessment of online reading comprehension will take place in 2009. The Program for International Student Assessment (PISA; Organization for Economic Cooperation and Development, n.d.) will provide important information about online reading comprehension to public policymakers around the world who are demanding it. Additional assessments of online reading comprehension are also beginning to be reported (see Bennett, Persky, Weiss, & Jenkins, 2007).

These data suggest that the Internet is now the defining technology for reading in a digital, socially networked, multimodal, hyperlinked, and multitasking world of information and communication (see also Bleha, 2005; Borzekowski, Fobil, & Asante, 2006; Livingstone & Bober, 2005; Ludlow, 2006; Pew Internet and American Life Project, 2005). The rate of growth in online reading has been exponential. In the history of literacy, no other technology for reading, writing, or communicating has been adopted so rapidly, by so many people, in so many places, and with such expansive implications for literacy. These changes have prompted research in online reading comprehension that seeks to understand what it means to read online and how best to support students in doing so.

RESEARCH IN THE NEW LITERACIES OF ONLINE READING COMPREHENSION

Research in online reading comprehension is informed by theoretical work in new literacies (Coiro, Knobel, Lankshear, & Leu, 2008a; Leu, Kinzer, Coiro, & Cammack, 2004). Broadly conceived, a new literacies perspective argues that the nature of literacy and learning is rapidly changing and transforming as new technologies emerge. Although there are many perspectives associated with the term *new literacies* (e.g., Cope & Kalantzis, 2000; Gee, 2003; Hull & Schultz, 2002; Kress, 2000; Lankshear & Knobel, 2003, 2006; New London Group, 1996, 2000; Street, 1998), the most recent theoretical review of this work (Coiro, Knobel, Lankshear, & Leu, 2008b) concludes that most share a set of common assumptions: (1) new skills, strategies, dispositions, and social practices are required by new technologies for information and communication; (2) new literacies are central to full participation in a global community; (3) new literacies regularly change as their defining technologies change; and (4) new literacies are multifaceted and benefit from multiple points of view. Results from investigations framed in a new literacies perspective have challenged existing classroom practices in literacy education (Beach & O'Brien, 2008; Dalton & Proctor, 2008; Merchant, 2008; Snyder & Bulfin, 2008; Unsworth, 2008; Wyatt-Smith & Elkins, 2008).

Within this broader context of new literacies theory and research, a new literacies perspective of online reading comprehension (Leu, Kinzer, et al., 2004) has also emerged to frame online reading comprehension as a problem-based inquiry process involving new skills, strategies, and dispositions on the Internet to generate important questions, and then locate, critically evaluate, synthesize, and communicate possible solutions to those problems online. This differs from earlier models of traditional print comprehension in that online reading comprehension is defined by not only the purpose, task, and context but also a process of self-directed text construction (Coiro & Dobler, 2007) that occurs as readers navigate their own paths through an infinite informational space to construct their own versions of the online texts they will read. During this process, both new and traditional reading comprehension skills are required. The overlap between online and offline reading not only enriches but also complicates our understanding of reading comprehension in the 21st century. Any model of online reading comprehension must begin with that basic observation.

What are the new skills and strategies for successful online reading comprehension? The answer is still emerging, though the outlines are becoming clearer. We know, for example, that the new literacies of online reading comprehension occur within a process that includes the skills and strategies required to identify an important question directing the reader to locate, critically evaluate, synthesize, and communicate information on the Internet (Leu et al., 2007).

Consider the initial phase of online reading comprehension: We read on the Internet to solve problems and to answer questions. How a problem is framed, or how a question is understood, is a central aspect of online reading comprehension. Recent work by Taboada and Guthrie (2006) within traditional texts suggests that reading initiated by a question differs in important ways from reading that is not. The fact that online reading comprehension always begins with a question or problem may be an important source of the differences between online and offline reading comprehension.

Locating information online, a second element of online reading comprehension, also requires new online reading comprehension skills, such as using a search engine, reading search engine results, or quickly reading a web page to locate the best link to the required information. Many students lack these skills (Coiro, 2007; Leu, Zawlinski, et al., 2007). Of those who do use a search engine, for example, many appear not to know how to read search engine results, instead clicking down the list of links in a "click and look" strategy (Leu, Zawlinski, et al., 2007).

Locating information during the online reading comprehension process may create a bottleneck for the subsequent skills of online reading comprehension (Henry, 2007); that is, those who possess the necessary online reading comprehension skills to locate information can continue to read and solve their problems; those who do not possess these skills cannot. In fact, this bottleneck may contribute to the lack of isomorphic performance between online and offline readers.

Critical evaluation is another area in which online reading comprehension requires a unique set of skills. Whereas important when reading offline information, it is perhaps more important online, where anyone can publish anything; knowing the stance and bias of an author become paramount to comprehension and learning. Determining this in online contexts requires new comprehension skills and strategies. For example, knowing which links take you to information about who created the data at a site (and actually choosing to follow these links) becomes important. So, too, is knowing how to check the reliability of that data with other information at other sites. Students do not always possess these skills. In one study (Leu et al., 2007), 47 out of 53 higher-performing online readers in seventh grade believed a site designed to be a hoax was reliable (*Save the Endangered Pacific Northwest Tree Octopus*), despite the fact that most students indicated in an interview that they did not believe everything they read online. Moreover, when told the site was a hoax, a number of students insisted that it provided accurate and reliable information.

Adults also appear to lack critical evaluation skills on the Internet, especially when it comes to search engine results. The Pew Internet and American Life Project (Fallows, 2005) found that whereas 92% of adults were confident about their searching abilities, 62% were unaware of the distinction between commercial and noncommercial results, and 68% said that search engines provide fair and unbiased sources of information. Clearly, many segments of our population have yet to acquire a full complement of online reading comprehension skills and dispositions to enable them to locate information effectively and think critically about what they have found.

The Teaching Internet Comprehension to Adolescents (TICA) project (Leu & Reinking, 2005) has been studying these and other skills essential to online reading comprehension. An evolving checklist of online reading comprehension skills in all of the areas required during online reading comprehension (understanding and developing questions, locating information, critically evaluating information, synthesizing information, and communicating information) is located in Appendices 22.1 and 22.2. Videos of students demonstrating these skills during online reading may be viewed at *www.newliteracies.uconn.edu/iesproject/videos*.

APPLYING RECIPROCAL TEACHING APPROACHES TO TEACHING THE NEW LITERACIES OF ONLINE READING COMPREHENSION

How should we begin to think about teaching online reading comprehension skills and strategies? A logical approach would be to review the research on comprehension to determine which instructional models appear to be most effective with teaching offline reading comprehension. The substantial effect sizes reported for one model of comprehension instruction, Reciprocal Teaching (Brown & Palincsar, 1989; Palincsar & Brown,

1984) would be especially noticeable in any review. Reciprocal Teaching has been shown consistently to improve students' comprehension of texts when implemented in intervention settings (Alfassi, 1998; Brand-Gruwel, Aarnoutse, & Van Den Bos, 1997; DeCorte, Verschaffel, & Van De Ven, 2001; Fung, Wilkinson, & Moore, 2003; Hacker & Tenent, 2002). A meta-analytic review of 16 studies (Rosenshine & Meister, 1994) showed that Reciprocal Teaching had a consistent, large, and positive effect on comprehension outcomes. Median effect sizes across the studies were between 0.34 to 0.60 on teacher-designed tests.

What defines the instructional approach Reciprocal Teaching? Key elements of this model include:

- The use of traditional, printed texts, which are often narratives.
- The reading of a common text.
- The teaching of a small group of students, often struggling readers.
- Teacher modeling of comprehension strategies.
- A focus on predicting, questioning, clarifying, and summarizing strategies.
- A gradual release of responsibility away from the teacher as students take on the modeling of comprehension strategies.
- Collaboration and discussion among all participants in each Reciprocal Teaching group.

While working in small groups, teachers and students take turns leading discussions of the text and demonstrate each strategy. Eventually, through continued practice and teachers' gradual release of responsibility, students begin to develop useful repertoires of metacognitive strategies for better understanding what they read. Over time, these strategies appear to become self-regulated and transfer to new reading contexts (e.g., Cooper, Boschken, McWilliams, & Pistochini, 2000; Palincsar, 1986b; Palincsar & Klenk, 1992).

Modifying Reciprocal Teaching for Online Reading Comprehension Instruction

To prepare students better for the unique challenges of reading on the Internet, we have begun to explore how best to frame instruction in online reading comprehension within middle school language arts classrooms (Leu & Reinking, 2005), middle school science classrooms (Leu et al., 2005), and in self-contained elementary school classrooms (Castek, in press). In each setting, our model of instruction has been informed by the well-established research in Reciprocal Teaching (Brown & Palincsar, 1989; Palincsar & Brown, 1984; Rosenshine & Meister, 1994). It has also been informed by research that has adapted this model to classroom learning contexts involving a wider spectrum of students (e.g., Hacker & Tenent, 2002).

Over time, our work has led us to modify a number of the elements of Reciprocal Teaching. Some changes have resulted from the differences between offline and online reading contexts. Others have resulted from moving a small-group instructional model, initially developed for teaching low-performing readers, to meet the needs of self-contained classroom teachers who confront both larger numbers of students and a wider range of reading proficiency.

Additional changes have resulted from our decision to adapt Reciprocal Teaching within classrooms in which students have their own laptop computers. We have found that it is important for each student to have a laptop computer with wireless access to the Internet. The desktop computers in most school computer labs make both interactive group work and discussions about strategy use quite problematic. Each is central to Reciprocal Teaching, as well as to our evolving model, which we call Internet Reciprocal Teaching (IRT). Other issues we have encountered with computer labs include the encroachment on instructional time necessitated by walking classes to the lab and back to the home classroom, as well as the limited times that computer labs are free. In addition, we are mindful that our work seeks to develop a model of instruction for the future, where we expect students to have their own laptops with wireless connections to the Internet, such as those found in Maine and an expanding number of districts around the United States (Dunleavy, Dexter, & Heinecke, 2007; Zucker, 2004). As a result of all these considerations, we have chosen to develop the model of Internet Reciprocal Teaching around the use of wireless laptop carts in a classroom. In the following sections, we compare and contrast Reciprocal Teaching and IRT.

The Use of Traditional Printed Texts, Often Narratives, versus Online Informational Texts

Reciprocal Teaching uses traditional, printed texts, often narratives, whereas Internet Reciprocal Teaching takes place with online resources, typically informational texts. Thus, somewhat different opportunities and challenges appear during lessons using IRT. Given the focus on expository texts, it is somewhat easier to integrate IRT lessons into other content areas. Alternatively, reading selections with this model often have more specialized vocabulary and are sometimes more challenging. Often, however, multimedia sources on the Internet are available to support reading comprehension in ways not possible with traditional texts. However, these additional media sources also require new reading skills and strategies to exploit their potential effectively.

The Reading of a Common Text versus the Reading of Unique Texts

Small-group Reciprocal Teaching instruction typically requires a common text that all students read linearly (Palincsar & Brown, 1984). With IRT readers typically construct individual texts through hyperlinks and the unique textual paths each chooses to follow on the Internet. As a result, strategy instruction during IRT focuses on both the common and the unique processes by which students navigate through multiple and different texts, rather than the reading of one, common text. Teachers and students model their choices about which links are most relevant to a group or individual question through think-alouds. They discuss how to locate information most efficiently within different kinds of websites, how to synthesize ideas across multiple texts and media, and how best to represent the answers to their questions. Instruction emphasizes choices about which sites to read, where to read on those sites, which links to follow to gather additional information, and when to conduct new searches.

Teaching a Small Group of Students, Often Struggling Readers, versus Teaching in Larger, Heterogeneously Grouped Classrooms

Reciprocal Teaching was initially developed for working with a single, small group of struggling readers (Palincsar & Brown, 1984). We work in diverse, urban and rural, heterogeneously grouped classrooms, with approximately 20–25 students in each class. Students come to our classrooms with a wide range of ability levels and backgrounds. They include English language learners (ELLs), as well as students who qualify for special services and those who struggle with reading, although they do not qualify for such services.

Because we work in self-contained classrooms, we have been required to adapt the basic context of Reciprocal Teaching—a single teacher working with a small group of struggling readers—to fit classrooms with one teacher for many more, and many different, students. The diversity of our classrooms provides a wider range of students with which to exchange a potentially wider range of online reading strategies. It also requires somewhat different organization and management in a classroom.

Greater Teacher Modeling of Offline Comprehension Strategies versus Greater Student Modeling of Online Comprehension Strategies

A key component of Reciprocal Teaching is that teachers model reading comprehension strategies, often by explaining their thinking during reading. IRT provides some degree of teacher modeling, but we also seek to take advantage of the online reading comprehension strategies that students bring to classrooms. There are two benefits. First, students frequently possess novel and potentially powerful online reading comprehension strategies with which teachers may sometimes be unfamiliar. Second, we have found that empowering students in this fashion—helping them to see themselves as experts with important skills to share—provides an instructional advantage. Often this approach generates greater involvement by students who might normally be thought to be weaker readers (Coiro, 2007; Leu et al., 2007; New Literacies Research Team, 2005a). We have found that honoring their contributions to the learning process encourages greater student investment in classroom activities and increases their engagement with texts and the learning process generally. Furthermore, we have observed that on several occasions, previously passive students, who were also weaker offline readers, took a leadership role in online strategy discussions.

A Focus on Predicting, Questioning, Clarifying, and Summarizing Strategies versus a Focus on Questioning, Locating, Critically Evaluating, Synthesizing, and Communicating Strategies

Reciprocal Teaching emphasizes four basic strategies: predicting, questioning, clarifying, and summarizing. The most important meta-analysis of Reciprocal Teaching studies (Rosenshine & Meister, 1994) indicated statistically significant gains in reading comprehension regardless of whether two, three, four, or 10 strategies were included, suggesting that gains may not be due to the type or the number of strategies taught but to cognitive processing that is made explicit during reading. We have followed this course in our development of IRT. Whereas IRT often includes the strategies used during Reciprocal Teaching, it focuses more on the somewhat novel online reading comprehension strategies required to develop or understand a question, then use that question to locate, critically evaluate, synthesize, and communicate information on the Internet.

In both, teachers gradually release responsibility as students take on the modeling of comprehension strategies. Both Reciprocal Teaching and IRT gradually transfer to students the responsibility for modeling comprehension strategies. With IRT, we have found it effective to provide the gradual release of responsibility using an instructional scheme with three phases: Phase 1 provides direct, whole-class instruction of basic skills and strategies of Internet use; Phase 2 provides group work and the reciprocal exchange of online reading comprehension strategies by students with their peers; Phase 3 provides online individual inquiry units, sometimes with collaborative efforts involving other students in other classes, perhaps even in other parts of the world, and periodic strategy sharing sessions with groups. We discuss these phases in more detail in a subsequent section. In the process, students assimilate strategies by engaging in explicit discussions about the online contexts in which these strategies appear to be most useful. Engaging in explicit discussions of strategy usage enhances students' awareness of their own thinking processes (Palincsar & Brown, 1984) and facilitates the application of these strategies in new reading contexts.

In both, collaboration and discussion take place among all participants in each Reciprocal Teaching group. Both Reciprocal Teaching and IRT take advantage of the potential that results from group conversations about reading strategies and the new strategies that appear to be especially helpful in various contexts. This posture is especially useful for online reading comprehension, because new technologies that continually appear online (e.g., new and revised search engine tools), require continually new online reading comprehension strategies to take advantage of their potential.

AN EVOLVING MODEL OF IRT

As we have come to understand the differences and the similarities between the contexts of Reciprocal Teaching and Internet Reciprocal Teaching, we have continued to investigate aspects of Internet Reciprocal Teaching during a yearlong formative experiment (see Reinking & Bradley, 2004, 2008) in five seventh-grade English language arts classrooms with a high proportion of low-achieving students. Instruction followed our three-phase model, seeking to develop online reading comprehension skills and strategies required to (1) generate online research questions; (2) locate information; (3) critically evaluate information; (4) synthesize information; and (5) communicate information among students.

Initially, the online reading comprehension skills that we sought to develop were informed by the patterns of strategy use demonstrated by approximately 50 proficient online readers, gathered during think-aloud sessions the previous year (see Carter & Henry, 2006; Coiro, Malloy, & Rogers, 2006; Leu & Castek, 2006; Leu et al., 2007). Throughout the year, we refined the structure of online reading experiences for students based on insights gained from an iterative cycle of data collection, including interviews and discussions among researchers, teachers, and sometimes students. We adjusted both *what* was taught and *how* it was taught, based on what appeared to enhance or inhibit the effectiveness of particular interventions in different classroom contexts (Castek & Reinking, 2006). Across the classrooms, we aimed to increase academic engagement, encourage active reading, and promote students as experts in online reading comprehension. These goals were based intentionally on those of Reciprocal Teaching (Palincsar & Brown, 1984). To achieve these goals, we encouraged student demonstrations of online reading comprehension to the maximum extent possible and supported strategy application across a wide range of online informational tasks.

Although we are still in the midst of analyzing the data collected in our formative experiment, we highlight here two important patterns that have begun to emerge from our work with students in urban and rural low-achieving school districts.

IRT Progresses through Three Phases of Online Reading Instruction

One important pattern that emerged from our formative experiments was that students required different levels of support at different points during the year in which we implemented IRT (Leu et al., 2007). Thus, we found it helpful to organize our thinking about online reading comprehension instruction into three phases that sought to accomplish the gradual release of responsibility for strategy instruction, which is a central aspect of Reciprocal Teaching (Palincsar, 1986a; Palincsar & Brown, 1984).

Phase 1: Teacher-Led Instruction

During Phase 1, students take part in teacher-led demonstrations designed to establish essential classroom routines and foundational Internet and computer skills. The teacher explicitly models online reading comprehension strategies and introduces procedures for conducting group discussions. Teaching procedures are designed to nurture collaborative group work skills among students. IRT lessons in this phase highlight foundational skills and strategies (e.g., handling laptops, opening and quitting applications, managing multiple windows) that serve as precursors to online reading comprehension. Instruction most often involves whole-class participation to facilitate think-aloud demonstrations. Toward the end of this phase, minilessons provide students with practice applying what they learned with a partner or two. Whereas the time spent in this phase may differ widely across classrooms, our work suggests that a gradual transition out of the teacher-led phase can be achieved when the majority of students demonstrate application of the skills and strategies listed on the observational checklist for Phase 1 (see Appendix 22.1).

Phase 2: Collaborative Modeling of Online Reading Comprehension Strategies

In Phase 2 of IRT, teachers and students begin to share the responsibility for introducing new strategies, and demonstrating how and when those strategies might be most useful. Lessons in this phase present small groups of students with common problems, often linked to key curriculum standards or goals, and designed to elicit important online reading comprehension skills. One day, for example, the groups in a class may be given these three problems and asked to solve them with the Internet:

1. How high is Mt. Fuji in Japan?
2. Find another, different answer to this same question.
3. Which answer do you think is most accurate and how did you determine that it was?

Students in each group are guided to discuss their solutions and to exchange reading comprehension strategies for locating information and critically evaluating information. Lessons are designed to minimize teacher talk and to maximize the time students engage with the task. An essential part of the lesson is time at the end of each period for students to debrief and to exchange strategies with the entire class after having already done so in their small groups.

Initially, lessons focus on locating and critically evaluating online information, and later, shift to synthesis and communication with a variety of online communication tools (e.g., e-mail, blogs, wikis, Google Docs, instant messages). Importantly, as this phase of instruction progresses, activities are carefully sequenced from more- to less-structured experiences to take maximum advantage of students' growing online reading knowledge and proficiency.

Because collaborative group exchanges of online reading comprehension strategies play an increasingly important role in this phase of instruction, students may sometimes be grouped homogeneously to contend collaboratively with an information challenge that targets a particular area of weakness. At other times, students may be heterogeneously grouped to share individual strengths while collaboratively solving online information problems. Consistent with the principles of Reciprocal Teaching, an important component of this second phase is working in groups to teach peers and their teacher(s) new strategies for navigating and comprehending information on the Internet. In this way, both teachers and students work together to document student progress on the observational checklist of Phase 2 strategies necessary for transitioning to Phase 3 (see Appendix 22.2). These activities reinforce students' growing independence as proficient online learners and prepare students for peer-teaching one another more regularly during Phase 3.

Phase 3: Inquiry

Finally, in Phase 3, instruction begins to move toward independent online inquiry related to the curriculum. Online work often takes place individually and in small groups, while the teacher acts more as a facilitator of online strategy use. Students develop their own questions to research or problems to solve using strategies introduced in Phase 2. Students are also encouraged to select what they believe to be the most effective means for communicating their findings, again applying strategies introduced earlier in instruction. Initially, in Phase 3, information is gathered and shared with reciprocal strategy support from students *within* the class. Later, the instructional focus shifts to provide support as students solve problems with students in other classrooms in their school or district, around the country, or even in other parts of the world via telecollaborative inquiry projects (Leu, Leu, & Coiro, 2004). Ultimately, students are invited to develop their own lines of inquiry related to their curriculum to demonstrate strategies spontaneously during authentic online reading experiences and to work collaboratively with others as they use the Internet to solve the important problems they have defined. It is especially at this point that students develop an understanding of how important it is to play an active role in their own learning about the curriculum and to experience firsthand the satisfaction associated with knowing how to question, locate, evaluate, synthesize, and communicate information on the Internet.

IRT Progresses from Simpler to More Complex Online Reading Comprehension Tasks

A second conclusion we have drawn from our formative observations of online reading comprehension instruction across five classrooms is that effective IRT lessons move progressively from simpler tasks that are somewhat similar to reading offline texts to more complex tasks that are quite different than reading offline texts. For example, we found it helpful to begin with demonstrations and strategy discussions that fostered skimming and scanning skills to locate specific information on a single Web page. Discussions centered around text features that lead readers to specific information on the page; students collaboratively shared strategies that helped clarify how good online readers strategically skim and scan a Web page, then check their facts by locating similar facts on other, reliable Web pages. Discussions that quickly led students to consider how to investigate an author's credibility and reliability provided a purpose for strategically skimming and scanning additional pages on a website where the information was found.

In turn, these discussions prompted students to search for information on other websites that they could use to confirm or to refute ideas by consulting additional sources. Discussions about the different types of search engines and how each worked prompted important new strategies for online reading comprehension. Amid these discussions, IRT lessons introduced tasks that offered students time to explore strategies for using keywords to narrow questions, using synonyms to revise searches on the same topic, and combining key words to refine searches effectively and locate specific information. Teachers and students modeled procedures for strategically reading search results and determining, for example, where to read for information on a search results page, how to determine when it was important to initiate a new search, or how to search more efficiently by attending to clues about the potential reliability of a website by examining the website's address as it appears in the results list. These types of lessons helped students learn how to make informed choices about where to read and how to navigate to reliable sites that contain information suited to their purposes for reading.

As students became more efficient with locating the information they sought, they had more time to read across multiple websites, summarize important information, and explore their options for communicating their findings to others. Reciprocal Teaching lessons then began to highlight strategies for organizing information into charts or idea webs, turning their collection of facts and multimedia resources into a cohesive summary, collaboratively editing their work, composing messages for particular audiences, and selecting appropriate communication tools. Small-group discussions focused on the skills and strategies required to use, among other technologies, instant messages, e-mail, blogs, and wikis. With support from the teacher and their classmates, students began to realize that each of these types of communication requires unique inferential reasoning skills to be used effectively. Students were given time to practice how to construct clear, appropriate messages for various contexts and purposes.

Over time, guided demonstrations of authentic research tasks aligned to the curriculum provided students with opportunities to apply different combinations of the online reading comprehension skills and strategies they had learned, and taught to others, in their Reciprocal Teaching discussions. Students were able to choose a related topic of interest, query search engines, locate relevant and reliable information, synthesize information from multiple sources, and communicate it to others using procedures appropriate to the type of communication tool they selected.

MEASURING THE POTENTIAL BENEFITS OF IRT

In addition to exploring new ways of thinking about new literacies instruction, we have begun to develop a number of different methodologies and instruments to measure proficiency in online reading comprehension. Although space does not allow for a detailed description of each assessment, we share below our think-aloud methodology and four broad categories of formal and informal instruments we have designed to evaluate the effects of IRT and, specifically, to determine whether instruction can improve offline and online reading comprehension and content area learning over time. Interested readers can see examples of these measures at *www.newliteracies.uconn.edu/irt*.

Student Think-Aloud Methodology

Process-based think-aloud methodologies (see Afflerbach, 2002; Pressley & Afflerbach, 1995) have provided an important window into the nature of online reading comprehension ability and how students respond to various online reading activities. Rich and complex think-aloud data have provided us information to systematically refine our evolving understanding of the online reading comprehension skills demonstrated by proficient and less skilled adolescent online readers. In a series of studies (see Leu & Castek, 2006; Leu,

Zawlinski, et al., 2007; New Literacies Research Team, 2005a), participants were asked to read online and to think aloud using both researcher- and student-selected reading assignments. Students' online reading sessions were recorded using Camtasia software (*www.techsmith.com/camtasia.asp*), which creates both a real-time movie of all online actions on the screen and an online recording of verbal think-aloud data.

Data from the Camtasia recordings were then transcribed, coded, and analyzed to reveal (1) the processes students use (or don't use) and (2) the understandings (or misconceptions) students may have about how best to compose task-related online questions, and to use a range of online contexts (e.g., search engines, informational websites, interactive images, e-mail, instant messages, and/or blogs) to locate, evaluate critically, synthesize, and communicate their answers to others. From our analyses, patterns of effective strategy use were systematically added to our evolving taxonomy of proficient online reading strategies. Likewise, patterns of ineffective online reading processes across several populations of adolescent readers helped to inform our decisions about the skills, strategies, and dispositions on which we might focus our sequence of IRT lessons.

Formative Assessments of Online Reading Comprehension Strategy Use

One fairly open-ended, easy-to-administer instrument is called the Formative Assessment of Students' Emerging Knowledge of Internet Strategies (FASEKIT). Once every 3–4 weeks, students are given approximately 15 minutes to list the most important strategies they employ on the Internet. They are also asked to explain why each strategy is important, and when they might use it as part of their online reading experience. This open-ended measure invites students to describe their online strategy use in their own words. A review of student responses can help to determine quickly the declarative, procedural, and conditional knowledge (Paris, Wasik, & Turner, 1991) that students may be acquiring from IRT lessons (and their interactions with peers), and highlight areas of misunderstanding that may be addressed in upcoming lessons.

Curriculum-Based Information Challenges

A second category of useful measures designed to assess online reading comprehension ability is challenges to find information that require a range of Internet technologies and link directly to a particular curricular theme or learning objective. As members of the TICA Project (Leu et al., 2007) we conducted a formative experiment of how IRT might help to accomplish its pedagogical goals. For example, we investigated the use of (1) leveled Jeopardy-style blog challenges to evaluate seventh graders' online reading proficiency while studying biographies; (2) a mystery e-mail challenge that integrated samples of descriptive writing and personal letters to evaluate the development of new literacy strategies as part of a unit on narrative writing; (3) a Wikipedia activity that challenged students to share information they researched about respiratory scientists with a worldwide audience; (4) an informational website challenge designed to prompt prediction and inferential reasoning skills as part of an interdisciplinary unit on the Holocaust; and (5) an interactive blog discussion that assessed seventh-grade students' ability to share their critical evaluation strategies to determine which informational websites were reliable and unreliable. In each case, observational data and feedback from students and teachers suggested that informal measures of online reading comprehension can be effectively integrated into authentic classroom literacy activities and aligned to grade-level objectives in reading, language arts, and content area curricula. Sample tasks and student responses can be found for each of these online informational challenges at *www.newliteracies.uconn.edu/irt*.

Performance-Based Assessments of Online Reading Comprehension Ability

A third type of instrument that has demonstrated the ability to estimate online reading performance validly and reliably among adolescent readers is called the Online Reading Comprehension Assessment (ORCA). In our work, we have developed several ORCA instruments (see Coiro, 2006) that invite students to solve a series of online information requests about middle school topics such as homelessness, the solar system, human body systems, and the Iditarod sled dog races. These rubric-guided measures have asked students to search for, locate, critically evaluate, synthesize, and communicate solutions to online information requests using instant messaging (ORCA–Instant Message; New Literacies Research Team, 2005a), e-mail and blog technologies (ORCA–Blog Human Body Systems; New Literacies Research Team, 2005a), and an online quiz interface (ORCA–Scenarios I and II [Coiro, 2007] and ORCA–Iditarod [Leu & Reinking, 2005]).

Data from these studies provided evidence suggesting that the ORCA instruments have demonstrated the ability to measure online reading proficiency and evaluate the potential of classroom instruction for increasing online reading comprehension over time. In one study (New Literacies Research Team, 2005a), scores on the ORCA–Instant Message and ORCA–Blog measures suggested that high Internet integration coupled with 12 weeks of strategy instruction yielded statistically higher scores in online reading comprehension and equivalent levels of science concept learning among seventh-grade students in one science classroom compared to a control group in another science classroom. In addition, a low correlation between scores on the ORCA–Blog and standardized reading scores provided preliminary evidence that online reading is not isomorphic with offline reading.

In a study from Year 2 of our TICA project (Leu & Reinking, 2005), results of paired t-test analyses indicated a statistically significant increase in mean scores on the ORCA–Iditarod from the beginning to the end of the year across at-risk students in five middle school reading and/or language arts classrooms. Data from a third study that used the ORCA–Scenarios I and II (Coiro, 2007) revealed additional evidence that online reading comprehension ability is not isomorphic with offline reading comprehension ability. Taken together, data from these three studies informed the development of a rubric-guided ORCA instrument called the ORCA–Iditarod—Revised. This assessment is being used in a randomized experimental study in Year 3 of the TICA project to evaluate the extent to which IRT instruction can improve students' comprehension and learning offline and online in four diverse classroom settings. These measures may be viewed online at *www.newliteracies.uconn.edu/irt*.

Objective Measures of Online Reading Comprehension Ability

A fourth category of measures involves the use of multiple-choice and short-answer items to estimate a student's level of online reading comprehension ability. Although we believe there are several limitations to estimating online reading proficiency with a set of isolated multiple-choice items, it would be useful to have valid instruments that require less time to administer and less time to score than performance based ORCA assessments. Initial efforts to measure online reading comprehension from a new literacies perspective with isolated skill items (Carter & Henry, 2006), as opposed to a series of scenario-based tasks, have demonstrated the potential for future work in this area. Henry (2007) revised this instrument to develop the Digital Divide Measurement Scale for Students (DDMS-S), which included 14 forced-response items that measured reading to locate and reading to critically evaluate online information. The items proved to be both statistically valid and reliable among scores of 1,768 middle school students, thus providing an objective alternative to a rubric scoring system for estimating skills in online location and critical evaluation.

Given the promising results of Henry's work, we have recently begun to develop a series of parallel, multiple-choice items to be used in a repeated-measures design to capture and track growth in online reading comprehension ability at four particular points over the course of a 20-week intervention. By collecting data with parallel objective items across four points in time, in conjunction with the pre- to posttest estimates of online reading comprehension proficiency measured with the process-based ORCA–Iditarod—Revised, we will then have the ability to accomplish several important goals. First, we will be able to more closely examine the relation of scores across the two types of instruments. Second, we will be able to compare possible gains and losses associated with each assessment. Finally, we will be able to consider the relative utility of each as a valid way of evaluating the potential of IRT to improve online reading achievement among adolescents at risk of dropping out of school.

PUBLIC POLICY FAILURES AND FUTURE RESEARCH

Most would agree that achieving high levels of online reading comprehension is an essential requirement for full participation in the age of the Internet. Unfortunately, however, little is being done to accomplish that goal in schools (Partnership for 21st Century Skills, 2004). Students seldom receive instruction in online reading comprehension (Henry, 2007) and no U.S. state systematically includes online reading comprehension skills in its state standards or in state reading comprehension assessments (Leu, Ataya, & Coiro, 2002). Indeed, the National Assessment of Educational Progress (NAEP), *The Nation's Report Card* in the United States (Lee, Grigg, & Donahue, 2007), fails to include any online reading comprehension skills, such as the reading of search engine results. Of even greater concern, however, the recently constructed *NAEP Reading Framework* (National Assessment Governing Board, 2004) includes no online reading comprehension skills. Because of this omission, online reading comprehension ability will not be evaluated in any of *The Nation's Report Card* reports until at least 2019, when a new framework will be developed (Leu, 2007).

Public Policy

The current No Child Left Behind (NCLB) legislation (U.S. Department of Education, 2002), with its focus on testing skills and strategies required for offline but not online reading comprehension may be exacerbating the very problem it seeks to solve. Economically challenged school districts currently have little incentive to include online reading comprehension skills in their instructional programs, because they are under the greatest pressure to raise reading test scores on assessments that have nothing to do with online reading comprehension. As a result, many students go unsupported in developing the literacies of online reading comprehension in school. This unfortunate omission is especially true for students who require our support the most—those who have access to the Internet at home the least (Leu, 2007).

This situation raises one of the most central questions for public policy in the United States: *Why are the new literacies of online reading comprehension not included in any national or state assessments of reading comprehension?* This unfortunate situation severely compromises the potential and the future of students in the United States. To continue ignoring online reading comprehension in reading assessments and during classroom reading instruction is to reify a static and increasingly less relevant understanding of reading comprehension in a world that has gone online, global, and networked. More importantly, this practice appears to harm the very students who are in need of our greatest assistance with reading comprehension.

Directions for Future Research

A more systematic integration of online reading comprehension into classroom instruction and assessment should be a high priority for future research. However, to be useful, that research must be conducted at multiple levels of our educational system, because profound changes are called for that affect multiple levels of education, including assessment, instruction, curriculum, teacher education, professional development, and school leadership, to name just a few. A number of important research questions need to be addressed to build on the emerging research base that is developing around the changing nature of reading comprehension:

1. *What are the most reliable and valid ways of assessing online reading comprehension to provide classroom teachers and school leadership teams with the most useful information to inform instruction?* The upcoming PISA International Assessment of Reading (Organization for Economic Cooperation and Development, n.d.) and the assessment approaches described in this chapter are just the beginning of efforts needed to determine optimal methods for assessing online reading comprehension. Much more work is needed in this area to understand more fully optimal assessment strategies for the variety of needs we have.

2. *How should IRT or other instructional practices be modified to support students, at all grade levels, to develop greater online reading comprehension ability?* Much more work needs to follow initial attempts to understand effective classroom instruction, including the use of a broader range of research methodologies, such as formative and design experiments. Furthermore, important work has yet to be conducted with younger students to determine the contexts in which their learning of online reading comprehension strategies is optimized.

3. *What curriculum resources best support the needs of teachers and students in developing online reading comprehension skills and strategies?* To support classroom instruction, we will require extensive curricular resources that promote the development of the new literacies of online reading comprehension, and important research efforts to evaluate optimal curricular materials designed to increase online reading comprehension.

4. *How might teacher education best support the development of new teachers who can effectively integrate the skills and strategies of online reading comprehension into classroom instruction?* A central aspect of change will be the effective preparation of new teachers in this area. An innovative study, such as the one being carried out in the University of Connecticut's secondary teacher education program, seeks to prepare a new generation of middle and high school teachers who are fluent with the new literacies of online reading comprehension, and integrate them into their subject area curriculum (Hartman, Leu, Olson, & Truxaw, 2005).

5. How might professional development be organized most effectively to prepare teachers for the changes in reading comprehension that have occurred during their lifetimes? An entire generation of teachers will require extensive professional development to manage the transition effectively from offline to online reading comprehension. Many teachers will need to acquire these new literacies themselves.

6. How might school leadership teams be prepared to provide the vision and leadership to direct the changing nature of reading comprehension instruction in their schools and districts? Change happens only in schools whose leaders have the vision to support that change. This will require retraining a generation of school leaders to understand the reading changes that have taken place in an online world.

7. What might be the impact of after-school "new literacies" clubs on the in-school reading comprehension proficiencies of struggling online and offline readers? Because many of the tools and much of the access to online content are available in out-of-school contexts, how could it impact the in-school comprehension skills of struggling readers?

As these questions suggest, a new and ambitious agenda of reading comprehension research is needed. That agenda will require all of us to devote our attention to the changing nature of reading comprehension, reading comprehension instruction, and reading comprehension assessment.

PROJECTIONS AND POSSIBILITIES FOR THE CLASSROOM OF 2030?

In a world of rapidly changing technologies, it is impossible to predict what might take place even just a few years into the future. Prediction in this area is a dangerous game because the landscape is rapidly and repeatedly changing. Who, for example, might have predicted the appearance of MySpace, Facebook, Second Life, Wikipedia, YouTube, or any other recent technologies just 5 years ago? Nevertheless, some possible outlines can be anticipated, assuming that public policies change to include the new literacies of online reading comprehension within increasingly important national and state assessments. First, it is likely that one-to-one computing and wireless access to the Internet will become a reality in every school. It is also likely that students and teachers will engage in important online reading projects to advance content area learning while they also develop greater proficiency with online reading comprehension. In addition, it is quite likely that as we begin to discover the potential of the Internet for increasing our understanding of the world around us, students will collaborate with other students around the world on common learning projects (Leu, Leu, & Coiro, 2004), increasing life's opportunities for every child. Based on the promise of emerging research on the new literacies of reading comprehension, our hope is that we will be insightful enough, and our public policies foresighted enough, to bring this world to reality sooner rather than later.

INTEGRATE, INVESTIGATE, AND INITIATE: QUESTIONS FOR DISCUSSION

1. Throughout Chapter 22 and in several other chapters in this book, authors have stressed the importance of online comprehension. From the information you read in this chapter and in others, describe the differences between online and offline reading comprehension. Write your description as if you were answering this question for parents and others outside of the education profession.

2. In this chapter, IRT research was presented. Several other chapters in this book have presented research on the use of traditional Reciprocal Teaching in reading classes and in content area courses. What are the most important differences of this method of comprehension instruction when presented in reading classes, content area courses, and through the medium of the Internet? Why are these distinctions important for students to experience?

3. Make a Letterman's Top Ten List of the Ten Most Important Ways in Which Online Reading Comprehension is Different from Offline Reading Comprehension. Rank-order your 10 items with number 1 being the most important difference, Explain your decisions.

ACKNOWLEDGMENTS

Portions of this material are based upon work supported by the Institute for Education Sciences and the U.S. Department of Education under Award No. R305G050154, the North Central Regional Educational Lab/Learning Point Associates, and the Carnegie Corporation. Opinions expressed herein are solely those of the authors and do not necessarily represent the position of either the U.S. Department of Education, the North Central Regional Educational Lab, or the Carnegie Corporation.

Important contributions to this work have been made by members of the Internet Reading Comprehension Research Team at Clemson University: Amy Carter, Jackie Malloy, Kathy Robbins, and Angela Rogers.

REFERENCES

Afflerbach, P. (2002). The use of think-aloud protocols and verbal reports as research methodology. In M. Kamil (Ed.), *Methods of literacy research* (pp. 87–103). Hillsdale, NJ: Erlbaum.

Alfassi, M. (1998). Reading for meaning: The efficacy of reciprocal teaching in fostering reading comprehension in high school students in remedial reading classes. *American Educational Research Journal, 35,* 309–332.

Beach, R., & O'Brien, D. (2008). Teaching popular culture texts in the classroom. In J. Coiro, M. Knobel, C. Lankshear, & D. J. Leu (Eds.), *Handbook of research on new literacies*. Mahwah, NJ: Erlbaum.

Bennett, R. E., Persky, H., Weiss, A. R., & Jenkins, F. (2007). *Problem solving in technology-rich environments: A report from the NAEP technology-based assessment project*. Retrieved October 5, 2007, from *nces.ed.gov/pubsearch/pubsinfo.asp?pubid=2007466*.

Bleha, T. (2005, May/June). Down to the wire. *Foreign Affairs* website. Retrieved December 15, 2005, from *www.foreignaffairs.org/20050501faessay84311/thomas-bleha/down-to-the-wire.html*.

Borzekowski, D., Fobil, J., & Asante, K. (2006). Online access by adolescents in Accra: Ghanaian teens' use of the Internet for health information. *Developmental Psychology, 42,* 450–458. Retrieved December 1, 2006, from *www.apa.org/journals/releases/dev423450.pdf*.

Brand-Gruwel, S., Aarnoutse, C., & Van Den Bos, K.P. (1997). Improving text comprehension strategies in reading and listening settings. *Learning and Instruction, 8,* 63–81.

Brown, A. L., & Palincsar, A. S. (1989). Guided cooperative learning and individual knowledge acquisition. In L. B. Resnick (Ed.), *Cognition and instruction: Issues and agendas* (pp. 393–451). Hillsdale, NJ: Erlbaum.

Carter, A., & Henry, L. A. (2006). *A survey of Internet usage and online reading: In-school and out-of-school settings*. In D. Reinking & D. J. Leu (Chairs), Studying the new literacies of online reading comprehension among adolescents at risk to become dropouts. Paper presented at the annual meeting of the National Reading Conference, Los Angeles, CA.

Castek, J. (in press). *An examination of classroom instruction that integrates the new literacies of online reading comprehension: Exploring the contexts that facilitate acquisition and the learning outcomes that result*. Dissertation being completed at the University of Connecticut, Storrs, CT.

Castek, J., Leu, D. J., Jr., Coiro, J., Gort, M., Henry, L. A., & Lima, C. (2008). Developing new literacies among multilingual learners in the elementary grades. In L. Parker (Ed.), *Technology-based learning environments for young English learners: In and out of school connections*. Mahwah, NJ: Erlbaum.

Castek, J., & Reinking, D. (2006, December). *Working with teachers in a formative experiment*. In D. J. Leu, Jr. (Chair), Studying the new literacies of online reading comprehension among adolescents at risk to become dropouts. An alternative symposium session presented at the National Reading Conference, Los Angeles, CA. Available online at *www.newliteracies.uconn.edu/iesproject/events.html*.

Coiro, J. (2003). Reading comprehension on the Internet: Expanding our understanding to encompass new literacies. *Reading Teacher, 56*, 458–464.

Coiro, J. (2006). *Measuring internet comprehension: Accessing, evaluating, and communicating information*. In D. Reinking & D. Leu (Chairs), Developing Internet reading comprehension strategies among adolescents at risk to become dropouts. Poster presented at the annual meeting of the American Educational Research Association, Chicago, IL.

Coiro, J. (2007). *Exploring changes to reading comprehension on the Internet: Paradoxes and possibilities for diverse adolescent readers*. Unpublished doctoral dissertation, University of Connecticut, Storrs. Available online at *www.newliteracies.uconn.edu/coirodissertation/*.

Coiro, J., & Dobler, E. (2007). Exploring the comprehension strategies used by sixth-grade skilled readers as they search for and locate information on the Internet. *Reading Research Quarterly, 42*, 214–257.

Coiro, J., Knobel, M., Lankshear, C., & Leu, D. J. (Eds.). (2008a). *Handbook of research in new literacies*. Mahwah, NJ: Erlbaum.

Coiro, J., Knobel, M., Lankshear, C., & Leu, D. J. (2008b). Central issues in new literacies and new literacies research. In J. Coiro, M. Knobel, C. Lankshear, & D. J. Leu (Eds.), *Handbook of research in new literacies*. Mahwah, NJ: Erlbaum.

Coiro, J., Malloy, J., & Rogers, A. (2006). *Patterns of effective strategy use among adolescent readers*. In D. Reinking & D. J. Leu (Chairs), Studying the new literacies of online reading comprehension among adolescents at risk to become dropouts. Paper presented at the annual meeting of the National Reading Conference, Los Angeles, CA.

Cooper, J. D., Boschken, I., McWilliams, J., & Pistochini, L. (2000). A study of the effectiveness of an intervention program designed to accelerate reading for struggling readers in the upper grades. In T. Shanahan & F. V. Rodriguez-Brown (Eds.), *49th yearbook of the National Reading Conference* (pp. 477–486). Chicago: National Reading Conference.

Cope, B., & Kalantzis, M. (2000). *Multiliteracies*. London: Routledge.

Dalton, B., & Proctor, C. P. (2008). Understanding understanding in a new literacies space: Changing the relationship of text, reader and activity in service of improving diverse learners' comprehension. In J. Coiro, M. Knobel, C. Lankshear, & D. J. Leu (Eds.), *Handbook of research in new literacies*. Mahwah, NJ: Erlbaum.

de Argaez, E. (2006, January). *Internet world stats news, 14*. Retrieved February 1, 2006, from *www.internetworldstats.com/pr/edi014.htm#3*.

DeCorte, E., Verschaffel, L., & Van De Ven, A. (2001). Improving text comprehension strategies in upper primary school children: A design experiment. *British Journal of Educational Psychology, 71*, 531–559.

Dunleavy, M., Dexter, S., & Heinecke, W. F. (2007). What added value does a 1:1 student to laptop ratio bring to technology-supported teaching and learning? *Journal of Computer Assisted Learning, 23*, 440–452.

Fallows, D. (2005). *Search engine users*. Pew/Internet and American Life Project. Retrieved July 1, 2006, from *www.pewinternet.org/ppf/r/146/report_display.asp*.

Friedman, T. L. (2005). *The world is flat: A brief history of the twenty-first century.* New York: Farrar, Straus & Giroux.

Fung, I. Y., Wilkinson, I., & Moore, D. W. (2003). L1-assisted reciprocal teaching to improve ESL students' comprehension of English expository text. *Learning and Instruction, 13,* 1–31.

Gee, J. (2003). *What video games have to teach us about learning and literacy.* New York: Palgrave.

Hacker, D. J., & Tenent, A. (2002). Implementing reciprocal teaching in the classroom: Overcoming obstacles and making modifications. *Journal of Educational Psychology, 94,* 699–718.

Hartman, D. K., Leu, D. J., Olson, M. R., & Truxaw, M. P. (2005). *Reading and writing to learn with the "new literacies": Preparing a new generation of teachers and researchers to develop literate American adolescents.* New York: Adolescent Literacy Preservice Initiative, Carnegie Corporation of New York.

Henry, L. A. (2006). SEARCHing for an answer: The critical role of new literacies while reading on the Internet. *Reading Teacher, 59,* 614–627.

Henry, L. A. (2007). *Exploring new literacies pedagogy and online reading comprehension among middle school students and teachers: Issues of social equity or social exclusion?* Unpublished doctoral dissertation, University of Connecticut, Storrs.

Hull, G., & Schultz, K. (Eds.). (2002). *School's out!: Bridging out-of-school literacies with classroom practice.* New York: Teachers College Press.

Internet world stats. (n.d.). *Usage and population statistics.* Retrieved October 25, 2005, from www.internetworldstats.com/stats.htm.

Kaiser Family Foundation. (2005). *Generation M: Media in the lives of 8- to 18-year-olds.* Retrieved September 15, 2007, from www.kff.org/entmedia/7251.cfm.

Kress, G. (2000). *Multiliteracies: Literacy learning and the design of social futures.* South Yarra, Australia: Macmillan.

Lankshear, C., & Knobel, M. (2003). *New literacies.* Maidenhead, UK: Open University Press.

Lankshear, C., & Knobel, M. (2006). *New literacies, Second edition.* Maidenhead, UK: Open University Press.

Lee, J., Grigg, W., & Donahue, P. (2007). *The nation's report card: Reading 2007* (NCES Publication No. 2007-496). Washington, DC: National Center for Education Statistics, Institute of Education Sciences, U.S. Department of Education.

Leu, D. J. (2007, May 12). *What happened when we weren't looking?: How reading comprehension has changed and what we need to do about it.* Invited keynote address to the Research Conference of the International Reading Association, Toronto, Canada.

Leu, D. J., Ataya, R., & Coiro, J. (2002, December). *Assessing assessment strategies among the 50 states: Evaluating the literacies of our past or our future?* Paper presented at the National Reading Conference, Miami, FL.

Leu, D. J., & Castek, J. (2006). *What online reading comprehension skills and strategies are characteristic of more accomplished adolescent users of the Internet.* In D. Reinking & D. Leu (Chairs), Developing Internet reading comprehension strategies among adolescents at risk to become dropouts. Poster presented at the annual meeting of the American Educational Research Association, Chicago, IL.

Leu, D. J., Castek, J., Hartman, D., Coiro, J., Henry, L., Kulikowich, J., et al. (2005). *Evaluating the development of scientific knowledge and new forms of reading comprehension during online learning* [Final report presented to the North Central Regional Educational Laboratory/Learning Point Associates]. Retrieved May 15, 2006, from www.newliteracies.uconn.edu/ncrel.html.

Leu, D. J., & Hartman, D. K. (2007, September). *What skills are required for successful online reading comprehension?: What do students who are high-performing, online readers tell us?* Paper presented at the annual meeting of the New England Reading Association, Augusta, ME.

Leu, D. J., Jr., Kinzer, C. K., Coiro, J., & Cammack, D. (2004). Toward a theory of new literacies emerging from the Internet and other information and communication technologies. In R. B. Ruddell & N. Unrau (Eds.), *Theoretical models and processes of reading* (5th ed., 1568–1611). Newark, DE: International Reading Association.

Leu, D. J., Jr., Leu, D. D., & Coiro, J. (2004). *Teaching with the Internet: New literacies for new times* (4th ed.). Norwood, MA: Christopher-Gordon.

Leu, D. J., & Reinking, D. (2005). *Developing Internet comprehension strategies among adolescent students at risk to become dropouts.* U.S. Department of Education, Institute of Education Sciences Research Grant. Retrieved June 20, 2006, from *www.newliteracies.uconn.edu/ies.html.*

Leu, D. J., Reinking, D., Carter, A., Castek, J., Coiro, J., Henry, L. A., et al. (2007, April 9). *Defining online reading comprehension: Using think-aloud verbal protocols to refine a preliminary model of Internet reading comprehension processes.* Paper presented at the American Educational Research Association, Chicago, IL. Available online at *docs.google.com/doc?id=dcbjhrtq_10djqrhz.*

Leu, D. J., Zawlinski, L., Castek, J., Banerjee, M., Housand, B., Liu, Y., et al. (2007). What is new about the new literacies of online reading comprehension? In A. Berger, L. Rush, & J. Eakle (Eds.), *Secondary school reading and writing: What research reveals for classroom practices.* National Council of Teachers of English, Urbana, IL.

Livingstone, S., & Bober, M. (2005). *UK children go online: Final report of key project findings.* London: London School of Economics and Political Science.

Ludlow, A. (2006, March 2). *Rolling out the national e-Mexico system.* Paper presented at the Digital Cities Convention, Houston, TX. Retrieved March 15, 2006, from *www.w2idigitalcitiesconvention.com/02282006/e_s/emexico.html.*

Matteucci, N., O'Mahony, M., Robinson, C., & Zwick, T. (2005). Productivity, workplace performance and ICT: Industry and firm-level evidence for Europe and the US. *Scottish Journal of Political Economy.* 52, 359–386.

Merchant, G. (2008). Digital writing in the early years. In J. Coiro, M. Knobel, C. Lankshear, & D. J. Leu (Eds.), *Handbook of research in new literacies.* Mahwah, NJ: Erlbaum.

National Assessment Governing Board. (2004). *NAEP reading framework.* Retrieved July 15, 2007, from *www.naepreading.org/.*

New Literacies Research Team (Castek, J., Coiro, J., Fogarty, E., Hartman, Henry, L. A., & Leu, D. J., Jr.). (2005a, December). *A methodology for studying the new literacies of online reading comprehension.* National Reading Conference. Miami, FL.

New Literacies Research Team. (2005b). *New literacies for learning.* In D. J. Leu (Chair), New literacies for learning. Paper presented at the Annual Meeting of the American Educational Research Association, Montreal, Quebec.

New Literacies Research Team. (2007). New literacies, new challenges, and new opportunities. In M. B. Sampson, S. Szabo, F. Falk-Ross, M. M. Foote, & P. E. Linder (Eds.), *Multiple literacies in the 21st century: The 28th yearbook of the College Reading Association* (pp. 31–50). Logan, UT: College Reading Association.

New London Group. (1996). A pedagogy of multiliteracies: Designing social futures. *Harvard Educational Review,* 66(1), 60–92.

New London Group. (2000). A pedagogy of multiliteracies designing social futures. In B. Cope & M. Kalantzis (Eds.), *Multiliteracies: Literacy learning and the design of social futures* (pp. 9–37). London: Routledge.

Organization for Economic Cooperation and Development. (n.d.). *The OECD programme for international student assessment.* Retrieved August 15, 2007, from *www.oecd.org/dataoecd/51/27/37474503.pdf.*

Palincsar, A. S. (1986a). Reciprocal Teaching. In *Teaching reading as thinking.* Oak Brook, IL: North Central Regional Educational Laboratory.

Palincsar, A. S. (1986b). Metacognitive strategy instruction. *Exceptional Children,* 53, 118–124.

Palincsar, A. S., & Brown, A. L. (1984). Reciprocal Teaching of comprehension-fostering and comprehension-monitoring activities. *Cognition and Instruction,* 1, 117–175.

Palincsar, A. S., & Klenk, L. (1992). Fostering literacy learning in supportive contexts. *Journal of Learning Disabilities,* 25, 211–225, 229.

Paris, S. G., Wasik, B. A., & Turner, J. C. (1991). The development of strategic readers. In R. Barr,

M. L. Kamil, P. Mosenthal, & P. D. Pearson (Eds.), *Handbook of reading research* (pp. 609–640). White Plains, NY: Longman.

Paris, S. G., Wasik, B. A., & Turner, J. C. (1991). The development of strategic readers. In R. Barr, M. L. Kamil, P. Mosenthal, & P. D. Pearson (Eds.), *Handbook of reading research* (Vol. 2, pp. 609–640). White Plains, NY: Longman.

Partnership for 21st Century Skills. (2004). *Learning for the 21st century*. Retrieved August 15, 2006, from *www.21stcenturyskills.org/reports/learning.asp*.

Partnership for 21st Century Skills. (2006). *Are they really ready for work?: Employer's perspectives on the basic knowledge and applied skills of new entrants to the 21st Century U.S. Workforce* [Report written in collaboration with the Conference Board, Corporate Voices for Working Families, the Partnership for 21st Century Skills, and the Society for Human Resource Management]. Retrieved December 9, 2006, from *www.21stcenturyskills.org/documents/final_report_pdf9-29-06.pdf*.

Pew Internet and American Life Project. (2001). *The Internet and education: Findings of the Pew Internet and American Life Project*. Retrieved October 15, 2002, from *www.pewInternet.org/reports*.

Pew Internet and American Life Project. (2005). *Teens and technology*. Retrieved April 15, 2006, from *www.pewinternet.org/topics.asp?c=4*.

Pressley, M., & Afflerbach, P. (1995). *Verbal protocols for reading: The nature of constructively responsive reading*. Hillsdale, NJ: Erlbaum.

Reinking, D., & Bradley, B. A. (2004). Connecting research and practice using formative and design experiments. In N. Duke & M. Mallette (Eds.), *Literacy research methodologies* (pp. 149–169). New York: Guilford Press.

Reinking, D., & Bradley, B. A. (2008). *On formative and design experiments*. New York: Teachers College Press.

Riley, T. (2003, August 4). *An overview of the knowledge economy*. eGov Monitor Weekly. Retrieved September 15, 2005, from *www.egovmonitor.com/features/riley07.html*.

Rosenshine, B., & Meister, C. (1994). Reciprocal teaching: A review of the research. *Review of Educational Research, 64*, 479–530.

Snyder, I., & Bulfin, S. (2008). Using new media in the secondary English classroom. In J. Coiro, M. Knobel, C. Lankshear, & D. J. Leu (Eds.), *Handbook of research in new literacies*. Mahwah, NJ: Erlbaum.

Street, B. (1998). New literacies in theory and practice: What are the implications for language in education? *Linguistics and Education, 10*(1), 1–24.

Taboada, A., & Guthrie, J. T. (2006). Contributions of student questioning and prior knowledge to construction of knowledge from reading information text. *Journal of Literacy Research, 38*, 1–35.

Unsworth, L. (2008). Multiliteracies and metalanguage: Describing image/text relations as a resource for negotiating multimodal texts. In J. Coiro, M. Knobel, C. Lankshear, & D. J. Leu (Eds.), *Handbook of research in new literacies*. Mahwah, NJ: Erlbaum.

U.S. Department of Commerce: National Telecommunications and Information Administration. (2002). *A nation online: How Americans are expanding their use of the Internet*. Washington, DC: Author.

U.S. Department of Education. (2002). *No Child Left Behind Act of 2001*. Washington DC: Author. Retrieved September 22, 2005, from *www.ed.gov/policy/elsec/leg/esea02/index.html*.

Van Ark, B., Inklaar, R., & McGuckin, R.H. (2003). ICT productivity in Europe and the United States: Where do the differences come from? *CESifo Economic Studies. 49*, 295–318.

Wyatt-Smith, C., & Elkins, J. (2008). Multimodal reading and comprehension in online environments. In J. Coiro, M. Knobel, C. Lankshear, & D. J. Leu (Eds.), *Handbook of research in new literacies*, Mahwah, NJ: Erlbaum.

Zucker, A. (2004). Developing a research agenda for ubiquitous computing in schools. *Journal of Educational Computing Research, 30*, 371–386.

APPENDIX 22.1. TICA Basic Skills (Phase 1) Checklist[1]

Most of the students and all of the groups in my class know how to:	
Computer Basics	**Comment**
☐ Turn a computer on/off.	
☐ Use the mouse/track pad.	
☐ Follow classroom and school rules for computer use.	
☐ Open programs and files using icons and/or the Start Menu (PC).	
☐ Log on and log off from individual file space.	
☐ Create/open a new folder/file.	
☐ Launch a word processor.	
☐ Open a word processing file.	
☐ Type a short entry in a word processing file.	
☐ Copy text.	
☐ Cut text.	
☐ Paste text.	
☐ Delete text.	
☐ Name a word processing file and save it.	
☐ Open a new window.	
☐ Open a new tab.	
Web Searching Basics	
☐ Locate and open a search engine.	
☐ Type key words in the correct location of a search engine.	
☐ Type addresses in the address window.	
☐ Use the Refresh button.	
☐ Use the "BACK" and "FORWARD" buttons.	
☐ Use a search engine for simple key word searches.	
General Navigation Basics	
☐ Maximize/minimize windows.	
☐ Open and quit applications.	
☐ Toggle between windows.	
E-Mail Basics	
☐ Locate and open an e-mail program.	
☐ Attach documents to e-mail messages.	
☐ Compose, edit, and send email messages.	
☐ Receive and reply to messages.	

---

[1] These skills and strategies inform and guide instruction during Phase 1, but they are not intended to limit instruction. New skill and strategy needs will emerge within each classroom. Each teacher must respond to (and document) those additional skill and strategy needs during the year. When most students and all groups can accomplish this list, the move to Phase 2 will take place.

APPENDIX 22.2. TICA Phase 2 Checklist[1]

Most of the students and all of the groups in my class know how to:	
Understand and Develop Questions	Lesson Evidence and Comments
Teacher-Generated Questions	
☐ Use strategies to ensure initial understanding of the question such as: • Rereading the question to make sure they understand it. • Paraphrasing the question. • Taking notes on the question. • Thinking about the needs of the person who asked the question.	
☐ Use strategies to monitor an understanding of the question such as: • Knowing when to review the question. • Checking an answer in relation to the question to ensure it is complete.	
Student-Generated Questions	
☐ Determine what a useful initial question is, based on a variety of factors that include interest, audience, purpose, and the nature of the inquiry activity.	
☐ Determine a clear topic and focus for questions to guide the search for information.	
☐ Modify questions, when appropriate, using strategies such as the following: • Narrowing the focus of the question. • Expanding the focus of the question. • Developing a new or revised question that is more appropriate after gathering information.	
Locate Information	Lesson Evidence and Comments
Locating Information By Using a Search Engine and Its Results Page	
☐ Locate at least one search engine.	
☐ Use key words in a search window on a browser that has this or on a separate search engine.	
☐ Use several of the following general search engine strategies during key word entry: • Topic and focus • Single and multiple key word entries • Phrases for key word entry	
☐ Use several of the following more specialized search engine strategies during key word entry: • Quotation marks • Paraphrases and synonyms • Boolean • Advanced search tool use	

[1] These skills and strategies inform and guide instruction during Phase 1, but they are not intended to limit instruction. New skill and strategy needs will emerge within each classroom. Each teacher must respond to (and document) those additional skill and strategy needs during the year. When most students and all groups can accomplish this list, the move to Phase 2 will take place.

☐	Copy and paste keywords and phases into the search engine window while searching for information.	
☐	Read search engine results effectively to determine the most useful resource for a task using strategies such as: • Knowing which portions of a search results page are sponsored, containing commercially placed links, and which are not. • Skimming the main results before reading more narrowly. • Reading summaries carefully and inferring meaning in the search engine results page to determine the best possible site to visit. • Understanding the meaning of bold face terms in the results. • Understanding the meaning of URLs in search results (.com, .org, .edu, .net). • Knowing when the first item is not the best item for a question. • Monitoring the extent to which a search results page matches the information needs. • Knowing how to use the history pull down menu.	
☐	Monitor the multiple aspects of search engine use and make appropriate revisions and changes throughout the process.	
☐	Select from a variety of search engine strategies to locate useful resources when an initial search is unsuccessful: • Knows the use and meaning of the "Did you mean . . . ?" feature in Google. • Adjusts search engine key words according to the results of a search. • Narrows the search. • Expands the search. • Reads search results to discover the correct vocabulary and then use this more appropriate vocabulary in a new search. • Shifts to another search engine.	
☐	Bookmark a site and access it later.	
☐	Use specialized search engines for images, videos, and other media sources.	
Locating Information within a Website		
☐	Quickly determine if a site is potentially useful and worth more careful reading.	
☐	Read more carefully at a site to determine if the required information is located there.	
☐	Predict information behind a link accurately to make efficient choices about where information is located.	
☐	Use structural knowledge of a Web page to help locate information, including the use of directories.	
☐	Recognize when you have left a site and know how to return back to the original site.	
☐	Know how to open a second browser window to locate information, without losing the initial Web page.	
☐	Know how to use an internal search engine to locate information at a site.	
☐	Monitor the reading of a Web page and knows when it contains useful information and when it does not.	

Critically Evaluate Information	Lesson Evidence and Comments
Bias and Stance	
☐ Identify, evaluate, and recognize that all websites have an agenda, perspective, or bias.	
☐ Identify and evaluate bias, given a website with a clear bias.	
☐ Identify and evaluate the author of a website whenever visiting an important new site.	
☐ Use information about the author of a site to evaluate how information will be biased at that site.	
Reliability	
☐ Investigate multiple sources to compare and contrast the reliability of information.	
☐ Identify several markers that may affect reliability such as: • Is this a commercial site? • Is the author an authoritative source (e.g., professor, scientist, librarian, etc.)? • Does the website have links that are broken? • Does the information make sense? • Does the author include links to other reliable websites? • Does the website contain numerous typos? • Does the URL provide any clues to reliability? • Do the images or videos appear to be altered?	
☐ Understand that Wikipedia is a reasonable, but imperfect, portal of information.	
☐ Identify the general purpose of a website (entertainment, educational, commercial, persuasive, exchange of information, social, etc.).	
☐ Identify the form of a website (e.g., blog, forum, advertisement, informational website, commercial website, government website, etc.) and use this information when considering reliability.	
Accuracy	
☐ Evaluate information based on the degree to which it is likely to be accurate by verifying and consulting alternative and/or especially reliable sources.	

Synthesize Information	Lesson Evidence and Comments
☐ Understand both the specific information related to the task as well as the broader context within which that information is located.	
☐ Synthesize information from multiple media sources including written prose, audio, visual, video, and/or tables and graphs.	
☐ Separate relevant information from irrelevant information.	
☐ Organize information effectively.	
☐ Manage multiple sources both on- and offline, including: • Choose tools to meet the needs of managing information (file folders, electronic file folders, notebooks, e-mail, etc.). • Cite sources. • Take notes with paper and pencil, when appropriate. • Take notes with a word processor, when appropriate. • Type notes using short cut strokes such as highlight/cut/copy/paste.	

Communicate Information	Lesson Evidence and Comments
☐ Understand that messages have consequences and will influence how others react.	
☐ Use a variety of offline writing/editing tools, such as a word processor spell checker, dictionary, thesaurus, pdf, etc.	
☐ Copy/paste text or URL to use in the message.	
☐ Know how to use e-mail, including attaching and downloading attachments, logging in, sending messages, and opening messages.	
☐ Know how to use instant messaging.	
☐ Know how to use blogs, including reading and posting information.	
☐ Monitor communication of information for audience or voice (i.e., formal vs. informal writing styles).	
☐ Use a wide array of Internet-based forms of communication, such as: • E-mail and attachments • Blogs • Wikis • Google Docs • Instant messaging • Websites • Presentation software	
☐ Are aware of the audience and the relationship between audience, purpose, medium, and message.	
☐ Know how to include multiple-media sources within messages.	
☐ Use formatting such as headings and subheadings to communicate the organization of information within informational text.	

23

Scaffolding Digital Comprehension

BRIDGET DALTON and DAVID ROSE

Learning without thought is labor lost; thought without learning is perilous.
—CONFUCIUS (551 B.C.–479 B.C.), *The Confucian Analects*

Successful readers are thinking readers. Depending on their purpose for reading, they are able to monitor their understanding and flexibly deploy an array of strategies to support their comprehension and goal attainment. They draw on a well-developed knowledge base about the world and reading as they make sense of text. Successful readers are also engaged readers, developing interests in topics, authors, and genres; setting goals; pursuing inquiry; and enjoying challenging texts and tasks.

Although much has been learned about how to teach students to comprehend printed text, far less is known about how to teach students to understand the tremendous range of print and digital texts that constitute today's literacy landscape. Our understanding of what it means to "understand text" is expanding to reflect the new literacies evolving on the Internet and in information communication technologies (Coiro, 2003; Dalton & Proctor, 2008; Leu, Kinzer, Coiro, & Commack, 2004). Of U.S. classrooms, 99% are connected to the Internet and 87% of youth today spend time on the Internet (Kaiser Family Foundation, 2005; Pew Internet and American Life Project, 2006). Digital tools, texts, and environments have an important role to play in developing students who are able to read with deep understanding in any context, digital or print. This chapter highlights the following:

- Brain research and the role of executive functioning in comprehension.
- Universal design for learning.
- Scaffolded digital literacy environments to improve comprehension processes, learning, and engagement.

RESEARCH FROM 1980s AND 1990s

The RAND Reading Study Group (Snow, 2002) developed a reading comprehension heuristic to describe how understanding occurs as a reciprocal interaction of reader, text, and activity. Furthermore, understanding of a specific text is constructed in a particular sociocultural context. If a reader is able to read with sufficient fluency, has the requisite background knowledge and vocabulary, knows when and how to apply reading strategies, and can generate interest in the learning goal, comprehension is likely to flourish. On the other hand, if the vocabulary and concepts are unfamiliar or the syntax is overly complex, comprehension suffers. It also lessens if the task is unclear or too difficult. Finally, comprehension may be impeded if the reader's peers view school literacy as irrelevant to their lives, or if the reader is distressed or distracted by recent events, such as a fight with a friend or an upcoming afterschool competition.

Research during the 1980s and 1990s demonstrated the potential of technology to support reading achievement and, more specifically, comprehension (for reviews, see Dalton & Strangman, 2006; MacArthur, Ferretti, Okolo, & Cavalier, 2001; National Reading Panel, 2000; Strangman & Dalton, 2005). Much of this work involved transforming the text to reduce learning barriers, such as allowing students to listen to digital text to bypass decoding or fluency issues, providing vocabulary and background knowledge support through embedded hyperlinks, and offering strategic reading prompts and model responses. Dalton and Proctor (2007, in press) adapted the RAND Reading Study Group heuristic to show how the inherent flexibility of digital environments and tools expands opportunities for comprehension in a strategic digital reading (SDR) framework (see Figure 23.1). The relationship of reader, text, and activity changes as aspects of each of these factors are offloaded to the text, thereby potentially increasing the comprehension potential (Edyburn, 2002).

Comprehension depends on fluent reading; students who struggle to decode, or those who have basic decoding skills but read haltingly, have a diminished capacity to read for meaning (Adams, 1990; Ehri, 1994). A series of studies has examined the effect of read-aloud functionality (either text-to-speech tools or digitized voice) on students' comprehension. Several studies have shown that reading with speech feedback positively affects comprehension (Aist & Mostow, 1997; Elbro, Rasmussen, & Spelling 1996; Elkind, Cohen, & Murray, 1993; Lundberg & Oloffson, 1993; Montali & Lewandowski, 1996), although only two of these studies found that improvement transferred to the comprehension of text without speech feedback (Aist & Mostow, 1997; Elbro et al., 1996). In contrast, several studies have shown that text-to-speech decoding support has no effect on comprehension (Farmer, Klein, & Bryson, 1992; Leong, 1995; Wise & Olson, 1995; Wise, Olson, Ring, & Johnson, 1998; Wise, Ring, & Olson, 2000).

Looking across these studies, the strongest evidence was obtained in studies with older students with reading difficulties and studies that took place over an extended period of class time with class reading materials (Elbro et al., 1996; Elkind et al., 1993; Lundberg & Oloffson, 1993). However, even for young students struggling to read, read-aloud tools provide access to the general education curriculum (Individuals with Disabilities Education Act, 1997), so that students are able to read and learn from grade-appropriate texts, while they are also taught word recognition and fluency skills.

Several key studies demonstrate the value of embedding multiple supports for comprehension in digital text, such as vocabulary definitions, additional background infor-

(a) RAND Reading Study Group's Reading Comprehension Heuristic (Snow, 2002)

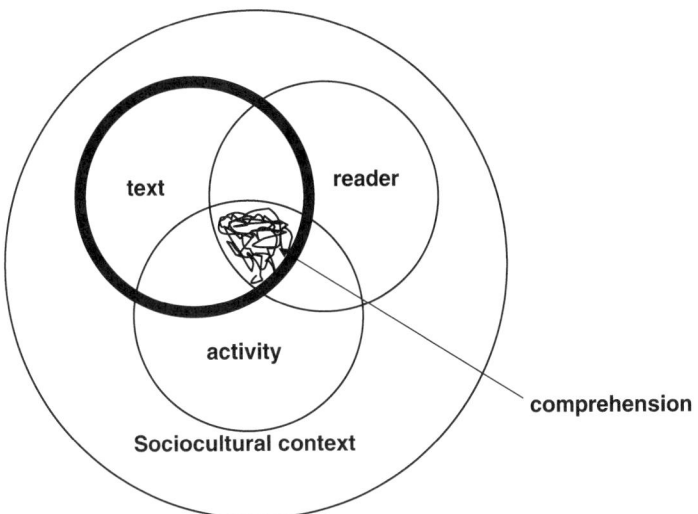

(b) Strategic digital reading heuristic

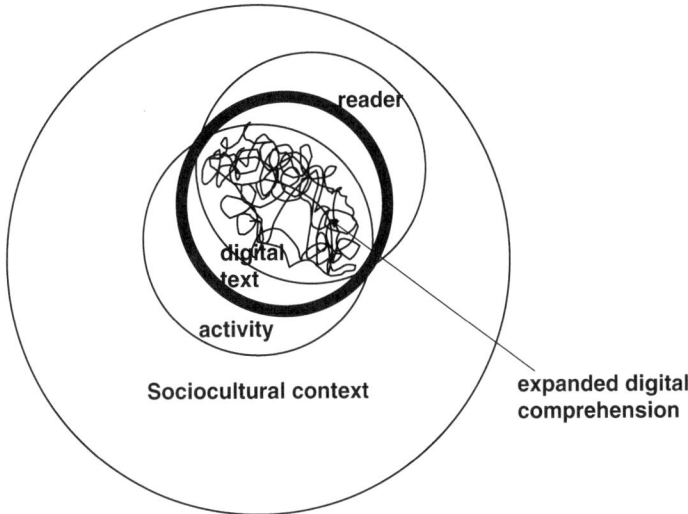

FIGURE 23.1. Expanding comprehension potential through scaffolded digital reading.

mation, highlighting of main ideas and critical information, and reading strategy prompts and models (Anderson-Inman & Horney, 1998; Higgins, Boone, & Lovitt, 1996; MacArthur & Haynes, 1995; Reinking, 1988; Reinking & Schreiner, 1985; Salomon, Globerson, & Guterman, 1989). Of particular interest is the work of Salomon et al. (1989) with the Reading Partner, a metacognitive tool for middle school students. Situated within a cognitive apprenticeship framework (Cognition and Technology Group at Vanderbilt University, 1993), these researchers compared three different versions of a supported hypertext: (1) Control students read a digital text without support; (2) the content question group read the texts with multiple-choice literal and inferential questions that were content related but not metacognitive; and (3) the Reading Partner group read texts offering metacognitive guidance in the form of self-guiding questions and examples on ways to be a good reader; to apply strategies (e.g., generate an inference from the title, identify by sequences, engage in mental imagery, and create summaries) and to self-monitor. Results favored the Reading Partner group, which outperformed the other two groups on a written essay, a standardized reading comprehension test, and a written test of metacognitive reconstruction. During this time, the Cognition and Technology Group at Vanderbilt (1993) developed a model reading environment based on cognitive apprenticeship principles of learning and found similar positive effects.

In summary, the research on hypertext and scaffolded literacy environments during the 1980s and 1990s showed promise, especially for struggling readers. Major advancements made since 2000 reflect recent advances in reading comprehension theory and practice, the neurological sciences, and information communication technologies. In the next section, we describe the role of executive functioning in reading comprehension, highlight promising research, and discuss classroom applications.

NEW DEVELOPMENTS: EXECUTIVE FUNCTIONING AND READING COMPREHENSION

Executive Functioning and Strategic Cortex

There has been a resurgence of interest in executive functioning and its role in learning generally, and in reading specifically. Just as reading comprehension involves all aspects of the reading process, all aspects of the reading process involve executive functioning (Rose & Rose, 2007). Executive functioning networks are located in the frontal lobes of the brain. This strategic cortex is responsible for students' knowledge of how to do things and act effectively in the world. Frontal strategic systems allow us to learn to read, compute, write, solve problems, plan and execute compositions, and complete projects (see Fuster, 2003; Goldberg, 2001; Jeannerod, 1997; Stuss & Knight, 2002).

Reading comprehension requires top-down, goal-directed processing. It is not enough to be able to read the words or to recognize the text structure. Effective readers tailor their approach to the text based on their purpose (reading a textbook end-of-chapter summary before a test is different from previewing that same text, and quite different from reading a mystery on the beach). The effective reader must also self-regulate, monitoring comprehension and taking action to resolve confusions. Executive function also plays a role in recognizing visual patterns, such as onsets and rimes in words, and in knowing how to sound out unfamiliar words or to deconstruct a poem. Brain imaging studies show that frontal cortex is active in skilled readers (e.g., Sandak, Mencl, Frost, & Pugh, 2004; Shaywitz & Shaywitz, 2004).

Executive Function and the Posterior Lobes: Recognition Cortex

Knowing how to do something is not just a province of executive functioning. Many systems work in concert with the frontal cortex (it has been said that the brain operates as a group of many committees that form and reform to accomplish varied tasks). Pattern recognition occurs primarily in the posterior (back) half of the brain's cortex as we process incoming visual, auditory, tactile, and olfactory stimuli (Mountcastle, 1998). Through recognition systems we learn to know basic patterns in orthography, phonology, and semantics, as well as the many higher-level patterns of written syntax, paragraph structure, story grammar, and style. Readers with recognition difficulties demonstrate atypical patterns of posterior brain activation (Shaywitz & Shaywitz, 2004). This difficulty with recognition networks may not only manifest as problems with recognizing words, structures, styles, and so forth, but may also influence executive functioning and comprehension. For example, brain imaging shows that people with dyslexia rely more heavily on the frontal cortex to recognize words, thereby decreasing available capacity for comprehension (Shaywitz & Shaywitz, 2004).

Executive Function and the Limbic System: Affective Cortex

Emotion and affect are situated in the extended limbic system at the core of the brain. These affective networks determine whether the patterns we perceive matter to us, whether they are important, and they help us decide which actions and strategies to pursue (Lane & Nadel, 2000; Ochsner, Bunge, Gross, & Gabrieli, 2002). They do not help us recognize bias in an editorial, but they do help us determine whether we care about the bias. They allow us to (1) prioritize reading and learning goals; (2) develop interests in topics, genres, and authors; (3) develop preferences for ways of learning with text; and (4) meet challenges with resilience and perseverance.

Affect provides a filter for action. Students who do not care about reading, and especially academic reading, or students who do care but are experiencing some emotional distress, find it difficult to act strategically to accomplish reading goals, or to monitor their comprehension. What may manifest as an executive functioning problem may in fact be due to negative affective issues.

DESIGNING AND TEACHING WITH SCAFFOLDED DIGITAL READING ENVIRONMENTS

Recent neuroscientific advances in how the brain learns reinforce research on reading comprehension showing the complex interaction of top-down and bottom-up processes that determine the outcome of any particular comprehension event. For the past several years at the Center for Applied Special Technology (CAST), we have been developing and applying universal design for learning principles (Rose & Meyer, 2002) to the design and use of scaffolded digital reading environments (Dalton & Proctor, 2007; Proctor, Dalton, & Grisham, 2007). The three basic principles are (1) provide multiple means of representation to support diverse recognition networks; (2) provide multiple means of expression within a cognitive apprenticeship environment to support diverse strategic networks; and (3) provide multiple means of engagement to support diverse affective networks (Rose & Meyer, 2002; to view samples of universal learning editions, go to *www.cast.org*). Reading comprehension involves executive functioning (strategic networks) in all aspects of reading, as well as recognition and affective networks. Thus, a universally designed learning environment includes supports in all areas that can be customized to meet the needs and interests of the individual learner.

In the next section, we provide an overview of CAST research on scaffolded digital reading environments (Dalton & Proctor, 2007), then highlight two other technology-based scaffolded approaches to improving reading comprehension that are obtaining strong results: McNamara's Interactive Strategy Training for Active Reading and Thinking (iSTART) program and Meyer and Wijekumar's Summary Tutor program.

Dalton and colleagues developed and researched the prototype version of Thinking Reader (Dalton, Pisha, Eagleton, Coyne, & Deysher, 2002), which was later published by Scholastic (Tom Snyder Productions, 2004). Thinking Reader applies Palincsar and Brown's (1984) Reciprocal Teaching approach to improving reading comprehension in a digital reading environment. A meta-analysis of Reciprocal Teaching (Rosenshine & Meister, 1994) indicates that it is a robust intervention leading to positive gains in students' comprehension of instructed text, as well as transfer text, and to modest gains on standardized measures of reading comprehension.

Reciprocal Teaching improves students' comprehension and self-monitoring skills through an apprenticeship model of learning. The teacher and students engage in an instructional dialogue about the text, coconstructing their understanding of the text as they apply several strategies: predicting, questioning, summarizing, and clarifying. Initially, the teacher plays the lead role, demonstrating, modeling, and providing feedback as students read a shared text. Students then take turns leading the discussion, with the teacher gradually releasing control as student competence increases. The goal of Reciprocal Teaching is not to teach strategies per se; rather, it is to teach students how to apply strategies in the service of developing deep understanding. Core to Reciprocal Teaching is the notion of scaffolding, in which supports are dynamically adjusted to meet the needs of the learner in relation to the demands of the task (Vygotsky, 1978; Wood, Bruner, & Ross, 1976).

The primary goal of scaffolded digital reading environments is to develop engaged, active, and strategic readers who are able to understand print and digital multimedia text. We have developed research prototypes of novels, folktales, informational texts, as well as a book maker tool and a web-based Strategy Tutor to support students' reading and viewing on the web (see Figures 23.2 and 23.3). The supported digital texts all offer a text-to-speech (TTS) tool that allows students to click on a word, phrase, or passage and have it read aloud; multimedia glossary hyperlinks; and embedded strategy instruction that adapts Reciprocal Teaching (Palincsar & Brown, 1984) to a digital context. In addition to the four Reciprocal Teaching strategies of predict, question, clarify, and summarize, we added visualization as a fifth strategy (Pressley, 2006) and a feeling response option to encourage students to make a personal connection to the text (Rosenblatt, 1978). As students read the text, they are periodically prompted to stop and apply a strategy. They enter their response in writing or audiorecording and save it to an electronic worklog that can be viewed at any time by the student and teacher.

The scaffolding of the text centers on students' strategy use. For example, the digital text offers five levels that move students from high support to low support to independent application of the strategies, ending with an open response option that can be used for any purpose (e.g., making a journal entry). Corrective feedback is provided for closed items. The scaffolding system manipulates the representation of the strategy task, students' response option, and the availability of three pedagogical agents who function as more able peer coaches, providing models, think-alouds, and hints. Level of scaffolding is

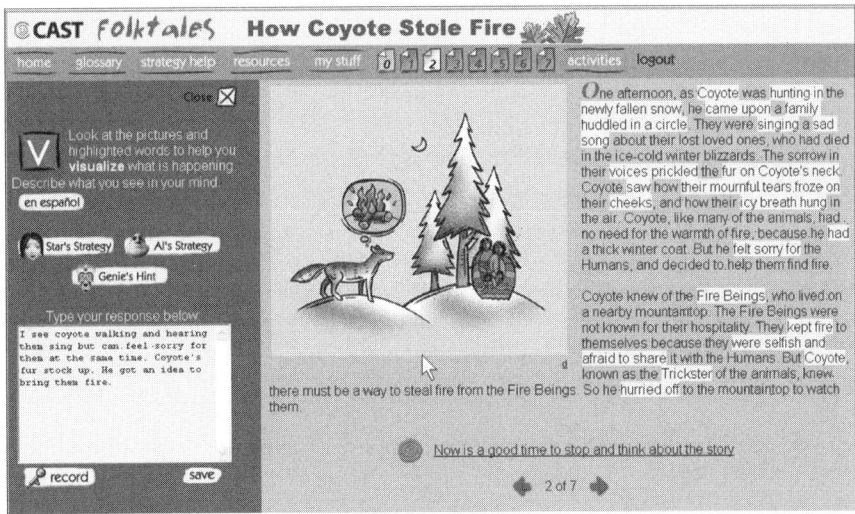

FIGURE 23.2. Screenshot of scaffolded digital folktale (CAST, Inc.).

also varied, so that more difficult strategies, such as summarization, offer more support than do easier strategies, such as prediction. Finally, students and teachers may access the Strategy Help section, which provides basic information about each strategy (What is it? Why should I use it? How do I use it? Tips). Another core feature is the focus on students' self-evaluation and embedded assessment. All of students' strategy responses are gathered in electronic worklogs that serve as artifacts of students' thinking.

All learning is filtered by affect (Lane & Nadel, 2000). As Guthrie and Wigfield (2000) state, engaged readers are strategic readers. We address engagement in several ways: scaffolding supports to vary the level of challenge; providing students' choice and

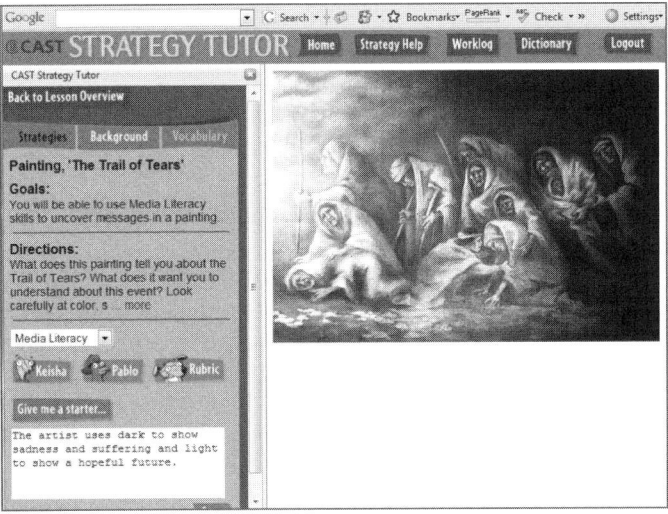

FIGURE 23.3. Screenshot of CAST Strategy Tutor showing student's summary response to information from a web page.

control over access of supports and options for response; embedding self-assessment, so that students can reflect on their progress and set goals; connecting reading to classroom discussion and peer interaction; selecting interesting literature and Web content, with options for student choice of extended reading and using multi-media.

Dalton et al. (2002) investigated the impact of traditional versus computer-supported strategy instruction in a quasi-experimental study with 102 middle school struggling readers. Students in both conditions used the Reciprocal Teaching strategies of predict, question, clarify, and summarize (Palincsar & Brown, 1984), as well as visualization (Pressley, 2006), to read and respond to three age-appropriate novels. Students in the control condition engaged in Reciprocal Teaching discussions as they read the novels in print. Students in the computer condition read Thinking Reader digitized versions of the novels, with supports for access to the content and strategic reading, as described previously.

After controlling for gender and pretest scores on comprehension and vocabulary, students in the Thinking Reader condition demonstrated significantly greater gains in comprehension on the Gates–MacGinitie Reading Achievement Test than did their peers in the traditional Reciprocal Teaching condition (note that Reciprocal Teaching itself is considered a robust intervention). The effect size was moderate, equating to approximately half a grade level of reading achievement gain. For these struggling readers who read at or below the 25th percentile prior to intervention, this was a meaningful increase. Qualitative analyses of student and teacher interviews and questionnaires indicate that students viewed the digital text as extremely helpful. Teachers' responses focused on the positive impact on students' engagement and self-efficacy, and the relative ease of integrating Thinking Reader into their curriculum and teaching.

Subsequent research using one of the universally designed scaffolded digital novels along with several folktales was conducted with three urban school reading language arts teachers and 103 students (Dalton, Pisha, Poniatowski, Concha, & Robinson, 2007). Teachers each taught two classes, one with the digital texts and the other with print-based Reciprocal Teaching. After controlling for initial comprehension scores on the Gates–MacGinitie Reading Achievement Test, students reading the scaffolded digital texts made greater comprehension gains than their peers in the Reciprocal Teaching print groups. Across conditions, struggling readers made significantly less comprehension gain than their typically achieving peers, and struggling readers in the print Reciprocal Teaching group made significantly greater comprehension gains than those reading the scaffolded digital texts. The latter result conflicts with other research and may be due in part to the use of teachers as their own controls (they reported feeling that they were in competition with the computer) and the reduced length of the intervention (students read one novel rather than three novels).

In addition to studying adolescents' reading of universally designed novels, Dalton and colleagues have continued to develop scaffolded digital reading environments and study their use with struggling and typically achieving readers in elementary and middle school classrooms, with the major focus on students in grades 5–8. In a descriptive study, Dalton, Schleper, Kennedy, Lutz, and Strangman (2005) adapted Thinking Reader for use with 14 deaf middle school students who were reading substantially below grade level. American sign language video and signing avatar technology were used to communicate instructional supports. The majority of students increased instructional reading level from one to two grade levels, as measured by an informal reading inventory administered pre- and postintervention. While causality cannot be inferred due to lack of a control group, this increase was substantially greater than their average yearly growth in previous school years (note that many deaf students graduate from high school reading at a fifth-grade level).

We recently expanded the scaffolded digital reading instructional supports to include interactive vocabulary and supports for bilingual students (Proctor, Dalton, & Grisham, 2007). Thirty fourth-grade students read several narrative and informational hypertexts that provided embedded vocabulary and comprehension strategy supports, along with TTS read-aloud functionality. Correlation analyses of pre- and posttest standardized reading vocabulary gain scores revealed that vocabulary gain was associated, though not significantly, with the frequency of access to hyperlinked glossary items throughout the intervention, and that lower pretest vocabulary knowledge was associated with positive vocabulary gains. A similar pattern was detected for comprehension gains that were significantly associated with the frequency of access of reading comprehension strategy coaching avatars. We are currently refining the prototype and testing it with a larger sample of fifth-grade students in a new project funded by the Institute of Education Sciences (Dalton, Proctor, & Snow, work in progress).

Two other lines of research have taken a similar tack in applying a well-validated instructional approach to improving comprehension with print materials. McNamara and colleagues have created and tested an intelligent tutoring system, iSTART, with positive results. Students learn key reading strategies and inferencing as they interact with pedagogical agents and receive ongoing feedback (McNamara, 2007; McNamara, O'Reilly, Best, & Ozuru, 2006). Meyer and Wijekumar (2007) have applied Meyer's extensive research on the structure strategy to an intelligent tutoring program that teaches through a series of leveled lessons with pedagogical agents and feedback. Again, the results of this research with secondary students have yielded strong positive gains in comprehension.

ONLINE TOOLS THAT SUPPORT COMPREHENSION AND STRATEGIC LEARNING

CAST Universal Design for Learning Book Builder

In addition to developing research prototypes, CAST has created two tools to support reading comprehension that are freely available on the CAST website. BookBuilder (*www.cast.bookbuilder.org*) allows teachers to create picture books and texts (or use public domain texts) with embedded pedagogical agents that prompt students to use reading strategies and to provide models and think-alouds. Resources for developing strategic reading supports and creating digital texts are offered, along with a coach to guide the authoring process.

CAST Strategy Tutor

With funding from Carnegie Corporation of New York, CAST has developed an open-source browser tool bar that provides reading strategy support to students as they read and conduct inquiry projects on the Web. In addition to reading strategies, students can get help from coaches in critical literacy and Web evaluation. The student site is accompanied by a teacher site that allows teachers to create their own lessons and customize support for vocabulary, background knowledge, and strategy instruction. A lesson database and other resources on comprehension, critical literacy, and Web evaluation are also offered. Teachers interested in using Strategy Tutor should contact Kristin Robinson at CAST (*krobinson@cast.org*).

INTEGRATING TECHNOLOGY IN READING COMPREHENSION INSTRUCTION

When reviewing research on technology-based educational applications, the question is often raised: Is there enough evidence to guide decision making? Does the evidence warrant the investment in technology and professional development necessary for successful technology integration? Palincsar and Dalton (2005) suggest that the rapidly evolving nature of information communication technologies makes it difficult to conduct multiple studies of the same intervention, and in fact, would be a waste of resources. Instead, it will be more productive to examine the principles underlying the design of the digital environment, and to consider how the design and content applies well-validated approaches to teaching comprehension with print materials. That is not to say that reading print is the same as reading a digital text or text on the Internet. However, there is much to learn and build upon as we simultaneously discover new ways of teaching and learning in digital contexts.

The research on scaffolded digital reading environments suggests its potential to improve reading comprehension instruction in several ways. First, using these tools and texts extends the capacity of the teacher to differentiate instruction and better meet the needs of todays' increasingly diverse classrooms. Second, these tools offer students the opportunity for extensive guided practice with multiple texts and over time. Third, they focus on strategic learning, while supporting other facets of the reading process that interact with strategic processes. This focus on "learning how to learn" becomes increasingly important in digital environments, where the support systems are evolving as technology moves forward. Fourth, they reflect a more expanded view of literacy, one that is more in tune with the realities of the workplace and community. And, fifth, they provide effective models for educational publishers and website developers.

DIRECTIONS FOR FUTURE RESEARCH

There is much to be done. There is a tremendous need for longitudinal research of students and teachers using scaffolded digital reading environments across multiple subjects. Much research on reading on the Internet has focused on the search and evaluation phases of inquiry; to develop effective teaching tools and instructional approaches, we need to understand better how students are making sense of the multimedia and interactivity options characteristic of the Web, and communicating their understanding in varied genres and media formats. The rapidity of technological change and the explosion of information heighten the learning demands and increase the importance of self-efficacy and resilience in the face of challenge. It will be important to develop and study digital tools and supports to address affective issues related to comprehension and learning. And finally, researchers in the field of technology and literacy tend to focus on reading or writing. Studies of the interrelationship of reading and writing in scaffolded multimedia environments are needed to address this gap, because it seems likely that both comprehension and expression might benefit from an integrated approach.

PROJECTIONS AND POSSIBILITIES FOR THE CLASSROOM OF 2030

It is hard even to imagine the technologies available in 2030, or the digital literacies that will be important to understanding text and living a literate life. The customization and personalization of literacy learning environments will begin in early childhood and continue throughout life, ensuring that all individuals successfully read, view, and interact with text (in whatever form it may be). Understanding will be integrally tied to producing and communicating in various media. Students will learn in a vast network of students, teachers, and experts from around the world. Just-in-time support will be ubiquitous and occur on-demand. Students will know that understanding depends on their ability to learn how to learn. Teachers will have the support and resources to reach every child. Teachers will take an active part in distributed learning communities. The reading–achievement gap will have become an historical anecdote.

SUMMARY

To summarize, scaffolded digital environments designed to improve reading comprehension abilities hold much promise for helping students improve their comprehension of both traditional and digital texts. The technologically based reading instruction programs discussed in this chapter are designed to use the same reading strategies, and to engage the same brain areas, used for traditional text comprehension. These include, but are not limited to, the frontal lobe of the brain (to engage higher-level thinking skills) and the limbic system (to engage positive affect). The inherent flexibility of digital environments and tools can provide immediate assistance for a variety of comprehension needs during reading. Such "on-demand" assistance includes (1) digitized read-alouds, (2) word definitions, (3) background information, (4) main ideas or other information critical to the understanding of the text, (5) reading strategy instruction, (6) self-guiding questions, (7) interactive scaffolding, (8) immediate corrective feedback, and so forth. Such technology-based instruction can effectively, and efficiently, help teachers to meet the diverse needs within their classrooms, without compromising quality instruction for anyone. The continued use and development of such programs hold promise to help all students become effective readers of both new and traditional literacies.

INTEGRATE, INVESTIGATE, AND INITIATE: QUESTIONS FOR DISCUSSION

1. In this chapter, the authors provide several examples of research-based digital approaches to improving reading, such as CAST's Thinking Reader and strategic digital reading environments, McNamara's iSTART program, and Meyer and Wijekumar's Summary Tutor. They also featured digital tools such as text-to-speech, the Universal Design for Learning Book Builder, and the Strategy Tutor. Identify one or two tools or programs that you believe would contribute to your students' literary achievement. How would you integrate them into your curriculum? What role could they play in helping your struggling readers? What kinds of support would you need to ensure a successful implementation?

2. Throughout this book, you have read several chapters that stress the need for increased scaffolding of digital comprehension and reading on the Internet. Please pause for a moment and jot down key information that you have learned about the role of technology in enhancing print literacy and developing new literacies. Then, consider your class, school, and district level approach to integrating technology and reading comprehension instruction. What insights do you have about the direction you are currently taking—is it consistent with the research and

emerging promising practices? Are there areas where you and your colleagues are in the vanguard?

3. Dalton and Rose ended their chapter by stating that in the year 2030, if educators continue their hard work in scaffolding digital comprehension, then "the reading–achievement gap will be a historical anecdote." What is the first step you envision yourself taking this week to help us reach this goal, based on what you have learned to date in this book and your reflections on its content?

ACKNOWLEDGMENTS

The CAST projects on universally designed digital literacy environments described here were funded in part by grants from the Office of Special Education Programs and the Institute of Education Sciences, U.S. Department of Education. The opinions expressed are those of the authors and do not represent views of the U.S. Department of Education. We thank Annemarie S. Palincsar, University of Michigan, C. Patrick Proctor, Boston College, Catherine Snow, Harvard University, and our CAST colleagues for their contributions to this work. We also thank the teachers and students who have participated in this research.

REFERENCES

Aist, G. S., & Mostow, J. (1997). *Adapting human tutorial interventions for a reading tutor that listens: Using continuous speech recognition in interactive educational multimedia*. Paper presented at the CALL'97 Conference on Multimedia, Exeter, England.

Anderson-Inman, L., & Horney, M. A. (1998). Transforming text for at-risk readers. In D. Reinking & M. C. McKenna (Eds.), *Handbook of literacy and technology: Transformations in a post-typographic world* (pp. 15–43). Mahwah, NJ: Erlbaum.

CAST Universal Design for Learning BookBuilder. (2006). Interactive book publishing program available for free at *bookbuilder.cast.org/* . Wakefield, MA: CAST, Inc.

CAST Strategy Tutor. (2007). Web browser tool bar application to support students' searching and reading on the Internet. Contact *krobinson@cast.org* or *bridgetdalton@vanderbilt.edu*. Wakefield, MA: CAST, Inc.

Cognition and Technology Group at Vanderbilt. (1993). Examining the cognitive challenges and pedagogical opportunities of integrated media systems: Toward a research agenda. *Journal of Special Education Technology, 12*(2), 118–124.

Coiro, J. (2003). Reading comprehension on the Internet: Expanding our understanding of reading comprehension to encompass new literacies. *Reading Teacher, 56*, 458–464.

Dalton, B., Pisha, B., Eagleton, M., Coyne, P., & Deysher, S. (2002). *Engaging the text: Reciprocal Teaching and questioning strategies in a scaffolded learning environment* (Final report to the U.S. Department of Education, Office of Special Education Programs). Wakefield, MA: CAST, Inc.

Dalton, B., Pisha, B., Poniatowski, L., Concha, S., & Robinson, K. (2007). *Strategic Learning Editions: Embedding flexible supports for learning comprehension strategies in digital text* (Final report to the US Department of Education, Office of Special Education Programs). Wakefield, MA: CAST, Inc.

Dalton, B., & Proctor, C. P. (2007). Reading as thinking: Integrating strategy instruction in a universally designed digital literacy environment. In D. S. McNamara (Ed.), *Reading comprehension strategies: Theories, interventions, and technologies* (pp. 423–442). Mahwah, NJ: Erlbaum.

Dalton, B., & Proctor, C. P. (2008). The changing landscape of text and comprehension in the age of new literacies. In J. Coiro, M. Knobel, C. Lankshear, & D. J. Leu (Eds.), *Handbook of research on new literacies* (pp. 297–324). Mahwah, NJ: Erlbaum.

Dalton, B., Schleper, D., Kennedy, M., Lutz, L., & Strangman, N. (2007). *A universally designed digital strategic reading environment for adolescents who are deaf and hard of hearing.* Manuscript submitted for publication.

Dalton, B., & Strangman, N. (2006). Improving struggling readers' comprehension through scaffolded hypertexts and other computer-based literacy programs. In D. Reinking, M. C. McKenna, L. D. Labbo, & R. D. Keiffer (Eds.), *Handbook of literacy and technology* (2nd ed., pp. 75–92). Mahwah, NJ: Erlbaum.

Edyburn, D. L. (2002, April–May). Cognitive rescaling strategies: Interventions that alter the cognitive accessibility of text. *Closing the Gap, 1,* 10–11, 21.

Ehri, L. C. (1994). Development of the ability to read words: Update. In R. B. Ruddell & M. R. Ruddell (Eds.), *Theoretical models and processes of reading* (4th ed., pp. 323–358). International Reading Association.

Elbro, C., Rasmussen, I., & Spelling, B. (1996). Teaching reading to disabled readers with language disorders: A controlled evaluation of synthetic speech feedback. *Scandinavian Journal of Psychology, 37,* 140–155.

Elkind, J., Cohen, K., & Murray, C. (1993). Using computer-based readers to improve reading comprehension of students with dyslexia. *Annals of Dyslexia, 43,* 238–259.

Farmer, M. E., Klein, R., & Bryson, S. E. (1992, March/April). Computer-assisted reading: Effects of whole-word feedback on fluency and comprehension in readers with severe disabilities. *Remedial and Special Education, 13*(2), 50–60.

Fuster, J. M. (2003). *Cortex and mind: Unifying cognition.* New York: Oxford University Press.

Goldberg, E. (2001). *The executive brain: Frontal lobes and the civilized mind.* New York: Oxford University Press.

Guthrie, J. T., & Wigfield, A. (2000). Engagement and motivation in reading. In M. L. Kamil, P. B. Mosenthal, P. D. Pearson, & R. Barr (Eds.), *Handbook of reading research: Volume III* (pp. 403–422). New York: Erlbaum.

Higgins, K., Boone, R., & Lovitt, T. (1996). Hypertext support for remedial students and students with learning disabilities. *Journal of Learning Disabilities, 29*(4), 402–412.

Individuals with Disabilities Education Act Amendments of 1997, Pub. Law No.105-17, 20 U.S.C. § 1400 et seq.

Jeannerod, M. (1997). *The cognitive neuroscience of action.* Boston: Blackwell.

Kaiser Family Foundation. (2005). *Generation M: Media in the lives of 8–18-year-olds.* Retrieved April 1, 2005, from *www.kff.org/entmedia/7251.cfm.*

Lane, R. D., & Nadel, L. (Eds.). (2000). *Cognitive neuroscience of emotion.* New York: Oxford University Press.

Leong, C. K. (1995). Effects of on-line reading and simultaneous DECtalk auding in helping below-average and poor readers comprehend and summarize text. *Learning Disability Quarterly, 18,* 101–116.

Leu, D. J., Jr., Kinzer, C. K., Coiro, J., & Cammack, D. (2004). Towards a theory of new literacies emerging from the Internet and other ICT. In R. B. Ruddell & N. Unrau (Eds.), *Theoretical models and processes of reading* (5th ed., pp. 1570–1613).

Lundberg, I., & Oloffson, A. (1993). Can computer speech support reading comprehension? *Computers in Human Behavior, 9,* 283–293.

MacArthur, C. A., Ferretti, R. P., Okolo, C. M., & Cavalier, A. R. (2001). Technology applications for students with literacy problems: A critical review. *Elementary School Journal, 101*(3), 273–301.

MacArthur, C. A., & Haynes, J. B. (1995). Student assistant for learning from text (SALT): A hypermedia reading aid. *Journal of Learning Disabilities, 28*(3), 50–59.

McKenna, M. C. (1998). Electronic texts and the transformation of beginning reading. In D. Reinking, M. C. McKenna, L. D. Labbo, & R. D. Kieffer (Eds.), *Handbook of literacy and technology: Transformations in a post-typographic world* (pp. 45–59). Mahwah, NJ: Erlbaum.

McNamara, D. S. (2007). *Reading comprehension strategies: Theories, interventions, and technologies.* Mahwah, NJ: Erlbaum.

McNamara, D. S., O'Reilly, T., Best, R., & Ozuru, Y. (2006). Improving adolescent students' reading comprehension with iSTART. *Journal of Educational Computing Research, 34,* 147–171.

Meyer, B., & Wijekumar, K. (2007). A web-based tutoring system for the structure strategy: Theoretical background, design, and findings. In D. S. McNamara (Ed.), *Reading comprehension strategies: Theories, interventions, and technologies* (pp. 347–374). Mahwah, NJ: Erlbaum.

Montali, J., & Lewandowski, L. (1996, May). Bimodal reading: Benefits of a talking computer for average and less skilled readers. *Journal of Learning Disabilities, 29*(3), 271–279.

Mountcastle, V. B. (1998). *Perceptual neuroscience.* Cambridge, MA: Harvard University Press.

National Reading Panel. (2000). *Teaching children to read: An evidence-based assessment of the scientific research literature on reading and its implications for reading instruction* (NIH Publication No. 00-4769). Jessup, MD: National Institute for Literacy.

Ochsner, K. N., Bunge, S. A., Gross, J. J., & Gabrieli, J. D. (2002). Rethinking feelings: An FMRI study of the cognitive regulation of emotion. *Journal of Cognitive Neuroscience, 14*(8), 1215–1229.

Palincsar, A., & Dalton, B. (2005). Speaking literacy and learning to technology; Speaking technology to literacy and learning. In B. Maloch, J. Hoffman, D. Schallert, C. Fairbanks, & J. Worthy (Eds.), *54th Yearbook of the National Reading Conference* (pp. 83–102). [Invited annual research address]. Oak Creek, WI: National Reading Conference, Inc.

Palincsar, A. S., & Brown, A. L. (1984). Reciprocal teaching of comprehension–fostering and comprehension–monitoring activities. *Cognition and Instruction, 1*(2), 117–175.

Paris, S. G., Cross, D. R., & Lipson, M. Y. (1984). Informed strategies for learning: A program to improve children's reading awareness and comprehension. *Journal of Educational Psychology, 76*(6), 1239–1252.

Pew Internet and American Life Project. (2006). *The Internet at school* [Report]. Retrieved July 30, 2007, from *www.pewinternet.org/ppf/r/163/report_display.asp*.

Pressley, M. (2006). *Reading instruction that works: The case for balanced teaching* (3rd ed.). New York: Guilford Press.

Proctor, C. P., Dalton, B., & Grisham, D. L. (2007). Scaffolding English language learners and struggling readers in a universal literacy environment with embedded strategy instruction and vocabulary support. *Journal of Literacy Research, 39,* 71–93.

Reinking, D. (1988). Computer-mediated text and comprehension differences: The role of reading time, reader preference, and estimation of learning. *Reading Research Quarterly, 23*(4), 484–498.

Reinking, D., & Schreiner, R. (1985). The effects of computer-mediated text on measures of reading comprehension and reading behavior. *Reading Research Quarterly, 20*(5), 536–552.

Rose, D., & Meyer, A. (2002). *Teaching every student in the digital age: Universal design for learning.* Alexandria, VA: Association for Supervision and Curriculum Development.

Rose, D., & Rose, K. (2007). Deficits in executive functioning: A curriculum-based intervention. In L. Meltzer (Ed.), *Executive function in education: From theory to practice* (pp. 287–308). New York: Guilford Press.

Rosenblatt, L. M. (1978). *The reader, the text, the poem: The transactional theory of the literary work.* New York: Appleton Century.

Rosenshine, B., & Meister, C. (1994). Reciprocal teaching: A review of the research. *Review of Educational Research, 64*(4), 479–530.

Salomon, G., Globerson, T., & Guterman, E. (1989). The computer as a zone of proximal development: Internalizing reading-related metacognitions from a reading partner. *Journal of Educational Psychology, 81*(4), 620–627.

Sandak, R., Mencl, W. E., Frost, S. J., & Pugh, K. R. (2004). The neurobiological basis of skilled and impaired reading: Recent findings and new directions. *Scientific Studies of Reading, 8*(3), 273–292.

Shaywitz, S. E., & Shaywitz, B. A. (2004). Reading disability and the brain. *Educational Leadership, 61*(6), 6–11.

Snow, C. (2002). *Reading for understanding: Toward a research and development program in reading comprehension.* Pittsburgh: Office of Educational Research and Improvement.

Strangman, N., & Dalton, B. (2005). Technology for struggling readers: A review of the research. In D. Edyburn, K. Higgins, & R. Boone (Eds.), *The handbook of special education technology research and practice* (pp. 545–569). Whitefish Bay, WI: Knowledge by Design.

Stuss, D. T., & Knight, R. T. (Eds.). (2002). *Principles of frontal lobe function.* New York: Oxford University Press.

Tom Snyder Productions. (2004). *Thinking Reader* [Software program]. Cambridge, MA: Scholastic.

Vygotsky, L. S. (1978). *Mind in society: The development of higher psychological processes.* Cambridge, MA: Harvard University Press.

Wise, B. W., Olson, R. K., Ring, J., & Johnson, M. (1998). Interactive computer support for improving phonological skills. In J. L. Metsala & L. C. Ehri (Eds.), *Word recognition in beginning literacy* (pp. 189–208). Mahwah, NJ: Erlbaum.

Wise, B. W., Ring, J., & Olson, R. K. (2000). Individual differences in gains from computer-assisted remedial reading. *Journal of Experimental Child Psychology, 77*(3), 197–235.

Wood, D., Bruner, J. S., & Ross, G. (1976). The role of tutoring in problem solving. *Journal of Child Psychology and Psychiatry, and Allied Disciplines, 17*(2), 89–100.

24

Technologically Based Teacher Resources for Designing Comprehension Lessons

JAN LACINA

> Mama, look! Look at the moon! I want to touch it! Can you help me touch the moon . . . PLEASE, PLEASE? I want to touch the moon.
> —GRACE LACINA, 2 years old (field notes, December 2006)

This quotation illustrates the natural curiosity of a young child as she views the magnificence of a full moon. In addition to natural curiosity, Grace's imagination and background in reading at a very early age are evident in the types of questions she asks. Day after day, she enjoys repeated readings of *Goodnight Moon, Hop on Pop, There Are Monsters Everywhere*, and numerous nonfiction picture books about beavers, zebras, and farm animals. She especially loves new informational texts about farms animals.

Because Grace's grandparents live on a Texas ranch, she has the background knowledge to make personal connections to the text and to ask a variety of questions while reading books about farms. According to Shanahan (2005), even very young children who cannot "read" yet can comprehend texts simply by listening to stories. Providing related background knowledge and experiences prior to and during reading, and exposing children to a variety of excellent fiction and nonfiction books to read and discuss with an adult, sets the stage for early success in school.

The purpose of this chapter is to provide a wealth of resources available to teachers, in both print and electronic forms, so that they can engage, motivate, and encourage children's curiosity. Coupled with teachers' genuine love for reading and learning, the resources in this chapter provide a backpack of tools for teaching well-crafted comprehension lessons, so educators can ensure that all children "reach for the moon."

Children today, "Generation Y" (Block, 2004), are distinctly different than children of the past. Over the past 10 years, children have become saturated with technology and media images. The way that we teach these tech-savvy children must mirror the times in which they live. Integrating technology into comprehension instruction is an important contemporary goal for educators. *New literacies* is a term used to describe the skills needed to locate, evaluate, and synthesize information on the Internet (Karchmer, Mallette, Kara-Soteriou, & Leu, 2005; Leu, Kinzer, Coiro, & Cammack, 2004; Street, 2003), and the integration of these new literacies of information and communication technologies (ICTs) is specifically a core foundation in a literacy community (International Reading Association, 2001; International Reading Association & National Council of Teachers of English, 2000; International Society for Technology in Education, 1998; Kinzer, 2003; Turbill, 2002). As teachers plan comprehension lessons, they must keep in mind today's children and their background knowledge, and even more importantly, prepare students for more than just print-based literacies (Labbo, 2002; Valmont, 2003; Van Leeuwen & Gabriel, 2007; Warschauer, 2006). Students today must be telecommunications literate, which means that a child can not only operate a computer, but that he or she can also locate and analyze multiple forms of information (Valmont, 2003). As Valmont explains,

> Students who use the new technologies effectively will be the new literacy "haves," while those who do not will be literacy "have-nots." As educators, we must be prepared to help all students become proficient in using advanced technologies in their development of literacy and thinking capabilities. In other words, we must do all we can to help our students become telecommunications literate. (p. 2)

With new technologies, new reading comprehension skills are necessary to engage students in learning opportunities on the Internet (Coiro, 2003a; Leu, 2001; Lewin, 1998; Snyder, 2002; Van Leeuwen & Gabriel, 2007).

Beyond a high level of exposure to good books, how can teachers provide vital comprehension lessons to reach a new generation of students who are growing up using iPods, e-mail, and instant messaging on a daily basis? Resources to integrate technology into comprehension lessons are discussed throughout this chapter, which highlights the following:

- Research and resources for finding exemplary children's literature.
- Lesson planning websites that teachers can use to develop comprehension lessons.
- Strategies for using technology for building background knowledge.
- Methods for discussing books online to build comprehension.

ESTABLISHED RESEARCH AND PRACTICE

Where should teachers begin when planning comprehension lessons? First, teachers must begin with good literature. Research supports teachers' use of interesting and appropriate texts to motivate and engage students (Block, Gambrell, & Pressley, 2004; Gambrell, Wilson, & Gantt, 1981). Hearing a peer or teacher talk about a book helps motivate young children to read a book (Palmer, Codling, & Gambrell, 1994). A variety of excellent Internet-based lists of high-quality literature are constantly updated so teachers can find the latest, best literature for teaching comprehension to today's students. The websites I recommend and use most often are the following:

High-Quality Literature Websites

- Children's Choices Booklist (*www.reading.org/resources/tools/choices_childrens.html*), sponsored by the International Reading Association (IRA), has been a well-regarded resource in finding excellent literature for children since 1974. IRA offers an innovative approach for selecting books on this list, because children themselves evaluate the books and provide reviews of their favorites. This list of favorites becomes the choices booklist for young children.
- Young Adult Choices (*www.reading.org/resources/tools/choices_young_adults.html*) is the IRA choices booklist for middle and high school youth. Since 1987, the IRA has developed this extensive list of books—based on adolescents' favorite, recently published book choices.
- Teachers' Choices Booklist (*www.reading.org/resources/tools/choices_teachers.html*) is the IRA annual annotated reading list of recently published books that educators have used to successfully encourage students to read.
- Young Adult Library Services Association (YALSA) (*www.ala.org/ala/yalsa/booklistsawards/booklistsbook.htm*) offers online booklists and book awards, such as books in the following categories: best books for young adults, great graphic novels for teens, popular paperback books for young adults, and quick picks for reluctant young readers. YALSA also offers an online search—to find books by title or subject.
- Newberry Medal (*www.ala.org/ala/alsc/awardsscholarships/literaryawds/newberymedal/newberymedal.htm*), named for an 18th-century bookseller, is awarded annually by the Association for Library Service to Children, a division of the American Library Association, to the author of the most distinguished contribution to American literature for children.
- American Library Association's Booklist (*www.ala.org/booklist/index.html*) magazine reviews both adult and children's books. Two highlights of this site are the "editors' choice" section, which lists top books and videos, and a section dedicated to interviews and essays about featured authors.

Although numerous other excellent lists and websites feature good books, the ones I have noted are among the most widely used. When choosing a booklist, teachers must first consider their students and the community in which their students live. What books would be most interesting and relevant to these specific readers? First, pupils' background knowledge and experiences should be considered when selecting books to introduce during a comprehension lesson, so students will be more engaged and motivated to read the book. Second, teachers need to consider the book's vocabulary level and density. Is the vocabulary appropriate for these children? Is the vocabulary too difficult? Language and syntax may also be taken into consideration as teachers analyze the difficulty of a book, and its grade-level appropriateness.

NEW RESEARCH SINCE THE NATIONAL READING PANEL REPORT: COMPREHENSION INSTRUCTION MUST INCLUDE MULTIPLE LITERACIES

In addition to its value in locating print resources, there are there are numerous benefits of using the Internet to teach comprehension and linking this instruction to writing development. Many websites online offer story animation, oral narration, or word pronunciation on demand. Giving children such choices allows students to take ownership of their own reading (McKenna, Labbo, & Reinking, 2003) and, as a result, reading becomes more enjoyable and relevant to their lives. Teachers can reference and bookmark the following sites to build online reading skills—and to locate resources for designing comprehension lessons.

High-Quality Online Literature Websites

- KidSpace @ the Internet Public Library (*www.ipl.org/div/kidspace/browse/rzn2000/*) offers numerous interactive picture book stories for children to read online—and links to additional, interesting websites with interactive K–3 appropriate stories, such as those about Clifford and Elmo.
- Bedtime Story (*www.bedtime-story.com/bedtime-story/indexmain.htm*) provides online, noninteractive, beautifully illustrated classic stories, such as *Alice in Wonderland*, *The Owl and the Pussycat*, and *Peter Pan*.
- The International Children's Digital Library (*www.icdlbooks.org*) provides a wealth of online, colorfully illustrated books that include interesting plots. The website does not charge a fee, and books from around the world are featured in multiple languages.

Online Read-Aloud Websites

- Storyline Online (*www.storylineonline.net*) is the best read-aloud booklist available on websites. This website offers books read aloud by popular actors from the Screen Actors Guild, such as Camryn Manheim, Haylie Duff, Amber Tamblyn, and Jason Alexander. Additional activities included with each book ask children to draw inferences and to retell the story. The website also has a phone line service in which children can call in and listen to an actor read a book.

Interactive Read-Along Stories Websites

- TumbleBooks (*www.tumblebooks.com*), offers one of the best websites for interactive read-along stories. Although the website charges a fee, it offers a trial issue. The books are engaging, interesting, and beautifully illustrated. Children can follow along with the reading as words appear on the screen and authors read them, and complete a paper-and-pencil quiz that assesses their comprehension of the story. The online interactivity of the read-along stories is the greatest benefit of this website. Figure 24.1 is a screenshot from one of the many interactive read-along stories features in TumbleBooks.
- RIF (Reading Is Fundamental) Reading Planet (*www.rif.org/readingplanet/content/read_aloud_stories.mspx*) website offers free access to interactive, online stories with musical accompaniment. The stories are not written by well-known authors or illustrators, but they are engaging. For example, the story, *Julia and the Big Wave*, includes ocean sounds, and one can envision being on the beach as a big wave approaches.
- The Amazing Adventure Series (*www.tosiproductions.com/%5famazingadventure/index_fl.asp*) offers children choices to enjoy interactive and online poems, cinema, and stories in many formats. For example, for the poem *Lazy Circles*, an interactive, talking happy face reads the poem.

In conclusion, similar to print books, teachers must take into consideration vocabulary, syntax, and students' background knowledge and experiences when selecting online

FIGURE 24.1. Tumblebus (*www.tumblebooks.com*).

books for students to view and read. Teachers may also evaluate the level of interactivity the site encourages between the child and the online book. When selecting online books for young children, it is best to choose books that include story animation, oral narration, or word pronunciation on demand. These types of books hold the greatest potential to capture our new Generation Y readers' interest and engage their high-level thinking.

TEACHING STUDENTS TO LET BACKGROUND BUILD

Block (2004) describes the importance of teaching students to build background rather than having teachers building background for them. As Block explains, comprehension is like building a bridge, because students learn how to comprehend material as they read, one paragraph at a time. Students must learn that each paragraph serves as a bridge of information to the next paragraph. Many readers are unable to make prior knowledge connections to what they are reading because their background experiences are too different from the school texts; the vocabulary is too difficult; or metacognition is not engaged and word errors are not corrected (Palincsar & Brown, 1984). To help students build their own background knowledge, teachers can use a variety of strategies mentioned in Block's book *Teaching Comprehension: The Comprehension Process Approach* (2004) and in the following technologically based resources.

Virtual Field Trips

Virtual field trips (VFTs) provide many resources to help students build background knowledge (Lacina, 2004). First, they offer a student-centered approach to instruction and integrate technology into content area comprehension instruction. Second, through them, children can interact with what they are reading, viewing people and places that they cannot view through print reading. To enable students to build their own background using a VFT during a comprehension lesson, teachers need to consider the following steps while planning and preparing for a lesson.

- Choose a topic or concept that cannot be studied well through print-based reading. VFT topics should extend print-based classroom comprehension instruction.
- Provide a clear guide throughout the VFT. It is best if the VFT is highly structured, so that students are not aimlessly wandering from website to website.
- Familiarize students with vocabulary they will need to know to read the VFT.
- Decide how students will participate in the VFT: small group, whole class, or individually (Lacina, 2004).

Teachers find that VFTs allow students to understand better the setting of a book prior to and during reading. For example, 7th-grade English teacher Daniel Spikes explains that he uses VFTs each year as his students read *Lupita Mañana*, by Patricia Beatty. He finds that students are better able to understand the book when they have a more in-depth understanding of the setting. Likewise, Mr. Spikes integrates geography into the VFT, and students can visit the same places that the main characters from the book visited (Lacina, 2004). Most importantly, VFTs can take students inside a cell, to environments around the world, or to meet historical characters from the past. VFTs provide numerous productive sessions in which students to learn to acquire background knowledge on their own, which in turn assists them better to comprehend other forms of reading material.

Many already developed, excellent resources can be used by teachers to create their own VFT. *How to Create a Virtual Tour* (*www.uen.org/tours*), which is designed and supported by the Utah Education Network, offers a step-by-step comprehensive tutorial on how to create a VFT (see home page in Figure 24.2).

Minnesota at Duluth also has a helpful page that describes how to create a VFT (*www.d.umn.edu/~hrallis/guides/virtualfieldtrips.html*). In summary, whether your students are preparing to read a book about mummies, colonial Williamsburg, or the Maya civilization, there are VFTs available on the Internet to help students acquire greater background on their reading topic.

WebQuests

WebQuests also help students learn how to build their own background knowledge bridges. A WebQuest is an inquiry-based technology activity designed by Bernie Dodge and Tom March at San Diego State University in 1995. WebQuests are an activity in which most or all of the information to be comprehended and used by learners is drawn from the Web. WebQuests are based on a constructivist philosophy, with cooperative learning and scaffolding of instruction as their essential instructional tools (Johnson, 2005). The design of the WebQuest provides the necessary scaffolds—because resource links are included within the WebQuest (Lacina, 2007). Teachers who design WebQuests emphasize higher-level skills, such as Bloom's Taxonomy tasks. Typically, the teacher

FIGURE 24.2. Virtual Field Trips (*www.uen.org/tours*).

serves as the facilitator, or guide, as students complete these (as well as other types of) computer-based activities (Labbo, 2004; Snyder, 2002). WebQuests provide background information for future assignments, because students work cooperatively to build their own background knowledge, to comprehend new knowledge, and to exchange information to understand a new topic.

Designing a WebQuest

A simple template for designing WebQuests is located at *webquest.sdsu.edu/webquest.html*. The WebQuest format comprises an organized structure of five essential components (see Figure 24.3). Each component is listed and briefly described below (Johnson, 2005; Lacina, 2007; Valmont, 2003).

Suggestions for Implementation

When beginning to design a WebQuest, teachers need to consider the time it will take to learn effectively about WebQuests, and to design and organize an effective WebQuest activity. The following advice is how a first-time WebQuest developer begins the planning:

Criteria	Description
The Introduction	The introduction should grab students' attention. WebQuest introductions typically list the goals for the project and include an introduction that builds on the reader's prior background knowledge.
The Task	This section requires students to synthesize information, take a position, or generalize. Students will use higher-level thinking skills to produce a culminating product.
The Resources	The various websites linked in this section will provide students with essential background knowledge to complete their task.
The Process	This section includes the process that students will need to go through to complete the WebQuest and to complete their final product.
The Evaluation	There are numerous templates online that teachers can use to evaluate student WebQuest products and participation, or teachers can create their own.

FIGURE 24.3. WebQuest framework.

- *Time.* You need to spend a large amount of time exploring various WebQuests prior to designing your own. It is easy to be deceived by appearances. When you explore and evaluate the site, you can determine which WebQuests are well designed.
- *Organization.* Follow Dodge and March's organization components. They are simple and easy for students to follow—and navigation of the site is clear to students.
- *Resources/Links.* Check links frequently since addresses change often. Also, too many resources can overwhelm students, and they may not try them all—or they may lose their enthusiasm for the activity.
- *Show—do not tell.* Show students how to use a WebQuest by guiding them through the process—using a computer to show them the process as they see each step on the computer screen. Just like any assignment, modeling and showing students the process is more effective than telling them about it.
- *Backup Plan.* I think most of us can tell numerous stories about technology glitches. Provide printed copies of the WebQuest, or be prepared with another activity in case there is a technology problem.
- *Be enthusiastic.* Your enthusiasm about inquiry learning, technology, and WebQuests will help excite the students about the project. (Lacina, 2007, p. 252)

In summary, WebQuests are a powerful instructional tool for helping students to practice building their own background for a comprehension lesson. Students learn new information that can better help them understand a text, and they learn to work collaboratively with their peers while acquiring new information. Most importantly, students become responsible for their own learning.

DISCUSSING BOOKS ONLINE TO BUILD COMPREHENSION

Newsweek recently reported (May, 2007) that children's book clubs are growing at school, online, and on TV (*www.msnbc.msn.com/id/18602858/site/newsweek*). By using technology to discuss books, teachers encourage new literacy opportunities, while familiarizing children with ICTs, as described earlier in the chapter (Castek, Bevans-Mangelson, & Goldstone, 2006). Using technology to discuss books enables children to learn skills they need in the future workplace, which includes being able to read, write, and communicate with others while using technology.

There are a number of excellent discussion boards teachers can access to allow students to participate in online discussion forums about books. Scholastic offers an excellent website, Flashlight Reader, which allows children to choose a book, then post a message to others about the book. Similarly, the Spaghetti Book Club at *www.spaghettibookclub.org* provides a discussion forum in which children can post book reviews or comment on what they are currently reading. The site is easy to navigate, and children can select the book title or authors' name to find the book on which they want to post a comment or review. Last, Book Raps (*www.rite.ed.qut.edu.au/old_oz-teachernet/projects/book-rap/index1.html*) is an additional online book discussion that takes place by e-mail, which is managed and developed by the Research in Information Technology Education Group (RITE), based in Brisbane, Australia. A Book Rap is a guided discussion in which individuals, or groups, can respond to a thought-provoking question or comment about a book they all have read. Raps are suggested and coordinated by classroom teachers, and the e-mail discussion is a closed discussion group or forum. In summary, there are a number of online sites where students can converse about books, located in safe online environments.

LESSON PLANNING WEBSITES TO CREATE COMPREHENSION LESSONS

There are a great number of excellent websites available to help teachers plan highly effective comprehension lessons. One of the best is Read Write Think, *www.readwritethink.org*, a joint effort between the National Council for Teachers of English (NCTE) and IRA. Lessons on this website are all peer-reviewed, aligned to national reading standards, and include Web resources and student material. The website contains many interactive graphic organizers online that can be used anytime, anyplace—because all teachers who have Internet access can use these graphic organizers. A few of the best graphic organizers to include in comprehension lessons are noted below:

- *www.readwritethink.org/materials/trading cards*. The interactive Character Trading Cards tool is a fun and useful way for students to explore a character in a book they are reading, or it can be used as a prewriting exercise when creating characters for original stories.
- *www.readwritethink.org/materials/plot-diagram*. The Plot Diagram is an organizational tool that focuses on a pyramid or triangular-shaped map to plot events in a story. This marking of plot structure or text features allows readers and writers to visualize the key features of narrative and expository text.

There are several other good lesson planning sites, although Read Write Think is probably the best one. Literacy Matters (*www.literacymatters.org/18under/index.htm*), a helpful site for teachers at the middle/secondary level, provides parents with ideas about how they can support literacy learning at home and offers students the opportunity to participate in interactive, online tutorials. The site also provides resources for teachers, including professional development activities and downloadable comprehension lesson plans.

The Vaughn Gross Center for Reading at the University of Texas at Austin offers a wide variety of online materials (*www.texasreading.org/utcrla/materials/primary.asp*), such as professional development guides, and videoclips of exemplary teachers.

In conclusion, the Internet offers a wide variety of lesson plan websites; however, teachers need to analyze the credibility of each site. Sites, such as Read Write Think, which offer peer-reviewed lesson plans connected to research and content standards, are the highest quality websites available for planning comprehension lessons. The other sites on the Internet first need to be analyzed for their quality and appropriateness before they are used to plan comprehension lessons.

HOW THIS NEW KNOWLEDGE CAN IMPROVE COMPREHENSION INSTRUCTION: TEACHING READING COMPREHENSION MUST INCLUDE THE INTERNET

As new technologies are integrated into comprehension lessons, teachers must be aware that such new literacies require students to possess a new set of skills. Searching for information on the Internet is a different task than searching for information in a printed book (Nachmias & Gilad, 2002), and this search process is a complicated one. For example, in a recent study published in *Reading Research Quarterly*, researchers found that successful Internet reading experiences required both similar and more complex applications of prior knowledge sources, inferential reasoning strategies, and self-regulated reading processes (Coiro & Dobler, 2007). For instance, Coiro and Dobler suggested that reading Internet text triggers a process of self-directed text construction, which may explain why online reading comprehension is more multifaceted than understanding print. Moreover, because information is often given at a rapid rate on the Internet, recent research suggests that students need to be taught effective information-seeking strategies to select search engines and search engine results adequately (Dreher, 1993; Eliopoulos & Gotlieb, 2003; Guinee, Eagleton, & Hall, 2003; Henry, 2006).

Additionally, Henry (2006) suggests that teachers teach students the different types of search engines and how they sort information. For example, Google searches for frequency and location of the key words typed, and the computer "crawls" the Web for results. Results are prioritized based on how often others type similar key words, and commercial sites often show up first on the list of results. Yahoo is similar, because the main results are also "crawlers," in which the main results are compiled after the computer crawls the Web. Not all search engines work this way. AOL, for example, uses third-party search providers for their results. AOL's search results come from Google's crawler-based listings. To determine which Internet search engines would be best for a particular type of search, Noodle Tools (*www.noodletools.com/debbie/literacies/information/5locate/adviceengine.html*) is an excellent site that categorizes various types of search topics and the most appropriate search engine to use.

Internet scavenger hunts also provide a way for students to learn the best way to search on the Internet. Such Internet scavenger hunts allow students to practice using key words and different search terms (Henry, 2006). A few examples of Internet Scavenger Hunts include Internet Treasure Hunts for ESL Students (*iteslj.org/th*), Internet Hunt Activities (*www.homepage.mac.com/cohora/ext/internethunts.html*), and Education World's site, which organize their scavenger hunts by month and theme (*www.education-world.com/a_lesson/archives/hunt.shtml*).

Beyond Internet activities to increase students' reading and navigation skills, Goldstone (2006) describes the importance of introducing children's books that mirror technological texts, as she explains the importance of Dr. Seuss's words, "Think left and think right/and think low and think high" (Seuss, 1975, p. 1). To comprehend digital texts, children must take in information from all over the computer screen. Literacy involves understanding nonlinear text structures, and the best way to prepare children for comprehending material presented in a nonlinear text is to teach students explicitly how authors uses such texts. Figure 24.4 highlights excellent books that are appropriate for teaching students about multiple story lines, multiple authors, and multiple spatial plans. This lesson shows students a variety of story and text structures to better prepare them for applying new comprehension skills needed to understand multiple literacies.

DIRECTIONS FOR FUTURE RESEARCH

Marc Prensky (2001) describes today's students as the digital natives, whereas today's teachers remain digital immigrants. Students today grow up using technology and go first to the Internet when searching for information, unlike their teachers, who often search for answers to questions by using print-based texts. As the Internet and newer ICTs are created and integrated into society, teachers must continue to find ways to teach students the new forms of reading and comprehending with those technologies—to advance future generations' comprehension abilities.

Based on what we have learned to date about the benefits of technology to increase (1) teachers' knowledge and use of high-quality literature and comprehension lessons, (2) students' comprehension, and (3) readers' multiple literacies, future research could advance our understanding in these areas in the following ways:

1. *How will the use of technology-driven texts change our understanding of reading comprehension?* The leading literacy organizations for teachers, the IRA and the NTCE (2000) endorse the necessity of teaching students how to use a variety of technologies. Similarly, the RAND Reading Study Group (2002) envisions that reading comprehension research will take another 20 years, because we live in an ever-changing world in which we are "experiencing an explosion of alternative texts" (p. xiv). It explains the complex skills needed in classrooms of the future: "Electronic texts that incorporate hyperlinks and hypermedia introduce some complications in defining comprehension because they require skills and abilities beyond those required for the comprehension of conventional, linear print" (p. 14). As a result, more research and practical professional development is needed on the comprehension processes necessary for reading on the Internet (Coiro, 2003b).

2. *How do exemplary teachers integrate technology into reading comprehension lessons?* Additional research is needed to assess how exemplary teachers integrate technology into comprehension lessons and, specifically, how teachers prepare students to search the Internet to become critical readers (Henry, 2006). Such research could inform school districts and teacher education institutions as they prepare new teachers to teach a tech-savvy group of students.

3. *How can we most effectively utilize WebQuest processes and inquiry learning using technology to teach English language learners and other diverse student populations (Ikpeze & Boyd, 2007)?* Such research could inform educators how multiple forms of representation impact language acquisition.

CHILDREN'S BOOKS THAT MIRROR TECHNO TEXTS
Bette Goldstone

"Think left and think right/and think low and think high," wrote Dr. Seuss in *Oh, The THINKS You Can Think* (first published in 1975). This is very wise advice for comprehending digital text and images, for traditional book comprehension skills are only a part of the skills repertoire today's students need. Literacy in hyperspace also requires understanding nonlinear text structure, taking on responsibilities of coauthoring—deciding what will be read, and in what order, and visually understanding the multiple screens (or spatial planes) and their interconnections. These literacy characteristics are not, however, solely relegated to screen-based texts. A form of children's book that has been emerging since the 1970s also uses these patterns. Sometimes called "postmodern," these books—which are becoming more prevalent each day—are nonlinear, require involved coauthoring on the part of the reader, and may have multiple spatial planes in the illustrations. Our students have to approach "technology text" and "postmodern text" thinking and viewing from high and low, right and left. They need to use skills that make them adept at being active coauthors and at maneuvering nonlinear texts and multiple spatial planes.

Explicit teaching, however, must occur. Every student is not necessarily comfortable or initially capable of using the latitude nonlinear texts offer. Deciding what to read on the page or screen, and in what sequence, and how to comprehend the seemingly disparate elements can be very confusing. Postmodern books can become a teaching tool to make transparent the needed thinking skills. Reading aloud a storybook quickly creates a shared experience and sense of community—computer use can be isolating. Books don't evaporate in cyberspace like some hyperlinks or websites—they are concrete, so they can easily be referred to again and again. Reading aloud books and investigating pictures as a group takes time—book time is slower than computer time and is thus easier to think about and reflect upon. These books also provide another venue for students to reshape, extrapolate, and apply important comprehension skills. Practicing skills in multiple contexts enhances and intensifies the learning experience.

Books with multiple story lines (told through words or illustrations) are excellent for understanding nonlinearity. The following are examples of such books:

- Burningham, J. (1978). *Time to get out of the bath, Shirley.* Ill. by the author. New York: Crowell.
- Browne, A. (1992). *Zoo.* Ill. by the author. New York: Knopf.
- Cherry, L. (1996). *The armadillo from Amarillo.* Ill. by the author. San Diego, CA: Harcourt Brace.
- Martin, J.B. (1999). *Snowflake Bentley.* Ill. M. Azarian. New York: Scholastic.
- Oppenheim, J. (1994). *Floratorium.* Ill. S. Schindler. New York: Bantam.
- Macauley, D. (1999). *Shortcut.* Ill. by the author. New York: Houghton Mifflin.
- Pullman, P. (1989). *Spring-heeled Jack.* Ill. D. Mostyn. New York: Knopf.
- Sis, P. (1996). *Starry messenger.* Ill. by the author. New York: HarperCollins.

Books that contain multiple voices, like multiple story lines, also provide greater insights and sensitivity to nonlinear texts. These also require coauthoring from the reader because connections are not explicitly apparent. The following are examples of these:

- Atkin, S.B. (2001). *Voices from the fields: Children of migrant farm workers tell their stories.* Ill. with photos. New York: Scholastic.
- Avi. (1993). *Nothing but the truth: A documentary novel.* New York: Morrow/Avon.
- Browne, A. (1998). *Voices in the park.* Ill. by the author. New York: Dorling Kindersley.

(continued)

FIGURE 24.4. Original list by Betty Goldstone from J. Castek, J. Bevans-Mangelson, & B. Goldstone (2006, April). *Children's books: Reading adventures online. The Reading Teacher, 59*(7), 714–728. Reprinted with permission of the International Reading Association.

- Creech, S. (2000). *The wanderer.* New York: Scholastic.
- Danzinger, P., & Martin, A.H. (2000). *Snail mail no more.* New York: Scholastic.
- Goldschmidt, J. (2005). *The secret blog of Raisin Rodriguez.* New York: Penguin.
- Hesse, K. (2001). *Witness.* New York: Scholastic.
- Konigsburg, E.L. (1999). *The view from Saturday.* New York: Scholastic.
- Sis, P. (2000). *Madlenka.* Ill. by the author. New York: Frances Foster.

Modern illustrators have been playing with multiple spatial plans, which make intriguing images and allow for interesting explorations of space and time. The following are examples of these:

- Banyai, I. (1995). *Zoom.* Ill. by the author. New York: Viking.
- Lehman, B. (2004). *The red book.* Ill. by the author. Boston: Houghton Mifflin.
- Lyon, G.E. (1996). *A day at Damp Camp.* Ill. P. Catalanotto. New York: Orchard.
- Raschka, C. (1997). *Mysterious Thelonious.* Ill. by the author. New York. Orchard.
- Rathmann, P. (1995). *Officer Buckle and Gloria.* Ill. by the author. New York: Putman.
- Sneed, B. (2002). *Picture a letter.* Ill. by the author. New York: Fogelman.
- Wiesner, D. (2001). *The three pigs.* Ill. by the author. New York: Scholastic.
- Yorinks, A. (1986). *Hey, Al.* Ill. by R. Egielski. New York: Farrar Straus Giroux.

Nontraditional postmodern children's books allow students to practice necessary comprehension skills. More important, they offer exciting new investigations into literary formats that resemble technology text but are unique unto themselves. They demonstrate that story structure is flexible and dynamic and that, similar to digital text, it will continue to be reconfigured and reimagined in the future.

FIGURE 24.4. *(continued)*

SUMMARY

In summary, comprehension lessons in the year 2030 will seamlessly connect literacy and technology. Teachers will have ready a backpack of teaching tools from which to teach comprehension lessons, such as turning to online read-aloud books, VFTs, and WebQuests to enable children to acquire background knowledge prior to reading a text. Teachers will explicitly show students a variety of texts that present multiple voices, stories, and structures, while enabling students to comprehend the nonlinear structure of Internet reading. As educators prepare for 2030, they must take into consideration those skills needed for their students to become productive and employable citizen of a technologically driven world. Educators today, and in the future, must continually find ways to engage and to create interest, so that their students possess the same type of enthusiasm as Grace illustrated in the quote that began this chapter. Reaching for the moon is just the beginning.

INTEGRATE, INVESTIGATE, AND INITIATE: QUESTIONS FOR DISCUSSION

1. Examine your school library or a library within your district. How would you change it to ensure that the information you learned in this chapter could be better incorporated into that setting to ensure that all students' needs can be met?
2. Visit one of the websites cited in this article and prepare a summary of the information you would use on this website to improve your instruction of comprehension.

3. Interview a school principal or a vice-principal about the most important features of technology- or print-based comprehension that exists in their school. Before you leave him or her, prepare a one page, bulleted summary of the information you have learned from reading this book that you would want to leave, so that he or she has improvements to consider in the future to improve the comprehension of all students. With each bulleted suggestion, include your reasons why that innovation would advance students comprehension from your perspective. Once these interviews have been completed, share the experiences with colleagues who conducted similar interviews.

REFERENCES

Block, C. C. (2004). *Teaching comprehension: The comprehension process approach*. Boston: Allyn & Bacon.

Block, C. C., Gambrell, L. B., & Pressley, M. (Eds.). (2004). *Improving comprehension instruction: Rethinking research, theory, and classroom practice*. San Francisco: Jossey-Bass.

Castek, J., Bevans-Mangelson, J. B., & Goldstone, B. (2006). Reading adventures online: Five ways to introduce the new literacies of the Internet through children's literature. *Reading Teacher, 59*(7), 714–728.

Coiro, J. (2003a). Rethinking comprehension strategies to better prepare students for critically evaluating content on the Internet. *NERA Journal, 39*(2), 29–34.

Coiro, J. (2003b). Reading comprehension on the Internet: Expanding our understanding of reading comprehension to encompass new literacies [Exploring Literacy on the Internet department]. *Reading Teacher, 56*, 458–464. Retrieved June 1, 2007, from *www.readingonline.org/electronic/elec_index.asp?href=/electronic/rt/2-03_column/index.html*.

Coiro, J., & Dobler, E. (2007). Exploring the online reading comprehension strategies used by sixth-grade skilled readers to search for and locate information on the Internet. *Reading Research Quarterly, 42*(2), 214–257.

Dreher, M. J. (1993). Reading to locate information: Societal and educational perspectives. *Contemporary Educational Psychology, 18*, 129–138.

Eliopoulos, D., & Gotlieb, C. (2003). Evaluating Web search results rankings. *Online, 27*, 42–48.

Gambrell, L. B., Wilson, R. M., & Gantt, W. N. (1981). Classroom observations of task-attending behaviors of good and poor readers. *Journal of Educational Research, 764*, 400–404.

Goldstone, B. (2006). Children's books that mirror techno texts. Reading *Reading Teacher, 59*(7), 725.

Guinee, K., Eagleton, M. B., & Hall, T. E. (2003). Adolescents' Internet search strategies: Drawing upon familiar cognitive paradigms when accessing electronic information sources. *Journal of Educational Computing Research 29*, 363–374.

Henry, L. A. (2006). SEARCHing for an answer: The critical role of the new literacies while reading on the Internet. *Reading Teacher, 59*(7), 614–627.

Ikpeze, C. H., & Boyd, F. B. (2007). Web-based inquiry learning: Facilitating thoughtful literacy with WebQuests. *Reading Teacher 60*(7), 644–654.

International Reading Association. (2001). *Integrating literacy and technology in the curriculum* (Position statement). Retrieved June 1, 2007, from *www.reading.org/downloads/positions/ps1048_technology.pdf*.

International Reading Association and National Council of Teachers of English. (2000). *Standards for the English language arts*. Newark, DE: Author.

International Society for Technology in Education. (1998). *National educational technology standards for students*. Eugene, OR: Author. Retrieved June 1, 2007, from *cnets.iste.org/students/s_stands.html*.

Johnson, D. (2005). Miss Rumphius as a role model for preservice teachers. In R. A. Karchmer, M. H, Mallette, J. Kara-Soteriou, & D. J. Leu (Eds.), *Innovative approaches to literacy education:*

Using the Internet to support new literacies (pp. 182–198). Newark: International Reading Association.

Karchmer, R. A., Mallette, M. H., Kara-Soteriou, J., & Leu, D. J. (2005). *Innovative approaches to literacy education: Using the Internet to support new literacies*. Newark, DE: International Reading Association.

Kinzer, C. K. (2003). The importance of recognizing the expanding boundaries of literacy. In *Reading Online*. Retrieved June 1, 2007, from *www.readingonline.org/electornic/elec_index.asp?href=kinzer*.

Labbo, L. (2002). Computers, kids, and comprehension: Instructional practices that make a difference. In C. C. Block, L. Gambrell, & M. Pressley (Eds.), *Improving comprehension instruction: Rethinking research, theory, and classroom practice* (pp. 275–289). San Francisco: Jossey-Bass..

Labbo, L. (2004). Author's computer chair. *Reading Teacher, 57*, 688–691.

Lacina, J. (2004). Designing a virtual fieldtrip. *Childhood Education, 80*(4), 221–222.

Lacina, J. (2007). Inquiry based learning and technology: Designing and exploring webquests. *Childhood Education, 83*(3), 251–252.

Leu, D. J. (2001). Internet project: Preparing students for new literacies in a global village. *Reading Teacher, 54*, 568–585.

Leu, D. J., Jr., Kinzer, C. K., Coiro, J. L., & Cammack, D. W. (2004). Toward a theory of new literacies emerging from the Internet and other information and communication technologies. In R. B. Ruddell & N. J. Unrau (Eds.), *Theoretical models and processes of reading* (5th ed., pp. 1570–1613). Newark, DE: International Reading Association.

Lewin, L. (1998). Taming the Web: Reading for comprehension. *Multimedia Schools, 5*, 50–52.

McKenna, M. C., Labbo, L. D., & Reinking, D. (2003). Effective use of technology in literacy instruction. In L. M. Morrow, L. B. Gambrell, & M. Pressley (Eds.), *Best practices in literacy instruction* (2nd ed., pp. 307–331). New York: Guilford Press.

Nachmias, R., & Gilad, A. (2002). Needle in a hyperstack: Searching for information on the World Wide Web. *Journal of Research in Technology in Education, 34*, 475–486.

Palincsar, A. S., & Brown, A. L. (1984). Reciprocal teaching of comprehension-fostering and comprehension-monitoring activities. *Cognition and Instruction, 1*, 117–175.

Palmer, B. M., Codling, R. M., & Gambrell, L. B. (1994). In their own words: What elementary children have to say about motivation to read. *Reading Teacher, 48*, 176–179.

Prensky, M. (2001). Digital natives, digital immigrants. *NCB University Press, 9*(5). Retrieved June 1, 2007, from *www.marcprensky.com/writing/prensky%20-%20digital%20natives,%20digital%20immigrants%20-%20part1.pdf*.

RAND Reading Study Group. (2002). *Reading for understanding: Towards an R&D program in reading comprehension*. Retrieved June 1, 2007, from *www.rand.org/multi/achievementforall/reading/readreport.html*.

Shanahan, T. (2005). *The National Reading Panel report: Practical advice for teachers*. Naperville, IL: Learning Point Associates.

Snyder, I. (2002). Literacy education in the digital age: Reframing curriculum and pedagogy. *Pedagogisch Tijdschrift, 27*, 145–157.

Street, B. (2003). What's "new" in new literacy studies?: Critical approaches to literacy in theory and practice. *Current Issues in Comparative Education, 5*(2). Retrieved June 1, 2007, from *www.tc.columbia.edu/cice/articles/bs152.htm*.

Turbill, J. (2002). The four ages of reading philosophy and pedagogy: A framework for examining theory and practice. *Reading Online, 5*(6). Retrieved June 1, 2007, from *www.readingonline.org/international/inter_index.asp?href=turbill4/index.html*.

Valmont, W. J. (2003). *Technology for literacy teaching and learning*. Boston: Houghton Mifflin.

Van Leeuwen, C. A., & Gabriel, M. A. (2007). Beginning to write with word processing: Integrating writing process and technology in the primary classroom. *Reading Teacher, 60*(5), 420–428.

Warschauer, M. (2006). *Laptops and literacy: Learning in the wireless classroom*. New York: Teachers College Press.

CHILDREN'S BOOKS CITED

Atkin, S. B. (2001). *Voices from the fields: Children of migrant farm workers tell their stories.* New York: Scholastic.
Beatty, P. (1992). *Lupita Mañana.* New York: Junior Books.
Beckwith, K. (2005). *Children of war* (L. Lyons, Illustrator). Tilbury House.
Browne, A. (1998). *Voices in the park.* New York: Dorling Kindersley.
Bunting, E. (1994). *Smoky nights.* (D. Diaz, Illustrator). New York: Voyager Books.
Cherry, L. (1996). *The armadillo from Amarillo.* San Diego, CA: Harcourt Brace.
Cole, J. (1995). *The magic school bus inside a hurricane.* (B. Degen, Illustrator). New York: Scholastic.
Fleischman, P. (1997). *Seedfolks* (J. Pedersen, Illustrator). New York: Joanna Cotler Books.
Frasier, D. (2000). *Miss Alaineus: A vocabulary disaster.* New York: Scholastic.
Goldschmidt, J. (2005). *The secret blog of Raisin Rodriguez.* New York: Penguin.
Greenfield, L. (2006). *When the horses ride by: Children in the times of war.* (J. Spivey Gilchrist, Illustrator). New York: Lee & Low Books.
Martin, J. B. (1999). *Snowflake Bentley.* (M. Azarian, Illustrator). New York: Scholastic.
Mayer, M. (2005). *There are monsters everywhere.* New York: Dial Books for Young Readers.
Naidoo, B. (2005). *Making it home: Real-life stories from children forced to flee.* Penguin Young Readers.
Oppenheim, J. (1994). *Floratorium.* (S. Schindler, Illustrator). New York: Bantam.
Macauley, D. (1999). *Shortcut.* New York: Houghton Mifflin.
Schotter, R. (1999). *Nothing ever happens on 90th street.* (K. Brooker, Illustrator). New York: Orchard Paperbacks.
Seuss, Dr. (1963). *Hop on pop.* New York: Beginner Books.
Seuss, Dr. (1975). *Oh, the thinks you can think!* New York: Random House.
Sneed, B. (2002). *Picture a letter.* New York: Fogelman.
Teague, M. (2002). *Dear Mrs. LaRue: Letters from obedience school.* New York: Scholastic.
Wiesner, D. (2001). *The three pigs.* New York: Scholastic.
Wise Brown, M. (1947). *Goodnight moon.* New York: HarperCollins.

VI

CONCLUSION

25

Summing Up

SHERI R. PARRIS and CATHY COLLINS BLOCK

> Do not go where the path may lead. Go instead
> where there is no path and leave a trail.
> —RALPH WALDO EMERSON

Our goal in this chapter is to summarize the research and best practices identified by the outstanding experts who authored chapters in this book. We identify commonalities between chapters that suggest future directions for comprehension investigations and instruction. We also synthesize the projections provided by each of the research teams represented in this book as to the future of exemplary instruction in 2030. You might enjoy noting the trends and common projections that you have identified and comparing your reflections to ours.

At the 2007 International Reading Association conference, John Kirby (Queens University, Ontario) reaffirmed the need for more research at all levels of processing in reading, from the neurological and genetic level to the higher levels of comprehension. He also confirmed the great need for more research in all contexts of reading, from early home to school to lifelong learning. This second edition of *Comprehension Instruction* takes steps in these directions. We look forward to the new directions that research will take us in the future.

There is virtually universal agreement among researchers and educators within and outside the realm of this book that to achieve complete comprehension, students need to decode words, understand vocabulary, read fluently, have adequate background knowledge, think critically, understand various text structures, and be motivated to read. Beyond these given domains of influence, other important, brain-based, theoretical discoveries are brewing in our field and drawing our attention toward a deeper understanding of individual students' comprehension needs. This volume looks at some of these current directions of new thought concerning reading comprehension. Effective and established instructional practices are also reconfirmed and investigated in greater depth.

In addition, this second edition of *Comprehension Instruction* contains input from talented researchers from countries outside of the United States. We welcome and acknowledge our international authors, who represent citizenship in Canada, China, Germany, and South Korea. It is always interesting when researchers from different cultural locales with distinct backgrounds gather to produce separate chapters on their topics of expertise, and produce a larger circle of influence through information that carries common underlying themes. Such overlapping of new data arises over and over throughout this edition of *Comprehension Instruction*. As you read and reread, you may have noticed some commonalities that piqued your attention. The most promising areas for future research, the best practices, and most prominent, newly evolving common directions for comprehension instruction and research from our perspective follow.

COMMON THEMES AND NEW DIRECTIONS FOR RESEARCH AND BEST PRACTICES

Nine of the newly emerging directions and needs in the field of reading comprehension, as presented in this book, are listed and discussed below:

- The need to continue and expand our global literacy discourse.
- The necessity to increase our research and instructional attention to technologically based, digital comprehension.
- The new obligation to partner with neuroscientists in the design of new comprehension research and instructional pedagogy.
- The requirement to explore the interactions between motivation and comprehension development.
- The new obligation to expand explicit comprehension instruction and teachers' professional knowledge base concerning comprehension pedagogy.
- The need to create more student-led, collaborative comprehension learning experiences.
- The exploration of new methods of learning to comprehend more effectively through multiple physical modalities.
- The importance of differentiating instruction for fictional and nonfictional texts.
- The call for more consistent schoolwide comprehension instructional frameworks.

Continuing and Expanding Our Global Literacy Discourse

There is a no longer a need for each country to study comprehension research and pedagogy separately. Rather, reading comprehension research is a universal issue in which all countries and all languages can share research and learn from each other. This global interpretation of new comprehension data is one of the most promising new directions for comprehension research that has emerged since 2002, and is described in depth in Chapter l (Parris, Gambrell, & Schleicher) of this volume. The numerous websites created within the last few years alone, as demonstrated by Parris et al., challenge all researchers to stay connected to our global research community. Parris et al. provide many directions that individual researchers and practitioners can take today to become instantly connected to global empirical and pedagogical conversations that are moving rapidly into new fields of fruitful exploration of how the mind learns to comprehend.

In addition to the direct evidence presented in Chapters 1 and 14 (Reznitskaya, Anderson, Dong, Kım, Kım, & Li) of this book, we can see this global footprint throughout many of the chapters. For instance, Cartwright (Chapter 4) discusses how cognitive flexibility theory is applicable across cultures, and discusses how this premise has been shown to be an important determinant for reading comprehension success among Chinese students. Baker (Chapter 5), meanwhile, discusses research conducted in various European countries. Moreover, Fisher and Frey (Chapter 18) note how adolescent students' comprehension increases when they share their responses to literature through Facebook, blogs, and fanzines (where geographic boundaries do not exist).

Parris et al. (Chapter 1) demonstrate how teachers can use many websites during comprehension instruction that contain current, global information. These classroom-based global communication infusions and others are present in at least one reading classroom program in almost every school district in America and around the world. Such international platforms for comprehension research and pedagogy were not widespread 6 years ago.

Through global assessments such as the Program for International Student Assessment (PISA) and the Progress in International Reading Literacy Study (PIRLS) (as described in Chapter l, this volume), and the efforts of the individual worldwide researchers represented in this book, we are finding the commonalities that bind us together in our search to improve reading comprehension for all. Finally, with the increasing presence of both technology and neuroscience in reading comprehension research, these borderless fields of study are increasingly blurring national and international borders within the reading community. The supremacy of technologically driven communication is the power that is enabling the world to become a smaller and more intimate place for us all to live, explore, and comprehend.

Increasing Our Research and Instructional Attention to Technologically Based, Digital Comprehension

Fisher and Frey (Chapter 18), Thompson (Chapter 11), Smolkin, McTigue, and Donovan (Chapter 13), and Castek et al. (Chapter 22) all point out that in addition to traditional texts, students need to be engaged with text in an ever-expanding variety of media (e.g., hypermedia, digital) to be fully literate in today's society. The term "new literacies" (see Jan Lacina's in-depth description in Chapter 24; see also Dalton & Rose in Chapter 23, and Castek et al. in Chapter 22) is used to describe the ability to find, use, and synthesize information on the internet and other technologies.

Several researchers throughout this book agree with Fisher and Frey (Chapter 18), Dalton and Rose (Chapter 23), and Castek et al. (Chapter 22) that traditional classroom instruction will soon evolve into a more technological experience, and a growing portion of comprehension learning experiences will take place through computer and other media devices. Lacina (Chapter 24) predicts that "comprehension lessons . . . will seamlessly connect literacy and technology" (p. 374). Dalton and Rose (Chapter 23) expand this prediction by stating that scaffolded digital literacy could lead us, by 2030, to the point that "the reading–achievement gap will have become a historical anecdote" (p. 628).

Additionally, Thompson (Chapter 11) points out that increased technology use in schools will also call for an increased need to instruct teachers as to how to use these new technologies effectively in their classrooms. As Lacina (Chapter 24) anticipates, the increased use of electronic and animated storybooks in the early grades, and the interactive nature of classroom storybook reading will enable teachers to "have ready a backpack of teaching tools from which to teach comprehension lessons, such as turning to online read-aloud books, VFTs, and WebQuests" (p. 660). This evolution will increase the need for students to learn how to synthesize and evaluate the abundant amounts of information, and communicate with others, regardless of distance and time constraints.

Fisher and Frey (Chapter 18) summarize a final directive made by several authors in this text: In the future, "knowledge transmission" will be replaced by "knowledge creation." They define "knowledge creation" as learners coming together to form new understandings, using key reading comprehension skills such as vocabulary knowledge, strategic learning, background knowledge, motivation, and engagement, with these elements being just as important for users of technology as they are for users of traditional text. To illustrate, Lacina (Chapter 24) found successful reading comprehension on the Internet also causes readers to engage in self-directed text construction, and these readers must be able to make their own decisions regarding what they want to read next. Thus, with "new literacies" will come new reading comprehension skills that students need to master, although the necessity to learn traditional strategies will remain. Lacina provides a rich and varied list of excellent Web resources to aid educators in improving the technological and text-based reading comprehension of their students.

Although Caccamise, Snyder, and Kintsch (Chapter 6) focus their discussion on new developments in constructivist theory, situation modeling, and assessment of reading comprehension, they demonstrate how integrative the field of comprehension research and practice has become within the last 6 years. They, like other authors in this book, demonstrate how technology has infused every component of comprehension investigation and instruction. Caccamise et al. eloquently describe how computer-mediated testing and advances in statistical and neuroscientific findings in natural language processing will soon make possible the delivery of more sophisticated testing protocols and scientific models of expert comprehension ability. These authors also include explanations of better ways to build on prior knowledge, to make student thinking visible, and to engage students in self-monitoring through technological advancements. As summarized in Chapter 6, today's assessments are in the process of being greatly improved through technological and neuroscientific advancements. The most important change is that comprehension assessment is becoming a dynamic, multipoint evaluation during learning and reading processes, and not simply a one-time snapshot.

Partnering with Neuroscientists in the Design of New Comprehension Research and Instructional Pedagogy

Throughout this volume, the use of neuroscience in assessing and teaching reading comprehension has been a recurrent theme. As Caccamise et al. (Chapter 6) and Block and Duffy (Chapter 2) point out, assessments are becoming increasingly flexible (unlike assessments of the past) and, according to Block and Duffy, are beginning to offer the capability to "adapt to students' mastery and instructional reading levels, control vocabulary levels, structure the presentation of questions, and query students' ability to construct not only coherence in their understanding of the content but also the ability to extend their understanding beyond explicit text content" (p. 180). The ease and efficiency of using these assessments will make them a much more "doable" component of reading instruction for all students, allowing both students and teachers to have more immediate feedback on progress and to incorporate these findings into instruction more quickly.

Similarly, Block and Parris (Chapter 8) inform us that advances in neuroscience are helping us to understand learning, in addition to many other implications specifically applicable to reading instruction. They also reiterate that reading instruction should be dynamic, exploratory, and interactive. Caine (Chapter 9) and Parris (Chapter 10) discuss how reading comprehension cannot be limited to simple acts of cognition, and how it is inseparable from all other brain-based functions, such as emotion, motivation, sensory, and real-life experience. Thus, learning is a wholistic experience from a neuroscientific perspective. All of the components of the brain are interconnected; thus, effective reading comprehension utilizes multiple brain areas simultaneously. Caine (Chapter 9) reports positive results when instruction is tailored to work with the way the brain learns naturally.

Making the most of neurological findings has led us to discover new methods to use in future comprehension lessons. Based on neurological data, Block and Parris (Chapter 8) recommend the following four instructional components: (1) personalized checklists to eliminate unproductive repetition of a particular thinking process; (2) fast mapping for long-term memory growth, (3) making reading a more positive emotional experience, and (4) creating an emotionally risk-free environment. These authors report that the field of reading comprehension still needs more research to create a bridge between brain processes and reading instruction. For example, more research is needed to delineate the neuroprocessing differences between different book- and technology-based environments.

Exploring the Interactions Between Motivation and Comprehension Development

Caine (Chapter 9) reported that the brain is naturally driven to learn, and that it is attracted to novelty and personally compelling situations. She presents 12 principles that maximize comprehension through the use of motivation, social interactions, pattern recognition, real-life experiences, reflection, engagement in multiple ways with text, meeting individual differences in maturation, as well as building challenging environments to extend individual student talents, abilities, and capacities. Likewise, learners who can generate their own, personally relevant questions are internally motivated to perform the research necessary to find the answer. Therefore, student- rather than teacher-generated questions should be used for reading instructional purposes whenever possible. Other successful methods were also described for adolescents by Parris (Chapter 10), and for elementary students by Thompson (Chapter 11).

Malloy and Gambrell (Chapter 16) offer other valuable solutions designed to increase student motivation (when motivation is lacking) to read certain texts. They present a theoretical piece that advises teachers on how to help readers to become engaged in a text. First, teachers must provide background information to help students find relevance and/or make personal connections to the topic. Second, students will be more motivated when they understand how learning outcomes are relevant to their own lives outside the classroom. Third, explicit instruction of comprehension strategies is motivating, because it lays a clear path for students to follow in overcoming their reading difficulties. Malloy and Gambrell provide the most comprehensive and up-to-date documentation of knowledge concerning the interaction of comprehension and motivation.

Similarly, as Gee (Chapter 21) points out, popular culture and the types of technology found in youth environments can also be effective tools to motivate students to learn reading comprehension skills. He discusses video games and other types of popular strategy games as examples. Such games, Gee remarks, are excellent sources for learning new vocabulary and critical thinking skills, especially because players of these games must master complex vocabulary and thinking processes to make progress in the game. Gee notes that these games typically use "specialist language" (language with an abundance of technical terms and/or formal words) and complex syntactic and discourse structures. He notes that content area courses are also infused with these same language features. Yet, Gee stresses that we should not simply rush to use pop culture devices as motivational or learning tools in and of themselves. Educators and researchers should take a hard look at the ways that pop culture engages children to learn and find ways to transfer these practices into today's classroom comprehension instructional programs.

Expanding Explicit Comprehension Instruction and Teachers' Professional Knowledge Base Concerning Comprehension Pedagogy

As discussed extensively in several chapters of this book (e.g., by Thompson in Chapter 11, relating to elementary students and fictional text; by Caccamise et al. in Chapter 6 and Parris in Chapter 10, relating to secondary students), today's readers need to be able to apply comprehension strategies consciously when necessary. Baker (Chapter 5) and Block and Duffy (Chapter 2) also confirm that explicit strategy instruction builds the metacognitive thinking processes that students need. Through explicit instruction, Baker and Block and Duffy demonstrate that teachers can show students appropriate strategies to overcome specific problems encountered during reading. Think-alouds (Block & Duffy, Chapter 2) and teaching students to recognize, and to be able to maneuver through different types of text structures (Duke & Martin, Chapter 17), should be something all students are taught to do.

This is especially true for expository text, which comes in a variety of text structures (for methods of providing strong comprehension instructional supports for these texts, see Williams, Chapter 12; Smolkin et al., Chapter 13). Also in Chapter 12, Williams provides examples of helpful strategies for expository text: (1) using clue words to identify the type of text structure; (2) using graphic organizers to lay out the information visually; and (3) answering a series of questions to help students focus on the important information in a text. Introducing strategies at the sentence level before proceeding to the paragraph level is recommended by Williams (Chapter 12).

Like Block and Duffy (Chapter 2), Smolkin et al. (Chapter 13) and Hock, Brasseur, & Deschler (Chapter 19) also emphasize the importance of think-alouds and of explaining the ideas found in both the text and graphics of a book. Helping students understand how to make sense of graphics and other visual aids that accompany text is important for all types of reading materials. All of these researchers agree that current research teams are viewing comprehension development with the complexity of perspectives/lenses that it deserves.

In almost every chapter, particularly in Reznitskaya et al. (Chapter 14), and Duke and Martin (Chapter 17), researchers today talk more about the importance of making comprehension strategies "transparent" and "transportable" for students than they did 6 years ago; that is, students should understand why a particular type of instruction is necessary (transparent) and how they can apply these strategies to other content areas (transportable) through a wide variety of activities, such as argumentation (Reznitskaya et al., Chapter 14), scaffolding group opportunities for metacognitive development through responding to text for struggling readers (Baker, Chapter 5), providing comprehension instruction all day long and across all content areas even for primary-age students (Duke & Martin, Chapter 17), and engaging in text structure analyses (Williams, Chapter 12). Overall, explicit instruction in its many forms (e.g., think-alouds, modeling, scaffolded instruction, strategy instruction, and guided reading) is an important component of effective reading comprehension instructional models throughout this volume. Reznitskaya et al. (Chapter 14) and Duke and Martin (Chapter 17) present new applications of argumentation schema theory and sociological theories of comprehension instruction and assessment, which are among the most promising paths for new, explicit pedagogical methods.

Creating More Student-Led, Collaborative Comprehension Learning Experiences

The importance of peer interaction in learning has become an increasingly important element on the menu of today's reading comprehension researchers, as so eloquently described by Dalton and Rose (Chapter 23) and Castek et al. (Chapter 22). Hock et al. (Chapter 19) discuss significant gains in test scores achieved through a ninth-grade reading course that includes ongoing peer discussion of text (along with engaging reading materials), in addition to regular reading instruction. Reznitskaya et al. (Chapter 14) discuss the benefits of argumentation for developing higher levels of reading comprehension ability.

Additionally, Fisher and Frey (Chapter 18) state that collaboration allows students to work together to "apply what they have learned in focus lessons and guided instruction" (p. 263). Their research has led them to understand that students need this peer interaction to "consolidate" their learning, and that doing collaborative work as a learning tool is most effective before students are asked to complete work individually.

Exploring New Methods of Learning to Comprehend Through Multiple Physical Modalities

Dual coding theory (described by Sadoski in Chapter 3 and Paivio in Chapter 7) informs us that the mental representations made during reading can activate, and are activated by, all five senses (i.e., seeing, hearing, tasting, smelling, and touching). Paivio reminds us that reading is "completely intertwined with and dependent on all other sensorimotor systems" (p. 103). Paivio (Chapter 7) also notes that the brain does need to "physically interact" with what is to be learned or understood.

These physical senses may be activated by the memories and experiences of the person during reading and can emerge as mental images, movements, or verbal associations. Sadoski (Chapter 3), Paivio (Chapter 7), Hock et al. (Chapter 19), and Parris (Chapter 10) all point out that creating visual images of what you read is an important component of reading comprehension. Sadoski and Paivio, through dual coding theory, explain that reading can be separated into two mental systems, linguistic and nonlinguistic, which work in unison to create mental images from text. Thus, educators must spend time to ensure that students develop the ability to create rich mental images during reading. Additionally, as Sadoski (Chapter 3) has proven, although it is easier to visualize concrete words, it is possible to help children learn to make visual or other modality associations to abstract words. These researchers, Sadoski (Chapter 3), Paivio (Chapter 7), and Block and Parris (Chapter 8), have found that this ability to create a mental image while reading significantly enhances reading comprehension.

Headley (Chapter 15) points out that writing and technology are efficient tools for both students' writing and the assessment of students' comprehension abilities. For example, Headley notes that both of these media build a physical, concrete, dual-coded activity to increase comprehension. Different modalities, through technology, can also be used for sharing and publishing student writing across classrooms, schools, and countries. She also points out that more than being just the "text-based products" of the past, writing should increasingly include graphics, images, and audio to complement the text. But, whether done through technology or traditional pencil and paper, writing in response to reading is found throughout this volume as an integral part of effective reading comprehension instruction. Headley also notes that writing with technology broadens teachers' conception of peer sharing and publishing, because peer feedback is available not only from classmates but also from students around the world.

Differentiating Comprehension Instruction for Fictional and Nonfictional Texts

With the increasing focus on accountability and standardized testing in the content areas, reading comprehension research has increasingly focused on best methods of understanding nonfiction texts (Smolkin et al., Chapter 13, summarize this body of research). Yet research also continues to show that nonfiction texts cannot replace the vitally important and different types of comprehension processes that must occur if students are to understand fictional texts. As Parris (Chapter 10) explains, literature and character studies, for example, enable students to use stories to develop their higher-level thinking and real-world problem resolution skills. Duke and Martin (Chapter 17) remind us that literature provides an abundance of opportunities to stimulate other such higher-level cognitive activities through its rich meanings, metaphors, and innuendos. In one example, Hock et al. (Chapter 19) discuss an effective reading comprehension program that uses engaging literature to teach students to use higher-level thinking processes.

The study of literature in general and/or character studies in particular can teach higher-level and abstract thinking skills such as grappling with complex concepts and thinking reflectively (even for English language learners, and adolescent learners; see Rueda, Velasco, & Lim in Chapter 20 and Parris in Chapter 10, respectively). Such lessons also develop cognitive flexibility (see Cartwright, Chapter 4) by creating opportunities for students to coordinate many meaning-making clues simultaneously. Another important type of flexibility in reading comprehension is the ability to consider semantic and graphophonological features of text simultaneously while reading. Specific cognitive flexibility abilities can be taught and measured as early as second grade. Lacina (Chapter 24) discusses how good literature provides teachers with an important source of interesting and motivating texts, especially when these texts are coupled with the exciting websites she cites, in which updated lists of high-quality literature are matched to pedagogical lessons.

In Chapter 11, Thompson provides three directives for using fictional texts that have remained sound and effective practices over the years: (1) Know your students and tailor lessons to their interests/needs; (2) plan effective, engaging instruction; and, (3) scaffold appropriately. Thompson also emphasizes the importance of finding creative ways of meeting students' needs. She cites a study in which puppets were effectively used in one kindergarten class to encourage children to become engaged with the text and to enhance classroom discussion. Recent research has demonstrated that each of the methods we have cited in this chapter, as well as numerous others cited throughout this text, may be modified when used to build comprehension of nonfiction. In essence, students must learn that some special comprehension skills are needed for fiction and others are needed for nonfiction, whereas still others can be used for both types of genres.

More Consistent, Schoolwide Comprehension Instructional Frameworks

Fisher and Frey (Chapter 18) call for more consistency among secondary teachers within each particular school. They use note taking as an example of how inconsistency can hinder secondary students' achievement. Because these students often have five or more class periods per day (each with different teachers), if each teacher demands that his or her students master a different set of note-taking strategies, then students can end up spending valuable learning time mastering each teacher's protocols rather than actually learning the course content. When this is multiplied by the myriad other protocols that may be different for each particular teacher, one can easily see how secondary students get caught up in trying to attend to the individual instructional styles of each teacher, and lose focus on what it is they need to learn.

When individual schools and districts adopt common instructional protocols that are transferable from course to course (also called "literacy frameworks" by Fisher and Frey), more of teachers' and students' time and mental energy can be focused on learning the content of the course. Fisher and Frey (Chapter 18) and Caine (Chapter 9) point out that educators must consistently collaborate and learn from each other to work effectively together to find the best ways to help the students in their own schools.

Rueda et al. (Chapter 20) point out that we have not tested enough culturally based interventions or studied the motivational factors that impact English language learners' comprehension. They propose that we must develop a comprehension theoretical framework that relates basic reading skills and comprehension processes to the multiple, complex dimensions of comprehension abilities and the social nature of classroom instruction. They also recommend that technology become a tool by which we begin to build a more consistent, schoolwide comprehension instructional program that addresses the special learning needs of English language learners. They cite a recent study that reports English language learners can effectively use digitally embedded instructional support to enhance reading ability. These tools include vocabulary supports, such as hyperlinked glossary definitions and text-to-speech, and read-aloud functions embedded into software. These enhancements to the reading experience have been shown to provide useful reading assistance for English language learners. Virtual environments can also be useful in providing English language learners with necessary background information prior to, or during, reading of particular texts.

Cartwright (Chapter 4) documents the need to teach all readers (especially those with special learning needs) cognitive flexibility. Research that supports these instructional programs has demonstrated that they can become a new way to help struggling readers overcome literacy challenges. She encourages the use of various programs already available at the adolescent levels, such as Fusion Reading. She also has data to suggest that after 2 years of such instruction, students who are more than two grade levels below their grade placements can close the achievement gap. As we reread Chapter 4, we became increasingly convinced that infusion of Cartwright's premises for cognitive flexibility theories throughout our curricula holds great potential to advance our comprehension knowledge base within the next decade.

PROJECTIONS AND POSSIBILITIES FOR THE CLASSROOMS OF 2030

We also synthesized the projections provided by each research team represented in this book as to the future of exemplary instruction in 2030. You might enjoy noting the trends and common projections that you identified, and comparing your reflections to ours. Among the 24 chapters, we tallied 92 predictions (we tallied those that were mentioned in at least two different chapters) regarding the future of comprehension instruction. We then collapsed these predictions into the following 16 categories:

1. widespread technology use (19 chapters),
2. increased peer interaction/collaborative learning experiences (11 chapters),
3. increased/improved professional development for teachers (8 chapters),
4. improved assessment to provide immediate, individualized feedback to inform learning (7 chapters),
5. increased use of neuroscientific evidence to inform research (6 chapters),

6. more attention given to student motivation and engagement (6 chapters),
7. comprehension instruction will become increasingly multimodal in nature (various discourses, texts, genres, types of media) (6 chapters),
8. increased attention to creating positive, emotionally supportive learning environments (5 chapters),
9. widespread participation in global literacy discourse (4 chapters),
10. comprehension instruction will expand to the early grades, including kindergarten (4 chapters),
11. increased use of explicit comprehension instruction (3 chapters),
12. increased use of metacognitively-oriented instruction (3 chapters),
13. increased use of authentic learning experiences (2 chapters),
14. comprehension instruction will merge with content area instruction (2 chapters),
15. additional benefits of using narrative text will continue to emerge (2 chapters), and
16. public policy will reflect the research (2 chapters)

Overall, the authors in this book agree that whereas classrooms will still maintain a need for rules and routines, they will be more flexible, with students working on assignments tailored to their individual needs. Increasing use of technology in classrooms will enable students to become more independent learners, with the ability to self-select the lessons they need and those that motivate them. This technology surge will also enable students to become part of a learning community that, without boundaries, literally reaches around the world.

In the future, all students will be metacognitively aware of the comprehension strategies they need for specific situations and flexibly apply these strategies when needed. This knowledge will come from both explicit instruction and digital technologies that will serve as individualized, personal tutors for each student. Technology will provide detailed, individualized assessments and immediate feedback regarding specific reading comprehension instructional needs. Future students will also have a basic toolbag of comprehension strategies, as well as a toolbag of strategies to use when maneuvering through multimedia texts. In addition, they will be adept at comprehending the meaning of the textual and graphical components of both traditional and digital texts.

Continuing, quality professional development will become a necessity for teachers to utilize these technology-rich environments effectively for instruction. They will assist students in creating knowledge rather than simply transmitting knowledge to students. In fact, students are already becoming knowledge creators through blogging, Facebook, and collaboration with peers overseas to compose fanzines and other digital products. Thus, a more creative, more collaborative atmosphere will be commonplace in the classrooms of tomorrow.

In summary, this volume shows us that as the world and the way we live our lives change and unfold, so must our explorations and teaching of reading comprehension keep up with these changes. There are daunting new challenges for both researchers and educators, whose vision is to ensure that students can read and comprehend all the texts that they encounter in school and in life. On our menu of reading comprehension practices are some reliable entrée's that must be a part of the balanced diet of reading comprehension instruction, yet new items are constantly being added to this menu. New types of texts, new technologies, and new colleagues from around the world continue to bring new items to the menu. Additionally, these items must be consistently refined to meet students' changing needs. Thus, while the world of reading comprehension is vast and changing, this very complexity makes it an exciting and interesting time to be a comprehension researcher and teacher.

Epilogue
What the Future of Reading Research Could Be

MICHAEL PRESSLEY

This talk is about what I hope will be the future of research in reading, especially reading education. I realize, however, that most research in reading education, like most science, will be incremental work, going a bit farther than the field has gone previously. Thus, a realistic, future-oriented talk about reading research must be grounded in past work.

For as long as people have studied or thought about anything, there has been the part–whole dilemma, whether it makes more sense to focus on the whole or its constituent parts. So it is with the reading education research of the recent past. There has been research on whole classrooms and schools that are making more of an impact than other reading educational settings, and thus, deserve our attention. As researchers study these situations, however, they inevitably spend a great deal of time focusing on the instructional components contributing to the achievement in these settings. And, for every study of whole classrooms or schools, there are dozens of studies directed at particular components of reading or literacy education, with many researchers making very good livings by analyzing particular components in great detail, turning their attention to how such instruction fits into whole educational settings only in the discussion sections of their articles.

Because whole classrooms and schools that work have been understudied relative to components, I am going to begin my talk by making the case emphatically that there is a need for a lot more research on whole educational settings that are effective. As I do so,

---

This speech, Michael Pressley's last, was presented at the annual conference of the International Reading Association on April 29, 2006. It is printed here by kind permission of Donna Pressley.

keep in mind that I will then follow with a discussion about particular reading education components that deserve additional attention in my view, for much progress has been made by studying individual components and more progress can be made by doing so.

I will not resist commenting on some of the wheat and some of the chaff now in the marketplace of ideas about reading education as I do this talk. It will be clear during this talk that I embrace research and the evidence produced by researchers as completely as I ever have. If you have read any of the three editions of my most complete appraisal of the research literature related to reading education, the book on balanced teaching, you know that. What will also be obvious is that I do not embrace the research uncritically, and I do not buy that all of the research findings that are being used to leverage practice, in fact, should be leveraging practice. So, implicit in what I say today is that I think you should look to research evidence for guidance in practice but do so with a sufficiently critical perspective that you will not be misled. This point is important, because there are researchers and policymakers who are willing to catapult reading practices that are not as well grounded in research as they could be. For those doing such catapulting, one message today is to do more research before foisting your perspective on the nation! Well, let's get started on this talk, thinking about the wholes first.

RESEARCH ON THE "WHOLES": STUDIES OF EFFECTIVE CLASSROOMS, EFFECTIVE SCHOOLS, ENTIRE LITERACY PROGRAMS, AND ENTIRE LANGUAGE WORLDS

To be perfectly honest, although I did some research on reading in the 1970s and 1980s, it was not the focus of my professional life then. It was not until the early 1990s that I took the plunge into reading completely, however, and literally was sucked into the vortex that was the reading war at the time—a war between whole language and those who thought that skills instruction needed to be driving beginning reading instruction especially. If you know my work from that era, I was studying classroom settings where comprehension instruction was being done impressively and effectively. That line of work put me in classrooms and schools a lot. It developed in me a real feel for what was going on in real schools. It prepared me to read the many pieces on the great debate that were floating around in the early 1990s with an informed opinion. One who recognized that was an editor named Carl Smith at ERIC (Educational Resources Information Center), who pulled me into the whole language versus skills fray as a discussant on an ERIC-published volume on the reading war that was then raging (Smith, 1994).

As I read both the pro-whole language and the pro-skills instruction great debaters in preparation for my summary comments in that volume (Pressley, 1994), I came to an important realization: None of them were describing what seemed to me to be the most engaging classrooms I had witnessed in the early 1990s. Indeed, as I read many of these authors, I found myself wondering if they had been in a first grade since the time when they were 6, for I could not recognize the environments they described at all. And, having visited both committed whole language and committed skills classrooms during that era, I did not remember the wonderfulness attributed to these classrooms by their advocates. But, the most important insight I had, along with my colleague and great friend, Ruth Wharton-McDonald, was that no one had ever taken the tactic of going out and studying grade-1 classrooms that were doing a really good job—that were producing better reading and writing achievement than other grade-1 classrooms. Yes, the whole language folks had studied classrooms they knew to be committed to whole language, and, similarly, the skills instruction enthusiasts watched and wrote about skills emphasis classrooms. But they studied these classrooms because of their commitment to a perspective or approach, not because they produced pretty good achievement. Ruth and I went on an odyssey to find grade-1 classrooms that were producing better reading and writing achievement than other grade-1 classrooms, classrooms where children could read and were reading more impressive books than the children in other classrooms, classrooms where children were writing more impressively than the children in other classrooms.

Effective Classrooms

As many of you know, we found those classrooms, and over a series of studies (for a review, see Pressley, 2006, Chapter 8), my colleagues and I documented the nature of whole grade-1 classrooms that work well. The finding I emphasize here is the main finding—there was remarkable consistency across the very best classrooms with respect to their instruction:

- There is a great deal of skills instruction, with it [being] common to see as many as 20 skills an hour covered, often in response to the needs of a reader or writer.
- Word recognition skills are explicitly taught, with students instructed to sound out words, including using letter–sound associations, as well as knowledge of larger chunks of words, including simply reading the whole word once it is known as a sight word. As these strategies are taught, students are also taught to coordinate their deployment, making sure the word sounded out makes sense given picture, story, and syntactic cues.
- Skills instruction is strongly balanced with holistic reading and writing, with students reading and experiencing substantial authentic literature and other texts that make sense for them to be reading given their needs (e.g., leveled little books). Students compose a great deal, typically in a plan, draft, and revise framework, with increasing demands with respect to coherence and mechanics as the year progresses. That is, most of the time, students are doing things academic in such classes . . . actual reading and writing rather than low-level workbook exercises or art.
- Comprehension strategies are taught.
- There is lots of teaching, in whole group and small groups, with a centerpiece of teaching being teacher scaffolding of students as they read and write. Students are doing reading and writing that is within their zones of proximal development, so that each student is challenged but not frustrated.
- There is high academic engagement in these classrooms, in part, because so much of teaching is aimed at motivating students. There is so much occurring to motivate students that Pressley et al. (2003) required a whole book to catalog the many different motivational tactics used by engaging, effective teachers.

As my colleagues and I did this work on effective classrooms, we often found ourselves in schools where it was clear that the student receiving exceptionally effective grade-1 instruction would not be so fortunate in subsequent years. You see, we peeked in other classrooms when we were in these buildings, often noting that instruction in many classrooms was not like the instruction in the most effective classrooms. Of course, we also studied enough not very impressive classrooms that were nominated to us as terrific to have lots of field notes that also made that point. (More about such nominees later!!)

Effective Schools

The realization that students in many schools did not have years of effective instruction led us to ask whether that happens anywhere. Beginning about 3 years ago we began a quest for schools where such consistency might occur. At this point, my colleagues and I are in the process of studying our fourth such school. We are finding a great deal of consistency, but I think the easiest way to talk about what we are finding is to discuss one such school.

Bennett Woods is an elementary school near the Michigan State University campus. What brought it to our attention is that in recent years it has produced more impressive state test scores in reading and writing than other schools in our area. For example, 95 to 98% of fourth graders pass the reading test, which is a solid 15% higher than the state average. More impressive, however, are the writing passing rates, which are always greater than 80% passing and sometimes greater than 90% passing, in a state where less than half the students pass on average. More than doing better than other schools in the state, the emphasis here is that this school does better than other schools in the East Lansing vicinity, which, in general, do better than state averages by very big margins.

Lisa Raphael Bogaert, Lindsey Mohan, Lauren Fingeret, and I spent a semester in Bennett Woods, observing teaching, interviewing teachers, and analyzing documents. This meant distributing more than 250 hours of observation across the 14 classrooms in the school, with the team seeing enough that we were very confident of our conclusions by the end of the study, conclusions that members of the staff confirmed by reading carefully and critically preliminary versions of our report. So, how does Bennett Woods do it?

- This is an academically focused school. The school days and weeks are routinized, with the routines all being in support of student learning, especially instruction of reading and writing. The district and school policies specify a rigorous academic program. There is frequent assessment, with assessments that are complete enough to inform in detail about student progress in reading and writing, with decisions about the curriculum and individual students informed by the assessment data.
- The principal and all of the teachers are committed to a strong reading and writing curriculum, as well as a strong curriculum in general. At the center of that commitment is a determination to get professional development that will permit better teaching of reading and writing in the school. An additional commitment is to prepare students for the reading and writing accountabilities they face, including the state tests, but to do so in ways that are consistent with a high-quality reading and writing curriculum, not simply getting students ready for the test. The regular classroom teachers work well and closely with support teachers, who are also committed to high-quality reading and writing instruction. Even special teachers (i.e., art and music) coordinate their efforts with the literacy program, with students frequently doing art projects connected to books they are reading and singing music that connects to readings in social studies. There is also a library specialist who puts together many activities (e.g., weekly read-alouds in the library for each class) intended to stimulate student interest in reading.
- At the center of the curriculum is a lot of reading, with students experiencing many books—ones read aloud to them in the classroom and library, ones they read as a class, ones that individual students elect to read. In support of such reading is much teaching of reading skills, including the letter–sound, phonics, word recognition, and spelling skills. Vocabulary instruction goes on continuously, as students hear read-alouds, as they read books, and as they experience content-area curricula. Students are taught to

use comprehension strategies. Reading instruction is complemented by writing instruction, most of which is in a plan–draft–revise framework, although there is explicit instruction of the skills required to transform a plan into words, sentences, and paragraphs (i.e., from teaching of handwriting to the grammar of sentences and the parts of a paragraph, and a five-paragraph essay). For both reading and writing, there are progressive demands across the years of schooling, with reading and writing expectations and instruction progressing in an orderly way. The faculty has thought long and hard about the progression through the grades and how to ensure that students are appropriately challenged at each grade level. Reading and writing also connect strongly to content area instruction at all grades, for example, with students experiencing many texts pertaining to social studies and science themes, and writing in response to those texts, as well as writing research papers that can be informed by such texts. Reading and writing also permits many opportunities to practice oral communications skills (e.g., through dialogues about texts, revision discussions).

- The school is an exceptionally positive environment, with many explicit attempts to motivate student literacy, from the many read-alouds in the library and classrooms to reading incentive programs to enthusiastic discussions about books being read by students in a class. Again, all the mechanisms covered in the Pressley et al. (2003) book happen daily at Bennett Woods. More than positive, Bennett Woods is virtually never negative. There is little sanctioning of students nor need for it. There is little failure, with students receiving supportive instruction that encourages them to grow from where they are at present, rather than be frustrated that they are not at some unattainable standard for them.

Of course, you will note that there are substantial similarities between the effective elementary classrooms that we studied and effective whole schools. A great deal of instruction of reading and writing in the context of substantial, authentic reading and writing occurs in great classrooms and most of the classrooms of a great school. Individual teachers and entire schools of teachers who succeed in teaching students to read and write well seek out and obtain professional development to support their work. There are increasing demands in excellent classrooms and across the years in excellent schools. These are exceptionally positive places, with excellent teachers and schools doing much to motivate literacy.

What this work accomplished was to provide visions of what excellent reading and writing instruction can be like, in individual classrooms and across whole schools. This was not a small accomplishment. For example, reflect on the vision of outstanding classrooms for a moment. Is this consistent with a vision of the outstanding classroom that is being thrust upon the nation, for example, through NCLB (No Child Left Behind)? I am certain that many of you immediately recognize that NCLB never mentions reading of lots of literature or composing. There is no concern in that framework for creating a massively positive learning environment. And, of course, the central role of testing in NCLB contrasts greatly with its role in effective classrooms and schools: Yes, excellent teachers and schools prepare students for the test ahead, but testing does not drive the curriculum.

More than not being a small accomplishment, one person close to the National Reading Panel (NRP) process that so informed NCLB informed me, off the record, that the work on effective classrooms was on the minds of some members of the NRP as they did their work. They were determined that this work would never see the light of print in the NRP! You might recall that only experiments made it into the NRP report, despite urgings at least by Panel member Joanne Yatvin that qualitative studies also should have informed the report. The one member of the Panel who chose to speak to me about this did so to inform me that my qualitative work on the nature of effective classrooms was particularly bothersome to some on the Panel, work with the potential to "mislead."

In 2006, my view is that this work on effective literacy instructional classrooms and schools should be leading much of the thinking about what should be done to improve reading education in this country. A hypothesis that definitely comes out of my work is that if we could produce more classrooms and schools like the ones I have studied, the literacy achievement of the nation would be higher. It is time to find out what is required to transform more classrooms and schools so that they are consistent with effective classrooms, and to determine just how much difference such transformation makes on the achievement and lives of children.

The need to do this research is urgent. Why? In the decade of studying effective classrooms, my colleagues and I always sought classrooms that were effective, typically, asking principals for nominations. Even with this bias toward being in classrooms that were very good, 20 to 30% of the time, we found ourselves in classrooms that I would not wish for any child. Along the way, we saw many classrooms where not much teaching of reading and writing skills occurred, not much reading and composing happened, children were often off-task or doing tasks with little to no academic value, and there was little encouragement of academic engagement. Visits to these classrooms—as well as many walks through schools peeking into classrooms—have made me very aware that many elementary students every morning experience teaching that is not too good.

It is time to find out if elementary teaching can be made much better. Of course, an obvious candidate for doing so is greater professional development. But, I am not certain that alone will do it. Let me tell you about one of the most consistent findings in our interviews of teachers over the years. It is always the most effective teachers who have told us that they have much more to learn. They are always the ones seeking the professional development. The weaker teachers are often very confident that they already teach well!! So, I think that rather than simply providing professional development, it may be necessary to select teachers who know they need to get better and are open to getting better, actively seeking ways to do so. As a teacher educator, I also know that there are young people who seem to have more talent for teaching than others . . . with one dimension of talent being greater openness to improvement. I think we have to get serious about figuring out who has talent for such work and doing all possible to keep them in the profession and provide professional development to them. On the other hand, for those who lack talent, we need to get serious about counseling them out, diverting professional development resources that might have been directed at them (which many of them feel they do not need) to those teachers who are hungry to learn more and improve. The main point here, however, is that a major research direction has to be the improvement of the teacher corps and whole schools.

With respect to whole schools, I am mightily impressed that often the principal will make a huge difference, a finding in my own work but also a classic finding in the effective schools literature (e.g., Reynolds, Creemers, Stringfield, Teddlie, & Schaffer, 2002; Teddlie & Reynolds, 2000). The effective principals encountered in my own research have done much to ensure they have excellent teachers who work together to create an environment that promotes the literacy achievement of all students in their school. But, recall that there are also principals who have nominated individuals as very effective teachers who are anything but effective!! Over the decade of doing this research, a very strong impression I have gained is that there are plenty of principals out there who are not providing anything like the leadership required to produce an effective literacy development environment in their school, who would not know an effective literacy teacher if they saw one. Of course, since such principals rarely venture down to the classrooms, they are not likely to see one!! Apologies for the cynical diversion, but it is on the way to an important point: We have to find out much, much more about principals who oversee effective schools and how they came to be effective. Then, we need research on what can be done to develop more of them, and what is required for them to be able to transform a school that is not impressive in its delivery of literacy instruction into a school that is.

So I have opened this talk on the research future that we need, making the case that we very much need research on how to develop excellent literacy teachers, as well as principals who can encourage effective literacy, that we need to do much to discover how to transform many more classrooms and schools into effective literacy education environments. This is important work to do, because classrooms and schools are the actual places where children experience much literacy instruction—what a child's classroom is like this year matters a great deal. Whether a child is in a school that consistently fosters literacy achievement will make a difference as well. Of course, I could have made the argument that we should be looking at whole school districts or states that succeed in fostering literacy better than other school districts and states. I did not, simply because I have not done such work. Somebody needs to do so, however, as a first step in figuring out how to transform many more school districts and states.

Effective Schools the Federal Government Way?

That first step—actually looking to see what goes on in an effective educational environment—seems critical to me. It is also a step that the current evidence-based administration seems to have forgotten. You are aware that the current NCLB approach favors teaching of phonemic awareness, phonics, fluency, vocabulary, and comprehension strategies, with basically no mention of anything else. Is there an effective classroom in the nation that is focused so heavily on those skills that nothing else even deserves mention? I doubt it. Indeed, I am not certain that I have ever encountered a classroom that is consistent with what was in the mind's eye of those who put together NCLB. Reid Lyon, have you ever been in a classroom that is so consistent with the NCLB envisionment? If you have been, might there have been a little something else going on besides reading skills instruction? Without work describing effective environments that provide high focus on the five NCLB skills, I cannot even imagine providing guidance to schools as to how to implement instruction that will work well. Of course, that did not stop the developers of some of the approaches to Reading First professional development. The bottom line is that never-validated approaches to professional development have enjoyed support from NCLB, despite the fact that this program wraps itself in an evidence-based flag!

At the very least, those who have forced on the nation an approach that emphasizes teaching of phonemic awareness, phonics, fluency, vocabulary, and comprehension strategies should evaluate it. And, recall that this is the group that has so vociferously made the case that evaluations, to be credible, should be true experiments. So where is the true experiment on the NCLB approach, which is most completely represented by Reading First? It does not exist and is not coming. Rather, the best the government can offer is what is called a regression discontinuity analysis (see *www.mdrc.org/project_28_65.html*). This type of study could be telling if nothing besides NCLB and Reading First had been happening at the same time with respect to literacy education in America's schools. But given that in most states there have been massive increases in reading and writing education standards during the same time period, any change could as likely be due to the shift in standards. Shame on the federal government for not effectively evaluating a whole-school reform model they have advanced as evidence-based. I think we should demand a true experimental evaluation of the Reading First intervention in the immediate future, and, if the government cannot provide it, their demands to move schools in the direction of their five-factor model should fall on deaf ears until they have produced data.

Shame on all the rest of us if we do not accelerate work to attempt to create more effective individual classrooms and schools based on broader models, based on what has been learned about the nature of effective classrooms and schools by spending time in them, by systematically observing and analyzing what goes on in such environments. Shame on us as well if, as we do so, we do not do research that permits evaluation of how our efforts to change classrooms and schools impact children and their literacy development. And, finally, shame on us if we do not evaluate the efficacy of the alternatives we create against the conceptions of others determined to change schools, for example, those so strongly identified with NCLB! The responsible way to challenge NCLB- and Reading First–type models is to create alternatives and then explicitly to pit the alternatives against NCLB/Reading First in as close to true experimental designs as possible.

Whole Reading Programs

Before leaving classroom-level and school-level interventions, I reflect on an important reality of American schooling. Many children experience contemporary reading programs, published by Houghton Mifflin, Harcourt, McGraw-Hill, and others.

Many of these contemporary programs have done all they can within the constraints of a published curriculum to incorporate evidence-based instruction, so that they can be sold in California and Texas, and across the NCLB-impacted nation. They include instruction of phonemic awareness, phonics, fluency, vocabulary, and comprehension strategies. They all go much farther, however, reflecting attention to other research-based practices, for example, plan–draft–revise composing instruction. They also go far in incorporating excellent children's literature. As they do so, they connect with the rest of the curriculum—social studies and science, in particular, as must be the case when so much of the elementary school day is taken up by language arts (i.e., typically 2½ to 3 or more hours of the 5½ hours or so of each day).

Given that there are many, many children who are experiencing years of such instruction, you might think that we would know what difference such programs make on children's literacy achievement. The bottom line is that we do not know for the most part. I think that we need to make a priority of evaluating these programs well to determine what these programs teach and whether students experiencing such programs become more literate or "different" literate than children who experience other forms of instruction.

As I make this recommendation in the context of an International Reading Association (IRA) research conference, I realize that my comments occur in a potentially hostile environment. After all, there have been prominent discussions in the *Reading Research Quarterly* about whether program evaluation should even be considered research (Reinking & Alvermann, 2005), with my clear sense that some members of IRA think such work is not research. I disagree and so do many other members, as Reinking and Alvermann made clear.

Many IRA members, however, seem concerned about conflicts of interest by creators of programs, if they also serve as evaluators of the program, especially if they stand to benefit financially from the program (Reinking & Alvermann, 2005). As I reflect on that concern, I am aware that many, many interventions are often first evaluated by those who invented them. Science has a natural corrective if the developer of an intervention tests it in a way that produces too-positive evaluations. When an investigator presents experimental or other data claiming effectiveness for an intervention, that is an invitation, one often taken, to do additional research on the intervention. I think we should be encouraging the developers of interventions to test them, report their tests in the literature, and be confident that there will be follow-up data that will confirm or challenge the conclusions that come out of the initial evaluations.

One analogy I have heard is that asking reading program publishers to evaluate their products is like asking the drug companies to evaluate theirs. Folks, a centerpiece of drug research is drug-company-conducted and -sponsored research. There would not have been nearly the progress in the development and evaluation of drugs that has occurred without it. I think it is perfectly appropriate to ask the publishers to conduct as good evaluations as possible of their programs and pay for those evaluations. As I make that call, I also think it is appropriate for the profession to establish professional standards for such evaluations, as well as for reporting and archiving them. If done well, such work will invite others besides the program producers to participate in the program evaluation process and, in doing so, lead to increased understanding about how such programs work, including how they might be refined to work better. Given the nation's history of using such programs, research aimed at improving them seems to me to be a moral imperative, for such programs are going to touch the lives of many children if history indeed predicts the future.

The Child's Language World

It has been known for a long time that from the earliest days of life, economically disadvantaged children are less likely to be immersed in supportive communications interactions than children who are better off economically (e.g., Bernstein, 1965). This is critical, because substantial progress in language development during the preschool years and beyond is an important correlate of later school success, especially with respect to literacy (see Scarborough, 2001; Snow, 1991). One study, in particular, has caught the attention of many in the last decade.

Hart and Risley (1995) observed 42 families carefully for 2 years, beginning when a child was between 7 and 9 months old. The researchers noted everything that went on, with especially careful coding and analysis of the language interactions. The outcomes of the study were striking: Both the quality and quantity of verbal interactions varied predictably as a function of social class. The higher the socioeconomic level, the more parents listened to their children, prompted children to elaborate their comments, talked to their children about what was worth remembering, and provided instruction about how to cope with situations, including verbally—teaching children how to let others know what they wanted and why. With respect to quantity, children in professional families sometimes experienced as many as 4 million verbal interactions in a year, compared to about 250,000 for children in lower class families. Not surprisingly, the children from professional homes had better developed language, indexed, for example, by the extent of their vocabulary, an association observed in other studies as well (e.g., Huttenlocher, Vasilyeva, Cymerman, & Levine, 2001; Naigles & Hoff-Ginsburg, 1998; Pearson, Fernandez, Lewedeg, & Oller, 1997). Most importantly for this discussion, in the Hart and Risley (1995) study, the quality of language interactions and language development during the preschool years predicted reading achievement 6 years later, with the more language-advanced preschoolers becoming better readers.

Of course, cause and effect cannot be inferred from such data. After all, there are a variety of alternative explanations for the associations between social class, language interaction, and child language and reading outcomes, most obviously, that there may be general intelligence differences as a function of social class, as well as differences in other important environmental variables as a function of social class, such as the quality of preschool and elementary school experienced by the children. Still, when there is a correlation, there is always a causal possibility that the richer language interactions during the preschool years, in fact, cause more complete language development and improved reading achievement.

At present this is an untested hypothesis. Yes, there are short-term interventions, such as the distinguished program of research carried out by Whitehurst and his colleagues, documenting that parents can be taught to interact verbally with their preschoolers over books with positive impact on the children's language development (see Whitehurst & Lonigan, 2001). But, I think it is time for a study of what happens when massive efforts are made to improve the language environments of disadvantaged children. Such an intervention would require long-term and substantial parental support and education, aimed at encouraging parents to talk more with their preschoolers and teaching them how to do it. It would help if efforts were made to ensure that the targeted preschoolers experience the cultural opportunities that provide conversational opportunities for many economically advantaged parents and their preschoolers, such as trips to zoos, museums, shows, bookstores, and even quality toy stores!! Provision of excellent preschool opportunities should be in the mix. Would such experiences impact children's language? Would such impact carry over to literacy achievement in the elementary schools? How long would such support be necessary? Although I am betting that it is likely to have maximum impact if there is sustaining support from birth through childhood, rather than support only during the preschool years? The work of Craig Ramey and his colleagues is very instructive on this point (Campbell & Ramey, 1994).

Concluding Comment on Whole Interventions

I am certain that there will be policymakers who are hearing/reading this address and simply bristling, believing that even if the work I have called for were carried out, the costs of the whole interventions that would promote literacy development would be too great in their view. A metamessage is that as we do research to discover the sufficient conditions to produce better literacy outcomes in children, we should be prepared for the likelihood, if I am right, that much is going to be required and that it is going to be very expensive. Another way of thinking about this, of course, is that the future of the country, if it is to be a great future, might be expensive. A better world might require that those of us who are advantaged are going to have to direct more of our income to supporting others, more of our income toward improving the lives of parents and children, and the world of schooling those parents and children encounter.

RESEARCH ON THE "PARTS"

Most research on reading and reading instruction is more modest in scope than the research I called for in the first half of this talk. Researchers typically have focused on parts in their work. Thus, what I am going to discuss in this section are "parts" of reading that most deserve attention, with my perspectives here, again, informed by research of the past. This section is about parts that are truly big ones in reading education, with each of these parts having the potential to transform much in many classrooms and schools.

Skills versus Holistic Instruction?: The Wrong Question

The skills-first versus whole-language reading war of the 1990s was fiercely contended. Although I think my own work identifying a balancing of skills instruction and holistic literacy experiences in the most effective primary grades classrooms went far in making the case that either extreme was missing the mark, extremes persist. Indeed, one reading of much that is offered in the name of Reading First is that skills-first instruction is doing pretty well, or, at least, commands a fair share of the federal dollars supporting beginning reading education in this country.

There is recent evidence, however, that reinforces considerably my position, and that of many others, that excellent primary grades teachers adjust instruction to the needs of individual children, balancing skills instruction and holistic experiences within their classrooms so that some children receive a greater dose of skills and others are more completely immersed in holistic reading and writing. The evidence come from Fred Morrison and his associates (Connor, Morrison, & Katch, 2004) and Juel and Minden-Cupp (2000). In both studies, students who entered grade 1 with low reading skills evidenced greater growth in reading during the grade 1 year if they experienced skills-emphasis instruction rather than more holistic instruction. In contrast, however, students entering grade 1 with good beginning reading skills benefited more from more holistic instruction than skills-oriented instruction.

This potential interaction between entering grade 1 reading ability and instruction deserves a great deal of follow-up, for, potentially, it is powerful evidence against one-size-fits-all instruction for beginning reading. And if the interaction is consistently replicable, there should be great impetus to develop more differentiated beginning reading instruction. One particularly great need will be to get serious about developing teachers who can balance skills and holistic instruction differently for each child in their classroom, depending on the child's level of reading accomplishment and current needs. Of course, one alternative would be not to promote balance but to segregate children who need skills instruction into classrooms that emphasize that, and place children who enter grade 1 with better skills in holistically oriented classrooms. That would be tracking, however, and I suspect strongly that such tracking is unacceptable to many because of the dangers of dysfunctions potentially associated with tracking, regardless of whatever positive benefits might occur for beginning reading. Thus, my guess is that the motivation for many to become balanced literacy teachers is going to increase as work on the interaction discovered by Morrison, Juel, and their associates continues. Exploring this interaction and how to develop instruction that provides the most benefit in grade 1 for the most children seems to me to be a highest priority in beginning reading instruction. I note that the importance of this direction will be recognized by IRA this week, with the Connor et al. (2004) paper being honored with the Dina Feitelson Award.

Fluency and the Practice Hypothesis

Beyond being able to sound out words, it is essential that students learn to read words fluently, recognizing most words as sight words, expending little effort to do so. My reading of the literature is that we know darn little for certain about how to develop fluency in children, although there are admirable compendia of volumes about instructional practices that good teachers believe are helpful in developing fluency. Tim Rasinski and his associates, in particular, have done a tremendous job in assembling this literature (e.g., Rasinski & Padak, 2006). As many of you know, the NRP (2000) provided the most support for repeated reading with teacher guidance and feedback, although I find Steve Stahl's thoughtful additional analyses and reflections on the Panel's position more helpful than the original Panel report on fluency (e.g., Stahl, 2004). For example, in Stahl's reanalysis, he identified that it really did not matter if students repeated reading of the same text or read new text. What seemed to matter was the total amount of reading. Practicing reading is what counts.

That said, there is remarkably little evidence on reading practice conducted in ways that convince the most conservative of the reading researcher community (i.e., few true experiments). The NRP's (2000) most noticed citation of this point was with respect to the practice of uninterrupted sustained silent reading (USSR) or Drop Everything and Read (DEAR) approaches, with the Panel not identifying enough experimental evidence to offer conclusions about these practices. This point was interpreted by some that USSR and DEAR, in fact, do not promote reading achievement, which is definitely a conclusion that goes beyond the information known based on available data!

I think a major priority in the quest for understanding instruction that increases fluency should be a great deal of experimentation on reading practice—not just USSR and DEAR, but reading practice of all types. Are there some methods that produce more impact than others, that are more likely to be carried out voluntarily by children and hence have more impact? For more than a century, with respect to a wide variety of tasks, there have been many, many confirmations that if practice does not make perfect, it makes better and faster (e.g., Ericsson, Krampe, & Tesch-Romer, 1993). We need to find out how much better and faster with respect to reading. As we do so and learn about fluency, there should be other reading measurements as well. For example, such studies would provide opportunity to determine how much practice of reading impacts vocabulary growth, as well as development of other world knowledge, with it certainly reasonable to hypothesize that if material being read is vocabulary- and knowledge-rich, readers might get substantially vocabulary and knowledge richer. I'll say a little more about this possibility in a few moments.

Before ending this comment on the need for a lot of research on fluency, I want to emphasize how distressing it is that speed of reading is so being emphasized in the current discussions of fluency. Millions of school children are now being tested for fluency several times a year with a measure that only taps speed of reading. Of course, I am referring to the DIBELS (Dynamics Indicators of Basic Early Literacy Skills), especially the oral reading measure. Some of you know about a study I did in which children read DIBELS passages, followed by immediate recall of the passages. Right after reading, they could only recall 15% of the ideas in the texts they read (Pressley, Hilden, & Shankland, 2006)! DIBELS oral reading is the ultimate in fast word calling.

I should add at this point that, as someone who did spend some time in his career studying very skilled readers, I am acutely aware that excellent reading often is anything but fast, but rather involves considerable reflection and reaction, sometimes rereading, and pauses to think about the images conjured by the text and the big ideas in the text (for a review, see Pressley & Afflerbach, 1995). In fact, those of you who are researchers, when you read research articles, that is exactly how you read, something I documented in a verbal protocol study more than a decade ago (Wyatt et al., 1993). You do not read anything like the little kids zipping through DIBELS passages!

As work on practice and other variables that might influence fluency proceeds, there needs to be very hard thinking about how to measure fluency much more meaningfully than it is measured by DIBELS. At a minimum, fluent readers can read words effortlessly and quickly, if they need to do so. But, as they do so, they are also accessing the meanings of the words read and constructing the meanings conveyed in phrases, sentences, paragraphs, and longer sections of text. Fluent reading involves more than word recognition processes, which are emphasized in DIBELS. It also involves meaning making at all the levels that meaning can be made as a text is read. Samuels and Farstrup (2006) have just published a book that collects the thinking of the best minds who have thought about fluency. I urge you to get the book and study it, reflecting hard on the ideas in there as you plan research on promoting fluency and measuring it. The essays in that volume give me hope there is better work ahead than the work we have at present. Even so, I stand by the message that opened this subsection: I suspect that the very simple variable of practice deserves a lot more attention as a powerful mechanism for promoting fluency. I'll add that I think it is irresponsible of anyone, in the name of evidence-based practice, to suggest children should be reading less, including doing less sustained silent reading. Rather, we should be doing work on what it takes to get children to really, really drop everything and read intently, measuring carefully the consequences of such reading practice!

Developing Children's Vocabulary

Over the years, I have said a lot about teaching vocabulary to children, including adding a chapter on vocabulary in the most recent, third edition of my book on balanced teaching (Pressley, 2006). As I reflect on the work that has been done, I keep coming back to Bob Sternberg's historic (1986) insight: Most vocabulary is learned in context, either encountered in written text or in oral interactions. Thus, although I applaud the efforts of individuals such as Andy Biemiller (e.g., 2005), who is attempting to identify the words that children at various age levels need to know (i.e., the words that most kids will have learned), as part of determining what words should be taught in school, I am not optimistic, however, that it is ever going to be the case that most vocabulary is taught through reading lessons. Even a very vocabulary-ambitious elementary reading program only attempts to teach 1,000 words a year, with 400 being learned considered a success (Biemiller & Boote, 2006). Even if lower-boundary estimates of vocabulary size are closer to accurate than upper-boundary estimates (i.e., high school graduates know 15,000–20,000 root words; Biemiller & Slonim, 2001), learning 400 words a year would not keep pace.

As I reflect on the various vocabulary learning hypotheses (e.g., see Chapter 7 in Pressley, 2006), I find myself not confident that any is likely to lead to a way of teaching that could keep the pace. So I am going to offer a new hypothesis, one that follows from the work of my colleagues and me in effective elementary classrooms and schools. In settings where literacy achievement is going well, teachers flood the classroom with vocabulary and vocabulary instruction! There is a great deal of reading of books filled with worthwhile vocabulary, with this reading prompting much instruction. Thus, in these classrooms, as a class reads a novel, they often will be held responsible for vocabulary in the novel, provided the words and expected to establish their meanings through context clues and use of resources such as dictionaries, followed by learning of the words, which often are tested. Current novels often inspire vocabulary word walls, with students also expected to use new vocabulary from the novels in their written responses to the novels. Some effective classrooms have charts or books of "wonderful words" that they can use in their writing—for example, all the different variations on the word "said," each of which expresses a nuance of meaning (e.g., shouted, whimpered, mouthed, and so on). Such charts and word books provide students with many exposures to words differing in shades of meaning, improving word variety in writing as it provides opportunity to provide vocabulary instruction in general. As teachers do read-alouds, novel words are noted, with the teacher often providing brief explanations of meanings. And, by the way, there are a lot of read-alouds in effective classrooms. Content-area lessons are chock full of vocabulary, with each social studies, mathematics, and science unit complete with a vocabulary list that students are expected to learn. In effective classrooms, dozens of novel vocabulary [words] are experienced each day, with teachers attentive to when an unfamiliar word is mentioned, flagging it for students, making certain there is some discussion of its meaning.

Of course, as I said earlier, I have been in many not-so-effective classrooms, and when I review the field notes from those classrooms, it is apparent that vocabulary is not as big a deal in these classrooms. So does vocabulary immersion make a difference in vocabulary development, as well as reading more broadly (i.e., comprehension)? We do not know at present, because no one has done a true experiment in which children randomly were assigned to classrooms receiving vocabulary flooding versus those not receiving such flooding. Such studies very much are needed, for they will provide critical information about whether a feature of teaching noted in effective classrooms is a large causal element for the achievement in those classrooms. If vocabulary flooding does promote vocabulary growth and reading achievement more broadly, there would be a strong case for encouraging much more flooding in the future. Such teaching would contrast considerably with some of the vocabulary instruction currently proposed as deserving more attention in classrooms, for example, the in-depth teaching of a relatively few words (e.g., Beck, McKeown, & Kucan, 2002). Flooding words should be tested relative to such an alternative. Of course, I am hoping that the flooding hypothesis also will lead to big bumps in reading achievement broadly defined (e.g., with respect to comprehension), something missing from most previous demonstrations that students can learn vocabulary (see Pressley, 2006, Chapter 7).

Building Conceptual Knowledge

Ever since the NRP report appeared, whenever Richard Anderson or David Pearson has been in the audience, I have jokingly asked them during my talk, "Did it tick you off, after all that work that your Illinois center conducted on the impact of prior knowledge on comprehension, that the NRP never mentioned prior knowledge in their report?" Of course, despite the fact that the case that prior knowledge is strongly associated with comprehension is overwhelming (see Anderson & Pearson, 1984), the work on prior knowledge effects on comprehension was not carried out in true experiments, studies in which readers were assigned randomly to conditions, with some readers then acquiring relevant knowledge and others not. In such a research design, it could be determined whether prior knowledge is actually causal in impacting subsequent reading. Although I find it quite a stretch to attempt to explain the many prior knowledge effects demonstrated in the reading literature as anything but causal, I recognize the logical possibility that they could be due to some third factors.

As I write this, reading and writing are demanding much more of the school day than was the case when Anderson and Pearson and their colleagues were doing their work. What that means is that social studies and science increasingly are being squeezed out of the school day, while at the same time, accelerating state standards demand students learn more social studies and science content than ever before. The only solution is that reading and writing are going to have to connect ever more completely with social studies and science. Of course, given that students must learn how to read and learn from social studies and science texts, this is a good thing in many ways.

It is also something that reading educators believe is possible. Reading educators have thought for a very long time that considerable social studies and science content can be acquired from reading high-quality literature (e.g., Morrow, Pressley, Smith, & Smith, 1997). For example, a book such as Jean Craighead George's *Julie and the Wolves* provides opportunities to learn about Alaska, Native Americans, and the survival of wolves, all topics that make sense for upper elementary students to learn about. And, of course, as expository texts become more common in the elementary reading curriculum (e.g., Duke, 2004), the opportunities expand for students to learn social studies and science as they experience the literacy morning.

Given the many opportunities for students to learn social studies and science from what they read, I think it is high time that researchers document the certainty and extent of such learning, and it can be done in true experiments in ways that are highly ecologically valid. My colleagues Katie Hilden and Lauren Fingeret are currently assessing what is learned as children experience novels and informational texts in their actual classrooms. They are making these assessments with respect to books that are part of the ongoing curriculum, so that it is possible to evaluate experimentally how much is learned about social studies or science content from experiencing a book. I do not want to give away the entire design, but suffice to say, we have come up with a design that permits estimation of between- and within-subject effect sizes and the variability in effect sizes that occur in elementary classrooms. In the very near future, we will be able to comment on the effects of experiencing novels and information texts on knowledge development in the short term. The goal is to continue such work to assess what difference such knowledge makes on subsequent comprehension of topic-related texts, as well as to assess long-term knowledge development. I suspect that Katie and Lauren are beginning a research program here that will at least take both of them to tenure!!

I hope very much that as my group turns its efforts to studies of knowledge development in children, others will do so as well, for this is very, very important work. Reflect for a moment on the consequences if it becomes clear in true experiments that exposure to literature and informational text substantially impacts children's knowledge in ways that impact their subsequent comprehension and other intellectual performances. That would strengthen considerably what is now simply an article of faith for many reading educators, that reading of authentic literature and informational texts should be at the center of reading instruction. That would strengthen considerably the position that reading policies only favoring phonemic awareness, phonics, fluency, vocabulary, and comprehension strategies have an unacceptable gap when they completely neglect what children are reading!

Comprehension Strategies Instruction

As one of the individuals who was one of the first to conduct research on strategies instruction (e.g., Pressley, 1976), I have been there from the beginning and witnessed the evolution of the approach. Pressley (2000) summarized that evolution. In that chapter, I discussed the many investigations of single strategies with potential to improve reading comprehension, reviewed the events leading to the insight that modeling and explanation of strategies followed by long-term scaffolded practice is the instructional approach with the most compelling support, and explained why the teaching of small repertoires of comprehension strategies is a more sensible approach than teaching of single strategies. In fact, by 2000, when the data on Reciprocal Teaching (Palincsar & Brown, 1984; Rosenshine & Meister, 1994) and Transactional Strategies Instruction (Brown, Pressley, Van Meter, & Schuder, 1996; Pressley et al., 1992) were considered together, the case was overwhelming in my mind for teaching small repertoires of comprehension strategies.

Unfortunately, some in 2000 paid little attention to the research progress, for example, the individuals responsible for the main comprehension section of the NRP report. The Panel basically generated a long list of comprehension strategies that they believed enjoyed experimental support (i.e., if you instructed children to use the strategy and arranged circumstances to maximize the likelihood they would do so, they did better on some comprehension test on some passages that were read). The implication was that sound teaching of comprehension was teaching these strategies. But the Panel was not the only group creating such a list: There would be several prominent books aimed at the professional development market, at least one of which has sold many, many copies. That book and similar ones basically provided brief coverage of any comprehension strategy found in the literature. The implication was that comprehension instruction was teaching all these strategies. The work conducted by my colleagues and me on complete teaching of a small repertoire of strategies, teaching through modeling and explanation, and scaffolded practice, was basically ignored from 2000 on.

Of course, before 2000, there was not much comprehension instruction, of strategies or otherwise, occurring in American elementary schools, something first documented by Dolores Durkin (1978/1979) and then reobserved several decades later, even after all that experimental work on comprehension strategies instruction (Pressley, Wharton-McDonald, Hampston, & Echevarria, 1998; Taylor, Pearson, Clark, & Walpole, 2000). Despite the urgings of the National Reading Panel, the 2002 mandating of comprehension strategies instruction in Reading First, and the massive sales of those professional development volumes aimed at comprehension instruction, the bottom line is that there is no evidence of much comprehension strategies instruction occurring extensively now and certainly no evidence of children being taught such strategies to the point that they use them in a self-regulated fashion, which is the goal of such instruction. Even in the classrooms of otherwise very effective elementary teachers, the ones showcased in the work of my colleagues and me on effective elementary instruction, there is little comprehension strategies instruction occurring. I might add that the lack of attention to comprehension strategies by teachers in this new century has been complemented by lack of attention by researchers, with research on the topic of comprehension strategies instruction simply not much evident in the journals in the past half-dozen years. When there has been research on comprehension strategies in recent years, much of it has been documentation that teaching comprehension strategies is very challenging and anything but a certain outcome of existing professional development targeting comprehension strategies instruction (e.g., Hilden & Pressley, in press; Klingner, Vaughn, Arguelles, Hughes, & Leftwich, 2004).

What to do? It is time to do some serious research on how to develop teachers who can provide comprehension strategies instruction that does produce students who learn to use and do use the strategies in a self-regulated fashion. Based on what is known from my previous work (see Pressley et al., 1992; Pressley & El-Dinary, 1997), I suspect that successful professional development is going to require at least a school year. Such professional development will require developing modeling, explanation, and scaffolding skills in teachers, as well as developing a commitment to teach and encourage comprehension strategies use every day. The task of comprehension strategies instruction can become manageable, in part, by developing the understanding in teachers that very effective readers actually use a small repertoire of strategies: They make predictions based on prior knowledge, inferential connections to ideas in text based on prior knowledge, construct mental images representing the ideas in text, ask questions and seek answers, reread and attempt to clarify when confused, and construct interpretive summaries of what they have read (see Pressley & Afflerbach, 1995). For students to acquire such skills to the point of internalization probably requires several years of instruction and scaffolded use, although comprehension gains should be quite pronounced even during the first year of use (Brown et al., 1996; Pressley et al., 1992). Yes, we have a vision of what it takes to create strategic elementary readers. What we now need is a lot of work to develop teachers who can create that vision, with as a starting point research on professional development of comprehension instruction teachers.

If you have not picked up that I believe the professional developers who are currently hawking such professional development do not know what they are doing, that, in fact, is my very strong, well-informed opinion about their work. If you want a five-page summary of what I think such professional development might look like, contact me and I will be happy to provide one for you, and I would be thrilled if someone would decide to do research on the professional development sketched in those five pages.

I'll add just one more comment. As is the case with effective teaching more generally, I am not optimistic that everyone can become an effective comprehension strategies instruction teacher. The only way to find out whether they can do it or not, however, is for them to try, receiving excellent professional development and support to do so. One anecdote provides some hope for me, however. The reading series that I codeveloped requires in every lesson that teachers model and explain and scaffold strategies use. Admittedly, this is not an ideal way to develop comprehension strategies instruction teachers, but I know of enough teachers who have learned a great deal of comprehension strategies instruction through teaching with the program to believe that many more teachers can learn to teach comprehension strategies than are teaching them at present.

Testing as a Stimulus for Reading Achievement?

Testing is a centerpiece of current educational policy, one that is at the heart of No Child Left Behind and publicly, openly embraced by President Bush and Secretary Spellings. One justification is that testing can inform educators about who needs additional instruction and even provide guidance about the particular type of instruction that children need. The assumption is that testing can, thus, ultimately produce improved achievement. The only problem is that testing does not seem to produce improved performance, except with respect to the particular test used; that is, being tested with one reading test produces improvement on that test (possibly a practice effect) but does not impact at all other reading tests (see Amrein & Berliner, 2002).

All right, Mr. President and Secretary Spellings, if you are as evidence-based and as committed to experimentation as a gold standard as you have claimed so often, it is time to put testing to an experimental test. It is very easy to imagine a true experiment in which children either receive all the testing that the federal and state governments want children to receive or they do not. After a year or two of such an experiment, using other measures of reading besides the tests the children have already experienced, if testing does promote reading achievement, the tested children should do better than the children who were not tested on the not previously experienced tests. The nation very much needs this experiment and needs to act on it. If testing is not producing increases in achievement, it is time to dispense with much of the testing and use the money for other educational inputs, for example, instruction and materials!

Just so no one misses my drift here . . . I think it is high time to call the government on its policy with respect to testing. This is a very, very expensive policy in terms of dollars and opportunity costs: Every minute spent testing is a minute not spent instructing, and every minute spent preparing for testing (and there are many, many of those across this land) is a minute not spent instructing something else. Then, there is very good reason to believe that the harm goes even farther, with testing potentially contributing to behaviors that really undermine student achievement, up to and including students deciding to drop out of school (Amrein & Berliner, 2003). The most constructive way to call them on their policy is to do telling research, true experimental research, and then, use the results of such inquiry to leverage for better policy in the future.

I cannot comment on the government and testing without saying at least a few more words about DIBELS. I already mentioned briefly one of the results from my own study of DIBELS (Pressley et al., 2006), which basically confirmed what DIBELS is revealing about reading speed when reading comprehension is low. So if you are interested in knowing about reading speed with low comprehension and memory of text, DIBELS is a great measure! I want to comment on another aspect of DIBELS, however.

DIBELS proponents make the case for it as a "dipstick" measure, a quick indication of whether the child is making progress in reading. Now, when I heard this description, it led me to expect quite a bit from DIBELS. After all, the height of the oil on my dipstick in my Honda correlates very highly with the actual volume of oil in the engine. Moreover, assuming the engine has just been turned off, the impurities in the drops of oil on the dipstick are very representative of the impurities in the oil in the crankcase. If the height of oil on the dipstick is low, I can be certain that I should add oil. If the oil on the dipstick is dirty, I can be certain I should change oil.

Not so with DIBELS. In my own study, DIBELS oral reading at the grade 3 level only predicted 20% of the variance on a more comprehensive reading test. If you go to the DIBELS website (*dibels.uoregon.edu/*) and read the predictive studies archived there, in the very best cases, DIBELS only predicts 50% of the variance in more comprehensive reading performance. What that means is that DIBELS often flags children as at risk who will do just fine on the comprehensive measure. It also means that it often signals that there is no problem when, in fact, performance on a more comprehensive test of reading would be troubling. DIBELS oral reading is a lousy dipstick!! DIBELS does not have the reliability of a Honda. Maybe it is a Yugo!

When the entire body of research on DIBELS is read, the only reasonable conclusion is that this is not a very completely validated test. But here is what really irks me. A claim is often made that DIBELS can be used to guide instruction. If you read the DIBELS manual, what you will find, however, that there is absolutely no guidance at all about what should be instructed for children to do better on the DIBELS . . . or become better readers if DIBELS flags them as at risk for reading failure.

This administration wraps itself in claims of being evidence-based, research-based. Nobody who is really respectful of evidence would recommend a measure such as DIBELS as a "dipstick" measure. Educators should demand evidence that administering DIBELS improves reading performance broadly measured before agreeing to continue administering the assessment. Again, the hypothesis that DIBELS administration can produce data that impact teaching so as to improve student achievement is easily testable in a true experiment and must be tested if a case is to be made that DIBELS should be prominent in reading education decision making.

Finally, before departing this subsection on testing, I must fulfill a promise that I made to Richard Anderson. To meet that promise, I'm going to ask you to read and reflect on a poem, "Introduction to Poetry," by Billy Collins[1]:

> I ask them to take a poem
> and hold it up to the light
> like a color slide
> or press an ear against its hive.
>
> I say drop a mouse into a poem
> and watch him probe his way out,
> or walk inside the poem's room
> and feel the walls for a light switch.
>
> I want them to water ski
> across the surface of a poem
> waving at the author's name on the shore.
>
> But all they want to do
> is tie the poem to a chair with rope
> and torture a confession out of it.
>
> They begin beating it with a hose
> to find out what it really means.

OK, now, I will test your comprehension of the meaning of the poem: Select the best answer: The poem "Introduction to Poetry" means

a. There is one best meaning to a poem.
b. Poems can be read and appreciated by animals, including mice.
c. Poems can be read at the beach.
d. Only stupid people think poems have one meaning that can be tapped with a multiple-choice item.

What Anderson wanted me to tell you is that progress in reading, and especially reading comprehension, is going to be severely handicapped by continuing to rely on multiple-choice testing. As I usually do, I agree with Professor Anderson on this point. There, in fact, is a great deal of new thinking emerging about comprehension assessment (see Paris, 2005), with this an active area of research, an area of research that I hope expands and leads to new thinking about how to measure comprehension. At present, testing probably is doing much harm, for example, prompting children and others to think that a Billy Collins poem could have only one best meaning, a long outdated notion of response to literature (Rosenblatt, 1938, 1978).

---

[1] Billy Collins, "Introduction to Poetry" from *The Apple That Astonished Paris*. Copyright 1988, 1996 by Billy Collins. Used by permission of the University of Arkansas Press, *www.uapress.com*.

I close by stating simply that testing, especially standardized testing, is not what it needs to be if it is to be helpful to educators. I also close by reflecting on the teaching of very effective teachers, something I have been doing for more than a decade. I have never once observed an effective classroom teacher use standardized test data in her or his decision making. I have seen effective schools do so to identify students in need of help, but I have never seen a school use the subscale scores of comprehension reading assessments to tailor instructional decision making, relying instead on clinical impressions and informal reading assessments to do so. As research on testing proceeds, there needs to be a lot of attention to the development of assessments that are truly helpful to educators, so helpful that effective educators will recognize that they should use the data provided by the test.

I know that as I made my closing point in this section on parts that many of you are bristling, recognizing that in the current environment, testing is being used to judge educators, as part of an approach to educational improvement intended to weed out ineffective teachers and schools based on test scores. Well, my response to that is that if testing is to continue for such a purpose, there needs to be scientific study that testing so used, in fact, does lead to better student outcomes. In fact, that could be tested scientifically in decidedly true experiments, and, if the current administration were truly evidence-based, they would be testing it. I see no sign, however, that this administration truly has an evidence-based perspective with respect to testing, and I truly believe that in the absence of such an evidence base, a very good case can be made for pulling back on testing considerably. I could go on for hours about the testing mess but will end now.

CLOSING COMMENTS

This talk started with a reflection on wholes and parts. I then made the case that we very much need to expand research on the nature of effective classrooms and schools, but, more importantly, how to create more effective classrooms and schools. As I talked about whole classrooms, curricula, language worlds, and schools, inevitably, I had to talk about parts. Given the limits of the human mind, it is the only way to conceptualize the complex in many ways. It is also a good way to think about the wholes, because reading educators and researchers are more experienced at focusing on parts, creating them, evaluating them, and improving them. The back end of the talk focused on some studies of parts that need to be done, and soon. Of course, as this work is done, the hope is that many educators will fold these components into whole classrooms. I am very confident that the future of schooling will be better if we come to understand better how to differentiate instruction, for example, providing more phonics to students who will most benefit from it, as well as more holistic instruction to students who will most benefit from it. Reading education will improve dramatically if better ways are found to improve fluency and vocabulary. Additional research on learning from literature and information texts has the potential to inform many teachers better about how to encourage children to get the most from the books they experience. Personally, however, I am most excited that it might be possible to make comprehension strategies instruction more appealing. Of course, there will be time to incorporate the new teaching insights into classrooms and schools if time and other resources are freed up by eliminating testing that is not promoting children's achievement. The work on parts I have proposed this morning has great potential for transforming whole educational worlds. I'm going to do my best to be part of this work, and I urge all of you to think hard about how you can contribute.

REFERENCES

Amrein, A. L., & Berliner, D. C. (2002). High stakes testing and student learning. *Education Policy Analysis Archives, 10*(18), 192–204.

Amrein, A. L., & Berliner, D. C. (2003). The effects of high-stakes testing on student motivation and learning. *Educational Leadership, 60*(5), 32–38.

Anderson, R. C., & Pearson, P. D. (1984). A schema–theoretic view of basic processes in reading. In P. D. Pearson (Ed.), *Handbook of reading research* (pp. 255–291). New York: Longman.

Beck, I. L., McKeown, M. G., & Kucan, L. (2002). *Bringing words to life: Robust vocabulary instruction*. New York: Guilford Press.

Bernstein, B. (1965). *Class, codes, and control: Vol. 1. Theoretical studies toward a sociology of language*. London: Routledge & Kegan Paul.

Biemiller, A. (2005). Size and sequence in vocabulary development: Implications for choosing words for primary vocabulary instruction. In E. Hiebert & M. Kamil (Eds.), *Teaching and learning vocabulary: Bringing research to practice* (pp. 223–242). Mahwah NJ: Erlbaum.

Biemiller, A., & Boote, C. (2006). An effective method for building meaning vocabulary in primary grades. *Journal of Educational Psychology, 98*, 44–62.

Biemiller, A., & Slonim, N. (2001). Estimating root word vocabulary growth in normative and advantaged populations: Evidence for a common sequence of vocabulary acquisition. *Journal of Educational Psychology, 93*, 498–520.

Brown, R., Pressley, M., Van Meter, P., & Schuder, T. (1996). A quasi-experimental validation of transactional strategies instruction with low-achieving second grade readers. *Journal of Educational Psychology, 88*, 18–37.

Campbell, F. A., Ramey, C. T. (1994). Effects of early intervention on intellectual and academic achievement: A follow-up study of children from low-income families. *Child Development, 65*, 684–698.

Connor, C. D., Morrison, F. J., & Katch, L. E. (2004). Beyond the reading wars: Exploring the effect of child–instruction interactions on growth in early reading. *Scientific Studies of Reading, 8*, 305–336.

Duke, N. (2004). The case for informational text. *Educational Leadership, 61*(6), 40–44.

Durkin, D. (1978/1979). What classroom observations reveal about reading comprehension instruction. *Reading Research Quarterly, 15*, 481–533.

Ericsson, K., Krampe, R., & Tesch-Romer, C. (1993). The role of deliberate practice in the acquisition of expert performance. *Psychological Review, 100*, 363–406.

George, J. C. (1972). *Julie of the wolves*. New York: Harper Collins.

Hart, B., & Risley, T. R. (1995). *Meaningful differences in the everyday experience of young American children*. Baltimore: Brookes.

Hilden, K., & Pressley, M. (in press). Stories of obstacles and success: Teachers' experiences in professional development of reading comprehension instruction. *Reading and Writing Quarterly*.

Huttenlocher, J., Vasilyeva, M., Cymerman, E., & Levine, S. (2001). Language input and child syntax. *Cognitive Psychology, 45*, 337–374.

Juel, C., & Minden-Cupp, C. (2000). Learning to read words: Linguistic units and instructional strategies. *Reading Research Quarterly, 35*, 458–492.

Klingner, J. K., Vaughn, S., Arguelles, M. E., Hughes, M. T., & Leftwich, S. A. (2004). Collaborative strategic reading: "Real-world" lessons from classroom teachers. *Remedial and Special Education, 25*, 291–302.

Morrow, L. M., Pressley, M., Smith, J. K., & Smith, M. (1997). The effect of a literature-based program integrated into literacy and science instruction with children from diverse backgrounds. *Reading Research Quarterly, 32*, 52–76.

Naigles, L., & Hoff-Ginsberg, E. (1998). Input to verb learning: Evidence for the plausibility of syntactic bootstrapping. *Developmental Psychology, 5*, 827–837.

National Reading Panel. (2000). *Report of the National Reading Panel: Teaching children to read:*

An evidence-based assessment of the scientific research literature on reading and its implications for reading instruction: Reports of the subgroups. Washington, DC: National Institute of Child Health and Human Development, National Institutes of Health.

Palincsar, A. S., & Brown, A. L. (1984). Reciprocal teaching of comprehension-fostering and monitoring activities. *Cognition and Instruction, 1,* 117–175.

Paris, S. G. (2005). Reinterpreting the development of reading skills. *Reading Research Quarterly, 40*(2), 219–231.

Pearson, B. Z., Fernandez, S. C., Lewedeg, V., & Oller, D. K. (1997). The relation of input factors to lexical learning by bilingual infants. *Appled Psycholinguistics, 18,* 41–58.

Pressley, G. M. (1976). Mental imagery helps eight-year-olds remember what they read. *Journal of Educational Psychology, 68,* 355–359.

Pressley, M. (1994). Commentary on the ERIC whole language debate. In C. B. Smith (Moderator), *Whole language: The debate* (pp. 155–178). Bloomington, IN: Educational Resources Information Center/Reading, English, and Communication.

Pressley, M. (2000). What should comprehension instruction be the instruction of? In M. L. Kamil, P. B. Mosenthal, P. D. Pearson, & R. Barr (Eds.), *Handbook of reading research* (Vol. 3, pp. 545–561). Mahwah NJ: Erlbaum.

Pressley, M. (2006). *Reading instruction that works: The case for balanced teaching* (3rd ed.). New York: Guilford Press.

Pressley, M., & Afflerbach, P. (1995). *Verbal protocols of reading: The nature of constructively responsive reading*. Hillsdale NJ: Erlbaum.

Pressley, M., Dolezal, S. E., Raphael, L. M., Mohan, L., Bogner, K., & Roehrig, A. D. (2003). *Motivating primary-grade students*. New York: Guilford Press.

Pressley, M., & El-Dinary, P. B. (1997). What we know about translating comprehension strategies instruction research into practice. *Journal of Learning Disabilities, 30,* 486–488.

Pressley, M., El-Dinary, P. B., Gaskins, I., Schuder, T., Bergman, J. L., Almasi, J., et al. (1992). Beyond direct explanation: Transactional instruction of reading comprehension strategies. *Elementary School Journal, 92,* 511–554.

Pressley, M., Hilden, K. R., & Shankland, R. K. (2006). *An evaluation of end-grade-3 Dynamic Indicators of Basic Early Literacy Skills (DIBELS): Speed reading without comprehension, predicting little*. East Lansing: Michigan State University, College of Education, Literacy Achievement Research Center.

Pressley, M., Wharton-McDonald, R., Hampston, J. M., & Echevarria, M. (1998). The nature of literacy instruction in ten grade-4 and -5 classrooms in upstate New York. *Scientific Studies of Reading, 2,* 159–191.

Rasinski, T. V., & Padak, N. (2006). *From phonics to fluency* (2nd ed.). Boston: Allyn & Bacon.

Reynolds, D., Creemers, B., Stringfield, S., Teddlie, C., & Schaffer, G. (Eds.). (2002). *World class schools: International perspectives on school effectiveness*. New York: Routledge-Falmer.

Reinking, D., & Alvermann, D. E. (2005). Editorial: What are evaluation studies and should they be published in RRQ? *Reading Research Quarterly, 40,* 142–46.

Rosenblatt, L. M. (1938). *Literature as experience*. New York: Progressive Education Association.

Rosenblatt, L. M. (1978). *The reader, the text, the poem: The transactional theory of the literary work*. Carbondale: Southern Illinois University Press.

Rosenshine, B., & Meister, C. (1994). Reciprocal teaching: A review of nineteen experimental studies. *Review of Educational Research, 64,* 479–530.

Samuels, S. J., & Farstrup, A. E. (Eds.). (2006). *What research has to say about fluency*. Newark, DE: International Reading Association.

Scarborough, H. S. (2001). Connecting early language and literacy to later reading (dis)abilities: Evidence, theory, and practice. In S. B. Neuman & D. K. Dickinson (Eds.), *Handbook of early literacy research* (pp. 97–110). New York: Guilford Press.

Smith, C. B. (Ed.). (1994). *Whole language: The debate*. Bloomington, IN: Educational Resources Information Center/Reading, English, and Communication.

Snow, C. E. (1991). The theoretical basis of the Home–School Study of Language and Literacy Development. *Journal of Research in Childhood Education, 6*, 1–8.

Stahl, S. A. (2004). What do we know about fluency?: Findings of the National Reading Panel. In P. McCardle & V. Chhabra (Eds.), *The voice of evidence in reading research* (pp. 187–211). Baltimore: Brookes.

Taylor, B. M., Pearson, P. D., Clark, K., & Walpole, S. (2000). Effective schools and accomplished teachers: Lessons about primary-grade reading instruction in low-income schools. *Elementary School Journal, 101*, 121–165.

Teddlie, C., & Reynolds, D. (Eds.). (2000). *The international handbook of school effectiveness research*. New York: Falmer Press.

Whitehurst, G. J., & Lonigan, C. J. (2001). Emergent literacy: Development from prereaders to readers. In S. B. Neuman & D. K. Dickinson (Eds.), *Handbook of early literacy research* (pp. 11–29). New York: Guilford Press.

Wyatt, D., Pressley, M., El-Dinary, P. B., Stein, S., Evans, P., & Brown, R. (1993). Comprehension strategies, worth and credibility monitoring, and evaluations: Cold and hot cognition when experts read professional articles that are important to them. *Learning and Individual Differences, 5*, 49–72.

Author Index

Aarnoutse, C., 58, 325
Abeel, S., 271
Abelson, R. P., 197, 198
Adams, G. L., 274
Adams, M. J., 50
Adendorff, R., 191
Adlof, S., 275
Afflerbach, P., 20, 24, 27, 50, 242, 247, 331, 402, 407
Ainley, M., 209
Ainsworth, L., 264
Aist, G. S., 348
Alao, S., 245
Alfassi, M., 274, 325
Allen, J., 259
Alley, G. R., 275
Allington, R. L., 28, 32, 231
Allison, T., 119
Almasi, J. F., 210, 230
Alvermann, D. A., 229, 230
Alvermann, D. E., 208, 221, 259, 287, 398, 399
Amanti, C., 302
Ames, C., 149
Ames, C. A., 228
Amrein, A. L., 407, 408
Anderman, E. M., 230
Anderson, A. A., 218
Anderson, D. K., 52
Anderson, E., 245
Anderson, J., 148
Anderson, J. E., 110

Anderson, R., 409
Anderson, R. C., 20, 39, 196, 197, 198, 200, 202, 206, 207, 242, 244, 244–245, 248, 313, 382, 404, 405, 409
Anderson, T. H., 244–245
Anderson, V., 23, 162
Anderson-Inman, L., 350
Andrews, G., 50, 51
Applebee, A. N., 245
Appleton, K., 185
Archer, J., 149
Ardila, A., 222
Arguelles, M. E., 406
Artiles, A. J., 300
Arya, P., 210
Asante, K., 322
Asgari, M., 119
Ashwell, S., 51
Ataya, R., 334
Atkin, S. B., 373
Atkinson, J. W., 228, 229
Au, K., 21
August, D., 248, 296, 300
Avi, 373
Avila, E., 109
Azar, B., 129

B

Bailey, A. L., 299
Baker, L., 66, 67, 68, 383, 386

Baker, S., 172, 272, 309
Baker, S. K., 313
Bakhtin, M. M., 196, 198, 199, 209
Bakken, J. P., 172
Baldwin, L. E., 173, 183
Bandura, A., 229, 263
Banilower, E. R., 185, 186
Banyai, I., 374
Barbosa, P., 247, 298
Barkovich, A. J., 144
Barksdale-Ladd, M. A., 29
Barnes, M. A., 180
Bauserman, K., 31, 76
Beach, R., 323
Beall, L. C., 68
Bean, T. W., 260
Beatty, A. S., 172–173
Beatty, P., 367
Beck, D. P., 244–245
Beck, I. L., 169, 207, 245, 310, 313, 404
Beers, K., 146
Begley, S., 127
Bell, N., 42
Bennett, L., 230
Bennett, R. E., 322
Bereiter, C., 67
Berger, A., 52
Berlin, L. J., 188
Berliner, D. C., 85, 407, 408
Berndorff, D., 209
Bernstein, B., 399
Best, R., 355
Betts, A. A., 160
Bevans-Mangelson, J. B., 369, 373
Bialystok, E., 50
Biancarosa, G., 221, 260, 272, 286, 287
Biemiller, A., 403
Bigler, R. S., 52, 53, 56
Billig, F., 185
Billings, L., 196
Binder, J. R., 110
Binkley, M., 14
Biondo, S. M., 250
Bird, M., 67
Birdyshaw, D., 260
Bivens, J. A., 198
Bjork, R. A., 197
Black, J. E., 127
Black, P., 82
Black, R. W., 309
Blake, A., 184, 187
Blakemore, S., 142, 146, 147, 148, 151
Blank, M., 188

Bleha, T., 322
Block, C., 76
Block, C. C., 4–5, 6, 19, 23, 24, 25, 26, 27, 28, 30, 31, 32, 33, 39, 43, 46, 68, 121, 122, 142, 149, 150, 159, 166, 243, 244, 286, 287, 363, 366, 384, 385, 386
Blommers, P., 52
Bloome, D., 9–10
Blumenfeld, P. C., 231
Blumenthal, P. C., 27
Bluth, G. J., 198
Bober, M., 322
Bock, A. M., 52, 54, 57, 59
Boerger, A. E., 52
Bogaert, L. R., 394
Bondi, J., 151
Bons, T., 109
Boone, R., 350
Boone, W. J., 185
Boonthum, C., 90
Boote, C., 403
Borman, G. D., 274
Borzekowski, D., 322
Boschken, I., 325
Bottge, B. A., 273
Bouchard, M., 294
Boulware-Gooden, R., 45
Boyd, F. B., 372
Boyd, S. E., 186
Boyle, B., 266
Braam, L., 52
Bradley, B. A., 328
Brand-Gruwel, S., 325
Brandt, D. M., 198
Bransford, J., 132
Bransford, J. C., 198
Brasseur, I. F., 285, 386
Braun, A., 111
Braunger, J., 25
Brewer, W. F., 197, 198
Brock, C. H., 247
Brooks, G. W., 216
Brophy, J., 231, 232
Brothers, L., 129
Brown, A., 67
Brown, A. L., 21, 66, 85, 132, 161, 162, 274, 324, 324–325, 325, 326, 328, 329, 352, 354, 366, 406
Brown, D. F., 151
Brown, J. S., 129
Brown, K., 21, 184, 187
Brown, K. J., 247
Brown, L. G., 172

Brown, R., 23, 67, 162, 167, 243, 406, 407
Brown, S., 274
Browne, A., 373
Brownell, M. T., 275
Brozo, W. G., 259
Brubaker, D., 185
Bruce, B., 246
Bruer, J. T., 145
Bruner, J. S., 161, 263, 352
Bryan, K. S., 70
Bryant, P., 69
Bryson, S. E., 348
Bulfin, S., 323
Bulgren, J. A., 274, 284
Buly, M., 276
Bunge, S. A., 351
Burack, J. A., 51
Burbules, N., 199
Burdenski, T. K., Jr., 45
Burningham, J., 373
Burns, M. S., 65, 142, 173, 241
Burton, C., 70, 75
Bush, G. W., 407
Buxton, C., 174
Byrd, D., 148

C

Caccamise, D., 85, 89, 90, 92, 384, 386
Cai, Z., 189
Cain, K., 69, 75
Caine, G., 128, 129, 133
Caine, R., 129, 133
Caine, R. N., 384, 385, 389
Calfee, R. C., 176
Calkins, L. M., 215
Cambourne, B., 231
Cammack, D., 221, 323, 347
Cammack, D. W., 246, 363
Campbell, F. A., 400
Campbell, J. R., 172–173
Campbell, M. L., 274
Campeau, S., 122
Caplan, D., 119
Capra, F., 129
Carey, J., 120
Carilgia-Bull, T., 20
Carlisle, J. F., 80
Carlo, M., 248
Carlo, M. S., 248
Carpenter, P. A., 110, 119
Carr, E., 21

Carretti, B., 91
Carter, A., 328, 333
Cartwright, K. B., 50, 51, 52, 53, 54, 55, 56, 57, 58, 59, 120, 382, 388, 389
Case, R., 52
Caseley, J., 175
Casey, B. J., 142
Castek, J., 321, 325, 328, 331, 369, 373, 383, 387
Catts, H., 275
Cavalier, A. R., 348
Caverly, D. C., 284
Cazden, C. B., 299
Celano, D., 230
Certo, J., 247
Chall, J. S., 25, 173, 183, 244
Chambliss, M. J., 176, 198
Changeux, J. P., 143
Chapman, J. W., 233
Chapman, M. L., 246
Chapman, S., 39
Chard, D., 24
Chen, R., 275
Chenery, H. J., 118
Cheng, P., 198
Cherkassky, V. L., 111
Cherry, L., 373
Child, D. A., 67
Chinn, C., 207
Chinn, C. A., 196, 200
Chodorow, M., 92
Choudhury, S., 142, 146, 147, 148, 151
Christian, W., 301
Chrostowski, S. J., 189
Chudowsky, N., 82, 83
Ciardiello, A. V., 179
Clark, F. L., 275, 284
Clark, K., 406
Clark, K. F., 243
Clark, L. F., 81
Clause, J., 55
Clay, M. M., 52
Cleveland, M., 24
Cocking, R. R., 132
Codling, R. M., 230, 234, 363
Cohen, C. L., 104, 105
Cohen, K., 348
Cohen, L., 105
Cohen, S., 28
Coiro, J., 221, 246, 321, 323, 324, 327, 328, 330, 333, 334, 347, 363, 371, 372
Coiro, J. L., 246
Collins, B., 409

Collins, C., 23, 162
Collins, J. C., 288
Collins, K. M., 245
Coltheart, M., 107
Colton, A. B., 263
Combs, A. W., 132
Concha, S., 354
Conlan, R., 127
Connor, C. D., 401
Cooke, C. L., 164, 165, 166, 167
Cooper, J. D., 325
Cope, B., 323
Copland, D. A., 118
Corrigan, S. Z., 149
Coulson, R. L., 52
Coutelet, B., 68
Cox, K. E., 230, 234
Coyne, P., 352
Craig, M. T., 184
Craighero, L., 127–128, 131
Creech, S., 374
Creemers, B., 396
Crévola, C., 265
Crosby, P. B., 168
Cross, D., 67
Crossman, G., 184
Crowell, S., 133
Crowhurst, M., 205, 207
Crowley, K., 311
Crump, W. D., 52
Csikszentmihalyi, M., 228
Cucchiarelli, A., 89
Cummings, C., 24, 25, 30
Cunningham, P. M., 231
Curtis, M. B., 272, 276, 286
Cusenbary, S., 284
Cutter, J., 245
Cutting, L. E., 272, 275
Cymerman, E., 399
Cziko, C., 262, 273

D

Dagher, Z., 184
Dahl, R. E., 142
Dalton, B., 248, 301, 323, 347, 348, 349, 351, 352, 354, 355, 356, 358, 383, 387
Dalton, L., 15
Damasio, A. R., 127, 129, 130
Dandy, K. L., 51, 54, 55
Daneman, M., 70, 75, 91
Danzinger, P, 374

Davin, D., 205
Davis, M. H., 247
de Argaez, E., 322
De Beni, R. D., 91
de Canis, J. S., 172
De Corte, E., 70
de Jager, B., 72, 75
De La Paz, S., 217
Deák, G. O., 50, 51
Deci, E. L., 132, 228
DeCorte, E., 325
deCourten, C., 143
Dehaene, S., 105, 143
Dejerine, J., 103, 105
Dellamura, R. Y., 28
Denis, M., 41, 110
Dennis, S., 89, 93
Denton, P. H., 275
Deshler, D. D., 271, 272, 274, 275, 278, 284, 285, 286, 386
Detterman, D. K., 197
Dewey, J., 197, 199
Dewitz, P., 21, 24, 27, 28, 31, 50
Dewitz, P. K., 50
Dexter, S., 326
Deysher, S., 352
Diamond, A., 51
Diamond, M. C., 127, 129
Dickinson, D. K., 190, 311
Dickson, S., 172
Dickson, S. V., 171
Dikli, S., 89, 91
Dillon, D. R., 208, 259
diSessa, A. A., 317
Dobler, E., 246, 321, 323, 371
Doige, N., 127
Dolch, E. W., 50
Dole, J., 21
Dole, J. A., 247, 278
Dolz, J., 205, 209
Donahue, P., 334
Dong, T., 196, 200, 382
Donovan, C. A., 173, 183, 185, 187, 188, 190, 245, 246, 383
Dooley, S., 89, 90
Dowdy, C. A., 52
Dreher, M. J., 371
Dressler, C., 248
Dromsky, A. J., 149
Druckman, D. Q., 197
Duffy, G., 30
Duffy, G. G., 19, 20, 21, 23, 25, 26, 27, 28, 30, 33, 161, 166, 243, 263, 278, 384, 386

Duggan, T. J., 220
Duke, N., 246, 405
Duke, N. K., 26, 183, 219, 241, 243, 245, 246, 247, 267, 386, 388
Dumais, S. T., 89
Dunleavy, E., 266
Dunleavy, M., 326
Durkin, D., 19, 29, 32, 243, 406
Dweck, C. S., 228
Dynarski, M., 180

E

Eagleton, M., 352
Eagleton, M. B., 246, 371
Eccles, J. S., 229
Echevarria, M., 406
Eckhoff, A., 89
Edelman, G., 144
Edelman, G. M., 114, 115
Ediger, K. M., 76
Edyburn, D. L., 348
Ehren, B. J., 275
Ehri, L. C., 348
Elbro, C., 348
El-Dinary, P. B., 406
Eliopoulos, D., 371
Elkind, J., 348
Elkins, J., 323
Ellis, E. S., 275, 278
Ellis-Weismer, S., 275
Ellsworth, R. A., 242
Elmore, R., 289
Eme, E., 68
Engel, H., 104–105
Engelmann, S., 274
Ericsson, K., 402
Everson, M., 245
Everson, M. G., 83

F

Faggella-Luby, M. N., 286
Fairbanks, M. M., 58
Fallows, D., 324
Farmer, M. E., 348
Farnan, N., 263
Farrar, M. J., 51
Farstrup, A. E., 403
Fawson, P. C., 247
Fearn, L., 263

Felton, M., 199
Feltovich, P. J., 52
Fernandez, S. C., 399
Ferretti, R. P., 174, 348
Ferstl, E. C., 117, 119
Festinger, L., 228
Fiebach, C. J., 118
Fiez, J. A., 119
Fingeret, L., 394, 405
Fisher, D., 219, 258, 259, 260, 261, 262, 263, 383, 384, 387, 388, 389
Fisher, J. B., 284
Fitzgerald, J., 196, 215
Fitzsimmons, S., 248
Flam, E., 247
Flavell, J. H., 66
Fletcher, J. M., 180
Fobil, J., 322
Foertsch, M. A., 245
Foltz, P., 90
Foltz, P. W., 89, 174
Forguson, L., 52–53
Franks, B. A., 24
Franzke, M., 89, 90
Frattali, C., 111
Freedman, A., 199
Freire, P., 199
Frey, B. B., 219
Frey, N., 219, 258, 259, 260, 261, 262, 263, 383, 384, 387, 388, 389
Friederici, A. D., 118, 119
Friedman, T. L., 321
Frisbie, D. S., 244–245
Frost, S. J., 120, 350
Frye, B. J., 274
Frye, D., 50, 51, 54
Fuchs, D., 67
Fuchs, L. S., 67, 172, 180, 272, 309
Fulbright, R. K., 117
Fullan, M., 265
Fung, I. Y., 325
Fuster, J. M., 127, 130, 350

G

Gabriel, M. A., 363
Gabrieli, J. D., 351
Gaines, P., 27, 32
Gaizauskas, R., 92
Galda, L., 199
Gallagher, G., 262
Gallagher, M. C., 24

Gallimore, R., 299
Gallini, J. K., 186, 187, 189, 190
Gambrell, L., 19, 28, 41
Gambrell, L. B., 149, 159, 226, 230, 234, 363, 382, 385
Gantt, W. N., 363
Garcia, G., 294, 295
Gardill, M. C., 24
Garey, L. J., 143
Garmon, A., 208
Garner, R., 66
Garnier, H., 299
Garrison, J., 23
Gaskins, I., 66, 76
Gaskins, I. W., 50
Gaskins, R. W., 50
Gavelek, J. R., 250
Gavrin, A. D., 301
Gee, J., 323
Gee, J. P., 309, 310, 311, 313, 314, 315, 316, 385–386
Geidd, J. N., 142, 143, 144
Gendlin, E. T., 130
Gentner, D., 197
George, J. C., 405
Gersten, R., 172, 173, 272, 274, 278, 309, 313
Gibbons, G., 187
Gick, M. L., 197, 201, 204
Gilad, A., 371
Gillam, R., 188
Gilliam, S., 90
Girardet, H., 205
Glaser, R., 83
Gleason, M. M., 206, 209
Globerson, T., 350
Goatley, V. J., 247
Goetz, E. T., 41, 45, 46, 109, 111, 120
Goff, L. S., 263
Gogtay, N., 145
Golbeck, S. L., 53
Goldberg, E., 130, 139, 350
Goldenberg, C., 296, 297, 298, 299, 300
Goldenberg, C. N., 244, 248
Goldman-Rakic, P. S., 144
Goldschmidt, J., 374
Goldstone, B., 369, 372, 373
Gonzalez, E. J., 189
González, N., 302
Good, R., 185
Goodlad, J., 260
Goodman, K. S., 52
Gopnik, A., 52–53, 129

Gore, J., 119
Gorin, J. S., 81
Goswami, U., 15
Gotlieb, C., 371
Gough, P. B., 59, 272, 275
Govier, T., 197
Grabe, M., 52
Graesser, A. C., 81, 83, 85, 90, 92, 183, 189
Graham, S., 217, 218, 220, 246, 284
Grandin, T., 111
Graves, B., 163, 164
Graves, D., 215
Graves, M., 163, 164
Graves, M. F., 165
Gray, J., 215
Green, C., 230
Green, S. J., 55
Greenberg, E., 266
Greene, D., 228
Greene, J. F., 273
Greenlaw, M, J., 243
Greenleaf, C. L., 262, 273
Greenough, W. T., 127
Gregg, M., 145
Grek, M., 274
Griffin, P., 65, 142, 173, 241
Grigg, W., 334
Grigorenko, E., 129
Grisham, D. L., 248, 301, 351, 355
Gross, J. J., 351
Guiffré, H., 52
Guinee, K., 371
Guo-Liang, Y., 57
Guterman, E., 350
Guthke, T., 119
Guthrie, J., 19, 173, 298
Guthrie, J. T., 68, 162, 169, 229, 230, 231, 232, 234, 245, 247, 259, 272, 323, 353
Gwinn, C. B., 246

H

Hacker, D. J., 325
Halford, G. S., 50, 51
Hall, K. M., 173
Hall, L., 247
Hall, L. A., 219
Hall, T. E., 371
Haller, E. P., 67
Halliday, M. A. K., 188, 190
Hamilton, L., 188
Hammett, L. A., 188

Hampston, J. M., 243, 406
Hancock, D. R., 149
Hannon, N., 91
Harlen, W., 185
Harris, A., 56
Harris, K., 284
Harris, K. R., 246
Hart, B., 244, 399
Hartman, D. K., 321, 335
Hartt, J., 69
Hasselbring, T. S., 273
Hawes, S., 220
Hawisher, G. E., 309
Haxby, J. V., 103
Hayes-Roth, B., 204
Haynes, J. B., 350
Headley, K., 387
Heath, C., 129
Heath, S. B., 205
Hebb, D. O., 102
Heinecke, W. F., 326
Henderson, V. W., 119
Heng, M. A., 248
Henk, W. A., 228
Henry, L. A., 321, 324, 328, 333, 334, 371, 372
Herber, H. L., 259
Heron, A. H., 287
Herrell, A. L., 294
Hesse, K., 374
Heward, W. L., 248
Hewes, G. M., 274
Hickman-Davis, P., 249
Hidi, S., 209
Hidi, S. E., 245
Hiebert, E. H., 309
Higareda, I., 300
Higgins, K., 350
Hilden, K., 243, 284, 405, 406
Hilden, K. R., 59, 402
Hildyard, A., 245
Hill, P., 265
Hirsch, E. D., Jr., 244
Hirschman, L., 92
Hobson, J., 129
Hock, M. F., 271, 272, 275, 276, 278, 284, 285, 287, 386, 387, 388
Hodges, J. R., 108
Hodgkiss, M. D., 54, 58
Hofer, B. K., 197
Hoff-Ginsberg, E., 399
Hoffman, J. V., 23, 24, 26, 172
Holcomb, A., 45

Holcomb, P., 109
Holcomb, P. J., 109, 110
Holmes, C. J., 143
Holroyd, C., 185
Holyoak, K. J., 197, 198, 201, 204
Hoover, W. A., 59, 272, 275
Hoppes, M. K., 24
Horney, M. A., 350
Hoskyn, M., 278, 284
Houtveen, A. A. M., 71, 76
Hsu, Y., 266
Huberty, C. J., 188
Hubisz, J., 184
Hughes, C. A., 275, 284
Hughes, M. T., 162, 406
Hull, G., 323
Hurt, H., 142
Hurt, N., 28
Hurwitz, L., 262
Huttenlocher, J., 399
Huttenlocher, P. R., 132, 143

I

Iacoboni, M., 127
Ikpeze, C. H., 372
Inhelder, B., 50, 52, 53
Inklaar, R., 322
Intrator, S. M., 250
Iran-Nejad, A., 145
Isaac, M. C., 51, 54, 55, 57, 58, 59
Israel, S., 30, 76
Israel, S. E., 19, 27, 31, 166
Ivey, G., 259, 262, 263

J

Jaccard, J. J., 275
Jackson, D. E., 144
Jacob, B. A., 258
Jacobs, M., 311
Jacobs, V. A., 173, 183, 244
Jacques, S., 51
James, W., 171
Jansen, M., 72
Jeannerod, M., 350
Jenkins, F., 322
Jenner, A. R., 119, 120
Jernigan, T. L., 143
Jessell, T. M., 149
Jewitt, C., 221

Jimenez, R. T., 295
Jin, Y., 266
Jitendra, A. K., 24, 27
Johns, A. K., 70
Johnson, C., 263
Johnson, C. J., 23
Johnson, D., 19, 367, 368
Johnson, M., 39, 129, 348
Johnson, M. K., 198
Johnson, N., 89, 90
Johnson, N. S., 172
Johnson, R., 27
Johnson, R. B., 122
Jones, J., 21
Jones, J. P., 149
Jones, M. N., 93
Jordan, M., 294
Joy, J. A., 27, 32
Juel, C., 401
Just, M. A., 110, 111, 119

K

Kaan, E., 118, 120
Kalantzis, M., 323
Kamberelis, G., 245, 246
Kame'enui, E. J., 171, 313
Kamii, C., 115
Kamil, M. L., 250, 272, 309
Kana, R. K., 111
Kandel, E. R., 121, 122, 123, 149
Kangiser, S., 41
Kapinus, B., 172–173
Kapp, B. S., 122
Kara-Soteriou, J., 363
Karchmer, R. A., 363
Karmiloff-Smith, A., 52
Katch, L. E., 401
Katz, L., 120
Kays, J., 245
Kealy, W. A., 42, 45
Kear, D. J., 234, 242
Keating, T., 274
Keene, E. O., 19, 27, 30, 32, 241
Keller, T. A., 111
Keller, T. A., 110
Kellough, N. G., 150, 151
Kellough, R. D., 150, 151
Kelly, A. E., 85
Kelly, D. A., 14
Kemeny, S., 111
Kendall, S., 90

Kennedy, M., 354
Kerawalla, L., 56
Kesidou, S., 184
Kim, A., 68, 73
Kim, H. S., 250
Kim, I., 200, 382
Kim, S., 196, 200, 382
King, K., 185
King, P. M., 197
Kingner, J., 162
Kinnucan-Welsh, K., 31, 76
Kintsch, E., 85, 89, 90, 91, 384
Kintsch, W., 40, 83, 86, 89, 91, 111
Kinzer, C. K., 221, 246, 323, 347, 363
Kipling, R., 309
Kirby, J., 381
Kirkham, N., 51
Kirsch, I., 259
Kitchener, K. S., 197
Kjos, B. O., 144
Klauda, S. L., 245
Klein, R., 348
Klenk, L., 325
Klimek, K., 129
Kline, F. M., 278
Kline, T., 276
Klingner, J., 67
Klingner, J. K., 248, 406
Knapp, M. S., 243
Knight, R. T., 350
Knipper, K. J., 220
Knobel, M., 323
Knowles, T., 151
Koda, K., 296
Kolb, B., 149
Konigsburg, E. L., 374
Koskinen, P. S., 41
Kosslyn, S. M., 109, 115
Kounios, J., 109, 110
Kouzekanani, K., 249
Krajcik, J., 184
Krampe, R., 402
Krashen, S., 173
Kress, G., 323
Kucan, L., 169, 245, 310, 404
Kucer, S. B., 294, 301
Kuhl, P., 129
Kuhl, P. K., 148
Kuhn, D., 50, 51, 58, 196, 197, 199, 202, 205, 209
Kuhn, M. R., 246
Kuiper, E., 246
Kukich, K., 88

Kumpulainen, K., 196
Kuo, L., 200, 202
Kuriloff, P. C., 222
Kurita, J. A., 21
Kurth, R. J., 243
Kutner, M., 266

L

Labbo, L., 228, 363, 368
Labbo, L. D., 246, 365
LaBerge, S. J., 59
Labouvie-Vief, G., 51
Lacina, G., 362
Lacina, J., 362, 367, 368, 369, 383, 384, 388
Lacina, J. G., 221
Laham, D., 89
Lakoff, G., 39, 129
Landauer, T. K., 89, 90
Landis, D., 216
Lane, R. D., 351, 353
Langer, G. M., 263, 264
Langer, J. A., 245
Lankshear, C., 323
Lauer, K. D., 173
Lave, J., 129
Laverick, C., 262
Lazarus, R. S., 132
Leach, J. M., 275
Leacock, C., 92
Leahy, S., 21
Leander, K., 246
LeDoux, J. E., 128, 132
Lee, J., 334
Lee, J. R., 119, 120
Lee, O., 174
Lee, S., 41, 111
Lee, S. W., 219
LeFevre, D. M., 74, 75
Leff, A. P., 105
Leftwich, S. A., 406
Leggett, E. L., 228
Lehman, B., 374
Lenz, B. K., 274, 275, 284
Leon, J. A., 183
Lepper, M. R., 228
LeRoy, K., 174
Lesaux, N., 296
Leu, D. D., 330, 336
Leu, D. J., 221, 246, 250, 321, 323, 324, 325, 327, 328, 331–332, 332, 333, 334, 335, 363

Leu, D. J., Jr., 330, 336, 347, 363
Leung, C. B., 183
Levin, J., 246
Levine, S., 399
Levinstein, I. B., 90
Lewandowski, L., 348
Lewedeg, V., 399
Lewin, L., 363
Lewis, J. P.,, 25
Lewis, S., 174
Li, Y., 196, 200, 208, 382
Liang, L. A., 165, 166, 167
Liben, L., 52, 53, 56
Liberman, A. M., 45
Lietz, S., 185
Lim, H. J., 388
Linan-Thompson, S., 249
Lindamood, P., 47
Lindquist, E. F., 52
Lipman, M., 207, 209
Lipson, M., 67
Livingstone, S., 322
Lizotte, D. J., 184
Locke, J., 80
Loera, G., 298
Long, D. A., 208
Lonigan, C. J., 400
Louwerse, M. M., 189
Lovitt, T., 350
Lubliner, S., 68, 72, 76
Luckin, R., 56
Ludlow, A., 322
Lundberg, I., 348
Luria, A. R., 108, 198
Lutz, L., 354
Lyon, G. R., 52, 180
Lyon, G. E., 374
Lysynchuk, L. M., 274

M

MacArthur, C. A., 221, 348, 350
Macauley, D., 373
MacDonnell, E. S., 244–245
Magliano, J., 90
Magnusson, S., 192
Magnusson, S. J., 192, 245
Maguire, T. O., 184
Maier, S., 128
Mallette, M. H., 228, 363
Malloy, J., 328
Malloy, J. A., 385

Mandler, G., 203, 204
Mandler, J. M., 172
Mangalath, P., 91, 93
Mangieri, J., 28
Mangieri, J. N., 243
Manning, M. L., 155
Marcovitch, S., 54
Marks, L. J., 221
Markus, H., 288
Marquis, J., 274
Marron, M. A., 174
Marrow, L. M., 32
Marshall, P., 19
Marshall, T. R., 54, 55, 57, 58
Marsiglia, C. S., 70
Martin, A., 103
Martin, A. H., 374
Martin, J. B., 373
Martin, M. O., 189
Martin, N. M., 267, 386, 388
Martineau, J. A., 183, 246
Martinez, M. G., 150, 151
Martins, I., 183
Marx, R. W., 184
Marzano, R. J., 259
Maslow, A. H., 228
Massengill, D., 219
Masson, M. E., 52
Mastropieri, M. A., 172
Mathes, P. G., 67
Matteucci, N., 322
Mattingly, I. G., 45
Mayer, R. E., 42, 46, 185, 186, 187, 189, 190, 192, 202
Maywall, K., 106
Mazoyer, B., 110
Mazzoni, S. A., 149, 234
McArdle, C. B., 144
McCandliss, B. D., 105, 106
McCann, T. M., 205
McCarthy, G., 119
McClelland, J. L., 107
McClintic, C., 129
McCombs, B. L., 235
McCormick, C., 172
McDaniel, B., 90, 92
McGivern, R., 148
McGoldrick, J. A., 21
McGough, K., 230
McGrath, C., 188
McGregor, T., 65, 66, 76
McGuckin, R. H., 322
McIntyre, L. D., 23, 27

McKelney, A., 110
McKenna, M. C., 234, 242, 365
McKeown, M. G., 169, 207, 310, 313, 404
McKiernan, K. A., 110
McLaughlin, J., 230
McMahon, K. C., 185
McNamara, D., 90
McNamara, D. S., 89, 90, 189, 191, 352, 355, 357
McNeill, K. L., 184
McRae, A., 245
McTigue, E. M., 183, 189, 383
McWilliams, J., 325
Mead, G. H., 196, 198
Means, M. L., 202, 205
Mecklinger, A., 119
Medler, D. A., 110
Meece, J. L., 231
Mehan, H., 299
Meister, C., 39, 67, 274, 325, 327, 352, 406
Mellard, D. F., 275
Mellet, E., 110
Melnick, S. A., 228
Meltzoff, A. N., 129
Mencl, W. E., 119, 120, 350
Meneghetti, C., 91
Merchant, G., 323
Mewhort, D. J. K., 93
Meyer, A., 351
Meyer, B., 352, 355, 357
Meyer, B. J., 198
Meyer, B. J. F., 171, 172
Meyer, M., 119
Mezynski, K., 58
Miall, D. S., 45
Midgley, C., 230
Miller, E., 185
Miller, J., 247
Miller, P. H., 52
Miller, S. D., 27
Millis, K., 90
Minden-Cupp, C., 401
Minshew, N. J., 111
Mishra, P., 197
Mitchell, D. C., 119
Moffett, S., 117
Mohan, L., 394
Moje, E. B., 287
Mokhlesgerami, J., 71, 75
Mokhtari, K., 66
Molfese, D. L., 118
Moll, L. C., 302

Monk, C. S., 146, 148
Montali, J., 348
Montaño, M., 52, 59
Montgomery, D. J., 221
Monzo, L., 302
Moore, D. W., 74, 260, 274, 325
Moore, V. K., 243
Morehouse, R., 204, 209
Moreno, R., 192
Morrison, F. J., 401
Morrow, L. M., 2, 405
Morrow, L. N., 28, 32, 230
Mosher, F. A., 82
Moss, G., 183, 185, 191
Mostow, J., 348
Mountcastle, V. B., 351
Moxley, K., 247
Mueller, F. L., 273
Mulhern, S. L., 24
Müller, U., 54
Mulligan, E. J., 91, 93
Mullis, I. V. S., 189, 245
Munsch, R., 199
Murdoch, B. E., 118
Murray, C., 348
Mutanen, M., 196
Mutter, K., 148
Myers, M., 66
Myers, P. A., 162, 163, 166, 167

N

Nachmias, R., 371
Nadel, L., 351, 353
Nagy, W. E., 313
Naigles, L., 399
Natriello, G., 267
Neri, F., 89
Neuman, S., 183, 244, 311
Neuman, S. B., 230
Neville, H. J., 145
Nevills, P., 127, 133
Newkirk, T., 246
Newman, A. D., 110
Newton, D. P., 184, 185, 186, 187, 188
Newton, L. D., 184, 185, 186, 187, 188
Nguyen, K., 207
Ni, W., 119
Niccols, A., 50
Nichols, S. L., 85
Nichols, W. D., 149
Nicholson, S. A., 284

Nisbeit, R. E., 228
Nobre, A. C., 119
Noppeney, U., 119
Norman, D., 144
Novak, G. M., 301
Nurius, P., 288
Nystrand, M., 208, 243–244

O

Oakar, M., 28, 142
Oakhill, J., 50, 69, 70
O'Brien, D., 323
O'Brien, D. G., 208, 259
Ochsner, K. N., 351
O'Flahavan, J. F., 210
Ogborn, J., 185
Ogbu, J., 299
Ogle, D., 21
Okamoto, Y., 52
Okolo, C. M., 174, 348
Oldfather, P., 230
Olivarez, A., 41, 111
Oller, D. K., 399
Oloffson, A., 348
Olson, M. R., 335
Olson, R. K., 348
O'Mahony, M., 322
O'Neal, S., 284
Oppenheim, J., 373
O'Reilly, T., 191, 355
Ormerod, F., 185
O'Rourke, T. B., 110
Osborn, J., 30
Osborne, J., 183
Otero, J., 183
Ouellette, G., 311
Overman, L. T., 274
Ozgungor, S., 173
Ozuru, Y., 90, 355

P

Paas, F., 190, 301
Padak, N., 402
Paivio, A., 40, 41, 43, 45, 46, 102, 105, 106, 108, 109, 111, 120, 123, 387
Paivio, M., 123
Palincsar, A., 21, 24, 67, 356
Palincsar, A. M., 85
Palincsar, A. S., 161, 162, 192, 245, 274,

324, 324–325, 325, 326, 328, 329, 352, 354, 358, 366, 406
Palmer, B. M., 230, 234, 363
Palumbo, T. J., 76
Panksepp, J., 128
Pappas, C., 28
Pappas, C. C., 173, 183, 245
Paris, S., 66
Paris, S. G., 67, 68, 226, 231, 232, 301, 332, 409
Park, A., 144
Park, G., 111
Parkinson, J., 191
Parodi, G., 216
Parris, S., 24
Parris, S. R., 25, 28, 43, 121, 142, 149, 150, 382, 383, 384, 385, 387, 388
Pasco, J. P., 122
Pasley, J. D., 186
Pass, L., 219
Patberg, J., 21
Patterson, E. T., 301
Patterson, K., 108
Paul, R. W., 207, 209
Pea, R., 129
Pearce, D., 56
Pearson, B. Z., 399
Pearson, D., 404
Pearson, P., 295
Pearson, P. D., 19, 24, 115, 243, 247, 262, 278, 309, 313, 404, 406
Pease, M., 50, 51
Pekrun, R., 149
Pellegrini, A. D., 199
Pellegrino, J. W., 81, 82, 83
Perencevich, K. C., 68, 245, 247, 272, 298
Perfetti, C. A., 174
Perin, D., 217, 218, 220
Perkins, D. N., 188, 196, 202
Perry, W. G., 197
Persky, H., 322
Person, N. P., 83, 85
Pert, C., 130
Peterson, C., 128
Peterson, C. A., 165
Peterson, C. L., 284
Peterson, F., 263
Peterson, S. E., 119
Piaget, J., 50, 52, 53, 115
Pichert, J. W., 198
Pinker, S., 311
Pintrich, P. R., 197, 298
Pisha, B., 352, 354

Pistochini, L., 325
Plant, G. T., 105
Poniatowski, L., 354
Pontecorvo, C., 205
Poon, L. W., 171, 172
Portes, P., 295
Possing, E. T., 110
Prensky, M., 372
Pressley, D., 391
Pressley, M., 2, 4–5, 6, 19, 20, 21, 23, 24, 25, 26, 27, 28, 30, 32, 33, 39, 41, 50, 51, 59, 66, 67, 68, 76, 159, 161, 162, 172, 173, 183, 214, 223, 242, 243, 244, 247, 272, 274, 284, 286, 287, 309, 313, 331, 352, 354, 363, 391, 392, 393, 395, 402, 403, 404, 405, 406, 407, 408
Price, C. J., 119
Price, G., 55
Price, L. H., 188
Pringle, I., 199
Proctor, C. P., 248, 301, 323, 347, 348, 349, 351, 352, 355, 358
Puce, A., 119
Pugh, K. R., 119, 120, 350
Pullman, P., 373
Purcell-Gates, V., 183, 219, 246, 247
Purnell, K. N., 42
Puustinen, M., 68

Q

Quirk, M. P., 299

R

Radvansky, G. A., 83
Ramey, C. T., 400
Ramsel, D., 52
Rankin, J. L., 243
Raphael, T. E., 247, 250
Rasch, G., 87
Raschka, C., 374
Rasinski, T. V., 41, 402
Rasmussen, I., 348
Rastle, K., 107
Rathmann, P., 374
Rawson, K. A., 91
Readence, J. E., 167
Reed, K. L., 24
Reed, S. K., 197, 198
Reese, L., 299

Reezigt, G., 72
Reffitt, K., 247
Reilly, J., 148
Reinking, D., 321, 324, 325, 328, 333, 350, 365, 398, 399
Renkl, A., 301
Renouf, K., 24
Rescorla, L., 275
Reutzel, D. R., 247
Reynolds, D., 396
Reznitskaya, A., 196, 197, 198, 200, 202, 382, 386, 387
Rice, M. E., 230
Rice, M. S., 80
Rich, S., 30
Rickards, D., 220
Rieber, L. P., 46
Riley, T., 321
Rinehart, J., 245
Ring, J., 348
Risley, T. R., 244, 399
Rissman, L., 274
Rizzolatti, G., 127–128, 131
Roberts, N. M., 41, 111
Robinson, C., 322
Robinson, K., 354
Rodgers, L., 27
Rodgers, L. L., 122
Rodney, D., 311
Roehler, L. R., 20, 30, 33, 161, 278
Roeschl-Heils, A., 69, 73
Rogers, A., 328
Rogoff, B., 198, 209
Roit, N., 23
Romance, N. R., 245, 247
Rong, Y., 57
Rose, 358
Rose, D., 347, 350, 351, 383, 387
Rose, K., 350
Rose, S. A., 188
Roseman, J. E., 184
Rosenblatt, L. M., 45, 243, 352, 409
Rosenshine, B., 39, 67, 274, 325, 327, 352, 406
Roser, N. L., 150, 151
Ross, G., 161, 263, 352
Routman, R., 215
Rowan, K. E., 191
Rubin, D., 199
Ruddell, R. B., 39, 243, 251
Rueda, R., 294, 297, 298, 300, 302, 388, 389
Ruff, T. P., 149
Rumelhart, D. E., 197, 243

Russell, T. L., 184
Rutherford, F. J., 184
Ryan, R. M., 132, 228
Rycik, J. A., 260

S

Saddler, B., 218
Sadoski, M., 40, 41, 42, 43, 45, 46, 101, 108, 109, 111, 120, 122, 123, 190, 387
Sakurai, Y., 105
Salazar, J., 300
Salomon, G., 188, 196, 202, 350
Samarapungavan, A., 52
Samols, D., 69
Samuels, S. J., 59, 76, 243, 403
Sanan, T., 296
Sandak, R., 350
Sandora, C. A., 169
Sapolsky, R., 132
Sarason, S. B., 260
Saunders, A., 159
Saunders, W. M., 244, 248
Scales, P. C., 150
Scarborough, H. S., 243, 272, 275, 399
Schacter, D., 131
Schaffer, G., 396
Schaller, J. L., 27, 32
Schank, R. C., 197, 198
Schiefele, U., 231
Schillinger, S. M., 24
Schleicher, A., 382
Schleper, D., 354
Schleppegrell, M., 311
Schmidt, K., 55, 56, 57, 58
Schmitz, J. G., 52
Schneider, W., 15, 69
Schoenbach, R., 262, 273
Schoon, K. J., 185
Schreiner, R., 350
Schuder, T., 23, 67, 162, 243, 406
Schultz, K., 323
Schumaker, J. B., 274, 275, 278, 284, 285
Schumm, J., 67
Schumm, J. S., 162
Schunk, D. H., 231
Schwanenflugel, P. J., 299
Schwartz, J. H., 149
Scruggs, T. E., 172
Seidenberg, M. S., 107
Selfe, C. L., 309
Seligman, M., 128

Senechal, M., 311
Seuss, Dr., 372, 373
Shaffer, D. W., 317, 318
Shanahan, T., 9, 215, 244, 248, 296, 300, 362
Shankland, R. K., 59, 402
Shaw, V., 199
Shaywitz, B., 119
Shaywitz, B. A., 350, 351
Shaywitz, S. E., 350, 351
Sheorey, R., 66
Shepard, L. A., 81, 82, 83, 85, 91, 92
Shin, L. M., 115
Short, D. J., 248
Shumow, L., 185
Shymansky, J. A., 185
Siegel, L., 296
Silva, C., 294, 301
Silverstein, A. K., 172
Simmons, D. C., 67, 171, 313
Singer, M., 83
Sinnott, J. D., 51
Sis, P., 373, 374
Skinner, B. F., 227
Sloane, F. C., 85
Slonim, N., 403
Smetana, L., 68, 72, 76
Smith, C. B., 392
Smith, J. A., 247
Smith, J. K., 405
Smith, L., 129
Smith, M., 405
Smith, M. W., 190
Smith, P. S., 185
Smith, S., 274
Smolkin, L., 183
Smolkin, L. B., 173, 183, 185, 187, 188, 190, 383, 386, 388
Sneed, B., 374
Snow, C., 295
Snow, C. E., 65, 142, 173, 221, 241, 248, 260, 272, 278, 286, 287, 348, 355, 358, 399
Snyder, B. L., 20, 21
Snyder, I., 323, 363, 368
Snyder, L., 85, 384
Solman, R. T., 42
Sommer, R., 45
Sousa, D., 127
Souvignier, E., 71, 75
Sowell, E. R., 143
Spaulding, C. L., 231
Spelling, B., 348

Spellings, M., 407
Spiro, R. J., 52
Spitsyana, G., 105
Squire, J. R., 25
Stahl, K. A. D., 243
Stahl, S. A., 58, 243, 402
Stanovich, K. E., 19, 145, 234, 244, 299
Stauffer, R. G., 160
Stein, N. L., 172, 207
Steinhauer, K., 119
Stenner, J., 86
Sternberg, R., 129, 130
Sternberg, R. J., 52
Stevens, R. J., 216
Stewart, M. S., 30
Stewart, M. T., 24, 25
Strang, R., 259
Strangman, N., 348, 354
Street, B., 323, 363
Street, B. V., 205
Stricker, A. G., 45, 46
Stringfield, S., 396
Stuss, D. T., 350
Stylianidou, F., 185
Sung, Y., 83, 245
Suzuki, N. S., 41
Swaab, T. Y., 118, 120
Swan, E. A., 262
Swanson, H. L., 278, 284
Swartz, S. L., 285
Sweet, A., 295
Sweller, J., 190, 301
Sylwester, R., 132
Symons, S., 20, 21, 23

T

Taboada, A., 247, 323
Taffe, S. W., 246
Tam, K. Y., 248
Tannock, S., 287
Taylor, B. M., 243, 274, 406
Teddlie, C., 396
Tenent, A., 325
Terwel, J., 246
Tesch-Romer, C., 402
Thelen, E., 129
Thomas, K. F., 29
Thomas, K. M., 142
Thomas, S., 55
Thompson, M. H., 159, 383, 385, 386, 388

Thompson, P. M., 143
Thompson, W. L., 109
Thorndike, E. L., 227, 258, 267
Thorndyke, P. W., 204
Thorne, M. T., 274
Tierney, R. J., 167
Todaro, S., 90
Toga, A. W., 143
Tollefson, N., 219
Tolstoy, L., 123
Tomesen, M., 58
Torgesen, J. K., 278
Toulmin, S. E., 197, 198
Tower, C., 219, 245
Trabasso, T., 83, 172
Trathen, W., 21, 247
Treyens, J. C., 198
Truxaw, M. P., 335
Tunmer, W. E., 233, 275
Turbil, J., 363
Turbill, J., 9
Turner, J., 226, 228, 231, 232, 234
Turner, J. C., 332
Tzeng, Y., 83, 245
Tzourio, N., 110

U

Udell, W., 205, 209
Ungerleider, L. G., 103
Unrau, N. J., 39, 243
Unsworth, L., 323

V

Valencia, S., 276
Valenti, S., 89
Valmont, W. J., 363, 368
Van Ark, B., 322
van de Grift, W. J. C. M., 71, 76
Van de Ven, A., 70
Van De Ven, A., 325
Van Den Bos, K. P., 325
van den Broek, P., 83, 245
van der Loos, H., 143
van Dijk, T. A., 83
Van Keer, H., 72, 75, 76
van Kleeck, A., 188, 190
van Kraayenoord, C. E., 69
Van Leeuwen, C. A., 363
van Merriënboer, J. J. G., 190

Van Meter, P., 23, 67, 162, 243, 406
VanLehn, K., 90
Vasilyeva, M., 399
Vaughn, S., 67, 162, 169, 248, 249, 406
Velasco, A., 388
Vellutino, F. R., 275
Verhaeghe, J. P., 72, 75, 76
Vernon, D. S., 285
Verschaffel, L., 70, 325
Viegut, D., 264
Virtue, S., 83, 245
Vispoel, W. P., 52
Vitale, M. R., 245, 247
Volman, M., 246
von Cramon, D. Y., 117, 119
VonSecker, C., 230, 245, 298
Vos, S. H., 118
Voss, F. J., 205
Voss, J. F., 202, 205
Vroom, V. H., 228, 234
Vye, N. J., 274
Vygotsky, L. S., 27, 67, 161, 196, 198, 209, 213, 263, 352

W

Wade, A., 25
Waggoner, M., 200, 207
Wagner, R. K., 52
Walberg, H. J., 67
Walczyk, J. J., 70, 75
Walker, B., 24, 27
Wallace, C. S., 127
Wallis, C., 144
Walpole, S., 183, 185, 243, 406
Walsh, M., 109
Walton, D., 197
Wang, D., 250
Wang, Z., 46
Warner, M. M., 275
Warschauer, M., 363
Wasik, B. A., 332
Waters, G., 119
Watkins, J. K., 185
Watson, J. B., 227
Webb, J. M., 42
Weimer-Hastings, K., 90
Weiner, B., 228
Weiss, A. R., 322
Weiss, I. R., 185, 186
Welch, M. W., 52
Welty, E., 214

Wendler, D., 243
Wenger, E., 129
Wernicke, K., 103
Wertsch, J. V., 198
West, C. K., 244–245
West, W. C., 110
Westbury, C. F., 110
Westera, J., 274
Wharton-McDonald, R., 28, 32, 243, 406
Whipple, G., 259
Whishaw, I. Q., 149
White, T. S., 46
Whitehurst, G. J., 400
Whiteley, C. S., 43, 121
Whitley, C. S., 24
Wiedenfeld, S. A., 128
Wiesner, D., 374
Wigfield, A., 68, 229, 230, 231, 245, 247, 259, 272, 298, 353
Wijekumar, K., 352, 355, 357
Wiles, J., 151
Wiles, M. T., 151
Wiliam, D., 82
Wilkinson, I., 9–10, 325
Wilkinson, I. A., 74
Willcutt, J. R., 76
Williams, D., 261
Williams, J. P., 172, 173, 174, 179, 183, 246, 272, 309, 386
Williams, K. T., 285
Williams, M., 204, 209
Willson, V., 45
Willson, V. L., 42, 43, 46
Wilson, M., 40, 43
Wilson, P. T., 242
Wilson, R. M., 363
Wise, B., 85
Wise, B. W., 348
Wise, R. J. S., 105
Witkin, M., 287
Wolfe, P., 127, 133
Wollman-Bonilla, J. E., 245–246
Wood, D., 161, 263, 352
Wood, J. M., 246
Woodcock, R. W., 55, 56
Worthy, J., 169
Wu, L., 208
Wyatt, D., 403
Wyatt-Smith, C., 323

X

Xu, J., 111

Y

Yancey, K. B., 221
Yatvin, J., 395–396
Yi, H., 200
Yokoi, L., 243
Yore, L. D., 184, 185
Yorinks, A., 374
Young, J. P., 230
Yuill, N., 50, 56, 58
Yurgelun-Todd, D., 147, 152

Z

Zeckler, L., 28
Zeiser, S., 208
Zelazo, P. D., 50, 51, 53, 54
Zentella, A. C., 295
Zhang, S., 246
Ziegler, J. C., 15
Zimmerman, B. J., 231
Zimmerman, C., 188
Zimmerman, S., 241
Zimmermann, S., 19, 27, 30, 32
Zinar, S., 69
Zucker, A., 326
Zwaan, R. A., 83
Zwick, T., 322
Zwiers, J., 142, 312

Subject Index

t indicates a table; *f* indicates a figure

Ability goals, motivation and, 228
Abstract language, neuroscientific knowledge and, 109–112
Academic Literacy course, at-risk students and, 273
Achievement motivation, 227–229. *see also* Motivation
Adelaide Declaration on National Goals for Schooling in the Twenty-First Century (Australia), 10
Adolescent students. *see also* Secondary students, teaching of
   instruction and, 149–152
   neuroscientific knowledge and, 142–153
   questions for discussion regarding, 153
   research regarding, 143–150, 144*f*, 145*f*, 152
Amazing Adventure Series website, 365
American Library Association's Booklist website, 361
Amygdala
   adolescent students and, 145–146, 148
   overview, 117
Angular gyrus, 107
Anticipatory activities, 261*f*
Apprenticeship model of learning, 352. *see also* Reciprocal teaching
Argument schema theory
   collaborative reasoning (CR) and, 199–200
   dialogic interaction and, 207
   future directions in, 208
   instruction and, 207
   overview, 196–199, 208–209
   questions for discussion regarding, 209
   research regarding, 199–207, 200*t*, 201*f*, 203*t*
Argument stratagems, 206
Artificial intelligence (AI), 88–89
Assessment
   close analysis of texts with structure (CATS) program and, 177–178
   collaborative analysis of student work and, 263–265, 264*f*, 265*f*
   future directions in, 92–94
   improving comprehension instruction and, 85–92
   Internet Reciprocal Teaching (IRT) model and, 331–334
   motivation and, 234
   overview, 80–81, 94
   questions for discussion regarding, 94–95
   research regarding, 81–85
   Teaching Internet Comprehension to Adolescents (TICA), 324, 342*f*–346*f*
   testing and, 407–410
At-risk students. *see also* Struggling readers
   family literacy and, 399–400
   future directions in, 286–289
   instruction and, 286
   overview, 271–272, 289

431

At-risk students *(cont.)*
  questions for discussion regarding, 289
  research regarding, 272–285, 277*f*, 281*f*, 282*f*, 283*f*, 284*f*, 286–288
Attention
  English language learners (ELLs) and, 299
  learning and, 131
Attribution theory, 228
Auditory logogens, 106–107. *see also* Logogens
Authenticity, instruction and, 246–247
Autism, neuroscientific knowledge and, 111
Automaticity, metacognition and, 76
AutoTutor tool, 90
AWARD Reading program, 13–14, 15

B

Background knowledge. *see* Prior knowledge
Balanced literacy, reading–writing connections and, 220*t*
Basal ganglia, working memory and, 118–119
Bedtime Story website, 365
Benchmark school, metacognition and, 76
Book clubs, online versions of, 369–370
BookBuilder website, 355
Brain imaging
  concreteness/imagery effects and, 110–111
  metacognition and, 76
  overview, 115–120, 116*f*, 117*f*
Broca's area
  research regarding, 106–107
  syntactic errors and, 119

C

CATS program, 174–179
Cause and effect structure of text, 174–179
Cell assembly theory, 102
Center for Applied Special Technology (CAST)
  digital comprehension and, 353*f*
  online tools from, 355
  overview, 351–352
Center on Education Policy, 174
Cerebellum, 117
Character studies, adolescent students and, 151–152
Children's Choices Booklist website, 361
Clarifying strategy, 327–328

Classification task, 53
Classroom environment
  at-risk students and, 288–289
  comprehension instruction and, 25–26
  motivation and, 226–227, 230, 234
  overview, 393
Classroom-based interventions, 70–73. *see also* Intervention
Close analysis of texts with structure (CATS) program, 174–179
Cognitive Complexity and Control theory of cognitive development, 51–52
Cognitive flexibility
  future directions in, 57–59
  improving comprehension instruction and, 56–57
  overview, 50–51, 60, 382–383, 388
  questions for discussion regarding, 60
  research regarding, 51–56, 54*f*, 55*t*
Cognitive neuroscience, 115. *see also* Neuroscientific knowledge
Cognitive strategy instruction. *see* Strategy instruction
Cognitive support, reading–writing connections and, 217–218
Cognitive theory, research regarding, 39–44, 43*f*
Collaborative analysis of student work, 263–265, 264*f*, 265*f*
Collaborative learning
  overview, 387
  secondary level instruction and, 263
Collaborative modeling, 329–330. *see also* Modeling
Collaborative reasoning (CR), 199–200
Collaborative Strategic Reading (CSR), 67
Colorado Student Assessment Program (CSAP), 42–43, 43*f*
Comprehension instruction. *see also* Instruction
  assessment and, 85–92
  cognitive flexibility and, 56–57
  dual coding theory and, 44–45
  fictional text comprehension and, 166–167
  future directions in, 30–33
  improving through research, 13–14, 29–30
  metacognition and, 74–75
  neuroscientific knowledge and, 120–123
  questions for discussion regarding, 33–34
  research regarding, 20–28, 22*t*
  technology and, 364–366, 366*f*
Comprehension monitoring. *see* Monitoring strategies

Comprehension Process motions (CPM) method, 43–44
Comprehension strategies, 22t, 29. *see also* Strategy instruction
Comprehension strategy instruction. *see* Strategy instruction
Computer-Assisted Collaborative Strategic Reading (CACSR) program, 73
Computer-based assessments. *see* Assessment
Concept-Oriented Reading Instruction (CORI)
  authenticity and, 247
  English language learners (ELLs) and, 298
  future directions in, 250
  motivation and, 230–231
  overview, 230–231
  prior knowledge and, 245
  secondary level instruction and, 262
Conceptual knowledge, 404–405
Concrete language, neuroscientific knowledge and, 109–112
Conscious processes, learning and, 131
Consistency in instruction
  overview, 388–389
  secondary level instruction and, 260–262, 261f
Constructivist theory
  future directions in, 92–94
  questions for discussion regarding, 94–95
  research regarding, 81–85
Content-enhancement routines, 274–275
Context, instruction and, 246–247
Cornell note taking, 260, 261f
Corrective Reading (SRA), 274
Cross-cultural research, argument schema theory and, 205
Cultural factors, English language learners (ELLs) and, 297–298, 300–301
Curriculum development
  motivation and, 232–233
  program evaluation and, 398–399

D

Decoding
  comprehension processes and, 83–84
  history of reading research and, 9
  intervention and, 75
  metacognition and, 75
  neuroscientific knowledge and, 119
Deep comprehension, assessment of, 91–92
Descriptive text, compared to explanatory text, 186t

Developmental processes. *see also* Vocabulary development
  adolescent students and, 145–146, 145f, 151–152
  cognitive flexibility and, 55, 55t
  expository text comprehension and, 173
  family literacy and, 309, 399–400
  learning and, 132
  literacy development, 215–216
  metacognition and, 66–67, 68–70
  overview, 385–386
  writing development, 218
Dialogic interaction, 207
Dialogic organization, 198
DIBELS, 59, 402–403, 408–410
Digital comprehension. *see also* Online reading comprehension; Technology
  executive functioning and, 350–351
  future directions in, 356–357, 371–372, 373f–374f
  instruction and, 351–355, 353f, 356
  online tools that support, 355
  overview, 347, 383–384
  questions for discussion regarding, 357–358, 374–375
  research regarding, 348–350, 349f, 356, 372
Digital Divide Measurement Scale for Students (DDMS-S0), 334
Dimensional Change Card Sort task, 53
Direct teaching of comprehension. *see also* Instruction
  future directions in, 31–32
  overview, 29–30
  research regarding, 24–28
Directed Reading Activity (DRA), 160
Directed Reading–Thinking Activity (DR-TA), 160
Disability, Transactional Strategies Instruction (TSI) and, 162
Discussion guides, fictional text comprehension and, 167
Drop Everything and Read (DEAR) approach, 402
Dual coding theory
  concreteness/imagery effects and, 109–112, 111
  future directions in, 45–46
  improving comprehension instruction and, 44–45
  motor logogens and, 107–108
  neuroscientific knowledge and, 101–103, 104, 104–108, 105f, 108–109, 120
  overview, 2, 38, 46, 387

Dual coding theory *(cont.)*
  questions for discussion regarding, 46–47
  research regarding, 39–44, 43f, 45–46, 104–108, 105f
Dual-coded instructional strategies, 2
Dynamic Indicators of Basic Early Literacy Skills (DIBELS), 59, 402–403, 408–410
Dynamic memory, 131–132

E

Educational Testing Service (ETS), 89
Electroencephalography (EEG), 116, 116f
Elementary Reading Attitude Scale, 234
Elementary students, teaching of. *see also* Instruction
  fictional text comprehension and, 160–167
  future directions in, 138–139, 250–252
  improving comprehension instruction and, 249
  neuroscientific knowledge and, 127–128, 133–139
  overview, 241–242, 252
  questions for discussion regarding, 139–140, 252
  research regarding, 244–249, 250–251
  science text and, 185–186
Elgin to Elgin project, 15–16
Embodied cognition, 39–44, 43f
Emotional experience
  neuroscientific knowledge and, 122–123, 128
  patterning and, 130
Empathy, adolescent students and, 147
Encoding, English language learners (ELLs) and, 299
Engagement
  classroom environment and, 393
  fictional text comprehension and, 166
  motivation and, 231–232
  secondary level instruction and, 259, 266
English language learners (ELLs)
  digital comprehension and, 355
  future directions in, 300–302
  improving comprehension instruction and, 299–300
  instruction and, 248–249
  Internet Reciprocal Teaching (IRT) model and, 326–327
  overview, 248–249, 294–295, 302
  questions for discussion regarding, 302–303
  research regarding, 295–299, 300–301
  secondary level instruction and, 266

Environment, classroom. *see* Classroom environment
Environment, learning and, 132. *see also* Classroom environment
E-rater assessment, 89
Error detection paradigm, metacognition and, 67
Event-related potentials (ERPs), 109–110, 116
Executive functioning, 350–351
Expectancy-value theory of motivation
  engagement and, 231–232
  overview, 229
Explanations
  overview, 26–27
  questions for discussion regarding, 192–193
  science text and, 183–193
  strategy instruction and, 407
Explanatory framework, 197
Explanatory text, compared to descriptive text, 186t
Explicit instruction. *see also* Instruction
  argument schema theory and, 201
  expository text comprehension and, 171–180
  future directions in, 179–180
  overview, 386
  questions for discussion regarding, 180
Exploration, adolescent students and, 151
Expository text comprehension
  explicit instruction and, 171–180, 386
  future directions in, 179–180
  motivation and, 233
  overview, 388
  questions for discussion regarding, 180
  research regarding, 172–179
External motivation programs, 227–228
Extrinsic motivation, 229. *see also* Motivation

F

Facial expressions, adolescent students and, 147–149
Family literacy
  importance of, 309
  secondary level instruction and, 259
  socioeconomic level and, 399–400
  specialist language and, 311–312
Fastmapping, 121–122
Fictional text comprehension
  future directions in, 167–168
  improving comprehension instruction and, 166–167

overview, 159–160, 169, 388
   questions for discussion regarding, 169
   research regarding, 160–162
First World Congress on Reading, 11
Flexibility, cognitive
   future directions in, 57–59
   improving comprehension instruction and, 56–57
   overview, 50–51, 60, 382–383, 388
   questions for discussion regarding, 60
   research regarding, 51–56, 54f, 55t
Flooding, vocabulary, 404
Fluency, 401–403
fMRI. *see* Functional magnetic resonance imaging (fMRI)
Formative assessment. *see also* Assessment
   Internet Reciprocal Teaching (IRT) model and, 332
   research regarding, 82, 82–83
   secondary level instruction and, 263–265, 264f, 265f
Formative Assessment of Students' Emerging Knowledge of Internet Strategies (FASEKIT), 332
"Fourth-grade slump", 183
Framework, instructional, 262–263
Friendship through education website, 15–16
Frontal cortex
   executive functioning and, 351
   research regarding, 106–107
Functional magnetic resonance imaging (fMRI)
   concreteness/imagery effects and, 110–111
   metacognition and, 76
   overview, 117
   working memory and, 118–119
Fusion Reading course, 278–285, 281f, 282f, 283f, 284f

G

Games
   future directions in, 316–317
   overview, 309
   questions for discussion regarding, 319
   research regarding, 316–317
   situated meanings and, 315–316
   specialist language and, 313–314
Gates–MacGinitie Reading Achievement Test, 354
Gender
   adolescent students and, 152
   prefrontal cortex development and, 152

Genre
   instruction and, 245–246
   technology and, 246
Global literacy
   AWARD Reading program and, 13–14
   future directions in, 14–15, 15–16
   overview, 382–383
   questions for discussion regarding, 17
Global Nomads Group (GNG), 15
Global Schoolhouse, 15–16
Goup processes, learning and, 133–138
Governance of Basic Education Act of 2001 (Philippines), 10
Graduate Management Admission Test (GMAT), 89
Grammar instruction, reading–writing connections and, 218
Graphic organizer
   close analysis of texts with structure (CATS) program and, 176, 177–178
   secondary level instruction and, 261f
   websites regarding, 370
Graphics in text
   future directions in, 192
   science text and, 184–185, 189–190
Graphophonological–semantic flexibility, 54–55, 54f
Group Reading and Diagnostic Evaluation (GRADE) test battery, 285
Guided instruction, secondary level instruction and, 263

H

History of reading research. *see also* Reading research
   overview, 9–10
   Programme for International Student Assessment (PISA) and, 11–13
   Progress in International Reading Literacy Study and, 13
Humanistic psychology, 228
Hypothalamus, 145–147

I

Identity development, adolescent students and, 151–152
IEA
   history of reading research and, 11
   latent semantic analysis and, 89–90

Imagens, 102, 103–104
Imagery
   dual coding theory and, 41–42, 45
   neuroscientific knowledge and, 109–112
Implicit memory, learning and, 131
Importance value, motivation and, 229
Independent learning tasks, secondary level instruction and, 263
In-Depth Expanded Application of Science (IDEAS) model
   authenticity and, 247
   future directions in, 250
   prior knowledge and, 245
Individual differences
   learning and, 132
   prior knowledge and, 244–245
Individuals with Disabilities Act, 348
Inference making, metacognition and, 69–70
Informational text. *see* Expository text comprehension
Informed Strategies for Learning (ISL), 67
Inquiry, 330
Instruction. *see also* Comprehension instruction; Elementary students, teaching of; Games; Secondary students, teaching of; Strategy instruction
   adolescent students and, 149–152
   argument schema theory and, 199–200
   cognitive flexibility and, 56
   dialogic interaction and, 207
   digital comprehension and, 351–355, 353*f*
   in the elementary classroom, 241–252
   English language learners (ELLs) and, 296, 299–300
   expository text comprehension and, 171–180
   fictional text comprehension and, 160–167
   Internet Reciprocal Teaching (IRT) model and, 329
   lesson design and, 362–375
   motivation and, 230–233
   neuroscientific knowledge and, 114–124, 116*f*, 117*f*, 118*f*, 133–138
   overview, 386
   reading–writing connections and, 219–221, 220*t*
   research regarding, 381–390, 392–410
   science text comprehension and, 190–191
   in the secondary classroom, 258–268, 261*f*
   technology and, 351–355, 353*f*, 356, 362–375
   vocabulary development and, 312–316
   whole reading programs and, 398–399
   in writing, 216–218
Instructional Conversations, 248–249
Instructional framework, 262–263
Instructional goals, 86–87
IntelliMetric assessment, 89
Interactive Strategy Training for Active Reading and Thinking (*iSTART*), 90, 352
Interactive Writing (IW), 219
Internal to external locus of control, 228
Internalization
   argument schema theory and, 198
   strategy instruction and, 407
International Association for the Evaluation of Educational Achievement (IEA), 11
International Children's Digital Library website, 365
International Literacy Year, 11
International Reading Association
   First World Congress on Reading, 11
   secondary level instruction and, 259, 259–260
   whole reading programs and, 398–399
Internet, 322. *see also* Internet Reciprocal Teaching (IRT) model; Online reading comprehension
Internet Reciprocal Teaching (IRT) model. *see also* Technology
   evolving model of, 328–331
   future directions in, 335–336
   measuring the benefits of, 331–334
   overview, 326–328
   questions for discussion regarding, 336–337
   Teaching Internet Comprehension to Adolescents (TICA), 324, 342*f*–346*f*
Internet scavenger hunts, 371
Intervention. *see also* At-risk students; Struggling readers
   metacognition and, 70–74
   overview, 272–275
   Scholastic Reading Inventory (SRI) assessment and, 88
   secondary level instruction and, 265–266
   using technology, 73–74
Intrinsic motivation, 228–229. *see also* Motivation
Intrinsic value, motivation and, 229

K

Kidlink projects, 15–16
KidSpace @ the Internet Public Library website, 365

Subject Index

Kinesthetic imagery, dual coding theory and, 43–44
Knowledge, conceptual, 404–405
Knowledge, prior. *see* Prior knowledge
K-W-L model of strategy instruction, 21

L

Language Experience Approach, 219
Language processing, statistical approaches to, 88–89
Language! program, 273
Language-processing areas, 111
Large-scale assessments, 85–88. *see also* Assessment
Latent semantic analysis (LSA)
  future directions in, 92–94
  overview, 89–91
Learning
  assessment of, 91–92
  neuroscientific knowledge and, 127–139, 129
  questions for discussion regarding, 139–140
  reading–writing connections and, 219–221, 220t
  from text, 91–92
Left hemisphere brain areas, 104–106, 105f
Lesson design
  building background knowledge and, 366–369, 368f, 369t
  future directions in, 371–372, 373f–374f
  questions for discussion regarding, 374–375
  research regarding, 363–366, 366f, 372
  technology and, 362–375
  websites regarding, 370–371
Literacy Decade–Education for All (United Nations, 2002)
  improving comprehension instruction and, 13–14
  overview, 10, 11
Literacy development, 215–216. *see also* Developmental processes
Literacy Initiative for Empowerment (LIFE), 11
Literacy Matters website, 370
Literacy motivation, 229–230. *see also* Motivation
Literature logs, English language learners (ELLs) and, 248–249
Locus of control, motivation and, 228

Logogens
  overview, 102, 103–104
  research regarding, 104–108, 105f
Long-term memory, neuroscientific knowledge and, 121–122
Lucidly functional language, 314. *see also* Vocabulary development

M

Magnetoencephalography (MEG), 116–117, 116f
Mastery goals, motivation and, 228
"Matthew effects", 244–245
Meaning, search for, 129–130
Meaning making
  assessment and, 84–85
  history of reading research and, 9
  neuroscientific knowledge and, 108–109
  overview, 103–104
  working memory and, 118–119
Measures of Academic Progress (MAP) assessment, 85, 86–87
Memorization, learning and, 131–132
Memory
  approaches to, 131–132
  comprehension processes and, 83–84
  learning and, 131, 131–132
  neuroscientific knowledge and, 121–122
Mental representations
  comprehension processes and, 83–84
  dual coding theory and, 41, 43–44, 45
  strategy instruction and, 407
Metacognition
  cognitive flexibility and, 52–53
  future directions in, 76
  improving comprehension instruction and, 74–75
  overview, 3, 65–66, 77
  questions for discussion regarding, 77
  research regarding, 66–74
Mirror neurons
  learning and, 131
  overview, 127–128
Modeling
  digital comprehension and, 352
  Internet Reciprocal Teaching (IRT) model and, 327–328, 329–330
  motivation and, 233
  neuroscientific knowledge and, 122
  overview, 26–27
  strategy instruction and, 407

Monitoring strategies, 69–70, 75, 76
Motivation
  Concept-Oriented Reading Instruction and, 247
  English language learners (ELLs) and, 298–299, 300–301
  future directions in, 233–235
  instruction and, 230–233
  metacognition and, 71
  overview, 3, 226–227, 235, 385–386
  questions for discussion regarding, 235
  research regarding, 229–230, 233–234
  secondary level instruction and, 259
  theories of, 227–229
Motivation to Read Profile, 234
Motor logogens, 107–108. *see also* Logogens
Multiliteracies, history of reading research and, 9
Multiple classification task, 53
Myelinization, 143–150, 144*f*

N

National Assessment of Educational Progress (NAEP)
  at-risk students and, 271
  future directions in, 14–15
  neuroscientific knowledge and, 115
  overview, 82–83
National Center for Education Statistics (NCES), 271
National Literacy Panel Report, 297–298
National Reading Panel
  adolescent students and, 147–150
  assessment and, 81
  changes since, 2
  comprehension instruction and, 24
  conceptual knowledge and, 404–405
  effective schools and, 395–396
  English language learners (ELLs) and, 294–295
  expository text comprehension and, 173
  fluency and, 402
  metacognition and, 65–66, 68, 70
  secondary level instruction and, 258–259
  strategy instruction and, 406
National Reading Research Center (NRRC), 229–230, 235
National Standards for all schools (Great Britain), 10
National Writing Project, 215

Natural language processing (NLP)
  assessment and, 88–89
  future directions in, 92–94
Neural plasticity, 127, 129
Neuroimaging
  concreteness/imagery effects and, 110–111
  metacognition and, 76
  overview, 115–120, 116*f*, 117*f*
Neuroscientific knowledge
  adolescent students and, 142–153
  concreteness/imagery effects and, 109–112
  dual coding theory and, 108–109
  instruction and, 114–124, 116*f*, 117*f*, 118*f*
  overview, 2, 101–104, 384–385
  questions for discussion regarding, 112, 124, 139–140, 153
  research regarding, 104–108, 105*f*, 128–133, 143–150, 144*f*, 145*f*, 152
  teaching elementary students and, 127–139
New Courses of Study (Japan), 10
Newberry Medal website, 361
No Child Left Behind legislation
  changes since, 2
  comprehension instruction and, 25
  effective schools and, 395–396, 397–398
  online reading comprehension and, 334–335
  overview, 10
  testing and, 407–410
Nonfiction text comprehension. *see* Expository text comprehension
Nonverbal representations. *see* Imagens
Northwest Evaluation Association (NWEA), 87
Note taking
  consistency in, 388–389
  secondary level instruction and, 261–262

O

Objective assessments, 333–334
Online reading comprehension. *see also* Digital comprehension; Internet Reciprocal Teaching (IRT) model; Technology
  future directions in, 334–336, 371–372, 373*f*–374*f*
  lesson design and, 362–375
  overview, 321–322
  public policy and, 334–335
  questions for discussion regarding, 336–337, 374–375
  reciprocal teaching and, 324–328

research regarding, 323–324, 334–336, 372
Teaching Internet Comprehension to Adolescents (TICA), 324, 342f–346f
Online Reading Comprehension Assessment (ORCA), 333
Organization of text
   close analysis of texts with structure (CATS) program and, 174–179
   expository text comprehension and, 171, 172, 179–180

P

Parietal areas, concreteness/imagery effects and, 111
Patterning, 130
Peer relationships, adolescent students and, 151
Peer-Assisted Learning Strategies (PALS), 67
Perception, learning and, 131
Performance goals, motivation and, 228
Performance-based assessments, 333
PET, 110–111
Phonological features, cognitive flexibility and, 54–55, 54f
Pilot 12-Country Study, 11
PIRLS, 13, 14–15
PISA. see Programme for International Student Assessment (PISA)
Popular culture, specialist language in, 313–314
Positron emission tomography (PET), 110–111
Predicting strategy, 327–328
Prefrontal cortex
   adolescent students and, 145–146, 147, 148, 151–152, 152
   identity formation and, 151–152
Prefrontal lobe, 119
Prewriting, 218
Prior knowledge
   close analysis of texts with structure (CATS) program and, 177
   English language learners (ELLs) and, 299
   instruction and, 244–245
   metacognition and, 70–71
   overview, 242
   secondary level instruction and, 259
   strategy instruction and, 407
   technology and, 366–369, 368f, 369t
Problem solving, adolescent students and, 150–151

Process learning circles, 133–138
Professional development
   comprehension instruction and, 23, 283
   future directions in, 32
   online reading comprehension and, 335–336
   overview, 396
   strategy instruction and, 407
Programme for International Student Assessment (PISA), 322
   future directions in, 14–15
   overview, 10, 11–13
Progress in International Reading Literacy Study, 13, 14–15
Progress monitoring, 88
Pruning, 143–145, 144f
Public policy. see also No Child Left Behind legislation
   online reading comprehension and, 334–335
   testing and, 407–410

Q

QAR (question–answer relationship) model of strategy instruction, 21
QSR Nvivo software, 202
Questioning strategy, 327–328

R

RAND Reading Study Group
   digital comprehension and, 348
   English language learners (ELLs) and, 294–295
Read 180 program, 273–274
Read Write Think website, 370
Readability level, 175
Read-alouds, 261f
Reading Apprenticeship, 273
Reading First program
   changes since, 2
   effective schools and, 397–398
   skills-first instruction, 401
   strategy instruction and, 406
Reading levels, brain differences and, 118
Reading research
   adolescent students and, 143–150, 144f, 145f, 152
   argument schema theory and, 199–207, 200t, 201f, 203t, 204t
   at-risk students and, 272–285, 277f, 281f, 282f, 283f, 284f, 286–288

Reading research *(cont.)*
  cognitive flexibility, 51–56, 55t
  comprehension instruction and, 20–28, 22t
  digital comprehension and, 348–350, 349f, 356
  dual coding theory and, 39–44, 43f, 45–46
  elementary level instruction and, 244–249, 250–251
  English language learners (ELLs) and, 295–299, 300–301
  fictional text comprehension and, 160–162
  future directions in, 14–15
  improving comprehension instruction and, 13–14, 29–30
  lesson design and, 372
  motivation and, 229–230, 233–234
  neuroscientific knowledge and, 115–117, 116f, 117f, 128–133
  online reading comprehension and, 323–324, 334–336
  overview, 9–10, 381–390, 392–410
  Programme for International Student Assessment (PISA) and, 11–13
  Progress in International Reading Literacy Study and, 13
  questions for discussion regarding, 17
  reading–writing connections and, 214–218
  science text and, 184–190, 186t
  secondary level instruction and, 259–260, 265–266
  vocabulary development and, 311, 316–317
Reading Research Quarterly, 9–10
Reading Strategy and Assessment Tool (R-SAT), 90–91
Reading–writing connections
  future directions in, 221–222
  history of reading research and, 9
  instruction and, 216–218, 219–221, 220t
  overview, 214, 222–223
  questions for discussion regarding, 223
  research regarding, 214–218
Reciprocal Teaching. *see also* Internet Reciprocal Teaching (IRT) model
  at-risk students and, 274
  digital comprehension and, 352, 354
  fictional text comprehension and, 162–163
  metacognition and, 67
  online reading comprehension and, 324–328
  overview, 161
  secondary level instruction and, 261f
  strategy instruction and, 406
Relationships, learning and, 129

Representations, mental
  comprehension processes and, 83–84
  dual coding theory and, 41, 43–44, 45
  strategy instruction and, 407
Research, reading. *see* Reading research
Response-oriented instruction, 165
"The rich-get-richer" phenomenon, 244–245
RIF (Reading is Fundamental) Reading Planet website, 365

S

Scaffolded Reading Experience (SRE), 163–165
Scaffolding
  argument schema theory and, 199–200
  classroom environment and, 393
  digital comprehension and, 347–358, 353f
  fictional text comprehension and, 163–165, 166–167
  overview, 27–28, 161
  questions for discussion regarding, 357–358
  reading–writing connections and, 218
  strategy instruction and, 407
Schema theory, 41. *see also* Argument schema theory
Scholastic Reading Inventory (SRI) assessment, 85, 87–88
Schools, effective, 394–398
Science Research Associates (SRA) Corrective Reading, 274
Science text comprehension
  explanations and, 183–193
  future directions in, 191–192
  instruction and, 190–191
  questions for discussion regarding, 192–193
Screening, at-risk students and, 271
Secondary students, teaching of. *see also* Adolescent students
  future directions in, 265–267
  improving comprehension instruction and, 260–265, 261f, 264f, 265f
  overview, 258–259
  questions for discussion regarding, 267–268
  research regarding, 259–260, 265–266
Self-determination theory, 228
Self-monitoring, 82
Self-regulation, metacognition and, 71
Semantic features, cognitive flexibility and, 54–55, 54f
Semantic representations, 103–104
"Semantic Web", 266
Sentence processing tasks, imagery and, 110

Shared reading, secondary level instruction and, 261f
Simple View of Reading model
  at-risk students and, 275
  overview, 59
Simultaneous sorting task, 53
Situated meanings of words. *see also* Vocabulary development
  overview, 314–315
  research regarding, 317
  video games and, 315–316
Situation model
  future directions in, 92–94
  neuroscientific knowledge and, 111–112
  questions for discussion regarding, 94–95
  research regarding, 81–85
Six Subject Study, 11
Skill instruction, 393, 400–410
Social activities, argument schema theory and, 198
Socioeconomic level, 399–400
Sorting task, 53
Specialist language
  family literacy and, 311–312
  overview, 310–311, 385–386
  in popular culture, 313–314
Speech process, motor logogens and, 107–108
Spelling, dual coding theory and, 45–46
Standardized testing, 407–410
Stanford Achievement Test (SAT-9), 273–274
Statistical approaches to language processing, 88–89
Storyline Online website, 365
Strategic behavior, 299
Strategic Instruction Model (SIM), 274–275
Strategy instruction. *see also* Instruction
  close analysis of texts with structure (CATS) program and, 177–178
  Concept-Oriented Reading Instruction and, 230–231
  digital comprehension and, 354
  future directions in, 30–33
  improving through research, 29–30
  metacognition and, 67
  motivation and, 230–231
  overview, 3, 405–407
  questions for discussion regarding, 33–34
  reading–writing connections and, 217
  research regarding, 21–23, 22t
Strategy Tutor
  digital comprehension and, 352, 353f
  overview, 355
Structural theories of cognition, 197. *see also* Argument schema theory
Structures of text
  close analysis of texts with structure (CATS) program and, 174–179
  expository text comprehension and, 171, 172, 179–180
Struggling readers. *see also* At-risk students
  cognitive flexibility and, 55, 55t, 57, 58
  comprehension instruction and, 25–26
  future directions in, 32
  intervention and, 75
  metacognition and, 75
  motivation and, 233–234
  neuroscientific knowledge and, 122
  research regarding, 233–234
Subjective task values, 229
Summarizing strategy, 327–328
Summary Street tool, 89–90
Summary Tutor program, 352
Summative assessment, 82–83. *see also* Assessment
Synaptic connections, 121–122
Syntactic errors, neuroscientific knowledge and, 119
Syntactic relations
  comprehension processes and, 83–84
  working memory and, 119

T

Task goals, motivation and, 228
Teacher characteristics
  adolescent students and, 149–150
  Internet Reciprocal Teaching (IRT) model and, 329
Teachers' Choices Booklist website, 361
Teaching. *see* Instruction
Teaching Internet Comprehension to Adolescents (TICA), 324, 342f–346f
Technology. *see also* Digital comprehension; Online reading comprehension; Websites
  assessment and, 82
  at-risk students and, 288–289
  AWARD Reading program and, 13–14
  building background knowledge and, 366–369, 368f, 369t
  fictional text comprehension and, 168
  future directions in, 94, 371–372, 373f–374f, 389–390
  as a genre, 246
  history of reading research and, 9
  instruction and, 246, 356
  lesson design and, 362–375

Technology *(cont.)*
  metacognition and, 73–74
  overview, 383–384
  questions for discussion regarding, 374–375
  reading–writing connections and, 221–222
  research regarding, 372
  secondary level instruction and, 266
Testing, 407–410
Text structure. *see* Structures of text
Thalamus, working memory and, 118–119
Theories of reading comprehension
  concreteness/imagery effects and, 109–112
  testing of, 109–112
Think-alouds
  digital comprehension and, 352
  fictional text comprehension and, 166
  Internet Reciprocal Teaching (IRT) model and, 331–332
  overview, 26–27
Thinking Reader program, 352, 354
Training, professional
  comprehension instruction and, 23, 283
  online reading comprehension and, 335–336
  overview, 396
  strategy instruction and, 407
Transactional Strategies Instruction (TSI)
  metacognition and, 67
  overview, 161–162
  strategy instruction and, 406
TumbleBooks website, 365, 366*f*

U

Unconscious processes, 131
Uninterrupted sustained silent reading (USSR) approach, 402
United Nations Educational, Scientific, and Cultural Organization (UNESCO), 10
Utility value
  instruction and, 232–233
  motivation and, 229

V

Vaughn Gross Center for Reading website, 371
Verbal meanings of words, 314–315. *see also* Vocabulary development
Verbal representations. *see* Logogens
Verbalizing–visualizing (VV) instructional program, 42

Video games. *see* Games
Virtual field trips, 367, 368*f*
Visual cortex, research regarding, 106–107
Visual logogens, 104–106, 105*f*. *see also* Logogens
Visual word form area (VWFA), 105–106, 105*f*
Vocabulary development
  digital comprehension and, 355
  family literacy and, 309, 311–312, 399–400
  future directions in, 316–317
  instruction and, 312–316
  overview, 403–404
  questions for discussion regarding, 319
  research regarding, 311, 316–317
  secondary level instruction and, 261*f*
  specialist language and, 310–311, 311–312
  types of words, 310
Vocabulary knowledge. *see also* Vocabulary development
  cognitive flexibility and, 58
  metacognition and, 69–70

W

WebQuests, 367–369, 369*t*
Websites. *see also* Online reading comprehension
  book clubs online, 370
  instruction and, 365–366, 366*f*
  lesson planning and, 370–371
  literature websites, 361
Wernicke's area
  research regarding, 106–107
  syntactic errors and, 119
Whole reading programs, 398–399
Word identification, neuroscientific knowledge and, 119
Word meanings, comprehension processes and, 83–84
Word recognition skills, metacognition and, 69–70
Words. *see also* Vocabulary development
  specialist language, 310–311
  types of, 310
Working memory
  metacognition and, 69–70, 74–75
  neuroscientific knowledge and, 118–119
WriteToLearn assessment, 86
WriteToLearn prompts, 261*f*
Writing, 45–46. *see also* Reading writing connections

Writing development, 218. *see also* Developmental processes
Writing instruction, 216–217
Writing workshop, 214–218. *see also* Reading–writing connections

X

Xtreme Reading program, 285

Y

Young Adult Choices website, 361

Z

Zone of proximal development
  classroom environment and, 393
  overview, 161

Contributors

Richard C. Anderson, EdD, Center for the Study of Reading, University of Illinois at Urbana–Champaign, Champaign, Illinois

Linda Baker, PhD, Department of Psychology, University of Maryland, Baltimore County, Baltimore, Maryland

Cathy Collins Block, PhD, College of Education, Texas Christian University, Fort Worth, Texas

Irma F. Brasseur, PhD, Center for Research on Learning, University of Kansas, Lawrence, Kansas

Donna Caccamise, PhD, Institute of Cognitive Science, University of Colorado at Boulder, Boulder, Colorado

Renate N. Caine, PhD, The Natural Learning Research Institute, Idyllwild, California

Kelly B. Cartwright, PhD, Department of Psychology and Office of the Provost, Christopher Newport University, Newport News, Virginia

Jill Castek, PhD, Graduate School of Education, University of California, Berkeley, Berkeley, California

Julie Coiro, PhD, School of Education, University of Rhode Island, Kingston, Rhode Island

Bridget Dalton, EdD, Peabody College of Education, Vanderbilt University, Nashville, Tennessee

Donald D. Deshler, PhD, Center for Research on Learning, University of Kansas, Lawrence, Kansas

Ting Dong, MA, Center for the Study of Reading, University of Illinois at Urbana–Champaign, Champaign, Illinois

Carol A. Donovan, PhD, College of Education, University of Alabama, Tuscaloosa, Alabama

Gerald G. Duffy, EdD, University of North Carolina at Greensboro, Greensboro, North Carolina

Contributors

Nell K. Duke, EdD, College of Education, Michigan State University, East Lansing, Michigan

Douglas Fisher, PhD, Department of Teacher Education, San Diego State University, San Diego, California

Nancy Frey, PhD, Department of Teacher Education, San Diego State University, San Diego, California

Linda B. Gambrell, PhD, Eugene T. Moore School of Education, Clemson University, Clemson, South Carolina

James Paul Gee, PhD, College of Education, Arizona State University, Tempe, Arizona

Douglas K. Hartman, PhD, Neag School of Education, University of Connecticut, Storrs, Connecticut

Kathy Headley, EdD, College of Health, Education, and Human Development, Clemson University, Clemson, South Carolina

Laurie A. Henry, PhD, College of Education, University of Kentucky, Lexington, Kentucky

Michael F. Hock, PhD, Center for Research on Learning, University of Kansas, Lawrence, Kansas

Il-Hee Kim, MA, School of Education, Indiana University–Purdue University at Fort Wayne, Fort Wayne, Indiana

So-Young Kim, PhD, private practice, Champaign, Illinois

Eileen Kintsch, PhD, Institute of Cognitive Science, University of Colorado at Boulder, Boulder, Colorado

Jan Lacina, PhD, College of Education, Texas Christian University, Fort Worth, Texas

Donald J. Leu, PhD, Neag School of Education, University of Connecticut, Storrs, Connecticut

Yuan Li, MA, Limited Brands, Columbus, Ohio

Hyo Jin Lim, MA, Rossier School of Education, University of Southern California, Los Angeles, California

Jacquelynn A. Malloy, MS, Eugene T. Moore School of Education, Clemson University, Clemson, South Carolina

Nicole M. Martin, BS, College of Education, Michigan State University, East Lansing, Michigan

Erin M. McTigue, PhD, Department of Teaching, Learning, and Culture, Texas A&M University, College Station, Texas

Allan Paivio, PhD, Department of Psychology, University of Western Ontario, London, Ontario, Canada

Sheri R. Parris, MEd, Department of Reading Education, University of North Texas, Denton, Texas

Michael Pressley, PhD (deceased), formerly of College of Education, Michigan State University, East Lansing, Michigan

Contributors

David Reinking, PhD, Eugene T. Moore School of Education, Clemson University, Clemson, South Carolina

Alina Reznitskaya, PhD, Department of Educational Foundations, Montclair State University, Montclair, New Jersey

David Rose, EdD, Center for Applied Special Technology (CAST), Wakefield, Massachusetts

Robert Rueda, PhD, Rossier School of Education, University of Southern California, Los Angeles, California

Mark Sadoski, PhD, Department of Teaching, Learning, and Culture, Texas A&M University, College Station, Texas

Andreas Schleicher, MSc, Indicators and Analysis Division (Directorate for Education), Organisation for Economic Co-operation and Development, Paris, France

Laura B. Smolkin, EdD, Curry School of Education, University of Virginia, Charlottesville, Virginia

Lynn Snyder, PhD, (Emerita), Department of Speech, Language, and Hearing Science, University of Colorado, Boulder, Boulder, Colorado

Mary Helen Thompson, MEd, Department of Reading, Texas Woman's University, Denton, Texas

Alejandra Velasco, EdM, Rossier School of Education, University of Southern California, Los Angeles, California

Joanna P. Williams, PhD, Teachers College, Columbia University, New York, New York